Role Theory

Expectations, Identities, and Behaviors

Role Theory

Expectations, Identities, and Behaviors

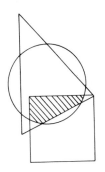

BRUCE J. BIDDLE

Center for Research in Social Behavior
The University of Missouri
Columbia, Missouri

ACADEMIC PRESS   New York   San Francisco   London
A Subsidiary of Harcourt Brace Jovanovich, Publishers

The quote on pages 329–330 is from J. H. Mann, Experimental evaluations of role playing. *Psychological Bulletin,* 1956, *53*: 227–234.
Copyright 1956 by the American Psychological Association. Reprinted by permission.

Case design by Patrick Turner and case artwork by Brooke Cameron.

ACADEMIC PRESS, INC.
111 Fifth Avenue, New York, New York 10003

United Kingdom Edition published by
ACADEMIC PRESS, INC. (LONDON) LTD.
24/28 Oval Road, London NW1   7DX

Library of Congress Cataloging in Publication Data

Biddle, Bruce Jesse, Date
    Role theory.

    Bibliography: p.
    Includes index.
    1. Role playing. I. Title   [DNLM: 1. Role.
HM131 B585r]
BF774.B52   158   79–6930
ISBN 0–12–095950–X

PRINTED IN THE UNITED STATES OF AMERICA

79 80 81 82   9 8 7 6 5 4 3 2 1

Contents

Contents

Preface

This book constitutes an integrative exposition of role theory. As is well known, the role perspective arose coincidentally in several disciplines in the late 1920s and early 1930s. Its central concern has been with patterns of human conduct—*roles;* with expectations, identities, and social positions; and with context and social structure as well as with individual response. As such, role theory offers a perspective that bridges social psychology, sociology, and anthropology. Thus it has generated interest among social scientists from many backgrounds.

Early proponents of the role concept differed in the assumptions they were willing to make about it. Anthropologists such as Ralph Linton saw roles as units of culture and tended to assume consistency of roles throughout the society. For Talcott Parsons, roles belonged to the social system and were to be explained through role expectations that were held by participants and were supported by sanctions. G. H. Mead saw role taking as a process essential to socialization and the development of the self, whereas J. L. Moreno assigned significance to role playing and saw the importance of this latter process for education and psychotherapy.

Given such diverse orientations, it is not surprising that role concepts have been applied to many research topics, among them to the analysis of consensus, conformity, role conflict, empathy, and the accuracy of social perception. They have also been applied to studies of small groups, families, communities, classrooms, kinship systems, formal organizations, and counseling. As a result, role theory has a wide following in education as well as in the clinical and helping professions.

Such breadth indicates the potential of role theory. But because role theory never generated an integrative theoretical statement, disagreement has appeared on the boundaries and assumptions of the field. For some, role theory is integral to functionalism in sociology, for others it is an expression of the symbolic interactionist perspective, or of cognitive social psychology; and proponents and critics have alternatively praised and damned role theory without being aware that they were often talking about quite different things.

I believe this work provides a long-needed synthesis for role theory. A single, overarching conceptual system is set for the role field which embraces other uses. Research involving role concepts is reviewed. Applications of role concepts are discussed for education, social work, and clinical practice. Advantages and shortcomings of the role stance are examined.

Two features, not always found in the social sciences, characterize this book. As readers may be aware, there is no standardized vocabulary for anthropology, sociology, or social psychology. Authors in these fields are likely to use terms without making explicit their meanings, and theorists may differ sharply over the assumptions that underlie work in the social sciences. This book meets such problems by providing a theory that evolves in explicit steps, each of which makes only the minimal assumptions necessary to discuss the concepts and processes being considered. As well, concepts central to the theory are each provided with consistent definitions that are built on previously considered material. (Terms indicating these concepts appear in boldface within the manuscript, and their definitions are repeated in a Glossary that follows the References.)

More than a decade of work has gone into preparation of this book. The work began as a series of algebraic notes from which seminars were conducted at the University of Missouri–Columbia during 1967 and 1968. In 1969 the manuscript was drafted into English while the author was at Monash University in Melbourne, Australia. It was redrafted in 1970, 1971, 1974, 1977, and 1978, in Columbia, Clearwater Bay (Ontario), and while the author was at the Australian National University in Canberra. In addition to the support I have received from students, colleagues, and administrators at three universities, four scholars were kind enough to provide me with detailed reviews of earlier drafts: Michael Banton, Irwin Deutscher, Ronald Taft, and Andrew Twaddle. My initial commitment to role theory was stimulated by Ted Newcomb (of course), but my recent thoughts about role matters have largely reflected interaction with Barbara Bank (of course). The complex tasks of preparing this book for publication fell onto various shoulders, but thanks are especially owed to Lorraine Elliott (for typing the first draft) and Sherry Kilgore (who prepared the last).

Role Theory

Expectations, Identities, and Behaviors

Chapter One

Relevance, Role Theory, and Ratiocination

Role theory has a splendid neutrality. . . . The importance of role theory is undeniable, its range of influence has been vast, research engendered in its name diverse and bountiful. . . . Role theory appears to have a remarkable specificity for our time.
                                               —Patricke Johns Heine

Role theory consists of pompous, nebulous and incredibly lengthy restatements of what has been common knowledge for a very long time.
                                               —Stanislav Andreski

It has been said many times: The proper study of human beings is humanity. Not only are men and women the most fascinating of all phenomena in our eyes, but their study is complex, difficult, and important. Yet how can persons be studied by persons? How can we apply the canons of science to such a task without dehumanizing ourselves, and thus fail through the very act of self-analysis?

For centuries we avoided the study of human beings. The history of science began with the investigation of distant and innocent events, with stars and geometry and the laws of physics. Only recently have we begun to turn the task of scientific investigation upon ourselves, thus creating the social sciences; and in so doing we run a perilous course. Social scientists are told by humanists that it is impossible to capture the complex essence of a person with crass science, by physical scientists that the scientific method is inapplicable to human beings, by disciples that human truths were dictated by Moses or Karl Marx, by philosophers that since

1

we are human ourselves we cannot presume to look at ourselves objectively, by politicians that our findings are trivial or inapplicable, by literary critics that our writings are incomprehensible, by moralists that our gathering of objective data concerning people is indefensible, and by anxious citizens that our knowledge is dangerous.

Apart from whether it is possible to be both trivial and dangerous, such criticisms reveal that we have yet to accommodate the social sciences in the folkways of our civilization. Even the voices of our critics are heard at but low volume—above all, the social sciences are ignored. Although all would agree that our civilization, our lives, our very planet are threatened by uncontrolled social forces, we are remarkably unwilling to involve social science data in making decisions concerning these events. We would not dream of constructing a bridge, distributing a new drug, or placing a person in a rocket to fly to the moon without careful research. However, we daily subject 30 million school children to instructional methods whose effects are largely unresearched. We also impose archaic and tragic methods of treatment upon prisoners in violation of findings already developed by social scientists; we consult representatives of the FBI in order to meet the challenge of campus disturbances rather than commission research on the subject; and we feed our children on a diet of televised violence in the face of social science evidence telling us of its evil effects. Since all persons are themselves human beings, all presume themselves equally expert in human affairs. Each of us *knows* what is best in education, in foreign relations, in the treatment of the poor or ethnic minorities—and we have little patience with the need to conduct research on these problems and but little interest in the recommendations of social scientists who have conducted that research.

The only difficulty with such private knowledge is that it is unreliable, and being unreliable it is often wrong. Surely "everyone knows" that to spare the rod spoils the child, that children learn to read more quickly with "sight-and-say" instruction, that the elimination of capital punishment will lead to more crimes of violence, that lack of parental discipline produces youthful rebellion, that the imposition of ceremonies of degradation upon the poor in connection with welfare payments will lead to their greater motivation to seek employment. Though each of these propositions is questionable, though research pertaining to each has appeared, though each is presumably in error—there are still many Americans who believe in the validity of each and are willing to plan social policy based on that belief.

What I am arguing, of course, is the relevance of social science. That we have a complex society, flooded with social problems, no one would argue. It is my contention that our best, and perhaps our only, hope for solving these problems is to apply the canons of science to their study and the evidence of that study to social policy. This does not mean that all social sciences are equally relevant, or indeed that all activities of social scientists meet the canons of science. Some social scientists might more properly be termed historians, social critics, social engineers, philosophers, or teachers. Some concepts of social scientists are irrelevant to current dilemmas, either because they concern obsolete or infrequent social forms or because they reduce human beings to mindless abstractions. Some (perhaps most) theories of social scientists are as yet untested with empirical data. And some social science research appears irrelevant because it is devoted to statistical model building, experimental design, techniques for interviewing, or other methodological issues having little apparent application to our needs.

Nevertheless, it is not only possible to construct a social science that is relevant, but the survival of our civilization depends upon our being willing to take this step. Among some physical scientists it is popular to distinguish between "natural" events and those that are induced through human agency. (Thus, some distinguish between the "natural sciences" and the "social sciences.") Such terminology is pejorative and suggests that human affairs are uncontrollable. What I shall argue in this book is that human affairs are not less "natural" than any other form of phenomena. Human behavior can be studied in both natural contexts—such as families, factories, and urban centers—and in the laboratory. And in making such studies we can generate evidence that is vitally needed if we are to solve the pressing problems of our society. Any knowledge is dangerous, and the findings of social science may surely be misused to control the behavior of others. But far more dangerous is the course of refusing to develop that knowledge, for then we must continue to blunder in the social decisions we take, and in so doing we will escalate the social problems that threaten to overwhelm us.

So much for the general argument. But this is a textbook for one specific field within the social sciences, role theory. In this work I shall argue not only that relevant social sciences are possible, but also that role theory illustrates that possibility. The task of this book, then, is to examine the concepts of the role field, to discover their applications to social problems of pressing concern, to review empirical evidence that has been developed within the role orientation concerning these problems, and to suggest additional research where we find it lacking. Thus, the general argument concerning the relevance of social science will be illustrated with the specific example of the role field.

This does not mean that other orientations within the social sciences are not also relevant. Nor is the only justification for role theory its relevance. (Other advantages of the role stance will be discussed later in the chapter.) But persons who enter the social sciences hoping to find relevance may find instead a diet of abstract and inapplicable concepts, statistical and methodological concerns, and evidence that seduces them away from their original concerns for human affairs. In role theory readers will find a field that preserves the humanity of human beings and allows them to examine the social problems that concern us all.

The Role Field

Role theory does not, as some wags would have it, concern the baking of buns or bagels. Rather, its focus is on persons and their behaviors. But how does one conceptualize persons and their behaviors? Different answers have been given to this question, depending on one's disciplinary orientation.

For the ethologist, humantity is but a single species, descended from the great apes and still bearing many of the impulses, physical characteristics, and instincts that were developed by our ancestors. For the anthropologist, the essence of humanity is culture, which is shared among all those within a given society, a culture that is studied best by contrasting its many variations among the wide assortment of societies around the globe. For the psychologist, persons are individuals, responding not only to their immediate environment, but also to their own peculiar history of socialization and characterized by both patterns of responses and phenomenal experiences which they only partly share with others. For the sociologist, the person is a product of his or her social world, not only a carrier of culture but also a representative of the assumptions and values of that person's community, social class, family, occupation, and social groups—conforming to the dictates of social systems, and responding to their challenges with behaviors that are functionally linked to other behaviors for the accomplishment of tasks.

These orientations are different in the explanations they offer for human conduct. They are similar, however, in that they are concerned with one basic set of phenomena—patterned human behaviors, or *roles*. Within each of these orientations it is assumed that persons are somewhat alike in the behaviors they exhibit and that the behaviors shown are more-or-less predictable once we know the person's identity and the context in which the person finds him or herself. They differ in the scope of roles each is willing to consider and in the grounds on which they would make predictions about those roles.

It is now possible to define the subject of this book. **Role theory**, then, is a science concerned with the study of behaviors that are characteristic of persons within contexts and with various processes that presumably produce, explain, or are affected by those behaviors. It is with the study of roles that this book is concerned, and with the many concepts with which roles are described, explained, predicted, studied, accounted for, learned, rationalized, perceived, and created.

Key Concepts

Let us examine briefly some of the key concepts that are used to discuss roles, their causes, and their effects. Although each of these concepts will be discussed in greater detail later in the book, it will help to anticipate some of our argument at the beginning.

Perhaps the most common notion in role theory is that roles are associated with *social positions* (or *statuses*). In general, a social position is an identity that designates a commonly recognized set of persons. The terms physician, school teacher, janitor, professional athlete, hermit, grandmother, and juvenile delinquent all refer to recognized sets of persons. Each constitutes a social position. But physicians, school teachers, janitors, and the like each behave in characteristic ways. Physicians write prescriptions, school teachers lecture in classrooms, janitors sweep up, and so forth. Thus, each social position is said to exhibit a characteristic role. In fact, when most of us think about roles, or write of roles in our professional publications, it is the roles of social positions that we have in mind.

The idea that social positions should have roles is deceptively powerful. On the one hand, we are asserting that at least some behaviors are associated with sets of persons, rather than with the entire society or with persons as individuals. On the other, we are also suggesting that persons who share roles are also likely to share a common identity. As we shall see, these assertions are problematic. But let us assume that they are justified in the main. Why should the members of a social position exhibit a common role?

Several explanations have been advanced. Perhaps the one most often heard is that roles are induced through the sharing of *expectations* for role behavior. Thus, those who exhibit the role are stimulated to do so because they learn what behaviors are expected of them, while others are stimulated through their own expectations to teach and enforce appropriate behaviors for those who are members of the position. For example, it is said that physicians wear white coats in the hospital ward because they (themselves) have learned expectations for the appropriateness of that behavior and because others (their instructors, nurses on the ward, even patients) have encouraged them to do so.

The idea that roles are induced through expectations is enormously attractive. It suggests that human beings are rational, thoughtful, perceiving beings. We are told not only that our phenomenal experiences are a useful guide to action, but also that our behaviors are controlled through those experiences. Emphasis is given to experiences of socialization through which we learn expectations, to the accuracy and adequacy of our expectations, and to the way in which our expectations lead to conforming behavior. Moreover, to the extent that our roles are shared, it is presumed that we also share (and can enunciate) expectations for those roles. Such an explanation is pragmatic, phenomenal, flattering, rational, ordered—indeed, as American as apple pie!

Unfortunately, it is also questionable. For one thing, exactly what do we mean by *expectation*? Some writers appear to mean *anticipation* when they use this term, others seem to imply *norm,* or *value,* or *feeling,* or even *thoughts about the feelings of others.* Clearly, these various kinds of expectations have different implications for behavior. For another, in some cases we are probably unaware of our role behaviors. For example, some teachers are more willing to tolerate poor answers from pupils they consider bright than from pupils they consider dull, but are unaware that they exhibit this characteristic, prejudiced behavior (Brophy & Good, 1970). Again, role expectations are simply not always shared (Gross, Mason, & McEachern, 1958). Idiosyncratic roles may also be recognized in the behaviors of individuals as well as in the behaviors of collectivities. And again, we do not always conform to our expectations in our behaviors. For instance, in situations of emergency we are likely to violate long-standing expectations in order to save lives or property. All of which suggest that one must view the expectational explanation of roles with a grain of salt. Surely many roles are induced through expectations, but some are not.

How else, then, are roles induced? Another type of explanation concerns the nature of the *context* in which the role is played out. As is widely observed, most role behaviors are contextually bound. Let us consider three contexts, all of which feature an audience: the football match, the church service, and the concert hall. In order to know whether to cheer, to sit in solemn silence, or to applaud enthusiastically the individual must know which of these three contexts he or she has entered. He or she must be provided with a "definition of the situation." Role expectations, then, may be associated with context as well as with social position. But contexts will affect roles in other, more primitive ways, as well. Consider the effect of equipment on role behavior. Without baseball bats it is impossible to play baseball, books in the home stimulate reading, pistols generate murder with handguns. Roles, then are facilitated by environmental equipment as well as by expectations.

Another explanation for roles concerns the consequences of role behavior. Roles are not without effects, rather they are likely to have characteristic effects, or *functions,* within the social system. The physician who wears a white coat in the hospital helps others to recognize him or her quickly and thus follow his or her orders in an emergency. The grandmother often provides baby-sitting services for her children and family history for her grandchildren. Even the criminal provides "employment" for policemen by his or her characteristic role behaviors. Many of the functions that are performed by roles are understood, and people may be motivated to continue in their roles because they desire and approve the function that they are accomplishing thereby. However, some functions of roles are inadvertant, accidental, or may be decried by all concerned. If these latter be the case, roles may still persist because those who perform them have not yet figured out a better way to get the job done. For example, our system of prison administration involves roles for prisoners, guards, wardens, parole officers and the like which have consequences that are often described as disastrous for the rehabilitation of criminals. And yet, we persist in these roles for want of a better system.

The last example also illustrates another property of roles. Many roles are imbedded within *social systems,* and role concepts may easily be used for the analysis of complex organizations and other social forms. Most factories, for example, have a table of organization that lists the social positions of those who are its employees. Each of these positions is assigned a job to do, and each exhibits characteristic role behaviors. The roles of the various positions are specialized and interdependent. Moreover, production will often depend on the sequential performance of many complex roles. In a production line, for example, performance of several thousand roles may be necessary to generate an automobile, a vaccine, or a computer. In such a context, individuals must learn to accommodate a specialized role if they are to remain members of the organization. At the same time, even within the formal organization, roles are not wholly determined by job descriptions (as we shall see). Moreover, some critics of the role concept have presumed that the same sorts of restrictions applying to roles in the formal organization also apply to other kinds of roles, which appears to be unjust.

Finally, the role concept is also used as a vehicle for discussing the socialization and adjustment of the individual. Consider the problem of initial socialization, which takes place in the family for most of us. Characteristic roles are performed in the family by fathers, mothers, older siblings, and even newborn infants. In time, however, the infant learns role behaviors that are deemed appropriate for his or her sex, social class, ethnic group, and other social poistions he or she is to occupy in life. He or she learns these through a variety of means, through *role playing* (that is, by practicing the roles he or she sees performed by others) and *role taking* (that is, by internalizing expectations that are enunciated for him or her by others). The child, thus, develops a *self-concept* that is composed of (among other things) a set of role expectations for him or herself as he or she assumes various identities and enters different contexts.

Adult life is not without its problems, of course, and some of these can be expressed in role terms too. Entrance into some social positions is governed not by abilities or desires of the person, but rather by accidents of birth or customs of the society. (For example, women and blacks are sometimes denied opportunities for employment, although they are fully qualified.) Moreover, positions are sometimes arranged in an age or achievement-graded sequence such that the person must first achieve membership in a given position of the sequence before he or she can be considered for membership in the next position. (Those without a bachelor's degree will not normally be accepted for postgraduate education at a university.) Problems may be encountered with the roles a person takes on, too. Some roles are difficult to perform and take great native ability or years of practice to learn. Sometimes the person is subjected to incompatible role expectations (or *role conflict*) wherein he or she is required to do two or more things that cannot all be done. Sometimes he or she suffers from *role overload,* when too much is asked of the person. Sometimes the role the person is asked to perform is inconsistent with his or her needs or basic values. Sometimes his or her role behavior is judged *deviant* by the society, and the person is subject to punishment or institutionalization until he or she learns more appropriate roles. And to help the person do this latter, he or she may be exposed to various professionals (such as doctors and social workers) whose roles are to aid in the relearning process.

By now, readers may have concluded that role theory is as broad as the ocean and as shallow as a mud puddle. A sovereign balsam against all evil, role theory may appear to be but a set of plastic concepts that can be applied to the superficial analysis of any individual and social system. And as a matter of fact, the plasticity of role concepts is one of the major reasons why the role orientation is popular. Since social scientists have rarely found it necessary to spell out exactly what they meant by *role, social position,* or *expectation,* these terms could be applied with impunity to almost any purpose. Role might be considered an identity, a set of characteristic behaviors, or a set of expectations; expectations might be descriptive, prescriptive, or evaluative; and so it goes. And given such a superficial level of analysis, it would be possible either to exalt or decry role notions with equal enthusiasm—since each of us would be talking about somewhat different things.

At the same time, role theory is based on several underlying propositions about which there is general, if informal, agreement. By way of summary, let us list five of these:

1. Role theorists assert that "some" behaviors are patterned and are characteristic of persons within contexts (i.e., form *roles*).
2. Roles are often associated with sets of persons who share a common identity (i.e., who constitute *social positions*).
3. Persons are often aware of roles, and to some extent roles are governed by the fact of their awareness (i.e., by *expectations*).
4. Roles persist, in part, because of their consequences (*functions*) and because they are often imbedded within larger social systems.
5. Persons must be taught roles (i.e., must be *socialized*) and may find either joy or sorrow in the performances thereof.

These are powerful propositions about which there is by no means agreement within the larger community of social scientists. Radical behaviorists would tell us that the concept of expectation is unnecessary and confusing; phenomenologists might deny the need for studying behaviors; psychoanalysts would stress the unconscious determinants of behavior; and Marxists would have us focus more on economic matters and historical imperatives. Despite such arguments, considerable enthusiasm has appeared for the posture suggested by role theory. Role concepts are widely accepted within the social sciences, and for many readers the five preceding propositions would appear to be self-evident. Perhaps this is because they so closely mirror the optimistic pragmatism that is the dominant philosophical orientation of Western societies.

Sources and Development

Unlike psychoanalysis or field theory, the role field did not begin with the contributions of a single great man. On the contrary, the role orientation has evolved gradually from related interests in several social sciences. This process of evolutionary coalescence has both advantages and disadvantages. On the positive side, role theorists have never suffered feelings of emasculation or found it necessary to develop their own ideas in opposition to those put forward by a Freud, Marx, or Beethoven. On the negative side, since the development of role ideas has proceeded from various sources, it should not surprise us to discover that those developments have sometimes taken place in ignorance or in violation of one another.

As is true for many fields within the social sciences, role theory owes some of its insights to the meanings of words common in the Indo-European languages. Terms such as *role, social position, status, expectation, conformity, consensus, function,* and the like appear in the common language, and use of these terms in role theory is clearly but a reflection of their use in everyday speech. An illustration of this general similarity is given in a table provided by Thomas and Biddle [B&T, pp. 10–12][1] in which the common-language meanings of role terms are contrasted with more limited uses to which they have been put within the role orientation. For example, the term *role* began life in Latin as "rotula," the round and wooden dowel on which sheets of parchment were fastened. Afterward, the same term was used to mean an official volume of papers for law courts, then later the parts of theatrical characters came to be read from "roles" (Moreno, 1960, p. 80). In current common usage *role* is either a part or character performed by an actor in a drama, or a function taken or assumed by any person or structure. In current social science the term *role* has come to mean a behavioral repertoire characteristic of a person or a position; a set of standards, descriptions, norms, or concepts held for the behaviors of a person or social position; or (less often) a position itself.

A second source for role concepts has been the terminology and ideas of several specialized fields, notably those of the theatre and the law. As was suggested in the previous paragraph, the term role had its origins in the vocabularly of the stage, and its extension to the description of patterns of behavior that are found in real-life situations constitutes a metaphor in which we compare behavior *in situ* with the make-believe of the stage. Some role theorists, however, have gone further and have sought to use additional terms and metaphors from the stage, the law, and other social forms. Such terms as *role enactment, role playing, coaching, performance, actor, mask, persona, psychodrama, presentation of self,* and *as-if behavior* imply the dramaturgical metaphor—which is perhaps best illustrated in the work of Goffman (1959) or in Messinger, Sampson, and Towne (1962). The theory of sanctioning, and terms such as *norm, law,* and *custom* stem from legal models, and in particular from the social contract theory of the Scottish moral philosophers.

Additional sources of insight have been provided by closely related disciplines

---

[1] Throughout this text, references given in square brackets apply to a collection of readings for the role field assembled by the author and E. J. Thomas [Biddle & Thomas, 1966]. This work also contains four chapters on the history and concepts of role theory by Thomas and Biddle.

within the social sciences. Structura! sociology and anthropology have focused our attention on persisting social forms, from whence have come such terms as *position, structure, network, relationship,* and the like. Personality theorists have discussed the *self,* the *ego,* and the development of *identity.* Social psychologists have contributed their concerns for *interaction* and *group norms.* But in the long run, some basic ideas within role theory stem not from the insights of social scientists, but rather from the semantic structure of the languages we share. For example, it is by now common to find role theorists discriminating among various modes of expectations—for instance, between *norms* and *anticipations*—but it is likely that our ability to make such distinctions stems from the fact that our language exhibits these semantic features, and we often express them when we speak about social behavior.

Some readers may want to learn about the history of the role field. For those seeking detailed knowledge, Anne-Marie Rocheblave-Spenle's excellent *La Notion de Rôle en Psychologie Sociale* (1962, revised 1969) is recommended. A shorter history was also provided by Thomas and Biddle [B&T, Chapter I]. In general, three stages can be discriminated in the development of the role field. The first was a *precursive* stage, which saw the gradual evolution of role terms, along with other vocabularies in the social sciences. The second was a stage of *conceptual development* in which role concepts were formalized, elaborated, and applied to the discussion of a variety of social events. The third (in which we are still involved) is a stage of extensive *empirical research* in which role concepts are being applied to research in many different contexts. In general, most of the research conducted in this third phase has concerned itself with practical problems (such as those associated with education, social services, mental health, or adjustment to occupations) rather than with basic propositions in role theory.

As a result of this pattern of development, role theory today exhibits three major features: (*a*) a vocabulary of terms and concepts that is widely used in several social sciences (albeit with some confusion); (*b*) a variety of books and monographs in which role concepts have been used to discuss social events; and (*c*) extensive empirical research applying role concepts to problems of interest to investigators. To date there have been few attempts to provide conceptual integration for the role field and still fewer to provide propositional syntheses or to conduct basic research on role matters.

Role Theory and Related Fields

It is possible to take three contrasting positions with regard to the place of role theory in the social scientific firmament. The first and narrowest interpretation is that role theory constitutes a subfield within anthropology, sociology, or psychology. Such a position is taken explicitly or implied by such works as Banton's (1965) anthropologically oriented text, Turner's (1974) review of theories in sociology, or Heiss' (1968) view that role theory can be partitioned into two contrasting fields, one stemming from symbolic interactionism and the other representing structural sociology. However, most of those who see role theory in this limited light seem to have concluded that it is a theoretical subfield of social psychology. This interpretation is suggested in both editions of the *Handbook of Social Psychology* (Sarbin, 1954; Sarbin & Allen, 1968). It also appears in the theoretically oriented texts of Deutsch and Krauss (1965) and Shaw and Costanzo (1970). It is also suggested by Rose (1962), who opposed the "psychologically oriented" field of role theory with the "sociologically oriented" field of symbolic interactionism. (Since I began my professional career as a social psychologist, my initial assumption was that role theory was indeed a branch of social psychology, and some of my earlier publications may be found to reflect this view—see Biddle, 1961.)

A second orientation suggests that role theory is a vehicle, perhaps even the major or only vehicle, presently available for integrating the three core social sciences of anthropology, sociology, and psychology into a single discipline whose concern is the study of human behavior. This claim for role theory has been advanced by various advocates. Rommetveit suggests that the concept of role is "the theoretical point of articulation between psychology and sociology," and is, moreover, "the largest possible research unit within the former discipline and the smallest possible within the latter" (1954, p. 31). Ackerman offers the concept of role "as a bridge between the processes of intrapsychic life and those of social participation" (1951, p. 1). For Sarbin, role theory "is an interdisciplinary theory in that its variables are drawn from studies of culture, society and personality" (1954, p. 223). For Cooper, Leavitt, and Shelly "the concept of 'role' is important in social psychology as well as in sociology and anthropology" (1964, p. 7), while Gordon suggests that "the concept of role is highly useful because it offers a means of studying both the individual and the collectivity within a single conceptual framework. Social scientists, therefore, have used role theory increasingly as a major, if not central, concept in their theoretical formulations" (1966, p. 21). In defense of this integrative position—which is the one adopted in this book—role terms are now used by social sciences representing a broad range of disciplinary commitments. Moreover, it is difficult to discover any other terminology that has quite this range of adoption, which led Thomas and Biddle to observe that "role concepts are not the *lingua franca* of the behavioral sciences, but perhaps they presently come closer to this universal language than any other vocabulary of behavioral science" [B&T, p. 8].

Still a third claim may also be made for role theory—that it is also a core concern for other social sciences beyond the boundaries of anthropology, psychology, and sociology. Such applications have surely been made. Role concepts have been used to study political, economic, legal, and other institutions. And yet, though role theory may be applied to economics or political science, it would be silly to claim that for these fields role theory has the central significance it has for anthropology, psychology, or sociology. Within the other social sciences human behavior is viewed more as an independent than as a dependent variable. For example, within economics assumptions about human behavior are used to generate models for the economic system. The same is true for political science, demography, and to a lesser extent the law. Role theory can contribute to these disciplines by informing us about the behaviors characteristic of people in the marketplace, the voting booth, the law court, and in matters procreational or migratory. It can, thus, help to provide the underpinnings for theory derivation—but its contributions should not be considered central.

When we turn to the helping professions, however, we find that role theory plays a more prominent role. Consider education. Given that teaching involves role behaviors on the part of both teachers and pupils, and that teaching goes on within a context of demands and beliefs, it is possible to view much of education within a role framework. And for this reason, scores of studies have now been conducted using role concepts in education. The same claim may also be made for such professions as psychiatry, clinical and counseling psychology, social work, community development, and leadership training. Role theory offers these latter, too, a vocabulary and the promise of empirical power; and once again research efforts have appeared within each of these fields using the role orientation.

Role theory, then, is of central importance in the disciplines of anthropology, psychology, and sociology. It is also useful in the helping professions that derive them. As for the other social sciences, role research can at least provide empirical evidence bearing on their assumptions.

Prospects and Problems

We may now list some of the reasons why role theory has provoked enthusiasm. First, role theory parades as a science. It has its own terms and concepts and has generated a healthy assemblage of studies in which these have received empirical study. And although propositional theory is hard to find within the role orientation, broad agreement exists concerning the basic arguments of the field. Second, role theory offers concepts for many of the events a social science should cover. Role theory differentiates individual behaviors, social activities, and the phenomenal processes that presumably lie behind them. Moreover, role theory accommodates symbols as well as nonsymbolic forms of behavior. And third, because role concepts are based on terms having surplus meaning within the common language, role theory appears to offer a means for expressing both the concrete thoughts of subjects and the abstract notions of investigators. For these reasons, role theory applies to human experiences in natural contexts, and hence to social problems of concern to citizens.

Role theory also appeals to social scientists because it offers a meeting ground on which the various social sciences can come together. Several reasons may be cited for this. For one, role theory provides many concepts, thus enabling investigators to study different and competing explanations for human conduct. For another, since many of the terms appearing in role theory are drawn from the common language, they appear natural and easy to measure. For this reason, also, role theory is methodologically neutral, and role concepts have been studied with nearly all of the tools used by social scientists—from participant observation, through questionnaires and interview schedules, to projective tests.

Role theory also appeals to practitioners, and in part the spread of role theory has been due not so much to calm decisions made by social theorists, but to the enthusiasm of those who seek individual or social change. Reasons may also be cited for this enthusiasm that are a source of some embarassment for role theory. For one, since role theory makes use of terms from the common language, it is easy to learn superficially, and many of the arguments within the theory can be carried by surplus connotation rather than by formal reasoning. For another, because of both its systematic stance in differentiating expectations from behavior and its conceptual sloppiness, role theory suggests a simple one-to-one relationship between the overt facts of social behavior and the subjective experiences of those who behave. And although role theory offers the promise of empirical evidence bearing on social problem fields, much of this research is not yet tied together by investigations of the basic propositions of the field.

Although it would be foolish to discourage the enthusiasm of anyone who is excited about role theory, readers should be cautioned concerning these latter "advantages" of the role orientation. As we shall see, the use of terms from the common language is a source of some misery within role theory; it is both necessary and difficult to separate concepts dealing with overt and covert events, and the relationship between these two realms is far from simple; and additional basic research is needed to lace the role field into a single discipline.

CONFUSION

The preceding observations suggest that role theory has problems as well as prospects. One such problem concerns confusion. Much of the discussion within role theory has used terms and concepts taken from the common language; therefore it is not surprising that some confusion has appeared concerning their use. Terms within role theory are used for many different concepts, and the same concept may be denoted by various terms. Moreover, some expositions of role ideas have been characterized by obscurity and superfluous assumptions.

These are harsh criticisms, but they are easy to document. To illustrate, more than a score of discriminable concepts have been denoted by the term *expectation* in different studies, while the concept of a covertly held prescriptive expectation

has received at least 15 different names in theoretical studies and more than twice
that number in empirical investigations (Biddle, 1961). Similar problems may be
found for such terms as *role, identity, position, status, consensus, conformity, role
conflict,* indeed, for most of the central terms of the role field. All is not madness,
of course, and there is some degree of agreement on the use of terms and concepts
within role theory. However, careful readers in the role field must always try first
to find out the concept intended by an author to apply a given term and whether
the operation chosen for its measurement is appropriate.

Obscurity is not less difficult to demonstrate, although one hesitates to do so
lest one appear to be waspish and quoting out of context. For these reasons, the
following examples of "clarity on the role front" are offered, with apologies, from
some otherwise excellent sources.

> [Role is] any position differentiated in terms of a given social structure whether the
> position be institutionalized or not. . . . The social position [is] given to the individ-
> ual. . . . These roles involve obligations, rights, and expected performances of the
> individuals who hold them. . . . An *ideal* role is an *institutionalized role.* Such a role
> involves normative standards, conformity with which is generally to be expected, and
> failure to conform with which is met by moral indignation. An *actual role* is the posi-
> tion in fact occupied by an individual (Levy, 1952, p. 159).

> Position: A location in a social structure which is associated with a set of social
> norms. . . . Role: A part of social position consisting of a more or less integrated
> or related sub-set of social norms which is distinguishable from other sets of norms
> forming the same position. . . . Norm: A patterned or commonly held behavior ex-
> pectation. A learned response, held in common by members of a group (Bates, 1956,
> p. 314).

> Roles are normative in that they involve some implicit shared expectancy among
> group members; and norms themselves, lacking visibility, may nonetheless dwell in
> expectancies. It is these expectancies, then, which may be normative, in the sense of
> typicality. Norms and roles are only distinguishable insofar as norms usually imply
> expectancies applicable to many persons, while roles are expectancies restrictive to
> one or a very few individuals in a group (Hollander, 1958, p. 118).

And, from more recent sources, we learn that

> The conceptual bridge between social structure and role behavior is the concept of
> *role expectations.* This is a cognitive concept, the content of which consists of beliefs,
> expectancies, subjective probabilities, and so on. The units of social structure are po-
> sitions or statuses. . . . These units are defined in terms of actions and qualities ex-
> pected of the person who at any time occupies the position (Sarbin & Allen, 1968,
> p. 497).

> A *role* is the set of system states and actions of a subsystem . . . including its interac-
> tions with other systems or nonsystem elements. . . . To amplify . . . if the subsystem
> is an individual the role consists of only those system states and interactions that are
> specified for his part in the organization. . . . A complete statement of role specifies
> the position and function in the larger organization—though the definition does not

require that all details of a role be explicitly stated or even understood (Kuhn, 1974, pp. 298–299).

The preference of the authors is to define role [using a] person–behavior matrix. . . . The matrix is composed of a set of behaviors ordered by a set of subjects and a set of behavioral classes. . . . Three segments of the total matrix are of interest because of their generic properties. The *person segment* is a vertical slice through the matrix consisting of all behaviors of a set of subjects. Analogously, the *behavior segment* is a horizontal slice consisting of behaviors of all subjects for a chosen set of behavior classes. Finally, the *person–behavior segment* is a set of behaviors of a selected group of subjects for a chosen set of behavior classes [Thomas & Biddle, B&T, pp. 29–30].

In defense of the preceding quotes, the authors who wrote them were at least struggling with the complex task of defining role concepts. Many examples can be found where authors have apparently abandoned this effort and have chosen to use role terms without explicit definition, often in self-contradictory senses.

Additional confusion appears when authors build questionable assumptions about social conditions into their definitions. Role theorists may assume, for example, that regularities in behavior are "caused" by shared norms that are held by members of the group. Hence, we may find definitions such as: "A social group is a set of two or more persons whose interaction is governed by shared norms." Such a definition appears simple until we ask ourselves how to handle cases when its assumptions about conformity and consensus are not met. What do we term a set of interacting persons whose behaviors are *not* governed by shared norms? Indeed, are we even allowed to think about the behaviors of group members that violate shared norms? Taken at its worst, such an approach overdefines concepts so that they apply only to an idealized form of the phenomenon discussed. For example,

A social group is made up of two or more status-positions, each of which is linked to every other position in the group by role reciprocality which is characterized by recurrent interaction over a period of time and directed toward the attainment of a common goal (Bertrand, 1972, p. 110).

Unfortunately, most of the entities we think of as "social groups" simply do not meet one or more of the assumptions within this definition. Moreover, no simple means are available to us to determine whether the assumptions are or are not met. Such definitions are difficult to apply to real-world events and are nearly impossible to use in research.

It is difficult to gauge the impact of these problems of conceptual and terminological confusion. They are not unique to role theory, of course, but appear throughout the social sciences. On the one hand, lack of clarity makes it difficult to read, understand, and cumulate empirical research from the role field. Moreover, theoretical statements involving role concepts are often obscure. On the other hand, it may be argued that during the formative stage of a discipline there is value in preserving connotative richness so as to suggest new realms of applicability. In addition, despite confusion, role theory also exhibits common interests and concerns. But it may be doubted that such rampant confusion as has characterized the role field to date is really useful. As we move from vagueness toward precision, generalized information, and explicit propositions, surely we must adopt for role theory a single, integrated structure of terms and concepts. Indeed, one task of this book is to offer such a structure.

INADEQUATE FORMALIZATION

A second criticism leveled at role theory is that it lacks propositional organization. Reviewers of role theory have noted that it is difficult to find examples of explicit propositions in the role field, let alone a propositional structure that ties the field together. Exceptions to this generalization may of course be found. Turner (1968) suggested a series of postulates for the role field concerned with the "normal" operation of role processes; Gross, Mason and McEachern (1958) advanced propositions concerned with role conflict resolution; Oeser and Harary (1962, 1964) [B&T, Selection 6] suggested propositions for "structural role theory" in the organization; Foa (1958) [B&T, Selection 40] tested an axiomatic, normative theory for the small group, and so on. And yet, the criticism seems justified in the main. Role theory exhibits the promise of relevance, richness of conceptual structure, and vigor of empirical research—but as yet only a few isolated examples of propositional structure. In Zetterberg's terms (1965), the role field seems a "taxonomy" struggling to become a "theory."

Why should this be so? As was noted earlier, role theory appears relevant to social problems, consequently stress has been given to the use of role concepts for solving those problems by both investigators and funding agencies. Such an emphasis leads to the neglect of basic processes. The concept of a distinct role field may also have been unclear in the minds of some social scientists, consequently they were unable to discriminate its basic issues. It is also true that there is a close relationship between the processes of defining and postulating, and confused thought about the former is not likely to facilitate the latter. Role theory also incorporates several levels of abstraction, and propositions about the individual may be deemed incommensurate with propositions about the group, the society, or social interaction.

Despite these problems, role theory would benefit from formalization of its assumptions and derived ideas. Fromal theory is easier to think about and to check with empirical evidence. Formalization is also necessary if we are to review knowledge or develop explanations for the appearance of regular social events. Let us hope that more efforts to formalize role theory will appear in the next decade.

AMBIVALENCIES

Finally, the role field has also received criticism because of conceptual ambivalencies stemming, in part, from the diverse training of its enthusiasts. Discussions of these ambivalencies may be found in Turner (1965), Thomas (1968), and my introduction to Chapter Five of this book. Let us take up some of these to see what has bothered the critics. For one thing, role theory has been viewed by some as concerned primarily with overt behavior (Davis, 1949), while others have seen it emphasizing covert processes (Newcomb, 1950). Another ambivalency has concerned whether or not role theory should limit itself to the study of phenomena associated with positional membership (Linton, 1936) or whether it is concerned with "any behavior pattern," be it cultural, social, or personal (Warren, 1949). Role phenomena have also been viewed as simply parts to be learned or played (Park, 1927), thus controlled primarily by internal variables (Child, 1963); whereas other authors have considered them to be a way of coping with the roles of others (Turner, 1962) and thus to be controlled in part by the responses of others (Cattell, 1963). If we accept the notion that role behavior is produced in part by covert processes, several other issues appear. Are these covert processes prescriptive, evaluative, or merely anticipatory in mode? Is role a conditioned response (Cottrell, 1942), or are roles associated with purposes, sentiments, and strategy (Parsons, 1942)? If we allow behavior to be controlled by internal processes, how are we to limit this phenomenon; is role theory anything other than an extension of the naive (anthropological) doctrine that individuals are taught their cultural norms and therafter exhibit them (Wrong, 1961)? Worse, can role theory be anything other than an extension of naive (sociological) functionalism that is merely a reification of existing social practices? How can role theory account for the evolution of roles (Turner, 1968), for deviancy, creativity, and the individual (Naegele, 1960)?

About This Book

These last criticisms are serious ones that challenge the basic posture of role theory. It is not my intention to answer them in this chapter; indeed much of the book may be considered to be a discussion of them, and they are considered explicitly at various points in the text. But in general, the posture adopted here will be to accept within role thoery the widest possible range of phenomena that fit comfortably under its conceptual roof. Thus, we will allow within the discussion both behaviors and expectations, both prescriptions and anticipations, both external and internal sources of control, both conformity and deviancy, both cultural similarity and individual differences, both accommodation and social change. As this posture is developed, readers who have prior experience with some portion of role theory may be surprised at the breadth of definitions or discussions offered here. But the alternative to this posture would be to restrict role theory to only a fraction of its range of potential applications—and indirectly to offend other readers who have used its terms in alternate ways.

The book is organized somewhat differently from most texts and monographs in the social sciences. Most texts aim for disciplinary coverage and offer readers a congeries of chapters that deal with independent matters. For example, the psychology text might offer chapters on "traits," "motives," "reinforcement," and "attitudes." Sociology texts offer such titles as "culture," "small groups," and "formal organizations." The chapters of such a text are largely independent of the others, and little effort is made to lace the chapters together. Social science monographs often feature essays on a common problem or discuss various implications of a central idea.

This book faces a quite different task. To date, no serious attempt has been made to provide a conceptual synthesis for the role field. Nevertheless, it should be possible to build for role theory a conceptual structure that is laid out as an integrated entity—and such is the core of this work. The organization of its ideas resembles more a physics text than most books from the social sciences. We begin with a set of basic elements that are crucial to role theory (human beings, their behaviors, their physical features). Though undefined, each of these elements is presumed to be observable, and Chapter Two builds a discussion of social behaviorism based upon simple assumptions concerning these elements. Chapter Three extends this discussion to encompass the role concept. Both chapters concern themselves with overt matters; neither makes assumptions concerning symbols, identities, phenomenal events, consensus, conformity, or other "assumptional baggage." Together they constitute an exercise in discovery, for it is an adventure to see how far we can go in building a role theory upon behavioristic assumptions alone.

Chapter Four makes an additional assumption. In it we take up the concepts of identity and social position. As will be discovered, these concepts take us into the realm of symbols and the relationship of symbols to those events symbolized, a realm that extends beyond behaviorism. At the same time, within Chapter Four it is not yet necessary to construct formal concepts for mind or phenomenal experiences; thus these are not yet allowed into the discussion.

Chapters Five and Six take up expectations and related matters. These chapters not only require that we make assumptions about mind, but in them we also discover that those persons whom we are studying make similar assumptions! Chapter Five covers the formal properties of the expectation concept. Chapter Six takes up ideas that are derived from the expectation concept, such as consensus, conformity, role conflict, and the notion of expected role. As may be appreciated, much of the empirical research of role theory to date has concerned these latter notions.

Chapter Seven concerns the application of role concepts to social system analysis. Once again, additional assumptions are made. Prior to this point in the analysis we were unwilling to grant assumptions about consensus, the association of roles with positions, and the assembly of both into social structures. Now these assumptions are examined, and a number of new concepts are developed.

Chapter Eight concerns individuals and their roles. No additional assumptions are required for the analysis, but a number of empirical propositions are advanced and additional concepts developed. The chapter has several interests: problems of socialization in children and adolescents, the self, love and deviancy, adult roles and role changing, adjustment, and the use of role concepts in therapy and the helping professions.

Finally, Chapter Nine attempts to provide some perspective on the role enterprise. Conceptual weaknesses of role theory are discussed, along with some suggestions for next steps in the development of the field.

ENVOI

Indeed, the proper study of human beings is humanity, and through appropriate means it is possible not only to apply the canons of science to human behavior but also to gain control of the social problems that threaten to overwhelm us. Well, then, why don't we do it? Why don't we fund a mammoth Manhattan District Research Program for the Social Sciences (preferably for role theory) and apply the results of that research to our society?

We have already noted some of the reasons why such a consummation is unlikely at the moment. For one thing, humanity is not only a complex entity, it is also ourselves, and looking in the mirror is a dangerous and anxious business. The collective enterprise of the social sciences is but two generations old, and its status is neither secure among the other sciences nor is it respected in the society at large. Moreover, many social scientists find it easier to pretend that human beings are but analogues of simpler animals, that their ahistorical problems can be solved by examining historical events, or that their phenomenal experiences can be conveniently ignored or modeled in some simple fashion. Even those of us who study human conceptualization are wont to confuse these events with the overt behaviors to which they somehow relate and spend much of our time in conceptual argument or in applicational research rather than in developing the propositional structure that will some day integrate our sciences. Still others who accept designation as social scientists are impatient with the slow pace and "immorality" of scientific investigations among human beings and view their professional jobs as the provoking of social change.

Such well-intentioned persons miss the point. Not only is it possible to build a social science that treats men and women as human beings, but also secure social planning is impossible without the empirically founded propositions such a science can offer. Moreover, role theory exemplifies such an approach. Role theory is but a young science at present—rich in promise and insight, as yet short in integration and basic research. We ignore its problems at our peril. But role theory offers us the potential for studying human beings as sentient, rational beings—and for gaining control of our precarious social existence. It is up to the new generation of young social scientists to solve the problems of role theory and realize its potential.

Chapter Two

The Study of Social Behaviors

Role theory concerns the study of roles, or patterns of behavior that are characteristic of persons and contexts. We begin, therefore, by discussing human behaviors and the other overt events that constitute the core subject matter for the social sciences.

Each of us is only too familiar with examples of behavior in our daily lives. This morning we awoke, dressed, brushed our teeth, and greeted others. Moreover, we watched others behaving too, as members of our families or roommates charmed, sulked, or snarled their ways through breakfast. Each of us is also convinced that beyond his or her immediate experience there exists a rich fabric of behaviors both within our society and elsewhere, for we are provided a daily diet of behavioral reports by word of mouth, books, newspapers, and television. We are also convinced that we know something about how to organize behavioral events. We know from our own experience how to influence others to accommodate our wishes, and we often presume that we could organize social affairs more efficiently than the bunglers who are portrayed on our television screens.

The major difficulty with personal experience is that it is so limited; whereas public information is biased, encapsulated, and sensationalized. Neither source provices truly reliable information concerning behavioral events, their antecedents, and consequences. For these, we must turn to the scientific study of human behavior. And when we do this, all sorts of surprising things turn up. Did you know that:

—Ideational and emotional leadership in small group discussions is usually provided by different persons?

—Eating meals with very young children is often a "disaster," and mothers spend much of their time during the meal disapproving either their children's activities or their children?

—Boys and girls are treated somewhat differently in the classroom, and while American boys (who are exposed to women teachers) do more poorly in reading than do girls, German boys (who are exposed to more men teachers) do better than German girls?

—Many people can be induced to deny the evidence of their senses in a group situation when they hear others testify to "objective facts" that appear to violate their own perceptions?

—Students in smaller high schools participate in twice as many activities as do students in larger high schools?

—Americans can be persuaded to place others who are strangers to themselves in "danger" and "pain" by the simple expedient of telling those Americans authoritatively that they must do so?

—Adolescents spend an average of more than 20 hours per week watching television, hours that used to be spent in reading (among other activities) before the advent of the boob tube?

Findings such as these are unexpected, not because they violate common sense, but rather because we have not thought much about the realms they represent. Each is a product of research on social behavior. Each is concerned with observable facts of social life and not with expectations or other cognitive processes presumed to lie behind or explain those facts. In this chapter and the one following we shall take up the study of the overt events that constitute our social world. In them, moreover, we shall pretend that overt events constitute the sole subject matter of role theory. Whereas in Chapters Five and Six we shall turn to expectations and other covert aspects of role phenomena, here our stance is explicitly and exclusively that of social behaviorism.

Some students who are unfamiliar with behaviorism may be offended that I begin the formal exposition of role theory with this orientation. Some social scientists (such as Dahrendorf, 1958) define their interests so as to exclude the study of behavior or to discuss role concepts strictly in expectational terms. Indeed, for some social scientists the term *behaviorism* is an anathema, since in the hands of some of its proponents (such as Skinner, 1971, 1974), a claim has been advanced that behavioristic concepts are sufficient for a science of human affairs. I shall not make this claim. Rather, it is explicitly denied in Chapter Five—for whenever we make assumptions about expectations we are clearly beyond the realm of behaviorism. However, role theory purports to discuss, predict, and explain the social behavior of human beings. Thus it is vital that we develop a clear vocabulary for discussing this arena of events. It is not less vital that we keep the terms and concepts used for discussing overt behaviors distinct from those used for talking about covert events such as expectations.

But why begin with behaviorism? Why not open the discussion by considering the concept of expectation? I have two reasons for the presentational order. The first is Occam's Razor. A behavioristic theory involves fewer assumptions than an expectational theory. It is surprising how far one can go in the social sciences on a behavioristic basis and how often our concepts of behavior and social processes are muddled because of the excess baggage of mentalistic redundancy.

My second reason concerns presentational logic. Many of our cognitive concepts are modeled after behavioral events, thus they are more easily discussed if the events that constitute their models are first considered. Role theory features an integrated structure of related concepts. Since this is so, we can begin with logically primitive ideas and then proceed to the derivation of more complex notions in simple, step-wise fashion, making clear our assumptions as we go along. If the reader should discover how powerful a tool is the concept of social behavior along the way, so much the better.

BEHAVIOR AND RELATED CONCEPTS

First we look, then we name, and only then do we see.
—Walter Lippman

What is meant when the social scientist says that he or she is "studying behavior"? How do we go about conceptualizing behavior, how do we measure examples of behavior, and how do we differentiate those concepts—and measurements—from the symbols expressed about behavior by citizens who must deal with it in their everyday lives? These are serious questions that have received many answers, not only in the social sciences, but also in philosophy and religion. I shall return shortly to alternate conceptualizations for behavior, but first let us set forth concepts for social behavior that are needed if role theory is to be an empirically based science.

As is true for any science, we begin by discussing primitive elements that are familiar to us through common experience. Three such elements are taken up here: human beings, their physical features, and behaviors.

HUMAN BEINGS

Let us assume that readers share with me experiences of a variety of phenomena that are termed **human beings** (or **persons**, **others**, and **individuals**). The class of phenomena so designated includes both you and me and other examples of the species *Homo sapiens* as well. Let us also assume that readers can recognize human beings when they see them and can differentiate human beings from inanimate phenomena or members of other species, such as dogs or cats.

Although many aspects of human beings can be studied, certain assumptions are normally made about persons in role theory that should be brought to light. For one thing, human beings are presumed to be discrete entities. Role theorists are not normally concerned with the parts of the human organism—with its liver, for example. Judgements made about persons are generally made about persons-as-wholes in role theory. For another, human beings are easy to discriminate from one another and from their environments. A set of persons may be numerated by the simple act of counting with positive integers. Human beings are also individually identifiable, and one can construct sets of persons using any analytic basis that offers a means for identifying persons as individuals. Finally, human beings persist for some time. It is characteristic, for example, to find human beings entering, and then later leaving, the sphere of our observations. Role theorists presume the persistence of human beings and must make special provision for their births and deaths (see Chapter Seven).

PHYSICAL FEATURES

When we observe human beings, we discover two types of phenomena that may be used to differentiate one observed person from another—their features and their behaviors. **Physical features** consist of relatively enduring states of the human organism, such as sex, age, coloration, body build, hairiness, facial contours, states of disability. Features and behaviors are alike in that they are both observable and may be unambiguously assigned to the individual human being who exhibits them. However, they are also distinct in at least four senses. We summarize these first as a series of assumptions commonly made about physical features. (We later take up the obverse of these assumptions in our discussion of behaviors.)

1. Features are slow to change. Because they are based on physiological conditions of the organism, and we have not yet developed a technology that allows us to change our bodily conditions at will, physical features are normally unchanging throughout the lifespan of the person or change only slowly with time.

2. Features are singular. Since they change only slowly, normally we need make but a single measurement in order to determine the sex, body type, or race of a given person. None of these is likely to change by the time of our next observation. Thus, judgements made about persons using any given classification for physical features will be made on a one-to-one basis, one judgement per person.

3. Features are passive and have no intrinsic effects. Although they can be hidden from view by appropriate behavior, physical features cannot be directed toward other persons, nor can they accomplish functions, nor do they deform the environ-

ment nor facilitate or hinder other features or behaviors. Features can, of course, be viewed and responded to by others, but they have no intrinsic implications, as do some behaviors. Reactions to features can reflect only the aesthetics of individual preference and cultural prejudice—despite assumptions that are sometimes made in science fiction about the "innate horror" of bug-eyed monsters.

The preceding three assumptions are strictly observable in their orientation; they refer to aspects of features as overt events. Another assumption is also made about features, however, that refers to their covert antecedence.

4. Features are inadvertent. The person is either presumed to be born with particular physical features or to have developed them through the aging process or prior experiences. These latter are not normally under the individual's control, except for the limiting case of deliberate mutilation or other surgical techniques entered into in order to change features. These experiences, however, are thereafter presumed to result in static or inadvertent conditions. And since features are inadvertent, they are not presumed to have resulted from covert processes now present in the mind of the person. Features are not motivated.

BEHAVIORS

A second type of phenomena associated with human beings are their behaviors. **Behaviors** consist of the relatively transitory, overt activities of human beings, such as bodily motions, speech content and manner, patterns of waking and sleeping, visible reactions to others, accidents such as stepping on another's toes, and neurotic or psychotic acts.

Once again, behaviors and features are presumed to be alike in that they are assignable to individuals and may be observed. However, we make assumptions about behaviors that contrast with those made about features.

1. Behaviors are transitory; they tend to change rapidly with the passage of time. Although some behavior patterns persist in cyclic rhythm for long periods or even for the lifetime of the person—such as cycles of sleeping, eating, breathing, or those associated with "character"—most of the behaviors of interest to us as social scientists change at a rapid pace. When we observe persons in a social context we are often struck by the extraordinary variety of behaviors they exhibit in even a short stretch of time.

2. Behaviors are not singular. Although behaviors are assuredly exhibited by a person, a given behavior may be performed either once or many times by the individual. Whereas it was necessary to make but a single observation in order to determine the person's status with respect to a feature, it is normally necessary to observe the person over some period of time to ascertain the probability of that person exhibiting a class of behaviors in some context. Behaviors are assignable to persons on a many-to-one basis. This is occasionally forgotten by citizens and

social scientists alike. We speak in sloppy fashion of the "number of airline passengers" when what we actually mean is the number of times airline flights were made by persons.

3. Behaviors are active and may have intrinsic effects. In contrast with features, behaviors can be directed toward others, can accomplish functions, can deform the environment, and can facilitate or hinder other behaviors. Indeed, some behaviors (such as a punch in the nose) have immediate and prepotent effects on others. We should not preclude the possibility of aesthetic judgements being made about behaviors, but behaviors have effects that may be observed directly and that exist whether or not the members of the social system are even aware of them.

4. As with features, a fourth assumption is often made concerning the covert antecedence of behavior—some, indeed most, behaviors are advertent. We do not often presume persons to be born with "instincts" or other characteristic patterns of behavior. Rather, we presume that most behaviors result from the operation of internal processes that are, in turn, learned through experience. The person is not, then, the passive vessel through which inherited behaviors are expressed, but rather the individual is conceived as an agent responsible for choosing among behavioral possibilities.

We have not always made this advertent assumption concerning behaviors in Western societies. During earlier centuries the differing behaviors of serfs and gentry were often assumed to reflect instincts. In more recent times, however, we developed a system of laws that presumed not only advertence but also that actions were "intended" by the behaver. This latter concept has, in turn, been challenged from a number of directions. Followers of Dr. Freud tell us of the "unconscious" processes that motivate behavior. Some geneticists are convinced that men inheriting an extra Y chromosome are more prone to violence. Ethologists argue that some inborn behavioral tendencies may have developed in the prehistory of human groups through Darwinian selection. School psychologists (and some British intellectuals) are convinced of the immutability of intelligence as a general capacity for adaptive behavior. Nazi ideologues were convinced that Jews inherited "undesirable traits" of behavior, and racial bigots argue for the "innate inferiority" of those with another skin color. Such exceptions run counter to the usual optimistic assumption made in the West that human affairs can be improved. At least some of them are presumably rationalizations for questionable social policies—such as racial segregation or the rigid tracking of pupils in schools.

The broad concepts of behavior and physical feature do not, of course, exhaust the realm of characteristics that may be associated with persons. In Chapter Four, when we turn to the classification of identities with which persons may be associated, other characteristics are adduced that are associated with the use of symbols. However, each of these latter is based on either behavioral or featural evidence. Indeed, much of this chapter and the material in the next two is but an extended set of deductions following from the assumptions set forth in this section.

Facets and the Measurement of Behavior

Behaviors are existential events, like stars and mountains and atomic explosions, and if we are to study them as scientists we must conceptualize them in such a way that they may be measured empirically. In so doing we run into problems. First, we must establish what aspects of behavior we are to study. When investigating stars, for example, the astronomer may measure their light, motion, temperature, or variability. In like manner, when examining a verbal discourse, the social scientist must decide whether to examine emphasis, warmth, syntax, manner, or other aspects. It turns out that there are many aspects of human behavior that can be studied, and social scientists have by no means agreed with one another over the basic catalogue of aspects that should be emphasized (Weick, 1968). Moreover, many of the concepts presently used for this purpose overlap concepts used by other investigators.

Second, it turns out that behaviors do not occur as discrete entities but flow and merge into other behaviors from which we would like to distinguish them. For example, it would be convenient if we could separate behaviors that were harsh from those that were loving. But it may turn out that the mother's instruction to her son begins by being harsh and then eases into being loving. Astronomers are lucky in that they deal with point entities (stars). Geologists and social scientists face a more difficult task, because the events with which they are concerned merge into one another.

Third, it is difficult to think about behavior without making assumptions about processes that are presumed to have caused behavior to happen. An action may be described as hostile, or motivated, but if we make such a judgement we are also implying something about the covert processes that lie behind the action.[1] Again, to judge a behavior as deviant or creative suggests that we share a standard against which such a judgement can be made. The only difficulty is that social scientists differ from one another on the assumptions they wish to make about the antecedents of behaviors.

At present, then, the social sciences offer us many concepts for studying behavior. Unfortunately, these overlap in meaning and in the assumptions they make concerning etiology. Further, many of them are difficult to apply to actual examples of

---

[1] Heider (1958) argues that it is difficult or impossible to perceive a behavior without making an assumption about the "intent" of its performer, and a similar assumption appears in common law. Although this may be a general tendency in our individualistic and achievement-oriented society, I will argue in this chapter that judgements can be made overt characteristics of behavior without involving ourselves with intent.

behavior, owing to the lack of discrete boundaries of behavioral events. This confused state of affairs cannot last forever, and there are signs of the appearance of order amid the confusion. One positive sign has been the development of the facet concept by Guttman (1954) and Foa (1965). Although the concept of facet is a general one applicable to all forms of measurement, its major use to date has been in the measurement of social behavior, and we will build our discussion of behavioral measurement around it.

FACETS

A **facet** is a scale or a set of categories that provides a tool for judging examples of behavior for some aspect they exhibit.[2] Suppose I wanted to discriminate verbal behaviors addressed to a target person for their degree of warmth. One way to do it would be to set up three categories into which behaviors might be sorted: warm behaviors in which the target person was addressed with positive euphemisms (such as "dear" or "honey"), neutral behaviors in which no form of address was provided for the target person, and cold behaviors in which a negatively loaded form of address was provided (such as "jerk" or "idiot"). Such a set of categories constitutes a facet for the measurement of target-address behavior, since it is formed from a mutually exclusive set of categories measuring but one aspect of behavior, and since we should be able to assign all examples of target-address behavior to the categories with reliability.

The fact that various facets may be chosen for studying behaviors means that behavioral measurement is in part arbitrary. Some social theorists have suggested that we confine our attention to facets that are socially meaningful. For Parsons and Shils (1951) "actions" are those behaviors that are oriented to the attainment of ends and are normatively regulated, whereas for Mead (1934) and Blumer (1969) the meaning of an act is indicated by the response of others to it and is a product of social interaction. In defense of this restriction, one notes that insight may be gained about why persons behave and respond by considering the facets they use for conceptualizing their own and others' behaviors. However, in the final analysis, such a restriction is not necessary. In fact, we may discover all sorts of useful things about behavior by considering facets that are not commonly thought about. Moreover, once we have conceptualized a facet, there is nothing at all arbitrary in the judgements we make about examples of behavior using that tool. Once we have decided to judge target-address behaviors for their warmth (for example), objective,

---

[2] In formal terms, a facet consists of a set of two or more categories into which events may be mapped, together with a mapping rule such that: (*a*) all examples of the events being studied may be mapped unambiguously into one and only one of the categories; (*b*) the mapping rule derives from a single, underlying aspect that conceptualizes some characteristic of the events being mapped; and (*c*) any two facets used for mapping the same events have conceptually independent mapping rules and aspects.

replicable, valid judgments may presumably be made about any such behavior for this quality.

The concept of facet is but a generalization of the common notion in the social sciences usually denoted by such terms as *variable, characteristic, dimension,* or *parameter*. Some consist of an interval scale (such as judgements made about "loudness"). Some are merely nominal classifications (such as judgements made about the identity of the speaker). Each facet measures but one aspect of behavior, and if we are to measure another aspect we must use an additional facet. To assess adequately the meaning of even a single behavior may require the employment of numerous facets.

The formal measurement of behavior, then, requires that we use one or more facets for judging observed behavioral events. In general, these facets must have been conceptualized and tested in prior research for us to accept their evidence as valid. If you like, we might think of formal research on behavior as going through three stages. In stage one, a concept is suggested that might be used for measuring behaviors. In stage two, the concept is expressed in the form of a facet and is found to be reliable. In stage three, the facet is used for measuring examples of behavior. Stages one and two are requisite before stage three can take place. Concepts for behavior must be developed before facet construction is possible, and the conceptualization of new concepts for behavior is an act of creativity. However, each concept proposed must also be operationalized, for if it turns out that we cannot make reliable judgements about behavior using that concept, no facet has appeared no matter how attractive was the original concept.

Several forms of facets may be recognized. As was suggested above, some facets consist of a set of nominal alternatives, some of ordered categories, and some even of interval or ratio scales. The simplest of all facets appear in our common language and consist of two verbal categories into which behaviors may be sorted—absence versus presence of the aspect discussed. ("I was *not* nasty just then." "You were *too* nasty." "I was *not*." "You were *too*.") Facets may also be sorted into two classes, those that contain a *vacuous alternative* (or *basket category*) which handles behaviors that cannot otherwise be judged within the facet, and those that do not. For example, a facet consisting of the three alternatives "movement toward," "not moving," and "movement away," consists of only meaningful alternatives. If we add to it a fourth alternative, "behaviors that cannot be judged for movement," we have created a facet with a vacuous alternative.

BEHAVIORAL MEASUREMENT

In order to study behavior, indeed even to speak of examples of behavior, we must map examples of behavior into facets. If we map but a single example of behavior into a facet, this means merely that we have selected the category into which that behavior fits. However, when we map a variety of behaviors into a facet, we thereby create a *distribution* consisting of the frequencies of behavioral mappings for each category of the facet. From examining such distributions we are able to assess the modal category for a particular set of behaviors or the range of behavioral alternatives exhibited. In such a fashion, the facet provides us with an operational measure of how the behaviors in which we are interested stack up against the aspect we have chosen for study.

It is difficult to overstress the importance of this process of mapping, indeed all techniques for measuring behavior used in the social sciences are based on it. Whenever the content analyst constructs a code for tabulating the number of lexical or content elements in a document, he or she is building a facet. Common scales for measuring attitudes, such as those of Guttman or Likert, constitute facets. Helson's investigations of adaptation level (1964) made use of facets that were constructed by the respondent, as did Kilpatrick and Cantril's (1960) research with "self-anchoring scales." Scores earned on achievement tests constitute a facet, as do ratings given on scales of maturity, adjustment, or interest inventories. Precategorized instruments for behavioral observation usually involve facets, as for instance does that of Bales (1950) [also see B & T, Selection 29]. However, some instruments used for behavioral observation do not constitute facets because their underlying aspect is not clear (see, for example, Flanders, 1970) or because several different aspects are used to construct the category sets in different portions of the scale (Smith, Meux, Coombs, & Nuthall, 1964). It is difficult to know what to make of findings reported for instruments that are not composed of facets, and presumably these will be abandoned as we learn more about studying social behavior.

Those interested in studying the behaviors that appear in a new context often begin by seeking to apply to them facets that had been found useful in other contexts. For example, by the mid-1950s social psychologists had developed various facets for observing behaviors in small discussion groups. Some of these same investigators, then, attempted to apply the same facets to studies of classroom behavior. In so doing, they discovered that facets applicable in one context might not be applicable at all elsewhere. For scientific purposes, facets are most useful when they generate a behavioral distribution across more than a single category, less useful when they generate a nonvacuous distribution in but a single category, and quite useless when they merely generate a vacuous distribution. (A classification for bananas is most useful when we have several types of bananas, less useful if but one type of banana is encountered, and utterly useless if we have only stringbeans, onions, cabbages, and scallions.) Unfortunately, some social scientists fall in love with their measuring tools and persist in applying them in contexts where they are not useful. ("Yes, we have no bananas.")

Where do the underlying aspects that generate facets for the study of behaviors come from? Whence cometh a Sigmund Freud, a Max Weber, a Kurt Lewin? Although a detailed answer to this question would involve us in the psychology of creativity, the conceptualization of new facets appears to be more likely when the investigator "wallows in data" and works closely with the basic, behavioral phenomena with which he or she is concerned. Recent creativity in conceptualizing new behavioral facets may be observed in the works of Barker and Wright (1955), Chomsky (1965), Goffman (1961b, 1967), and Smith and Geoffrey (1968).

The concept of facet, then, provides us with a basic tool needed for the study of behaviors, and from here onward when I speak of *behaviors* it should be understood that my reference is to their mappings in one or more facets as well as to the raw phenomena that produced those mappings. Given a facet, we can study a behavior set to establish how those behaviors "stack up" in terms of the aspect expressed by the facet. However, there is nothing in the concept of facet which guarantees that a given facet will generate other than vacuous distributions when assessed against a given set of behaviors.

Before leaving the subject of facets we should take a last look at the use of this concept for the study of features. Categorical systems that express variations in sex, age, and race also constitute facets. However, featural distributions are simpler than behavioral distributions. Featural distributions normally consist of only one observation per subject (since features do not change). Not so behavioral distributions. A single person may exhibit various behaviors during our period of observation, so the number of observations in a behavior distribution may be larger than the number of persons studied.

Problems with the Concept of Behavior

As with other major concepts in the role field, the notion of behavior has generated controversies and confusion. We review some of these briefly in the form of questions.

1. Are behaviors always overt? Some psychologists use phrases such as "covert action" or "internal behavior" to refer to presumed thought processes taking place in the person that stand behind his or her actions. While not denying others the right to use the term *behavior* in this way, such usage is specifically avoided here. For this book behavior refers only to overt activities, events that can be observed by trained personnel and usually also by others in contact with those who behave.[3]

2. Are behaviors fit subjects for scientific inquiry? Challenges to study of behavior have appeared from several sources. Some physical scientists, noting that human behavior is evanescent and multifaceted, have concluded that it is useless to study such phenomena, hence that the social sciences are a fraud. At a more sophisticated level, some philosophers suggest that the act of studying behavior is

---

[3]Concerned about this problem, Thomas and Biddle [B & T, Chapter III], used the term *performance* in their discussion of behavior. But the term *behavior* has wider acceptance outside of psychology.

itself a form of behavior—and that the social sciences are logically akin to such chimeras as perpetual motion machines. Those who preach free will have found the study of behavior offensive, for it suggests that behaviors might be determined by causes other than those emanating from within the individual (which, indeed, is obiously the case from time to time). Finally, other philosophers, concerned with the development of social perception, have doubted that evidence for the independent existence of social behavior exists apart from the shared facets with which we approach behaviors in our (necessarily biased) social science community. To all of these well-intentioned critics let us reply that human behaviors are among the most pressing and obvious of events, and although they are complex, their complexity is no greater than that of many physical phenomena. Moreover, although we cannot expect behaviors to generate the aspects with which we shall study them, once a facet has been suggested we surely can observe whether or not it applies to the behaviors in question. It certainly was true that before the vocabularies of the social sciences existed it was more difficult to study behavior, but this is true for the phenomena of any science.

3. Why bother to study behavior? One recurring controversy in the social sciences concerns whether it is reasonable to study human behavior at all or whether we should concentrate our efforts on how behavior is conceptualized and reacted to by persons. For the phenomenologist, behaviors may be merely the nonmeaningful, raw stimuli to which human beings are exposed; and for an appreciation of why individuals act the way they do it is necessary to appreciate their symbolic reconstructions of those stimuli. In contrast, it is here presumed that human behaviors are meaningful events in and of themselves and that a profitable study can be made of them and their effects. Moreover, since role theory concerns relationships among both overt events (behaviors) and covert events (expectations), it is necessary to establish means for conceptualizing and studying both realms in order to establish these relationships.

4. How are we to go about studying behavior? For many social scientists the appropriate way to study behavior is to ask people about it. For anthropologists of an earlier age, behavior was conceptualized as the culture of a society and was discoverable through interviewing informants concerning the beliefs, values, and norms they held and assigned to others in the society. Sociologists, too, have often presumed that untrained citizens were capable of reflecting behavior accurately in their reports, expectations, or attitudes. Sometimes this belief is even verbalized,[4] but often it is merely assumed when a questionnaire or interview schedule is drawn up in the hope that subject reports of behavior will be equivalent to the actual behaviors they purport to mirror. Surely it cannot be denied that when a respondent

---

[4]Soles (1964), for example, has suggested that "an index designed to measure role expectations . . . is assumed to give a somewhat better than chance prediction of actual role behavior." See also Getzels (1958) or Sorenson, Husek, and Yu (1963).

answers a question we have asked, he or she is "behaving." We may, in fact, be interested in his performance as a respondent—whether he uses good grammar, whether he stammers, whether he speaks with emphasis, whether he answers our questions or engages in evasion. But if we move beyond these interests and accept the "content" of his statement about behavior as equivalent to the behavior it references we are on slippery grounds. To make such a naive assumption is to presume that Baron Munchausen was an honest man or that one should take political propaganda at its face value—but perhaps the latter is now water over the gate.

The position taken in this book is a simple one. *The best way to study behavior is to observe it*; and if we are to measure behavior, this means that we must train ourselves to classify examples of observed behaviors into well-conceptualized facets. Reports given by those whom we study—whether1made *in situ* or given in response to questions or interviews—represent the phenomenal world of that person. Such reports are interesting in their own right, and many matters of concern to us are best approached through their study (as we shall see in Chapter Five), but whether or not they relate to the real world of behaviors is a matter for empirical investigation.

It should not be contended, however, that the observation of behavior is a simple task. Careful studies of behavior usually involve the use of both recording techniques and formal coding systems. In addition, behavioral events often occur with surprising rapidity, and we can choose from a literally endless choice of facets for their observation. Moreover, even the choice of behavioral units for observation is still an open question. Are we to observe gestures, sentences, interactive "moves," strategic postures, or even units of multiperson behavior such as group activities? These issues are too complex to be entered into here, although they are discussed elsewhere (e.g., Weick, 1968, Dunkin & Biddle, 1974). However, to repeat, the best way to study behavior is to observe it.

THE COMPARING AND LINKING OF BEHAVIORS

> *Civilization is nothing else but the attempt to reduce force to being a last resort.*
>
> *—Ortega y Gasset*

A single measurement of behavior is of little intrinsic interest. After all, of what use is it to us to know that Alice Smith eats cold cereal for breakfast? It is only when such data are related to other types of events that they become interesting. How then are we to relate behaviors to one another and to other events? This topic is explored in the next four sections of this chapter, which discuss behavioral comparability, behavioral effects, behavioral linkage, and complex linking concepts for behaviors.

Comparability of Behaviors

The existence of a system of facets for mapping behaviors also provides us with a method for comparing behaviors with one another. Let two behaviors (or any other events) be mappable into a given facet. Provided that both are mapped nonvacuously in the facet, we will say that they are **comparable** (for that facet). If they should have exactly the same, nonvacuous mapping in that facet, we will say that they are **identical** (for that facet). Should they have nonidentical mappings that are insignificantly different from one another (in statistical terms), we will say that they are **similar** (for that facet). If their mappings are significantly different, although still nonvacuous, we will say that they are **distinct** for that facet. The fact that two behaviors may be comparable, similar, or even identical for a given facet does not mean that they are even comparable for another facet.

Let us take some examples. A sneeze and an exclamation of "ouch" are comparable for the facet measuring *loudness*. They are, however, noncomparable for a facet indicative of *pain expressed*, for only the "ouch" has a nonvacuous mapping into such a facet. If we were to utilize a decibel meter—one measuring the loudness of tones—we might discover that the sneeze and the "ouch" had identical, similar, or distinct measurements for loudness. If the measurements turned out to be similar we would want some sort of criterion to tell us how close they had to be before we would consider them identical and how far apart they would have to get before we would consider them distinct. I shall pass on this question for the moment, although we return to it in the discussion of consensus in Chapter Six. For now, it is merely assumed that we will have some statistical criterion, appropriate to the scale upon which the alternatives of the facet are displayed, with which we can make a discrimination of this sort. It should also be noted that when the facet consists of but nominal alternatives, the judgement of similarity cannot be made.

Let us now expand the notion of similarity so that it cuts across a number of facets. Two or more events will be said to **correspond** if their mappings in an arbitrarily chosen set of facets are either similar or identical. Technically, their correspondence is limited to the facets we have chosen for examination; in other facets they may or may not correspond. If events do not correspond, they are said to be **differentiated** (for the facets chosen). Various types of events may be compared for correspondence: behaviors, physical features, roles, functions, contexts, sanctions, and others. For example, if two roles are to correspond, then the majority of their characteristic behaviors must also correspond (see Chapter Three). It turns out that many other terms are used by social scientists as synonyms for *correspondence*, depending on the types of events that are compared. For example, overt characteristics of persons, such as their behaviors or features, are often said to be **uniform** if they correspond. Thus it would not be strange to hear such statements as "The soldiers were all doing push-ups in a uniform fashion," or "All their children had hair of a uniform color." Additional synonyms for correspondence will be given in Chapter Six.

The Effects of Behavior

One of the difficulties in discussing social behaviors is that behavioral events may be related to two different persons—the person who exhibits the behavior and the other upon whom it impinges. Of these two relationships, only the first is provided for by definition. (It is almost impossible to observe behavior without also observing the person who did the behaving.) The second relationship, that between the behavior and the other upon whom it impacts, requires exploration.

BEHAVIORAL PRESENCE

In general, there are three conditions of **behavioral impact** that are discriminated in the social sciences. Each of these appears in definitions of more complex concepts, and each is based upon a model of observable events. The first and weakest condition is that of **behaviors occurring in the presence of another**. If the other is physically present, in the room or close to the person who is behaving, we conclude that the other is capable of acquiring knowledge of the person's behavior, whether or not he or she actually does so. Under this weak condition, we say that the other is an **audience** for the behavior. It should also be noted that features also occur in the presence of others, thus the other can also be an audience for featural display. It is necessary for behaviors to occur in the presence of others before we can ask others to respond to those behaviors, even to the point of telling us how they perceive those behaviors.

BEHAVIORAL DIRECTION

A second and stronger condition of effect is that of behavioral direction. Sometimes a person is observed to "cast" his or her behaviors toward one or more others, in which case we shall speak of **behaviors directed toward another**. Speakers may address only a few others among a larger assembly; whispers are intended only for the person whose ear is at hand; mothers often insist that children who are not addressed "mind their own business." Behavioral direction is here assumed an observable characteristic of behavior and not one of actor intent. If we cannot observe that the behavior has been directed toward some specific other or others, there is no directionality to the behavior, regardless of the intent of the actor.

Those persons to whom a behavior is directed constitute the **target** for the behavior; features cannot, of course, be directed.[5]

BEHAVIORAL EFFECT

The third and strongest condition is that of **behaviors affecting another**, who is then referred to as the **recipient** of the behavior. Under this third condition, the other is known to have "received" the behavior and to that extent at least to have been affected by it. But under what conditions would we judge behavioral recipience? Certainly not all behaviors occurring in the presence of others nor even those directed toward targets are received by the other. Upon what grounds would we judge that behaviors had been "received"?

Three conditions for concluding recipience have appeared in the literature. First, if the other volunteers a report of perceptual awareness of the behavior, here termed a **recognition response**, we tend to judge behavioral recipience. To have a subject volunteer that he or she has observed the same behavior we have also seen is an "unlikely" event, unless he or she had in fact encountered that stimulus. However, in extreme, experimental conditions, where the number of behavioral alternatives has been reduced and subjects have been told what to look for, this criterion is somewhat less useful. If the subject, for example, were given the task of discriminating between only two behavioral alternatives, and the discrimination required considerable acuity, we might expect errors of reporting to occur.

Second, we also judge behavioral recipience if the behavior involved is prepotent. **Prepotent behaviors** (or other stimuli) are those whose force is so great that we presume that no human being receiving them and having normal faculties can be other than aware of them. In formal terms, a prepotent behavior is a member of a behavioral class that has in the past elicited similar recognition responses from a wide variety of persons regardless of context. Examples of prepotent behaviors include shouting loudly at another who is close-by, punching the other in the nose, stroking the other's forehead, or the provision of universally desired goods to the other. Once again, judgements made about behavioral recipience on the basis of prepotency have their limitations. If the other is deaf or blind, or if he or she is psychotic or severely distracted, it is possible that even a prepotent behavior may be passed over.

[5]The concepts of actor, target, and audience constitute only a fraction of the transitory behavioral roles that can be observed in face-to-face interaction. Many are unique to a specific context: "emotional leadership" appears in discussion groups, "teacher's pet" in the classroom, and so forth. Other transitory roles may be discriminated in many contexts. For example, we sometimes find that a speaker addresses one target person but keeps an eye on a second "indirect target" who is also supposed to receive the message; or again, two interactors may put on an impromptu performance for the entertainment of others. Such transitory roles have received little study to date (however, see Goffman, 1961b).

Third, behavioral recipience is also judged if the other provides a **behavioral response**, that is alters his or her subsequent behavior in such a way that it is reasonable to presume recipience. This third condition, in turn, breaks down into several alternatives.

1. Some behavioral responses are *reflexive* and inadvertent, such as blinking or ducking from a thrown ball.

2. Some responses are so constrained by situational alternatives as to be *unambiguous*. For example, when the batter strikes at a pitched ball, it is reasonable to presume that he or she has been affected by the behavior of the pitcher in throwing it.

3. Still other responses are *probabilistic*. Depending upon context or the state of the other's digestion, the other "may" respond in such-and-such a way.

Establishing a probabilistic relationship between behavior and response requires research. We must examine various examples of behaviors similar to the one in question to see how likely it is that they will be followed by responses of the given sort and what contextual features affect this contingency. If it is likely that a response of the given type will be elicited by this behavior, and if no other stimulus change is present that would reasonably have elicited the response, then we conclude that the other has been affected. For example, the farm manager calls to his taciturn, hired hand that the latter should grease the tractor that afternoon. No immediate response from the hand. Did he receive the message? We watch him and observe that he is kicking clods of dirt out of his path. We have observed in the past that he does this when annoyed over an order given him by the manager. But this was the only time the manager has spoken to him this morning; *ergo*, recipience has taken place.

From the foregoing discussion it would appear that judging behavior for its recipience by others is a risky business. In actual situations of interaction we are usually presented with a multitude of cues telling us whether behaviors have been received by the other or not. The mother tells her teen-age son to "clean up your room, immediately." Her son says, "I did—last week," and then ambles off in the general direction of his room. We conclude that recipience has taken place because there was both a recognition response and a behavioral response. In passing, features can also generate recognition or behavioral responses. Behaviors in an all-male group will often change sharply upon the appearance of a woman in the company, blacks may be treated differently from whites, and so on. We do not often theorize about the effects of features, however, possibly because features themselves do not change and cannot respond to anything. (A feature can be a stimulus, but not a response.)

Behavioral Linkage

In the previous section we were concerned with the impact of behavior upon the other; whether the other was in a position to observe, whether he or she was a target of behavior, whether or not he or she was affected by it. We now extend this discussion to the relationship between the behavior of the person and the behavior of the other, or **behavioral linkage**. In formal terms, two behaviors are said to be *linked* if the performance of the first affects the probability of the performance of the second. In the previous section we discovered that probabilistic linkage was but one criterion we might use for judging behavioral recipience. Now we turn this problem around and look at behavioral linkage per se. Before leaving it, however, let us note two things about the definition of linkage. First, behavioral linkage is defined as a one-way process. Nothing whatsoever is said about the possible effects of the behavior of the other upon subsequent behavior by the person. Second, if the person's behavior alters the probability of behavioral elicitation in the other, it must either increase or decrease that probability. As we will see, the twin phenomena of enabling and disabling have generated separate and opposed terms for various forms of linkage.

FACILITATION[6]

Facilitation occurs when one behavior affects another by means of environmental manipulation. Alexander the Great (presumably) facilitated Diogenes' observations by moving his shadow. The assembly line worker facilitates another's behavior by placing the nut that is next to be tightened. The hod carrier facilitates the mason by bringing the latter his bricks, etc. In those cases where one behavior increases the probability of another we will speak of *facilitation*, where the probability is decreased it is common to speak of *hindrance*.

In the preceding discussion the concept of environmental manipulation is undefined. Throughout this book I have given little attention to concepts having only peripheral usefulness to the role orientation, such as those of real time and space. To treat these in detail would be to open a can of worms, although environmental concepts, for example, would have to appear in a complete social science. However, if we are to define environmental manipulation formally it is necessary to introduce minimal notions of the physical world.

Let us assume that our physical world includes any number of disjoint **environmental units** that are presumed to have the following (logically primitive) properties:

---

[6]In Thomas and Biddle [B & T, Chapter II] the term *facilitation* was used for the concept I have here termed *linkage*.

(*a*) they are *locatable* in the Euclidean three-dimensional space we inhabit; (*b*) they may be *deformed* (special cases of which include their assembly and destruction); (*c*) persons can move or deform them through their behaviors; and (*d*) deforming them or shifting their locations can affect the probability of subsequent behaviors in others.

At this point in the discussion we place no further restrictions on the concept of environmental unit (although later we will do so). For example, there is nothing in the definition that precludes the use of a human being as an environmental unit. Human beings can surely be deformed or moved, and behaviors of a person can be affected by such actions just as they can be by deforming or moving a nonhuman object. To illustrate, it has been known for years that behaviors of persons are affected by the presence of an audience, a phenomenon termed *social facilitation* by Floyd Allport (1924). Again, when young men and women of different ethnic groups are made proximal, love and intermarriage result. For members of an older generation this may appear a tragedy, and some parents go to great lengths to remove their adolescent offspring from the vicinity of tempting but "inappropriate" young persons of the opposite sex.

Given the concept of environmental unit it is possible to define facilitation formally. A given behavior **facilitates** or **hinders** another behavior if it relocates or deforms an environmental unit in such a way as to raise or lower the probability of eliciting the latter. Placing crayons in the hands of young children raises the probability of walls being drawn upon; selling guns to the public facilitates murder. As defined, facilitation is a one-way process. Few would argue that drawing on the walls by children brings on the purchase of crayons. However, some *have* argued that murder also brings on the purchase of handguns. Thus, it is possible to discover behaviors of the person and the other so that they facilitate one another. For example, we occasionally read in the literature that the husband and wife's behaviors were "mutually facilitative." Applying the above definition, we conclude that some of the husband's behaviors manipulated their mutual environment in such a way as to facilitate the wife's behaviors, and vice versa. A special case of mutual facilitation is provided by some multiperson machine systems. For example, two men on the opposite ends of a long, cross-cut saw are capable of mutual facilitation or hindrance, depending on whether or not they can pull in alternating rhythm.

Extensive research has now been carried out on facilitation under the aegis of engineering and industrial psychology, and a good deal is now known concerning the effects of noise, vibration, illumination, and other environmental characteristics on human behavior (Alluisi & Morgan, 1976). Studies of facilitation in interactive contexts are harder to find, possibly because it seems so "obvious" that a person can affect another through environmental means. Studies of social facilitation have appeared regularly, however, possibly because it seems "strange" that a person's behavior would be affected by the mere presence of an audience. Some of these studies have found the audience to hinder behavior, others have found it facilitative. In an influential review, Zajonc (1965) concluded that the learning of new responses was impaired and the performance of previously learned tasks was enhanced through provision of an audience.

REWARD

The concept of reward provides us with a second type of behavioral linkage. In contrast with facilitation, rewards are presumed on a basis of behavioral prepotency. Thus we know (from whatever source) that candy is a reward for the child and that spanking is a punishment (or a "cost," to use another term). Formally, the definitions of reward and punishment depend on our being able to discriminate two types of prepotent stimuli, those that reliably elicit the recognition responses of *pleasure* (such as smiles, or statements such as "good" or "yum") from those of *pain* (such as frowns or "ouch"). Prepotent stimuli (including behaviors) that elicit responses of the former type are termed **rewards**, whereas those eliciting the latter are termed **punishments.**[7]

The relationship between rewards and punishments and their defining criterion responses is also that of a behavioral linkage. However, as was not true for the concept of facilitation, in reward we presume the behavioral linkage of prepotency regardless of whether a recognition response is obtained in the specific instance or not. For example, we presume that candy rewards the child even when the child does not crack a smile when given it. This presumption is equivalent to our assuming that motivational forces are operating in the child regarding candy, whether or not he or she reveals those forces to us via recognition response. Thus, while facilitation is mediated through environmental manipulation, rewards and punishments are assumed to be induced through motivation.

Needless to say, motivational assumptions are upsetting to the convinced behaviorist, and it is not surprising to find authors such as Skinner (1957) and Premack (1962) inveighing against the use of reward and punishment concepts or going to some lengths to avoid their use. But there is a stronger reason for regarding the reward notion as suspect. To assume, for example, that praise is always to be classified as a reward leads us into difficulties when attempting to account for the behavior of "pathological" individuals who react negatively to instances in which they are being praised. In fact, it is difficult to find stimulus classes to which human beings always react with signs of pleasure or aversion.

This difficulty has led some investigators to substitute concepts of positive and

[7]This discussion is not meant to preclude further differentiation of recognition responses or of prepotent stimuli; indeed, various additional classifications have been suggested for them. Foa and Foa (1971), for example, suggest the differentiation of rewards into six categories: love, status, information, service, money, or goods. However, the basic differentiation of rewards from punishments is made widely in the role literature.

negative reinforcement for reward and punishment (see the following section on reinforcement). However, the reinforcement concept too has its shortcomings, and there is little evidence of acceptance of the reinforcement doctrine outside of those who have been trained in experimental psychology. Perhaps this is because—as is true for so many concepts in role theory—the concepts of reward and punishment are modeled after beliefs that are widespread in Western societies. Thus, the mother spanks her child because she "knows" that this is a punishment; the instructor "knows" that a good grade will reward the pupil; and an American President "knows" that bombing will punish the North Vietnamese. And each person who delivers such a reward or punishment believes firmly that it will have a salubrious effect on the other, that a hoped-for behavioral change will take place.[8] How often are we surprised with such assumptions? It would appear to depend on the sophistication of our choice of rewards and punishments. Only the very innocent person believes that if—as in the Western morality play—we beat up villains they will either die or recant their villainy.

An enormous mass of research has now been conducted on the effects of rewards and punishments on human behavior. Not surprisingly, much of this research shows that persons will choose behavior that tends to maximize rewards and minimize punishments. However, unrestrained pursuit of immediate gratification would lead to a war of all against all. Thus, human beings also develop rules for the distribution of rewards and punishments in social situations as well as notions concerning the equitable distribution of gratifications. These latter processes have interesting implications, and theories concerning them have been suggested by several investigators (Adams, 1963; Blau, 1964; Homans, 1961; Thibaut & Kelley, 1959). Research stimulated by these theories appears under several terms, *equity*, *social exchange*, *distributive justice*—and good summaries of the effort may be found in Berkowitz and Walster (1976) and Walster, Berscheid, and Walster (1973).

REINFORCEMENT

The awkward assumptions involved in the concept of reward have suggested to some psychologists that another linking concept be proposed in which observed stimulus-response linkages are designated. We review this usage now.

We have already discussed the concept of behavioral response. A response is said to occur when a stimulus appears (which might be, for our purposes, either a behavior or a physical feature of a person) and there is subsequent alteration in the behavior of the other such that we presume recipience by the latter. We have also

---

[8]The application of rewards or punishments to another "in order to change his or her behavior" constitutes an act of sanctioning and is discussed in more detail later in the chapter.

discussed various types of responses: those that are reflexive, those unambiguous, and those that are probabilistic. For the latter, it was pointed out that we establish relationships between the stimulus and response by observing a class of similar stimuli and a class of responses in a known or controlled context to determine the probability of behavioral elicitation or suppression.

Let us now clothe these concepts with additional terms. Let us presume that we have ruled out any possibility that a class of stimuli exhibited by the person either facilitates or hinders a class of responses exhibited by the other. Nevertheless, the former are known to affect the probable appearance of the latter. Under these conditions, we will say that the former **reinforces** the latter.[9] (For purposes of this definition, I shall also assume that reflexive and unambiguous responses are merely probabilistic responses that have high probability.) As with other linkage concepts, it is also common to distinguish among those reinforcing stimuli that increase, and those that decrease, the probability of the other's response. The former are termed **positive reinforcers**, the latter **negative reinforcers**. As an example, we observe several instances of quarreling between a man and his wife. In time, we discover that comments by the wife concerning her husband's mother and sarcasm by the husband concerning his wife's housekeeping abilities are both likely to provoke anger. In contrast, reference by the wife to her husband's gentleness or by the husband to his wife's smart dressing are likely to reduce anger. In this case, the former are positive reinforcers, the latter are negative reinforcers, for the response of anger.

What is the relationship between the concepts of reward and reinforcement? As the preceding example illustrates, the relationship is not really a close one. For one thing, reinforcement is defined to be situationally specific. Those stimuli that reinforce one person positively may reinforce another negatively and provoke no response at all in a third. For another, many behaviors that turn out to reinforce responses in another would not normally be considered to constitute rewards or punishments. Worse, in some contexts a reward or punishment may turn out to have quite an unexpected effect in reinforcement (as when the teacher discovers, to his or her despair, that repeated punishing of a given pupil for misbehavior is only stimulating more of the same). This suggests yet another aspect of the reinforcement concept. As we know, it is necessary to specify a criterion response before we are able to make a judgement about whether a reinforcing stimulus is positive or negative. As it turns out, we may not approve the appearance of some responses (such as anger or disruptive behavior by pupils) and may wish to reduce them. This may involve either the reduction of positive reinforcers or the increasing of negative

---

[9]Those with psychological background will recognize that this discussion is confined to *operant* conditioning. *Classical* conditioning concerns associations among stimuli and is less relevant to role theory (except, perhaps, to the learning of expectations—see Chapter Five).

reinforcers for that response. Or, to make matters worse, it may involve reinforcing another response that precludes the one we wish to extinguish. Each of these strategies has advantages and disadvantages (Bandura, 1969).

There are at least three difficulties with the concept of reinforcement. First, many persons are confused about the relationships between reward and reinforcement. These confusions are abetted by the use of such terms as "primary reinforcement" or "positive control" as synonyms for the use of reward. As can be seen, the concepts of reward and positive reinforcement are independently defined. Both are legitimate, but findings for one should not be confused with findings for the other. (Nor should we confuse negative reinforcement with punishment, despite the fact that the latter may be termed "cost," or "aversive control.")

Second, it seems less useful to describe the behavior of human beings in stimulus and response terms than it is to describe the behavior of lower animals in this way—not only because human behavior is more complex, but also because of the more complex internal processes presumably taking place within the person. There is no question that human beings can learn through reinforcement, but there is considerable question as to whether their complex responses in real situations are adequately described with this simple paradigm. The creative artist, for example, may spend several years producing popular works for which he or she is enthusiastically reinforced by an adoring public. Then, tiring of the adulation he or she receives for "superficiality," the artist turns to producing works for which there is no reward other than his or her own satisfaction. It is difficult to describe situations such as these using the reinforcement model. Nor is it easy for the reinforcement theorist to handle learning that follows from the exchange of complex symbols between persons.

Third, contingencies of reinforcement for human beings are presumably quite complex, and simply have not been studied in most situations. In many contexts the physical environment, the identity of the person who exhibits behavior, the identity of the other, the unique use of symbols by the other, and the sequence of previous behaviors may all be of equal or greater importance in determining response than the class of reinforcing behaviors emitted by the other.[10] This suggests that the concept of reinforcement may be too microscopic for application to problems of human interaction, and in fact studies of human reinforcement in natural contexts are hard to find. Thus, although substantial research has now been conducted on the modification of human behavior through reinforcement (Bergin & Suinn, 1975; Kanfer & Philips, 1970; Krasner, 1971; Yates, 1970), most of this

---

[10]To illustrate this complexity, Schachter and his associates have shown that the eating behaviors of normal and obese persons are controlled by somewhat different mechanisms. While normal persons appear to eat when they are hungry (and to cease eating when they are full), obese persons are likely to eat whenever they enter a food-eating situation. Such situations provide positive reinforcement for the obese person but not for the normal eater (Goldman, Jaffa, & Schachter, 1968).

effort is confined to artificial contexts in which stimuli can be tightly controlled—such as mental hospitals, prisons, or therapy sessions. Natural contexts are anything but tightly controlled.

This problem is especially exemplified in the writings of Skinner, who begins his discussions of human reinforcement with straightforward expositions of the reinforcement paradigm but then slides into the concepts of reward and punishment when he runs out of data concerning human behavior (see Chomsky, 1959). However, if reinforcement theorists have had difficulty describing the complexity of real social situations in reinforcement terms, they have not lacked in seeking to improve on those situations by designing contexts in which the environment is simplified to the reinforcement model. The best example of this appears in the field of computer-assisted instruction—in which crisp, unambiguous, machine-administered reinforcements are substituted for the vagaries and complexities of the classroom (see, for example, Skinner, 1960). Reinforcement enthusiasts are not the first social scientists who have sought to reconstruct the world in the overly simple images of their theories. Marxists and Freudians have played this game for years, but reinforcement theorists seem the first to have tried it with computer assistance!

In summary, three forms of behavioral linkage have appeared within the role literature: (*a*) facilitation, which involves environmental manipulation; (*b*) reward, which depends upon stimuli that are judged prepotent; and (*c*) reinforcement, which depends on our ability to establish stimulus–response contingencies. Of these, the concept of reward appears more frequently and is often used for defining other concepts, as is exemplified in the next section of the chapter. All three forms of linkage have been used, however, to discuss ways in which behaviors (and features) can influence the behavior of others, and through such influence set up systems of social behavior.

Complex Linking Concepts

We now turn to the definition of several concepts involving complex linking phenomena—including imitation, influence, injunction, sanctioning, power, function, and context. Each of these has a central place in the galaxy of role concepts, and assumptions made about them stand behind many propositions stated for role behavior. Each has also attracted research efforts, and reviews of those efforts are in order. However, some of these efforts are tangential to role theory, so our reviews here are brief.

IMITATION

One of the simplest of complex linking concepts is **imitation**. English and English suggest that imitation is any "action that copies the action of another more or less exactly, with or without intent to copy" (1958, p. 253). In short, imitation involves only judgements about the overt qualities of behavior and not judgements about its etiology or internal dynamics.

In formal terms, imitation involves the co-occurrence of two processes we have already defined: correspondence and linkage. A behavior will be said to *imitate* another if it is linked to and corresponds with the other. This definition makes no distinction between whether the two behaviors compared are emitted by one person or two. Normally we think of imitation as a product of interaction, but it is also possible for a person to imitate him or herself—as when the person repeats a successful joke in order to generate additional rewards from an audience.

The concept of imitation has attracted considerable attention and research over the years. Early theorists such as Morgan (1896), Tarde (1903), and McDougall (1908) regarded imitation as an instinctive process, and recent research suggests that spontaneous imitation can actually be observed in human infants who are less than a month old (Meltzoff & Moore, 1977). However, most investigators have considered imitation problematic, and research has concentrated on conditions under which imitation was more or less likely to occur. Unfortunately, this research has been conducted using various terms for the imitation concept, terms that imply hypothetical processes that are used to "explain" imitation. Let us consider some of these terms and their connotations.

The term **behavioral contagion** has had considerable use since the pioneering work of Polansky, Lippitt, and Redl (1950) and Lippitt, Polansky, Redl, and Rosen (1952). For our purposes behavioral contagion may be considered imitation wherein the mechanism operative is reduction of expected sanctions that normally restrain behavior (see Chapter Six). To illustrate, when boys in a summer camp observe other boys "getting away" with deviancy, they are more likely to engage in deviancy themselves.

Another term, *conformity*, is also used to indicate imitation within the small group context. Since the term conformity is also used for other purposes (see Chapter Six) it is helpful to speak of its use as a synonym for imitation as **behavioral conformity**. Ever since the early studies of Sherif (1936) and Asch (1956) it has been known that persons were likely to imitate others in the group, particularly if others spoke with one voice. So striking is the effect that some persons can be led to deny the evidence of their own senses when this evidence comes into conflict with the testimony of the rest of the group; hence people tend to "conform." Why should a person conform to the group? Most investigators presume a mechanism in the form of social pressure that is imposed on the person or that is presumed by the person to be likely for conformity. Thus, behavioral conformity is imitation that is presumed to be induced through some form of social influence (see the following section). Reviews of research on behavioral conformity may be found in Allen (1965, 1975) and Bass (1961).

Another term that may be used for imitation is **social facilitation**. As we already know, social facilitation is said to occur when the behavior of a person is affected by the presence of an audience. Not all socially facilitated behavior is imitative, but some may be. An example is provided by Bandura and Walters (1963, p. 79) in "cases in which an adult, who has lost the idioms and pronunciation of the local dialect of the district in which he was raised, returns for a visit to his home. The original speech and pronunciation patterns, which would take a stranger years to acquire, may be quickly reinstated." Why should imitative social facilitation occur? Because of the enabling effect of the stimulus behaviors as cues, which release associations, solve a problem, or provide relief from ennui for the person who then imitates.

Yet another term used for imitation is **modeling**. In modeling the other who is to be imitated is someone with whom the person can identify (see Chapter Eight). The father combs his hair in a certain way, and so then does his son. The charismatic leader has certain personal mannerisms that appear in the behaviors of his or her followers. The employee aspiring to a higher position in the organization apes the behaviors of those who are presently members of that position. Modeling may or may not be consciously engendered, but in either case, it results in the person taking on the behaviors characteristic of the other—that is, his or her role. For this reason, modeling is often advanced as an explanation for the appearance of roles, a problem to which we shall return in Chapter Eight. One distressing example of modeling occurs in the tendency of children to imitate aggressive behavior they see portrayed on their television screens (Bandura, 1973; Berkowitz, 1962; Geen, 1977; Geen & Quanty, 1977; Goranson, 1970). An even more distressing example is provided by those cases of severe and systematic destruction of the person's personality so that he or she is left with few options other than modeling behavior after that of his or her tormentors. Illustrations of this latter have appeared in Orwell's *Nineteen Eighty-Four*, in Bettelheim's (1943) discussion of the Nazi concentration camp, and in the "brainwashing" of Korean war prisoners.

The difficulty with using these several terms (and others) for the imitation concept is that investigators are led to believe that they are studying different phenomena. In fact, studies of behavioral contagion may be operationally indistinguishable from studies of social facilitation or modeling. This tends to confuse both investigators and reviewers of imitation. To add to the confusion, competing theories have now been advanced for imitation based on classical conditioning, operant conditioning, sensory feedback, stimulus contiguity, and catharsis, each of which has generated somewhat independent literatures (Bandura, 1965; Parton, 1976). Moreover, studies of imitation have concerned not only aggression, but also altruism (Berkowitz, 1972; Krebs, 1970; Macauley & Berkowitz, 1970), alcohol use (Alexander & Campbell, 1962; Biddle, Bank, & Marlin, in press a,b; Forslund & Gustafson, 1970), drug use (Jensen, 1972; Kandel, 1974), school achievement (Kandel & Lesser, 1972), therapy with adults (Rosenthal, 1976) and children (Kirkland & Thelen, 1977), and other content fields. Thus, although interest in imitation remains high, research on imitation is diffuse, and no recent summaries of the field as a whole seem to have appeared.

INFLUENCE

We turn next to that most common term one encounters in discussions of face-to-face interaction, *influence*. What is meant when someone "influences" another—when the mother influences her child, the boss his secretary, the motorist a traffic officer who has stopped him or her for speeding, the advertiser his or her client? In some authors' uses, the term influence is substituted for the general concept of behavioral linkage—thus if we know that a behavior of the person has affected the other, the other is said to have been influenced. Such uses seem superfluous and confusing. However, a more restricted meaning for the influence concept is available that involves judgements made about the intent of the person. In this latter usage, if the behavior of the other is affected through actions taken by the person, and we have evidence of advertence on the part of the person, we judge that **influence** has occurred. But what constitutes evidence of advertence?

By **advertence** we mean that the person evidences intention or design upon a behavior of the other. Advertence can be indicated in either of two ways. The person may tell us—as a separate act, out of context—that he or she intends to influence the other. Or the person's behavior may be such as to provide *prima facie* evidence for attempts at influence. I shall suggest three forms of behavior that provide such evidence: direct injunction, indirect injunction, and sanctioning.

A **direct injunction** occurs when the person exhibits behavior in the form of an overt *demand* or *assessment* made for the other's behavior.[11] The mother says, "Sally, eat your peas"; the boss pontificates, "You must improve your spelling"; the motorist comments, "Your sergeant wouldn't want you to write out so many speeding tickets this weekend"; the advertiser demands, "Buy our toothpaste!" But **injunctions** may also be indirect—the motorist might have said, "But officer, I was only speeding up to pass that truck"; or the advertiser may claim, "Our toothpaste cleans whiter and brighter than any other!" **Indirect injunctions** are behaviors that reference other phenomena than the behavior of the other but that nevertheless have logical implications for the other's behavior or its functions. (There is even a third form of injunction that I shall not attempt to define formally wherein the person reveals his or her feelings about the other's behavior through gesture, flinching, blushing, or other nonverbal action.)

Note, please, that the definitions given of direct and indirect injunctions are strictly behavioral. Although it is claimed that they offer evidence of advertence on the part of the person, hence of his or her "intent" (a hypothetical construct), that

---

[11] Demands and assessments are overt expressions of expectation and are given formal definition in Chapter Five.

evidence is strictly overt. It is also common to find authors speaking of **positive** injunctions, in the case wherein the other's behavior was approved or demanded, and of **negative** injunctions, wherein the other's behavior was disapproved or decried. Given these definitions, it is also possible to judge whether the behavior of the other that is referenced subsequently changes, and if so in what way. If the behavior of the other changes in such a way as to be consonant with the injunction— that is, if the injunction is positive and the frequency of the other's subsequent behavior increased, or if it is negative and subsequent behavior decreased—we will say that the injunction was **successful**. In all other cases the injunction is termed **unsuccessful**. For example, if the mother has told her daughter to eat her peas and there was no effect on the latter's behavior, or if the eating of peas subsequently slowed down, we would say that her injunction was unsuccessful.

A second form of evidence acceptable for conclusions of advertence is the use of sanctioning. What is a sanction, and how does it differ from an injunction? As is true for many role phenomena, it is possible to define sanctioning in overt, behavioral terms or by use of expectations for behavior. We deal here with the former and delay until Chapter Six the latter. Behavioral sanctioning involves a relationship of contingency between the exhibition of a stimulus behavior by the other and the probability of soliciting rewards or punishments from the person. Thus, behaviors of the person are termed **sanctions** if they constitute rewards or punishments for another and if their exhibition by the person is more or less likely depending on the appearance of a stimulus behavior in the other (Radcliffe-Brown, 1934). As was the case with reinforcement, the provision of rewards or the cutting off of punishments are termed **positive** sanctions, whereas the provision of punishments or the cutting off of rewards constitute **negative** sanctions. It is also correct to say that the stimulus behavior of the other is "sanctioned."

Sanctions, like injunctions, can be judged for success against subsequent change in the stimulus behavior of the other that gave rise to them. If a positive sanction for behavior is followed by an increase in similar, subsequent behaviors by the other, we will say that the sanction was **successful**. A negative sanction would be successful if it succeeded in decreasing the probability of similar stimulus behaviors by the other. All other sanctions are **unsuccessful**, including both those that had no effect and those that "backfired."

Examples of sanctioning are easy to find. The child draws on the wall of his or her room and is spanked. Or, conversely, the parent refuses a child a raise in his or her allowance and is whined at. In both cases the person doing the sanctioning presumes that with the provision of sufficient punishment a change in the stimulus behavior is likely to come about. Or again, the instructor gives an "A" to the student who writes an excellent paper and a "D" to another whose paper is seriously below standard.

Sanctions are sometimes confused with threats and promises. In the **threat** (or **promise**) a sanction has not actually been exhibited, but an indirect injunction has been given, warning that a sanction is likely, and making clear its contingency relationship with the stimulus behavior of the other. (Threats warn of negative sanctions; promises concern positive sanctions.) The parent might say, for example, "If you draw on that wall again I will spank you." Threats and promises are not sanctions (unless we presume that a threat or promise constitutes a prepotent stimulus in and of itself, which seems dubious). Rather, the threat or promise is formally similar to other forms of indirect injunction that warn of environmental consequences (such as, "If you touch that hot kettle you will burn your fingers"), the only difference being that in the threat or promise it is the speaker who will "bite" rather than the impersonal forces of nature. In deciding whether to change behavior following receipt of warning of environmental consequences, the other decides whether the feedback effect is likely and what its reward or punishment value for him or her might be. If the effect warned of is deemed unlikely or that it will make little difference, he or she will not change behavior. When responding to a sanction, the other has already experienced a "taste" of the consequences.

Why would anyone want to impose a sanction on another? Why would we bother to reward or punish another person? The sanctioning act is normally entered into, of course, to get the other person to change his or her behavior, in order to influence the other. Since the sanctioning act involves the use of prepotent stimuli (about which it is reasonable to presume knowledge on the part of both those who administer and those who receive them), we shall normally presume that the application of sanctions constitutes *prima facie* evidence of advertence. In other words, sanctions are normally "intended" (Lockwood, 1964).

There are several limitations to this presumption (Turner, 1973). For one, it occasionally happens that the sanctioning act and the stimulus behavior it is designed to influence are sufficiently separated in time so as to confuse the sanctioning paradigm for either the person or the other. For example, a child who is spanked some hours after the infraction has occurred may be genuinely confused as to why he or she was being so treated; or family members occasionally "explode" at other members for trivial matters, some hours after the event that actually created the loss of temper occurred.

For another, some contingent rewards or punishments may be administered inadvertently. The young bridegroom makes a wry face upon tasting his bride's dinner, reducing her to tears; the alcoholic husband cannot stop drinking to excess, though his drunken weekends constitute a serious punishment for others in his family. Although these events are surely punishing to other members of the family, hence are likely to affect the latters' behavior, it is apparently unreasonable in such cases to conclude advertence or that sanctioning was intended. However, to conclude that the administration of reward or punishment is not an act of sanctioning can be a tricky business. The bridegroom or drunken husband may, indeed, have intended to sanction their spouses. The person who loses his or her temper regularly, and just as regularly tells those who were offended that he or she is sorry and "did not mean it" is probably engaging in self-deception.

Again, some sanctions seem to be employed as much for the edification of the audience as for the control of target-person behavior. Teachers will sometimes "make an example" of a deviant pupil in order to establish the limits of misbehavior that they will tolerate and to demonstrate their own willingness to control it. The police will sometimes conduct token raids on houses of prostitution or known drug pushers, either to keep these activities from becoming blatant or to persuade the public that they are "doing their job." Regardless of these exceptional cases, those who are sanctioned and others observing the act are likely to presume advertency on the part of the person who sanctions. We are probably on safer grounds if we begin by assuming that the contingent administration of rewards and punishments is advertent and then be willing to allow for exceptions when they are clearly indicated.

However, it should not be assumed that sanctions are the only way in which people affect one another. This assumption is only too prevalent in role theory. It is usually associated with assumptions about the existence of shared norms for behavior and presumes that all concerned are aware not only of the norms, but also of the likelihood that sanctioning will follow from deviations from those norms. For example, according to Homans (1950, p. 123) a "norm, then, is an idea in the minds of the members of a group . . . specifying what the members or other men should do . . . [provided also that] departure of real behavior from the norm is followed by some punishment" [also see B & T, Selection 11]. From this point, some theorists proceed to the assumption that it is only through norms and sanctions that social behavior is organized. In actual fact, of course, behavior may be organized by any of several means, among which sanctioning is but one of the options available.

If there be any doubt about this point, let us consider the various ways in which direct and indirect injunctions, threats, promises, and sanctions can be combined by the person in attempting to get another to do his or her bidding. Direct injunctions can appear alone ("Please close the window"); so can indirect injunctions ("It would be warmer in here if the window were closed"), threats or promises ("If that window is left open, I shall become cross"), sanctioning (the provision of a smile and a "thank you" to one who has just closed the window), or any combination of these. Nor do these alternatives exhaust the possible strategies for behavioral control of the other (Skinner, 1953) [B & T, Selection 39]. In fact, persons seem to employ sanctions for influencing others only in certain, limited situations (Leventhal, 1976). Moreover, to influence others through sanctioning is surely less civilized than to influence them through persuasion.

Very well, if sanctions are not always used for influencing another, how *does* the person go about achieving influence? What strategies are open to the person, and when does the person choose one strategy over others? Research on this question is surprisingly unsatisfactory. The question has been recognized by many theorists, and schemes for classifying influence tactics have been suggested by various authors (Dahl, 1957; Davis, 1965; Gamson, 1968; Marwell & Schmitt, 1967a, b; Rapoport, 1960; Singer, 1963). These schemes seem unsatisfactory in the main, for they largely reflect ad hoc classification rather than explicit theory. Also, additional concepts for viewing influence tactics have been suggested by authors such as Weinstein and Deutschberger (1963) or Jones (1964) that have yet to be integrated into general schemes for discussing influence strategies. Choice of influence strategy has occasionally been investigated in questionnaires (Marwell & Schmitt, 1967b) and in laboratory studies (for a summary, see Leventhal, 1976), but it is difficult to find studies in which influence strategies were observed in natural contexts. Thus, today we know very little about the strategies that are actually chosen for influencing others.

A more positive report may be given when we ask the questions: Which influence strategies are more successful? When is the other more likely to be influenced by injunction, threat, sanction, or other strategies? These latter questions have been studied endlessly by social psychologists, not only under the topic of influence, but also in studies of power, conformity, compliance, bargaining, leadership, persuasion, and a host of related topics. Rather than attempt a review of this broad effort here, we delay until later when specific reviews will be given of several types of influence (see especially Chapter Six).

In summary: Direct injunction, indirect injunction, threats and promises, and the use of sanctions all constitute *prima facie* evidence of advertence. However, these forms are by no means the only strategies by which influence is effected. It is also possible that we have additional knowledge (from some other source) of intent to influence on the part of the person and may judge *any* behavior he or she exhibits for its influence potential. Consider the man who tells us privately that he is trying to cure his son of biting his fingernails. We may thereafter observe him rewarding or punishing the son (thus using sanctions), discussing the problem (employing injunctions), buying him a nail clipper (using environmental manipulation), modeling the behavior he hopes his son will imitate, or even attempting to condition his son's behavior. Since we know from outside information the father's intent, all of these actions are judged to be influence attempts. But had we not such an external source of information, only his use of sanctions or injunctions would have been clear in their meaning as regards influence. Nor are all cases where the person affects the other necessarily due to influence. Behaviors of the person may affect the other though such an effect was not intended, nor in some cases even recognized.

FUNCTIONS AND CONTEXTS

As we have seen, it is possible to affect units of the physical environment by means of behavior. Moreover, relocations or deformations of environmental units may, in turn, affect subsequent behaviors. Analysts of role systems are often concerned about the antecedents or effects of behaviors in the environment and use the terms *function* and *context* to express these relationships.

The introduction of the term *function* into our discussion involves some problems, since this term has generated confusion among role theorists and other social scientists. Let us clear up this confusion. The simplest concept of function appears in mathematics, where a function is merely a statement of relationship. Provided that variable A appears to affect variable B in some way, or A is mappable onto B, we say that "B is a function of A." The interesting thing about this usage is that the variables are reversed. Whereas A is presumably the independent, and B the dependent, variable, the functional sentence lists them in reverse order. As a result, our attention is diverted from the relationship to the dependent variable or consequent B.

This peculiar reversal was retained in the second use of the function concept that first appeared in physiology. Early anatomists were puzzled by a number of organs in the body whose "function" they did not at first understand. For example, the pineal gland was known for many years before the effects of its endocrine secretions were understood. Thus A (the organ) was known, and it was presumed that if A existed that there must be a B (the function) that it accomplished. When carried to its extreme, speculations of this sort lead to the teleological fallacy; namely, that whenever we find A (an organ) there *must* be a B (its single function)—since evolution (or God) would not have been so sloppy as to provide otherwise. The difficulty with such assumptions is that the world is more complex than our simple faith insists. The veriform appendix appears to have no contemporary "function" in the body whatsoever, although in prehistoric times it may have had one for the ancestors of men and women. And numerous organs appear to have many "functions" that interact with those of other organs in complex chains of cause and effect.

These same problems appear in the sociological uses of function. We observe A (for example, a custom within a society) and then presume the existence of a B (the function that must be accomplished through that custom). In so doing we are tempted to assume either the teleological fallacy (that A would not have existed unless there were a B that was being accomplished) or that those who perform A are aware of or intend B. In one of its worst forms, the teleological fallacy has been embraced by some sociologists who appear to suggest that whatever forms of social behavior exist are "functional," hence necessary ("requisite") for the survival of the society. This leads in turn to embracing all existing social forms and inveighing against proposals for social reform.

But apart from such teleological nonsense, we need a concept that deals generally with social effect. The fact is that events *are* influenced by behavior. Personal violence in America *does* have consequences, although most of us disapprove and decry them. So a general term is set forth to deal with the consequences of action—**function**, any condition or state of affairs that results from behavior (Levy, 1952). This definition is a broad one, for subsumed under function are such diverse effects as deformations of the physical environment, alterations in the social behavior of others, production of symbols, and even covert responses.

If we restrict the concept of function to events we have already assumed to be observable and affected by behaviors, one may discriminate *behavioral functions* and *physical functions*. An example of the former would be the appearance of applause following a speech. Among the latter we would include any artifact that is constructed through human endeavor.

Nothing in the above definition suggests that functions are necessarily intended or perceived by social participants. Although these latter stipulations take us beyond the realm of behaviorism, a vocabulary has sprung up extending the concept of function to them. Those functions recognized may be termed *social functions*, those intended are *manifest functions*, and those unintended are *latent functions* (Merton, 1949). Nor should functions be confused with individual goals or group tasks. As used here, functions are states of affairs that actually occur, whether or not they were intended. However, for other purposes we may be interested in conceptualizing states of affairs that are intended by actors, whether or not they ever eventuate. It is common to use the terms "goal" or "task" to refer to such states, together with the modifiers "individual" or "group" to indicate that the intention is idiosyncratic or shared (see Chapter Seven). Given such usage, it is evident that a manifest function must always reflect a "goal" or "task."

We also need a concept that denotes units of the environment that have an effect on our behavior, for who can deny that behavior is environmentally dependent? Battles generate killing, churches praying, football games cheering, highways speeding and traffic accidents. Each of these four surroundings is a complex environment consisting of physical, behavioral, or symbolic events. Each exemplifies a **context**, any condition or state of affairs that affects behavior. Functions and contexts are similar in that both are general as regards content, and both are tied to behavior by links of cause and effect. Contexts, however, are independent variables, while functions are dependent variables—which does not preclude the possibility of a given function becoming a context for subsequent behaviors. The violin maker produces a fine instrument, which is thereafter used by the violinist to produce fine music.

Several forms of contexts may also be discriminated. As with functions, *behavioral contexts* may be differentiated from *physical contexts*. The field of collective behavior is largely concerned with such behavioral contexts as crowd behavior, whereas environmental psychology and industrial design are focused on physical contexts. In addition, a third type of observable context consists of the *complement of persons* who are present. As was suggested earlier, human beings are one type of environmental unit. Consider a small group that is composed entirely of men or women. Should a member of the opposite sex now appear, interaction in that group will often change sharply. Political discussions have a quite different character when members of the press are present or absent. Clearly, persons can form part of the context.

Finally, some contexts consist of sheer time itself. Time has already entered our discussion in several informal ways. For example, we have distinguished between behaviors facilitating and those facilitated, and between stimuli and responses in terms of a temporal sequence of events. In a strict formalization of role theory it would be necessary to deal explicit with time, for differentiating between more than a single example of a given type of behavior exhibited by one person requires observations over time. For the present, however, we need merely note that time exists, and that events—including human beings, behaviors, and features—are laid within it. A *temporal context* consists of a time (or sometimes a class of times, such as the "evening hours") whose presence affects behaviors. It seems unreasonable to extend this concept to functions, however, since to the best of our knowledge and philosophy, objective time cannot be affected by our behaviors. (Like features, time may be a stimulus but not a response.)

In summary, then, behaviors can be linked to their surroundings in various ways. A unit of the surroundings that affects behaviors is known as a context, whereas something that is affected by behavior is termed a function. Some types of functions and contexts have been discussed, including behaviors, the physical environment, person complements, and time itself.

ENVOI

In this chapter we have examined some of the basic concepts used by role theorists for studying social behaviors and other overt events. The chapter began by considering three logically primitive notions—human beings, physical features, and behaviors. Thereafter we discussed the measurement of behaviors and the ways in which behaviors could be compared, their effects on other persons, and the ways in which behaviors could be linked with other behaviors. The chapter ended with a discussion of complex linking notions, including influence, injunction, sanctioning, function, and context.

We have merely scratched the surface of behavioral analysis, of course. Many concepts in the social sciences turn out to have little meaning beyond that of a specific pattern of behaviors. Behavioral definitions may be given for such concepts as conflict, discrimination, rumor, assimilation, aggression, migration, social mobility, and a host of other terms. Such concepts are powerful tools for describing the complexities of our social world. Moreover, much of the empirical effort of experimental psychology may be described in behavioristic terms, including research on behavioral modification and verbal learning that are specific to human beings.

Despite such great potential, however, many readers may feel that studying social behaviors is a dry business, that to consider human beings as merely the loci of features and behaviors is to convert them into automatons, and that insights and predictions cannot be gained for human behavior without recourse to information about how the world looks, feels, tastes, and smells to its participants. This contention illustrates what is probably the greatest difficulty with the behavioral orientation as applied to human beings. Concepts used for behavioral analysis are analytic and abstract. However, most social behaviors in which we are interested concern themselves with symbols that are familiar and concrete. To put it another way, much of human interaction is mediated through the use of shared symbols that have meanings—and unless we understand those meanings we have difficulty in understanding or predicting behaviors. Worse, it is difficult to presume that subjects are capable of learning and using shared symbols without also presuming that they are sentient—that their behaviors are in part generated by the conceptions that they hold about behavioral events. But if we make these assumptions, we will also be tempted to incorporate the familiar and concrete symbols used by our subjects into our scientific vocabularly, thus confusing events with conceptions about events, and concepts for behavior with concepts for conceptions about behavior. Many social scientists despair of finding a solution to this dilemma and restrict their interests to behaviors alone or to conceptions alone. The role orientation presumes to offer concepts for both the behavioral and conceptual realms and to study the relationship between these two sets of phenomena.

It should also be recognized that only a handful of social scientists today are truly concerned with the empirical study of human behaviors in real-life contexts. Those who make this effort are often astonished at the evidence uncovered. Investigations of interaction in small groups, jury trials, classrooms, industrial settings, cocktail parties, or families have revealed behaviors of amazing density and complexity. Reports given of those behaviors by subjects who participate in them tend to be summative, simplified, ideologically bound, and are often distorted by desires or values. In short, the real world of behaviors is a complex environment that is only partially mapped by the conceptions of subjects. And if we are to study behaviors (and we must) the concepts we use for this purpose must be clearly separated from those used to express the conceptions held about behaviors by participants and others.

Chapter Three

Roles

One man in his time plays many parts—some of them grossly under rehearsed.

—Sean O'Casey

We turn now to *the* central concern of role theory—the study of roles—and immediately find an enigma. In any reasonably ordered science one would expect minimal agreement among its practitioners regarding the central concepts of that science. Astronomers, chemists, and anatomists usually have little difficulty agreeing on their basic concerns. But if role theory is to concern itself with the study of roles, what then is a role? Unfortunately this question has generated many answers, and much energy has been generated by confusions involving the role concept.

Consider the following, only too typical, definitions one may encounter for the term *role*. Depending on whom one reads, a role may be conceived as:

. . . "[a] position differentiated in terms of a given social structure" (Levy, 1952, p. 159);

. . . "what the actor does in his relations with others" (Parsons, 1951, p. 25);

. . . "an internally consistent series of conditioned responses" (Cottrell, 1942, p. 617);

. . . "[an] integrated or related sub-set of social norms" Bates, 1956, p. 314);

or, if this were not sufficient,

... "[the] sum total of the culture patterns associated with a particular status. It thus includes the attitudes, values and behavior ascribed by the society to any and all persons
occupying this status" (Linton, 1945, p. 77).

To say the least, role must be a plastic concept to accommodate such a wide range
of phenomena. Alas, there is more. Roles may also be conceived as limited to:

... " some specific external problem or . . . special class of other persons" (Thibaut &
Kelley, 1959, p. 143);

... what persons do as "occupants of the position" (Newcomb, 1950, p. 280);

... "what the actor does . . . seen in the context of its functional significance" (Parsons,
1951, p. 25);

... "complementary expectations concerning . . . others with whom [the person] interacts"
(Parsons & Shils, 1951, p. 23);

or even

... "activities which in combination produce the organizational output" (Katz & Kahn,
1966, p. 179).

To have such an array of different meanings accommodated by a single term seems
unreasonable. Small wonder that Neiman and Hughes complained (in 1951) that
"the concept role is at present still rather vague, nebulous, and non-definitive." One
wonders to what extent two succeeding decades have served to reduce this
confusion.

It is easy to curse the darkness, but what about lighting a candle? Surely these
theorists had some central idea in mind or they would not have chosen the same
term. Moreover, the role term appears endlessly in the writings of social scientists
and seems to communicate a core meaning without obvious pain. What is that
meaning? For our purposes, I shall assume that the role concept centers upon
behaviors that are characteristic of persons in a context. Thus when the social
scientists writes "the man was performing a role," readers would generally understand that the individual described as behaving in a manner similar to others in such
a place and time. Why, then, so many disparate definitions? Because social scientists have chosen to focus on different phenomena that may cause, be associated
with, or result from the performance of roles. Thus, for some investigators roles
are not conceived of as patterns of behavior but rather are seen as expectations that
are presumed to cause those patterns. For others, roles may be conceived of as
limited to a context, to interaction with other persons, to be approved, or to be
those behaviors that accomplish functions. None of these conceptions is "wrong."
Each focuses our attention on a set of phenomena often associated with roles. But

each is limiting, and to examine "the whole ball of wax" we should begin with the broadest meaningful definition of the role concept. This chapter, then, concerns itself with roles as behaviors. (For those concerned with such a concept, *expected roles* are taken up in Chapter Six.)

Roles occur in everyday life, of course, and are of concern to those who perform them and others. Children are constantly enjoined to act in a more grown-up fashion; new recruits into the armed services must learn roles of deference and deportment; the young lady who is to make her debut will adopt the style and manners of the event; predictable patterns of behavior appear within the school, the factory, the office, the sports arena, the hippie pad, the summer camp. Some of us, in fact, spend a good deal of time talking about roles. Parents, teachers, psychiatrists, social workers may sometimes feel as if there are no other topics of conversation at the end of their working days.

Roles, too, are portrayed in novels and in the theater. Much of what we know about life in earlier times is acquired through dramatic portrayals of roles, be they of Brutus and Cassius or the generations of the Forsytes. Occasionally we are even treated to self-conscious discussions of their roles by the characters who are portrayed. In *Pygmalion* Eliza Doolittle comes to recognize that if she behaves as a lady, and is treated as a lady by others, that she *is* in fact a lady. A similar revelation destroys Willy Loman in *Death of a Salesman,* for when Willy finally discovers that he is nothing apart from his occupational role he kills himself. In contrast, *The Admirable Crichton* is led by the challenge of circumstances to assume a wholly new role (thus saving his own life and that of others), but when the situation reverts to its former condition so does Crichton's role.

Dramatic portrayals are a mere shadow of the complexity of real-life role phenomena. Consider the role of the teen-age girl. Her behavior is surely determined in part by the expectations she holds for herself, as well as by those she attributes to her parents, her friends, her teachers, her siblings. But she will also be constrained by the sanctions offered her by others and by the models suggested in the behaviors of both adults and peers. Moreover, some of her behavior will be controlled by environmental conditions, such as the social class of which she is a member and the amount of available cash her parents can invest in her wardrobe. Nor does our interest stop with the prediction of her role behavior, for that behavior too has functions in the environment, as she is a model for her younger sister, an influence on others in her school, a source of worry to her parents, and a consumer within the marketplace.

These illustrate the realm of the role concept. This chapter begins with a discussion of roles and related concepts, continues with sections on role identification and common variables applied to roles, and concludes with a discussion concerning the study of roles.

THE CONCEPT OF ROLE

> *The ruler rules, the minister ministers,*
> *the father fathers, and the son sons.*
> *—Confucius*

As suggested in the previous pages, we now define a **role** to be those behaviors characteristic of one or more persons in a context. This definition hangs on four terms—behavior, person, context, and characteristicness—three of which have already been defined. Let us sort out their implications.

1. Roles are behavioral. Involved in the definition of role are only those overt actions or performances that may be observed and that characterize the persons observed. (The role of the policeman presumably includes the wearing of a uniform, directing traffic, arresting criminals, finding lost pets, giving directions to pedestrians, filling out forms, saluting superiors, and selling tickets to policemen's balls.) *(Example)* Specifically included in this concept are those things that policemen characteristically *do*—whether or not those things are expected, valued, or approved either by policemen or others. Excluded from the definition are nonbehavioral characteristics of policemen (such as their sex, race, or national origin) and the concepts, attitudes, norms, values, sanctions, and reactions of either policemen or civilians that may serve as a context for the policeman's role or may affect it in some way.

2. Roles are performed by persons. As used here, the role concept is confined to the behaviors of human beings (although later we shall briefly review the application of this concept to nonhuman animals). Excluded from role are "forces of nature," acts of God, and other presumed actions of nonhuman agents. However, any number of persons may be studied for the roles they exhibit, from John Q. Dokes to the sum total of all human beings. We normally think of roles as applying to some limited set of persons, but the role concept can be (and has been) applied to as few as one person and as many as the entire species *Homo sapiens*.

3. Roles are normally limited in some way by contextual specification and do not represent the total set of all behaviors exhibited by those persons studied, on stage and off stage, at work and at home, 24 hours a day or 365 days a year. As we shall see, the choice of context is important in two senses: some roles are defined contextually; others are limited in their applicability by contextual boundaries. It will surprise no one if we assert that roles may change radically from context to context. At the same time, the term *context* is a collective noun (like *forest* or *people*), and we normally think of roles as applying to classes of places or occasions rather than to specific context examples. Thus we speak of "community roles" rather than of "roles in Middletown," although the role concept might easily be applied to the latter use as well.

4. Roles consist of those behaviors that are *characteristic* of a set of persons and a context. Thus, it might be characteristic of one set of persons that they smoke a

great deal or of another that they smoke a moderate amount. Each would be judged characteristic if we could validate these statements by appropriate behavioral observation. In contrast, those behaviors not characteristic of the persons and context studied do not form part of their role. Cheering wildly is *not* characteristic of church congregations, nor is nakedness of school teachers in their classrooms, nor the wearing of winter wraps in Tahiti, nor expectorating during a job interview, nor public admission of a mistake by a politician. Each of these behaviors might be characteristic of other persons or other contexts—but they are not parts of the roles nominated.

It is possible to provide a formal definition for the concept of *characteristicness*. Let us assume that we have observed behaviors that are emitted by persons in a context. It is possible (but by no means certain) that some of these behaviors will be found to correspond for an arbitrarily chosen set of facets. Provided that "a significant proportion" of them are found to correspond for those facets, we shall say that the corresponding behaviors are **characteristic** of those persons and that context—hence a role. Note also that by definition a set of characteristic behaviors generates a nonvacuous distribution in at least one of the facets chosen for study. We will also refer to the statistical parameters of these distributions (e.g., their modal categories) as the *characteristics* of the role. Normally we describe a role by simply listing its characteristics. For example, we say that "characteristically, the mother's role involves the succoring of children."

The preceding discussion leaves open the question of what constitutes "a significant proportion" of the behavior set emitted by those whom we study in context. No formal criteria have yet been advanced for making this judgement. Clearly some roles are discriminated even though they involve but a small percentage of the behaviors of the set. This is particularly true when those behaviors constituting the role are unique. If we discovered that only a small proportion of businessmen in Indianapolis practiced Yoga, whereas businessmen from elsewhere did not, we would tend to conclude that "Yoga was characteristic of businessmen in Indianapolis," hence part of their role. But clearly, also, there are limits to this process. Two accidentally corresponding behaviors surely do not constitute a role (even *two* swallows do not constitute a summer). As formal studies of roles become more sophisticated, we should expect to find explicit criteria appearing for what constitutes "a significant proportion."

It should also be noted that a role depends on our discovery of both a set of behaviors and a set of facets, thus roles are bounded by both our observation of events and our choice of content for thinking about or measuring them. There is nothing in the definition that prohibits our discovery of a second (or third, or fourth) set of facets for which other significant proportions of the behavior set may turn out to correspond; hence more than one role can be unearthed for a given set of persons within a context. Roles are constrained by our concepts as well as by the behaviors we observe. Like the concepts of personality and culture, the role concept has no natural boundaries as far as content is concerned.

Role, then, is a collective noun. We normally use the role concept to apply to several persons, a classification of contexts, a range of facets, a set of behaviors. (A role is bigger than a breadbox.) Of these four assumptions, only the last is required by our definition. Roles *may* be exhibited by one person, in one example context, and may be confined to but a single aspect of behavior. Roles *must* be based on the observation of several behaviors, because only by so doing is it possible to detect those behaviors that are characteristic.

Roles need not be socially significant. The mere fact that we have observed a role does not mean that it is desired or expected by anyone, nor that it accomplishes functions, nor that it be institutionalized into a social system. Some roles *are* important in these or other senses. Some roles are so trivial that their performance is not consciously recognized, either by those who perform or those who witness them. On the other hand, the fact that roles are often characteristic of several persons or a range of contexts means that similar forces are probably at work or such uniformity would have been unlikely. And when a role is found to involve various facets of behavior, those aspects are presumably interrelated and suggest to us a role that has internal dynamics as well as statistical parameters. These latter topics are subject to empirical investigation, and we return to them in the final section of the chapter.

Concepts Related to Role

ROLE AND ROLE SECTOR

Three concepts are closely related to the notion of role and are sometimes confused with it. One of these is the concept of role sector. It turns out that some, but not all, roles that are of concern to us are those associated with persons who have a clear identity (or "occupy a social position") within a social system.[1] For such persons, it is sometimes possible to differentiate among the behaviors they characteristically direct toward others (or that affect others) having different identities within the social system. For example, within American families fathers characteristically engage in sexual relationships with their wives but not with their daughters or sons; whereas on the other hand they also characteristically teach their sons to play baseball but not their wives. Such portions of roles may be termed **role sectors** (after Gross, Mason, & McEachern, 1958; also see Hage & Marwell, 1968; Marwell & Hage, 1970).

It is sometimes claimed that roles are composed of nothing else than a set of mutually exclusive role sectors, and that social systems can be analyzed in terms of

[1] The concepts of identity and social position are examined in Chapter Four.

the role-sectored behaviors of their constituent members.[2] Apparently, Radcliffe-Brown saw society in such terms, and studies of social structure by British anthropologists have generally followed this insight. Actually, this model is too simple. For one thing, it is not an easy task to isolate those behaviors of the individual that affect another, nor is there a one-to-one relationship between behaviors that are directed toward others and those that actually affect the others. For example, in the family the way a husband treats his wife at dinner may also turn out to affect their children. Thus, role sectors are neither mutually exclusive, nor are they easy to measure. Moreover, they would appear to be inapplicable to roles that are not defined in terms of positional membership. Nevertheless, the role sector notion leads to some interesting mathematical models for social structure (Foa *et al.*, 1966).

ROLE AND PROFILE

Occasionally the role concept has also been expanded to include nonbehavioral characteristics of a set of persons. For example, we learn that a disproportionate percentage of combat troops in Vietnam were black, or that large numbers of primary teachers in America are women, or that numerous immigrants are to be found in New York City. Is being black, a woman, or an immigrant part of a role? If we include these nonbehavioral characteristics in the role concept we run the risk of confusing both others and ourselves, for nonbehavioral characteristics are usually not bounded by context. Instead, let us use the term **profile** to denote the nonbehavioral characteristics of a set of persons.

In such usage, a profile might include physical features, background experiences, and any other human characteristics that are context-free. Many sociologists have an interest in profile variables (which they consider to be independent variables), and social surveys often include a battery of questions designed to elicit profile information from respondents. The investigator then analyzes the data to see whether such profile variables as sex, race, age, or social class are associated with the behavior being studied. For example, we learn that men are more likely to be aggressive than women, or that black pupils do less well than white pupils in school work. Such findings are conundrums. Profile variables are not presumed to have intrinsic effects, and the only way in which we can explain their ability to predict behavior is by positing an association between profile and experiences encountered by respondents. Thus men are "taught" to be more aggressive than women, or black pupils presumably suffer from environmental handicaps not encountered by white pupils.

[2]In fact, some authors have defined *role* to be a role sector. This is implied in Parsons (1951) and Nadel (1957), and is made explicit by Foa, Triandis, and Katz (1966) and Benedict (1969). Such definitions are needlessly restrictive.

ROLE AND TREATMENT

It is common in discussions of the role concept to differentiate between *obligations* (those behaviors expected of a position member) and *rights* (those behaviors that others are expected to direct toward him or her). Although the concepts of rights and obligations are usually defined expectationally, one may also give a behavioristic interpretation of them. The behavioristic analogue of obligations is simply the role concept itself—those behaviors characteristic of position members. However, the concept of rights involves us in a new realm.

For our purposes, a **treatment** will be defined as those behaviors characteristically directed toward persons in a context. Let us explore some implications of this definition. First, note that treatments may involve behaviors directed toward a set of persons either by others or by themselves. Within the public settings of the school, for example, teachers are usually called formal names ("Mrs. Peterson") by pupils, the school principal, and other teachers alike. Second, the treatment inevitably constitutes a role in its own right. If we are to establish that a characteristic pattern of treatment behaviors exists, then by definition those persons who accord this treatment must also be performing a role. However, it is *not* implied that the treatment constitutes the totality of the latters' role; those others providing a treatment may well have other characteristic behaviors that are not directed toward the person in question. Nor need the others all have the same identity, nor will the treatments they accord the person always be homogeneous. In mob action, "all" others will take similar actions regarding a target person— cheering him (or her), cursing him, or lynching him. However, in more organized social systems it may be possible to recognize differentiation of a person's treatment into constituent roles that are performed by specific others who share identities with one another. Within the university, for example, students receive one type of treatment from professors, a somewhat different type of treatment from departmental secretaries, and still another treatment from janitors. If this latter is the case, we may term the specific treatment a person receives from one set of others a **treatment sector**.

The concept of treatment sector clearly mirrors that of role sector, and either concept can be viewed as the other, depending on one's perspective. To illustrate this, let us consider a family composed of a father, a mother, two sons, and a daughter. It is not unreasonable to presume that the father directs behaviors toward his sons that are characteristic and different from those he directs toward his wife or daughter. Moreover, the sons reciprocate and direct behaviors toward dad that are also characteristic and unique. If our attention is given to the father, his behaviors constitute a role sector and those of his sons a treatment sector. But if we turn our attention to the sons, their own behavior is a role sector and that of the father a treatment sector. For this reason, we may analyze the interactive behavioral structure of the family either as a set of role sectors or as a set of treatment sectors and will obtain an identical analysis. However, the totality of the father's role and treatment are different from the totality of the son's role and treatment.[3]

One of the more interesting concepts generated by the treatment notion is that of rolecasting. In **rolecasting** (or **altercasting**, to use the term of Weinstein & Deutschberger, 1963) the other encourages or projects a role for the person as a part of the treatment given the latter. Weinstein and Deutschberger suggest that rolecasting is a basic technique of interpersonal control and offer evidence that subjects are more likely to engage in rolecasting when confronted by negative reinforcement from others. Rolecasting is engaged in consciously by parents, teachers, and other socializing agents, of course. But we are not always aware of the degree to which our own needs and beliefs are generating treatments on our part that help to shape the roles of others. Rosenthal and Jacobson (1968) have suggested that teachers inadvertently treat pupils differentially, depending on the expectations they hold for pupil ability, thus unknowingly encouraging some pupils and discouraging others (see Chapter Six). Smith and Geoffrey (1968) have explored rolecasting in the classroom and see the evolution of pupils' roles as a process that reflects both the context and the needs of teacher and pupils.

Criteria for Role Identification

As has been indicated in the discussion, the role concept is normally associated with defining criteria that limit its application. Two such criteria are suggested in the definition given to role: Roles may be associated with persons or with contexts. A role may also be defined in terms of its content or a function that is performed by the role, and we review these criteria too. Of course, roles may be identified through several criteria simultaneously (for example, we might study the teacher's role in the classroom versus the teacher's role in the lunchroom), but for purposes of exposition it is interesting to consider roles that are identified in terms of only a single criterion. We begin, however, with a noncriterion.

SPECIES-WIDE ROLES

Some roles are characteristic of human beings as a species. These may be sorted into roles that are induced through our biological inheritance and those that result from common experiences of socialization or the necessities of joint, social living. To the best of my knowledge, human beings characteristically walk on two legs, breathe, ingest food through their mouths, blink, and cannot fly—and these poten-

---

[3]Collections of role sectors and treatment sectors are called role sets (after Merton, 1949), and a discussion of them appears later in this chapter.

tialities seem to be given in the biological structure of our bodies. Other behaviors also appear to be universal, such as socialization through the nuclear family, the existence of religious institutions, and kinship systems—although biological mechanisms for producing these roles have not been discovered. For these latter, then, we are inclined to seek "explanations" based on common experiences of socialization or theories of the "functional requisite" sort that posit universal problems that must be solved for human social systems to prosper (see Chapter Seven).

In an earlier era I might have been tempted to explain these latter roles by citing "instincts"—species-wide and physiologically generated modes of response to environmental cues, usually associated with states of physical maturation. At present most social scientists doubt whether instincts exist for the human species. Perhaps the strongest advocates for human instincts today are ethologists, such as Ardrey (1961, 1966), Lorenz (1963), or Eibl-Eibesfeldt (1970), but speculations about the innate "territoriality" or "aggressiveness" of human behavior are merely fanciful metaphors based on animal observation until they are assessed against cross-cultural evidence and until the biological mechanisms responsible for the presumed instinct are discovered. Unfortunately (for the argument) many societies persist in which "territoriality" and "aggression" are either unknown or appear in a form vastly different from that normally encountered in Western countries (Montagu, 1968).

Nevertheless, the role concept has been applied to the description of animal, as well as human, behavior (Benedict, 1969; Reynolds, 1970). Since this is so, it might be wise to summarize briefly the major differences presumed to distinguish human from infrahuman roles.

1. Animal roles are assumed to be instinctively generated, whereas human roles tend to be learned through socialization. Thus, we are "surprised" to find that socialization takes place in colonies of baboons (Ardrey, 1966), and we are "offended" when the ethologist suggests that humans might also be driven by instincts.
2. Whereas human roles appear to be differentiated among socially generated populations of persons, animal roles are presumed to be characteristic of the species as a whole.
3. Humans share a symbolic culture, hence it appears reasonable to posit the existence of symbolic role expectations in the cognitive structures of persons that help to account for their roles. Such an assumption seems less tenable for animals.
4. The social systems of which animal roles are a part are presumed to have evolved due to phylogenetic processes, usually Darwinian selection, whereas at least some human social systems are surely "planned" and "adjusted" by their participants (see Chapter Seven).

In fact, each of these assumptions may be questioned. Socialization obviously takes place among colonies of primates, and some of it is positionally differentiated

(Altmann, 1962; Reynolds, 1968). Some primates also appear capable of symbol learning (Premack, 1971), although evidence for the initiation and transmission of symbols among naturally occurring groups of primates has been skimpy. And although most animal social systems appear to be genetically induced, primitive game forms are invented by some animals (such as dogs) that are specific to a given context and set of animals. In short, though each of the preceding assumptions may be statistically true, and although in sum they describe a human society that is vastly different from animal society, the primitive seeds of socialization, symbol usage, positional differentiation, and planned social systems appear also among infrahuman species.

Come to think of it, each of these assumptions is but an explanation for role behavior, not a definition of the role concept. If we confine the definition of role to be that of an observed pattern of behavior that is characteristic of individuals in a context, there is no reason why this definition should not also apply to animals. The use of the role concept for describing animal behavior is not only legitimate, but it focuses our attention on those nonsymbolic aspects of behavior that may also characterize human roles.

PERSON-ASSOCIATED ROLES

One of the simplest ways of defining roles is in terms of behaviors associated with a specific set of persons, or **person-associated roles**. Definitions of this sort range from macro-roles, which are characteristic of whole societies, to micro-roles, which we associate with individual human beings.

It is certainly true that men in contemporary, Western societies are aggressive toward their fellows and tend to defend their "turf." These, then, are examples of **societal roles**—patterns of behavior that are characteristic of persons who are members of a given society. The best known example of a societal role is that of a common language that is spoken widely in the society, but societies also exhibit unique role elements in such fields as religion, recreation, socialization, utilization of the physical resources, and methods of insulting or complimenting one another. It is presumably part of the role of the Bedouin, for example, to belch copiously to show his appreciation of a meal; of the Indian woman to marry at an early age; of the Australian man to participate in sports; of the American to "date" in adolescence. It is possible, in fact, to so expand the role concept to include all of those behaviors characteristic of a society, and if we do this the role concept becomes equivalent to that of "behavioral culture." However, we normally think or roles as being somewhat smaller units of behavioral similarity than are cultures, and for this reason use of the role concept in connection with societies is usually confined to some institutional or functional context. Thus, one may read of the "religious role of the Burmese," or of "productive roles among the Bantu."

Although roles may be associated with any arbitrarily chosen set of persons, the commonest use of the role term is that of **positional role**, which may be defined as behaviors characteristic of those sharing a commonly recognized identity or social position (see Chapter Four). In our society, dominance and mechanical interests are characteristic of men, succorance and social sensitivity of women. Accents, life styles, patterns of consumption, family relationships, and even forms of criminality vary among persons whose race or ethnic membership differs. Infants, adolescents, adults, and the elderly behave in ways that are somewhat distinct. Roles vary for those having different occupations, caste memberships, or kinship designations.

As these illustrations suggest, some positional roles have great generality and are likely to appear regardless of context. Most positional roles are presumed to be context dependent, however. Thus, those who study occupational roles have usually confined their attention to observing behaviors in contexts wherein the person is recognized as a member of the position. Sports officials are studied on the sports field, business executives in their offices, physicians in the hospital and consulting room, soldiers in the barracks or on the battlefield. Such restrictions may not always be reasonable. There is no a priori reason why the behavior of a businessman, for example, may not be somewhat different from that of other men at home or at the meat market. We are all familiar with the cheery, optimistic patter that appears to characterize the speech of nursery school teachers regardless of context. Thus, role behavior may or may not generalize beyond the context in which one's positional membership is recognized.

To say the least, we are somewhat ambivalent about roles (and treatments) that generalize across a wide range of contexts. Differentiation of age and sex roles appears to be characteristic of all known societies, and yet such roles may be resented by persons whose interests or abilities run counter to the roles prescribed for his or her age, sex, or race. Professionals, such as ministers or doctors, are likely to resent it when they encounter pressures to take their professional roles into nonrelevant contexts, such as their homes, and professional associations are active in seeking to limit role performances to office hours and the work setting. All of us enjoy a change of pace, and recreational contexts or summer vacations enable us to perform roles that are normally impossible in our lives. On the other hand, none of us can be Everyman, and positional roles provide us a series of convenient behavior patterns to which we can become habituated that free us from the necessity of deciding constantly among the trivial details of living.

At the other end of the continuum, it is also possible to recognize **personal roles** in the behaviors characteristic of an individual. Joe Doakes characteristically takes a nap after dinner in the evening, whereas his neighbor characteristically works in his garden, and their friend across the street plays golf. As we noted earlier, it is possible to expand the role concept so that it becomes equivalent to that of behavioral culture. Just so, it is also possible to restrict the compass of role so that its coverage is identical to that of "personality."[4]

---

[4]Thomas (1968) provides a discussion of the major ways in which the concepts of role and personality are usually differentiated.

In fairness, the majority of social scientists do *not* use the role concept when speaking of the behaviors of individuals, however characteristic. Rather, roles are more often assumed to be common to sets of persons who share an identity or social position. (Thus, we sometimes encounter the assumption in "popular" social science that performing a role is antithetical to self-expression.) However, some social scientists, particularly symbolic interactionists, have for years insisted that roles should be conceived in personal terms (Vickers, 1971). Turner (1962) argues that personal roles are less often coerced than they are evolved through the interaction of situational demands and the needs of the person who exhibits them.

Another example of personal roles is provided when someone comes along whose behavior is sufficiently forceful or archetypical as to cause us to discuss it as a model for characteristic behaviors, hence in role terms. In such a way we become familiar with the roles of a Christ, a Napoleon, a Hitler, a Lincoln. Though such roles are retained in our vocabulary through association between a person's name and a set of expectations for behavior, originally there was such a person as Napoleon or Lincoln who actually exhibited the behavioral role after which our expectations are modeled.

A related concept is that of *social type*, which consists of a bundle of associated behaviors that embody not the prior role of a specific individual but rather the values of the society. Klapp (1962), who discusses this concept, lists such social types for American society as those of "fool," "hero," and "villain" and discusses the roles of individuals who have apparently cast themselves in these molds. Thus social type roles, too, are person associated, but the progenitor for the type is absent. Occasionally also a person-associated role appears through portrayal in literature rather than in real life. We are familiar with the roles of a Pollyanna or a Walter Mitty and can identify patterns of behavior in real persons that match these models, although the roles involved were originally portrayed in fiction.

CONTEXTUAL ROLES

Roles may also be defined in terms of context (**contextual roles**), and various contextual cues may be associated with certain roles. For example, some roles are *periodic* and are associated with clock hours or with daylight or darnkess. Nearly everyone washes upon first awakening; we are more likely to eat at noon than an hour earlier; traffic accidents are at their height in the evening; crime soars at night. Periodic roles also appear within other types of contextualization. When strangers are first introduced they are likely to shake hands; during the opening phases of a formal meeting the minutes of the previous meeting are likely to be read or approved; mothers are likely to weep when their children are leaving for camp for the first time.

Another type of contextualization is that associated with the physical context or *setting* in which behavior takes place. Open spaces are more likely to generate large-muscle behavior than confined areas; people normally drop their voices when entering a dark room; rioting from causes other than panic is unlikely to occur in crowded quarters, and so forth. These are all examples of constraints or facilitations of behavior due to the physical characteristics of spaces. But settings are also familiar to us through a vocabulary we share that is used to classify settings for various purposes, and once we enter a setting that is given a social designation we recognize, our behavior is likely to change appropriately. Pupils become noticeably quieter when entering the door of a school building;[5] transactions concerning automobiles are likely to take place at the filling station; sports activities are engaged in within the fieldhouse or on the football field.

Still another type of context is the **activity**, which I will define as a temporary but characteristic co-occurrence of two or more interdependent roles.[6] Like positions and settings, activities can also be recognized and designated. Examples of recognized activities include a football game, an orchestral concert, a ceremonial greeting, a jury trial, a church mass, a lynching. Examples of activities that are not socially recognized are harder to find, but Goffman's (1961b) concept of the "encounter" is a good example (also see Berne, 1964). The fact that roles are differentiated within an activity is provided for in the definition of this concept. However, it is also true that activities provide a context for roles that are not performed in other activities. A good example of this is the annual office party in which we may find staid execcutives singing, drinking, and telling risqué jokes in a manner that is foreign to their everyday behavior. The existence of activities also allows us to identify roles within a physical setting used for various purposes. A municipal auditorium, for example, may be used for a concert one night, a rodeo the next, a political convention, or a boxing match. Each of these activities involves distinct roles, and if we know what activity is going on, we will have less difficulty in planning our behavior to fit into it.

Yet one more type of context consists of the *positional complement* of those who are physically present (see Chapter Four). To illustrate this type of context, let us take a social structure whose positions are set—a baseball game—and examine the roles when one of the positions is not filled or when a representative of an additional position appears. If a player is missing—for instance the pitcher—members usually stand around and wait for a replacement. If the manager walks out onto the field—that is, if a position is added—either a conference occurs on the

---

[5]This illustration, and the term *setting*, are taken from Barker and Wright (1955), although these authors use the term to refer to all aspects of a context. Barker suggests that a setting "coerces" behavior! The concept of setting is defined formally in Chapter Seven.

[6]The concept of interdependence is defined formally toward the end of this chapter. An activity is a simple type of social system and is discussed in greater detail in Chapter Seven. Some authors define roles in such a way that they can only be conceived of as components of social systems. Such discussions are needlessly restrictive and tend to be logically circular, since system may then be defined as an organization of roles!

pitcher's mound or a dispute ensues between the manager and one of the umpires. If only the "normal" complement of positions is present, none of these roles or activities is likely. Or to take another example, Goffman (1959) points out that many settings have a "backstage" region where the players may "let their hair down" and relax from the rigors of overly strict role performance. But should a stranger enter the backstage region, roles will quickly become formalized again. Goffman illustrated this by describing the kitchen of a Hebridean resort, but something similar occurs when a woman enters a previously all-male group or when the school principal appears in a classroom.

Of course, the concepts of time, setting, activity, and positional complement do not exhaust the subject of contextual impact on role differentiation. Roles may be affected by the weather, the sequence of prior events, the larger social context, and so forth. We are only beginning to understand the effects of contexts on behavior, and careful studies of overt human behavior in many contexts have yet to be performed.

The concept of contextual role allows us to consider an important point. Some readers may be surprised to learn that roles need not be associated with membership in social positions. Perhaps half of all definitions of the role concept one finds in textbooks link the concepts of role and position together. And yet, this limitation on the role concept (which began with Linton, 1936) simply is not useful. To illustrate, let us consider the research of Bales (1950) in which various patterns of characteristic behavior were observed in discussion groups [B & T, Selection 29]. Bales identified several discussion roles to which he gave names such as "ideational" and "emotional" leadership. These roles were contextualized, for they were more likely to appear during certain phases of the group discussion than at other times. In addition, these roles were not always exhibited by the same persons but could be rotated from person to person as the discussion proceeded. In time, however, individuals became more likely to "specialize" in one or another of the roles described.

Findings of this sort suggest a phylogenetic ordering for role and positional phenomena in unplanned social systems. In the most primitive case, roles are primarily contextual, and different behaviors may be performed by those available or by "anyone" upon different occasions. For example, any or all members of a primitive society may fish in the morning and weave in the afternoon; greeting or departure roles may be performed by "anyone" who arrives or leaves, or "child care" may be accomplished by the nearest available adult. At a somewhat more advanced state of role evolution, specialists will appear who perform only a subset of the roles in the system. For example, in the research on jury trials by Strodbeck (1957; Strodbeck & Mann, 1956) roles were isolated and their performance was found related to the age, sex, and occupations of members. Again, Wahlke, Eulau, Buchanan, and Ferguson (1962) [B & T, Selection 28] discovered that different roles were, characteristic of majority and minority members of the legislative systems. In neither of these examples, however, were participants fully aware of the roles that were differentiated, nor were they aware of the fact that they were being performed by specialists. Finally, as roles become more complex and require more skill and training, not only will they be differentiated more clearly from other roles, but also their practitioners will come to be positionally designated and differentiated from others. Karl Marx, for example, suggested that only when the proletariat becomes self-aware will socialist revolutions take place.

Another illustration of a role as yet in its nascency is that of "soap pasting." When bathing, it turns out that there are only a few things one can do with the last little sliver of soap. One can throw it away, shove it down the drain, save it with others of its kind in a jar, or paste the sliver to the next bar of soap. It turns out that a surprising number of Americans do the latter on a regular basis, usually while bathing. This, then is the "soap-pasting role," which has presumably passed through the stages of contextualization and specialization. There is little evidence, however, to suggest that soap-pasters are self-identified or are cast into a social position by others (let alone evidence that their role is controlled by norms or sanctions). One can only speculate as to the far-reaching social consequences of self-awareness among soap-pasters—consumer strikes in favor of lower soap prices, public bathing, riots, and the like. Soap-pasters of the world arise; you have nothing to lose but your stains!

FUNCTIONAL ROLES AND TASK ANALYSIS

Somehow, despite my enthusiasm for soap pasting, I doubt that many readers will take this as a serious example of the role concept. Why not? Why should soap pasting appear so trivial in our eyes? Presumably because it appears to have so few effects. Until this point in the discussion we have ignored the consequences of roles. But clearly, roles are not isolated phenomena. Rather they are tied meaningfully to those social situations that imbed them. Indeed, many roles are performed because people are motivated to behave in that characteristic way, and roles tend to interlock with others and are related to the general phenomena of social accomplishment.

Roles, then, can accomplish functions. Moreover, if it can be shown that various elements of a role contribute to two or more distinct functions, then the role can be partitioned into its functional components. It is possible, for example, to establish those behaviors of the teacher's role that contribute to "instruction of pupils," versus those organized about "pupil counseling," "maintaining the physical setting of the school," "keeping satisfactory relationships with superiors," and "advancing the profession of the teacher" (Fishburn, 1962). In so doing we gain insight as to why a role is organized the way it is and how it integrates with other roles in a social system.

Several comments should be made about functional partitioning, however. For one, those portions of a role associated with one function may not be distinct from those associated with a second. Some of the teacher's classroom behaviors may well contribute to both "instruction of pupils" and "pupil counseling," though we can differentiate these functions clearly in our thinking. For another, there is no convenient way of setting forth a list of functions that clearly exhausts the effects of a role. Social events (such as roles) have the annoying habit of creating ripple effects that extend indefinitely in all directions, and just when we presume to have pinned down the functional significance of a given role with a list of impressive-sounding outcomes, a more insightful observer comes along to show us other functions that we had not considered. Thus, any list of functions that are accomplished by a given role tends to be merely a set of arbitrary insights.[7] In addition, we occasionally find authors who actually define the role concept in functional terms. For example, we sometimes hear definitions such as, "the role of the physician is to cure the ill." Such definitions exhibit two difficulties: they leave us with no way to talk about those persons who fail in the functions assigned (e.g., the doctor who loses a patient despite mammoth efforts), and they blind us to other functions also accomplished by the behaviors characteristic of those discussed (such as participation by American doctors in union activities that have led them to become the most highly paid professionals in the world).

The concept of **functional role** directs our attention to a legitimate problem, however. Occasionally we want to limit the role concept so as to apply only to a limited range of behaviors. Thus, one finds authors speaking of occupational, recreational, or economic roles, or of roles in the use of language. Such uses illustrate roles that are **content-specific**. This latter concept is more useful than that of functional role, since it points our attention to behaviors we can observe rather than to functions that may eventuate. At the same time, there is no reason why two content-specific roles need be mutually exclusive. Some behaviors may be both occupational and recreational.

Finally a special case of functional analysis obtains for those social systems in which it is reasonable to presume the existence of tasks. For example, in a modern organization we often find that tasks are assigned explicitly to each position making up the complement of positions in the organization. A foreman is expected to: supervise certain persons, maintain equipment, submit specific reports, attend certain meetings, etc. Under these conditions we are provided with specifications that make the functional partitioning of these positional roles an easier job. However, the fact that tasks are specified does not prevent us from discovering additional functions that are also accomplished by roles performed that were not intended and that sometimes are not even recognized by members of the system. A discussion of this problem appears in Homans (1950), where the author differentiated between

---

[7]To illustrate, contrast the functions listed for the teacher's role by Fishburn (1962) with those offered by Furst (1965), Lindgren (1962), and Sorenson, Husek, and Yu (1963).

the "official system" of tasks and officially expected roles that were specified by the formal organization on the one hand, and the "informal system" of functions, behavioral roles, and group expectations that existed side by side with it on the other. We return to this problem and to that of formal task analysis in Chapter Seven.

CONCEPTS AND VARIABLES FOR ROLES

The inhabitant of a country has at least nine characters: an occupational character, a national character, a civic character, a class character, a geographical character, a sex character, a conscious character, and an unconscious character, and perhaps a private character as well.

—Robert Musil

Roles have been discussed extensively, of course, and many concepts have been advanced that would differentiate roles from one another. Some of these have also been studied as variables, although roles are more often theorized about than studied directly. Some distinctions commonly made for roles are easier to apply to expected roles, and we delay a discussion of these until Chapter Six. Many may easily be applied to behavioral roles, however, and we now turn to a sample of these. (A related discussion appears in Marwell & Hage, 1970.)

Concepts Applying to Single Roles

GENERALITY

Roles have greater **generality** when they are performed by a wide group of persons or upon many occasions. At one end of the generality scale we find roles that are characteristic of "everyone" and "all occasions," such as the use of spoken language and bipedal locomotion. Only slightly less general are those roles associated with age, sex, or nationality (see Chapter Seven). Patterns of deference, aggression, flirtation, and even choice of vocabulary are usually sex-specific within a given society, and men and women tend to exhibit these characteristic behaviors in most contexts. Similarly, the behaviors of children are often distinct from those of adults and the aged. In contrast, at the other end of the generality scale lie roles that are performed by only a few persons and only on rare occasions, such as the role of the astronaut.

Generality of roles involves two dimensions that are sometimes treated independently. The first of these is contextualization. **Contextualized** roles are those whose behaviors are circumscribed by the boundaries of a context, whether that context be a setting, an activity, or whatever. Earlier in the chapter we discussed the fact that occupational roles are normally assumed to be differentiated only in those contexts where positional membership is relevant. In fact, occupational roles may or may not be contextualized by the work situation. Professors may be generally absent-minded, generals dominant, prize fighters pugnacious, servants obsequious, ministers unctuous—regardless of context. On the other hand, many roles are sharply contextualized, as is illustrated by our differential behaviors as audience members at a football match, at a concert, and in church.

The second dimension is personalization. **Personalized** roles are those whose performance is limited to but a single individual. Somewhat less personalized are those roles that are performed by a small set of persons (presidents of the United States, generals of the army). Less personalized yet are roles of professional or occupational positions, whereas at the other end of the continuum we find roles that involve most, if not all, of the persons in a given population.

Contextualization and personalization are rarely studied as variables. Most investigators specify the role in which they are interested by nominating persons or contexts which pins down one or both of these characteristics. There is no reason why one should not study the contextualization of a person-associated role, however, nor the personalization of a contextual role. To illustrate the former, popular accounts appear frequently that are concerned with the degree to which the jobs of public figures intrude upon their home life. Would that we had better data on this topic. As well, contextualization and personalization can both be studied for content-specific roles, as is illustrated in the work of Bales (1950).

The obverse of role generality is sometimes assumed to be *specialization*. Interestingly, a nongeneral role is not necessarily specialized. As we shall see later, role specialization refers to the differentiation of roles within a social system. Some quite general roles, such as that of directing traffic, may nevertheless be specialized within the social system of the street corner. In contrast, the role of the astronaut is assuredly a nongeneral one, although there is little specialization of the role, since all astronauts are taught to perform the duties of others, lest the mission fail if one of their number becomes ill.

COMPLEXITY

Roles vary in terms of complexity. Simple roles may be observed in the behaviors of infants or when persons are greeting or departing from one another. Complex roles appear in formal organizations and are characteristic of the professions. As it turns out, **complexity** in roles is composed of several different aspects that may or may not appear together. Let us consider some of these.

The first aspect of role complexity is **breadth**, or the range of characteristic behaviors appearing within the role. In a confused or routine situation, or one in which persons from many backgrounds are present, roles may appear that exhibit but few characteristic behaviors. However, given time and familiarity, broader roles

Roles spilling over [handwritten]

tend to appear. Turner (1968) calls this process "role accretion." Breadth of roles should also be inversely related to contextualization, since roles that "spill over" into other contexts should tend to exhibit a broader range of characteristic behaviors. Narrow roles are often felt to be constraining, and several studies have found positive relationships between breadth of occupational roles and job satisfaction among workers (Vroom, 1969).

A second aspect of role complexity is **difficulty**, the degree to which skill and energy are required to perform the role. By all accounts, the roles of the surgeon and professional athlete are difficult, while those of the street sweeper or janitor are presumed less difficult. As these illustrations suggest, status and power are often accorded those who perform difficult roles, which suggests that we will strive to accomplish roles of increasing difficulty. At the same time, difficult roles exact a toll, and we may eventually decide that the ulcers, high blood pressure, or torn knee cartilage which accompany the difficult role are not worth it.

A third aspect is **coherence**, the degree to which the components of a role fit together. Roles that cohere consist of behaviors that can be performed easily, either simultaneously or in sequence. Less coherent roles are characterized by behavioral disjuncture, by mutually inconsistent behaviors, by lack of self-facilitation, or by roughness of the behavioral flow. Coherent roles are felt to be "natural" by those who perform them, whereas less coherent roles take more practice. Noncoherence may appear when an individual attempts to perform two roles that are normally performed by different persons—the creative professor who attempts to chair a department, the accountant who also takes on sales management. Coherence of occupational roles should also be positively related to job satisfaction, which would parallel the effect obtained for breadth. [handwritten: Questionable—Not sure whether to add]

Breadth, difficulty, and coherence are but a few of the variables that make for comfort or discomfort for those who perform a role. Other variables include role conflict, role ambiguity, role discontinuity, role overload, and so forth. These will be discussed in Chapter Eight.

UNIQUENESS

Discussions of breadth have often dealth also with **uniqueness**, by which we mean the proportion of behavioral elements making up the role that are dissimilar to the behavioral elements of other roles. We are delighted (or appalled) to discover the breadth of unique behaviors that characterize the personal role of an iconoclast such as George Bernard Shaw or Bertrand Russell. Note that judgements of uniqueness require the existence of at least one alternate role against which the role to be judged is compared. A role is unique only in comparison with other roles. Popularized reports of roles are usually confined to those behaviors presumed to be unique without specifying the other roles against which uniqueness has been assessed. In addition, uniqueness is not an issue when we are discussing roles that were initially identified through the discovery of differentiated behaviors. These latter are unique by definition. Roles need not be unique, however; indeed, we may be interested in investigating whether two roles are or are not similar. Data collected by Blood and Wolfe (1960) [B & T, Selection 31], for example, suggest that the roles of husband and wife are more similar during the honeymoon than they will be later in the marriage.

VISIBILITY

Visibility is the degree to which a role is performed in the presence of an audience. Some professional roles, such as those of the psychiatrist, are performed in privacy or with but few others present. Other occupational roles, such as those of the bus driver or assembly-line worker, are performed in public. Visible roles are subject to direct feedback from others, and thus to sanctioning and problems of reciprocity with other roles. For this reason, role behavior is more likely to conform when it is visible (Argyle, 1957); Asch, 1956; Deutsch & Gerard, 1955). Roles low in visibility are less subject to feedback from others, which increases the importance of internalized controls within their performers. This is one of the reasons why professional associations tend to enforce a code of ethics on their members. Visibility also has the property of familiarizing others with the role, and several studies have demonstrated that nonvisible roles are more likely to be misunderstood (e.g., see Schanck, 1932).

Role System Concepts

ROLE DIFFERENTIATION

Some role concepts apply not to single roles but rather to role systems. Of these, the simplest is **role differentiation**. Two or more roles are said to be differentiated if they have but few behavioral elements in common (thus each tends to be unique when compared with the others). Role differentiation is a general notion that may be used not only to separate performances of persons who occupy different social positions, but also behaviors of a single person in various contexts. Several conditions have been suggested that lead to greater differentiation of roles. Roles of social positions, for example, seem more likely to be differentiated when: (*a*) specified by a static social tradition; (*b*) closely tied to the accomplishment of tasks; or (*c*) the positions have different statuses (Warner, Meeker, & Eells, 1949).

Role differentiation is one of the major conditions of modern, urban society, and it would be difficult to conceive of formal organizations without differentiation of its roles and jobs (see Chapter Seven). When roles are both differentiated and complex, they are also likely to become specialized, routinized, and differentially rewarded. For these reasons, some critics find role differentiation a questionable state and seek to amalgamate the roles of men and women, teachers and students, managers and workers. Role differentiation may take place without specialization, however. A surgeon, for example, exhibits differentiated roles when opening up a patient, when performing corrective surgery within the body cavity, and then in closing up the patient again. These three roles can be performed by specialists, although usually they are not. Role diff~~~~~~~~ ~~~ ~en, is neither a blessing nor a curse, although quite d~~~~ when roles are differentiated.

ROLE SETS

It is convenien~ ~~~~~~~~~~~~~ es. A set of roles that is perfo~~~ rton).[8] For example, a man m~ ~t his desk" when in the office, ~, and "per-form as a lover" lat~ ~ as the use of spoken English) ~ , a role set normally consists of ~~~~~~ ~ometimes argued that a compl~ ~n for the person, although this ~ ~l Salmi, 1970; Sieber, 1974; Sn

Role sets should be ~ithin a social system. For ex: ~ ~f roles made up of the behavi~ ~~~er, and children. The usual term denoting su~ ~~~ ~~ *division of labor*, but this is pejorative since labor may or may not be divided. (All family members may pitch in and do the dishes.) It is quite possible for a given person to perform several, distinctive roles within a social system.[9] Within the small business, for example, a single man may perform the roles of clerk, bookkeeper, and stockboy on successive after-noons, although his positional title is given as vice president of the firm. If we assume that terms of identity are normally given to persons whose roles are differentiated, it follows that most social systems will exhibit at least as many differentiated roles as social positions. Exceptions to this generalization may be found, however, wherein persons whose identities differ are actually doing the same job.

ROLE SPECIALIZATION

The concept of a role complement relates closely to that of specialization, for when differentiated roles of the system are performed by different persons, they

[8]Actually, Merton (1949) used the term *role set* to refer to expectations. A somewhat different usage is intended here.

[9]The concept of social system is defined in Chapter Seven.

(Handwritten note: Role sets link to role conflict, loads of roles being performed at once.)

are specialized. In formal terms, let us assume that persons in a social system may be classified in some manner and that each set of persons so classified exhibits a role. (For example, let us assume that all persons in a given office have either the title "secretary" or the title "executive," and the role of each so-designated set of persons can be established by observation.) Now, should the roles of the system also be differentiated, we say that the roles are **specialized**.

Thomas and Biddle [B & T, p. 34] suggested that the concept of specialization involves two facets, which I shall here term *diffuseness* and *singularity*. A **diffuse** role is one that involves many or all of the domains of behavior encountered within the social system, whereas a nondiffuse role is one involving only a limited domain. The role of the general practitioner is diffuse, whereas the role of the neurosurgeon or child psychiatrist is nondiffuse. A **singular** role is one that is performed by a single person within the social system, whereas a nonsingular one is performed by several persons. Within the large primary school there are often several third-grade teachers, whose role is nonsingular—but only a single music teacher.

In a rather sloppy way, we associate the term *specialization* with both nondiffuseness and singularity. Thus, it is often assumed that the more restricted the role you play, and the more it is played by you alone, the more "specialized" you are. Nevertheless, diffuseness and singularity have different implications for the system. Diffuse roles are harder to learn, to supervise, and to evaluate; they therefore tend to be eschewed by the formal organization, despite the fact that they are generally felt to be more rewarding to persons who perform them. But the greater the number of nondiffuse roles, the more one needs a system of control and integration (Parsons, 1951). Singular roles are generally performed by those who have special qualifications or training and may be quite necessary in the formal organization. Nevertheless, such persons are more sorely missed when ill or when their positions are vacated.

ROLE INTEGRATION AND RELATED CONCEPTS

Several concepts have also been suggested for describing the ways in which the roles of a system relate together. The general term describing a well-ordered social system is **role integration**; when we say a system is role integrated we are saying that its roles fit well together. There are various ways in which malintegration may be generated. Performers of different roles may find their duties overlap, that their roles are functionally interrelated although they have inadequate means for communicating, that they are competing against one another for scarce resources needed for role performance, that differing standards of reward or demand apply to their several roles, and so on. It is common to find malintegration within social systems where several competing sources of authority prevail (again, see Chapter Seven). For example, malintegration of roles within dockyards appears endemic in port cities because of the competing demands of shipping companies, unions, importing houses, and the public. A general discussion of the phenomena of role integration appears in Warren (1949).

Among conditions affecting role integration is complementarity. **Complementary** roles are those that fit together in that specific functions are accomplished through their occurrence. The function of child socialization, for example, is accomplished more easily when the roles of both father and mother are performed in the family than when either is missing—thus mothering and fathering are complementary. Roles in ceremonial occasions are also complementary, such as those of priest and congregation; the military reviewer, his subordinates, and their troops; or those of judge, jury, defendant, and attorneys in a criminal trial. In each case, the functions of the activity in which the several roles are imbedded are accomplished more easily owing to the presence of all roles than if one or more were missing. By definition, complementary roles must be at least partially differentiated, but total differentiation is neither necessary nor useful. Should roles be so specialized that their performers did not even communicate with one another, it would be difficult to see how they would have many jointly effected functions.

Another condition affecting role integration is interdependence of roles. **Interdependence** concerns the degree to which roles are mutually facilitative or hindering of one another. The performance of a sports team certainly stimulates cheering on the part of the spectators, and it is claimed that the cheering in turn stimulates extra effort on the part of the sports team—thus the roles of sports performance and audience cheering are interdependent. Interdependence can also be demonstrated for roles performed by the same actors. For example, some persons find that regular sports competition facilitates their office work, and, in addition, that their performance on the tennis court, handball court, or golf course depends on work accomplishment. Once again, roles must be minimally differentiated in order to be judged for interdependence.

Interdependence and complementarity are in theory defined independently, but it is difficult to conceive of interdependent roles that are not also complementary. However, many interdependent roles interfere with the accomplishment of set tasks. The wearing of sexy clothing on the part of young women and flirting behavior on the part of young men are probably interdependent roles, but it may be doubted that either contributes much to the accomplishment of work tasks.

A special case of interdependence is that of **reciprocity**. Roles are said to be reciprocal when some of the characteristic behaviors of one act as sanctions for the other and vice versa. Children and their parents commonly exhibit reciprocal roles. We are well aware of the rewards and punishments parents mete out to their children, but children too have means for sanctioning their parents and use them to good effect. Reciprocity is obviously only one type of interdependence, for roles may be interdependent for other reasons than sanctioning. It is also interesting to note that reciprocal roles are likely to be specialized and to be performed by nonoverlapping sets of persons.

ON THE EMPIRICAL STUDY OF ROLES

*Some social scientists will do any mad thing rather than study
men at firsthand in their natural surroundings.*
                                                    —George C. Homans

Suppose we wanted to study a role. Presuming that we knew but little about
the role to begin with, how would we begin? How would we collect detailed information about the role? And what criteria would we use to tell ourselves that we
had succeeded in our quest?

As was suggested in Chapter Two, the best way to study behaviors is to observe
them. Consequently, the best way of studying roles is to observe the characteristic
behaviors of persons as they cope with real-world problems and contexts. Although
there are other ways of gathering information about behaviors in contexts than by
observation, surely the best way of studying any observable phenomena is to
observe directly the events with which we are concerned.

Let us assume, for example, that we are interested in the role of the teacher in
the classroom. Then our best strategy at the beginning is to sit in classrooms with
an open mind and try to get a feel for what is going on there. In this exploratory
phase we are likely to adopt a posture similar to that advocated by anthropologists
when they speak of "participant observation." That is, we will enter the context
with as few preconceptions as possible and try to observe a wide range of examples
of the role we are interested in, taking copious notes, and trying out various ways
of conceptualizing behavior in our minds to see which of these allow us to differentiate the role we are interested in from other roles. A good example of such
participant observation in the classroom is in fact provided by Smith and Geoffrey
(1968).

However, if we are true empiricists, we soon discover that there are limitations
to the data generated by participant observation. For one thing, human behaviors
are emitted at a rapid pace that often exceeds our ability to note by informal
means. For example, classroom observers such as Jackson (1968) and Adams and
Biddle (1970) report that teachers can emit several hundred discriminable sentences
in interaction with pupils in a given class hour! Then, too, we become aware that
each behavioral event is a bundle of complex bits of information, and we have
difficulty trying to comprehend all of the implications of its symbols, logic, emphasis, warmth, aggressiveness, syntax, humor, and so on. In fact, once we think about
it, we discover that each behavioral act can be judged from an almost endless array
of conceptual viewpoints, many of which are capable of generating useful information about the role with which we are concerned. When acting as participant
observers we are conducting a selective integration and filtering task, for we sort
through this amazing mass of data generated by thousands of behavioral units
(which can be viewed from many conceptual vantage points) and emerge with

conclusions concerning those behaviors we believe are "characteristic." But since the processes of filtration and integration are performed internally, the conclusions we have reached may be biased, nor can we adduce objective evidence to substantiate them. Participant observation, then, is an excellent means for generating hypotheses but not for testing them.

For these reasons, most investigators of behavioral roles have eventually decided that they needed detailed records of behavior and some formal means for coding them. Prior to the advent of electronic recording devices, the major way in which behaviors were studied required the observer to take notes and then to dictate a "specimen record" of behavioral events (Barker & Wright, 1955). However, with the advent of portable tape recorders it is now possible to collect accurate audio or video recordings of behavior in field situations. When the person in whom we are interested is physically mobile (as is the manager in a factory, for example), data may be collected by means of a two-channel, audio recorder. Such a device is fed by two microphones: one broadcasting microphone that is hung around the neck of the subject, and a supplementary stenomask into which the observer dictates a running account of supplementary information. When the person who interests us is immobilized in a physical setting, as is true for the teacher in the classroom, videotape recordings may be used to good advantages (Kounin, 1970). Video recordings provide more information than audio recordings, since nonverbal gestures and context-relevant responses can be interpreted more fully.

A question is often asked concerning behavioral observation. "Aren't people affected when you observe them, and doesn't the fact that they are being observed also change their behaviors?" The answer to this question is, of course, "yes." Since we will presume (in Chapter Five) that human beings are sentient, the persons whom we study should be capable of detecting the act of observation and may adjust their behaviors as a result. Some social scientists have been so concerned with this problem as to recommend that we study the nonreactive "traces" of behavior rather than behavior itself whenever possible (Sechrest, Webb, Campbell, & Schwartz, 1966). However, most behaviors that are of interest to us leave no "traces" of their passing, thus we *must* observe behavior and the game is to minimize the effects of that observation. Sometimes this is done by concealing from persons the fact that they are being observed—by use of one-way mirrors or concealed microphones. Sometimes the observer "lies" to those he or she wishes to observe and offers a fictitious rationale for his or her presence in the situation (Festinger, Riecken, & Schacter, 1956; West, 1945). More often the observer offers a scientific rationale to subjects, encourages them to act naturally, promises that data will be kept inviolate, pledges that participants will never be identified as individuals in reports, and so forth. Moreover, if human observers or television equipment are placed unobtrusively in the room, do not appear to move, and do not respond to the behavioral overtures of those present—subjects appear eventually to forget that they are under observation (Barker & Wright, 1955).[10] It is also true that some subjects "haven't a clue" as to how to make themselves "look good" when under observation. Nevertheless, as is the case with Heisenberg's electron, the act of observing human subjects is likely to have some effect on them. Since there is no truly valid alternative to observing behavior, we are stuck with seeking to minimize this effect.

Our task does not end with the obtaining of a behavioral recording, however. The raw data provided by recordings are simply frozen records of behavioral events. These must then be subjected to formal analysis to detect which behaviors are characteristic of the persons in whom we are interested, thus development of codes and behavioral coding are also part of the process of studying roles (Weick, 1968). Through use of such formal tools, behavioral roles have now been studied in many contexts such as the home, the school, the factory, the office, the business conference, the psychiatric session, the jury trial deliberation, and others.

So much for the ideal case. But formal behavior observation is both time consuming and expensive, and most social scientists avoid it like the plague. Is it not possible to find a simpler method for studying behavioral roles? Indeed it is—provided only that we are willing to make assumptions. Three different strategies have been proposed by social scientists for gathering "cheap" data that could be substituted for direct behavioral observation. One of these has already been mentioned in the use of nonreactive "traces" of behavior, such as available public documents or indices of wear. The difficulties with this method are twofold. Most behaviors in which we are interested leave no traces, and we are at the mercy of biases that may have been introduced by those who originally assembled the records for their own purposes. Nevertheless, for roles that have been played out in the past, or for such realms as voting, migration, or economic behavior, this method may prove an acceptable (or the only available) substitute for direct behavioral observation.

A second strategy for studying behavioral roles has been advocated by experimental social psychologists concerned with testing hypotheses for human interaction under controlled, laboratory conditions. Observation of behavior in the laboratory is simpler than in real-life contexts. One-way mirrors may be used more freely, and extraneous subject behaviors can be minimized with appropriate controls. But to equate subject behavior in the laboratory with subject behavior in real-life contexts requires our willingness to accept the controlled stimuli of the laboratory as a fair representation of the complex stimuli of the real world. Real-life roles are normally

---

[10]The author was once an observer at a summer camp for boys where he witnessed acts of serious delinquency by both campers and staff members, including behaviors that destroyed camp property and threatened the health of others. At one point he actually abandoned his dispassionate stance and intervened—when a counselor sat on a camper while the latter slowly turned blue from lack of oxygen!

performed under the impact of a complex stimulus environment for which the laboratory appears to be a poor model. So far few studies of roles have as yet come out of the laboratory, except those of roles in face-to-face groups (see Chapter Seven).

The third strategy, by far the most popular for studying roles to date, is to administer a questionnaire or to conduct an interview that asks respondents to describe their own role or those of others. Literally hundreds of roles have now been studied by such means, ranging from occupational roles to personal roles, societal roles, contextual roles, content-specific roles, indeed the entire panoply of role types. In asking subjects to tell us about roles we are presuming that their descriptive accounts of role behavior are a fair reflection of those behaviors that have actually occurred. Although the issue of the equivalence of these two realms is taken up in detail in Chapter Five, in general there is little evidence to support the notion that behavioral reports by untrained subjects is an adequate substitute for actual observation. If behavioral events are too complex for the trained observer to handle, they are surely no less complex for the naive participant. Respondents inevitably select only certain aspects of behavior to remember; they also tend to distort evidence, filter out contradicting details, and integrate experiences into their own assumptional systems. This does not mean that testimony is a totally un-reliable guide. On the contrary, where questions are framed as simple matters of fact, in terms that are familiar to the respondent, and where the respondent is not emotionally involved in the answer and has had a chance to observe the behaviors in question, the respondent may well provide accurate information about a role. And it must be granted (albeit wryly) that most of what we think we know about roles to date has been gathered by this third technique.

Whether we study by observation or by substitute techniques, our strategy is likely to vary depending on whether the role is assumed to be person- or context-associated. When studying the former, we are rarely unsure of the identity of our subjects. Rather, the question to be answered is whether those persons *have* a role, and if so whether that role varies from context to context. To illustrate, studies of occupational roles usually begin by observing the behaviors of members of that occupation or by gathering descriptions of those behaviors from members or others. These data are then sorted to see whether the behaviors of members are character-istic, and if so, whether those characteristic behaviors vary depending on context. In contrast, when studying contextual roles, subject identity is very much at issue. As we know, contextual roles may be observed apart from knowledge concerning the identity of subjects. Separate investigations may then be conducted to find out whether those roles are performed by "everyone" or by specific persons. If it is the latter, then we have to find out who those specific persons might be and whether they are given a recognized identity. In recent years the campus of my university, like others, has been entertained by several outbursts of "streaking." Clearly, "streaking" is a contextual role. It also appears to be associated with maleness, with being an undergraduate, and with springtime. To bare other asspects of this phenomenon, however, would require research, for I do not yet know whether "streakers" constitute some specific subset of the male, undergraduate population nor whether they are as yet identified for their role. (For their sakes, I hope not.)

To discover a role is fun. But the study of roles goes a long way beyond the simple act of discovery. Let us review some of the other phenomena one might study that are associated with roles. Some roles may be partitionable into subroles that are associated with subsets of persons or contexts. Again, the behaviors found characteristic for the role may well affect one another, in which case the role may be studied for its dynamic properties or coherence. Most roles of interest are also imbedded within a wider social context, produce functions, are responded to by other roles, and may even be planned for. Thus, the discovery of a role is often merely a prelude to the study of other events with which the role is associated.

But how do we know when we have succeeded in studying a role adequately? What criteria would we use for establishing whether we had exhausted the range of behaviors that was characteristic of a set of persons in a context? This question can only be answered in a limited sense. In order to assure ourselves that our results are unbiased, we can study a representative sample of the persons and contexts in which we are interested. Moreover, if we set out to study only a small number of facets with which to conceptualize behavior (such as those offered by the typical formal coding scheme), it is certainly possible to establish whether none, any, or all of the behaviors mapped by these tools are characteristic of the persons and context studied. But there is no way on earth to guarantee that other investigators will not shortly come along who discover other aspects of the same role, using different conceptual tools of which we had not conceived. In this sense, then, trying to conduct an exhaustive study of a role is similar to the problem of making an exhaustive study of a personality or a culture.

Studies of these latter phenomena, however, are generally more sophisticated than studies of roles. Investigators such as Cattell (1946, 1950) have concerned themselves not only with a wide range of behaviors that might prove characteristic of individual personality, but also with the dynamics and evolution of those characteristic behaviors. Similar sophistication attends anthropological explorations of the range and dynamics of behaviors characterizing a culture, as exemplified by work with the Human Relations Area File (Murdock, 1957). Unfortunately, studies of roles have not yet appeared with this degree of sophistication. Most empirical research to date has concerned role components rather than the breadth of behaviors that should characterize a role. When such studies are at last available we will have better grounds for concluding that any given study deals with "important" aspects of role behavior.

The difficulty of setting boundaries for the role concept has been noted by other commentators. Occasionally a discouraged proponent will call for the abandonment of such terms as role, culture, or personality because of their asymptotic unreachability. Such pessimism is misplaced. Although a "complete" role may be impossible to establish, it is easy to discover salient portions of one; and we need a concept that denotes the behaviors characteristic of persons in a context. Truly, if the role concept did not already exist, those of us concerned with human behavior would have to invent it!

ENVOI

It has often been claimed that role theory offers a way to bridge the gap between the micro-science of psychology and the macro-sciences of sociology and anthropology. We have seen in this chapter that the role concept, at least, offers a link between the related concepts of personality and culture.

Overt aspects of personality, on the one hand, involve those behavior patterns characteristic of the individual, as he or she moves from situation to situation. Behavioral culture, on the other, concerns patterns of behavior that are common throughout a society. In between these two concepts stands role, focusing our attention on behavior patterns that are multi-individual and context relevant. In contrast with personality, when we look at a role we are normally concerned with behavior rather than with those who perform it, and we usually focus on some specific set of performing persons or a context for behavior. In contrast with culture, role analysis allows us to partition the realm of behaviors in a society so that we can isolate patterns characteristic of persons or contexts. Role truly bridges the gap between these micro- and macro-concepts, and it is small wonder that the role concept has gained wide acceptance.

At the same time, the role term suffers from many of the same defects as do the concepts of personality and culture. For one thing, each is an elastic concept with indefinite boundaries, easy to speculate about but difficult to operationalize, and subject to various interpretations. Each is also a high-level abstraction with no intrinsic content—a vessel waiting to be filled. All three have also been characterized as abstractions of stability. Personality presumes the persistence of individual behaviors; culture presumes that the society is to some extent homogeneous and static; role presumes that behaviors remain characteristic of persons and environments. How then can we deal with the phenomena of change?

Let us begin by asking whether these assumptions of stability are reasonable. We should take care in answering this question, because as citizens of a complex society we are surely motivated to view our world as stable, even if it is not so. Homans (1950) has suggested, as a general proposition, that the norms we hold for behavior are usually less variable than the actual behaviors to which they apply, and it seems reasonable to extend this proposition to our perceptions of most social phenomena. Nor have social scientists been free of guilt in this field. Role investigators have often taken the "role perceptions" or "role concepts" of untrained observers as an adequate way to study role behavior, despite repeated evidence suggesting that these two realms are only partially related.

But to deny the persistence of personalities, roles, and cultures is to deny both our own phenomenal experiences and the evidence of predictability in the social sciences. Surely there is a tendency for personal behaviors to persist, for the society to exhibit today and tomorrow some of the characteristics it exhibited yesterday, and for roles to form a semistable differentiation of the social system. It remains for us to discover, by appropriate empirical means, what behaviors are in fact characteristic of people in contexts and then to ask as auxiliary questions how these roles are perceived and how the perceptions in turn affect the behaviors of those concerned.

How then can role theory accommodate change in the social system, and to what extent can we predict, or even control, the processes of change so evident in contemporary society? This question is difficult to answer at the abstract level of the role concept. Propositions concerning changes in roles—for example, their specialization, differentiation, merging, and the like—are difficult to substantiate for all types of roles. However, when we turn to specific types of roles—for example, the roles of formal institutions, or roles associated with selected activities, or professional roles—we should be able to generate propositions concerning both role persistence and social change (see Chapter Nine).

There is also at least one more "defect" of the role concept that deserves mention. As is true of both personality and culture, role is modeled after a class of referential concepts that appear in the common vocabularies of Western cultures. Thus it is that Eliza Doolittle and her friends can discuss her role and those of others—presuming, in epistemological innocence, that their referential statements can be taken for the actual role behaviors after which they are presumably modeled. What then is the role: the actual behaviors that they are discussing; or the concepts, norms, values, or attitudes they express for that behavior? (For that matter, what is culture: the actual pattern of behaviors characteristic of societal members; or the concepts shared within that society for those behaviors? What is personality: the behaviors characteristic of the person; or the motives, values, and expectations presumably standing behind those behaviors?)

The position taken here is that the central concern of the role concept is with characteristic behaviors. Later (in Chapter Six) we will extend the role concept to expectations, but this latter discussion is based on the assumption that real roles exist in the behavioral world about which one might form expectations. It is an open question whether the role concept would have appeared at all in our social science had not examples of it conveniently appeared in the common language we share. It may even be that some of us who do not speak Indo-European languages may not use role expectations to organize our behaviors. But roles-as-behaviors must appear in all contexts and among all peoples. Not only is their study *the* central topic of the social sciences, but their contemplation is the joy, frustration,

anxiety, and concern of all humanity. One should not despise such a useful concept, even if it is home-grown.

Chapter Four

Identities and Social Positions

Tolerably early in life I discovered that one of the unpardonable sins, in the eyes of most people, is for a man to go about unlabeled. The world regards such a person as the police do an unmuzzled dog.

—T. H. Huxley

In Chapter Three we discovered that some roles are associated with sets of persons who share a common identity. Each of us knows personally but a small number of others—our spouse, parents, children, personal friends, close associates. But each of us is also able to interact appropriately with many others because these latter indicate that they hold identities which are commonly recognized—pedestrians, policemen, fishermen, the elderly—and because we, and they, know how to behave with those so identified. When persons share an identity that is widely known, we say they are members of a *social position*. Although the concept of social position may be a new one to some readers, the phenomena of shared identities appear in all societies and are a prominent feature of the human experience.

Let us exemplify the use of social positions by following a neighbor of ours while he is on his way to work.

At 7:46 on Monday morning, Urban Dweller kissed his *daughter* goodbye at the door of his home. He then climbed into his car and, together with his *wife*, drove to the nearby suburban station. While on the way there he discussed the evening menu with his wife and also negotiated interactions with various other automobiles—containing *drivers* and *pas-*

87

sengers. Upon arrival at the station, our hero purchased a commutation ticket from an *agent,* spoke briefly with two *acquaintances,* and ignored 43 other *commuters* who entered the train with him. Settling behind his newspaper, Dweller appeared to be oblivious to all outside events (including the slums through which his train was passing), but when the *conductor* and his *assistant* came down the aisle, Dweller fished out his commutation ticket and held it up for punching. Upon arrival at the city, he proceeded from the station, via a short bus ride, to his office—while en route recognizing and reacting differentially to a *bootblack,* a *beggar,* a *Salvation Army street band,* a covey of *nuns,* a *bus driver,* several thousand *pedestrians,* a *taxi driver* who nearly drove him down, a *black porter,* a *white elevator starter,* eleven *fellow passengers* (*male*) and one *fellow passenger* (*female*) in his elevator, a *typist* from his office pool, one of the *senior partners* from his firm, and his *secretary.* At 9:06 Urban Dweller settled behind his desk, having negotiated successful contacts with more than 5000 persons in the space of 1 hour and 20 minutes.

The interesting thing about this tale is that Mr. Dweller had no difficulty in interacting with this surprising number of persons. Only a mere handful of them were actually known to our protagonist, or had indeed been seen by him before this very morning. And yet, none of them were truly strangers, since each could be identified by membership in a social position with which our hero was familiar, and this identity enabled him—and them—to negotiate one anothers' presences.

It is also instructive to consider the variety of identities recognized by our hero. These included:

his daughter and his wife	a beggar
drivers and passengers	a woman
nuns	a black porter
commuters	a senior partner of the firm

Some of these classifications referred to a single person; others referred to larger groups. Some were based on behavior, others referred to such physical characteristics as sex or skin color. Some classifications could be entered easily; others would require years of training or careful selection. Some could be easily identified because of the wearing of a uniform; others could be identified only through the physical setting or characteristic behaviors of their members. However, each of these classifications referred to people, and each was recognized and given a common designation in the society of which Dweller and they were jointly members. Each is an example of a social position.

In this chapter we begin the process of relaxing the strictures of behaviorism under which we have labored in Chapters Two and Three. Readers will recall that in Chapter One we set forth rules for this text in which we would accept only the simplest assumptions needed to deal with each of the major concepts of role theory. As we have seen, one needs only the concepts of social behaviorism in order to deal with roles. In fact, the role concept can be (and has been) applied to animals that do not use symbols. This is not true for concepts such as identity and social position. These latter require, at a minimum, that subjects recognize and use symbols for the designation of persons. Thus in this chapter we shall add the assumption of symbol utilization to those we have considered heretofore. We shall not, however, concern ourselves with the complex task of representing the total range of symbols that are used by human beings, but merely with symbols that are used to designate persons. Other uses for symbols are considered in the chapters that follow.

CONCEPTS OF IDENTITY AND POSITION

> *There may be said to be two classes of people in the world: those who constantly divide the people of the world into two classes and those who do not.*
> *—Robert Benchley*

The term *identity* is another one of those protean words that has acquired nearly as many meanings as it has authors to write about it. Although used informally by social scientists for some years, modern enthusiasm for the identity concept seems to have been generated largely by E. H. Erikson (1956, 1968). Erikson used the concept of identity as a vehicle for discussing the problems of self-awareness and personal identification. Others have viewed identity as the means by which the person situates him or herself in social relations (Gross & Stone, 1964; Stone, 1962), as a source of motivation for the person (Foote, 1951), or as a way of providing meaning for individuals in mass society (Klapp, 1969; Stein, Vidich, & White, 1960).

In the broadest sense, identity may be said to encompass "all things a person may legitimately and reliably say about himself—his status, his name, his personality, his past life," thus "any generally satisfactory answer to the question, Who am I? (Who are you?)" (Klapp, 1969, p. 5). Such uses tend to incorporate entire theories of personality or interaction into the concept of identity. However, there is also a more limited use for the term *identity*, which relates to the act of labeling. To illustrate this latter use, let us assume that we are introduced to a person who is a stranger to us. He has mannerisms and an accent we cannot place at first. We watch him closely, however, and then, suddenly, we identify him as a "Frenchman" or whatever. He now has an *identity* for us, and to some extent we can use this information to plan appropriate behaviors with regard to him.

It is this latter, more limited, use of the identity term that we shall adopt in our discussion. In formal terms, then, an **identity** is a symbol that is used to designate one or more human beings. "Jimmy Carter" is such a symbol; so are titles like "President," "Justice of the Supreme Court," and "Congressman"; so are "woman," "author," "criminal," "adolescent," and "hermit"; so are private nicknames used by lovers to refer to each other. Any term or gesture may be considered an identity, provided only that it is used consistently to refer to one or more persons. It is true, of course, that common identity terms carry with them a host of expectations, attitudes, motives or whatnot concerning the behaviors of those who are so designated, or of others toward them, but we will delay discussion of these latter matters until later chapters. For now, to assign an *identity* to someone means only that we have given him or her a label.

Considerable overlap exists between the concepts of identity and social position. Depending on training, one author will use the term "identity" where another would use "position" (and others "role" or "status," etc.). However, the concept of position is somewhat more restricted than that of identity. Most of the identity terms mentioned in the preceding paragraph would serve also to illustrate social positions, but some would not. Let us see which would not and why.

Identities may be differentiated from one another in at least four ways.

1. Some identities apply to but a single person, such as the name of one's spouse, private nicknames, and secret designations that are used (I am told) for identifying agents of international espionage. Other identities apply to collectivities of persons, such as occupational and kinship designations. In general, identities that designate positions are applied to collectivities. "Jimmy Carter" does not exemplify the position concept; "President" does.

2. Identities may be differentiated in terms of their clarity. Some identities refer to unclear sets of persons. For example, Americans are familiar with such political epithets as "communist sympathizer" or "radical-liberal," yet even those who use these terms are probably uncertain as to their exact meaning—which makes it very easy to defame others through their use. Similar unclarity surrounds those who claim to be "saved" at a religious revival, those who are presumed to hold "public opinion," or members of a "plot" that is dreamed up in someone's paranoiac fantasy. In general, we shall say that identities are *clear* when the criteria for establishing their membership have an overt base (a topic to which we return later in the chapter), and for all practical purposes an identity must be clear in order to be considered a *position*. The interesting thing about this stipulation is that when we have met it we can thereafter assume a one-to-one relationship between the identity term and those persons it designates. Thus, our concept of social position includes both the term *grandmother* and those women who meet the overt criteria defining membership in the set designated. To put it another way, membership in social positions is rarely assumed an "interesting" topic for research.

3. Identities may be widely recognized within a society or may be familiar to only a few persons within a small social context. The terms, "father," "policeman," and "student" are probably recognized throughout American society. However, only those familiar with the Lions Club (a service organization) are likely to recognize the identity of "Tail Twister," which refers to those persons who are appointed for a season to serve as sergeant-at-arms and to enliven the proceedings of meetings. Again, all sorts of arcane occupational specializations may appear within a given

industry that are not recognized elsewhere. In general, identities involved in *social positions* are recognized throughout the population we are studying.[1] If this condition is not met, the identity will be said to designate a *membership position*. A special kind of membership position is the *analytic position* of the social scientist, such as Riesman's concept of "other-directed persons," psychoanalytic classifications for persons, demographic categories, and the like. Social scientists are sometimes tempted to presume that their analytic classifications are understood by citizens, thus to use identity terms with which they are familiar in constructing questionnaires or explaining their findings to others. Giving way to such temptations leads to confusion. There is a gradual drift of identity terms from the social sciences into the general vocabulary, however. For example, at one time the social class designations used by Warner, Meeker, and Eells (1949) were known to only a few social scientists. Today, such distinctions as "upper-middle class" are coming to have common usage among educated Americans.

4. In some authors' treatments of social positions it is stressed that positions are imbedded within and specified by a social structure (see Chapter Seven). This stipulation certainly holds for positions set forth in the rules of a game or within a kinship or formal organization. Without a quarterback there can be no American football team, and the manager's position within the organization is set forth in its charter and table of organization. However, this stipulation simply does not hold for other recognized positions, such as those of race, ethnicity, or occupational classifications. These latter were not created through rational discussion but rather have arisen through the vagaries of historical accident, and it is no wonder that ethnic positions, for example, do not form a mutually exclusive or exhaustive categorical system. (We return to this point later in the chapter.) However, some positions are assuredly stipulated by social structure, and when they meet this additional criterion we shall term them *structural positions*.

The concepts of familiarity, clarity of membership, and structurality are all defined independently. This suggests that it should be possible to form an eightfold classification for collective identities in terms of these three dimensions. Such a classification is presented in Table 4.1. According to the definitions suggested here, those identities falling within the left half of the table are the only ones that should be termed *positions*. Those within the far-left column are *social positions*, the next column constitutes *membership positions*, whereas structural positions appear within the top left quadrant only.

To summarize the discussion, then, a **position** is an identity used for designating two or more persons who presumably share one or more overt characteristics (also, by convention, those persons so designated). A **social** position is familiar; a

---

[1]Thus, although the concept of social position is both abstract and arcane, examples of social positions are both concrete and familiar. This contrasts with the role concept, for which we do not presume familiarity.

Table 4.1

A CLASSIFICATION FOR COLLECTIVE IDENTITIES

	Positions (clear rules exist for establishing membership)		Nonpositions (rules for establishing membership are unclear)	
	Social (familiar)	Membership (arcane)	Social (familiar)	Membership (arcane)
Structural (specified by a social structure)	Organizational positions	Social classes (in America)	Those "saved" at a revival	"Those who are against me," according to the deluded person
	Kinship positions	Identities within a secret society	"Participants" in a in a riot	
	Game positions			
Nonstructural (only incidental part of a social structure)	Race Religion Ethnicity	Psychiatric classifications	"Communist sympathizers" "Radical-liberals"	Various terms for persons appearing in *Finnegan's Wake*

membership position is arcane; an **analytic** position is recognized by social scientists. A **structural** position is one that is stipulated by social structure.

Confusion and Related Concepts

The concept of position has been designated by various terms in the role litera-ture and has been confused with several related concepts. Let us look at some of these problems.

The first person to discuss the concept of position formally was Ralph Linton (1936) who used the term "status" to refer to it. Some social scientists, particularly anthropologists, continue this usage. For example, one might read that "his status was that of chief," or "her status was that of mother-in-law." The only difficulty with this usage is that "status" has additional meanings which make such state-ments unclear. This problem is succinctly summarized by Hammond (1952), who suggests that status has "two additional connotations—statistically that of magni-tude on a single dimension, and socially that of respect." Since neither of these connotations has anything to do with the basic notion of person classification, the term *position* is to be preferred and will be used throughout this book. (Thus, we will say that "his social position is that of chief.") However, the "status of social positions" (that is, their ranking in terms of some criterion) is a legitimate field of inquiry and will be discussed later in this chapter.

Positions are also sometimes confused with roles. Many positions imply roles and vice versa, but positions are classifications of human beings; roles are classifications of behavior. This confusion (which also began with Ralph Linton) is a reasonable one, since we often classify people in terms of their behaviors, and one of our motives in making classifications of people is to predict their behavior. However, many common classifications of people are made on nonbehavioral bases, indeed do not reflect any identifiable roles. In addition, some roles are simply not associated with positions (such as those related solely to context or function, as we saw in Chapter Three). As a result, it is necessary to keep the concepts of position and role conceptually distinct. This places a burden upon the student, who will have to disentangle a certain amount of confusion in the role literature regarding positions and roles. Some authors, for example, use the phrase "role occupant" when it would be clearer to speak of *position member*. Other authors (for example, both Parsons and Nadel) attempt to elide the concepts of position and role, using the latter term for both concepts interchangeably. Still others, apparently despairing of conceptual clarity, have adopted a sloppy dualogism, "status-role," to refer to persons, their identities, their behaviors, expectuations for same—Old Uncle Tom Cobbley and All. This seems foolish.

Another type of confusion is generated by definitions given to the concept of position. Some authors define positions in terms of their relationships with other positions or in terms of a social structure that imbeds various positions. For example, we might find such definitions as: "*Status* . . . a position within a division of labor. It should be understood, of course, that a status is not a physical position. It is, rather, a set of cultural definitions that specify how a person is supposed to perceive and respond to objects and people when he is in a particular relationship with them" (Bredemeier & Stephenson, 1962, p. 30). Such definitions are not wrong, they are merely unclear—or in some cases logically circular. To define a social position as a "location" or a "niche" in a social structure simply does not tell us what it is that is being located (although we find out from subsequent examples that human beings were intended). In addition, if we define the social position to be a "location in a social structure" and then a social structure to be an "assembly of positions" we have ended up defining neither term. Finally, not all positions are defined in relationship to other positions or in terms of a social structure. True, it is difficult to conceptualize the position of mother without also conceiving of child, or of pitcher in baseball without catcher and batter, but the positions of wanderer, artist, or redhead have no clear counter positions involved in their conceptualization, unless it be that of all other human beings lumped into one vast basket category. The easiest way out of the dilemma is to recognize that the position concept invariably refers to identities, that is, to classifications into which people may be fitted. Then, if the author intends additional meaning to inhere in his or her usage—such as that positions are to be related to other positions or are imbedded in a social structure—this limitation can be spelled out.

Characteristics Used for Defining Positions

Two elements are involved in defining a position: the *symbol* (or identity) given the position and those *characteristics* position members are presumed to have in common. Positions differ in these elements, and we turn now to a discussion of them.

BEHAVIOR AS A CRITERION

Many types of human characteristics have been used for conceptualizing social positions. Probably the most common criterion used is *behavior*. Musicians are identified because they play an instrument or sing, athletes because they perform a sport, politicians because of their political activities, and so on. Many behaviorally identified positions receive designations that reveal the origin of their classification— teachers "teach," students "study," bakers "bake." Other behaviorally based positions have arbitrary designations whose origins are lost in the mists of time— tinkers repair pots and pans, barkers sell wares using their voices, authors write books.

Several things may be noted regarding behaviorally identified positions. For one thing, membership in them is transitory. Since behaviors change, membership in a behaviorally identified position normally depends upon situational context. An architect in his (or her) office, for instance, is "on stage" and normally performs differently from when he is "off stage" at home. In fact, no one (except perhaps the social scientist) would classify him as an architect in the latter context; there he is a husband, father, or gardener.

Behaviorally identified positions may also be transitory in another sense; they are entered only when some condition in the individual or environment is fulfilled. For example, some behavioral positions are only entered when a sufficient skill level is reached. One must practice many hours before becoming a professional athlete, and entrance into a clinical profession follows years of training and examination. Other behavioral positions may be entered only when the person has reached a given age or has gone through a ceremony. Still others require the maintenance of social conditions or of behavioral skills for retention of membership. The prime minister, for example, is subject to discharge following a vote of censure upon his or her government and policies.

It is also commonly assumed that entry into behaviorally identified positions is voluntary—that human beings enter them because they choose to do so. In the law, for instance, a criminal is assumed to have decided upon a criminal act and to be punishable for this decision. However, this may be a tenuous assumption. Some behaviors—for example stammering or neurotic inabilities—seem beyond the immediate control of the individual. And although other behaviors may be volitional, accidents of socialization or problems in the current environment may make it difficult for the person to conceive or consider alternative behaviors.

PHYSICAL FEATURES AS A CRITERION

Another common way of classifying human beings reflects the *physical features* they share. All societies recognize differences between the sexes and among age categories. It is also common to recognize racial distinctions based upon physical features that are presumably (although not always actually) correlated, such as skin color, hair texture, shape of the lips, epicanthic folds, and distribution of body hair. We also recognize aberrant physical features such as deformities or the loss of limbs. In addition, positional classifications are made for selected physical features that presumably bear relationships to personality traits or treatment by others—blonds are presumed to have more fun, redheads are hot tempered, little men are pugnacious, and so on.

In contrast with behaviorally based positions, positions based on physical features are inadvertent and relatively immutable. A person's sex, for example, normally does not change from situation to situation, nor does the person enter his or her sexual classification upon the fulfillment of conditions, nor is a person "responsible" for his or her sexual identity. Rather, membership in a featurally based position is assigned to the individual because of accidents of heredity, illness, or the aging process. Such membership may be advantageous, when persons of one sex, age, or race are given privileges or allowed more freedom than others. But when inadvertent membership subjects one to ridicule or prejudice, then such positional classifications are pernicious. There is a great deal of difference between denying freedom to the criminal and denying it to the black, or between restricting entry to a profession to those who pass a qualifying examination versus restricting it to men alone. At least in theory, criminals and those who lack qualification can adjust their behavior so as to achieve better treatment from others—blacks and women have no such options open to them.

Let us also note that some physical features are *not* used for positional classification. In our society, for example, we do not classify people in terms of their ear shape, despite the fact that ears are easily visible and manifestly different from person to person. Surely we could work up prejudices or stereotypes concerning flat or batlike ears if we put our minds to it. (Heyerdahl, 1950, reports that the Easter Islanders used ear shape for purposes of racial classification!) In other societies racial distinctions may be made on different physical bases or may be absent altogether. But positional distinctions seem always to be made in terms of age and sex categories, presumably because of the central importance of these features in determining interaction within the nuclear family and kinship system.

TRAITS, PRIOR EXPERIENCES, AND TREATMENT BY OTHERS AS CRITERIA

Another group of positional classifications stand somewhere between those based on behaviors and those based on physical features. As with behaviorally based positions, these classifications are organized around transitory evidence, however the positions created are treated "as if" they were immutable. Several kinds of positional classifications may be recognized with these characteristics.

The first method is classification by behavioral **trait**. Depending on the society, some behavioral traits are presumed to transcend situations, and thus to be generally characteristic of those persons who exhibit them. In our society we speak of intelligent or stupid persons, or of those who are hot tempered, or of good athletes. Other societies have presumed that different traits were transcendent and have recognized such positions as that of the dervish, orator, homosexual, or moribund person. Whether or not such situationally general traits actually appear in a given society is not germane to the discussion. The fact is that certain behavioral traits are presumed within a society to transcend situations, and social positions are erected upon this assumption.

The second method is classification by **prior experience** (or background). Those who have had the "misfortune" to have been born in another country are "aliens" until they have passed through a naturalization ceremony, but even as "naturalized citizens" they may not have the same rights as those of the native born—such as the right to be elected president of the United States. Such positional classifications as alien and naturalized citizen are behaviorally irrelevant, and nothing the person so classified can do—no matter how noble or self-sacrificing—will undo his or her membership in a position based solely upon prior experience. Castes in India have the same quality of behavioral irrelevance, as did membership in the Jewish ethnic community in Nazi Germany.

Still a third method of classification is through *treatment* accorded by others. A matinee idol or "sex goddess" is often distinguished from other, less fortunate (sic) movie stars more by the adulation he or she receives than by anything particular that was done to deserve the treatment. Despised members of a minority group may be behaviorally or featurally indistinguishable from the majority. Pupils with a "reputation" may be treated quite differently from their contemporaries in school, despite the fact that their actual behaviors or features are indistinguishable from those of others. Some common terms used to designate positions reflect treatment accorded—individuals may be "despised" or "well liked" or "looked up to," or "no 'count."

The three criteria of traits, prior experiences, and treatments by others will sometimes interact. A "minority group" is presumed to exhibit unique behavioral traits, will often be characterized by common background experiences, and will be treated differentially by the majority. Minority pupils with a "reputation" may acquire that reputation through behavioral traits that reflect their background experiences, but the fact that their "reputations" precede them does little to aid their integration into the majority culture. This is a particularly vicious cycle when positional membership is also based on physical features, such as race. The black child from the slum is coerced into academic failure not only by his or her background experiences, but also by the treatment others give him or her by virtue of membership in a racial position from which he or she can neither resign nor hide.

SOCIAL STRUCTURE AS A CRITERION

The last criterion for positional identification that we shall discuss is *social structure*. Some positions appear as part of a complement of positions necessary for organized activities. In a baseball game, for example, someone must be "pitcher" and someone else must play "left field." Should there be no pitcher there would be no baseball game, since our very concept of baseball depends upon an interaction among the positions of pitcher, catcher, batter, and fielders.

It is only in certain forms of social systems that abstract social structures appear—wherein the concept of the system requires the filling of social positions whose members are replaceable. In more primitive social system forms, such as in the family or community, persons are allocated to positions by virtue of their physical features, behaviors, or prior experiences. Moreover, these bases may form sufficient foundations for the entire complement of positions making up the system, be it family or kinship; and should the person leave the system, the system will be redefined. However, in games and organizations (and sometimes in small groups) the complement of positions is abstracted from its performers, any of several persons may perform within a position, and our concept of the structure of the system is that of a complement of positions rather than of a complement of persons. (Chapter Seven provides an expansion of this discussion.)

It is characteristic of structural positions that they are filled by public assignment. Normally the manager of a baseball team assigns who will pitch tonight, who will catch, who will play left field—and the left fielder of tonight may well play third base tomorrow night. Similar processes of assignment appear in the organization, where some are nominated to be workers, others foremen, others vice presidents, accountants, or personnel managers. The reason for public assignment within a social structure is that all concerned recognize the transitory nature of positional membership in such situations and need to know, clearly, "who is to pitch tonight." Thus, agreed-upon assignment procedures become necessary for structural positions, and positional assignment is generally accepted by both the member assigned and others in the system.

When structure is the sole criterion for positional classification, we must have either written instructions or an oral tradition that specifies the positional complement of the system. It is necessary that we agree on a complement of 9 positions in order to field a baseball team—rather than 10 players as in softball, or 11 as on a cricket team. Historically, our concept of the pitcher developed from the observation of a role—in this case the role of throwing a ball toward a batter in innumerable sandlot games of rounders, one- and two-old-cat, and other precursors of the modern game of baseball. But membership in the position of pitcher today does not depend on role performance. A pitcher is a pitcher because he (or she) is assigned to that position. The pitcher may in fact perform brilliantly, poorly, or monstrously—he is still the pitcher until someone else is assigned in his place.

Positions identified through social structure are similar to behaviorally identified positions in that they are limited to a situational context. However, the former are laid within an agreed-upon social structure, persons are assigned to them, and the behavior of the positional incumbent is irrelevant to the fact of his or her positional membership. In contrast, a person enters a behaviorally based position simply because of his or her behavior, and behaviorally based positions appear only incidentally within social structures. This does not deny, of course, the relevance of behavior for tenancy in a structurally based position—those who do poorly in a job often lose it. Nor is it denied that a strong person may create a social structure as a complement to his or her own behaviorally based position. Freud created the psychoanalytic movement to imbed his new ideology, Hitler a cancerous and violent analogue of Western civilization, Bonaparte a hundred institutions to mirror his genius.

SUMMARY: THE FOUNDATION OF A POSITION

Membership in social positions may be confirmed through various criteria. Thus, blacks are identifiable through racial signs (physical features), through characteristic accents (behaviors), or through treatment accorded them by others. However, one of these criteria defines the position, whereas the others are only incidentally characteristic of its members.

It is useful to distinguish between the criterion that defines a position and those that are only incidental characteristics. Let us call the defining criterion the **foundation** of the position.[2] In terms of the example given previously, regardless of his (or her) own behavior or treatment by others, a black is considered a member of a racial position because he or she exhibits the foundational physical features defining it. (Even this apparently clear stipulation is sometimes violated by state laws that define "Negritude" in terms of ancestry, which is a paranoiac confusion of positional foundation with condition of entry. We will return to this problem shortly.)

Many positional foundations are unambiguous. A baker is a "baker" by virtue of his or her occupational activities; an uncle remains one as long as he and his

[2] For an additional discussion of the foundation problem see Hughes (1945).

nephew remain alive; an alien remains "an alien" regardless of accent; a vice president holds membership in his position even if he beats his wife. However, occasionally there is confusion between the foundational and incidental characteristics of a position. Personal characteristics of forceful or long-tenured positional incumbents are sometimes presumed to inhere in the position and to be *de riguer* for their successors. Social scientists are not immune to this latter problem and are capable of confusing the definition of a position with some convenient operation by which they would assess positional membership in an investigation. Thus we occasionally read such self-defeating statements as "intelligence is that characteristic measured by an IQ test," or "blacks in America are those who so identify themselves and are so identified by others."

VARIETIES OF POSITIONS

> *The rich man in his castle, the poor man at his gate, God made them, high or lowly, and order'd their estate.*
> *—Cecil Alexander*

Types of Positions

Many typologies have been proposed for social positions. Linton (1936) distinguished positions that were "ascribed" from those that were "achieved." "Status" and "office" were differentiated by Hughes (1937). "Caste" has often been opposed to "class," occupations to professions, and so on (Davis, 1949) [B & T, Selection 1]. Most of these distinctions are actually points along variables that apply to positions and are somewhat awkward when used for constructing typologies. However, some basic typologies are useful in helping us to distinguish among positions in social analysis.

FOCAL AND COUNTER POSITIONS

It is possible to define a position in such a way that it includes all human beings, for example, "breathers"—all persons who regularly inhale and exhale. Such definitions are not particularly useful. Normally the foundation of a position enables us at least to partition the universe of all persons into two sets: those who are members of the position and those who are not; for example, "redheads"—all persons whose hair is red (versus all persons whose hair is either some other color or absent). Any position so defined may be termed a **focal position**, the term focal indicating that we focus on this position in our analysis. (It is also common to term a member of a focal position **ego**.)

It is likewise possible that those who are not members of a focal position may be analytically indistinguishable from one another; for example, "non-redheads."

However, should it be possible to partition those who are not members of a focal position into one or more additional positions whose membership is not residual, these others may be termed **counter positions**. (Members of counter positions are commonly termed **alter**.) For example, if the focal position is that of "redhead," it is possible to recognize the counter position of "blond"—all persons whose hair is yellow. Note, however, that in order to make such partitions it is necessary to utilize foundations for defining the counter positions that are closely related to that used for defining the focal position. Although it is possible to define counter positions by simply partitioning the residual set of persons (for example, contrasting the focal position of "men" with the counter positions of "young girls" and "old women") it is more common to differentiate focal and counter positions by use of foundations that form mutually exclusive categorical sets. Red hair and yellow hair, for example, are mutually exclusive categories.

Let us presume also that it is possible to continue on in this fashion, defining counter positions in such a way that they are mutually exclusive, until the set of focal and counter positions exhausts the universe of all persons in the system. In such a case the positions so defined constitute a facet. I will presume, for example, that the positions of "redhead," "blond," "brunette," "grey," and "bald" form a facet, since it would be difficult to imagine a person whose crowning glory was not roughly encompassed by such a classificational scheme. Similarly, a listing of the job titles for most organizations provides us with a facet of positions.

Given such definitions, a focal position may turn out to have none, one, or many counter positions; and the focal position may or may not form a facet together with its stated counter positions. In those cases where a facet is formed, it is common to speak of the set of positions forming the facet as a **complement of positions**, and those interested in the analysis of social systems often begin their study by trying to ascertain its positional complement, if any. For example, those interested in studying a primitive society or game or organization often begin by asking the participants to list for them the titles of the players. Another reason for enumerating counter positions for a selected focal position is to establish who the "others" are to whom a positional incumbent must accommodate. For example, in the research of Gross, Mason, and McEachern (1958) it was shown that much of the role of the superintendent of schools was taken up with relationships between himself and representatives of such counter positions as school principals, teachers, school board members, and the like. However, many focal positions simply do not have commonly recognized counter positions.

POSITIONAL SETS AND SEQUENCES

Whereas in simple social systems it may be true that a person occupies only one social position, it is more common in urban civilizations that we have many memberships. Urban Dweller was a father, a husband, a motorist, a commuter, a pedestrian, a member of his firm. But he is surely only a piker when it comes to positional membership. Some active businessmen hold membership in dozens of volunteer organizations, and concerned public figures, such as an Eleanor Roosevelt or a Dr. Benjamin Spock, may be at least nominal members of several hundred organizations! This suggests another concept, that of the **position set** (termed a "status set" by Merton, 1949), consisting of the collection of social positions characterizing a person.

Position sets are sometimes confused with position complements, and both with a third concept, the **alter position set** (termed a "role set" by Merton), which consists of a listing of the positions within a social system with whom a person has role relationships. To illustrate these three concepts: The *complement* of positions within a typical primary school includes pupils, grade teachers, specialty teachers, the principal, a secretary, and the janitor. The *position set* of the typical grade teacher includes the identities of teacher, union member, church member, mother, wife, citizen, and so forth. Within the school, however, the teacher normally has *role relationships* with her pupils, specialty teachers, the principal, and his secretary—but only occasionally with the janitor.

As the preceding examples suggest, the fact of multiple identities need not cause hardship for the person who holds them. However, in some cases the positions held are associated with multiple roles, in which case the person may find him or herself flooded with expectations and conflicting demands. Pooh-Bah in *The Mikado* complains of such conflicts for his several identities. Killian (1952) suggests that "latent" conflicts may appear in times of disaster among expectations for identities that normally fit well together. Thus, the concept of position set relates closely to that of role set and to problems of person–role fit. (We return to these problems in Chapter Eight.)

Some position sets are co-temporal. For example, I am both an American and a professor in a university; neither identity precludes the other. In contrast, some identities not only preclude one another but may actually be preconditions for entry into other identities. In some fields a person must first serve as an apprentice before he or she can be qualified as a journeyman. At most American universities it is necessary to pass through the positions of freshman and sophomore before one can enter the position of junior. In many societies a strict sequence of age-graded positions is imposed on members, with ceremonies or rites of passage provided to announce changing from one position to another. When positions are arranged in sequence so that membership in one is a requisite for entry into the next, we shall say that they form a **positional sequence** (after Merton, 1949) [B & T, Selection 2]. The concept of positional sequence has attracted both discussion and research (and is also discussed further in Chapter Eight).

POSITIONAL DIFFERENTIATION

As was suggested in the introduction to the chapter, positions are not always differentiated. Apart from age, sex, and kinship positions (which appear to be universal), many types of positions are simply not differentiated in preliterate societies. And in "innocent" activities, such as the games invented by young children or in hippie colonies, the classification of persons by generic titles of identity may be missing or deliberately repressed. By **positional differentiation**, then, we mean simply that a particular set of collective identities is socially recognized and used clearly within a population. When we discuss positional differentiation we must make clear what type of positions we are speaking of. For example, within aboriginal societies in Australia there was little differentiation of occupational positions, although vastly differentiated kinship terms were recognized.

When does positional differentiation take place? Structural positions defined for a game or organization must be differentiated, for we have planned it that way. But when are societal, kinship, or community positions differentiated? Little research has been conducted on this problem, although it would appear that positional differentiation is more likely to take place following role differentiation (see Chapter Three).

EMPTY POSITIONS

Given that a position is a classification for human beings, it is possible to find **empty positions** under certain circumstances. Except in a vacuous sense, empty positions cannot be defined by behaviors or physical features. (The position of "men with green skin" is meaningful, but what have we gained by making such a statement?) Empty positions may easily be defined, however, by using such criteria as treatment by others and social structure. The position of Vice President in Charge of Sales may persist in a firm even after the death or discharge of its most recent incumbent. The empty position attracts treatments from others— memos are addressed to it, letters pile up at its desk, and so on. Additionally, the firm begins to search for a new incumbent, describing the job to candidates, advertising in trade journals, seeking suitable applicants. Finally, a new incumbent may be appointed with considerable ceremony. ("The King is Dead. Long live the King.")

We should restrict use of the empty position concept to identities for which an incumbent was recently available or another will shortly appear. The referential terms "ghost," "spirit," "Visigoth," and the like are not normally assumed to be social positions because one will not find living human beings whose behaviors, features, or other characteristics match those specified for the classification. Positions may be temporarily empty, but only so long as others accept the imminent tenancy of the position and continue to direct their behaviors toward that position in anticipation of its complementation.

Variables Applying to Positions

Many variables have been suggested for the analysi⟋
membership, only a few of which will be discussed here. In a⟍
applying to roles may also, with some stretching, be applied to po⟍⟍
versa. Consequently, the reader interested in further pursuit of variables app⟍⟍
to positions is urged to review Chapter Three.

CONDITIONS OF ENTRY, MAINTENANCE, AND EXIT

Following Linton (1936), the distinction between ascribed and achieved positions has appeared widely in both anthropological and sociological literature. In general, **ascribed** positions are those into which one passes through accidents of birth, social experience, or maturity—for example, sex, nationality, or ethnic identity. **Achieved** positions are those attained through skill or effort—such as professional positions, military ranks, or public honors. Thus, membership in ascribed positions is presumed inadvertent, whereas one enters an achieved position for advertent reasons.

Nadel (1957) and Banton (1965) have criticized Linton's distinction, suggesting that ascription and achievement are not antonyms of each other, thus some positions might be neither ascribed or achieved. In fact, once we think about it, Linton's distinction applies more to the conditions by which a person enters a position than to the foundation through which the position is defined. If these coincide, then Linton's distinction is easy to make. When they do not, we have problems. This insight led Thomas and Biddle [B & T, p. 50] to suggest that **entry**, **maintenance**, and **exit conditions** might exist for some positions that are independent of each other and of the foundation that defines the position. A public school teacher, for example, is defined as a person who is hired by the school system and who instructs pupils within a school. The teacher becomes one by taking a prescribed course of instruction, by passing certain examinations, and by virtue of state certification. The person remains a teacher provided that he or she performs his or her job adequately and does not violate regulations concerning personal conduct. He or she departs from the position through resignation, retirement, or being discharged for cause. Thus, in the case of the teacher, the defining foundation is conceptually independent of conditions for entry, maintenance, and exit from the position.

However, none of these conditions is capricious—all relate to the social system in which the position of the teacher is imbedded. This suggests that conditions of entry, maintenance, and exit may be distinct from those defining the foundation when the position is imbedded within a social structure. This does not mean that structural positions will always have elaborate conditions for entry and maintenance of membership. Mack (1956) calls those that have such qualities **determinate**

.ions and advances a series of hypotheses contrasting positions that are deter-
.nate from those that are indeterminate. Nevertheless, one characteristic of our
bureaucratized society is a tendency for the proliferation of entry and maintenance
conditions for positions. Indeed, once lawyers, accountants, pressure groups, and
public opinion have all had their say, it may someday be impossible to fill positions
of public responsibility!

Another example of the differentiation of entry, defining, and maintenance
conditions is provided in labeling theory (Becker, 1963; Erikson, 1962; Lemert,
1951, 1967; Scheff, 1966). This perspective is concerned with membership in
positions that are normally considered "deviant," such as those of addiction, retar-
dation, delinquency, or mental illness. Such positions are defined by traits that are
punished within our society. According to proponents of labeling theory, one
enters such positions by exhibiting one or more acts of "primary deviance" and by
being labeled by others, often in a public "ceremony of status degradation" (such
as a court trial). Once labeled, it is argued, the person may thereafter exhibit
"secondary deviance" because of social pressures placed on those who bear such
pejorative labels, thus confirming membership in perpetuity. Labeling theory is
attractive because it suggests that underdogs may be victims rather than perpetrators
of their misfortune, hence underdoggedness may also be "cured." Unfortunately,
empirical support for this perspective is weak (Gove, 1975). Again, we return to
this topic in Chapter Eight.

In summary, Linton's distinction is best applied to positions having coincidental
conditions of entry, maintenance, and exit that reflect the foundation of the
position. Thus, behavioral positions are likely to be *achieved*, whereas positions
defined by features or in terms of past events or treatment by others are generally
ascribed. Structural positions and those defined by traits are often difficult to
classify in Linton's terms.

RELATIONALITY

As has been suggested, some positions are defined in ways that pair them with
other positions. Kinship positions have no meaning by themselves but must be
imbedded within a kinship structure containing additional positions; rivals must be
paired, judges require advocates, and so on.

Other positions, such as those of artist, banker, prophet, or tramp are not
defined explicitly in relationship with others. Thus, **relationality** is a variable with
which positions may be distinguished from one another.

At least two aspects of relationality may be discriminated. First, we may
distinguish those positions that are paired with *none*, versus those paired with *one*,
two, or *many* others. A husband requires only one wife for complementation (in
our society), a teacher only pupils, an orator only an audience; but a cuckold needs
two positional partners, as does a referee or marital counselor; and a defense

counsel requires the whole panoply of positions found in the courtroom—judge, prosecuting attorney, client, baliff, jury, and so on.

Second, even positions that are not defined relationally may yet be found paired with one or more counter positions within some contexts. Professional singers, for example, are often paired with their managers, corporation executives with secretaries, political candidates with speech writers, and so forth. Thus, relationality may appear either because of interdependence of foundational definitions or because of functions accomplished.

STATUS

As we know, some human characteristics provoke sanctions. Some (such as telling the truth, intelligence, or desired accomplishments) are likely to be rewarded; others (such as criminality or homosexual behavior) will be punished. Many forms of sanction may be given: on the one hand, praise, money, honor, or deference; on the other, physical punishment, censure, or imprisonment. Sometimes treatments are given to an entire position that involve sanctions not given to other positions. When this happens it is possible to rank positions in terms of the characteristics they (presumably) possess or the sanctions they are (presumably) given. By convention, a position has higher **status** if its members have (or are presumed to have) more of some characteristic that is positively sanctioned, or it regularly receives (or is presumed to receive) more of some positive sanction, than some other position.

Many criteria are available for establishing status involving both the characteristics of and sanctions given to position members. Classic discussions of status have tended to focus on three of these criteria: prestige, wealth, and authority, claiming that these tend to subsume or to determine other criteria (Benoit-Smullyan, 1944 [B & T, Selection 3] ; Lasswell, 1936). Let us see what these discussions are about.

Some positions have higher **prestige** than others; that is, they are more likely to attract deferential behavior from others who are not their members. In most societies members of the professions have more prestige than do janitors or ditchdiggers. The president of the firm normally attracts more deference than does the foreman or worker. It is possible, of course, for prestige to inhere either in the person or in the position of which he or she is a member. The creative scholar, famous athlete, or successful politican acquires prestige in his or her own right. However, a position may also be accorded deference, and the person can acquire prestige merely by joining it. The colonel who has been told that he will shortly "receive his star," the designate for a Nobel Prize, the newly elected vice president of a bank—all are likely to receive increased deference from others. Societies differ in the degree to which prestige is attached to positions. Whereas the American university professorship confers little additional prestige beyond that given to an assistant professor, to be a professor in a British university confers a great deal of deference.

Nevertheless, the overall prestige ranking of occupational positions is quite similar among most Western countries (Inkeles & Rossi, 1956).

Positions also differ in their **wealth**—in the number of commodities its members are given or allowed to control. Businessmen, physicians, movie actors, and trial attorneys are likely to be wealthy in our society, whereas dictators, shamans, or army officers may be wealthy elsewhere. Within societies possessing a currency it is possible to measure wealth in monetary terms (see Chapter Eight). When no such currency is available, wealth may be indicated by the size of one's dwelling, the number of cattle owned, or one's ability to destroy property at a potlatch (Benedict, 1934). Wealth is different from prestige in that the number of commodities is finite at any given time within the society. To have differential distribution of those commodities requires acquiescence, thus extremes of wealth must appear "inevitable" if not "right and proper" to both the millionaire and pauper. Within our society we deem it "proper" to inherit wealth or to acquire wealth through sharp business transactions. Other societies deem these avenues "improper," and wealth may be accumulated through military conquest or political subterfuge (which we deem "improper"). Wealth and prestige may vary independently, of course. The member of an "old family" usually receives deference, although he or she may not have much wealth. Americans tend to think of wealth as the single, most important criterion of status, but then Americans are hung up on money.

Another criterion for status is **authority**—the degree to which others follow the dictates of position members. Those belonging to certain positions can tell others what to do. Policemen, judges, sages, university presidents, community leaders—all can get others to do their bidding by virtue of positional membership. Authority is sometimes confused with power, charisma, and legitimacy, and we should separate these four concepts in our thinking. **Power** is the general ability to exert influence. One person has power over another if that person can get the other to do what he or she wants. Power stems from many sources—control of resources, love, personal or positional qualities, terror, persuasion, force, and others (Dahl, 1957; French & Raven, 1959; Goldhamer & Shils, 1939; Harsanyi, 1962; Schopler, 1965). When power is associated with positional membership, we term it *authority*. Power may also be associated with the person as an individual, in which case it is **charisma** (after Weber, 1925; see also Shils, 1965). To illustrate the difference between authority and charisma, consider American versus British forms of political democracy. British politicians run for office through party nomination and may not even reside in the district they represent; their power is authoritative. American politicians campaign on their abilities to solve local problems through personal intercession; their power is charismatic.

Authority and charisma may be based on rational considerations. I am a fool if I do not obey the policeman who directs traffic or listen to the warnings given me about my sick automobile by an expert mechanic, since negative consequences are likely to follow if I do not. On the other hand, some positions acquire authority through social structure rather than because of functions produced. Persons having grandiose titles and uniforms are likely to be obeyed by others, though no clear consequences of disobedience are known. This latter phenomenon is referred to as **legitimacy**, and it is useful to note that formal organizations probably could not exist without some form of it (see Chapter Seven). Prestige and wealth are normally associated with authority. However, some positions are authoritative in the teeth of contradictory evidence. A court jester has little prestige and less wealth, nevertheless he has the "right" to order even his monarch around in certain realms of behavior.

As the preceding examples suggest, criteria for status need not coincide. The bishop normally has considerable prestige and authority, although he may lack wealth. The robber baron may have wealth and power but lack authority. Despite these examples, many persons confuse criteria for status or tend to generalize from one criterion to others. Thus, a person or position known to have one rewarded characteristic will be assumed to have others as well, thus those who are known to have accumulated wealth may also be accorded prestige and authority, or vice versa. This process is termed **status equilibration**, and a practical example of it occurs when advertisers use the face of a sports hero to advertise cigarettes or other commodities. Considerable research has now been conducted on status equilibration (Sampson, 1969), and formal, propositional theory has been stated for it (see, particularly, Berger, Zelditch, & Anderson, 1966).

This discussion does not exhaust the subject of status. The status concept may be applied to persons as well as to positions. To illustrate, those interested in sociometry may say that a person has "high status" when he or she is chosen frequently for friendship by others (see Chapter Eight). Many grounds may also be recognized for sanctioning positions (Foa & Foa, 1971, 1974; Moore, 1969). Some sanctions given to positions are idiosyncratic to the viewer or are bounded by context. The grounds upon which sanctions are given may change from time to time and are certainly different from one society to another. Nevertheless, quite apart from who you are as a person and what you do, as long as you hold membership in a social position you will be accorded status in terms of that membership. Some of us garner self-esteem by clutching to our bosoms the rewards given, anonymously, to high-status positions of which we are members. And those of us who were born with the "wrong" skin color or who persist in attending the "wrong" church may be inclined to hate others (and ourselves!) for the venomous punishments given, again anonymously, to those positions from which we cannot escape (Asher & Allen, 1969; Clark & Clark, 1947; Goodman, 1952).

GENERALITY

Like roles, positions also differ in **generality**. Some positions are specific to a limited range of persons or situations—for example, astronauts. Other positions include large portions of the human species and appear relevant to nearly all situations, such as sex or age classification. In between these two extremes one finds positions that involve many persons but are limited to rare occurrences (bridegrooms) or positions involving only a few persons who are nevertheless indispensable in various situations (chairpersons of meetings, referees). We are more familiar with positions of high generality, recognize their members more readily, and have personal knowledge of the roles we are to play with them and vice versa. Of necessity, our relationships with positions of low generality tend to be controlled more by stereotype and formal specification. Most of us attend only a few weddings in our lives and would be somewhat confused about the identities of the actors in one if we were not guided by those more familiar with the ceremony. When we first encounter it, the behaviors of foreigners in their own lands appears to be quixotic and colorful. As we become more familiar with the positions used for classifying these former strangers, their behaviors become not only more predictable but also more "ordinary."

AMBIGUITY

Positions also differ in **ambiguity**. One type of ambiguity has already been mentioned—lack of a clear foundation for defining the position. We have considered examples of identities—such as "communist sympathizer"—whose foundations are so unclear that we would have difficulty establishing even a single person as a member of them. Contrast this with the position of "adulterer," whose common definition is not only unambiguous but is also backed up by legal specifications. It is possible to sue another for slander when one has been called an adulterer, but suits based upon accusations of communist sympathy have not been tolerated by the courts.

In addition to foundational unclarity, there are other ways of generating ambiguity for a position. One of these occurs when two distinct positions happen to have the same identity term within a given language. Consider the term *father*. In English this applies to male persons who are also parents, and also (confusingly) to priests of certain churches. For this reason, statements such as "Patrick O'Boyle is a father" are ambiguous. We are not sure what has been communicated to us until the speaker provides additional information. Again, the term *Yankee*, is used by foreigners to apply to all Americans, by southerners to apply to northerners, by northerners to apply to New Englanders, and by New Englanders to apply to white Protestants of early migration.

Closely related to this type of ambiguity is another that occurs when a position is given two or more identity terms depending on context. Several terms are used in English to refer to those who teach, for instance, including "teacher," "instructor," "master," and so forth. Ambiguity also occurs when the mode of address for a given position changes depending on who it is within the social system who is speaking. Within the nuclear family, for example, the same person may be both a father and a husband. Multiple identity terms generate problems, and in most preplanned social systems, such as organizations and games, this type of ambiguity is avoided (see Chapter Seven). However, multiple designations are often found in nonplanned systems.

Ambiguity may also appear when members of a social system are aware of a given classification of persons but have not yet given a name to that position. Americans are manifestly aware of social classes and class differences, but for ideological reasons they may refuse to entertain a terminology that would enable them to discuss these differences systematically.

Still another type of ambiguity occurs when inadequate means are available for detecting members of the position, although its foundational definition may be clear. In the paternity suit, the accused may truthfully answer that he does not know whether or not he is the father of the child. Although the accused may be presumed familiar with the theory of conception (!), evidence may not be available to assign responsibility to him alone. Similar problems may appear for any position whose membership is based on a past event for which evidence has been lost.

Two kinds of problems are connected with positional ambiguity. On the one hand, those who might be members of such positions may be unsure of their membership. It is not clear to these people whether they will be subject to role expectations associated with that position or not. On the other hand, the ambiguity of a position interferes with crisp thinking about the position by those who would use the positional designation as a reference term. It is possible for the orator to wax eloquent about the evil character of "radical-liberals," for instance, without ever saying anything; or we may be confused when another uses the term, Yankee, without specifying a context.

CUE CLARITY AND POSITIONAL SIGNS

How do we go about telling whether one is a member of a social position? In the simplest case the actor establishes his or her membership by public exhibition of the foundational characteristics with which the position is defined. On other occasions membership may simply be announced by the incumbent or by others who address him or her. When, for example, an accident has taken place and a stranger rushes up announcing "I am a doctor," his or her self-identification is usually taken without question. However, it may be inconvenient or illegal (or immoral, or fattening) to exhibit foundational characteristics publicly or to make continuous announcements about positional membership. For many positions, then, membership is announced by means of **positional signs**—the wearing of uniforms, the display of gestures, or the maintenance of an accent—which clearly tell the onlooker who one is.

Positions vary in the degree to which positional signs are associated with their membership—in their **cue clarity**. When persons of various backgrounds may enter the position and positional membership must be established unambiguously and instantly, the wearing of uniforms is *de rigueur*. This is why uniforms appear in the hospital, the military post, and the courtroom. On the other hand, on the university campus there are likely to be more behavioral cues differentiating the undergraduate from his or her professors, so that although only the latter are likely (if they are men) to be wearing a white shirts and ties, this uniform is not required and may be violated by professartorial deviates.

Many positional signs are inadvertent, however. Different styles of language persist among different ethnic groups and social classes and are a major cue by which "one of us" or "the stranger" may be identified. This is particularly true for static and status-oriented societies such as those of New England or Britain. British accents differ not only from social class to social class, but also from county to county, and the sensitive Englishman listens carefully to the other's speech manner-isms before committing him or himself to an appropriate style of interaction (as in Shaw's *Pygmalion*). Indeed, positional cues may achieve such importance as to be confused with the foundation of the position in the minds of innocent people. A "gentleman," for example, becomes one who has excellent table manners, rather than one who has good breeding and chivalrous behavior.

Whether advertent or inadvertent, the cues by which one presents one's mem-bership in a position are necessarily part of the role associated with that position. They should not, however, be confused with the foundation that defines a position. Sexual positions are defined physiologically, although usually we confirm member-ship in the male or female position by means of clothing, gestures, and speech patterns. When positional signs are unclear, it usually means that membership in the position is unambiguous or that instant identification of the actor's position is unimportant in the situation involved.

THE STUDY OF POSITIONS

> *We know of no attempt at the compilation of an inclusive inven-tory or classification of either positions or role-relations.*
> *—G. Marwell and J. Hage*

Suppose we were interested in studying a social position, how would we pro-ceed? Surely our first concern would be to establish the existence of the position. To do this we would want to learn whether the identity label in which we are interested was recognized by our subjects. Then we should find out whether sub-jects shared definitions for membership in the position designated by that label. Perhaps we might also want to learn whether subjects used similar cues for iden-tifying those who were members. Surprisingly, these basic issues are seldom studied by those interested in social positions. Nomination of positional titles is occasionally studied by ethnographers or those interested in small communities, such as Lynd and Lynd (1929, 1937), but it is difficult to find studies concerned with positional definition or with the cues that are actually used for establishing positional membership. In effect, most investigators appear to take identification and membership in social positions for granted.

How reasonable is this stance? Presumably most Americans recognize common labels for age, sex, and racial positions. Moreover, membership in these positions is not often deemed problematic, and cues that are used for establishing membership are normally quite obvious. But once we move away from these general positions, such assumptions become questionable. How many Americans recognize occupational or political identities? What criteria would various subjects use to define membership in such positions as "alcoholic" or "hyperkinetic child"? Through what cues are "homosexuals" recognized, and are all persons equally able to recognize those cues? Surely these are interesting topics for study, and we are remiss if we make unexamined assumptions about them. Moreover, studies concerned with the existence of social positions should be easy to conduct, since they require only that we ask questions of subjects. In this sense, to study a position is much easier than to study a role, for as we saw in Chapter Three the latter should involve the observation of behavior. Be that as it may, studies concerned with the existence of positions are hard to find.

Few of us would be content merely to establish the existence of a social position. Great interest is given to positional variables and to events associated with positional membership, and most research on positions has in fact concerned these latter. Some investigators have studied entrance, maintenance, and exit conditions for various positions (see Gove, 1975; Money & Ehrhardt, 1972; Thomas, 1968—or Chapter Eight). Others have concerned themselves with the prestige, wealth, or authority accorded position members (Goldman & Fras, 1965; Hodge, Siegal, & Rossi, 1964; Lenski, 1954; Raven & French, 1958a, b) or with the phenomena of status equilibration (Sampson, 1969). Still others have focused their attention on positional roles or the treatments that are given to position members (Berelson & Steiner, 1964; Caldwell, 1964; Sears, 1969). And others have dealt with the evolution of positions (Caplow, 1954; Hughes, 1958; Wilensky, 1964) or the integration of positions within a social context (Habenstein, 1970). Studies of these various topics have involved a wide range of methods, from informal and formal observation of behavior through sample surveys and manipulative experiments. Each of these study forms concerns an important aspect of positional phenomena. None really subsumes any of the others. To study a social position well, then, may involve a battery of research tools and a lifetime of effort.

If all of this sounds complex, it should. As was suggested earlier in the chapter, the concept of social position involves assumptions not involved in the concept of role—among others, the shared use of identity terms among a group of subjects as well as their unambiguous application to a real set of persons. The fact that the social position concept involves more complex assumptions than does the role concept is not recognized by most writers in the field, but this has had little consequence as yet, given the lack of studies concerned with the existence of social positions.

ENVOI

What, then, are the advantages of positional classification? Why do we categorize human beings, and what are the advantages and disadvantages of categorization?

Some forms of positional classification are universal. All of us share membership in sex- and age-based positions. And in most societies positional differentiations exist that are based on food production, warfare, maintenance of order, and magic or religion. In some instances these classifications are based on physiological differentiation or facts of birth—women bear children and are their mothers; the old are more likely to be infirm and the young inexperienced; sexual maturity begins sharply during adolescence. However, in other cases positions appear to be differentiated by chance. In one society, for example, all members of the society may take turns at fishing and weaving, whereas in another society the positions of "fisherman" and "weaver" are differentiated, named, and have nonoverlapping membership. However, within the primitive society or small community positional membership is not divorced from personal knowledge. The shaman, warrior, mother, and aged grandfather are all known personally, and their personal characteristics interpenetrate and humanize the positions of which they are members.

When we consider positional phenomena, the modern, urban civilization contrasts with the primitive society in several ways. For one thing, positional differentiation is more complex in the urban society. Not only are there more roles within an urban civilization, but also the roles are so complex that to perform more than a few of them is beyond the capability of most persons. (Whereas it is possible to fish in the morning and weave in the afternoon, most people would find it impossible to perform as a scientist in the morning and as a trial attorney in the afternoon.) For another, positional membership tends to become divorced from personal knowledge, thus much of our interaction with others is based on their membership in positions and not on their personal characteristics. This trend is produced by several forces in urban situations: by the sheer volume of persons with whom we must interact, by the numbers of positions with whom we must strike up minimal relationships, and by the replaceability of persons in positions defined by social structure. Returning to Urban Dweller for a moment, one of the reasons why his firm has corporate stability is that it is efficient in recruiting candidates for secretarial positions—since the turnover rate of secretaries in Dweller's city is high.

The fact that interaction within an urban context tends to be positional rather than personal has been noted by many social scientists. Tönnies (1887) differentiated between *gemeinschaft* and *gesellschaft* forms of association, the former being based on personal relationships, the latter on instrumentality. Durkheim (1897) asserted that the urbanite suffered from *anomie*, a state of normlessness in which the individual is cut off from the supports and controls associated with close, primary relationships. On the other hand, it is difficult to imagine how else an urban civilization could be organized without enormous positional differentiation and the defining of positions in terms of social structure. As Weber (1925) has suggested, the concept of formal organization is essential to urban society, and at the base of the organizational notion stands a social structure of related positions.

Let us turn the coin over, however, and see how Urban Dweller deals with the positions in his life—how he copes with the advantages and problems engendered by positional membership and differentiation. Surprisingly, Dweller copes quite easily with positional differentiation. Only rarely is he conscious of worry over who the other might be, and once the other is identified he has few second thoughts about the possibility of reclassification or concerns about roles expected of himself or the other. Nor was he formally instructed in the complex, positional, classification system he shares with others in the society; he learned it easily and rarely questions its bases for classification. (Since he is a humane man, Dweller does not believe in discriminatory behavior toward women, blacks, and Jews; but since he is a WASP, Dweller does not question that some "unfortunate" people bear these identities.) In short, positional classifications enable Dweller to identify others, thus to organize appropriate behaviors toward them, a task that he accomplishes with ease and rarely questions.

But Urban Dweller, too, occupies positions. He is also a father, motorist, commuter, and a member of his firm; moreover, he is well aware of these identities, and in many instances his behavior is as much determined by his membership in these focal positions as by the counter-position membership of others. Positions, then, also serve as a source of self-concept for the person. Primitive persons or those living in small and simple communities have not only a simpler self-concept but also one built of more idiosyncratic, personalistic elements. For Urban Dweller, there is a tendency that his self-concept will include little more than the complex roles of the many positions of which he is called upon to be a member over time.

Is this a good thing or a bad thing? It depends on what we are looking for. Holmes (1966) has pointed out that positional identification and the performance of stereotyped roles within a familiar ceremony promote security for the individual. And yet, there must be for all of us a time of repose, of surcease from the everlasting necessity of being "someone." Perhaps Urban Dweller maintains his balance in an urban society precisely because he has a home to return to, where he can do all kinds of foolish and irresponsible things, simply because he wants to do them. To construct personality out of fragments of positions and their roles is to confuse individual motivation with the maintenance of the social system. Positions are merely classifications, and membership in them may be rewarding or galling. In particular, structured positions within an organization are created not to please their members, but rather to accomplish organizational tasks. To identify oneself with such a position is to repress individual motives in the service of organizational purposes.

It is also true that there are positions, and then there are positions. "Being upper class" has intrinsic rewards, whereas "being a secretary" or "vice president" of a firm accomplishes worthy goals within the society. But racial positions serve neither individual needs nor those of the society. And although "being a southerner," or "a Swede," or "from the 'best' people" may be comforting, it is doubtful that such classifications are in the interests of a rapidly changing society. Some positional classifications, then, are iniquitous—are but monstrous holdovers from the past—and deserve nullification. But how to nullify the prejudiced classifications of an insecure public is not yet clear; nor is it clear how self-concept is to be built without the archaic crutches of race, social class, ethnicity, and nationalism.

Chapter Five

Expectations

> Remember, our conduct is influenced not by our experi-
> ence but by our expectations.
> —George Bernard Shaw (on his 90th birthday)

So far so good. We know what a role is and are willing to grant that some roles
are exhibited in common by persons who share membership in a position or appear
within a given context. But *why* do they behave in that way? Why does the older
person tend to be conservative and the younger person idealistic? Why do mothers
keep house while fathers work at the office? Why do we cheer at a football game
and not in church? Let us assume that we have ruled out explanations based on
linkage. Some roles are not facilitated, rewarded, or reinforced in any obvious way
—yet they persist. Why?

Most social scientists answer this question by suggesting that persons carry in
their minds some sort of hypothetical construct that accounts for and predicts their
behavior. The psychologist might say that those who perform similarly hold similar
motives. The anthropologist might say that they share a symbolic culture. The
sociologist might say they have a common definition of the situation. The role
theorist says that they "share expectations" for their own behavior and that of
others. Thus, family members "expect" the father to work in an office and the
mother to cook meals and succor children, whereas both spectators and players
"expect" the audience to cheer at a football match and would be surprised if they
did so in church.

The choice of the phrase *shared expectations* is a deliberate one for role theorists, for these terms suggest connotations that are different from those suggested "motivation," "symbolic culture," or "definition of the situation." The term *expectation* connotes awareness, thus suggesting that persons are phenomenally alive and rational in their orientations to events. Expectations should also be time binding. Presumably they were formed as a result of prior experiences and represent, in some sense, a distillation of those experiences into a meaningful whole for the subject. To say that role behavior is controlled or predicted by expectations suggests that persons conform in their behavior to expectations they hold. Moreover, persons should become unhappy when their expectations are not met, thus be willing to influence others toward conformity. To say that expectations are shared implies that at least some aspects of persons' conceptual experiences are held in common among those who exhibit the same roles.

These are exciting ideas, and much of the emotional appeal of role theory stems from them. It flatters us and makes as feel warm when roles are explained in such a manner, thus the phrase *role expectations* has caught on widely in the social sciences and is used by practitioners and lay persons alike. At the same time, evidence for these ideas is—frankly—spotty, and some of them are undoubtedly inapplicable in many situations. Worse, authors differ in which of these implications they choose for providing formal definitions of the expectation concept. For these reasons, it is necessary for the serious role theorist to disentangle the basic concept of expectation from the auxiliary ideas with which it has been associated in various presentations.

The concept of role expectation began with the dramaturgical analogy. Hamlet, Juliet, and Prince Hal persist for us because their roles are set in specifications drafted by Shakespeare. However, more is connoted by the concept of role expectation than merely a theatrical part.

The extension of the dramaturgical concept of role expectation into real-life situations may be dealt with in three stages, each one of which involves additional assumptions beyond those of a theatrical script. First, analogies to theatrical scripts appear in the form of written rules for conduct that occur in the literate society. Codebooks are assembled for competitive sports, laws are enacted by legislatures and are interpreted by courts, directives are issued by companies specifying productive activities, standards are set out for student conduct in university catalogues. By extension of the analogy, then, behaviors of the tennis player, the law-abiding citizen, the production-line worker, and the student may be controlled by the written specifications set forth for them—in much the same sense that the behavior of an actor playing Falstaff is controlled by his script.

ch an extension of the dramaturgical concept requires an assump-
cifications may involve explicit threats for sanctions should some-
ply with the behavioral specifications set forth—fines, jail sen-

tences, discharge from employment, or ceremonies of humiliation (such as cutting off one's buttons). Such threats to sanction are not part of the theatrical script. No sanctions are set for the poor performer of Falstaff, although in the real world of a performance he may either cause a bad review to be given to the play or disrupt other actors. We are confused, then, as to whether the law-abiding person conforms to prescriptions of the law because of internal motivations (as is true for the actor) or because he or she is threatened by sanctions. Such confusions are manifest in our ambivalent attitudes toward law enforcement. On the one hand, violation of the law (even civil disobedience) is seen as immoral, while on the other we are hostile to the police or other agents who actually apply sanctions specified by the law to ourselves or others who violate them. To take another example, visitors to Petrified Forest National Park in Arizona will be amused to discover signs urging them to refrain from taking souvenir pieces of petrified wood on grounds that: (*a*) it would be immoral to so destroy the resource; *and* (for good measure) (*b*) they will surely be apprehended and punished.

A second extension of the theatrical analogy takes place when we use spoken injunctions as a model for behavior. For example, in preliterate societies (and Boy and Girl Scout meetings) we find ceremonial occasions when all those present chant together a code of beliefs and ethics. Rules for conduct are often enunciated by parents for their children. Small groups sometimes discuss rules for the conduct of their members, and so on. In cases such as these, the behaviors of preliterates, children, or small-group members may be judged for conformity or nonconformity to the injuctions that have been stated for their behavior.

This extension too has a hidden assumption. Written injuctions are permanent; spoken injunctions are evanescent, and what a speaker demands today another may not demand tomorrow. Thus, in order to extend the analogy, we must assume injunctive correspondence on the part of speakers. All who enunciate injunctions must speak with one tongue. Father and mother, for example, must prescribe corresponding behaviors for their children. If this condition is met, then we may speak of *shared expectations* that are enunciated for a particular social system and that have the functional equivalence of written prescriptions. This extension of the dramaturgical analogy is perhaps the most common in anthropological approaches to role theory, which almost always exhibit assumptions about correspondence.[1]

The third and last extension of the analogy places the concept of expectation in the mind of the performer. The journeyman carpenter builds a beautiful cabinet not because written instructions have been given him (or her) nor because of injunctions spoken by others, but rather because of his own internalized standards. Once we have learned them, most of us no longer need specifications from others in order to dress ourselves properly, greet others with polite phrases, exhibit punctuality,

---

[1] Gross, Mason, and McEachern (1958) call this assumption "the postulate of concensus."

and assume the responsibility of complex tasks. We do these things, presumably, because we have taken up standards for behavior within ourselves and no longer need the guidance of an external control system. Moreover, we maintain standards not only for ourselves but also for others with whom we are in contact. We learn to expect deference from some others, complementary behavior from our work associates, conformity to traffic customs from motorists, and so forth. In addition, these expectations are events of which we are aware. We experience, and enunciate for others, if asked, standards of etiquette, work performance, and methods of greeting and leave-taking.

This last extension is an exciting one, for with it we have taken up one of the major promises of the social sciences—the lure of making sense out of the social world in terms that are meaningful to its participants. In one fell swoop we are promising to explain both observable events and the way events look to people, to account for both behavior and thought.

However, this extension too is based on assumptions. For one, it is assumed that role expectations are phenomenal events—that people are aware of role expectations and can enunciate them for us if we ask them to do so. For another, it is assumed that role expectations produce conforming behavior—that if we knew someone holds an expectation, it also follows that he or she will behave in conformity with it (if the expectation is for own behavior) or will take action to ensure conformity in others (if the expectation is for another's behavior). Finally, it is also assumed that expectations are simply formed—that they are either modeled after injunctions for behavior that have been enunciated by others, or are set up by observing the behaviors of others, or (confusingly) both. Those using this third extension of the dramaturgical analogy have included social scientists of nearly all persuasions, but it is interesting to note that investigators have often accepted only one or two of these latter assumptions and have either questioned or in effect ignored the others.

Altogether, five **assumptions** have now been suggested that are sometimes applied to the concept of role expectations: **sanctioning, correspondence, phenomenal equivalence, conformity**, and **simple formation**. One or more of these assumptions usually appear in nearly all discussions of role expectations, but there is little agreement among authors as to which of these assumptions they will make, and there is but minimal evidence for any of them! Earlier it was suggested that one of the major sources of confusion for the role field was our inability to separate concepts for persons from concepts for behavior. We have now uncovered a second source of confusion in the lack of agreement among authors as to which assumptions they will attach to the expectation concept. Each of these assumptions is questionable, and whether or not they hold for a particular social event is a matter for empirical investigations. Let us begin by stripping the concept of expectation of these assumptions. Then we will consider occasions when each is likely to hold and what difference it makes to subjects when this does or does not occur.

SIMPLE EXPECTATIONS

England expects every man will do his duty.
—Horatio Nelson

OVERT EXPECTATIONS

We begin our discussion by considering expectations that are expressed overtly. What do statements of behavioral intention, evaluations of another's actions, or demands have in common? Surely each of these expresses expectations. But why do we recognize them as expectations, and thus differentiate them from other events such as sunsets, sonatas, or sneezes?

First of all, expectations involve the use of *symbols*. Like identities, expectations are expressed in symbols, although the latter involve more complex symbols than do the former. Second, expectations concern *human beings*. Their focus is upon human affairs and not upon impersonal events. (We ignore, for these purposes, those who would discuss expectations for tomorrow's weather.) Third, expectations reference *human characteristics*. Not only do they focus upon behaviors, features, traits, or other human characteristics, but they also reference those characteristics. Finally, expectations express some sort of *reaction* to those characteristics referenced. An expectation is not neutral. Rather, it asserts, or approves, or evaluates human characteristics.

Formally, an **expectation** is a statement that expresses a reaction about a characteristic of one or more persons.[2] In terms of this definition, overtly expressed expectations (or **enunciations**) include testimony concerning human events, past, present, or anticipated—demands expressed by a person for his own or others' behavior, or evaluative remarks concerning behavior, skin color, or any other human characteristic. To say the least, enunciations are a common form of behavior. Human beings are forever talking about one another's characteristics, particularly in such contexts as the home, the classroom, or the gossip session. Enunciations are also a simple form of statement. It takes only a single clause to express an overt expectation. Indeed, once we have learned it, the expectation concept appears so obvious that we are lulled into assuming we had known it all along or that it is unnecessary. Big deal, expectation! Alas, as is so often true in role theory, such apparent simplicity cloaks a set of problems for the theorist.

COVERT EXPECTATIONS

Enunciations are a type of behavior, and were they the only form of expectation of concern to us we could handle them within the general compass of behavior-

---

[2]An expanded definition appears at the end of this section of the chapter.

ism. However, expectations need not be uttered overtly. Our personal experience suggests that sometimes we hold an expectation but do not utter it. Moreover, it appears likely to us that others also hold expectations covertly. Consider the mother who threatens and then later punishes her children for not cleaning their plates at dinner time. We may also observe that she rewards her children when they do clean their plates, is careful to clean her own plate, avoids serving foods that seem to cause difficulty, discusses the matter with her husband, or is observed to consult a book on child psychology for advice. These several actions become explicable when we assume that the mother thinks her children should clean their plates. In short, we posit the existence of a covert expectation in her mind in terms of which she takes action. Moreover, if she is able to verbalize this expectation for us, we will also assume that she is aware of it.

The concept of a covertly held expectation is radical, and in allowing such a concept we abandon—from here onward—our previous commitment to behaviorism. Such a concept involves at least two assumptions, one obligatory and one optional. To speak of covert expectations at all means that we have accepted the existence of hypothetical constructs in the mind of the person. Most role theorists go further, however, and assume that subjects are aware of their expectations. To say the least, this latter assumption is controversial. Each of us is aware of his or her own phenomenal awareness, but to assume that awareness exists in the other is an act of faith. For all I know, each of you may be a Martian robot and I am the only being in the universe who is sentient! Despite its attractiveness, let us try to avoid making this assumption just yet. (In a few pages we shall discover other reasons for making it.)[3]

The idea of covert expectation is leagues ahead of any other expectation form in popularity among social theorists. It is not surprising that this is an accepted concept among social psychologists, but sociologists, anthropologists, and other social scientists are also likely to use the covert expectation concept as a means for explaining behavior. Covert expectations are also widely studied empirically, as we shall see through the rest of the book. Indeed, role theory may be said to rest on the concepts of *role, position,* and *covert expectation;* whereas role research is

---

[3] Readers will recognize this latter as the assumption of phenomenal equivalence. Most theorists making it also assume that thoughts are efficacious; that the person is rational, is capable of thinking about expectations and of making conscious decisions that affect subsequent behavior (Dewey, 1922). This latter is also controversial. One's thoughts may be epiphenomenal, a mere rationalization of decisions one has already made through mind processes of which one is not aware (Skinner, 1974). This issue stirs souls, despite the fact that it cannot be resolved empirically. Nevertheless, many propositions in role theory presume efficacious thoughts, and should we presently assume phenomenal equivalence I will also make this additional assumption.

mostly concerned with the latter. Where necessary to differentiate them from other forms, I shall term covert expectations **conceptions**.

WRITTEN EXPECTATIONS

A third form of expectation also appears in role theory, although this form exists only in literate societies. Conceptions have no overt existence. Enunciations are spoken and have only a transitory effect on the environment. (Except when we use recording devices, the environmental effects of speech die away in fractions of a second.) The literate society, however, has communications media that enable a more permanent record of symbols. Among these records one finds written expectations such as commandments, rules of law, or journalistic accounts. I shall refer to these latter as **inscriptions**.

Symbols that are recorded on papyrus, paper, or stone have a permanency that transcends the accomplishments of those who exhibit them. Writing binds time, and the person who inscribes his or her thoughts in the public record has earned a form of immortality impossible in the preliterate society. Small wonder, then, that inscriptions have received attention and reification. For the gullible or illiterate person, the mere fact that an expectation has been written down suggests that we should give it credence. But even for the sophisticate (such as the author and his readers) written expectations have an importance beyond that of their spoken equivalents. Our reverence for the written word appears in the law, in our belief in the veracity of religious documents, in conventions concerning freedom of the press, in our national practices concerning "security," in the Nazi fiction that by burning books one can do away with unpopular ideas. (Also consider our superstitious belief in the efficacy of written curses, such as that presumably inscribed over the tomb of King Tutankhamen, which was supposed to have "caused" the death of the entire party who opened the grave.)

Written expectations have different properties than those covert or overtly expressed. Inscriptions have continuing existence and are easier to study than are enunciations, since their expression is more permanent. However, the person who authored the inscription is no longer with us and thus may be unknown. Even if we know who he or she is, the motives of the author will vary depending on how he or she expects the inscription to be used. Contrast, for example, the private letters studied by Thomas and Znaniecki in *The Polish Peasant* (1918) with documents designed for consumption by a specific public, such as war propaganda (Berelson, 1952). Expectations appearing in the former were designed for self-expression or to influence intimates; expectations in the latter are to influence an entire population, often in devious ways. In addition, reactions to written expectations depend on the context in which they are presented. Reactions to a prescription found in the law, the church bulletin, the newspaper known for its hysterical news reporting, and the ancient Runic inscription are likely to be quite different.

Symbols and Person Characteristics

Expectations involve the expression of symbols. As such, expectations are capable of either being understood or misunderstood by those who encounter them. When visiting a foreign country we may or may not comprehend expectations that are addressed to us there. Normally, however, the enunciated expectation is assumed to be understood by those who use and respond to them. (Expectations, like social positions, are assuemd to be familiar.) This does *not* mean that expectations are shared. One parent may encourage his or her child to ride a bicycle, while the other discourages the same behavior. However, the symbols used by both parents are normally assumed to be understood by parents and child alike.

What kinds of symbols constitute an expectation? In minimal terms, an expectation involves the juxtaposition of symbols for characteristics of persons and symbols that express a reaction. Let us consider the first of these classes. Wherever found, expectations discuss the behaviors, features, experiences, ancestry, impulses, or some other characteristics of one or more human beings. In so doing, expectations involve different sorts of symbols than those used to express identities. Identity terms are mainly *nouns*—mother, author, Australian, Barbara. Terms used to reference characteristics are *verbs* or verb phrases—smoking, behaving deviantly, being curly headed, receiving deference. Identity terms tell us who we are talking about; terms referencing characteristics tell us what they are *doing* or who they might *be*. Terms referencing human characteristics must appear in the expectation; indeed there is no expectation without them. Identity terms, in contrast, may or may not be found in an expectation, although when they are absent the context will often provide clues as to whom the expectation applies. Contrast two signs that might appear on the wall of a public room—"No drinking allowed!" and "No drinking by minors!"

The fact that persons (may) and person characteristics (must) be referenced in expectations has various implications. For one, the person who holds an expectation may or may not be the person whose characteristics are referenced. Contrast the following two expectations:

(a) *I will go to the store this afternoon.*
(b) *John will go to the store this afternoon.*

In the first case the speaker is referencing him or herself, but in the second he or she is referencing someone else. It is convenient to adopt terms for differentiating the speaker from the person referenced. I shall refer to one who enunciates or holds an expectation as the **subject person**, whereas the referenced person(s) whose characteristics are at issue in the expectation shall be called the **object person**. The subject person is a real, observable human being. The object person appears only as a referenced identity and may not be present, may have lived only in the past (or will live in the future), or may even be fictitious—from our viewpoint as social analysts.

Several distinctions have also been made concerning expectations that depend on subject- and object-person characteristics. Of these, the most signifcant is the distinction between individual and shared expectations. Expectations may, of course, be held or expressed by a single person. However, some authors specify that role expectations are those that are shared. For example, in the definition suggested by Homans (1950) [B & T, Selection 11] "a norm, then, is an idea in the minds of the members of the group . . . specifying what the members or other men should do do. . . ." Such definitions suggest that it is possible to detect when expectations do and do not correspond. Those expectations that are held uniquely by a single subject person are termed **individual expectations**, whereas those that correspond among subjects are termed **shared expectations**. It is quite possible to study expectations for whether or not they correspond, and we shall take up this issue in Chapter Six. However, most authors who write about shared expectations have merely assumed sharing and have not bothered to discover whether or not this was the case. As was pointed out at the beginning of the chapter, the assumption of correspondence does not always hold for expectations, and different forms of behavior are likely to result when persons share or do not share expectations. Family quarrels, for example, may hinge on the fact that expectations for one anothers' behaviors are not shared and are resolved when members sit down to examine their expectational disparities.

Why, then, is such importance attached to the sharing of expectations? The theory goes like this: When two or more persons share expectations for their joint behavior, behavioral uniformity is likely to result. Moreover, when they share expectations for the specific behavior of one of their members, not only will that member understand what he or she is to do, but others will treat him or her in a uniform fashion, thus reinforcing that person's special role. This is a powerful argument for face-to-face interaction, and evidence has accumulated concerning the effects of shared expectations within small groups and families (see Chapter Seven). The argument is weaker for larger social systems, such as formal organizations or communities. Not only are workers in an organization ignorant of the details of other workers' roles, but they could not care less. When we come to think of it, there are at least three kinds of limits to the proposition that expectations should be shared. First, the sharing of expectations is nearly always bounded by the limits of the social system. Norwegians surely know more about the details of Norwegian life than do Americans, and citizens used to Western notions of political freedom feel that others "have no right" to details concerning their personal and family roles. Second, some roles are kept secret because of the needs of their performers, as is true of spies and con men. And third, some expectations are restricted as a structural feature of the social system. Many complex roles can only be performed when persons have latitude to perform them in ways that reflect their own styles (Katz, 1968), and the right to maintain secrets concerning clients is guaranteed in law to confessors, attorneys, and physicians. The theory concerning shared expectations is an attractive one, but we must always remember its limitations.

A second distinction concerns expectations that are held for individual object persons versus expectations that are held for object-person positions. The term for the former of these is **personal expectations** and for the latter **positional expectations**. Each of us holds personal expectations for the behaviors of members of our family and for our close friends. Each of us also holds positional expectations for the behaviors of politicians, teachers, physicians, grandmothers, blind persons.

In the definitions given by some authors, role expectations are limited to those applying to positions. For example, Gross, Mason, and McEachern (1958) define "role [to be] a set of expectations . . . applied to an incumbent of a particular position." The reason for this restriction is that the role and position concept are often assumed to be tied together. But as we have already seen, role and position are defined independently, and many roles are not associated with positions at all. If we are to use the expectation concept to discuss the latter, it would seem unwise to adopt this limited definition.

The distinction between personal and positional expectations is a meaningful one, however, and expectations of these two forms are somewhat different in their origins and consequences. Personal expectations are more likely to be developed through direct experience with oneself or another, hence should be more concrete and context-specific. Positional expectations are more likely to be abstract and context-general, and the subject may have difficulty applying them to members of the position (particularly if the position lacks cue clarity) or in recognizing examples of characteristics that are referenced in the expectation. Personal expectations are also more likely to be cognitively isolated, whereas positional expectations are tied to other cognitive information, such as presumptions about values or the functions of roles (see Chapter Eight). The distinction between personal and positional expectations is conceptually independent of the distinction between individual and shared expectations. A personal expectation may be either individual or shared, as may a positional expectation. However, positional expectations are probably more likely to be shared.

Still another distinction concerns the relationship between *subject* and *object persons*. It is possible for the subject and object persons to be one and the same (when the subject holds an expectation for him or herself), or for an object position to be one in which the subject holds membership (as when a minority group member speaks of "our people"). In other cases, the object person will be someone else or will consist of a position of which the subject is not a member (such as a civilian speaking of the army, or Americans discussing actions by Russians). In the former case we shall refer to **expectations for self** and the object position as an **own posi-**

Table 5.1
A CLASSIFICATION FOR SIMPLE EXPECTATIONS IN TERMS OF SUBJECT- AND
OBJECT-PERSON CHARACTERISTICS

	Individual expectations		Shared expectations	
	Personal	Positional	Personal	Positional
Expectations for self	A student talks about his or her own characteristics	A student talks about the characteristics of "students"	(Students agree about their own individual characteristics)[a]	Students agree about the characteristics of "students"
Expectations for other	A student talks about the characteristics of of his or her professors	A student talks about the characteristics of "professors"	Students agree about the characteristics of one of their professors	Students agree about the characteristics of "professors"

[a]In technical terms this classification is empty. Two or more students talking about "themselves" are actually speaking about different persons!

tion, in the latter case **expectations for other** and the object position as an **alien position.**

We have now taken up three distinctions commonly made for types of expectations; *individual* versus *shared* expectations; *personal* versus *positional* expectations; and *expectations for self* versus *expectations for other.* These distinctions are conceptually independent of one another. Lest there be any doubt of this, the reader may want to look at Table 5.1, which presents a classification for simple expectations in terms of these three distinctions.

Expectations for self and other differ in their implications for the subject. The former apply to the subject's own behavior, and it is commonly argued that subject behavior will usually conform to expectations for the self. Expectations for another do *not* apply to the subject's own behavior, and it is not often argued that subject behavior will conform to them. However, it *is* argued that subjects will take action to influence the other(s) to conform to expectations they hold for the latter. Within the traditional family the father attempts to conform to his expectations that he will work hard at his job and provide for his family; at the same time, he also exerts influence on his wife to keep up their home and take proper care of the children. Though each of these arguments is plausible, the fact is that we have but weak evidence for them at present, and clearly each does not hold in some situations. When sorely pressed, the subject may ignore expectations he or she holds for him or herself (witness the movie *High Noon*), and we are unlikely to attempt to influence another who has considerable power and appears willing to use it on us, whether or not that other meets our expectations for his or her behavior.

Which raises a point that will be made several times in this chapter. Although "reasonable" propositions can be advanced concerning individual versus shared expectations, personal versus positional expectations, and expectations for the self versus expectations for others—and although these are often made a basis for deriving more complex ideas in role theory—empirical evidence for these basic propositions is hard to find. Investigators have not often thought it worthwhile to investigate such basic notions, and the limits of their applicability are not known. Moreover, when such investigations are conducted, the "reasonable" proposition may turn out to have many exceptions.

Reactions and Modality

As indicated earlier, expectations involve not only symbols that reference person characteristics but also symbols that express a reaction. Expectations are not neutral with regard to the referenced characteristics they discuss. Rather, they describe these characteristics, anticipate their occurrence, insist upon them, or devalue them. This second feature of expectations is here termed **modality**. Expectations are modal in that they express a prescription, cathexis, or description of some characteristic of an object person; and it is the appearance of modality that enables us to differentiate expectational forms from other types of symbolic activity that also refer to human characteristics. Contrast, for example, two statements: (*a*) "Will John sing in the audition?" and (*b*) "John should sing in the audition." The first is reactively neutral. Unless given further clues one does not know whether the speaker advocates, desires, or anticipates John's singing. The second provides a reaction; the speaker has advocated that John sing. The first is not an expectation; the second is.

The concept of modality takes us into new realms with regard to the use of symbols. Heretofore we have considered only symbols whose use was denotative. Whether used for designating human beings or their characteristics, until now we have considered only those symbols that are used for pointing and naming. With modality we take up a different class of symbols—those that express a subject response. No longer is the subject a passive observer and designator. To express an expectation the subject must *react*, must commit him or herself in some way with regard to that event. Should the subject *approve* or *request* the characteristic, we shall say that the expectation exhibits the **prescriptive** mode ("Johnny, you should eat your peas"). Should the subject tell us how he or she *feels* about the characteristic, we shall say that the expectation exhibits the **cathectic** mode ("I dislike it when little boys do not eat their peas"). Should the subject make *objective* statements about the characteristic, we shall say that the expectation exhibits the **descriptive** mode. Descriptive expectations may be further subdivided into those that report about presently occurring events ("I am eating the peas, Mother"), those that

Table 5.2.
MODES OF PERSONAL EXPECTATION

Prescriptions (demands)	Cathexes (assessments)	Descriptions (assertions)		
		Present	Past	Future
		Expectations for self		
I should (or should not) smoke pot	I like (or dislike) smoking pot	I now smoke (or do not smoke) pot	I have (or have not) smoked pot	I will (or will not) smoke pot
		Expectations for other		
He (she or you) should (or should not) smoke pot	I like (or dislike) him (her or you) smoking pot	He (she or you) now smokes (or does not smoke pot	He (she or you) has (or has not) smoked pot	He (she or you) will (or will not) smoke pot

describe things past ("Yesterday I ate all my peas"), and those that anticipate things to come ("Tomorrow I will eat everything").

Expectations have different implications, depending on their mode. In addition, implications vary depending on whether the expectation is enunciated for self or for another. Again, little research has been conducted on these implications, although in sum they constitute part of the basic folk wisdom of role theory. To illustrate, Table 5.2 provides a series of enunciations that are concerned with the smoking of marijuana. Let us consider their implications.

When speaking prescriptively of him or herself, the subject might say "I should smoke pot," whereas a prescription for the other might be phrased "He (she or you) should smoke pot." Such statements reflect consequentiality, thus we presume the speaker to have notions about what is likely to happen if the prescription is or is not followed. However, unless it is made clear to us, we know little about the speaker's notion of consequence—whether it reflects physical, social, or moral outcomes—whether the speaker learned of it through hearsay or personal experience. Regardless of this unclarity, the person who utters a prescription is normally assumed to be encouraging behavior. Thus, prescriptions for the self are assumed to be self-motivating, whereas prescriptions for the other should be associated with the encouragement of compliance. As was suggested in Chapter Two, to utter a prescription for another is evidence for attempted influence. In fact, prescriptive utterances for the other are common features of interactive discourse, however demands for the self are less often uttered (except perhaps by followers of Dale Carnegie). Since there is a need for at least some uniformity of behavior in social systems, prescriptions have some likelihood of being shared. Prescriptions are also more likely to be enunciated for behaviors than for nonbehavioral characteristics, since it seems futile to issue demands for events that are not under advertent control.

Cathexes announce what would or would not please the subject, thus "I dislike smoking pot," or "I like him (her or you) smoking pot." Such assessments reveal the subject's affective response to events and are presumably based on personal experience. Thus, cathexes should be formed when the person experiences rewards or punishments associated with the characteristic referenced. In contrast to prescriptions, cathectic enunciations may be given about either behaviors or nonbehavioral characteristics. Cathexes are probably less often shared than are prescriptions, since their implications for compliance are less direct. (Given adverse consequences, one may end up advocating a course of action that will cause pain.) Cathexes for the self are quite likely to appear and may be used by the subject to encourage another to try out a new behavior. ("I like mango chutney; therefore you should at least try it.") Cathexes for the other are more problematic, nevertheless in Chapter Two it was suggested that enunciation of these latter, too, constitutes evidence for attempted influence. Why should this be so? Why should we be concerned when someone else tells us he or she dislikes our behavior? Because such announcements are not mere curiosities. Normally, the speaker will voice such preferences in the hope of eliciting a change in our behavior through altruism or fear of sanctioning. Thus, cathexes may also imply sanctions to follow. (Of course, when the other is in the dentist's chair or is our prisoner, we may not make this assumption.)

Descriptions set in the present are more often encountered than those of the past and future, and in many ways the latter are simply specialized cases of the former. Nevertheless present-oriented descriptions pose a conundrum. Since the real present is an evanescent slice of time, expectaions phrased in the present tense involve assumptions about the stability of ongoing events. When the subject says "I now smoke pot," or "He now smokes pot" the subject announces the existence of an event the boundaries of which extend, indefinitely, into both the past and furture. Such assertions also imply the unspoken assumption, "all things being equal." However improbable such an assumption may appear, we all make it, and probably *must* make it in order to cope with the chaotic details of living. Assertions concerning ongoing events pepper our speech in real-life contexts. Social scientists frequently ask subjects to make such assertions as a means for assessing the subject's ongoing phenomenal experiences. Assertions of the present may or may not match prescriptions or cathexes, of course. Disapproved others may be viewed as likely to behave in ways that are disliked; and educators and parents spend considerable time encouraging behaviors in the young that are not presently in evidence. Because of their quasi-stationary assumption, descriptions set in the present are more valid when made about nonbehavioral characteristics. Nevertheless they *are* made about behaviors too, which leads to such topics as stereotyping (taken up later in this chapter), labeling, and deviancy.

Descriptions may also be set in the past—"I have not smoked pot," "She has smoked pot." Such assertions are normally assumed to be truthful, to represent events that actually occurred. For this reason, assertions of the past (**reports**) are used by social scientists in lieu of observational evidence, and similar assertions constitute the major source of evidence in criminal trials. Since actions are planned on the basis of such assertions, sanctions are likely to be assessed against those whose words are found to be false. But this implication is contextually bound. The person may or may not have observed the events he or she reports, and some contexts (such as a liars' club) may call for creative falsehoods. We are all fascinated by extended fiction such as the utopian novel (*Erewhon* or *Islandia*) or the wholly fictitious other (*The Man Who Never Was* or *Lieutenant Kije*).

Finally, descriptions may also be set in the future—"I will smoke pot," "You will not smoke pot." Future descriptions for oneself (**intentions**) may represent rational processes and, if honestly given, are probably the best form of expectation for predicting subsequent behaviors of the subject (Fishbein, 1973). Such expectations also appear frequently in legal contracts and may lead others to make substantial commitments of effort or money. For this reason conformity to promises is important, and sanctions are likely to be assessed against welchers. Future-oriented descriptions for the other are useful also, for they tell us what the subject thinks likely in the behavior of the other, hence what he or she must take into consideration in planning behavior. When spoken to the other they may also lead to modification in the other's subsequent behavior—a topic to which we will return soon.

Prescription, cathexis, and description—how do we know that these three modalities exhaust all possible reactive stances? Is it always reasonable to distinguish these three modes from one another? Can other modes be distinguished? No simple answer can be given to these questions. These same three modes appear with remarkable frequency in the theories of social scientists (e.g., Bredemeier & Stephenson, 1962; Deutscher, 1967; Fishbein, 1967; Rokeach, 1968; or Triandis, 1977).[4] On the other hand, some theorists appear to differentiate only two of the three expectational modes and to ignore the third. Skinner (1957), for example, distinguished "mands" from "tacts" (which I take to be *prescriptions* from *cathexes*; also see Bem, 1964). Some social psychologists (e.g., Fishbein & Raven, 1962; Goethals & Nelson, 1973; Jones & Gerard, 1967) differentiate "beliefs" from "values" (i.e., *descriptions* from *cathexes*). In contrast, sociologists (such as Dahrendorf, 1958) are more likely to distinguish "opinions" from "norms" (i.e., *descriptions* from *prescriptions*).

I am not aware of any theorist who differentiates more than three basic modes for expectations. However, modal distinctions are sometimes made for *other* phenomena, and these may be confused with modes for expectations. Criteria used for

---

[4] For that matter, Freud (1933) viewed the libido as divisible into "id, superego, and ego," whereas Berne (1964) viewed game-playing roles as those of "child, parent, and adult," although these latter concepts take us beyond the modality of expectations.

establishing status are occasionally stated modally. Again, users of the Semantic Differential (such as Heise, 1973; Osgood, 1962; or Osgood, Suci, & Tannenbaum, 1957) may differentiate "evaluation, potency, and activity" as modes of affective responses to words. One of these concepts (*evaluation*) appears to coincide with the *cathectic* mode, but the others do not.

What, then, is the basis for discriminating these three modes and none others for expectations? As far as I can tell, this discrimination is based in part on historical accident and in part on semantic convention. The historical accident was the initial discrimination of mental functions into *cognition, affect,* and *conation* by Plato and Aristotle. This distinction was formalized by Tetens and Kant and has proved to be popular among social psychologists (such as McGuire, 1969) who use it to express modality for the attitutde concept.[5] In the long run, however, the discrimination of three modes appears to be based on semantic features that occur frequently in Western languages. When we speak of the characteristics of others or ourselves, we often discriminate those things we believe in from those we advocate and those that would please us. There is no intrinsic reason why additional modes should not be discriminated. Indeed, additional modes might be generated in several ways: (*a*) by extending the expectation concept to include notions of consequentiality or contingency; (*b*) by differentiating "moral" expectations from those that are "expedient"; or (*c*) by subdividing modes of cathectic response. (For example, characteristics that "sickened" might be differentiated from those that caused "terror.") That these latter distinctions are not often recognized in theory may mean simply that they appear less often and less consistently in the natural speech of those who use Western languages.

Has any evidence yet appeared demonstrating that it is useful to discriminate three modes of expectation? Under what conditions are these modes amalgamated by users? Under what conditions are three (or perhaps more) modes differentiated? Few studies have yet appeared on the modality of either spoken or written expectations. Griffin (1972) showed that teachers' demands for pupil behavior could be differentiated from their assessments and assertions, but it is difficult to find studies in which differential response to these forms of enunciation were examined. However, considerable research has been conducted on subjects' covert discrimination of expectational modes. Some of these studies have failed to establish subject discrimination of modality (Blumstein, 1973; Campbell, 1947; Campbell, Converse, Miller, & Stokes, 1960; Kahn, 1951; Vidulich & Krevanick, 1966). Other studies have found that subjects discriminated modes for various topics (Bank, Biddle, Keats, & Keats, 1977; Biddle, Rosencranz, & Rankin, 1961; Cheong & Devault, 1966; Fishbein & Raven, 1962; Goethals & Nelson, 1973; Kothandapani, 1971; J.

---

[5] In fairness, *conation* is not always assumed to be prescriptive in mode. In the hands of some investigators conation becomes *motivation* or even *behavioral intention*. We return to relationships among these latter concepts in Chapter Nine.

H. Mann, 1956; Rodman, 1966; Smith, 1965; Westie, 1965). Taken together, these studies suggest that modes of covert expectation will be discriminated by subjects only when the situation requires this of them. So far no study seems to have explored modal discrimination for a wide range of topics.

The fact that the three expectation modes may or may not be discriminated has not prevented social scientists from pursuing each of these modes in apparent ignorance of research on other modes. More than 100 studies of clients' expectations for the role of the professional counselor have now been published by psychologists in which descriptive expectations were examined (Corsini, 1966). In contrast, most sociologists concerned with expectations have assumed a prescriptive mode, whereas anthropologists have given greater attention to cathectic expectations. Since few of these authors have bothered to examine other modes of expectation, it is not known whether their findings are correctly interpreted. To illustrate a given study may have established covariation between the appearance of a prescriptive expectation and some other variable. But if that prescriptive expectation were also accompanied by an unmeasured expectation in the descriptive or cathectic mode, it is possible that the latter would be the real cause of the reported finding. Worse, some authors have theorized about expectations in one mode and then have constructed research instruments that measured a different one.

All of which raises yet another problem concerning modality distinctions. It turns out that there is no standard terminology for making modal distinctions. Descriptive expectations are sometimes called "beliefs," "social perceptions," "anticipations," "opinions," or "cognitions." Prescriptive expectations may be termed "norms," "demands," or "request forms." Cathectic expectations may be called "values," "evaluations," or sometimes "preferences." Moreover, if the issue is not already sufficiently confused, *all* of the expectational forms have been termed "expectations" by different groups of investigators, or worse, have been given that universal sobriquet in social psychology, "attitude."[6] Given this confusion, students must be careful when reading in the role field to establish for themselves the modality an investigator intends by the term he or she has selected. Readers might also want to follow the author's practice of "translating" all theoretical arguments and findings from expectational research into a standard modal vocabulary (see the following section).

In sum, three modes of expectation are here distinguished: prescription, cathexis, and description. This distinction is arbitrary, although it is made by a

---

[6] As we shall see shortly, the concepts of expectation and attitude are similar though not identical. Nevertheless, attitude research is plagued by the same kind of modal confusion as research on expectations, thus Louis Guttman's despairing definition: "An item belongs to the universe of attitude items if and only if its domain asks about behavior of a cognitive [or] affective [or] instrumental modality toward an object, and its range is ordered from very positive or very negative towards that object" (Gratch, 1973, p. 36).

number of theorists, and clearly expectations in these three modes have differing implications for the subject. Evidence is spotty concerning when these modes are distinguished or amalgamated, but sometimes they *are* differentiated. Investigators have used may terms to refer to these modes, and scholars must read carefully to find out the modality an investigator intends by the term he or she has chosen. We should not force a choice among these modality concepts; rather we should recognize the legitimacy of each, adopt standardized terms for them so that we do not confuse ourselves and our readers, design our measuring instruments so that they reflect the modality we intend, and be prepared to entertain questions as to whether subjects do or do not discriminate among modes in the context we are studying.

A Vocabulary of Expectations

It is now possible to give a somewhat more formal definition of the expectation concept. **Expectations** consist of subject-held or emitted statements that express a modal reaction about characteristics of object persons. It follows that expectations may be differentiated from one another in at least five ways: (*a*) in the subjects who hold (or emit) them; (*b*) in the object persons to whom they refer; (*c*) in the referenced characteristics that specify their content; (*d*) in their modality; and (*e*) in their form. It is common to use different terms for expectations that differ in modality and form, and Table 5.3 presents a tabulation of the terms I shall use.

Table 5.3.
TERMS FOR EXPECTATIONS

EXPECTATIONAL MODES	EXPECTATIONAL FORMS		
	Conceptions (covertly held)	Enunciations (overtly expressed)	Inscriptions (written)
Prescription	Norm	Demand	Rule
Cathexis	Preference	Assessment	Appraisal
Description	Belief	Assertion	Representation

Examples of these expectation types are easy to provide. **Norms** are privately held prescriptions ("I think that my boss should not smoke so much"). **Preferences** are private reactions to characteristics ("I dislike shrill, nasal voices"). **Beliefs** assess human characteristics against the criterion of subjective probability ("I think, privately, that blacks are more musical than whites"). **Demands, assessments,** and **assertions** are overtly enunciated forms of expectation. ("Son, go upstairs and make your bed immediately. You know that when you don't make your bed it makes me unhappy. This is the third day in a row it wasn't made.") **Rules** are prescriptive forms of inscription and appear in laws, in manuals of etiquette, or in job specifications in industry. **Appraisals** are less often encountered, but a good example would be the literary or musical review. **Representations** include all attempts to describe human characteristics that appear in literate records, such as in newspaper accounts or histories. Terms appearing in Table 5.3 are arbitrary, of course.[7] As suggested earlier, alternate terms have been used for each of these specific concepts by others, many of which are used for more than one concept by different authors (Biddle, 1961). In particular, the term *norm* has received a wide variety of uses.[8] However, it will reduce confusion if we hold to just one vocabulary in this book, and the terms listed in Table 5.3 are used whenever a specific form of expectation is intended. When a less specific term is needed, I use the more generic term, expectation.

The Measurement of Simple Expectations

The notion of expectation is seductive, and the concept of expectation has appeared centrally within both role theory and other theoretical orientations in the social sciences. In most of these applications the expectation concept is used as a hypothetical construct that predicts or explains other phenomena. Expectations are used to account for behavioral uniformity, for influence attempts, for conformity, for the organization of instrumental efforts, for the persistence of social systems. In such arguments it is not necessary to discuss the measurement of expectations; indeed the expectation concept may be used in a quite vague way without disturbing the force of the argument. However, expectations may be studied as events in their own right, and we now turn to a discussion of methods for so doing.

ENUNCIATIONS

Enunciated expectations are a form of behavior and may be studied, as may any other behavioral form, by observing and classifying them. As we have seen, an enunciation has at least four properties: the *subject* who enunciates it, the *object person* to whom it refers, the *referenced characteristic* that specifies its content, and its *modality*. The concepts of subject and object person are clear enough, but how do we go about studying referenced characteristics and modes that appear in enunciations?

[7] In Thomas and Biddle the concept of belief was termed a "conception," and preference a "value" [B&T, pp. 26–7]. Both changes represent a need for using these terms elsewhere in role theory, and the uses of the present book are to be preferred. Thomas and Biddle also proposed the neologism "transitor" for the generic concept of expectation. To the best of my knowledge, the intervening years have not generated even a single adoption of this term by other authors. Perhaps they were put off by an electronic homonym.

[8] *Norm* has two core meanings in the social sciences. It is used synonymously with "mode" or "average," and it refers to a standard for conduct. For the latter usage (which is adopted in this book) it is probably the least ambiguous term. Nevertheless, readers beware! (For other uses, see Rommetveit, 1954.)

To study referenced characteristics it is necessary to detect and understand the symbols in which they are expressed—thus the language of the enunciation. Two distinct judgments are then required of the investigator. First, the investigator must detect the class of object-person characteristics being discussed. Second, he or she must be able to assign the enunciation to one of the categories constituting a facet for expresssing alternatives for that characteristic. This latter task may be facilitated by assuming that the subject "had in mind" a facet of alternatives when he or she spoke. Although this sounds like a reasonable assumption, the information provided by the subject may not provide many clues concerning facet use. For example, the subject volunteers, "I smoke too much." How much is "too much"? Into how many categories is his or her scale of smoking divided: two, three, or many? All that we have been told is that there exists a point along a scale concerned with "amount of smoking," and that above that point is the region of "too much." Several alternatives are available to us for solving this problem. If possible, we may wish to interview the subject or others similar to him or her concerning the alternatives recognized for "amount of smoking." If not, our general knowledge of the language may provide clues as to what alternatives would be recognized by the typical subject. However, in order to compare two or more enunciations concerning "amount of smoking" we must have a facet for categorizing the symbols with which this characteristic is discussed.

The measurement of modality involves similar assumptions: on the one hand at least three types of modality may be recognized in enunciations, while on the other each of the modes exhibits variations in its magnitude. Prescriptive enunciations provide a degree of advocacy or prohibition. Cathectic enunciations tell us not only that subjects are pleased or displeased, but also how pleased or displeased they are. Descriptive enunciations provide more than merely a report; they tell us that the characteristic described is or is not likely.

The most convenient way of thinking about such problems is to conceive each of the modes as a scale of alternatives. The scale that establishes a prescription I shall term **approval,** which ranges from "strongly approve" through "neutrality" to "strongly disapprove" (of the characteristic discussed). Since a given characteristic may either be approved or disapproved, it is convenient to consider the scale of approval as having both positive and negative values, with neutrality occupying a value of zero in the middle. For example, should a mother say to her teen-age son, "You must not wear that tie," we would code her behavior as having a negative score for approval, whereas the prescription "You should be home by midnight" has a positive score. The scale that establishes a cathexis I shall call **liking,** and it is also capable of being assigned either positive values ("strongly liking"), zero values ("neutrality"), or negative values ("strongly disliking"). The scale that establishes a description I shall call **subjective probability,** and we normally assume that subjective probabilities are like real probabilities and can only be assigned positive values and zero. For example, should the mother have said to her husband "I think he will

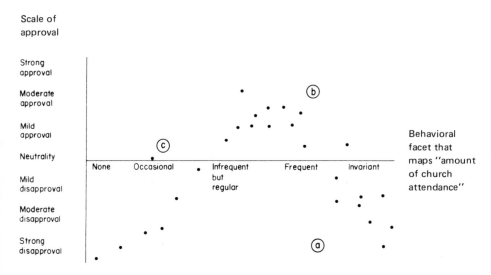

Figure 5.1. Illustrative two-dimensional space for mapping demands voiced by community members for "church attendance by teen-agers" (fictitious data).

drive carefully," we would have assigned a positive value to her expression of subjective probability, but her statement, "It is beyond belief that he will be home before midnight" would have received a zero score.

It is convenient to conceive of the measurement of enunciations as a process of assigning them to a two-dimensional space, one dimension consisting of the facet of alternatives for the human characteristic discussed, the other consisting of one of the modality scales. Such a two-dimensional space is illustrated in Figure 5.1, which concerns itself with demands expressed by community members for "church attendance by teen-agers." Each enunciation that is of the proper modality and content can be mapped as a point within this space. For illustration, three different demands have been identified within Figure 5.1. The first one (a) was spoken by an atheist and went, "I strongly disapprove frequent church attendance by teen-agers." The second one (b), provided by a minister, said, "Teen-agers probably should attend church frequently." The third (c), provided by a bystander, went, "Frankly, I don't care whether teen-agers attend church occasionally or not." Figure 5.1 also maps a number of additional demands for teen-age church attendance, and as we can see from the general pattern of these demands, most subjects (from the population studied) favored a moderate amount of church attendance. The notion of mapping expectations in a two-dimensional space defined by mode and object-person characteristic is basic to most methods of measuring expectations, and we shall return to it presently (also see Chapter Six).

INSCRIPTIONS

A major problem we will encounter in studying enunciations is in spotting them among the rich and rapid flow of symbolic utterances. This problem is solved, in part, when we make audio or video recordings of the discourse stream that contains enunciated expectations. The study of inscriptions is equally straightforward and, if anything, an easier task. Inscriptions are "frozen" within a medium and need no prior recording. They are already in a form that facilitates formal study. Let us contrast two views on the subject of chastity. According to St. Paul, "Ye should abstain from fornication; that every one of you should know how to possess his vessel in sanctification and honour, not in the lust of concupiscence" (First Thessalonians, King James version). According to Nietzsche, "Do I counsel you to chastity? Chastity is a virtue with some, but with many almost a vice. These are continent, to be sure: but doggish lust looketh enviously out of all that they do. . . . To whom chastity is difficult, it is to be dissuaded" (*Thus Spake Zarathustra,* Modern Library ed., p. 56). The first of these two rules counsels against fornication, the second is neutral on the subject; one demands chastity, the other adopts a more tolerant view. The two inscriptions are not similar, although they concern the same behavior and are both prescriptive.

As previously suggested, in one way the study of inscriptions is more difficult than that of enunciations. Whereas the subject person is usually clear to us when we have witnessed an enunciation, the subject responsible for an inscription may not be clear. How do we know that Saul of Tarsus actually wrote First Thessalonians? The evidence is weak, although to examine it in detail would take us into the methods of historiography.

CONCEPTIONS

Most role investigators are not satisfied with studying overt expressions of expectation. As we have seen, the notion of expectation is exciting precisely because it suggests the existence of a covert event within the subject that may be used to explain his or her behavior. If we now seek to discover whether this notion is right or not we must study conceptions. However, conceptions are presumed to be covert, and covert processes cannot be observed directly. Instead, we study them by measuring something else that presumably relates to covert processes and then inferring the presence of covert events. In general, covert events may be measured by making input, output, or phenomenal assumptions; by measuring the prior experiences or stimuli that presumably lead to their formation, by measuring the behaviors that are presumably generated by them, or by asking persons to report about them as phenomenal events. (These three routes are symbolized in Figure 5.2.) Let us examine each method of measurement.

If we assume that conceptions exist because of *prior experiences* (or stimuli)

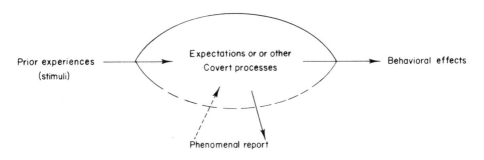

Figure 5.2. Ways of operationalizing covertly held expectations.

the person has experienced, then we must know how conceptions are formed. Three broad propositions have been advanced concerning the origin of conceptions. The first states that conceptions are formed through personal experience. Preferences may be learned through pleasant or unpleasant experiences, for example, or norms may be acquired because others have sanctioned the person. The second suggests that conceptions are formed through observation of others' characteristics, through social perception. When we visit a foreign country, for example, we learn conceptions about the likely behaviors of its residents by observing them. The third states that conceptions are formed by exposure to others' messages. Stereotypes, for example, are presumed learned through exposure to those who express them.

Broad support may be cited for each of these three propositions. Confirmation for the idea that conceptions are learned from *personal experience* is provided by research from the reinforcement tradition (Krasner, Knowles, & Ullman, 1965; Scott, 1957, 1959a, b; Staats, 1964; Staats & Staats, 1963). Moreover, personal experience is argued to determine conceptions by authors representing psychoanalytic theory (Adorno, Frenkel-Brunswik, Levinson, & Sanford, 1950; Erikson, 1963), by those interested in religious conversion (Davis, 1930; Lofland & Stark, 1965), and by investigators studying brainwashing (Lifton, 1963; Schein, 1961). In support of learning through *observation,* Heider (1958) suggests that most persons seem willing to form conceptions from minimal observational evidence, an assertion that has been supported by various investigators (Helmreich, Aronson, & LeFan, 1970; Jones, Davis, & Gergen, 1961 [B&T, Selection 17]; Thibaut & Riecken, 1955; Walster, Aronson, & Abrahams, 1966). Long-term contact with others has also been shown to affect conceptions (Deutsch & Collins, 1951; Festinger & Kelley, 1951; Minard, 1952; Mussen, 1950), whereas persons also seem to respond to others' nonverbal cues (Hall, 1959; Rosenthal, 1967; Sebeck, Hayes, & Bateson, 1964). Support for the impact of *messages* on conceptions is provided by the massive literature on persuasion and attitude change (Eagly & Himmelfarb, 1978; Greenwald, Brock, & Ostrom, 1968; Himmelfarb & Eagly, 1974; Insko, 1967; Kiesler, Collins, &

Miller, 1969; McGuire, 1969; Rosnow & Robinson, 1967; Zimbardo & Ebbesen, 1969; Zimbardo, Ebbesen, & Maslach, 1977).

In many situations, two or more of these processes may operate and may complement one another (see Zimmerman & Rosenthal, 1972). In other cases, evidence for conceptions may be available from only one source. If we have never seen Hottentots, our conceptions of them are likely to be based solely on hearsay. In contrast, when we meet a stranger for the first time, we are likely to form conceptions about him or her from observing his or her characteristics. But what governs the formation of conceptions when experience, observation, and enunciation do not coincide? How many of our conceptions are actually learned through each of these three mechanisms? These are complex questions, and ones for which insufficient research has yet been conducted. Doob (1940) provided data suggesting that conceptions are more likely to be affected by messages than personal experience. Prejudicial stereotypes seem more likely to be learned when the actual characteristics of those others are not observed (Amir, 1969); but once learned, conceptions that are closely tied to other beliefs and values seem likely to be defended rather than to change in the face of disconfirming behavioral evidence (Rokeach, Smith, & Evans, 1960). (To illustrate, prejudiced whites may respond to a clean, moral, intelligent, and well-educated black man by considering him an "exception.") On the other hand, research on impression formation suggests that persons try to accommodate both messages and observational information when forming conceptions about strangers (Kang, 1971; Rosenberg, 1968; Tagiuri, 1969; Zimmerman & Rosenthal, 1972).

In short, then, although personal experience, observation, and messages are all known to affect the formation of conceptions, how these three kinds of processes interact is not well undestood. One shortcoming of much of the applicable research has been its modal ambiguity. This is a shame, since preferences, norms, and beliefs seem likely to be learned through somewhat different processes. (Preferences should respond more to personal experience, norms to messages, beliefs to observation.) Other variables also affect the learning of conceptions, such as the sequence of presented experiences (Rosenthal, Rogers, & Durning, 1972), associated beliefs (Dienstbier, 1972; Rokeach *et al.*, 1960), and subject abilities (Tagiuri, 1969). Moreover, some conceptions surely result from thoughtful reasoning on the part of persons rather than from exposure to specific stimulus experiences.

In sum, it is theoretically possible to reach valid conclusions about conceptions by knowing about the subject's prior experiences, but we do not yet know enough to make the method work well. Worse, in field studies it is rare that we have sufficient information about the subject's background to make it work at all. Only in the laboratory is it possible to provide subjects with experiences that presumably induce covert expectations, and most investigators appear unwilling to employ such experiences without also checking subjects (by means of phenomenal reports) to see if the latter have acquired the desired expectation.

To measure conceptions through their *behavioral effects* is also difficult, al-though Dahrendorf (1967) recommends this method. It is certainly true that when a subject enunciates an expectation *in situ*, we normally presume that he or she is mirroring a conception. (When the boss gives an order to a subordinate, we presume that he or she "means it.") But we may have to observe a given subject for hours or days before he or she gets around to verbalizing the exact expectation we are look-ing for. Moreover, should we assume that other forms of behavior exhibited—threats, sanctions, influence attempts, rationalizations, and the like—are good evi-dence for the holding of specific conceptions, we are indeed opening a can of worms. Although considerable research has now been conducted on subject confor-mity to expectations for the self (see Chapter Six), little is now known about how subjects go about gaining compliance in others. In addition, behavioral effects of expectations seem to vary depending on context. And though we may be convinced from behavioral evidence that a person holds a conception, the modality of that conception may not be clear. Will persons sanction others for violation of beliefs? Maoist literature suggests that this will happen, although it seems reasonable to pre-sume that sanctioning is more likely when norms or preferences are violated. Once again, then, to judge the presence of a conception because of behavioral effects is a dicey matter.

The third method for measuring conceptions makes use of *phenomenal reports.* In this method we ask subjects to respond to our questions concerning their con-scious experiences. We ask subjects to tell us what they remember, what they fear or desire, or what they perceive in stimuli we present to them. In so doing we are asking respondents to play *our* game, to respond to our questions in a forthright and honest manner. To the extent that subjects are capable and willing to do this, the method offers an advantage over the two we have just reviewed in that we can control the topic to which the subject is asked to respond. Instead of combing through endless evidence concerning irrelevant stimuli to which the subject has been exposed, or equally irrelevant behaviors he or she may have committed *in situ*, we can come directly to whatever may be our topic: "Tell me, Mr. Jones, do you or do you not like the way your wife serves dinner?" Experience suggests that middle-class Americans are quite willing to play this game, although there are certain taboo topics with which even Americans have difficulty. Subjects of other nationalities may be less willing to play the game (Lerner, 1961), and primitive people may not understand it at all.

Assuming that we can apply the method, what then is the relationship between the subject's response and the conception we wish to measure? Two answers may be given to this question, depending on whether one considers the conception an experience of which the subject is fully aware or whether it is some other sort of mind concept. If the latter, we will probably opt for an *indirect technique* for mea-suring the conception from phenomenal report data. Many such techniques are available to the social scientist, and nearly all have been used to measure conceptions by one investigator or another. Musgrove (1961) coded responses to open-ended questions, Anderson and Anderson (1961) used projective techniques, Friedman and Gladden (1964) employed the Semantic Differential, and a host of investigators have utilized multi-item attitude scales for the measurement of conceptions.

Indirect measurement has several advantages. We may choose such techniques if the subject is presumed to hold a diffuse conception, if he or she is unused to verbalizing conceptions or might hesitate to reveal the conception held, or if the conception is presumed to be a process that affects behavior, even though the subject may be unaware that he or she holds it. Indirect techniques may offer the investigator greater reliability of measurement, since they often provide several items that bear on a given conception. On the other hand, indirect techniques have their disadvantages. Most are cumbersome tools and may be difficult to administer. Since they normally involve multiple measures for a given conception, indirect techniques are inefficient. Many also make additional assumptions about the effects of conceptions that may not be valid. In addition, they imply a role relationship between the investigator and the subject in which the latter is to reveal information about him or herself of which he or she is not aware. Such a relationship is not always tolerated by the sensitive subject or investigator.

These disadvantages have led most investigators to avoid indirect measurement in favor of *direct techniques* in which subjects are asked to speak in a forthright manner about their conceptions. Such techniques presume that the subject is fully aware of conceptions he or she holds and offer a number of advantages. For one, direct measures are similar to judgements we would make concerning the equivalence of an assertion and a conception that caused the subject to utter it. For another, to make direct measurements is to embrace fully the assumption of phenomenal equivalence. As we know, this is one of the more attractive features of role theory. Indeed, if we make this assumption explicitly, we are encouraged to conduct depth interviews with subjects to ascertain their views of social reality and their interpretations of the actions of themselves and others. Such a posture not only flatters the subject and casts him or her into the role of an honest reporter, but it can also lead us into additional insights about his or her personal dynamics. Direct techniques are also more efficient, and by using them the investigator can cover more issues in a given length of time than the investigator can with most indirect techniques.

At the same time, this method too suffers from shortcomings. Some subjects may not be aware of the conceptions that we (the investigators) conclude on other grounds are affecting their behavior. Subjects are not always willing to discuss their conceptions with us in full candor, particularly conceptions concerning touchy areas of life, such as sexual behavior, financial status, expression of aggression, or occasions of embarrassment. Also, it is difficult to measure conceptions directly without affecting the clarity of those conceptions by "educating" the subject to pay attention to a conception he or she has held only vaguely up until the moment you asked him or her about it. Direct measurement is thought of as being equivalent to opening a window in the mind of the subject. In fact, you must provide a stimulus to the subject in order to provoke him or her into opening that window, and in so doing you cause the subject to react to you, the investigator, as yet another stimulus in context. The game of direct measurement may have fewer assumptions than the game of indirect measurement, but it is a game nevertheless, and subjects may or may not be willing to play.

Clearly, if their use is possible, we are better off measuring conceptions through phenomenal reports than through prior experiences or behavioral effects. Such a procedure allows us to provide an operation for conceptions that is independent of stimulus and response. It also means that the role theorist studies the influence of stimuli-upon-conceptions and of conceptions-upon-behaviors as analytically separable processes. Conceptions, then, are not merely a hypothetical process standing between stimuli and behavior. Rather, they are to be measured directly by independent processes.

Moreover, where warranted, we should measure conceptions through direct rather then indirect phenomenal procedures. Such procedures embrace the assumption of phenomenal equivalence and imply that role theory is, among other things, a vehicle for discussing the thoughts of subjects concerning social events. This means that what a subject says to us will normally be taken by the role theorist at face value, and (to paraphrase Deutscher, 1973) role theory becomes a means for studying the relationship between *experiences, words,* and *deeds.* Only when it is suspected that subjects hold "unconscious" expectations or that deliberate distortion of phenomenal reports is likely should we insist on indirect techniques for measurement of conceptions.

CLASSIC TECHNIQUES

So far so good, Conceptions "may" be measured by any techniques used for examining phenomenal reports and have, in fact, been studied by many different tools. In this sense, the study of conceptions is methodologically neutral, and role theory has not had to develop unique techniques for its empirical research. However, most investigators of conceptions have used methods that were modeled after the assumptions expressed in Figure 5.1. Thus, it is assumed that subjects retain in their minds a facet for expressing object-person characteristics and a modality scale, and questions are asked of subjects relating to these assumed conceptual features.[9]

[9] Once again, these assumptions are not often checked empirically. Subjects may or may not recognize the symbols the investigator uses for expressing a facet, and they may or may not hold a conception concerning them for a given object person. (Upon asking respondents what they expected a teacher to do at a track meet, the author was once given the answer, "Tie the tracks back together when they are broken!" In answer to what a teacher should do at a play rehearsal, another subject opined, "Enjoy the children at play.") Examples of errors that are introduced into data when scaling conditions are not met appear in texts on scaling. Yet we are often impatient and prefer to use a precategorized scale rather than "waste" the extra 6 months it would take to explore subjects' conceptualization of the problem at hand. Implications of this posture are discussed by Cicourel (1970).

Three systematic techniques have been used for asking these questions. The first, which I shall call the **complete method**, asks subjects to provide a modality rating for each point of the facet expressing alternative characteristics of the object person. To illustrate, subjects who are married might be asked to provide responses indicating the norm they hold for smoking by their spouses. In the complete method, an approval rating is asked for each behavioral alternative conceived. Usually, Likert-type scales are used for expressing both modal and facet alternatives. This method generates a response distribution for each subject, as is illustrated in Figure 5.3. Such distributions have several aspects that may be scored for each subject: the modal point of the distribution, the range of positively scored alternatives, the maximal and negative scores given, and so forth. Each of these scores has meaning, and theories have been advanced concerning their use (Jackson, 1960, 1975) [B&T, Selection 9]. Scores may also be summed for samples of subjects to provide a collective response distribution (Santee & VanDerPol, 1976; Stouffer, 1949). The complete method has advantages, then, and is the method of choice for measuring conceptions. It is also cumbersome, however, and is usually replaced by one of two short-cut techniques.

The first of these techniques, the **modal strength method**, asks questions of the subject that are closely akin to the format he or she might use in enunciating an expectation. A phrase is given the subject that represents an amalgamation of categorical alternatives for the facet he or she presumably uses, and the subject is asked to assign a value for some modal scale to that phrase. For example, the subject is given the phrase "smoking a good deal," and is asked to tell how much he or she approves, likes, or thinks this behavior likely for the object person. A typical format for such a question provides the subject with a Likert-type scale of response alternatives:

How much do you approve or disapprove of "smoking a good deal" by your wife?	I approve it strongly. . . . . ( )
	I approve it moderately . . . . . . ( )
	I approve it mildly. . . . . ( )
(Place an "X" next to the response that most closely corresponds with the degree of approval you give this behavior.)	I feel neutral about it . . . . ( )
	I disapprove it mildly . . . . ( )
	I disapprove it moderately. . . . . ( )
	I disapprove it strongly. . . . . . . ( )

Responses to modal-strength questions are termed **strength scores**. Thus, should a husband "disapprove strongly" of smoking on the part of his wife, we would say that he held a *strong expectation* on this issue, whereas the husband who only "disapproved moderately" or felt neutral about the issue would be said to hold a *weaker expectation*.

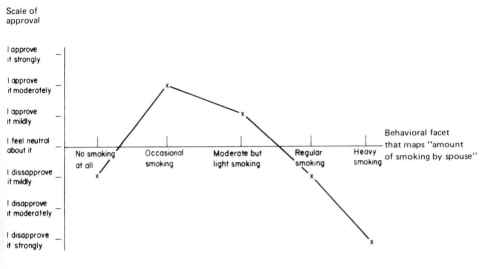

Figure 5.3. Two-dimensional space for mapping subject-held norms for "amount of smoking by spouse" measured by the complete method. Illustrated are responses obtained from a single subject (fictitious data).

The second technique, the **facet alternative method,** makes different assumptions. Instead of asking subjects to choose among modal alternatives, the subject is asked to pick among facet categories representing the object-person characteristic. For example, the subject might be asked to choose among various amounts of "smoking" that he or she most approved.

How much smoking do you approve on the part of your wife? (Place an "X" next to the response that corresponds with the amount of this behavior you most approve.)	No smoking at all . . . . ( ) Occasional smoking . . . . ( ) Moderate but light smoking. . . . ( ) Regular smoking . . . . ( ) Heavy smoking . . . . ( )

Scores that are generated by the facet alternative method are termed **amount scores.** Thus, should a husband choose the alternative of "heavy smoking," he is said to approve a greater amount of smoking than another respondent who chooses "occasional smoking" or "no smoking at all." (Of course, the phrase *amount score* would be a misnomer if the response alternatives did not fall into an ordered set.)

These two short-cut techniques appear to give similar information, and if we make some assumptions it is possible to equate strength scores with amount scores. For instance, a husband who tells us that he "disapproves strongly" of "smoking a good deal" by his wife will probably also tell us that he "approves" of the response alternative of "no smoking at all." Which is the better method? It depends on what one wants to do with the data. For example, should one want to compare several norms for their degree of approval, or should one want to discriminate between subjects who "felt strongly" versus those who "did not care" about an issue, the modal strength method would be chosen. In contrast, the facet alternative method is indicated if one wants to discover the range of modally selected alternatives within a subject population, or to discover whether or not two populations exhibit the same norm in consensus, or to compare norms with preferences or beliefs.

In summary, one measures *enunciations* and *inscriptions* as one does other overt events—by observing them and classifying them by using facets that express their subjects, object persons, characteristics, and modalities. One studies *conceptions* by measuring overt events presumed to relate to conceptual formation, effects, or (preferably) companionate phenomenal experiences. Many methods are available for the latter, nearly all of which make assumptions about the conceptual processes of subjects. However, three techniques have predominated in published studies of conceptions—the complete, modal strength, and facet alternative methods. The first of these methods offers more data but is cumbersome, the latter two are short-cut techniques and are more often used.

COMPLEX EXPECTATIONS AND PRESUMPTIONS OF SENTIENCE

> . . . *for filth, I'm glad to say, is in the mind of the beholder.*
> —*Tom Lehrer*

Until this point in the discussion we have been dealing only with **simple expectations** (sometimes termed **own expectations**)—referential events that involve but a single modal reaction about one characteristic of an object person or position. But expectations may take on more complex forms, and we should also explore these latter.

Non-Simple Expectations

A **non-simple expectation** is one containing one or more modality or reference components that may be analytically decomposed into simple expectations without loss of semantic content. For example, a speaker might have said, "I like John's haircut," and "I like Bill's haircut." Instead he said, "I like both John's and Bill's haircuts." We presume that the latter statement can be decomposed into the former two without semantic loss, hence it is a non-simple assessment. In this case the referenced person was twinned. Non-simple expectations can also exhibit modality multiplication ("You are *too* wearing that red skirt which I hate!") or expansion of the referenced characteristic to include several nominative elements ("You must not scream and curse!"). Examples of non-simple expectations are easy to find in both everyday speech and in public documents. Legal proscriptions, for example, often contain long lists of forbidden behaviors that are gathered together to make a single, non-simple rule.

Contextualization

It is also easy to find expectations in which references are made to other phenomena beyond those of person and characteristic. For example, we often find a contextual restriction placed upon the expectation ("While in the woods you must not speak above a whisper," or, "But during the final round of the fight his performance became erratic"). These illustrations are of **contextualized expectations**, which may be defined as those whose applicability is circumscribed by stated conditions. As is true for other expectational characteristics, contextualization may sometimes be provided by environmental embedding. The sports announcer, for example, normally need not tell his radio or TV audience over and over that he or she is describing a specific sports event and not another. However, environmental cues may be insufficient to allow us to judge contextualization with reliability. It may be unclear to the child, for example, whether a parental demand was made for "this week only" or whether it is to apply to other weeks in the future as well. In Chapter Three we discovered that some roles may be contextualized. Expectations for these roles may be similarly restricted.

Another related form of expectational complexity is provided by contingency relationships that tie an expectation to other referenced events. Sometimes referenced events are given as causes or occasions for the elicitation of an expectational response ("If you do that, Johnny Williams, I'll scream, I really will!"), but this type of contingency is little more than another form of contextualization. A more interesting form appears in the enunciation wherein an expectation becomes a cause or occasion for the appearance of another referenced event. For example, the primitive says, "We hold our monthly rain dance in order to ensure sufficient rainfall for our crops"; or the student rebel says, "We must destroy this rotten university in order to bring down the rotten society"; whereas the spouse who is tired of fighting says, "I am apologizing in order to bring our quarrel to a stop"; or the critic pontificates, "His shoddy performance appeared to disrupt the entire orchestra." An extended discussion of the various forms of *contigent expectations* is beyond the scope of this work,[10] but each exhibits relationships of stated contingency with other referenced events.

Extended Expectations

A third type of expectational complexity appears in the extended expectation. In order to generate this concept, let us examine the class of human characteristics that may be referenced within an expectation. Since we have given no limitations to this class, it is possible that an expectation may reference symbolic behavior, or even other referential forms such as the enunciation of an expectation! In such a fashion, it is possible to generate *expectational chains* in which an expectation is enunciated about an expectation, or even an expectation about an expectation about an expectation. . . . These are not difficult to illustrate in everyday speech. The mother says to her husband, "You must not condemn Johnny about his haircut"—thus demanding cessation of a cathexis. Or again, the reporter tells us, "The union representative demanded an increased salary for workers"—which is a statement about a demand for differential treatment. Or the lover, "I just adore it when you tell me you like my eyes"—an assessment of an assessment.

We are now in a position to define the concept of **extended expectation**, which consists of two or more simple expectations arranged in a chain so that later expectations in the sequence are the referenced characteristics of those that precede it. Some additional verbal conventions are also useful when speaking of extended expectations. The **length** of an extended expectation consists of the number of expectations in the chain. (Simple expectations have length one; nonsymbolic forms of behavior have length zero.) Extended expectations of length greater than three are rarely encountered ("I know, that you know, that I'll go, where you go" to the contrary notwithstanding). It is also convenient to use ordinal numbers to refer to the simple expectations of the chain, the *first* or *leading expectation* being the one that is capable of direct enunciation, the *last* or *terminal expectation* being the one that concludes the reference sequence.

The concept of extended expectation is deceptively simple and generates new problems for us to unravel.

1. Although the leading expectation of the chain can receive overt enunciation, the remaining expectations are always referenced and should not be confused with the actual events they discuss. We illustrate this with an earlier example. The mother's enunciation, "You must not condemn Johnny about his haircut," is simply not the same event as the actual condemnation by the father, nor is either to be confused with the actual hair-cutting behavior of the son (if any). For purposes of re-

---

[10] However, see the discussion of expected sanctions in Chapter Six.

search we may, in fact, be interested in the effects of either the father's condemnation upon his son's behavior or of the mother's adjuration upon either the father's subsequent behavior or the son's willingness to go to the barber. All of us maintain covert extended expectations in our minds concerning the expectational behavior of others, and some investigators have naively assumed that data gained from subjects about others' expectations will provide reliable data about the actual expectations held or enunciated by those others. This assumption is one of *veridicality*, which may or may not obtain.[11] Sometimes subjects are reasonably veridical in the expectations they attribute to others, while under other conditions expectations attributed simply do not match those of others (Biddle, Rosencranz, Tomich, & Twyman, 1966 [B&T, Selection 37]; Foskett, 1967a,b; Musgrove & Taylor, 1965; Schanck, 1932; Wheeler, 1961).

2. Extended expectations may involve references about not only the overt enunciations for others, but also expectations for covert events. A person may say, for example, that "John dislikes me," which describes a covert cathexis held by another. This extension of the expectational concept involves something that has not entered our discussion heretofore, and that is presumptions about the *sentience* of others. As has been noted on several occasions, role concepts are often modeled after beliefs that are found in Western culture. This is no less true for the concept of extended expectation. Our everyday language reveals that most of us form expectations of sentience on the part of others. Indeed, we will argue in Chapter Eight, with G. H. Mead, that presumptions of sentience are necessary both for adequate adjustment to the complexities of social behavior and for the development of a self-concept. But whether or not this latter argument is accepted, it is an empirical fact that people behave as if they assumed sentience on the part of others, and we shall now explicitly allow this extension of the expectation concept.

3. Extended expectations vary in their implications depending on modality. To date, the majority of studies of extended expectations have concentrated on those having the descriptive mode for their leading expectation (e.g., "I *believe* that you want [like, think] Stephen to eat his peas.") Moreover, this form appears frequently as an enunciated expectation, and it is reasonable to believe that it is frequently held as a conception, too. Let us call it an **attributed expectation**. Within two-person interaction, attributed expectations tend to have implications that mirror their simple counterparts. For example, it is reasonable to presume that the subject will attempt to *conform* to prescriptions he (or she) holds for his own behavior and to bring *sanctions* to bear on the other for failure to conform to expectations he holds for the latter. In contrast, the person will expect *sanctioning* from the other for failure to conform to expectations for himself that are attributed to the other, whereas the other will be presumed likely to *conform* to expectations at-

---

[11] This concept and the related concept of expectational *accuracy* are also discussed in Chapter Six.

tributed to him or her for own behavior. Implications will vary, however, for more complex forms of attributed expectations. And although they may be less encountered, extended expectations may easily be found where the initial modality is prescriptive or cathectic ("Thou shalt not covet thy neighbor's ass," or "I like that idea!"). These have implications that are quite different from those of attributed expectations.

4. For every simple expectation in the chain (after the first), it is possible to find another referenced person or position. Thus, for the overused example, "You must not condemn Johnny about his haircut," the mother has referenced both her husband ("you") and her son ("Johnny"). It is useful to adopt another verbal convention concerning these referenced persons. Consequently, I shall extend the earlier definition of **object person** so that now it is also applicable to the terminal expectation of the chain—in the preceding example, "Johnny" is the object person. I also define a new term, the **sentient person,** to be someone whose expectations are referenced in an extended expectation—in the same example, "you" (the father) is a sentient person. It is possible for both the sentient and object persons to be positions rather than individuals ("We Americans disapprove of communist hypocrisy"). In such cases, it is also useful to distinguish between object positions that do and do not include the subject, and sentient positions that do and do not include the subject. Terms for such distinctions are presented in Table 5.4 together with a classification for expectations of lengths one and two based on positional membership of the subject. (Expectational sequences of greater length generate even more complex possibilities that are not reviewed here.)

Object and sentient positions are examples of *reference positions,* a concept that has had considerable attention. By **reference position** is meant any term of identity for two or more persons that appears as a referential element within an expectation. The commonest term for this concept in social psychology is *reference group* (after Hyman, 1942; also see Hyman & Singer, 1968), but this is a poor usage, for it leads us to confuse the term of reference (which might refer to totems or to persons dead or even fictitious) with a real *group* of human beings.[12]

The concept of reference position is an important one in role theory, for it turns out that we use reference positions both for building self-concepts and for learning standards of behavior that fit us for later life. However, there is a difference between "any old" reference position and reference positions with which we identify. Typologies for the classification of reference positions have been suggested by both Merton (1957b) and Turner (1956) [B&T, Selection 14]. These have re-

[12]As may have been noted, the term *group* has been avoided in this book. We will continue to do so until Chapter Seven, where it is used to designate a set of real persons who interact.

Table 5.4
A CLASSIFICATION OF LENGTH-ONE AND LENGTH-TWO
EXPECTATIONS IN TERMS OF RELATIONSHIP
AMONG SUBJECT, SENTIENT, AND OBJECT POSITIONS[a]

	Length-one (simple) expectations (no sentient position)	Length-two expectations		
		Sentient position is also own	Sentient position is alien and conjoint with object position	Sentient position is alien and disjoint from object position
	Expectations for self	*Pluralistic expectations*	*Reflexive expectations*	
Object position is own	Student subjects talking about student characteristics	Student subjects talking about student expectations for student characteristics	Student subjects talking about professors' expectations for student characteristics	
	Expectations for other	*Pluralaxive expectations*	*Projective expectations*	*Complex expectations*
Object position is alien	Student subjects talking about professors' characteristics	Student subjects talking about student expectations for professors' characteristics	Student subjects talking about professors' expectations for professors' characteristics	Student subjects talking about professors' expectations for administrators' characteristics

[a]*Note:* Illustrations chosen are for *positional* expectations. The distinction between *individual* and *shared* expectations is ignored.

cently been synthesized by Cain (1968) whose usage I shall follow here (with modification). Readers may also want to consult the even more recent and comprehensive treatment provided by Schmitt, 1972.

The classification is based on a series of conditions that make the reference position *important* for the subject person, and for convenience the presentation is organized in terms of presumed ascending order of importance. In the general case, a reference position will have no importance to me, for what care I for the opinions of idiots and scoundrels? However, because I am involved in a social system in which they are also present, some reference positions hold power so that I must take them into account in accomplishing my own goals. These are *authority posi-tions*[13] (an example of which would be, for the writer who is a university professor, the administration of his university). However, it is not guaranteed that members of authority positions will be able to see (and hence to evaluate) my behavior. If this latter be the case, they are termed *audience positions* (exemplified by my profes-sorial colleagues at the university).

These conditions are still weak ones, for they involve only my accommodation to others and not my acceptance of their norms. If I should also accept for myself norms I attribute to others (see Chapter Eight), they become a *comparative posi-tion*[14] (for the author, those who write English with grace and fluency, such as E. B. White). However, members of comparative positions are not always able to set and maintain standards for my behavior. Should this be the case, they are termed a *nor-mative reference position*[15] (exemplified by the police in my community or the pas-tor of my church). Finally, some reference positions assume even greater impor-cance in that I seek their acceptance as a member of the position (exemplified by my professional colleagues in the social sciences). These latter are *identification po-sitions* and are discussed in greater detail in Chapter Eight.

Clearly, the five concepts defined in the preceding paragraphs involve more connotations than does the simple concept of reference position. These surplus connotations have generated much of the enthusiasm for the reference position no-tion. Consider the classic study of "reference groups" by Merton and Kitt (1950). Reworking materials from *The American Soldier*, these authors showed that sol-diers did not view their chances for advancement objectively but rather in terms of chances enjoyed by a "reference group" (actually, a comparative position). When members of the comparative position were promoted, respondents felt "relative de-privation" even though they might have recently enjoyed a promotion themselves. Americans are also likely to feel "relatively deprived" when siblings buy a new car, or (even worse) when their brothers-in-law get a promotion—a fact that is widely exploited by advertisers. Thus, comparative positions are an important part of our social environment. But so also are authority, audience, normative reference, and identification positions. The only difficulty is that authors are apt to write about all of these concepts as "reference groups," thus confusing both their readers and themselves.

Although theoretically more complex than simple expectations, extended ex-pectations have usually been measured using methods similar to those used for their

---

[13] Turner (1956) calls this concept an "interaction group."
[14] And this one a "valuation group."
[15] The term is Merton's (1957b).

simple analogue. To illustrate this, let us take the typical study of "social perception." Such a study might concern whether subjects (husbands) were or were not capable of estimating the norms of sentient others (their wives). Using the facet alternative method, for example, a wife might be asked to indicate how much smoking she approved for herself. Her husband would then be asked to estimate his wife's norm, using the same scale of facet alternatives. The wife's response is a simple expectation, the husband's an extended expectation, and each response is presumed to be an amount score.

Actually, an additional assumption must be made before we measure an extended expectation in such a manner. Since an extended expectaion (of length two) has two modality scales and a facet of behavioral alternatives, it should be conceived as a figure in a *three*-dimensional space. To use either the facet alternative or modal strength methods, we must agree to focus our attention on the second modality scale and reduce the leading modality scale to a single alternative. Usually this is done with appropriate question wording, asking the subject to provide an answer he or she thinks most likely.

Many studies of extended expectations may be found in which subjects' beliefs are reported. In contrast, only a few studies are reported of extended norms or preferences, and vanishingly few studies in which overt or symbolic record forms of extended expectations are studied formally. Either these latter forms are less often encountered in the real world, or social scientists have yet to take up the empirical challenge they represent.

It is difficult to overstress the importance of keeping the distinction between simple and extended expectations clear, as well as the necessity to distinguish among the various forms of simple and extended expectations and the human characteristics with which they are concerned. Unfortunately, some of those who have studied expectations have not done so. Some authors theorize about "role behaviors," for example, and then operationalize their interests by asking subjects to describe, prescribe, or evaluate either their own or others' behavior. Other investigators talk knowledgeably about simple expectations and then operationalize this interest by asking naive subjects to report on the expectations held by others. Still other authors speak of prescriptive expectations but ask respondents to discuss their beliefs, or presume that because someone prescribes another's behavior he or she also considers it likely to occur. For these reasons, when we read empirical studies of expectations we may discover that the theory stated is inapplicable to the data displayed, or that we are unable to interpret the findings reported—simply because investigators were unclear about the events they were investigating. This problem becomes worse when investigators are not studying expectations by themselves but rather the more complex phenomena that are defined in terms of expectations, such as role conflict or sanctioning. We return to this problem again in Chapter Six.

VARIABLES OF EXPECTATION

> *The famous French skepticism is, at bottom, a defensive measure*
> *for avoiding future deprivation by maintaining deliberately low*
> *expectations.*
>
> *—Daniel Lerner*

The concept of expectation is a complex one, and many variables have been suggested for it. Some of these have already been discussed and are related to the basic properties of expectations. Others involve connotations of the expectation concept not yet considered. Some expectational variables are also based on concepts that were defined earlier for roles or positions.

Basic Expectational Variables

MODE AND FORM

Expectations differ in their mode and form, and sometimes these differences are expressed as variables. For example, some authors speak of the "degree of prescriptiveness" of an expectation, or of the degree to which it is "expressed overtly." None of these variables has yet achieved much acceptance, and in my presentation it was assumed that readers would want to use different terms for expressing expectations that differed in mode and form (as was suggested in Table 5.2). However, expectations *are* differentiated within a given mode in terms of their **strength**. We say that one person holds a *strong* expectation and another a *weak* one, referring to the degree of approval, liking, or subjective probability expressed. This variable appears frequently in both theory and research. In fact, it is one of two variables central to the study of expectations, and the modal strength method of expectational measurement is designed to reflect it.

REFERENCED CHARACTERISTIC

The second central variable for expectations is **amount**, or the degree of the referenced characteristic that is preferred, anticipated, or approved within the expectation. When Daniel Lerner suggests that Frenchmen hold "low" expectations, he is attributing a judgement about amount. When we say that the parents hold "high expectations" for their children, we are using the amount variable. The difference between amount and strength is that amount refers to object-person characteristics, whereas strength reveals the degree to which the subject is committed to the expectation. "Demands" are stronger than "requests," and demands for allowance tend to become "higher" as the child gets older. The facet alternative method for measuring expectations is designed to generate amount scores.

OBJECT PERSON

Several expectational variables are associated with the object person, most of which are modeled after variables that were also defined for roles. The first of these is **generality**. Expectations that are general refer to many object persons and contexts. Codes of morality, for example, are usually quite general, whereas game rules are limited to a context and may be position-specific. As is also true for roles, the expectational variable of generality breaks down into two components: *personalization* and *contextualization*. Personal expectations are those applying to but a single object person, positional expectations to a designated reference position, universal expectations to all persons. Contextualized expectations are those whose applicability is constrained to a physical or social environment. We have also suggested that contextualization either can be stated as an explicit component of the expectation or can be implicit.

This suggests another variable, **clarity**. Occasionally we find expectations whose object person is unclear. We are all familiar with the injunction "Thou shalt not kill," but who art thou? Does this expectation apply to all people or only to civilians? The statement itself is simply unclear as to whom it applies, and debate has been generated among Christians as to whether its implications are those of a universal, or merely a limited, pacifism. But the variable of clarity can be applied to other components of an expectation. The mother's injuction, "Now, Johnny, you must be a good boy" is clearly an injunction, but we may be forgiven some confusion (as may her son) over exactly what behaviors were enjoined. Sometimes expectations are enunciated in a context that helps us to understand their referential unclarity. The classroom teacher who says "Don't do that!" is apparently uttering a denunciation of behaviors unspecified by object persons unknown. However, if two pupils are having a tussle together in the back of the room, and the teacher delivers her injunction in a sharp tone and looks directly at the miscreants, few would doubt the identity of either the targets or behaviors proscribed. Clarity, then, can refer to object person, referenced characteristic, context, or mode. However, simple expectations are rarely unclear in both object person and referenced characteristic. One does not often find statements such as "I disapprove"—outside of political posters or poetic imagery.

A special case of unclarity appears in the concept of attitude. Some theorists presume that persons organize their thinking using conceptions that are not specific in content but are applied to a range of associated characteristics. To illustrate, the person who is racially prejudiced may find distasteful any or all behaviors and features (and for that matter, artifacts) that are associated with the disliked race.

Such conceptions are unclear as regards content, and I shall term them **diffuse**. For some theorists (such as Thurstone, 1931; or Doob, 1947) the attitude concept is preferential in mode. Thus we may define **attitude** as a diffuse, preferential conception. For other theorists (such as Allport, 1935; or McGuire, 1969) attitudes are also diffuse as regards modality. I find this latter notion questionable. Lack of clarity in normative expectations has been found to be a source of disruption and discomfort for those who interact (Smith, 1957). Evidence is available to indicate that norms, preferences, and beliefs need not coincide (see Chapter Six). It would appear unwise to build a concept upon the assumption that they did. But even the preferential concept of attitude may be questioned. Evidence suggests that persons are more likely to conform to preferential statements when the latter are expressed clearly (again, see Chapter Six).

Since attitudes are assumed to be diffuse, they are usually measured with instruments consisting of various items that are presumed to co-scale for a subject population. Most of these items constitute direct measures of expectations, although some may concern nonhuman events that are presumed associated. Some instruments are confined to the preferential mode, whereas others may also feature items worded as norms and beliefs. Instruments are normally assumed to co-scale, thus to demonstrate the "existence" of an attitude, when items are intercorrelated for a subject population. This criterion has been challenged (Bank, Biddle, Keats, & Keats, 1977). Nevertheless, given similarities between the expectation and attitude concepts, some research on attitudes may be interpreted for application to expectations and vice versa.

SUBJECT PERSON

Other variables are associated with the subject person who holds or enunciates the expectation. Perhaps the most important of these is the notion of **sharing** (or **consensus**). Expectations may be held, uniquely, by a single person or may be shared among a subject population. As was suggested earlier, sharing is more often assumed by social scientists than it is studied. Anthropologists, particularly, are apt to assume that expectations are shared within the society or to confine their interests to expectations for which sharing may be assumed. If we do not make this assumption, it is possible to define a second variable, **ambiguity**, which refers to our uncertainty over whether a given set of persons does or does not hold or enunciate an expectation. Inscriptions are more likely to be ambiguous than are other expectational forms. However, the anthropologist who makes use of an informant must always be concerned with whether the expectations reported are held uniquely by that informant or are shared within the community.

In terms of their definitions, the concepts of sharing and generality are independent. (Sharing concerns the number of subjects who hold an expectation; generality, the number of object persons to whom it applies.) Recently, however, some investigators have begun to consider expectations that are *both* widely shared and generally applicable to the population. Let us term expectations of this sort **constituting expectations** (after White, 1972). An example of a constituting expectation would be the *norm of reciprocity,* which states that: "(a) people should help those who have helped them, and (b) people should not injure those who have helped them" (Gouldner, 1960 [B&T, Selection 12]; also see Homans, 1961). Evidence has now accumulated that this norm is widely held and is applied by at least American subjects to many object persons and contexts (Berkowitz & Walster, 1976; Staub, 1972). Despite this evidence, Americans would probably have some difficulty enunciating the norm of reciprocity in its simplest form, hence the norm is unclearly held—which is probably true of most constituting expectations. Gouldner argues that some constituting expectations (such as the norm of reciprocity) are cultural universals, whereas others are presumably limited to a given subject population. For example, Americans seem to share expectations concerning egalitarianism and populism that are not necessarily shared in other Western countries. Other constituting expectations include notions about social responsibility (Berkowitz & Daniels, 1963), altruism and rationality (Meeker, 1971), deference, authority, cleanliness, and the like. In fact, when it comes right down to it, the five assumptions for role theory with which we began the chapter (sanctioning, correspondence, phenomenal equivalence, conformity, simple formation) are probably all modeled after constituting expectations that are held within American society, at least. To illustrate, in their study of state police officers, Preiss and Ehrlich (1966) found that subjects felt sanctions were likely to be applied to them if they violated norms of conduct, but they really had no idea as to the form those sanctions might take nor who would apply them.

SENTIENT PERSON

Several variables already discussed for object person may also be applied to sentient person, particularly personalization and clarity. A **sentient-personalized** expectation is one that is attributed to but a single person, whereas an extended expectation exhibits **sentient clarity** when we know for certain to whom the expectation is attributed. For example, a child may be told "Everyone expects you to be clean and neat, John," but most children discover sooner or later that "everyone" is an ambiguous term of reference. Clarity of referenced characteristic, object person, and sentient person may all vary independently, thus the extended expectation may provide us various types of information or confusion. And whereas simple expectations for which the object person and referenced characteristic are both missing are rare, this is not true for extended expectations. An extended expectation may provide information about the speaker's reaction to another expectation, but not what the latter is about. Hence the lover says, "I just love what you love!"

Another set of variables is generated by the relationships among subject, object, and sentient persons. As has been suggested, simple expectations wherein the object position is alien may be differentiated from expectations wherein it is the subject's own. One may convert this distinction into a variable. Simple expectations may be judged for their **applicability** to the subject. Children in American families are sometimes offended, for example, when standards are enunciated for their behavior by parents which the parents do not follow themselves. Parents claim that these standards are for children and are inapplicable to adult behavior. Similarly, the sentient position may also be judged as conjoint or disjoint with either the subject position or the object position. This generates two more variables for extended expectations. **Self-reference** measures the degree of similarity between subject and sentient position; **other-reference** refers to similarity between sentient and object persons. When a member of the Roman Catholic laity speaks of lay opinion among Catholics, his or her enunciations have high self-reference. They would have less self-reference if he or she spoke of the opinions of Catholic priests, still less if he or she spoke about the opinions of Protestant Americans, and even less if the discussion was about Hottentots. If he or she spoke of the norms held by priests for priestly behavior, his or her enunciation would have high other-reference.

Variables of the above type illustrate a general notion that we shall term **consonance.** Whenever we encounter an expectational form having more than one element of a given type, it is possible to judge whether those two elements are similar to each other. For example, it is possible to judge an extended expectation for modality *consonance.* A *modally consonant* expectation is one wherein all of the modes stated are similar in classification and sign. Dissonant modes differ either in classification or sign. The statement, "I want what you want," exhibits consonance. "He spoke, saying, 'Thou shalt not kill,'" is modally dissonant because it involves a description of a demand, "I approve your disapproval of Johnny's eating habits," is dissonant because the preferences expressed differ in sign. It is also possible to study *form consonance* in extended expectations, such as a norm for a norm (consonant versus a norm for a demand (dissonant).

Additional Expectational Variables

Other variables have been suggested for expectations that involve ideas beyond those defining the expectation concept. For example, **formality** is characteristic of some expectations whose enunciation is long winded, full of semantic qualifications, exact, and rule expressed. In contrast, informal expectations are those whose specifications are vague, general, or are not codified in written form. Formal expectations are characteristic of contexts in which it is felt that roles must be controlled exactly, as in ceremonies or situations of danger. Formal specifications are set for the military review, the coronation, and the celebration of mass. Another illustration of formality is found in regulations governing the roles of pilot, co-pilot, and flight engineer in a modern aircraft. Each such person is provided an explicit check list of duties, and each must perform them in the exact order indicated, integrating his or her efforts with those of he others, lest the aircraft be placed in danger. Useless formality of expectations is resented by nearly everyone. However, it is difficult to imagine complex social systems without formal expectations. In addition, most of us get a kick out of performing well those roles that are formally specified, if we have accepted the systems of which they are a part.

Another variable is **legitimacy**, or the extent to which an expectation is viewed as "right and proper" by members of the social system. Legitimacy of expectations is related to legitimacy of positions. When expectations are enunciated by persons who are legitimate, they acquire legitimacy through association. We are also trained to honor certain classes of expectations—such as laws or commandments—without any initial understanding of why such honoring is advisable. Eventually, for some of us, such expectations are integrated into a value system, and legitimacy is replaced by *autonomy* (see Chapter Eight).

Yet another variable is *stereotypy*. Since its first introduction by Walter Lippman (1922), the term stereotype has accumulated many connotations. In its most general use, stereotypes are "beliefs about classes of individuals, groups, or objects which are 'preconceived,' i.e. resulting not from fresh appraisals of each phenomenon but from routinized habits of judgement and expectation" (Jahoda, 1964). As examples, stereotypic beliefs would have it that blacks are lazy and musical, women timid and dependent, Scotchmen penurious, Italians excitable, Latins romantic. Such beliefs may be false, of course. Some are also rigidly held or may be imbedded in general attitudes of prejudice concerning those who share a sexual, racial, or ethnic identity. Thus, stereotypes are also conceived as beliefs that are false, rigidly held, and prejudicial. Indeed, so disparate are the uses to which this term has been put that Ehrlich (1973) reduces his definition of stereotype to any "set of beliefs and disbeliefs about any group of people." Such a counsel of despair is not necessary. Earlier in the chapter it was suggested that conceptions might either be learned through exposure to enunciation by others or through the observation of others' characteristics. Stereotypes are expectations that are learned through the first of these means. **Stereotypy**, then, is the degree to which an expectation is based on hearsay rather than evidence. Expectations of all three modes may be stereotypic—although usually we are concerned with the stereotypy of beliefs. Stereotypes may be held for individuals or for positions—although more attention has been paid to the latter. Of studies concerning stereotypes there appears to be no end. Good general reviews of this literature are provided by Brigham (1971), Cauthen, Robinson and Krauss (1971), and Ehrlich (1973), while Broverman, Vogel, Broverman, Clarkson, and Rosenkrantz (1972) reviewed studies of sex-role stereotypes. Each year brings a new crop of stereotype studies, however, probably because stereotypes are so often associated with prejudice and discrimination.

Other variables that have received empirical attention focus upon ways in which the person reacts to holding an expectation, such as the degree to which the expectation is **central** in the person's self-concept, the degree to which the expectation is **imbedded** in a belief or value system, and the degree to which the expectation is **internalized**. (We return to variables of these sorts in Chapter Eight.)

Nor have we yet exhausted the list of variables that has been suggested for expectations. Blake and Davis (1964), for example, suggest the following additional variables for shared norms: "societal requirement involved," "whether the norm relates to a goal or to the means," "strength, sign, and specificity of sanction (if any)," "mode of transmission (primary versus secondary socialization)," "source of imputed authority for the norm," "mode of origination," and so forth. A related discussion also appears in Morris (1956) [B&T, Selection 8] and another in Gibbs (1965). It is also possbile to analyze systems of expectations for their logical relationships to one another, and these relationships generate additional variables for study (Anderson & Moore, 1957 [B&T, Selection 10]; Rescher, 1966).

ENVOI

At the beginning of the chapter we discussed five assumptions that are involved in extending the dramaturgical concept of role expectation to real-life situations: phenomenal equivalence, simple formation, conformity, sanctioning, and correspondence. It is possible to take a formal position now with regard to the first two of these.

I have explicitly endorsed the assumption of *phenomenal equivalence.* Indeed, this is the only one of these assumptions I will accept without qualification. This assumption was embraced for empirical reasons, among others. As long as the concept of (covertly held) expectation remains hypothetical, unmeasurable, or of explanatory value only, then no problem arises. But once we are faced with the problem of measuring norms, preferences, or beliefs, we are forced to make a choice among operational alternatives. As we have seen, measuring conceptions by use of prior experiences or behavioral effects has disadvantages. Both techniques make questionable assumptions, and both mask interesting research problems. This leaves us with the alternative of measurement through phenomenal report and causes us to accept the assumption.

Such a decision has implications. In assuming that subjects are capable of reporting conceptions we tend to ignore other mind concepts that may determine behavior of which the subject is unaware. In assuming that they will report conceptions we are casting them as aware and honest citizens. Both postures are characteristic of American pragmatism, which assumes of human beings that they are (or can become) masters of their own fate and that social relations are both understandable and rationally conducted. It is small wonder, then, that role theory has flowered in the New World, or that its major applications have been to the exposition of "normal" social relations in such settings as the home, church, school, or business place. In accepting phenomenal equivalence, we make it more difficult for role theory to accommodate intuitive processes, the unconscious, and theories of motivation that place stress upon physiology. Social scientists concerned with these latter are apt to discuss how a "drive" or "impulse" is perceived by the subject; role theorists write about whether or not a conception the subject reveals to us will result in appropriate behavior. This means that role theorists tend to ignore motivational concepts, and explanations cast in role terms may leave the reader in doubt over why the subject takes action.

The assumption of *simple formation* concerns the origin of covert expectations and suggests that these are learned either through experience, observation, or through hearing expectations expressed by others. Each of these notions has some empirical support, but extensive research has yet to be reported on them, and the conditions under which one or the other will hold are not yet known. Consequently, this assumption is not yet useful. Covert expectations are surely formed from experience, but as yet we know little about the processes involved in their formation. Some theorists suggest that thoughts are a form of subvocal speech and that their learning is similar to the learning of ideas that we express vocally. While all would agree that conceptions are modeled after enunciated expectations, I sincerely doubt that the two forms are learned through similar means. Among other differences, conceptions are not subject to corrective feedback from others when formed. This means that reinforcement theory is less applicable to their learning.

Let us wait a bit before commenting on the assumptions of conformity, sanctioning, and correspondence. Chapter Six reviews evidence bearing on each of these. We will, however, return to these five assumptions—and to the prospect of propositional theory concerning expectations—at the end of Chapter Six.

Chapter Six

Comparison Concepts and Expected Roles

It is commonly supposed, although there is very little evidence to warrant such a supposition, that there exists a simple and logical relation between what a person says and what he thinks.
—Roethlisberger and Dickson

This chapter continues the discussion of role expectations begun in Chapter Five. Up to now we have dealt with the expectation concept itself. We now turn to derivative concepts in which role expectations are involved. Many such concepts have appeared in the role literature, and once again most of these concepts are modeled after notions that are found in the structure of our language or in beliefs of Western societies.

Consider *role conflict*. Role conflict is said to occur when someone is subjected to two or more contradictory expectations whose stipulations the person cannot simultaneously meet in behavior. Borodin's only opera, *Prince Igor,* concerns a situation of role conflict. The hero, Igor—Prince of Seversk—is captured by an invading army, the Polovetsi. Rather than slaughter Igor, the invaders importune him to join their cause and give him the run of their camp, asking only that he pledge his word not to escape. Shortly, however, Igor is offered an opportunity to escape under circumstances that will lead to his resuming command of the Russian armies. At this point he must choose between honor and patriotism. He chooses patriotism but is ambivalent about the choice.

Role conflicts are among the classic ingredients of tragedy. In *The Red and the*

Black, Stendahl's hero is destroyed between conflicting expectations of church and state. Rhadames is caught between love and duty; Cio-Cio San is victimized by the values of a traditional society and the demands of her foreign husband; Tristan must choose between his love for Isolde and his responsibility to King Marke. In each of these latter examples the protagonist is unable to resolve role conflict, and death ensues. But the resolution of role conflict can appear to us a heroic act, particularly when associated with physical disability or an impoverished background. Those who immigrate to a new society suffer role conflicts too, and must reconcile the expectations of their new home with those they learned as children in their country of origin, an experience that can be seen as tragic, heroic, or even funny, as in *The Education of H*Y*M*A*N K*A*P*L*A*N.*

Since they are modeled after ideas that are widely shared, concepts such as role conflict have "caught on" rapidly among social scientists and have been applied to practical problems. Consider the early history of role conflict investigations. The first empirical study published using this concept was that of Stouffer (1949), which concerned problems of student adjustment in the university. But within the next three years role conflict was applied to problems of multiple-position occupancy (Warren, 1949), marital adjustment (Ort, 1950), complex organizations (Jacobson, Charters, & Lieberman, 1951), personality analysis (Mishler, 1951), the industrial foreman (Charters, 1952), a military rank (Karcher, 1952), and social class conflict (Ort, 1952). And given this focus upon practical applications, we should not be surprised to discover that *role conflict* was given a number of differing definitions in these studies, indeed almost as many definitions as there were investigators.

Role conflict is not the only concept that can be formed by apposing expectations and other role notions. Other such concepts include conformity, consensus, accuracy of expectations, veridicality, and the concept of expected role itself. These latter, no less than role conflict: have generated considerable research, have proven popular as much for their intuitive appeal as for their theoretical significance, and have been characterized by conceptual confusion. Indeed, most of the empirical research in role theory to date may be said to have concerned such derivative concepts, but it may be doubted whether this research has yet been adequately integrated.

Thomas and Biddle suggested that the role vocabulary is only "partially articulate" in that role terms connote many things to many people, thus generating enthusiasm but not much cumulative knowledge [B&T, Chapter I]. This is a basic dilemma of contemporary role theory—if not of American social science in general. Role theory implies a wealth of applications to the solution of social problems. Consequently it is accepted with enthusiasm by educators, clinical psychologists, and social workers—and by social scientists who are interested in solving problems—as well as by funding agencies that hope to place their limited resources behind research that will pay off in solution to these problems. But random acquisition of facts does not a science make. And investigations of processes in the role field will not cumulate until they are based on agreed upon conceptual distinctions and are accompanied by research on basic assumptions. Two things are badly needed in the role field today: social scientists who will do its basic research, and funds to support their efforts.

COMPARISON CONCEPTS

> *He that complies against his will,*
> *Is of his own opinion still.*
>   *—Samuel Butler*

Many concepts in role theory involve the comparison of expectations (and sometimes behaviors) for their similarity. For example, the concept of *consensus* means that two or more persons are judged to hold similar expectations. In addition, some (but not all) concepts that concern the similarity of expectations also involve a second idea, determination. To define the concept of consensus requires only the idea of similarity. However, to define *conformity* involves two ideas: similarity, and the fact that it is the expectation that is presumed to determine the behavior and not vice versa. Let us consider what are meant by similarity and determination

SIMILARITY OF EXPECTATIONS

Until now we have used the concept of comparison to apply to overt characteristics only. In Chapter Two it was noted that two behaviors could be *compared* if both were mapped into the same facet, and if comparable, their traces in that facet might be identical, similar, or distinct. Concepts such as these may be applied easily to overtly enunciated expectations. For example, demands might be compared for the volume or forcefulness of their expression, or for the clarity of their enunciation. However, enunciated expectations are most often compared for what they "say"—for what they describe, prescribe, or evaluate in the characteristics of object persons. And once we conceive of making comparisons among enunciated expectations for their content, it is but a small jump to apply these same concepts to inscriptions and to covertly held expectations.

Once again, the basic notions involved in comparing expectations appear in our common experience. The mother says to her child, "Honey, I know just what you are thinking"; the prelate differentiates between legal and moral codes; critics may differ in their evaluation of a performance; parents may become aware that they hold differing standards for the behaviors of their children. These examples illustrate two limitations that are commonly placed on the comparison of expectations. First, expectations are normally compared with one another (or with object-person behavior) for their distributional forms. We are usually concerned, for example, with whether various subjects give approval to the same behavior or whether the object person is exhibiting behavior that is approved—rather than (let us say) with whether subjects are talking about the same object-person characteristic or are using the same referential assumptions in doing so.

Second, other nonspecified aspects of expectations (or behaviors) are normally held constant. When two subjects respond to a question concerning their norms, we assume that both accept the facet alternatives for those characteristics specified, both are using the same mode of response, and both accept whatever contextual specifications are set forth and have no others in mind. When comparing expectations and behaviors, we assume both to involve the same facet, the person who exhibits the behavior should be a member of the object position, and the exhibition of behavior must not violate contextual specifications set forth in the expectation. When comparing a simple and an extended expectation, both must involve the same (terminal) modality, the other must be a member of the sentient position, etc.

Let us state these limitations formally. Two or more expectations will be termed **comparable** if they agree in: their object persons, the characteristic they discuss and the facet in which this is expressed, their modality, and their context. If comparable, they may be found to have identical, similar, or distinct distributions. Comparable expectations will be termed **identical** if they have the same distributional form, **similar** if their distributional forms are "not too different," and otherwise **distinct**. To illustrate, the enunciations "John has not washed his ears," and "Mary must not sing so loudly" are not comparable since they differ in object person, characteristic mapped, and modality. However, another descriptive utterance concerning John's ear-ablutive behavior—namely, "John has, indeed, washed his ears"—is comparable with the first statement. Again, Orthodox Jews are enjoined to fast on Yom Kippur. Provided that we observe (*a*) the eating behavior, (*b*) of a known, Orthodox Jew, (*c*) on the occasion of Yom Kippur, we can make a meaningful judgement as to whether or not a behavior has occurred that is similar to the injunction.

To judge whether or not expectations are similar is more complex than judging whether behaviors are identical, similar, or distinct. This is because a single behavior generates but *one* score for any given facet, whereas an expectation is defined as a *distribution* of scores for that facet. Statistical conventions have not yet been adopted for judging the similarity of expectations. Indeed, most authors have ignored the issue completely and have either simply asserted that expectations were similar (or distinct) or have set arbitrary criteria for making such judgements. (I return to this problem in my discussion of consensus later.)

DETERMINATION IN EXPECTATIONS

Some concepts that are generated by comparing expectations involve more than the notion of similarity. As suggested earlier, the concept of *conformity* involves both the idea of similarity between an expecation and a behavior and the idea that the former determines the latter. As we shall see, notions concerning determination appear in several comparison concepts.

Formally, one expectation (or behavior) is said to **determine** another if its appearance affects the occurrence of the other in some way (usually unspecified). As used here, the concept of determination is similar to behavioral linkage but is sloppier in usage and less often subject to empirical investigation. Behavioral linkages may be observed and are judged to exist only when specific conditions are found involving a sequence of behaviors (see Chapter Two). Determination, in contrast, is often an assumption made by the investigator without benefit of empirical evidence (or clergy).[1] Let us assume, for example, that expectations held by husbands for their wives' behaviors are similar to the behaviors actually exhibited by their wives. Does this mean that the husbands' expectations were modeled after the wives' behavior—or that the wives, aware of their husbands' expectations, have modeled behavior after the expectations which occurred first? One process generates *accuracy*, the other *conformity*. Too often investigators have ignored problems of this kind, measuring both sets of phenomena concurrently, and making an assumption about determination without evidence. (For an exception to this generalization see Dinitz, Angrist, Lefton, & Pasamanick, 1962) [B&T, Selection 41]. This does not mean that concepts involving determination are useless. However, assumptions about determination may or may not be legitimate.

To summarize, derivative concepts have appeared in role theory that involve the comparison of expectations and object-person behavior for their *similarity*. Some of these concepts involve an additional assumption, *determination*, but others do not. I shall refer to this class of ideas as **comparison concepts**. We turn now to the major comparison concepts that have been discussed or investigated empirically. For convenience, these concepts are reviewed as they are used by others. At the end of the section, however, a formal discussion is provided of the events one might reasonably include among comparison concepts.

Conformity and Expected Sanctions

Few terms in the social sciences have been used in so many senses as has *conformity*. Some of these many uses are reviewed in Rokeach (1962) and Allen (1965). Among others, conformity has been used synonymously with the general concept of determination; to designate whatever results from socialization, acculturation, adaptation, adjustment, or learning; to describe any process of successful influence

---

[1] In fact, two different kinds of assumptions seem to underlie determined concepts. In some concepts, such as *conformity* or *alignment*, the investigator assumes a causative relationship between the elements compared. In others, such as *accuracy* or *veridicality*, one element is merely judged for whether it matches the other. These two uses should be separated, although at present they are entangled.

or injunction; as a marker for situations involving coercion; as an antonym for creativity or—in other contexts—as an antonym for deviancy; to describe concept formation, and more particuarly perceptual learning; as an epithet for denigrating the personality of Americans; and on and on. Needless to say, to require of one term that it encompass all of this territory is ridiculous. In the present discussion I will restrict the discussion of conformity to those meanings associated with expectations and behaviors.

Conformity is a determined concept. As Walker and Heyns (1962), (p. 5) put it, "Conformity and non-conformity always involve movement or change. This is true even when only a single observation is possible and change is not directly observable. To describe a person or a group as conformist on the basis of a single observation implies an earlier state in which the degree of agreement with the norm was not so great." In general, then, conformity is judged when a "model" appears after which one might pattern a response, and an example response occurs that has been determined by and is similar to that model. But what constitutes the model? And what the response?

At least four answers have been given to this question. For some investigators, such as Sherif (1936) or Asch (1956), the "model" constitutes behaviors that are emitted by others, whereas the response is a similar behavior emitted by the person. As we know from Chapter Two, this is one form of imitation. Studies of *behavioral conformity* differ from others concerned with imitation in two respects: the behavioral stimulus is presented by group members, and investigators have presumed "conformity" to occur because subjects had formed and responded to expectations for their own behavior. Whether this "explanation" for conformity holds is problematic (Asch, 1956), thus studies of behavioral conformity may represent several different processes. I shall generally avoid them here, although good reviews are provided by Bass (1961) and Allen (1965, 1975).

In contrast, for many investigators the "model" for the conforming act is an expectation that is held or expressed for the object person, either by others or by him or herself. But even for these latter, some confusion exists concerning the nature of the response. For a few theorists (such as McGuire, 1969) the conforming response may be a covert process, a shift of expectation or "attitude change." Given that this is a minority position, I shall review it later on under the term *acceptance*. In contrast, for most investigators the conformity term refers to overt responses, to shifts in behavior. In formal terms, then, a behavior will be said to **conform** to an expectation if it is both similar to and determined by the latter. But even this position breaks into several research traditions, depending on the nature of the expectation that determines the conformity response. Some investigators have concerned themselves with the person's conformity to his or her *own* expectation, to expectations the person holds for self (but is willing to tell us about). Other scholars have studied the person's conformity to expectations held or expressed by *others.* Conforming to one's own expectations has different implications from those of conforming to the expectations of others, and studies of these two

Table 6.1
MAJOR TYPES OF CONFORMITY

		Form of expectation serving as the "model"		
		Covertly held	Overtly expressed	Written down
Identity of the person holding or expressing an expectation	The object person	Type A. Consistency of response to own conceptions	Type B. Consistency of response to own enunciations	Type C. Consistency of response to own inscriptions
	One or more others	Type D. Compliance to others' conceptions	Type E. Compliance to others' enunciations	Type F. Compliance to others' inscriptions

processes have constituted separate enterprises in the main. I shall refer to the former as *consistency* and to the latter as *compliance*.

Additional distinctions concerning conformity may also be made in terms of the length and mode of the expectation conformed to, the content and context of the behavior to which it refers, and the form of its expression (also see Bass, 1961; Campbell, 1961). The last is particularly useful for examining studies of conformity, since clear distinctions may be made among studies in which conceptions are measured, enunciations are expressed, and inscriptions are used to elicit conformity. The distinctions between consistency and compliance, and among the three forms of expectational expression, are used in Table 6.1 to sort out studies of conformity. My review concentrates on the different types of conformity listed in this table.

In operational terms, studies of conformity should involve the independent measurement of two events: an expectation and a behavior that may be determined by it. In field studies these two events will generally be measured concurrently, and the fact that the expectation determines the behavior will simply be assumed. In experimental studies the presence of the expectation should be manipulated as an independent variable, whereas the conforming behavior should appear as a dependent variable. Such designs appear to be straightforward. In practice, however, many studies of conformity have departed from them. Most of these departures have involved substituting another variable for the expectation or behavior that the investigator really wanted to study. To illustrate, some studies of conformity have not measured behavior directly but instead have asked subjects to indicate their behavioral intentions and have assumed that these would predict behaviors. To what extent such design faults have spoiled the findings of conformity research is not now known. Behavioral intentions often do predict behaviors (Liska, 1974). But studies have also appeared in which they did not (for examples, see Leventhal, Jones, & Tembly, 1966; Leventhal, Singer, & Jones, 1965; Leventhal, Watts, & Pagano, 1967). To accept the findings of research having such faults it is necessary to establish when their assumptions are and are not valid—which requires additional research.

CONSISTENCY OF RESPONSE TO CONCEPTIONS

A person's behavior is judged **consistent** when it is similar to and determined by an expectation that is held for it by the person him or herself. Nearly all studies of consistency have concerned conformity to covert expectations, and thus should be placed in Type A of Table 6.1. Such studies should involve the apposition of some sort of phenomenal response from the person indicating his or her conception and an independent observation of what he or she does *in situ*. Thus, such studies are presumed to concern the relationship between "thoughts and deeds," although in operational terms they have concerned "words and deeds" (Deutscher, 1966).

Consistency of response to conceptions is one of the key concerns of role theorists. As we know, consistency is a flattering idea, and the assumption of correspondence is often built into social theories. Moreover, literally hundreds of social scientists are regularly involved in the measurement of opinions, attitudes, values, and intentions, assuming that these measurements will predict behavior in some simple way. Nor should we be surprised to discover that many studies have now appeared on this topic. The first of these seems to have been the classic investigation of discriminatory practices among hotel and restaurant proprietors conducted by LaPiere (1934); whereas several excellent summaries have recently appeared for the field (Abelson, 1972; Deutscher, 1966; Fishbein & Ajzen, 1975; Liska, 1974, 1975; Schuman & Johnson, 1976; Thomas, 1971; Wicker, 1969).

Much, but by no means all, of this research has made use of the concept of *attitude*, and thus it suffers from the conceptual and operational difficulties that have plagued attitude research generally. Let us briefly review four of these.

1. The attitude concept is applied to a wide range of reference objects and not simply to persons and their characteristics. For this reason, some attitudinal studies have used questions that were not directly concerned with the behavior of the person but rather with other events that were presumed to be associated with behavior. For example, white subjects' willingness to behave prejudicially toward blacks has occasionally been "measured" by assessing their preferences for "black music" or "soul food."

2. Attitudes are usually "measured" by instruments that consist of items presumed to co-scale for a subject population. This procedure poses problems. For

one, the items may not co-scale for a given subject. For another, subject-held conceptions are often contextualized, whereas the items of the attitude scale usually feature no contextualization or, sometimes, a variety of confusing contexts.

3. Attitudinal instruments may involve items of more than one modality. Although theorists may (or may not) assume "attitude" to be a diffuse, preferential expectation, items appearing in attitude scales are likely to feature all three modes of response.

4. Attitude scales normally concern only the subject's own conceptions. Persons often conceive and respond to extended expectations, but this fact is ignored in most attitude research.

Bearing these problems in mind, what has so far been discovered concerning conformity to conceptions held by the person for him or herself? Perhaps the most pervasive finding is that conceptions held for oneself do *not* always predict the person's behavior! Time and again, investigators have reported—to their apparent surprise—that consistency was not obtained in their study or was obtained for only a minority of subjects. Why on earth should this finding have appeared? Surely, all things being equal, a person's expectation should predict his or her behavior. Why should this type of conformity have proven elusive ?

Several answers may be given to this question. First, inconsistency is not a universal finding. Some studies report consistency, or consistency for certain classes of persons (Brannon, Cyphers, Hesse, Hesselbart, Keane, Schuman, Viccaro, & Wright, 1973; DeFleur & Westie, 1958; Freedman, Hermalin, & Chang, 1975; Juster, 1964; Kelley & Mirer; 1974; Schwartz & Tessler, 1972). Second, some of the apparent lack of consistency appearing in early studies seems to have reflected poor methodology. Recent studies have demonstrated more consistency when subjects were asked specific rather than vague questions, when questions provided contextual specification, and when questions concerned subject behavior rather than other content (DeFleur & Westie, 1963; Fishbein & Ajzen, 1975; Heberlein & Black, 1976). Third, consistency appears more likely when stronger, more salient expectations are studied (Sample & Warland, 1973).

At a deeper level of analysis, conforming to one's own preferences may be quite a different thing from conforming to one's norms or beliefs. Norms are rooted in beliefs about consequences, so conformity to norms should appear when consequences are deemed severe and likely. In contrast, preferences reflect hedonic experience, and conformity to them should be more likely when the person experiences strong and predictable rewards. (To illustrate this difference, let us take a case where norm and preference contradict each other—when a person who enjoys smoking learns that smoking may lead to lung cancer. Whether that person continues to smoke thereafter will depend on the strengths of the opposed expectations; that is, on how much the person enjoys the physical and social rewards of smoking, and how certain and fearful he or she is about the consequences of doing so.) Beliefs should generate conformity only under certain conditions. Reports of past behavior may have little relevance for the future if the person is to enter a new context or intends to change his or her habits. On the other hand, if given honestly, a behavioral intention may be the best of all conceptions for predicting behavior in a known situation (Fishbein, 1973; Liska, 1974).

The preceding propositions seem reasonable and suggest that consistency will vary with modality of expectation. Unfortunately, evidence bearing on them is spotty. Modality is an emerging concept, and as we know, some investigators are unaware of it. Even those who are aware may debilitate their research through use of modally ambiguous instruments.[2] Nevertheless, various studies have now examined two or more modally distinct expectations as predictors of behavior (for examples, see Ajzen, 1971; Ajzen & Fishbein, 1970; Carlson, 1968; Kothandapani, 1971; Ostrom, 1969, Schwartz & Tessler, 1972). These studies suggest that the relative effectiveness of norms, preferences, and beliefs for predicting behavior will vary depending on content and context. Other studies have shown consistency to be greater when expectations of one modality are accompanied by concordant expectations in other modes (Norman, 1975).

Evidence is also weak concerning conformity to extended expectations. Conformity to attributed norms, for example, should be more likely when the other has more legitimacy, more opportunity to observe behavior, and greater power to levy sanctions against the person. Apart from research on role conflict resolution (reviewed later in this chapter) these propositions seem not to have been investigated systematically. In addition, it is not now known whether persons conform to attributed norms for external reasons or because they have internalized those norms as their own (however, see Biddle, Bank, & Marlin, in press a,b). Some of the available research has concerned the relative influence of two or more reference others for a specific problem (for examples, see Alexander & Campbell, 1962; Bowerman & Kinch, 1959; Brittain, 1963; Herriot, 1963; Riley, Riley & Moore, 1961; Rosen, 1955). Other studies have found attributed expectations to have effects that were independent of respondents' own "attitudes" (Acock & DeFleur, 1972; Ajzen, 1971; Ajzen & Fishbein, 1969, 1970, 1972; Bowers, 1968; Brannon *et al.,* 1973; DeFriese & Ford, 1969; Ewens & Ehrlich, 1972; Fendrich, 1967; Sample & Warland, 1973; Warner & DeFleur, 1969).

The preceding arguments suggest that conformity to any single expectation may actually be *unlikely.* If we truly want to predict what the person will do next, perhaps our best strategy would be to assess several of the expectations he or she holds and attempt to predict from the set. In line with this thinking, several models have now appeared that predict behavior from a combination of simple and ex-

---

[2]To illustrate, Ostrom (1969) studied relationships among four, modally distinct "components of attitude," but three of the scales used in the study involved items worded as beliefs.

tended expectations in several modes. The best known of these models is that of Ajzen and Fishbein (1970), although other models are suggested in Calder and Ross (1973), Liska (1974), and Triandis (1977). Building upon the expectancy-value theory of Dulany (1961, 1968), Ajzen and Fishbein predict behavior from *behavioral intention,* which is predicted, in turn, from *attitude* (presumably preference) and *attributed norms.* This model has now been tested in numerous studies (Fishbein & Ajzen, 1975) and has been found to be a good predictor of behavior in the laboratory.

In part, the Ajzen–Fishbein approach may have caught on because of the Law of the Instrument, which may be stated, in this case, that "any model is better than no model." Nevertheless, the Ajzen–Fishbein model makes quite specific assumptions that appear to be limiting. Why, for example, is the model limited to attitude and attributed norms as predictor variables? In an earlier version of the model, the authors also predicted from *own norm* (Ajzen & Fishbein, 1969; Fishbein, 1967). They have since abandoned own norm, claiming to have found it "essentially equivalent" to behavioral intention. This claim has not been supported in others' research (Gabrenya & Biddle, 1978; Schwartz & Tessler, 1972). Other expectational forms, such as attributed preferences or associated beliefs, seem not to have been considered by Ajzen and Fishbein, nor have these authors yet taken up issues suggested by role conflict research (discussed later). Effectiveness of the model depends on establishing "weights" for predictor variables, but little is yet known concerning conditions that would affect those weights. As well, the model hangs on the concept and measurement of attitude. Ajzen and Fishbein are among those who consider attitude to be a diffuse, preferential expectation. Within their research, however, they have chosen to measure attitude with a Semantic Differential based on items that exhibit several modes.

This last issue brings us back to what has been the major problem for research on consistency. Given confusions in current concepts and methods for measuring attitude, one has difficulty in interpreting results from much of this research. It seems time to clean up attitude research. Let us begin by abandoning the idea that attitudes subsume several modes of thought. While this may have been a useful way of thinking about racial prejudice (Allport, 1935, 1954) it seems less useful for other arenas of human affairs. As we know, preferences, norms, and beliefs need not coincide—and often do not if we are to believe the evidence. But even the concept of attitude as a diffuse, preferential conception bears thought. Under what conditions will such a conception be maintained, and what does an attitude scale measure when the person holds only specific preferences? Surely much of our behavior is generated by specific preferences, and for these latter an attitude scale would appear a poor predictor. And even if we grant some usefulness for a diffuse attitude concept, it seems resonable that one should measure attitudes with scales whose items are phrased as preferences. If this were done faithfully, perhaps then one could begin to cumulate research on conformity to attitudes.

CONSISTENCY OF RESPONSE TO ENUNCIATIONS
AND INSCRIPTIONS

Types B and C of Table 6.1 concern consistency of response, respectively, to enunciations and to inscriptions. Studies of these latter types should involve an observation of the enunciation or inscription of an expectation by a person and an independent observation of his or her behavior that may be judged for conformity. Once again, these are socially significant forms of conformity. Persons who utter promises are supposed to keep them. Words of self-encouragement are presumed by both coaches and counselors to induce greater effort on the part of clients (Caplan, 1968). Parents or teachers may ask the child to verbalize a norm for conduct on the assumption that conformity will be more likely thereafter.

These assumptions seem reasonable, moreover public disclosure of intentions has been found to increase conformity (Schofield, 1975; Wankel & Thompson, 1977). Nevertheless, direct evidence bearing on the conditions under which consistent response to enunciations and inscriptions will and will not hold is hard to find. As we know from the preceding, most studies presumed to concern consistent response to conceptions actually feature a design that compares "words with deeds." As a result, their findings might be interpreted for application to enunciations. But this is not really fair, since phenomenal responses given to an investigator are not presumed by the subject to be "public." Public espousal of an expectation is more often studied for its effect on acceptance than on conformity, and we shall return to this latter topic later in this chapter (however, see Kiesler, Mathog, Pool, & Howenstine, 1971). In the absence of evidence, it seems reasonable to believe that persons will respond to public declarations of their beliefs, norms, and preferences in much the same way they will respond when they hold those conceptions privately. Nevertheless, public espousal should generally produce more conformity. Public declaration probably "commits" the person more strongly to act (Kiesler, 1971), may have a self-persuasive effect (Collins & Hoyt, 1972; Janis, 1968), and should allow others to act with greater assurance to support conformity.

In sum, *consistency* of response to expectations is not a simple phenomenon. Persons may conform to what they tell us they ought to, prefer to, or are likely to do—or to what they presume others think about the same topic—but on other occasions they will not. They are more likely to conform if: (a) they are familiar with the context and are competent to perform; (b) the words they use refer clearly to the behavior to be observed; (c) the behavior in question appears shortly after their words are given; (d) the conception they report is strongly held and other conceptions are not present that would lead to contradicting behaviors; and (e) social supports are present that would favor conformity. They may also be more likely to conform if their expectations appear as enunciations or inscriptions. It is important for us to learn the conditions under which a person's expectations will be matched by his or her deeds. Research on this topic is of abiding interest, and readers should be alert for future studies and theories concerning it. But as for the assumption of consistency being a universal truth, forget it!

COMPLIANCE TO CONCEPTIONS

Behaviors are judged **compliant** when they are similar to and determined by the expectations of one or more others. Many studies have also dealt with compliance, a fair portion of which concern conformity to others' conceptions (Type D of Table 6.1). In operational terms, studies of this type should feature the independent measurement of both a conception held by another and a behavior by the person that is matched to it. In fact, many studies of compliance to conceptions have exhibited this straightforward design (e.g., Dinitz, Angrist, Lefton, & Pasamanick, 1962 [B&T, Selection 41], or Simmons & Freeman, 1959). On the other hand, some studies presumed to concern compliance have not measured others' conceptions but have instead asked the respondent to *attribute* expectations to others (Ehrlich, Rinehart, & Howell, 1962; Gross, Mason, & McEachern, 1958 [B&T, Selection 35]). Studies of this latter design may be interpreted to provide evidence for consistency wherein the expectation serving as the model for behavior is attributed to another. To interpret them as studies of compliance requires that we assume subjects have correctly attributed expectations to others. As we shall see shortly, this assumption is not always justified. When it is, this substitute technique will provide results that compare favorably with those provided by the proper design. When it is not, results may still be interesting, but they will not provide simple information concerning compliance.

Compliance is more problematic than consistency. Since the other is *not* the person, the former must take some sort of action to induce the latter to conform, an action that is distinct from the subsequent act of conformity. Despite this problematic feature, many studies have now appeared demonstrating compliance to conceptions. A superficial reading of these might lead one to conclude that compliance was *more* likely than consistency. This would be an error. Studies of both phenomena will report moderate correlations between conceptions and behavior. Authors investigating consistency are then likely to bemoan the fact that their findings are not stronger, whereas investigators of compliance seem delighted to have found any effect at all. Compliance to others' conceptions may be demonstrated. It is certainly less likely than conformity to one's own conceptions.

Studies of compliance to conceptions have reflected three research traditions in the main: research on small groups, positions in formal organizations, and classroom teaching. Interest in compliance in small groups began with the pioneering work of Festinger, Back, Schachter, Kelley, and Thibaut (1950) and with Homans' (1950) interpretation of results from the Hawthorn Studies. These early authors claimed that face-to-face groups will take action to enforce conformity to group-held norms upon group members. In support of this argument, many studies have appeared showing relationships between norms held by group members and group-member behavior (Allen, 1965; Walker & Heyns, 1962). Thus, compliance to shared norms seems likely when persons interact regularly.

How do group members go about inducing compliance? Most investigators have assumed members to be aware of group norms and to *intend* influencing others to conform to them. As we know from Chapter Two, various strategies are open to the other for influencing the person. Some of these strategies reveal the other's intention: direct injunctions, indirect injunctions, threats and promises, or the use of sanctions. Other strategies are more subtle, such as modeling or environmental manipulation. These strategies will differ in their ability to effect compliance, as well as in their implications for other aspects of the relationships among group members. How likely are they to be used in the group? Few studies have yet taken up this question, although it has been discussed extensively (Davis, 1965; Marwell & Schmitt, 1967a; Rapoport, 1960; Schelling, 1966). In brief, then, it seems likely that others will bring pressure to bear on the person to comply with their norms, but what they will do to create that pressure is not now known in any detail.

Assuming the other has done "something" to communicate his or her norm to the person, why does the person comply in a group context? Surely the most likely reason is that the person will have found out about the other's norm through actions taken by the other and conforms because of that information. This argument implies that within the group: (*a*) persons are likely to attribute accurate norms to others; (*b*) the norms attributed will generate matching norms for each person; and as a result (*c*) norms will come to be shared.

This argument is tidy, but is it correct? It does not appear to handle cases where group members are in conflict over norms. Alternate reasons have also been suggested for the appearance of group conformity (Allen, 1965; Campbell, 1961; Kelman, 1958). Apparently conforming behaviors may in fact be accidental. Compliance also can result from facilitation, hindrance, or physical coercion. Compliance may appear because of positive evaluation of the behavior by the person. (The behavior may be pleasurable or may be seen as a legitimate alternative to boredom or confusion.) Again, the person may comply for instrumental reasons or may be conditioned so that behavior results from environmental cues although he or she does not understand what is going on. Or, compliance may result from the person having a positive evaluation of the other. (The other may be liked or may belong to a social position having legitimacy.) And if these were not reasons enough, compliance may also take place because the person holds a constituting norm favoring the act of conformity.

This last explanation is intriguing, since it suggests that some of us learn to comply regardless of whether or not there are obvious reasons for doing so (Jones, 1967). Presumably this latter reflects response generalization from past situations when compliance was rewarded and called to our attention. (Perhaps the critics are right, and ours *is* a conformity-ridden society. But then again, what society is not?)

These several reasons for compliance differ in their implications, and research is now available concerning the effects of some of them (Allen, 1965; Walker & Heyns, 1962). Unfortunately, most studies do not make clear the mechanisms responsible for compliance in groups, so at present we do not know when compliance will be produced by conformity to norms correctly attributed and when it will appear for other reasons.

What about others with whom the person does *not* interact? Will persons comply with the expectations of nonintimates, and if so under what conditions? To answer these questions we turn to a second research tradition reflecting the formal organization. This second effort began with the study of Gross *et al.* (1958) [B&T], Selection 35], which concerned responses by school superintendents in Massachusetts to norms they (correctly) attributed to other positions in their school systems, such as members of their school boards, teachers, community leaders, and the like. School superintendents were unlikely to interact with some of these others. Nevertheless superintendents were found to comply with the expectations of these latter—under certain conditions.

What are these conditions? This question has generated considerable research (van de Vliert, 1979), and two conditions are now believed to make compliance likely. First, persons are likely to comply with the norms of others whom they perceive as powerful—who have the ability to find out what the person is doing and who will exert sanctions against the person for conformity. To illustrate, industrial workers should comply to the norms of their supervisors (and not vice versa). Second, persons are also likely to comply with the norms of others having legitimacy—those who have the "right" to order the person's behavior. Thus, parishioners should conform to the norms of their pastors in matters of morality (and not vice versa). The only trouble with these two conditions is that they have not been cleanly separated in studies to date. Most studies have been field surveys, and the referent others studied have tended to be both powerful and legitimate. For that matter, they were also likely to have wealth and to be intelligent, forceful, and charismatic as individuals. So whether these two conditions are sufficient as explanations for compliance in the organization is not yet clear. Good experimental research is needed to untangle these matters.

This second research tradition stimulates an additional thought about sanctions. One often finds arguments suggesting that compliance occurs "because" of sanctions the person expects from others. In these arguments the concept of sanctioning is used somewhat differently from its usage given earlier. In Chapter Two we defined sanctions as behaviors that constituted rewards or punishments and were more or less likely to appear depending on the exhibition of a stimulus behavior by the object person. To cover our new usage it is now necessary to presume that the object person will form expectations for the sanctioning activities of others. I shall refer to these latter as **expected sanctions**. Thus, when persons and others are not interacting, conformity by the person may be "explained" by assuming that the person fears being "found out" and sanctioned by the other.

But do persons always comply through fear or hope of sanctions they expect from others? In light of our discussion above this appears doubtful. We have already criticized the theory of sanctioning as a description of actual behaviors. It also appears that compliance may be induced through custom, values, habit, or love of the other (rather than through expected sanctions) or may be generated by cognitive processes learned at an early age. Indeed, if compliance is a constituting norm, some of us will think that conformity is generally a good thing and will be offended by persons who break an unjust law in order to call our attention to it. There can be no doubt that sanctioning and conformity to the other's norm are related processes in certain situations. But it seems improbable that sanctioning is either likely—or that it is perceived to be likely or that it leads to conformity—in some civilized settings. Studies of capital punishment (for murder) and sterilization (for sexual offenses) suggest that these sanctions are ineffective for controlling the crimes for which they are levied. Philosophers such as Martin Buber stress that willingness to forego sanctioning is integral to relationships of trust and love. Clearly, we should reject the sanctioning–compliance postulate as an invariant.

The rejection of this postulate has ramifications. Among others, it causes us to avoid a terminology that was first suggested by Rommetveit (1954) but has since been adopted by Kahn, Wolfe, Quinn, Snoek, and Rosenthal (1964) [B&T, Selection 33] for the differentiation of positions in formal organizations. Rommetveit refers to members of alter positions as "norm senders" and provides four operations for the "norm-sending" process, including the holding of norms, the overt expressing of norms, and the sanctioning of others. In terms of the viewpoint argued here, these processes are only likely to imply one another in settings where sanctioning prevails, hence to presume their equivalence within a single concept is unwise.

So far we have considered compliance to norms. Is there any evidence that persons comply to others' preferences or beliefs? The former are rarely studied for compliance, however evidence concerning the latter is provided by a third group of studies concerned with classroom teaching. These studies began with a controversial experiment by Rosenthal and Jacobson (1968) in which fictitious information was provided to teachers in a primary school. Early during a school year an unfamiliar test was administered to pupils at the school. Although the test was designed to measure intelligence, teachers were told it was an instrument that predicted which pupils were likely to "bloom" or "spurt ahead." Moreover, teachers were provided with a list of pupils who were said likely to "spurt ahead"—although in fact the pupils who appeared on these lists were a random selection of one out of every five pupils. Thus, teachers were provided plausible information predicting extra achievement on the part of randomly selected pupils.

At the end of the year the investigators returned and readministered the original test of intelligence. Most pupils showed normal gains in intelligence, but in the first and second grades those children who had been singled out as "spurters" showed greater gains! Rosenthal and Jacobson interpreted this finding (dubbed the "Pygmalion Effect") as a demonstration of compliance to teacher-held beliefs. In short, when teachers believed a pupil likely to achieve, teachers would treat those pupils "appropriately" and pupils would conform. Moreover, teachers were unaware that they were treating pupils differently and could not even recall the names of those nominated to be "spurters" when interviewed subsequently! In short, compliance was produced although teachers did not intend (or even understand) the effect.

To say the least, the Pygmalion thesis has aroused controversy. Educators were offended to learn that pupil achievement (and measured intelligence!) would reflect teacher beliefs. The Pygmalion study was attacked for poor methodology (Elashoff & Snow, 1971), and hundreds of studies have been conducted attempting to replicate it (Braun, 1976; Brophy & Good, 1974; Dusek, 1975). Enough of these latter were successful to suggest that the Pygmalion Effect *will* appear for certain teachers. Why? What does a teacher do when convinced that a pupil is bright? How does that same teacher behave when convinced that the pupil is dull? Observational studies have addressed these questions, and good summaries of their findings appear in Good and Brophy (1977) and Cooper (in press). Results suggest that some teachers sanction pupils whom they presume to be "bright" for effort expenditure, whereas sanctions are given to "dull" pupils to control their class participation. This pattern of treatment leads "bright" pupils to expend more effort, while "dull" pupils learn helplessness in academic tasks. As a result, those pupils assumed to be "bright" shoot ahead. Studies also suggest that this pattern of teacher behavior is characteristic of only certain teachers and that teachers can learn to avoid it if given appropriate training. Nevertheless, the Pygmalion Effect provides a striking example of compliance induced inadvertently.[3]

COMPLIANCE TO ENUNCIATIONS

Studies concerned with compliance to expectations that are enunciated by others would appear as Type E in Table 6.1. Operationally, such studies should feature comparisons between two classes of behavior: the enunciation of one or more expectatons by the other, and conformity to those expectations by the person. Folk wisdom has it that this is a powerful form of conformity. We are used to the ideas of persuasion and encouragement, and it is reasonable to believe that much of

[3] Other examples of compliance to beliefs may also be cited. Thoughtless social scientists may induce subjects to conform to beliefs they hold for the latter through design of studies, instrumentation, or inadvertent treatment (Rosenthal, 1966). Compliance to beliefs may also be induced deliberately. One technique often used for this purpose is role casting (see Chapter Four), and others are reviewed in Chapter Eight.

our behavior is induced through injunctions from others. Indeed, our forms of political democracy are based on such premises. And yet, we surely do not always comply to the dictates of others. When do we, and when do we not?

Given the history of research into persuasion by social psychologists, one would expect to find a host of Type E studies. In fact this is not the case. Most studies of persuasion turn out to have concerned acceptance ("attitude change") rather than compliance. Why this should be so is not quite clear, except that it is obviously easier to ask an experimental subject to provide a verbal response than it is to observe his or her subsequent behavior. However, a handful of studies of compliance are available from research on persuasion. In addition, one can find studies of compliance to enunciations in at least four other research traditions, those concerned with small-group interaction, behavioral modification, response to authority, and hypnotic suggestion.

Probably the strongest finding from the persuasion literature is that others who are able to control sanctions can induce compliance in the person. Example studies supporting this finding include Bennis, Berkowitz, Affinito, and Malone (1958) and Raven and French (1958b); whereas a good review of research bearing on the topic appears in McGuire (1969, pp. 194-196). Experimental studies have shown greater compliance when those who place demands upon the person can control sanctions, when they are deemed likely to apply those sanctions, and when they are given opportunity to scrutinize the behavior of the person. (Clearly, experimental subjects are not fools!) Interestingly, other characteristics of those who place demands upon persons have so far not been found closely associated with compliance. We might expect that those who are liked by the person, who have status, approval, or legitimacy—all would have more ability to exact conformity to their demands than those lacking these qualities. Evidence for these latter propositions is as yet weak (however, see Collins & Raven, 1969). Perhaps the stress upon sanctions in the persuasion literature is a reflection of the artificial character of laboratory experiments—in which subjects are asked to interact with strangers. As persons learn to know and trust one another, compliance should have less to do with sanctions and more to do with respect and mutual accommodation. (We return to this argument in Chapter Eight.)

Observational research on human interaction is a young field. Instruments for studying human communication *in situ*—audio and videotape recorders—are barely two decades old. Coding systems used for unraveling the details of human exchange are as yet primitive tools (Weick, 1968), and few systems have yet focused on the enunciation of expectations. Studies of enunciations to date have concentrated on the "effectiveness" of professional communications rather than on enunciations and compliance among peers. (It is as if the details of persuasion and influence among consenting adults were too obvious for investigation!) A small group of studies *has* appeared in which teacher demands, pupil responses, and teacher assessments were studied in classrooms (Dunkin & Biddle, 1974, pp. 274-295). These studies have found that most teacher demands are conformed to, that clearer demands are more likely to be obeyed, and that teacher assessments of conforming reactions were erratic. (Apparently teachers are more often interested in encouraging pupils to respond than they are in assessing that response.) Another set of studies (Kounin, 1970) have concluded that teacher influence is not so much a product of the enunciation of specific demands as it is the management of group activities. Clearly, we need additional research on both the use of differing forms of enunciated expectations in live situations and their effects on compliance and other forms of response.

Additional studies demonstrating compliance to others' enunciations have appeared within the behavioral modification tradition (for examples see O'Leary & O'Leary, 1971; Staats, 1964; Staats & Staats, 1963). Most of these studies have involved the experimental manipulation of incentives for persons by a powerful other (the experimenter or his or her associate), and *assessments* have generally been studied rather than either demands or assertions. Several contexts for interaction have been studied (mental hospitals, group therapy sessions, classrooms), and modification of various forms of behavior has been achieved through manipulation of assessments. In general, positive assessments (praise) have been found more effective than negative assessments (criticism) for inducing compliance. (This is probably because for some persons even negative assessments are preferable to being ignored, thus they serve as positive reinforcers.) Also, compliance is more likely when assessments are used frequently and predictably. In addition, positive assessments appear to be more effective when delivered by a stranger, whereas negative assessments are more effective when given by a friend. In sum, there appears little reason to doubt that compliance can be developed through the use of assessments as reinforcers. What may be doubted is whether this is always the most efficient way of achieving compliance or whether many of us would have the patience to use assessments as our sole strategy for achieving conformity in most situations.

To illustrate the power of *demands,* let us turn next to studies concerned with compliance to authority. We are all appalled by atrocities committed by barbarians, and yet when those responsible for a My Lai or Dachau are brought to trial their primary defense has been that they were "ordered to do it." What would *we* do if "ordered to do it"? That this is not a simple question is illustrated by the research of Milgram (1965, 1974). Imagine, if you will, that you are brought into a laboratory and asked to participate in "research on learning." The study design calls for you to administer increasing doses of electric shock to "another subject" who is strapped into a chair and cannot get away. (In fact, the experimental conditions are "rigged," and the other "subject" is a confederate who is not being shocked at all. However, the confederate grunts, moans, and begs to be let out of the experiment, and eventually screams in "pain" as the level of shock is raised.) You begin by administering only "mild shock"—identified as 15 volts, but, if willing, you must administer increasing "voltages" ending with 450 volts or "severe shock" to the apparent victim. The experimental conditions are realistic in the extreme (most subjects are convinced of its authenticity), and the experimenter vigorously urges you to "go on" with the experiment. Nevertheless, the experimenter has no power to sanction you should you choose to stop. Would you "go on"?

The major finding of Milgram's research has been that many subjects *did* go on! Moreover, the effect has been obtained both with college students and with citizens, within the United States as well as in other countries. In short, many persons were found to comply with forceful and realistic demands even though the demands were for behavior that was odious and morally questionable! (For the love of heaven, why should we be willing to comply with such demands? Apparently we have learned to respond to the demands of authority as part of the price of living in a society that is controlled by formal organizations. Once again, then, compliance appears as a constituting norm, and many of us have learned to conform to the demands of authority even when they contradict our own preferences, norms, and values.) Not all subjects conformed in Milgram's studies, of course. Moreover, conformity was found to vary with relationships between the subject, the victim and the authority figure. In brief, subjects were less willing to punish a victim whom they could see than one who was in the next room. The authority figure also had more influence when physically present than when his or her demands arrived via tape recordings. Thus, even compliance to demands depends on the context.

So much for assessments and demands. But what about assertions? Has evidence appeared for complicance to expectations of this mode? Conformity to descriptive enunciations would seem to be unlikely, and yet the model offered by the hypnotic trance is almost exclusively one of control by assertion. In general the hypnotist does not demand or assess but rather tells the bemused subject who he or she is, what is going on, and what he or she will presently be doing. As has been suggested elsewhere (Sarbin, 1950) such states of ego abdication are simply extensions of normal social relations in which persons allow others to define the situation. Indeed, one condition for the success of the self-fulfilling prophecy (Merton, 1957b) is that the hearer believe in its inevitability. In short, compliance may also be induced through assertions, particularly when the subject is suggestible or when the situation makes belief in the other's assertion a reasonable reaction.

COMPLIANCE TO INSCRIPTIONS

Compliance to written records of others is also a significant topic for study. Studies of Type F in Table 6.1 pair the appearance of an expectation in written form with a behavior that either conforms or does not conform to it. Compliance of this type is vital in a civilized society. One cannot imagine a complex social order without enacted laws, game rules, and the written regulations of formal organizations. Rules of these sorts are supported by both sanctions and moral codes, and it is reasonable to believe that they generate conformity. Nevertheless, compliance to them is rarely studied (for exceptions, see Allport, 1934; Stech, McClintock, Fitzpatrick, & Babin, 1976), and surely conformity does not appear in all circumstances. Criminals do not obey the law, card sharks cheat on game rules, and some industrial regulations may be ignored for reasons of safety, convenience, or conventionality.

Prescriptions for behavior also appear in the mass media that are supported by neither sanction nor morality. These are vital in the fields of marketing and political propaganda, and considerable research has now been conducted on compliance to them (Berelson, Lazarsfeld, & McPhee, 1954; Hovland, 1954; Katz & Lazarsfeld, 1955; McGuire, 1969). By far the major finding of this research is that the mass media produce little compliance! In contrast to most other forms of conformity studied, compliance to prescriptions appearing in the mass media appears uncertain. Some innovative advertisements are known to have induced compliance, but most such efforts have little effect—if we believe the published research.

Given the billions of dollars that are spent on advertising and political propaganda in this country, why continue the effort? Several answers have been advanced for this question, each suggesting limitations of the published research. First, not all research on the topic is published. Regular studies are conducted on the effectiveness of advertising throughout the industry by newspapers, advertising agencies, and marketing research organizations. Most of these studies have *acceptance* ("attitude change") as their dependent variables, but some concern *compliance*. Vanishingly few are ever published, since they concern the effectiveness of trade matters. This suggests that evidence for successful compliance may actually be suppressed. Second, most advertising is concerned with products that are highly similar. If three bakeries are marketing the same type of bread and all are advertising their products heavily, small wonder that their messages produce little compliance. Advertising of this kind is generated by fear over what would happen if it were withdrawn rather than by hope of gaining customer conformity. In contrast, we might expect more compliance to prescriptions for a new and different product. Third, some persons seem more likely to comply to written messages than do others, and in the mass situation even compliance by one person out of a hundred may be sufficient to justify an advertisement. Fourth, though the basic message intended by the advertiser or propagandist may be prescriptive ("*do* such-and-so"), this message may be either delivered directly or implied by preferential ("I like such-and-so," or " you will like such-and-so") or belief-oriented ("such-and-so will leave your breath smelling sweeter") messages. Systematic research seems not to have appeared concerning the differential effects of these modes. Finally, it is often argued that advertising and political propaganda have other useful effects in addition to compliance, such as keeping a "brand name" before the public. These latter effects may be thought of sufficient importance to justify the expense, even if immediate conformity is not induced.

Compliance to written prescriptions is also studied in research on the diffusion of innovations (Coleman, Katz, & Menzel, 1966; Rogers, 1962). Studies in this latter tradition concern the spread of new ideas and techniques. For example, adoption of new drugs by physicians may be studied, or acceptance of agricultural innovations among farmers. Findings from these studies tend to confirm those of research on advertising or political propaganda. Most innovations are spread through information gained from interaction with others and not through written sources.

The evidence, then, suggests that persons are less likely to comply with prescriptions appearing in the mass media than they are with prescriptions that are held or enunciated for them by other persons. If compliance to prescriptions is a constituting norm, that norm seems to apply more to interaction than to public messages. What about public inscriptions in the cathectic or descriptive modes? Is there any evidence that these generate compliance? Surely bad reviews of plays affect some members of the public; and if Pope Paul was right, publication of results from social surveys concerning the use of contraceptives among Catholics is likely to encourage even more of their use. One suspects, however, that these forms of compliance are no more likely than compliance to prescriptions, although little evidence is yet available concerning the issue.

Compliance seems more likely when a written expectation is given privately to the person. Bosses leave written instructions for their secretaries; doctors write prescriptions for pharmacists; husbands and wives leave notes for their spouses—all are likely to be followed. Indeed, so "obvious" is this form of compliance that little attention has been paid to it in research to date. However, it often appears in laboratory studies that are concerned with other phenomena (for examples see Schlenker, Bonoma, Tedeschi, & Pivnick, 1970; or Schopler & Thompson, 1968).

In sum, the study of compliance is a complex affair. The prevalence of many forms of compliance is by now well established, although persons do not always comply and may in fact resist compliance under certain conditions (Allen, 1975). Conformity to the expectations of others has been found related to many factors: to the mode and form of expectation, to the topic, to the context, to the form of interaction between the person and others, to the personality of the person, and so forth. However, many interacting aspects of the compliance problem have not yet been studied at all. Compliance may be either a curse or a blessing, depending on context, and social critics have alternately damned or praised the conformer. Perhaps a more useful approach would be to establish when conformity is and is not useful, and to formalize our knowlege about when it is and is not likely to be exhibited.

ACCURACY AND ALIGNMENT

Instead of being determined by expectations, sometimes the behavior of the person may determine an expectation that describes, prescribes, or cathects it. For example, the child does poorly in school, and in time the mother learns to demand little of him or her scholastically; or industrial workers discover, to their chagrin, that high productivity on their parts is followed by higher quotas for their piecework. To refer to effects such as these with the term conformity is misleading, for such a use would suggest that it was the behavior that was determined. Instead, I define two new terms. A descriptive expectation is said to be **accurate** when it is similar to and determined by an object-person characteristic that serves as its model. A prescriptive or cathectic expectation is said to be **aligned** when it is similar to and determined by an object-person characteristic.[4] Accuracy and alignment are wholly parallel concepts that differ only in the modality of the expectation being judged. Both are determined concepts—although (as is true for conformity) some studies of accuracy or alignment provide little evidence bearing on the assumption of determination.

The concept of accuracy is a pervasive one in psychology, and the definition offered here covers only part of the phenomena that have been discussed under this term or its synonyms. For example, memories are described as being "accurate" or "inaccurate," perceptions may be "selective" or may suffer from "distortions," clinicians analyze thoughts as being "reality oriented" or "autistic." (The term *accuracy* has also been used in studies of social perception, but such studies involve comparisons between expectations attributed and expectations actually held. Comparisons of this latter sort involve different methods and assumptions, and their results are handled later under a different term, *veridicality*.)

For some reason, empirical research on the accuracy of expectations has appeared infrequently. Apparently this is an "uninteresting" concept for investigators, although assumptions about accuracy appear widely in social theories—and are attacked with enthusiasm by both psychologists and social critics. Moreover, one can find innumerable social surveys of the objective characteristics of doctors, policemen, teachers, alcoholics, fathers, lower-class persons, or other positions—and many studies also of the expectations, attitudes, or sterotypes that are maintained for these same persons, either by themselves or by others. What one cannot readily find are studies in which the objective characteristics and stereortypes are paired, and the latter are judged for accuracy. Indeed, so striking is this lack that neither Cauthen, Robinson, and Krauss (1971) nor Ehrlich (1973) considered the accuracy of stereotypes as a topic for discussion in their excellent reviews of research on prejudice.

The concept of alignment is rarely discussed in the role literature (in fact, there is no standardized term for this concept), and research on it is even rarer than research on accuracy. A few writers have, however, been aware that norms or preferences might be adapted to the performance they reference (for example, Freeman & Simmons, 1963) [B&T, Selections 39 and 42]. The process of alignment is, however, discussed in related fields such as balance theory (Heider, 1958) and the cog-

---

[4]In contrast with conformity, *accuracy* and *alignment* may be judged for both behaviors and nonbehavioral characteristics. Thomas and Biddle used the term "adjustment" to refer to alignment [B&T, p. 40].

Table 6.2
TYPES OF ACCURACY AND ALIGNMENT (BY MODE OF EXPECTATION DETERMINED
AND IDENTITY OF PERSON EXHIBITING BEHAVIOR)

		Mode of expectation determined	
		Beliefs	Norms or preferences
Identity of person exhibiting behavior	The subject person	Type A. Accuracy of beliefs for self	Type C. Alignment of norms or preferences for self
	One or more others	Type B. Accuracy of beliefs for others	Type D. Alignment of norms or preferences for others

nitive dissonance literature (Festinger, 1957), and part of our review must be drawn from such sources.

As was the case with consistency, studies of accuracy and alignment have been confined to covert expectations in the main. Few investigators have yet concerned themselves with the accuracy or alignment of either assertions or representations in empirical research. This is too bad. Accuracy of assertions is of concern to jurists, for example, although little research seems to have been conducted on it. Accuracy of representations is a classic concern of both journalists and historiographers, but both problems are more often discussed than investigated empirically. And surely studies of the realignment of standards for literary criticism or sexual conduct would be of interest. Nevertheless, the fact is that most studies have concerned the accuracy and alignment of conceptions, and my review will be centered on them (see Table 6.2).

Studies of Type A in Table 6.2 concern the accuracy of beliefs about one's own characteristics. In operational terms, such studies would compare an observed characteristic of a person with a report he or she later gave about that characteristic. As was the case for conformity to one's own conceptions, studies of this form have not always reported accuracy (Deutscher, 1966). However, a recent reviewer (Liska, 1974) suggests that more studies have found accuracy than have found inaccuracy in reports of own behavior. In fact there is a good reason for suspecting that self-reports of behavior are more likely to be *accurate* than are reports of behavioral intentions likely to generate *consistency*. The former are reports of events that have already occurred, and the only reasons for inaccuracy are those associated with internal processes in the subject. The latter are predictions of events that have yet to occur, and in making them the subject must also contend with contextual factors he or she has not yet encountered.

What processes induce inaccuracy in self-reports? A good discussion of inaccuracy appears in Cannell and Kahn (1968), who also review relevant studies. According to these authors, processes likely to induce inaccuracy may be sorted into three classes: those of accessibility, cognitive conditions for the interview, and motivation as a condition for the interview. Processes of *accessibility* concern whether the person may have forgotten or repressed the experience and whether he or she conceptualizes the experience in terms sufficient to answer questions put to him or her by the interviewer. *Cognitive processes* concern whether the person understands the interviewing situation and the roles appropriate for interviewer and interviewee. *Motivational processes* concern whether accuracy or dissimulation is conceived the best course of action by the person. Some findings are now available for each of these classes. For example, accuracy would appear more likely when the person is reporting on recent events, on events that were not greatly unpleasant, or on events that are conceived in simple terms. Subjects who do not understand the interviewing "game" are less likely to report accurately, and special care must be taken to ensure accuracy when interviewing persons about matters of money, embarrassment, or sex (Kinsey, Pomeroy, & Martin, 1948). In general, then, accuracy of reports about one's own characteristics appears more likely than not, although inaccuracy is likely with certain types of information and may be countered by careful interviewing techniques.

Studies of Type B in Table 6.2 concern the accuracy of beliefs about others' characteristics. Studies on this topic should compare an obseved characteristic of another with a report given later about that characteristic by the person. As a rule, we would expect somewhat less accuracy for this type than for Type A, since in Type B the person is being asked to report on events that he or she may or may not have witnessed personally. For this reason, studies of this problem have usually reported greater accuracy for situations in which the person and other were in interaction, or when the person was known to have observed the other's characteristic directly. In contrast, inaccurate beliefs may appear when these conditions do not obtain (Biddle, Rosencranz, Tomich, & Twyman, 1966 [B&T, Selection 37]; Jessor, Graves, Hanson, & Jessor, 1968). Apart from this, many of the same problems attending accuracy obtain in this type as in Type A (again see Cannell & Kahn, 1968).

The concept of accuracy is a simple one, and studies of accuracy should have a straightforward design—at least in theory. In practice, the accuracy paradigm may also be mangled by investigators. An example of this appears in research on the "accuracy" of judging emotional states. This research began with Charles Darwin's (1872) interest in the way in which emotions are mirrored in facial expressions. Darwin studied this problem by asking persons to estimate emotions by studying the facial expressions portrayed by models (in photographs). Some photographs were judged "correctly," others not, and the results were interpreted to mean that some emotions were easier to "perceive" than were others. This research design has since been replicated, with variations, by dozens of investigators (Tagiuri, 1969). As has been suggested by Hastorf, Schneider, and Polefka (1970), such designs confuse two problems, the problem of how emotions are expressed facially, and the problem of the perception of facial expressions. It is only this latter that is an accuracy issue, and because of the confusion, little can be said to be known today with certainty about either problem. Surely these two problems will be seperated in future research.

Let us turn now to studies of alignment. Studies falling into Type C of Table 6.2 concern alignment of either norms or preferences to one's own characteristics. In operational terms, such studies would compare the behavior of a person with the report of a norm or preference concerning that characteristic that was given by the person at some later time. When we first think about it, self-alignment may appear an unlikely phenomenon. After all, why should one automatically approve one's looks or prescribe one's own behavior? And yet, those of us who do not hate ourselves will surely align our expectations to many of the things we have come to be or do. If not, we would come eventually to hate ourselves. Thus alignment should appear frequently, and nonalignment should be the exception rather than the rule.

Illustrations of alignment are provided by studies of forced compliance (Festinger & Carlsmith, 1959; Helmreich & Collins, 1968). Studies of this phenomenon concern instances when the person is called upon to testify concerning attitudes that are at variance with those he or she is known to have held originally. Under certain conditions the attitude subsequently reported by the person is found to have shifted so that it is aligned with his or her testimony. In general these conditions are such that the person believes the decision to testify was his or her own and was not forced on him or her by others. Thus, the person is led by his or her apparent willingness to testify to discover his or her "true" attitude, which is at variance from the one the person previously thought was held.

Forced compliance sounds disquieting, for of such events are built the plots of movies concerned with secret persuasion. If this bothers you, consider studies falling into Type D which concern alignment of norms or preferences to the characteristics of others. Perhaps the best known example of such alignment is that reported by Bettelheim (1943) in which it was recounted that Jews in concentration camps sometimes substituted for their own norms of conduct those expressed behaviorally by the brutal Nazi guards who were their tormentors. Why this form of alignment? In some cases it appears that the victims felt this was the only way they could survive at all; whereas in others they may have been so deprived of the original contextual props for their values as to be willing to accept a completely different set of standards. This latter explanation leads to the theory of "brainwashing" portrayed vividly in Orwell's *Nineteen Eighty-Four* and various horror movies since. Appallingly, there is some evidence that this form of "brainwashing" has already been practiced by totalitarian regimes (Lifton, 1963; Schein, 1961).

In addition to these specific examples, the concept of alignment bothers us because we feel that behaviors "should" be generated by our standards instead of the reverse. After all, if there is any integrity to ourselves as independent agents, surely that integrity leads us to generate behaviors through the preferences and norms we hold. To imply that our preferences and norms are themselves generated by behavior is to suggest that we are the victims, not the authors, of our experiences. And yet, little evidence has so far appeared to tell us under which conditions we conform and under which we align. As was previously noted, some apparent evidence in studies of conformity comes from field studies and might have been generated by processess of accuracy or alignment. And clearly under some conditions our norms and preferences are generated by the behaviors we observe. More research is needed on these questions.

We must not leave the phenomena of conformity, accuracy, and alignment without commenting on the social system models of Talcott Parsons (1951). As has been suggested by critics, Parsons appears to contend that all forms of social relations operate best when people hold adequate expectations for their own behavior and that of others, and when behaviors of both themselves and others is in conformity with those expectations. There are several reasons for supposing that this view is too simple. For one thing, it tends to ignore the needs of individuals who must accommodate to the system. As has been suggested by Goffman (1959) and Wrong (1961), the performance of roles may be demanding, exhausting, or may lack intrinsic rewards for the person who performs. Under these circumstances it is reasonable to presume that persons will seek to limit role performance to an "on stage" context and to forego it elsewhere. However, those who are customers or audiences in the system must be kept unaware of the staging of roles, hence systematic deception is engaged in, and those being deceived are not allowed to hold accurate or aligned expectations. In addition, some types of social sytems pit persons against others whose needs are diametrically opposed. It is not surprising, for example, to discover that deception, inaccuracy, and secret nonconformity are common occurrences in the prison (Mitchell, 1966) [B&T, Selection 22], in the industrial bargaining room, and at the peace negotiation table. It should be possible to analyze social systems so as to discover the conditions under which honesty is in fact the best policy versus those in which inaccuracy or nonconformity are likely to occur, but to the author's knowledge this has not been done systematically (however, see Moore & Tumin, 1949).

Verdicality, Empathy, and Role Taking

Closely related to the concept of accuracy is *veridicality*. As I use the terms, accuracy relates to comparisons between someone's overt characteristics and the expectations that describe them. Veridicality, in contrast, refers to the relationship between another's expectations and attributed expectations that purport to describe them. In formal terms an attributed expectation is said to be **veridical** when it is similar to and determined by the simple expectation it purports to describe. Most studies of veridicality have concerned simple expectations that were held covertly, thus have involved measuring a conception attributed by the person to another and the matching simple conception actually held by the latter. As with accuracy, veridicality judgements are confined to the descriptive mode, as far as the person's extended expectation is concerned. (In theory, it is possible to judge extended expectations whose leading expectation was normative or preferential for their alignment, but nobody has yet discussed such a concept to my knowledge.) As we know, studies of accuracy may concern either the person's own characteristics or the characteristics of another. Studies of veridicality, in contrast, "should" concern only judgements about the expectations of others—after all, what could be sillier than asking a person to estimate his or her own expectations? But believe it or not, one or two studies have actually appeared in which subjects were given the task of estimating the expectations of persons who were anonymous, among whom were included themselves (Huntley, 1940; Wolff, 1933, 1935, 1943)!

Veridicality has generated a long history of empirical research. Most, but not all, studies have represented a single tradition concerned with "social perception" or "empathy." **Empathy** refers to a presumed general ability of some persons to judge others' expectations veridically. The idea that persons might vary in empathic ability seems to have developed in the 1930s and represented the thinking of such theorists as Cooley, G. H. Mead, Dewey, Sullivan, and Cottrell. If it should, indeed, turn out that some persons have more empathy—that is, are better judges of the thinking of others—such persons would surely make better group leaders, counselors, therapists, or confessors. Accordingly, a research tradition was spawned in which the task was to search for the personality correlates of empathy.

Studies of empathy have had similar designs. A group of subjects are given the task of judging the personality characteristics of others. Usually a number of personality characteristics are included, and usually the others judged are strangers to the subjects. Personality characteristics studied have included both expectations and other phenomena. Subjects are given access to the others by various means—through films, handwriting samples, voice recordings, and so forth. In addition, several means are used for measuring the "actual" personality characteristics of the others, including not only their own reports, but also judges' estimates, projective procedures, and so forth.

By the mid-1950s enough of these studies had appeared that reviews of their findings were in order (Bruner & Tagiuri, 1954; Taft, 1955). However, results were equivocal, and it was not then clear whether or not a general trait of empathy could be discriminated. At about this same time, a series of critical papers began to appear that questioned the assumptions and methods of the research. Cronbach (1955, 1958) and Gage and Cronbach (1955), in particular, challenged most previously published studies by noting that "empathy scores" might represent at least four

different components. These included: (a) *elevation,* or the tendency for subjects to use a low, middle, or high region of the judgement scale for making their ratings; (b) *differential elevation,* or the ability of subjects to estimate the average
score for the others rated (across all items); (c) *stereotypic accuracy,* or the ability
of subjects to estimate the average score for each item (across the others rated); and
(d) *differential accuracy,* or the ability of subjects to estimate individual trait scores
for each other rated. The last three of these components all appear to be of interest
to those concerned with empathy, but would these three components appear in the
same subjects? Cronbach thought they might not but noted that it was impossible
to tell from most published studies because of poor techniques used for data analysis. Since the appearance of these critical papers somewhat fewer studies of empathy have been conducted, but those appearing have evidenced more sophistication of design (for example, Cline, 1964). Recent reviews of their findings may be
found in Tagiuri (1969) and Hastorf, Schneider, and Polefka (1970). As of this
writing it would appear that Cronbach was right and that empathy is *not* a single
trait.

Studies of empathy have also evidenced other design faults. For one, they have
lumped together estimates of several personality characteristics, including both expectations and other phenomena, and in particular expectations of various modes.
For another, subjects were called upon to rate strangers rather than those whom
they knew, thus ignoring questions that might be raised concerning the growth of
veridicality. For another, they studied only subjects' ability to rate others as individuals and ignored the possibility that some subjects might be expert at judging
social positions. Also, many used indirect means for measuring the actual expectations of others, thus introducing neddless error. In all, these studies seem to have
avoided many of the really interesting problems associated with veridicality!

These criticisms apply less to veridicality research from outside the empathy
tradition. For example, studies are now available in which veridicality was examined for each of the three modes of expectation: for beliefs see Chowdhry and
Newcomb (1952), for preferences consult Howells and Brosnan (1972), for norms
see Biddle, Rosencranz, Tomich, and Twyman (1966) [B&T, Selection 37]. In studies such as these, work associates, family members, or other closely related persons
are asked to estimate one another's expectations, and then these estimates are compared with the simple expectations revealed by the others nominated. Such studies
suggest that some findings for accuracy are also likely to hold for veridicality. For
example, persons who interact or who have similar training and outlooks are usually
better at estimating one another's expectations. On the other hand, interaction does
not guarantee veridicality, since the other may not choose to reveal his or her expectation to the person. Thus, factors that would cause the other to withhold this
information are likely to interfere with veridicality. (We return to this problem
shortly.)

Another concept related to veridicality is *role taking.* The term "role taking"
was coined by G. H. Mead (1934) who argued that adequate development of the

self and participation in social interaction both depended on the person's ability to "take the role of the other." In Mead's usage, role taking was a "sequential, self-correcting process through which one individual can experience another's subjective state" (Scheff, 1967). But as is true for so many of Mead's concepts, role taking has been interpreted in various ways (Shibutani, 1961; and Turner, 1962) and has more often been theorized about than studied empirically (Kuhn, 1964). For our purposes, **role taking** means that a person holds veridical expectations in which he or she (correctly) maps the expectations of a sentient other.[5] Why is role taking important? Given the ability to take the role of another, it is argued, the person can then predict and understand the other's reactions in various situations. Accordingly, inability to take roles presumably handicaps the person in complex situations, and clinically disturbed persons should be less able to take roles than those who are not disturbed. In addition, leaders seem more able to take the roles of others than do persons who are not leaders (Chowdhry & Newcomb, 1952; R. D. Mann, 1959).

Role taking should not be confused with **role playing.** This latter term, first suggested by J. L. Moreno (1934), means that a person (correctly) imitates another's role. (Role taking concerns the veridicality of thought, role playing the imitation of behavior.) Role playing is a basic strategy for learning. It appears spontaneously in the behaviors of children and is formalized among adults as theatrical performance. It has also been argued (by Moreno and his associates) that to play roles in psychodramatic therapy has many benefits—among them increasing role-taking ability. We will consider the evidence for this claim, along with others form research on role taking, in Chapter Eight.

Acceptance

A few pages back it was pointed out that many studies of persuasion have concerned covert rather than overt response. In such studies the subject is presented with some sort of persuasive message, say the presentation of a demand from another, and we use a standardized instrument (usually an "attitude scale") to see whether the message has caused the subject to change his or her opinion. Such studies involve the comparison of two forms of expectation for similarity and determination. Interestingly, no common term has yet appeared for comparisons of this sort, unless it be "attitude change" which encompasses other meanings as well. Following usage suggested by McGuire (1969), I shall refer to such comparisons with the term *acceptance.* To provide a definition, an expectation is **acceptant** if it is both similar to and determined by another's expectation.

[5] Symbolic interactionists tend to argue that role taking involves the expression (and correction) of attributed expectations through behavior and social feedback. Nevertheless, studies of role taking have generally used a definition based on veridicality (Stryker, 1957, 1962). Thus research on role taking differs from research on empathy mainly in that it focuses upon the person's ability to estimate the expectations of a single sentient other (Thomas, Franks, & Calonico, 1972).

Acceptance involves comparisons between two expectations, and one might expect that most studies of it would involve expectations that were identical in form and mode. Interestingly, this has not been the case. Most studies have apposed the presentation of an overt stimulus (either a spoken or written expectation) with the report of a covert response. Most have also used modally ambiguous instruments for their dependent variables. (i.e., attitude scales), although modal distinctions have been retained for the expectations that were enunciated as independent variables. One can think of few good reasons for these conventions, but within their limitations a vast body of research has appeared. Those interested in findings from this research are urged to consult recent reviews such as those of Eagly and Himmelfarb, 1978; Greenwald, Brock, and Ostrom (1968); Himmelfarb and Eagly (1974); Insko (1967); Kiesler, Collins, and Miller (1969); McGuire (1969); Rosnow and Robinson (1967); Zimbardo and Ebbesen (1969); or Zimbardo, Ebbesen, and Maslach (1977), since my coverage here will be confined to a handful of findings.

As we know from research on conformity, some studies of persuasion have concerned themselves with characteristics of the other who enunciates the stimulus expectation. Following distinctions originally suggested by Kelman (1958, 1961), many of these studies may be conceived as focusing on one of three characteristics of the other: credibility, attractiveness, and power. Each is argued to induce influence for somewhat different reasons: *credibility* because the person internalizes the other's expectation; *attractiveness* because the person identifies with the other; *power* because the person expects the other to use sanctions upon him or her. As it turns out, both credibility and attractiveness have been found to induce acceptance, but not power. As may be recalled, this contrasts with findings for conformity. To put it another way, those who are powerful seem more able to impose (overt) compliance on the person than they are to induce (covert) changes in the person's expectations. This makes sense. After all, if sanctions are likely, the other will surely impose them only as a function of the person's overt behavior. By keeping expectations to him or herself, the person may well escape retribution.

Such findings provide evidence that acceptance and compliance are different processes of response. On the other hand, they are also likely to imply one another, given appropriate circumstances. Surely acceptance sometimes leads to compliance. Similarly, when conformity is induced, the person may eventually align expectations to match his or her own behaviors. The only difficulty with these propositions is that we do not yet know when they will and will not hold, and until we do the relationship between compliance and acceptance will remain problematic (Deutsch & Gerard, 1955).

Many studies of acceptance have used messages that were in the prescriptive mode, and a good deal of research has now gone into studying the conditions under which prescriptive messages will or will not induce expectational change. For example, findings are now available concerning the use of prescriptions with and without threats, other forms of consequences, the refutation of prescriptions, and the repetition of the prescriptive message. Other studies have made use of cathectic messages, either for the reinforcement of conforming behaviors that match the expectation to be patterned or as an intrinsic component of the message (Weiss, 1962). In general, then, demands and assessments are both known to induce acceptance, although these two modes have not often been studied in opposition, and their competitive advantages are not well understood. Studies of acceptance using descriptive messages have appeared but rarely.

Acceptance studies have used both overt messages and messages that were presented in written form. Both are known to induce acceptance. In addition, a number of studies have appeared in which the same message was presented using these two forms to different groups of subjects. As with compliance, these studies have tended to show that overt expression induced more acceptance than did written expectations. Why should a message have greater verismilitude when its author is present? At present there is no answer for this question, although various explanations may be suggested. But for all practical purposes, if you want to change another's ideas, talk to him or her personally.

Consensus

Acceptance is not the only concept that has appeared in which expectations held by two or more persons are compared. A second major concept, *consensus,* has a definition that is similar to acceptance, although its implications are different. In general, expectations held by two or more persons are said to be **consensual** when they are similar. Note that this definition involves no assumptions about determination. It is possible that consensual expectations have "spread" from one individual to others in a group, but we are not interested in etiology. Consensus is judged when expectations are found to be similar, regardless of how they got that way. (It will also be recalled from Chapter Two that behaviors which correspond are said to be uniform. The term *consensus* is usually confined to expectations, whereas *uniformity* is applied to behaviors.)

Varieties of consensus have been discussed in role theory using many terms including "consensual validation," "social reality," "shared expectations," and consensus itself paired with modifiers. The antonym of consensus—dissimilarity of expectations—has been termed "role conflict," "norm conflict," "dissensus, " "marginality," and so forth. Many distinctions have appeared in the literature differentiating types of consensus and dissensus. My aim here is to discuss some of the major types of consensus; dissensus forms are dealt with in the next section.

One of the easiest ways of distinguishing among types of consensus is by reference to the modality of the expectations being compared. For instance, consensus may exist among norms, beliefs, or preferences; or it may be noted among enunciated expectations of various modalities. It is also possible to speak of consensus for covert, overt, and written forms of expectations. Each type of consensus thus differentiated exhibits properties basic to the expectational form being compared. For instance, consensus among overtly expressed expectations may be established by direct observation, whereas covert consenses are typically studied by questionnaire or interview techniques.

A related distinction may be made among common consensus, attributed consensus, and shared consensus. **Common consensus** (or simply consensus as defined previously) consists of an extant condition of expectational similarity for a given set of persons. Nothing whatsoever is implied about awareness of that consensus on the part of these persons; indeed, members may be unaware that they share the same prescriptions, descriptions, or evaluations. A commonly cited example of this phenomenon occurs in American social class groups that are generally unaware of the degree to which they share preferences for recreation, demands for specific behaviors on the part of their children, and so forth. An **attributed consensus** (or "perceived consensus") occurs when a person assigns to others the same expectation that he or she holds. Technically, of course, attributed consensus is not a form of consensus at all, nor does it imply that consensus actually exists. Nevertheless, examples of attributed consensus are easy to find and assumptions are often made by persons about the consensually held expectations of others. Much of socialization, for instance, may be described as the acquistion by the child of preferences, beliefs, and norms that he or she (rightly or wrongly) ascribes to adults and significant others. A **shared consensus**, finally, combines the two foregoing conditions. Persons sharing a consensus hold the same expectations and (correctly) attribute those expectations to one another. For additional discussion of these distinctions, see Angell (1958) and Newcomb (1959b). Expansion of these concepts and formal theories based on consensus typologies may also be found in Laing, Phillipson, and Lee (1966), Scheff (1967), and Stryker (1962).

A special type of consensus is that which is either inaccurate, nonaligned, or nonveridical. Usually we assume that inaccuracy and nonveridicality are individual events, deviations from the conditions required for social stability, and soon to be cured. This tacit assumption fails when we discover groups of subjects who share inaccurate or nonveridical expectations. The first example of the phenomenon appeared in a study by Schanck (1932) who termed it **pluralistic ignorance**. Schanck found that members of an isolated, strictly religious community shared similar norms prohibiting such behaviors as smoking, drinking, playing cards, and so forth—expectations that were at odds with the actual behaviors engaged in by these same persons in the privacy of their homes. Since the publication of Schanck's original study other examples of pluralistic ignorance have been uncovered by investigators such as Wheeler (1961) and Biddle, Rosencranz, Tomich, and Twyman (1966) [B&T, Selection 37].

It is possible to categorize the forms of pluralistic ignorance. For example, let us examine relationships among a person's own expectation, the expectation of the sentient other, and the expectation attributed to the latter by the person. Five Types of pluralistic ignorance may be discriminated (see Table 6.3). Different con-

Table 6.3
TYPES OF PLURALISTIC IGNORANCE

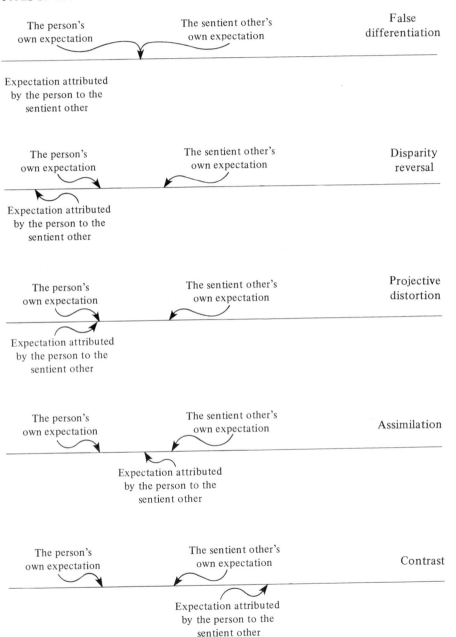

ditions are likely to generate, and different effects are likely to result from each of these forms. For example, *projective distortion* is more likely when the subject is truly ignorant of the other; *assimilation* is more likely when the subject likes or identifies with the other; whereas *contrast* is more likely when the other is disliked (Sherif & Hovland, 1961).

One of the intriguing implications of pluralistic ignorance is that sometimes it will generate social mechanisms that guarantee its perpetuation. Let us assume that two social positions are in interaction. Normally we assume that members of these two positions will discuss their expectations and thus tend to rectify mistaken expectations held. When this does not occur, we look for an explanatory mechanism. Sometimes this mechanism is built into the system—for example, traditional sex mores proscribe the discussion of sexual matters between men and women, which nearly guarantees that pluralistic ignorance will develop in this arena. However, pluralistic ignorance may also generate its own supportive mechanism. Over estimation of the conservative norms concerning desegregation in the American South appears to keep some southern liberals from speaking out on desegration, thus helping to perpetuate pluralistic ignorance on this topic. Similar ignorances appear likely whenever social change is taking place or when civil servants are called upon to represent what they conceive as "public opinion" without adequate means for discovering what the public actually wants. Pluralistic ignorance is probably more likely, also, when social distance is high between positions and when observation of object-person behavior is difficult.

When is consensus likely to occur? When are pesons likely to hold the same expecations or assume that they do? Functionalists in sociology argue that a minimal degree of consensus is either necessary for social stability or at least conducive of social order; and surely to have agreement within a population for basic roles such as those applying to public behavior, upholding of the law, and table manners is a good thing. But we probably overstress the need for consensus in our theories of social stability, and as is so often the case with role phenomena, consensus is more often assumed than empirically established.[6] There are many reasons beyond consensus why behavioral uniformity may result within a social system—because only limited number of artifacts are available providing for only a narrow range of responses, or because of danger, habit, ennui or physical limitations of the body. To assert that all regularities of behavior, then, result from holding consensual expectations is to extend a limited explanation to the status of a total, explanatory theory.

Nevertheless, the idea that "everyone thinks as I do, and that is why they behave the way they do" is popular among citizens as well as role theorists. To discover that people agree in their expecations is not normally considered "news." Newcomb (1947) suggested that persons often engage in the process of *consensual validation* – seeking out at least one other who can be counted on to agree with them. Festinger (1954) argued that persons seek to compare and validate their opin-

---

[6]That consensus is not often studied may reflect the fact that few texts offer statistics that can be used for making this judgment. However Leik (1966) has designed a statistic for estimating consensus using the modal strength method.

ions with those of others who are presumed similar. In addition, studies have now appeared in which conditions of consensus were associated with higher groups productivity, cohesiveness, and morale (Festinger *et al.,* 1950), family integration (Jacobson, 1952) [B&T, Selection 36] and other good effects. However, endless demonstrations of dissensus have also been established, which raises questions about the universality of the consensus assumption. There can be no doubt that common consensus appears in many social systems. What we do not know are the limits of this assumption—the boundaries of consensus, and the conditions under which consensus becomes unlikely or deleterious to the system. And for this reason, role theorists should avoid the concept of *shared expectation* (or its euphemisms, "group expectation," "group norm," "cultural norm," and so on) unless the actual condition of consensus can be established.

If the assumption of simple consensus is suspect, what about the assumptions of perceived and shared consensus? No simple answer can be given to these questions either, although some theorists assume their validity. This also appears unwise. As Goffman (1959) suggests, some social situations require the systematic deception of others, who may or may not be aware that they are being deceived. In the theater, for instance, the audience are aware that there is a "backstage" where things happen to which they are not witnesses, but they prefer to enter into the deception. Within the "con game," in contrast, the victim is unaware that he or she is being conned until the game is over, and then the con artist must take care to "cool the mark out" so that he or she does not blow the whole matter to authorities (Goffman, 1952). One's expectations may be formed not only by internalization, but also by behavioral observation, or even by cognitive restructuring on the part of the subject. As was suggested earlier, expectations may be judged for their accuracy or alignment—implying that they may be affected by object-person behavior. Moreover, the creative novelist, legislator, or moralist is quite capable of constructing expectations out of the fabric of his or her imagination.

Nevertheless, most people assume that expectations they attribute to others are veridical (surprise!) and appear to be most comfortable when their own expectations are more-or-less similar to those attributed to others. Moreover, these same assumptions appear explicitly in both anthropology and sociology (for example, see Bredemeier & Stephenson, 1962). It is too bad that we know so little about the limits of these assumptions.

Dissensus and Role Conflict

Consensus need not exist, of course, nor do persons always presume that others will share expectations. It is useful to define a new term, **dissensus,** which denotes conditions when nonconsensual expectations are found or are presumed to exist. Dissensus is often opposed to consensus, and some distinctions applying to one of these terms may be used with the other. To illustrate, should a mother and father differ over norms they hold for their son's behavior, we might cite this as an example of *common dissensus.* Should the son assume that his parents disagree, we would have an example of *attributed dissensus,* and so forth. Nevertheless, consensus and dissensus are not wholly parallel concepts. To illustrate their differences, let us consider two alternatives to consensus. If members of a group, for example, differ in expectations they hold, it is possible for those expectations to vary widely with no clear modal categories. In other cases, expecations may fall into two or three distinct sets that are held by different persons. Let us refer to the first of these cases as **diffuse dissensus** and the second as **polarized dissensus.**

Of studies of polarized dissensus there is literally no end. For example, if we review the literature reporting expectations held for a single professional role—that of the school teacher—we find reports of polarized dissensus among expectations held by the following: teacher educators and experienced teachers (Drabick, 1967); student teachers and school principals (Finlayson & Cohen, 1967); teachers and administrators (Fishburn, 1962; Washburne, 1957); younger teachers and older teachers (Fishburn, 1966; Getzels & Guba, 1955b; Smith, 1965); differing pupil groups within the school (Cobb, 1952); teacher–trainess and other university students (Biddle, Twyman, & Rankin, 1962); students from differing social classes (Phillips, 1955); administrators from schools in differing social areas (Turner, 1965); parents from differing social classes (Koopman, 1946; Musgrove, 1961); teachers and non teachers (Smith, 1965); rural communities and urban communities (Haer, 1953); pupils, teachers, parents, school officials, and school board members (Biddle, Rosencranz, & Rankin, 1961); teachers in various countries (Adams, 1970); and many others.

What can we make of such findings? In some cases the teacher will be worried if differing expectations are held for his or her conduct. Should those expectations lead others to place pressure on the teacher, then he or she will have problems. Suppose the administrator wants the teacher to spend more time in mathematics instruction while parents want less time spent on this subject. The teacher may then be faced with conflicting demands, complaints, or sanctions for mutually contradicting behaviors. To reflect this type of thought, role theorists often refer to polarized dissensus as *role conflict.* In so doing they imply that dissensus always leads to problems for the person to whom it applies. But is this true? Surely the person may sometimes be unaware of the fact that others hold differing expectations for his or her conduct. And even if the person is aware of dissensus, he or she may not worry about it in some conditions. (The American southerner may take delight in discovering a polarized dissensus between norms held by his or her friends and those held by "Yankees.") For these reasons, the term role confict appears an ill-chosen one. Nevertheless, it has received wide acceptance and will presumably be retained in the role vocabulary. So I shall define **role conflict** as any condition of common or attributed polarized dissensus that poses (usually unspecified) problems for the object person.

This definition does not denote the characteristics over which role conflict exists. Object persons may feel discomfort because polarized expectations are held for their features, conditions for entrance into their positions, treatments given to them, or even functions for which they are responsible. However, the study of role conflict has usually concerned object-peson *behaviors.* As well, role conflicts might be defined for expectations in the cathectic or descriptive modes. Nevertheless, most studies of role conflict have dealt with *norms,* reflecting a general stress on prescription in functionalist theories of social integration (Parsons, 1951) [B&T, Selection 32]. Also, nearly all studies of role conflict have dealt with expectations that are held for *social positions,* rather than expectations for individuals. These three restrictions are not required by the concept of role conflict, but studies using this concept have generally exhibited them.

Many forms of role conflict have been suggested. As with other types of dissensus, *common* (or *extant*) *role conflict* may be differentiated from *attributed role conflict.* One may also distinguish cases in which the object person is a member of one of the subject positions holding expectations from other cases when the object person belongs to a separate position. Again, dissensus may arise because the object person is simultaneously a member of two postions for which distinct expectations are held (sometimes called "inter-role conflict") or because the object person belongs to a single position for which others simply hold differing expectations ("intra-role conflict"). (To illustrate the former, military chaplains may experience role conflicts because they are both ministers and commissioned officers (Burchard, 1954). The latter is illustrated by our previous example, when administrators and parents differ over stress to be given to mathematics by the teacher.) If we put these variables together, we arrive at a rough tabulation of the major forms of role conflict that have been studied to date (see Table 6.4).

As Table 6.4 suggests, normative role conflict for the behavior of position members may be quite common. Gross, Mason, and McEachern (1958), Kahn, Wolfe, Quinn, Snoek, and Rosenthal (1964) [B&T, Selection 33], and others have advanced data suggesting that role conflict is a major source of dissatisfaction among organizational employees. Why should this be so? Why should polarized norms for behavior cause distress to position members to whom they apply? As was suggested in Chapter Five, norms that are held by others are assumed to be associated with the encouragement of compliance. In the case of extant role conflict, this means that object persons would be subject to conflicting social pressures (although they might not understand why those pressures appeared). In the case of attributed role conflict, object persons would assume that conflicting social pressures were likely (although the latter might not eventuate). In either case, normative role conflict should be more bothersome when others have opportunities to observe the person's behavior, when they are powerful, and when they are deemed likely to take action to enforce their norms. However reasonable these propositions,

Table 6.4
MAJOR FORMS OF ROLE CONFLICT IN EMPIRICAL STUDIES

	"Intra-role conflict"				"Inter-role conflict"	
	The object person belongs to one position, and polarized norms for behavior of its members are				The object person belongs to two positions, and polarized norms for behaviors of those two positions are	
	Held within the object position	*Held within another position*	*Held by the object position and another position*	*Held by two other positions*	*Held by object persons*	*Held within another position*
Extant role conflict	Doyle (1958) Wispé (1955)	Getzels & Guba (1957) Gullahorn & Gullahorn (1963) Seeman (1953)	Doyle (1958) Dunkin (1966) Gullahorn (1956) Jacobson et al. (1951) Karcher (1952) Sommer & Killian (1954) Twyman & Biddle (1963)	Borgatta (1955) Charters (1952) Gullahorn (1956) Laulicht (1955) Mishler (1953) Stouffer & Toby (1951) Sutcliffe & Haberman (1956)	Getzels & Guba (1957) Rosen (1955)	Getzels & Guba (1954, 1955a,b)

	Attributed to the object position	Attributed to another position	Attributed to the object position and another position	Attributed to two other positions	Attributed to other object persons	Attributed to another position
Attributed role conflict			Biddle (1970) Ehrlich et al. (1962) Gross et al. (1958) Miller & Shull (1962) Stouffer (1949) van de Vliert (1974)	Biddle (1970) Ehrlich et al. (1962) Gross et al. (1958) Miller & Shull (1962) van de Vliert (1975)		

may seem to be, little evidence has yet appeared to test them, apparently because most investigators assume that one may take for granted the bothersomeness of role conflicts. Interesting exceptions to this generalization were provided by Getzels and Guba (1955a,b), who established that the degree of "bother" experienced is affected by both structural and personal factors.

What do persons *do* when they experience role conflict? Several theories have been proposed concerning this problem, the most influential of which was stated by Gross *et al.* (1958) [B&T, Selection 35]. The theory suggested three strategies for *resolving* role conflict: conformity to one or another of the polarized expectations, compromise between them, and avoidance of the issue. Adoption of one or another of these strategies was predicted, in turn, from three factors: expected sanctions, legitimacy of the expectations held, and whether the object person is "moral" or "expedient" in his or her orientation. (Those who are "moral" will presumably place greater stress on legitimacy, those who are "expedient" should focus more on expected sanctions.) This theory has been tested both by its original authors and subsequently by numerous others (van de Vliert, 1979). In general, these studies found considerable support for the influence of expected sanctions on resolution of role conflict, less support for legitimacy, and little or no support for a moral-versus-expedient orientation.[7] Nevertheless, impact of these factors on role conflict resolution seems to vary depending on context. Biddle, Bank and Marlin (1978) found legitimacy to have little impact on the prediction of adolescent drinking. Ehrlich, Rinehart, and Howell (1962) found difficulty in predicting role conflict resolution among police officers from either sanctioning or legitimacy.[8] Apparently, response to sanctioning and legitimacy depends on whether object persons are familiar with these concepts and whether they think reflectively about the resolution of role conflicts.

The concept of normative role conflict has generated enthusiasm among both investigators and practitioners and is often used to discuss problems that are faced by persons who are caught between traditional and newer standards for conduct. To illustrate this use, women who attempt both a professional career and to be a homemaker and mother are often beset by role conflicts (Hunt & Hunt, 1977; Myrdal & Klein, 1956; Paloma, 1972; Rapoport & Rapoport, 1969, 1971). On the one hand, to perform a professional role adequately as a homemaker and mother requires time, attention, and involvement. On the other, to perform adequately

---

[7] In fairness, the theory of moral-versus-expedient orientation has not been adequately tested, since most studies have used a test for this construct that has questionable validity (see van de Vliert & Cottrell, in press).

[8] Instead, Ehrlich *et al.* suggested that role conflict resolution could be predicted by knowing which groups of referent others were "important" to the object person (Preiss & Ehrlich, 1966). This latter theory was challenged by Bank (1968) with data from advertising salespersons who found subjective "importance" unimportant.

as a homemaker and mother also requires time, attention, and involvement. What does the professional woman do when she has a sick child, for example? How does she cope when her professional job requires overtime work that conflicts with the needs of her husband and children? How does she meet the opposed demands of her professional associates and her more traditional neighbors? Such conflicts are only partly resolved when she is fortunate enough to marry a spouse who is willing to share equally in homemaking and parenting, for within her professional career she is often in competition with others who are supported by a full-time house-spouse. I do not know how to solve this dilemma, any more than I know how to counsel someone who is caught between the demands of a traditional, ethnic or religious, background and the requirements of our secular society. I do know that such problems may be described as normative role conflicts and that they are a source of deep concern and stress.

Despite enthusiasm for the concept of normative role conflict, research on this topic suffers from many of the same problems we have noted for other comparison concepts. Role conflicts may be defined for preferences or beliefs, but these are rarely studied. Problems faced by the object person in role conflict are usually assumed and rarely studied. Definitions offered for role conflict differ, and it is not yet clear whether these "matter" or may be ignored. Adequate theories for role conflict resolution have not yet been tested in a variety of contexts, and so forth. Nevertheless, role conflict is an intuitively attractive idea, and research concerning it seems likely to continue.

Consistency and Cognitive Dissonance

Role conflict is sometimes confused with cognitive dissonance. Both involve inconsistent expectations and in both concepts it is presumed that someone "suffers" because of that inconsistency. However, in role conflict the inconsistency may involve two or more subject persons, whereas in cognitive dissonance the inconsistencies are held by a single person; in role conflict it is the object person who "suffers," whereas in cognitive dissonance the "sufferer" is the subject person; and role conflicts are "resolved" behaviorally, whereas in cognitive dissonance "resolution" is assumed to involve changes of expectation.

We turn now to a formal presentation of these ideas. Two expectations will be defined as **inconsistent** if one of them implies some event that is denied by the other. We would judge it inconsistent if a person told us on Monday that he or she loved to eat peanut butter and on Tuesday that he or she hated the stuff. The commandment "Thou Shalt Not Kill" is presumably inconsistent with prescriptions demanding that we kill our enemies in war time. A report that a person is a physician is inconsistent with another report that the same person is also an undertaker.

These examples illustrate the fact that inconsistency may be judged for all modes of expectation. They also indicate several types of inconsistency. The first example (assessments of peanut butter) exemplifies **logical inconsistency**, which is yet another type of comparison concept. Two expectations are judged logically inconsistent if they are identical in form and distinct. By this definition, role conflicts always involve logical inconsistency. But, as the preceding example suggests, expectations that are held or uttered by a single person may also be logically inconsistent. The person who both wants and hates something, who thinks that he or she should both do and not do some act, who believes in and does not believe in another's testimony suffers from logical inconsistency.

The second example (prescription for killing and not killing) illustrates **inclusional inconsistency**. This is not a comparison concept in the strict sense. As we know, expectations may be judged for comparability if they agree in mode of expression, object person, content, and context. Occasionally two expectations may not meet this stipulation, although one may apply to conditions that are a subset of conditions to which the other applies. One might be stated for a single object person, for example, whereas the other applies to a position of which the object person is a member. Or one may be stated for a limited content or context, whereas the other applies to a larger content or context which includes the former. We shall say that the less inclusive expectation *exemplifies* the more inclusive one. Two expectations are inclusionally inconsistent, then, if they agree in mode, are distinct, and one exemplifies conditions appearing in the other for object person, content, or context.

The third example (reports that a person is both a physician and an undertaker) illustrates **functional inconsistency**. Once again, this is not a comparison concept, for functional inconsistency depends upon physical or social limitations appearing in the culture. A human being cannot simultaneously swim and climb stairs, and prescriptions calling for the joint performance of these two acts would be functionally inconsistent. Although it is logically consistent for a person to be both a physician and an undertaker, and further, although it is possible that this combination of callings might appear in some societies, social forces common in our society conspire against it. Thus, expectations are functionally inconsistent if their joint performance would produce effects that are logically inconsistent or if their joint performance requires meeting logically inconsistent conditions.

A number of different concepts have appeared that are based on assumptions about inconsistency. One of these is **cognitive dissonance**, which is presumed to appear when a person holds inconsistent conceptions, at least one of which concerns that person's behavior. According to Festinger (1957), the result of holding such conceptions is a feeling of discomfort that leads the person to any of several strategies for rectifying the situation, including seeking reasons for changing or discounting one or both of the conceptions. To illustrate this point, I recently decided to buy a new car. Like most people, I considered several different makes and models before making my purchase. Having decided on one car, I quickly rationalized that decision by finding reasons why my choice was best and why all the other choices were less desirable. Whereas once I held inconsistent preferences for purchasing a car, these made me uncomfortable, and once I had made my decision I took steps to remove the inconsistency. (By now, my new Olds is old news.)

The phenomena of cognitive dissonance have been subjected to intensive research (Aronson, 1969; Brehm & Cohen, 1962; Chapanis & Chapanis, 1964; Festinger, 1964; Zajonc, 1966), and scores of demonstrations have appeared suggesting that inconsistent conceptions for oneself may be altered. At the same time, a number of attempts to demonstrate cognitive dissonance have failed, and it appears at a minimum that this phenomenon varies depending upon content, context, and characteristics of the person who experiences the inconsistency. To illustrate a common case where inconsistency is apparently tolerated, many of us pay lip service to standards for conduct on the Sabbath that we proceed to violate in our conduct on weekdays. Thus, although cognitive dissonance may be a common experience, one doubts that it is as inevitable as has been claimed by some enthusiasts. Moreover, modality problems have also plagued dissonance research. Festinger's original statement of the dissonance proposition involved beliefs, but examples he cited for dissonance could easily have been interpreted as inconsistencies between preferences or opposition between preferences and norms. Moreover, classic demonstrations of the dissonance effect also may be interpreted as providing experiences leading to the opposition of preferences (Aronson & Mills, 1959; Brehm, 1956) or of preferences and norms (Aronson & Carlsmith, 1963).[9] At this writing it appears unlikely that inconsistent, self-relevant beliefs will produce dissonance unless they are also supported by preferences or norms. One wonders also why so little attention has been given to normative inconsistencies in dissonance research. Surely we may be bothered upon discovering that we hold inconsistent prescriptions for our own behavior.

Other applications of the consistency concept appear in balance theory. Heider (1944, 1946, 1958), Osgood and Tannenbaum (1955), and Rosenberg and Abelson (1960) have suggested that we are made uncomfortable when we believe that someone whom we like (or approve) holds expectations that are inconsistent with our own—or when someone we dislike (or disapprove) holds expectations that are consistent with ours. This discomfort will lead us either to change our expectations or to restructure our relationship with the other. Once again, considerable research has been reported supporting these propositions (Brown, 1962; Feather, 1967; Osgood, 1960; Zajonc, 1960, 1966) most of which has concerned preferences. And once again, support has appeared to vary depending on content, context, and characteristics of the person who experiences inconsistency. Why should persons tend to "balance" their thoughts about their own and others' preferences? Heider (1960)

---

[9] Comparisons between expectations that differ in mode involve the concept of concordance and are dealt with in the following section.

argued that such processes are akin to Gestalt principles of perception and are essentially unlearned. Other authors, such as Hovland and Rosenberg (1960), have suggested that tendencies to "balance" expectations are learned from prior experiences in which inconsistencies have led to disliking others and consistencies to liking.

This latter explanation is related to a second major proposition in balance theory. Newcomb (1953, 1956, 1959a) has argued that persons who like one another will come to hold consitent expectations, and that those who hold inconsistent expectations will come eventually to dislike one another. Why? Because inconsistencies lead to the imposition of reciprocal punishments, whereas consistent expectations lead actors to reward one another. This latter extension of the "balance" concept has attracted somewhat less research, but several studies have also tended to support it (Burdick & Burnes, 1958; Newcomb, 1961, 1963). Once again, the research has tended to focus upon preferences. One of the more striking aspects of research on consistency within balance theory has been formalization of propositions by means of graph theory (Feather, 1967; Harary, Norman, & Cartwright, 1965). As we shall see in the next chapter, this same form of mathematics has also been applied to the analysis of role relationships in formal organizations.

Yet another application of inconsistency appears in the psychoanalytic concept of *ambivalence*. According to Freud (1922), the Oedipal Conflict begins when the son develops feelings of hatred and fear for his father (because of sexual fantasies, fears of castration, and concern over the power of the father). Eventually these negative feelings are "repressed" (because they are dangerous) and are replaced by love and respect for the father. However, somewhat ambivalent feelings about the father continue into adulthood and may be applied to any authority figure who is considered a substitute for the father. To illustrate, Fromm (1941) hypothesized that enthusiasm for Nazism in Germany was a product of ambivalence toward authority induced through authoritarian child rearing in German families (also see Adorno, Frenkel-Brunswik, Levinson, & Sanford, 1950). Once again, then, it is assumed that inconsitent preferences lead to no good end.

Despite extensive research that has appeared during the past two decades, the phenomena of consistency also seem to be inadequately explored. As we have seen, most research has involved the preference mode, and yet theories of consistency are usually stated so that they would apply also to norms and beliefs. Logical, inclusional, and functional inconsitency probably have somewhat different effects, and yet these concepts are usually combined in theories and research summaries. Most theories concerning the effects of consistency are stated as if they had universal applicability, and yet much of the evidence suggests that they apply only in certain contexts. Despite these objections, consistency is also an attractive concept, and research on it appears to hold potential for understanding a wide range of human responses .

Concordance

Another concept sometimes confused with role conflict concerns expectations that differ in modality. For example, in psychotherapy we may be concerned that subject's aspirations and "reality evaluation" of him or herself come into agreement. Or, we may worry when a child reports to us that his or her parent fails to come up to standards held by the child. These are examples of nonconcordance. To define this concept formally, **concordance** occurs when comparable expectations of contrasting modalities are found to be similar. However, this definition involves a modification of our concept of comparability. Earlier I stressed that comparable expectations were assumed to be similar in object person, content, modality, and context. For purposes of defining concordance (only) I modify these assumptions by abandoning the requirement of identical modality and substituting for it another stating that the expectations being compared must be held by the same subject person. (And in so doing I brush aside the question of how it is that we go about comparing expectations that differ in modality—see Chapter Five.) Generally, concordance is not presumed to be determined.

Clinicians have considerable interest in concordance and generally presume that persons will be healthier or better adjusted if their beliefs about themselves are aligned with "ideals" they hold for themselves. This propostition was argued in Rogers and Dymond (1954) had supported by a study showing that concordance was greater for patients who had completed therapy than for those who were just beginning it (Butler & Haigh, 1954). Assuming this proposition to be true, a number of attitude scales have appeared or been adapted that include measures of concordance between beliefs and ideals for self as measures of "self-esteem" (Bills, Vance, & McLean, 1951; LaForge & Suczek, 1955; Miskimins & Braucht, 1971; Worchel, 1957). Moreover, validating studies have tended to show positive, albeit weak, relationships between concordance as measured by these instruments and measures of mental health (for an exception, see Hamilton, 1971).

Despite this support, several questions have been raised concerning the supposed reajtionship between "self-ideal" concordance and adjustment. It has been suggested: that a curvilinear relationship obtains between these variables (Block & Thomas, 1955); that differences in concordance may be unrelated to adjustment (Levy, 1956; Wilcox & Fritz, 1971); that older and more intelligent persons may tolerate more nonconcordance (Katz & Zigler, 1967); and that concordance scores are poorer indicators of self-esteem than simple measures of satisfaction (Robinson & Shaver, 1973; Wylie, 1974). A serious question can also be raised concerning the meaning of ratings that are provided by a person for his or her "ideal" self. Does "ideal" refer to preferences or to norms, and what does the subject do when he or she would prefer to be or do one thing and thinks he or she ought to be or do another? In short, studies of self-ideal concordance have tended to confuse the concepts of preference and norm and to ignore the possibility that nonconcordance might appear between these two modes. One can only guess at the problems this has raised for research on concordance and adjustment. (I shall have more to say about the self in Chapter Eight.)

Whatever one may think about research on "self-esteem," there can be little doubt that nonconcordance is often an unpleasant experience. One would predict it to be so on theoretical grounds, and it has been found associated with lack of satisfaction in more than one study (Cheong & DeVault, 1966; Rodgers, 1959). Once again, however, we do not yet know the limits of this propostion, and surely some forms of nonconcordance are welcomed. The athlete may enjoy setting standards for achievement that he or she has not yet attained and then striving to meet them. Moreover, experiences of nonconcordance are presumably common in certain situations. J. H. Mann (1959) demonstrated nonconcordance for beliefs and preferences concerning racial discrimination. Kothandapani (1971) found a similar form of nonconcordance for the use of contraceptives. Biddle, Rosencranz, and Rankin (1961) and Smith (1965) demonstrated nonconcordance between beliefs and norms held for school teachers by teachers and others.[10] Rodman (1966) was able to resolve apparent inconsistencies in earlier research concerning "attitudes" toward nonlegal marital unions in the Caribbean by showing that norms and preferences were at odds. Westie (1965) demonstrated norm-preference nonconcordance for the treatment of blacks by white Americans. To date, however, no formal theory has been advanced for concordance, nor has agreement yet appeared on what term to use for this concept, and my choice of *concordance* is presumably new. Clearly, this is a concept deserving additional work.

The Set of Comparison Concepts

We have now examined several concepts that are used by role theorists to discuss the affairs of human beings. All have been defined by comparing expectations (or expectations and behaviors) for their similarity. Some have also involved the condition of determination. In many ways these notions, *comparison concepts,* constitute the empirical heartland of role theory.

As readers may suspect, there is only a limited number of comparison concepts. Not all comparison cencepts have yet been studied by role theorists, however, and it is useful to look at the set as a whole. For convenience, I have included two tables that display all concepts generated by comparisons between two elements (that is, two behaviors, two expectations, or an expectation and a behavior). More

---

[10] Respondents in both of these studies believed that some teachers fail to live up to high normative standards, and in both studies respondents who were teachers thought that failure was likely. One is tempted to suggest that teachers, at least, see their own profession through Dewey-colored glasses.

Table 6.5
COMPARISON CONCEPTS INVOLVING EXPECTATIONS AND BEHAVIORS[a]

	Concepts involving behaviors	
Comparisons between behaviors	$B \longleftrightarrow B'$ Uniformity $B \rightarrow B'$ Imitation	
	Concepts involving behaviors and simple expectations	Concepts involving behaviors and extended expectations
Comparisons between expectations and behaviors	$B \rightarrow E$ Accuracy or alignment $B \longleftrightarrow E$ Concurrence $E \rightarrow B$ Conformity	$B \rightarrow E^*$ Attributive accuracy $B \longleftrightarrow E^*$ Attributive concurrence $E^* \rightarrow B$ Attributive conformity

[a]Legend: B =   A behavior
           B' =   Another behavior
           E =   A simple expectation
           E^* =   An extended expectation
           $\longleftrightarrow$ =   A nondetermined comparison
           $\rightarrow$ =   A determined comparison with arrow pointing to the element determined

complex concepts may be generated by comparisons among three or more elements, but these are seldom discussed.

Table 6.5 conerns concepts generated by comparing expectations with behaviors. At the top of the table we find two concepts which, because they concern behaviors only, were defined in Chapter Two: *uniformity* and *imitation*. To the left, below we find three concepts: *accuracy* (or *alignment*), *concurrence,* and *conformity.* The second of these three is a new term that refers to nondetermined comparisons between a behavior and a simple expectation. Should one want to assert that a behavior and an expectation are similar to each other without implying that either caused or matched the other, the "correct" term to use for this purpose would be *concurrence.* This term is my own, and to the best of my knowledge the concept it denotes has neither been discussed nor investigated to date. To the right, below we find three additional concepts, each the analogue of those to the left but defined for extended rather than for simple expectations: *attributive accuracy, attributive concurrence,* and *attributive conformity.* Of these, only attributive conformity has received much attention (as a methodological artifact in studies of role conflict resolution, and as an element in models for consistency). The other two concepts are viable, however, and readers may enjoy thinking up applications or research designs that would employ them.

Table 6.6
COMPARISON CONCEPTS INVOLVING SIMPLE AND EXTENDED EXPECTATIONS[a]

	Concepts involving expectations held by one person		Concepts involving expectations held by two persons	
Comparisons between simple expectations	$E_1 \longleftrightarrow E_1'$ $E_1 \rightarrow E_1'$	Consistency (or concordance Generalization	$E_1 \longleftrightarrow E_2$ $E_1 \rightarrow E_2$	Consensus (role conflict) Acceptance
Comparisons between simple and extended expectations	$E_1 \rightarrow E^*_{1.2}$ $E_1 \longleftrightarrow E^*_{1.2}$ $E^*_{1.2} \rightarrow E_1$	Projection Attributed consensus Incorporation	$E_2 \rightarrow E^*_{1.2}$ $E_2 \longleftrightarrow E^*_{1.2}$ $E^*_{1.2} \rightarrow E_2$	Veridicality Matched attribution Suggestion
Comparisons between extended expectations	$E^*_{1.2} \longleftrightarrow E^*_{1.3}$ $E^*_{1.2} \rightarrow E^*_{1.3}$	Attributed agreement Attributed acceptance	$E^*_{1.3} \longleftrightarrow E^*_{2.3}$ $E^*_{1.3} \rightarrow E^*_{2.3}$	Matched agreement Matched acceptance

[a] Legend:
E_1 = A simple expectation held by the person
E_1' = Another expectation held by the person
E_2 = A simple expectation held by another
$E^*_{1.2}$ = An extended expectation attributed by the person to the other
$E^*_{1.3}$ = An extended expectation attributed by the person to a third person
$E^*_{2.3}$ = An extended expectation attributed by the other to the third person
$\longleftrightarrow$ = A nondetermined comparison
$\rightarrow$ = A determined comparison with arrow pointing to the element determined

Table 6.6 concerns comparison concepts that involve simple and extended expectations. At the top left we find concepts for simple expectations held by one person: *consistency, concordance,* and *generalization.* Of these, only the latter concept has yet to be discussed. Generalization occurs when one forms a second expectation that is similar to another, as for example when one assumes that a younger brother will behave as did his older sibling. This concept is often discussed, but to the best of my knowledge it is seldom studied. At the top right we find two concepts that involve comparisons between simple expectations held by two persons: *consensus* (and one of its antonyms, *role conflict*), and *acceptance.* Neither needs additional discussion here. At the middle left we find three concepts for comparing simple and extended expectations that are held by one person: *projection, attributed consensus,* and *incorporation.* Of these, projection and incorporation are the directed analogues of attributed consensus. The former concerns instances when the person forms ideas about the other's thinking form his or her own; the latter occurs when the person takes into his or her thinking expectations that the person originally found in others. Both concepts are widely discussed, although little research seems to have appeared for them. The middle right cell provides another three concepts: *veridicality, matched attribution,* and *suggestion.* All three concern comparison between a simple expectation held by one person and an extended expectation held by another. Of these, only veridicality has received attention. I am unaware of either discussions or studies representing the latter two concepts. The two cells at the bottom both concern comparisons among extended expectations. At the left we find two concepts concerned with comparisons within a single subject: *attributed agreement* and *attributed acceptance.* To the right we find two concepts formed by comparing extended expectations between two persons: *matched agreement* and *matched acceptance.* All four concepts deserve further work.

EXPECTED ROLES

> *In any case, social positions are a Danaän gift from society to the individual. Even if he has not acquired them by his own effort, even if they have been ascribed to him from birth, they demand something from him; for every position carries with it a social role, a set of expectations addressed to the behavior of its incumbent and sanctioned by the reference groups of its field.*
> —*Ralf Dahrendorf, Homo Sociologicus*

We turn now (at last) to that concern which for some theorists is the core concern of role theory—the study of *expected roles.* Although logically complex, the basic notion of an expected role is familiar enough. For almost every identity we recognize, we also carrry in our minds a set of conceptions concerning the behaviors of those who are its members. Our parents, spouses, and children behave in ways that are chacteristic, and we are able to predict those behaviors because we hold beliefs concerning them. Similar beliefs are held concerning the behaviors of infants, adolescents, and the aged; whites, blacks, Jews, and Chicanos; businessmen, generals, farmers, and politicians; radicals, mystics, and drunkards. Moreover, for most of these same identities we maintain not only beliefs but also norms and preferences. Many of these conceptions are also overtly enunciated on occasion, and some of them are reflected in the inscriptions that constitute our laws and codebooks. In many cases the expectations that we hold are also likely to be held by others, and out of the threads of our shared expectations is woven a cloth of social structure that is our common heritage as members of a given society, community, or organization.

It is this latter condition that so often appears as a general assumption in anthropological and sociological discussions of role theory. As we know, this assumption does not always hold; in fact, the cloth of social structure is a coat of many colors. However, to discuss this problem intelligently it is necessary first to define expected role.

Expected Role Defined

Several assumptions are normally made in defining the concept of expected role. To begin with, such a role is made up of expectations that are applied to an object person or position. These expectations may either be held by subject persons or may be attributed by them to others. Expected roles may also be shared among subject persons who form some subset of the population. And like behavioral roles, expected roles are usually limited to some context. We meet these assumptions by defining an **expected role** to be the set of expectations for the behaviors, in context, of an object person (or position) that are held consensually by one or more subject persons (or are attributed by them to others).[11]

This definiton covers various contingencies. For example, several different roles may be held for persons of a given identity by differnt subject subsets. Expectations held for us by our close friends are usually somewhat different from those held by strangers—the former hold a "private role" for us, the latter hold "public role" expectations. Expected roles also differ depending on context. We are expected to behave differently in our homes, in the university, on the city streets, in the commune, on a battlefield—each of these expected roles is distinct, although they all contain some overlapping elements. Or let us take the case where the father attributes to the mother expectations for their son. Are these attributed expectations part of the role of the mother or of the son? The answer is, of course, that they are a part of both roles. The son's role includes expectations that are attributed (to others) for him; the mother's role includes expectations that are attributed to her (for others).

On the other hand, expectations held for the behaviors that others direct toward object persons are not part of the expected role, given the above definiton—rather, they are part of *expected treatments*. (In other discussions, expected treatments may be termed *rights*, to distinguish them from expected roles, which are called *obligations*. Both may be associated with a given identity, but in any technical sense the expected treatment an object position is to receive constitutes an element of the expected role of whomever is to administer that treatment.) Note also that we have not specified modality or expectational form for an expected role. Under our definition, expected roles may be descriptive, prescriptive, or cathectic—or all three. Moreover, they may be held covertly, expressed overtly, or appear as inscriptions—or all three.

The concept of expected role is obviously more complex than that of behavioral role. In one sense, however, it is conceptually simpler. When establishing a behavioral role, we must examine an unbounded range of facets to discover those for which characteristic behaviors appear. As was pointed out in Chapter Three, this is a difficult task and suggests that the concept of behavioral role is more useful for

[11] Such a definition may also be extended to **expected profile**, and without ceremony I shall presume that we have done so.

boundary setting than for strict denotation. This difficulty is less troublesome for expected roles. In order to establish an expected role that is held by a single person it is "merely" necessary to interview him or her exhaustively until the person has told us all that he or she can describe, prescribe, or evaluate concerning the object person and context in question.[12] The expected role held by a plurality of subjects is even more restrictive, since we demand that expectations appearing in the role be consensually held. Nevertheless, it is still difficult to establish the limits of an expected role, and in fact few investigators have yet attempted to inventory one.

Of what use are expected roles? Common experience suggests that behavioral and expected roles are similar. Two hypotheses have been advanced to explain this apparent similarity. The usual argument "explains" behavioral roles by positing that members of the system share expectations for those behaviors and that these expectations were learned through common experiences of socialization (Parsons, 1951). An alternative hypothesis has been advanced by Turner (1968), who argues that the behavioral role may well appear first (generated by contextual constraints or personality factors) and that the expected role is then built up as a rationalization of behavioral reality. The first hypothesis asserts that the expected role is the independent variable; the second presumes it to be dependent. These two hypotheses relate to theories of expectational learning that we reviewed in Chapter Five. Both probably have some applicability, depending on circumstances. Pre-existing expectations surely constrain behavior, but when they are weak or the object person is forceful, rationalization of roles undoubtedly occurs.

Expected roles are also similar to behavioral roles in that additional criteria may be used to specify or circumscribe them. I suggested one of these, *uniqueness,* in Footnote 12. Expected roles are also normally constrained by contextual boundaries, although contextual assumptions are rarely investigated empirically. It is also possible to constrain an expected role in functional terms (Fishburn, 1962) or to conceptualize it in terms of tasks with which the role is to be associated (Oeser & Harary, 1962) [B&T, Selection 6]. Still other authors have presumed additional processes to inhere in the expected role concept—for example, conformity or expected sanctions.

What, then, is the necessary relationship between a behavioral role and an expected role? The answer, of course, is that there need be no relationship whatsoever! In the case of the stereotypic role, the expectations held may bear no relationship to the way in which members or the focal position actually behave. Expected roles held by ignorant or bigoted persons bear little relationship with behavioral reality. Four conditions must be met before an element of an expected role will be similar to its behavioral counterpart. First, subjects must maintain the facet

---

[12] In so doing, we may help the person if we confine attention to those expectations he or she presumes are unique. By specifying that we are interested in unique behaviors, the subject is relieved of the necessity of telling us that object persons breathe, eat, brush their teeth, and despise social scientists who ask foolish questions!

for judging behavioral alternatives we have in mind. Second, they must use that facet in expressing expectations for the object person and context specified. Third, those expectations must be consensual. Fourth, the expectation must be similar to the behaviors exhibited by object persons. Given these strict conditions, it seems an unlikely event that any elements of an expected role will be accurate! But of course, many expected roles are accurate in the main, particularly those that concern behaviors of well-known, well-observed, well-liked others. In fact, one of our major reasons for maintaining expected roles is that in so doing we obtain predictive control over our environment. And if they were really inaccurate, most expected roles would be quickly abandoned.

Variables of Expected Roles

Since expected roles are modeled after behavioral roles, all of the variables discussed in Chapter Three that were defined for the latter concept may be applied to its expected analogue. Moreover, since expected roles are assembled from expectations the variables discussed for expectations in Chapter Five may also be applied to expected roles. Some of these earlier variables have additional significance when applied to expected roles, and it is worthwhile discussing these briefly. A few variables are also definable only for expected roles.

CONTEXTUALIZATION

Expected roles are more likely to be contextualized than are their behavioral analogues. As an example of this, our prescriptions for the behaviors of occupational positions are nearly always restricted to work-relevant contexts. We are so used to this form of contextualization that we resent it when others hold expectations that would restrict the after-hours behaviors of teachers, ministers, or statesmen (and their spouses and children). Nevertheless, noncontextualized prescriptions may be set for those who are "supposed" to constitute models of sobriety, rectitude, or accomplishment for the general public (for examples, see Greenhoe, 1940; Haer, 1953).

LEGITIMACY

Like the expectations of which they are composed, expected roles may be legitimate, and the example of contextualization we have just considered in the preceding paragraph also illustrates legitimacy. Consider the teacher's role: teachers usually accept as legitimate prescriptions that are set for their performance within the school; but school board members have in the past imposed standards of dress, decorum, and even marital status upon teachers that applied to nonschool contexts. Teachers resented these as illegitimate. Again take the policeman's role in the ghetto community: residents usually accept as legitimate police activities involving the direction of traffic, apprehension of criminals, and the rescuing of drowning children; but they consider it illegitimate when police officers attempt to tell them how to dress, whether or not to loiter on street corners, or inflict discriminatory treatment on them because of their color or accent. Why? Why are some role expectations legitimate and other illegitimate? The usual explanation offered is that we are all familiar to some extent with the theory of social organization and are willing to accept (or give) direction from others within a given social system in order to facilitate operation of that system (Weber, 1925). Thus, teachers are willing to accept mandates of the school board within a school context because they believe that such rules are necessary for school operation, but they are unwilling to accept rules pertaining to after-hours conduct. Citizens view the direction of traffic and apprehension of criminals as necessary for order maintenance, but not bigotry. (School boards and police officers may hold somewhat different definitions of the situation.) Studies of the legitimacy of role expectations may be found in Gross, Mason, and McEachern (1958) and Ehrlich, Rinehart, and Howell, (1962), and we discuss the theory of social organization in greater detail in Chapter Seven.

BREADTH

Almost by definition, expected roles are likely to be less broad than behavioral roles. No person carries within his or her mind more than a fraction of the facets that can usefully be applied to behaviors, and it is unlikely than any expected role will encompass all of the facets that would be found to map characteristic behaviors of object persons. In fact, most expected roles are quite limited in their coverage, particularly those that are specified in inscriptions.

FORMALIZATION

In small groups and simple, traditional societies it is common to find that the expected roles of position members are well integrated, broadly agreed upon, and conformity inducing. For example, the duties of the mother in the family are generally understood by everyone. Moreover, her role is integrated with that of her husband, her eldest son, her daughter—so that the necessary functions of family life are accomplished. In addition, there is likely to be a close relationship between her expected role and its behavioral counterpart, for with general consensus concerning roles an understanding of their integration and functions (and with no competing roles available as models), simple pressure will be exerted upon members to conform to roles.

These conditions are less likely to be present in formal organizations or in rapidly changing, urban societies. The latter are more complex social systems and are likely to produce conflicting pressures upon participants. For this reason, crucial roles within contemporary social systems tend to become **formalized** over time. As organizations, games, nation-states, and other social systems mature, the duties of its crucial members tend to be written down, to become complex, to be endlessly qualified. Several types of events accelerate formalization. One is the appearance of a dangerous or incompetent member of the position who forces us to think about what we should require of those who occupy that slot. (Recently we experienced this process regarding the American presidency.) Another is technological innovation that leads to adjusting the range of functions that can be accomplished through the role in question. Still another is the need structure of persons who are members of that position, for each of us would like to redefine our roles so as to achieve maximum satisfaction from them.

Our reactions to the progress of role formalization vary, depending on context. In those contexts we enter for the fun of participating in them, such as games and ceremonies, we are likely to revel in formalization. For example, the rules of baseball have gradually become more and more complex over the years, and with each coronation ceremony in Britain the pomp becomes more impressive. On the other hand, we tend to resent formalization in contexts that are instrumental, such as organizations, and to denigrate it as "excess red tape." Progressive role formalization does not go on forever, of course. It is limited by our unwillingness to force incumbents to conform to overly precise restrictions, our belief that "local initiative" is better than "constraining rules," and our intolerance for "red tape." We return to this process of role formalization, too, in the next chapter.

STEREOTYPY

In Chapter Five we noted that expectations are stereotypic to the degree that they are based on hearsay rather than on evidence. Expected roles may also be **stereotypic**, in which case a substantial portion of the expectations of which they are composed are stereotypic in origin. As we also noted earlier, stereoptypic expectations may or may not be accurate. However, stereotypic roles are more likely to form when interaction is prevented between subject and object persons, and as a result are likely to be associated also with inaccuracy. Stereotypes are also sometimes funny or tragic and can lead to setting up social forms that guard them from change. (When shared, stereotypic roles often constitute examples of pluralistic ignorance.) Stereotypes concerning minority groups, for example, may prevent others from interacting with minority group members and thus discovering that the stereotypes held are invalid. Other stereotypes—such as those pertaining to sexual, ethnic, religious, and national differences—seem to reflect the subject's own sense of identity (Duijker & Frijda, 1960). American social scientists are vitally interested in stereotypy and prejudice, and substantial research has been published on role stereotypes. A perticularly good review of their findings appears in Ehrlich (1973) together with a propositional summary for the field.

SALIENCY

One more characteristic associated with role expectations is occasionally used to set boundaries for expected roles. Let us suppose that we have asked subjects an open-ended question: "Tell us all of your expectations for the behavior of professional golfers." The first expectation volunteered by the subject is the most salient for him or her. The next expectation he or she volunteers ranks behind it in **saliency**, and so on throughout all of those he or she volunteers. Sooner or later, the subject will run down, of course. It is likely that he or she holds additional expectations in his or her mind—moreover we may later attempt to elicit these by probing with additional questions—but they are sufficiently nonsalient that the subject did not feel it necessary to volunteer them to us at the time.

What determines saliency? Salient expectations are likely to reflect formalization, legitimacy, importance to the subject, and recent experiences the subject has had with members of the object position. In addition, minor changes in the way we word our question to the subject can radically change expectational saliency. For example, when asked to volunteer negative norms subjects come forward with concrete complaints against specific members of the object position, whereas a request for positive norms generally provokes more abstract content (Biddle, Rosencranz, & Rankin, 1961). In addition, contextualization of the question affects saliency.

Saliency is sometimes employed within pilot studies to generate a set of facets that will later be used for measurement of role expectations within a larger population. To illustrate, suppose we wanted to study the expected role of an occupational position. One way to begin our study would be to ask a few members of that position, and others concerned with it, to volunteer their salient expectations for it to us. We would then choose facets that were volunteered by various respondents for further study with a larger, more representative, sample of subject persons.

The Study of Expected Roles

As has already been suggested, it is difficult to establish the limits of an expected role, since to do so we would have to explore "all" of the possible expectations that might be held in consensus among those persons concerned with a given object person. Nevertheless, several authors have made broad attempts to investigate expected roles (for example, see Biddle *et al.,* 1961; Foskett, 1967a,b; Gross *et al.,* 1958; Habenstein & Christ, 1955; Karcher, 1952; Preiss & Ehrlich, 1966; Trahair, 1968, 1969, 1970). How does one go about studying an expected role?

Such studies have begun by making restrictions of coverage. One common restriction made is contextualization—one decides, for example, to study only those expectations that are held for work-relevant contexts. Another restriction is to limit coverage to certain functions—one studies only those expectations associated with certain accomplishments or tasks of position members. Other restrictions may concern modality of expectations, identities of subject and sentient persons, and so forth. It is possible to study these restricting conditions themselves as features of the role. For example, subjects might be asked (in a pilot study) to discuss the contexts in which object persons are likely to be found or the functions they associate with behaviors of the object position. Restrictions such as these are usually made arbitrarily, although most authors who have studied expected roles have recognized that they were making them and have discussed the implications of restrictions.

Once restrictions have been accepted, the next step is to set up a listing of facets that may be used for asking respondents about their expectations. As indicated above, such a listing may be obtained from object persons using the criterion of saliency. (Some studies of expected roles have in fact published results at this point, content to deal only with the volunteered responses of those who are also members of the object position.) Other criteria may also be used for suggesting facets, such as the official rules stated for the object position (if any), newspaper accounts or other public documents concerned with the behaviors of position member, and the insights of "experts" who have thought or taught about the position.

The penultimate step in the study of an expected role is canvassing respondents concerning their expectations to determine which (if any) are held in consensus, which generate role conflict, and so forth. To do this, the investigator constructs a standardized instrument from the facets that were generated in the second step, mentioned previously. He or she must also make decisions concerning the format of the questions to be asked—usually a choice between the modal-strength method and the facet-alternative method although the investigator might opt for a more sophisticated methodology if he or she is willing to study just a few facets of behavior. The instrument developed must be pretested, and a sample of respondents must be selected that represents the universe of those whom the investigator wishes to inventory for their role expectations.

Of what practical value is the study of an expected role? If we go to all the trouble that such a study entails, have we produced anything worthwhile as a result? Several answers may be given to this question. Often we are interested in information concerning the expectations that are maintained for a given object position for their own sake. To what extent do members of a subject population agree or disagree in the expectations they hold? Do they exhibit role conflict, and if so, for what issues? Are their expectations bounded by contexts, or are they associated with certain functions, and what facets do they cover? If we plan action to rectify difficulties suffered by members of an object position, such information is vital to our plans. In a larger sense, however, we may be interested in an expected role because we wish to study decision making concerning that role or may want to study (or make assumptions about) behavioral roles that relate to that expected role. Sooner or later the role field will mature so that we will know the conditions under which role expectations will produce conforming role behavior, but even at present it is reasonable to presume that some relationships exist between these two realms.

Thus, information generated by studies of expected roles is often interpreted to reflect the behavioral roles of object persons, and many investigators have presumed that the simplest way of studying a behavioral role was to ask expectational questions.

Like behavioral role, the expected role concept has its major use in providing a "ballfield"in which investigations may be carried out. In any exact sense, we know little as yet about expected roles as wholistic entitites. But studying expected roles is both feasible and useful, and empirical information concerning expected roles will surely continue to appear.

ENVOI

At the beginning of Chapter Five we discussed five assumptions that are involved in extending the dramaturgical concept of role expectation to the real world. Two of these assumptions, *phenomenal equivalence* and *simple formation*, were re-examined at the end of Chapter Five. Let us now review the assumptions of *conformity, sanctioning*, and *correspondence*.

The assumption of *conformity* says that if someone holds an expectation it also follows that he or she will behave in conformity with it (if the expectation is for his or her own behavior) or will take action to ensure conformity in others (if the expectation is for the other). In brief, this assumption is probably a good beginning for theory, but it does not tell the whole story. Preferences seem likely to generate conformity in many conditions; norms and attributed norms may or may not do so, depending on the likelihood of consequences; beliefs probably generate conformity only under special conditions. Conforming responses should only appear when the person is capable of giving them and the environment allows such responses. Little seems to be known now about the conditions under which persons will attempt to influence others, nor is there much knowledge about the various strategies they might choose for attempting such influence. Nevertheless, considerable evidence has been amassed concerning the person's conforming responses, and on balance it appears that conceptions *are* likely to generate appropriate behavior in many situations. Research on conformity is sophisticated, and it appears that we are close to stating formal theories on this topic. Once such theories are available, we will know when to accept and when to reject assumptions about conformity.

The assumption of *sanctioning* states that object persons conform in their behavior to role expectations because of sanctioning they are exposed to or because they anticipate the imposition of sanctions from others supporting conformity. By now it should be clear that this assumption is not generally needed and may be in error for many forms of interaction. In saying this I am not asserting that sanctions are *never* useful. On the contrary, we have all been successful in controlling others through promising or imposing sanctions, and some of us spend considerable energy worrying about possible punishments or rewards that we are likely to receive for transgressions or achievements. Moreover, sanctioning characterized much of the pedagogy to which we were exposed during our early school years—which is one of the reasons why most of us hate mathematics. But is all behavior controlled by sanctions? On the contrary, some behavior responds to preferences (for which sanctions are largely irrelevant), some reflects physical or moral consequences, some is affected by environmental constraints, persuasion, or concern for another's welfare. In fact, sanctioning is one of the least civil ways we have of controlling one another, and I suspect that it tends to disappear in relationships of affection and love. Nevertheless, sanctions surely characterize the army, the prisons, the formal organization, and most relationships based on authority. Many role theorists are concerned with these latter and make legitimate assumptions about sanctions. But we must beware of extending these to other contexts!

The assumption of *correspondence* is even more questionable. There can be no doubt that citizens often assume consensus—often, if Newcomb (1947) is correct, on the barest evidence imaginable. The isolated anthropologist who has a limited budget with which to study a primitive tribe for the first time may also find it necessary to presume correspondence of expectations. Moreover, that assumption may be justified when the topic at issue is kinship, residence patterns, or tribal leadership. But the limits of this assumption are not yet known. Nor are the rest of us justified in making the assumption of correspondence when we do not have to make it. Subjects may or may not agree in expectations held; object persons may or may not exhibit uniform behavior; conceptions may or may not be accurate or veridical. Such conditions of noncorrespondence are likely to occur and are frankly more interesting to study than the dull condition of correspondence.

As we know, assumptions about correspondence are often made in functionalist theories of social integration. Moreover, correspondence is probably common in face-to-face interaction where persons have an opportunity to respond directly to one another's expectations. Correspondence is surely less likely in larger social systems, except for issues of conduct that are deemed crucial for the operation of the system. Roles and activities may (or may not) appear within the system, but when they do they are probably supported through other processes as well as through shared expectations. Thus, a more fruitful model for analyzing the social system would allow for "local" models of consensus and the "negotiation" of roles and activities. (We return to this question in Chapter Seven.)

A Phantom Propositional Theory

As critics have noted, role theory lacks formally stated, integrative propositions. Nevertheless, expectations (particularly conceptions) are advanced by role theorists to explain the appearance of roles. Moreover, expectations form the base for derived concepts that have generated much of the research that has appeared in this field. Surely role theorists have propositions in mind when giving expectations this central focus. Surely, also, we now have sufficient evidence to review those propositions. Herewith a brief, informal summary of the phantom propositions that I consider the core of role theory. What can we believe about conceptions, their origins, and their effects?

To give conceptions a central, explanatory focus suggests that persons hold thoughts in their minds about their own and others' actions. Those thoughts are presumed learned through appropriate experiences, and persons are presumably aware that they hold conceptions and can express them for us if asked. Since these thoughts are conscious, persons are also capable of contemplating and changing them if needed. As well, these thoughts lead persons to behave appropriately, to structure their responses intelligently, to cope. Stress is therefore given to rationality, to the person as a processor of information about the social world, to meaningful and responsible action.

This does not mean that all thoughts are identical. The role theorist presumes that a number of different conceptions may be held. Some are *preferences,* by which we mean feelings of pleasure or aversion associated with states of behavior. Some are *norms*—conclusions that one should or should not behave in a given way. (Norms are associated with consequences rather than with gratifications, although the person may be unclear in his or her thoughts about the matter. Consequences of concern may involve others or the person, may be physical or social in origin, or may involve concepts of morality and the deity.) Some are *beliefs* about the likelihood of behavior. Some are conceptions that are *attributed* to others. Moreover, each of these conceptions may be held for the person's own behaviors or may be held for the behaviors of others. Each may also be applied to individuals or to groups of persons, particularly to social positions.

Where do these conceptions come from? What leads a person to form conceptions? Several answers are suggested. For one, persons may form conceptions through their own experiences. The person who encounters a bitter taste when biting into a new food will likely form a negative preference for it. One may also form conceptions through observing the experience of others—through seeing another make a wry face upon tasting a new food. Conceptions may also be learned from the words of others—from hearing another warn us of the bad taste of a new food. Finally, if these were not sufficient, conceptions may also be developed through thoughtful reasoning. We may, for example, decide that a given food is likely to taste bad because of our knowledge of its ingredients or chemical composition.

It is likely, also, that we learn different conceptions from somewhat different experiences. Preferences seem likely to appear following personal experience, particularly experience that is proximal to the act of behaving. Norms are more likely to follow when behavior produces consequences or when others warn of consequences to follow. Beliefs seem more likely to result when one observes oneself or others behaving, or when one has time to reason thoughtfully about the functions of behavior. Attributed conceptions are more likely to appear when others report about their own thoughts or when those others are observed to behave. This listing suggests that more than one conception might be formed from a given experience, and in fact we must also assume that conceptions will be diffuse unless the person has a good reason to differentiate them. Thus, in the absence of contradicting events, a given experience might generate both a preference and a norm; a norm attributed to another will often be matched by a norm the person holds for him or herself, and so forth. On the other hand, when gratification and consequences are opposed, the person should form preferences and norms that are distinct. If another pressures me to do something I consider unwise, it is unlikely that the norm I attribute to that other will be matched by my own.

What does the person *do* when holding a conception? How do conceptions affect behaviors? Preferences may be considered intrinsically motivating, thus to produce appetitive or avoidance responses. In the case of preferences for one's own behavior, this means that the person should strive to engage in behaviors that are liked and to avoid behaviors that are disliked. When another's behaviors are at issue, the person should seek to influence the other to engage in liked behaviors and to avoid disliked ones. (How will such influence be exerted? As we know, various strategies may be employed depending on context and the identities of the person and the other.) In contrast, norms are motivating only when the person feels that consequences are likely. Thus, a person will also exhibit appetite or avoidance responses when holding a norm, but only if positive consequences are deemed likely for so doing or negative consequences for not so doing. (Among other things, this means that the person may use similar means for influencing another, whether that person holds a preference or a norm. But the reasons and conditions for exerting influence will be quite different.)

Beliefs are not generally motivating, therefore they have no simple implications for the person's behavior. Nevertheless, they provide contingencies affecting choice of action. To illustrate, should a person believe a desired behavior state can be reached, he or she is likely to strive for it. If the person believes that such a state cannot be reached, he or she is likely to despair and try to restructure thought. If another is deemed powerful, the person will be more concerned about sanctions the other may use than if the other is deemed weak.

Conceptions attributed to another are likely to generate responses predicated upon the assumption that the other will respond as if he or she were another person. Thus, the person anticipates that the other, also, will strive to engage in behaviors that are liked or approved and will avoid behaviors that are disliked or disapproved. Should the other be presumed to hold a preference or norm for the person, the other is also presumed likely to attempt to influence the person to conform. (This suggests that observations of attempted influence are a major source of evidence for the formation of attributed conceptions. Moreover, since the person has scant evidence from most such attempts for determining whether the other holds a preference or norm, the conceptions attributed will often be ambiguous.. Clearly, explaining our conceptions to one another is a good idea.)

Why, then, does our behavior as individuals tend toward consistency? Why do we exhibit roles? Because we have developed preferences, norms, and beliefs that tend to structure our behaviors over time; because our behaviors are constrained by contexts; because others bring patterns of influence to bear upon us; and because we attribute conceptions to those others. Why are the behaviors of those who are members of a social position somewhat similar? Why do positional roles appear? Because position members have tended to develop similar conceptions for their own behaviors through common experiences; because they enter similar contexts; because others bring similar patterns of influence to bear upon them; and because they attribute similar conceptions to others.

So much for uplift. As we also know, empirical support for this phantom, propositional theory is inadequate. I reserve the right to modify any or all of the above declarations of faith if they should be contradicted by evidence—and you should too.

Chapter Seven

The Analysis of Social Systems

"Stability," said the Controller, "stability. No civilization with-
out stability. No social stability without individual stability." His
voice was like that of a trumpet. Listening, they felt larger,
warmer.

—Aldous Huxley, Brave New World

This chapter concerns the use of role concepts for analyzing social systems. It focuses on the systematic units that make up our complex social world and on the role concepts that enable us to discuss those systems, their components, and their effects. Of necessity, its stance is sociological or anthropological. In answer to the question, "Wherein lies the *real* environment?" this chapter answers, "Within the social system." In response to the query, "Which came first, the system or the individual?" in this chapter we assert, "The system."[1] Basic to our concern here is the idea that much of our lives are played out within social contexts—families, gangs, offices, churches, schools, social clubs, factories, armies, political movements. Such contexts have predictable components and structure greatly the lives of those who participate in them. And, as we shall see, role concepts may be used for discussing such systems to good effect.

Given this orientation, a somewhat different posture will be adopted than has prevailed in earlier chapters. As readers are aware, those who have used role con-

[1] For contrasting answers to these questions, see Chapter Eight.

cepts for social system analysis have often found it convenient to build assumptions concerning sanctioning, consensus, accuracy, veridicality, or conformity to role expectations into their theories. This means that individuals have tended to disappear from their analyses, and one is tempted when reading their work to conclude that the social systems discussed are immutable juggernauts to which participants must accommodate in their behaviors. For example, one might read that a "social group is a set of two or more persons whose interaction is governed by shared norms." Such a definition appears simple until we ask ourselves how to handle cases when its assumptions about conformity and consensus are not met. What do we term a set of interacting persons whose behaviors are *not* governed by shared norms? Worse, are we even allowed to think about the behaviors of group members that violate norms?

Let us guard against such uses. Questionable assumptions need not be built into definitions of social systems, nor need the system be conceived as an immutable mold. Social systems not only structure constraint, they also structure opportunity. No social system can survive unless it provides for individual variation. Above all, if there is one thing invariant in our contemporary world it is that our social systems are changing. Whether control over these changes can remain in the hands of participants is moot. But we are shortsighted if we allow ourselves to build untenable assumptions concerning homogeneity or immutability into our discussions of social systems. As before, such assumptions will be kept to a minimum here.

It is difficult, however, to discuss social systems without making additional assumptions. As will be seen, two such assumptions will now be built into the system, assumptions concerning the *characteristicness* and *interdependence* of social system components. These two assumptions are discussed in the section that follows. Once these assumptions have been made, we take up formal definitions for the concepts of structure and social system.

Later sections of the chapter take up three types of structure and provide examples of social systems that are defined through structured components. As will be discovered, some social systems are defined through observable events such as roles, some through social positions, and some through expectations and other conceptual components. Each of these three sections begins with conceptual distinctions and then turns to social systems in which those concepts are applied. The chapter then closes with a discussion of theories of social system integration.

Social Systems and the Concept of Structure

We are all familiar with social systems. A nuclear family is a social system, but so is an orphanage, a bookmaking joint, a gang of delinquent boys, a metropolitan transportation system, a church mass, a preliterate community, a nation-state. What makes each of these phenomena a social system? What can such disparate events have in common that cause us to discuss them as examples of a common genus? In general, social systems exhibit two kinds of properties: they are composed of social elements, and those elements are structured.

We will examine these two properties in turn. Of what social elements may a social system be composed? Strikingly different answers have been given to this question by various theorists (Blau, 1975). Some theorists (for example, Homans, 1974; Katz & Kahn, 1966; or Levy, 1952) see social systems primarily as behavioral structures and devote their major energies to analyzing roles, activities, integration, contexts, and functions. Other theorists (Bredemeir & Stephenson, 1962; Dahrendorf, 1958) view social systems as assemblies of shared conceptual elements (such as role expectations) that tie people together in a joint definition of the situation. Nor do these two stances exhaust the possibilities. Barker considers social systems ("settings") to consist of both behavioral and physical components (Barker & Wright, 1955). Parsons and Shils (1951) assume that systems of social action involve behavioral and conceptual components, as well as a shared, symbolic culture. Some anthropologists (for example, White, 1949) stress not only behavioral and conceptual components for social systems, but also technological components. Indeed, White asserts that technology forms the ultimate constraint for both behaviors and conceptualizations—a thesis with which we are becoming more aware as we continue to uncover details of our ecological and energy crises. And so its goes.

None may doubt but that social systems "may" exhibit structural components such as these. However, one type of component appears crucial for defining the social system concept. Social systems are difficult to conceive without characteristic *behavioral* elements. (Football fields may constitute the characteristic venue for football games, but no game exists without running, passing, and kicking. A corporation cannot be said to have become a social system until its documents of incorporation have produced behaviors in its members.) Social systems are minimally characterized, then, by the appearance of structured behavioral components; they may be (and often are) characterized by other structured components as well.

So far so good, but what do we mean by *structure?* Here again is one of those wonderful words that is used for many purposes by role theorists and other social scientists. In the hands of various users, structure may connote the appearance of characteristic roles or role expectations, a fixed set of positions, a formal system of written regulations, a set of tasks that are collectively assumed or functions that are accomplished, or other presumed features of the social system. Such disparate uses are rooted in the history of social thought. Early functional analysts in sociology, such as Hobbes and Spencer, saw social systems as analogues of biological entities. By analogy, if the physiologist was able to find organic "structures" in the body (such as the liver), then surely the social analyst is also entitled to note and label the invariant, structural features of the social system with which he or she is concerned. Thus various characteristic features of each social system were noted or were termed "structured." But the analogy is a poor one. Elements of social structure are not grounded in a physical body whose components are largely invariant.

They are more likely to vary over time, their boundaries are more diffuse than those of biological structures, and (as we have noted elsewhere) the functions of a given social structure are more problematic.

Nonetheless, it remains true that at least some elements of a given social system form are structured, otherwise we would not recognize examples of that form as they appear. First, then, to say that the elements of a social system are **structured** means that they are *characteristic* of the system—using the term *characteristic* as it was used in Chapter Three. To say that social systems are structured is to assert that the typical system exhibits a characteristic (although not invariant) complement of behaviors, persons, contexts, functions, expectations, or what-have-you. Classrooms are structured in that they typically feature a teacher and several pupils, each of whom exhibit characteristic roles. Hospitals feature doctors, nurses, patients, orderlies, and administrators, each with characteristic roles—and as well a building, means of support, written rules for operation, and characteristic functions in the realm of health.

But more is denoted by structure than mere characteristicness. The classroom roles of teacher and pupils are not independent entities; to the extent that one of these elements varies, the other is likely to vary also. Thus, structural features of the social system are not only characteristic, they are also *interdependent*. As we know from Chapter Three, roles are interdependent when they are mutually facilitative or hindering of one another. We now extend this usage to other features of social systems. A social system is no adventitious collection of accidental elements. Rather, its characteristic components are to some extent locked together with bonds of interdependence.

Such uses are sufficient to enable a definition of the social system concept. For our purposes a **social system** will be said to comprise a structured set of behavioral elements—or, in more familiar terms, a characteristic set of interdependent roles. In addition, most social systems also feature other structured elements that are associated with its roles, such as a complement of positions, shared expectations for the behaviors of members, functions that are characteristically performed within the system, and the like. The latter do not always appear, however, nor are they required for us to recognize the appearance of a social system form.

So much for the problem of what a social system *is*. As defined, the concept of social system is an abstract one, and is generally unfamiliar to those who have not studied sociology or anthropology. It is possible to provide examples of social systems in our society with which participants are not generally familiar, and some social scientists delight in doing so. For example, Eric Berne (1964) describes the "Game of Alcoholic" as a social system, although few of us would have heretofore considered this activity form in such a light. However, most discussions of social systems make use of examples that are familiar to us, thus those discussions usually deal with such things as games, communities, families, or organizations rather than social system forms that may not be familiar to readers. In accepting this restriction the social analyst generates a problem that is not always recognized. To state this problem simply, readers already have preconceptions concerning the nature of games, communities, families, and organizations, and those preconceptions may not match the features of these systems the analyst wishes to discuss. What does the analyst do to meet this problem? In most cases he or she simply "defines" the system so as to focus the attention of readers on those elements in which the analyst is interested and hopes that readers are sufficiently tolerant to abandon their preconceptions in favor of his or her definition. Such procedures lead to chaos, for eight different texts may present eight different definitions for the "Family," despite the fact that they are all presumably talking about a social system form with which we are reasonably familiar. Moreover, research using one of these definitions may be incommensurate with research using the others.

How to solve this problem? Let us begin by recognizing that as long as we choose to discuss social systems that are familiar to readers, the "definition" of those systems will lie with the public rather than with the analyst. Analysts may convince themselves and their students that the family *is* what they have defined it to be, but as long as analysts choose to speak of a system denoted by that familiar term, "family," most readers will persist in thinking that they knew what a family was all along. Best we should find out how members of the public view the family. Lacking this information, better we should adopt the definition for family that makes the fewest assumptions. Accordingly, I shall adopt a solution such as that used in Chapter Four, where similar problems were faced in defining concrete social positions. As long as we are to discuss concrete examples of social systems, I shall assume that the systems in question are defined by *foundations* of structured elements that are recognized among persons concerned with those systems. Such foundations may or may not be composed of behavioral elements. Thus, although all social systems will be assumed to have behavioral components that are structured, in some cases the foundational definition for a given social system will focus on other things than behaviors.

This solution implies that I cannot provide an adequate review of findings from research on the "family" in this chapter, nor can I do justice to theoretical debates concerning the nature of the family, the organization, or other social system forms. To do either of these tasks would require that I review in detail the assumptions that are made by others, a task that would greatly expand the chapter.[2] Instead, this chapter focuses on the discussion of social systems using role concepts that make minimal assumptions and on the interesting implications of such a stance.

In sum, for our purposes a social system *is* characterized by structured behaviors, it *may* also feature other structured elements, and concrete examples of social

[2] To illustrate, recent reviews of assumptions and findings from research on the "classroom" have constituted monographs (see Dunkin & Biddle, 1974; or Rosenshine, 1971).

systems will be *defined* through foundations of structured elements that may or may not include behaviors but that make minimal assumptions.

OVERT STRUCTURE

> *A camel is a horse assembled by a committee.*
> *(Anon.)*

We turn now to discussions of elements that may be structured within social systems. For convenience, we begin with **overt structure**—structured elements that can be observed directly. Several such elements are discussed in this section. In addition, some social systems are also defined by foundations that involve overt elements. Examples of such systems include small groups, communities, and societies (which are reviewed shortly)—and cocktail parties, riots, lynchings, campus confrontations, pedestrian traffic, office parties, political gatherings, kava-drinking ceremonies, the British pub, and encounter groups (which are not). In each of these cases, the term with which we identify the social system form is associated with a pattern of overt events with which we are familiar and which enables us to recognize examples of that form when we encounter them.

Although exceptions may be found, most social systems that are defined by overt structure are not planned; rather they occur "naturally" within a given society in response to pressures that are indigenous to that society. In the usage of Sumner (1906), such systems are "crescive" and appear within all known societies, preliterate as well as urban. Such systems evolve as a result of environmental challenges or to accommodate the foibles of forceful persons, and in many cases a given system form has been in existence for some years before participants become aware of it. In time, however, participants tend to develop structured conceptions for such systems which, in turn, help to stabilize its behavioral components. In literate societies such systems may also develop structured elements in the form of symbolic records that enshrine their histories or set forth rules for the conduct of their members.

This does not mean that we are always aware of the overt components of a social system. Even simple social systems normally evidence a complexity of roles, activities, and functions that is only vaguely understood, and the more complex the system, the less likely we are to be aware of its overt details. Such knowledge is useful. For example, the roles now characteristic of a given social system may be stressful, dangerous, or immoral. Accordingly, field studies of the overt components of social systems are increasing in popularity and have recently led to the appearance of "systems analysis" as a field.

Components of Overt Structure

ROLES AND ACTIVITIES

Let us now consider some of the components of overt structure, beginning with roles and activities. By definition, all social systems exhibit roles, and in most such systems these roles are also assembled into activities. For example, it is characteristic of American families that meals are cooked, beds are made, lawns are mowed, and decisions are taken following discussion. Moreover, roles such as these are clustered together to form activities. Dinner is cooked and then eaten, and discussion often takes place during the latter.

As we know from Chapter Three, a *role* constitutes those behaviors that are characteristic of persons in a context, whereas an *activity* is defined as a temporary but characteristic co-occurrence of interdependent roles. By such definitions, an activity is in and of itself a simple social system form. However, most of the entities we think of as social systems are large enough or have sufficient duration to subtend several characteristic activities. Within the hospital, for example, a number of characteristic activities appear such as operations for appendicitis, preparation of patients' bills, and monthly meetings of the hospital board. Each of these activities is, in turn, composed of characteristic roles. In this sense, roles are the smallest unit of behavioral structure with which the analyst is normally concerned, activities are intermediate in size, and the system itself is the overarching unit.

It is sometimes assumed (by other authors) that the structured roles of social systems are always specified in role expectations that are shared among system participants or are set forth for participants in the form of symbolic records. Such assumptions are silly. Some roles (or activities) may be specified in expectations, whereas others may not be recognized at all in expectations or are even proscribed. Organizational rules, for example, normally specify roles for productive behavior (which are followed), have little or nothing to say about behavior during coffee breaks (although characteristic activities occur at these times), and may set forth obsolete and unworkable rules that are regularly ignored by employees except during work-to-rule strikes.

It is also sometimes assumed that the structured roles of social systems are always those needed to accomplish tasks assumed, or specific functions accomplished, for the system. This is also silly. Most long-standing or complex social systems develop a variety of roles and activities, many of which are independent of task or function. The baseball club, for example, develops any number of activities in addition to baseball games: father-and-son dinners, promotional events, personnel-management procedures, recreational activities, and the like. Many of these have no effect on the production of a winning baseball team; others interfere with it.

Several variables have been suggested for the activity components of a social system. For example, a **primary activity** (or **relationship**) is one in which interaction is face-to-face, is frequently repeated among the same actors, and involves many behavioral facets. **Secondary activities** are those in which participants are separated from one another and must communicate via hearsay or by mechanical means, in which interaction takes place among persons recognized as positional members rather than as individuals, and in which interaction is confined to a limited sphere of behavioral facets. The classic example of primary activity occurs in the family (Cooley, 1902), although long-standing work and recreational groups are often considered to exhibit primary activities too. Secondary activities are more characteristic of the organization, the urban community, and the large society.[3] Other activity distinctions will be discussed later on.

PHYSICAL CONTEXTS

Many, but by no means all, social systems are associated with elements of the physical environment. Some systems appear only within a single location or class of locations. Others are associated with specific equipment or facilities. Participants are often aware of these environmental associations, and some environmental units may actually be used to provide a foundation for defining a given system. For example, the social system of Jefferson Junior High School may be defined as the structured events taking place within and around a single school building. Let us now examine some of the basic concepts used for expressing physical structure.

In Chapter Two a general term was introduced, *context*, that refers to any condition or state of affairs that is found to affect behavior. This concept may easily be extended for use in social system analysis. To say that a **context** is **structured** for a given social system form means that it appears characteristically with other elements of that system and is found to affect one or more of the roles of that system. Such usage covers a lot of territory. As we know, some contexts may consist of behaviors. Others may consist of time or a complement of persons or position members. However, some contexts constitute units of the nonbehavioral environment, and to these latter—*structured physical contexts*—we now turn.

The distinction most often made for physical contexts is that between *settings* and *artifacts*. As the terms are commonly used, settings are larger and more stable units of environment that tend to enclose behavior and are not themselves transformed. In contrast, artifacts are smaller and less stable units that may be moved or transformed by behaviors. Although this distinction seems to be obvious, it is often difficult to apply because the same physical features may be a setting for one activity and an artifact in another. To illustrate, for several days before "the big game" workmen are busy preparing the stadium. Bleachers are erected or repaired, the playing surface is manicured, press facilities are cleaned and checked out. Comes the day of the game, however, and these physical features become a fixed context

---

[3] The primary–secondary distinction is also sometimes applied to social systems (as in the German distinction between *Gemeinschaft* and *Gesellschaft*, see Tönnies, 1887).

in which the game is played. The artifacts have become a setting—particularly the bleachers. Within a given social system, however, some physical units are likely to be structured as settings, others as artifacts. Let us consider each of these concepts formally.

For our purposes a **setting** will be defined as a structured physical context for one or more associated roles that is *not* characteristically relocated or deformed by those roles. (Like the chemical catalyst, the setting is an unmoved mover.) So defined, a setting might either be large or small. Some settings are tiny indeed. Consider the structured events that suddenly appear when a small sample of fissionable material is lost in shipping from one part of the country to another. Specially equipped search teams spring into action, including some that are airborne. Warnings are given to the public. Activities of the police, the national guard, and other organizations are set into motion. Responsibilities for coordination are assumed by one or more federal agencies, and so forth. And all for one small container of a highly dangerous, toxic substance. Most settings are larger than this example, however, and many constitute venues in which roles are characteristically found. Some of these latter were "designed" for a specific activity form, such as sports arenas, shopping centers, or filling stations. In other cases, certain locations may be associated with a given class of roles or activities, although we may be largely unaware of the fact. (We return to this latter case later on when discussing the community.)

By way of contrast, an **artifact** constitutes a structured physical context for one or more associated roles that *is* characteristically relocated or deformed by those roles.[4] Artifacts are not incidental to the activities of a social system, nor are they independent environmental stimuli. Rather, their appearance, relocation, and deformation are intrinsic to activity forms, and without them those forms would be difficult to accomplish. For this reason, artifacts are often used by archeologists to indicate the types of activities characteristic of a prehistoric community. Like settings, artifacts may be large or small. Among examples of large artifacts we might consider the Pyramid of Cheops or the Grand Coulee Dam. Among smaller examples, consider tools for the surgical manipulation of chromosomes. Such examples suggest that manipulation of artifacts is always intended within the social system. Such is not the case, of course. Artifact use may be inadvertent, and transformation of artifacts may produce poisonous wastes whose effects we become aware of only after some years of pollution.

The fact that settings and artifacts may be structured does not mean that this is true for all social systems. Simple systems, such as rituals to be performed when greeting or leaving another, may appear in nearly any setting and require no artifacts at all. The more complex the social system, however, the more likely it is to be associated with settings and artifacts. This does not mean that these contexts are invariant. Limited variation in setting and artifact characteristics is no less likely than

---

[4] By this definition, the characteristic relocation or deformation of the artifact is also a function of the social system.

variation in the other structured components of social systems, and variations in these contexts are likely to affect other components of the system.

FUNCTIONS

It would be difficult to imagine a social system that did not accomplish functions. The management conference makes decisions; the assembly line produces refrigerators; the community distributes goods and services for its members. Even simple social systems produce satisfaction, alarm, or fatigue for their participants.

It is useful to review briefly what is meant, and is not meant, by our use of the term *function* (see Chapter Two). What is meant is that behaviors may be observed to have objective effects, functions, which can be seen by the researcher and which are often (although not always) understood by the participants. Should these effects be perceived by the latter, we will term them *social functions*. We may also distinguish between those functions that were intended (*manifest functions*) and those that were not (*latent functions*). What is not meant is to equate functions with goals or tasks. As we shall see shortly, these latter may also appear within some social systems, but many functions appear that are not recognized by system participants or that violate the needs or tasks shared by members. Some social clubs, for example, adopt constitutions with but limited objectives—only to discover, at a later stage of their development, that they engage in activities whose functions are irrelevant or antithetical to the intent of their constitutions. Functions may be associated with roles, activities, and social systems. If the latter, they may occur rarely or may, in contrast, be characteristic of the social system studied. If characteristic, we will say that such **functions** are **structured** for that system.

Many suggestions have been given for the analysis of functions. Basic distinctions may be made between functions that have the form of (other) behavioral states and functions that are conditions of the physical environment. To give an example of the former, the functions of "coaching" usually include the improvement of a performance by the client (Strauss, 1959) [B&T, Selection 43], whereas the efforts of those who are building a home are more likely to result in a physical product. It has been suggested by several commentators (notably Katz & Kahn, 1966; and Rhea, 1964) that social systems may be sorted into those whose functions are largely concerned with *processing people* (for example, social systems concerned with education, medicine, human transportation, or entertainment) and those concerned with *products* (such as factories or newspapers).

Another implication of this distinction lies in the possibility of analyzing *functional sequences*. When functions appear in the form of (subsequent) beavioral states, it is possible for these latter, in turn, to have additional functions. The analyst may discover for complex social systems that long, structured sequences of functions appear. In the basketball game, for example, sequences of behavior appear in the form of "plays" on the part of the offensive team, which are only interrupted when one of the team members fails to perform his or her role or opponents intrude into the system. It is also possible for environmental functions to appear within a functional sequence. The journeyman's assistant characteristically performs a continual round of roles that have such functions for the carpenter, painter, or plumber who is his (or her) supervisor.

Another way to classify functions is to differentiate those that are "requisite" for the survival or maintenance of the social system. For our purposes, a *functional requisite* may be defined as a state of affairs whose attainment or maintenance is necessary for the survival or continued operation of the social system. For example, social systems that persist must make provision for the recruitment, replacement, and socializing of new members. If they cannot perform this function, as their old members die or drop out of the system, the system itself will wither.

As defined here, functional requisites cover a broad range of events, from activities and roles through environmental conditions, and even the maintenance of conceptual structure. For this reason the concept of functional requisite is sloppy, and most of the lists of functional requisites that have bee proposed for social systems are but ad hoc collections of insights (Aberle, Cohen, Davis, Levy, & Sutton, 1950; Levy, 1952; Parsons & Shils, 1951) [B&T, Selection 27]. However, insightful classifications of functional requisites based on explicit theory can be found in several places (see Bredemeier & Stephenson, 1962; Buckley, 1967; Katz & Kahn, 1966).

Which brings up yet another point to make concerning functions. Schemes for functional analysis are used not only for classifying the roles and activities of the system, but also for making an analysis of the place of a given social system within a larger context. To illustrate this, let us return to the functional requisite of member socialization. One of the major reasons for conducting the public school is the socializing of young persons, thus this social system serves the function of member socialization within the larger society. But new members must also be socialized into the public school, thus new teachers normally meet together for a preschool workshop before the school year opens. As can be seen, the phrase "member socialization" describes two quite different functions, one internal and the other external to the school.

The confusion between the *internal* and *external* functions of the social system illustrates a trap characteristic of functional analysis. It seems unlikely that the functional requisites of the small social system will be identical with those of the larger social system that encloses it. (What is good for General Motors may *not* be good for the country.) And yet, functional analysts are sometimes guilty of suggesting that social systems persist only because they have positive consequences for the society. In fact, many social systems appear to persist accidentally or because they serve the needs of their participants—despite the fact that their consequences in the society are dangerous or disastrous. The Mafia is surely a social system, but only a madman would argue that it has positive consequences for the society at large.

In summary, social systems may exhibit a variety of structured features that are overtly observable. Three of these have been discussed: behavioral aspects (roles and activities), physical contexts (settings and artifacts), and functions accomplished by the system. Of these, we require the appearance of structured and interdependent roles to establish the existence of a social system. Contexts and functions may or may not appear within a given social system, although all three types of elements are sometimes used by lay persons (or social scientists) to define a given system form.

Social Groups

We now consider several social systems whose definitions are based on overt structure. We begin with social groups. As noted previously, the term *group* has connotations beyond those of simply a set of elements or population of persons. When we say that persons are formed into a group, visions of frequent interaction, we-feeling, mutual commitment, sharing, and primary relationships float through our heads (*vide* Mary McCarthy). To use all of these ideas in a definition is unacceptable, for some may not characterize one or more "groups" we choose to study. What, then, is the minimal condition we would accept for a definition of the concept of social group? Clearly a group involves more than one person. But two or more persons do not constitute a group unless they interact. By minimal definition, then, a **group** (or **social group**) constitutes a set of two or more persons who are linked through interaction.

The concept of interaction is easily defined as a form of behavioral structure. We recall from Chapter Two that persons are able to behave in such ways that they affect other persons. Let us now define **interaction** to be a condition existing between two or more persons such that each exhibits one or more behaviors which affects the other(s) during the period of our observation. To extend this definition to sets of three or more persons, we require merely that *all* pairs of persons of the set interact with each other. A social group, thus, is defined and identified in terms of behavioral structure. Since the number of interactive pairs in an N-person group is $[N(N-1)]/2$, it is easy to see that the defining condition that "all" pairs must interact becomes progressively more difficult to meet with increasing group size, and most social groups are in fact small entities. For this reason, the condition of interaction normally does not apply to extended social systems (such as formal organizations) which are more weakly connected.

Some authors assume that social groups appear only among those who meet on a face-to-face basis, but this is neither a necessary nor a sufficient condition. Two persons may be working in a room; if either appears oblivious of the other's behavior no group exists, even when the other is directing his or her behavior toward the person we are observing. In addition, given such mechanical aids as the telephone, radio, or television, groups of persons may be assembled who interact, even though they are separated by many miles. However, the condition of interaction seems to develop in most face-to-face relationships that persist over time.

Examples of naturally occurring groups are easy to find. The nuclear family constitutes a group when it asssembles around the dinner table, the work group in the factory, the service club during its weekly noontime luncheon, the classroom, the political rally, the encounter group—all meet the defining criterion of interaction. And yet these several examples exhibit a wide range of social positions, roles, and functions. Thus we discover that the defining criterion for social groups, though strict, leaves many aspects of structure unspecified, and that many different kinds of events are collected together under the term *group*.

A number of variables have been suggested for differentiating among groups. Two of these have been mentioned previously: number of participants and physical propinquity. Another is the "age" of the group in terms of the number of hours its members have interacted or the frequency with which the group has assembled. A special type of "young" group is one that is composed of strangers who are brought together for some specific task. In such a group persons neither know one another personally, nor are they usually aware of the positions each occupies within the general society. This type of group is rare in the real world—with the possible exception of the trial jury or the therapy group—but it has figured extensively in experimental studies within social psychology.

One of the basic processes that can be observed with a "young" group is the gradual differentiation of its behavioral structure. Bales (1950) [B&T, Selection 29], Sherwood and Walker (1960), Slater (1955), Marwell (1968), and others (see Tuckman, 1965) have demonstrated that within such groups there is a gradual appearance of differentiated roles. Several studies have suggested that two roles predominate in groups: a role focusing on "task" performance, and another concerned with "social emotional" support (Bales, 1958; Bales & Slater, 1955) [B&T, Selection 29]. Moreover, these roles tend to be performed by different persons, and role conflict may be experienced when one person attempts to provide both task leadership and support (Hutchins & Fiedler, 1960; Seeman, 1953). Other studies have identified a third group role—that of the "joker" (Cloyd, 1964a; Davis, Gebhard, Huson, & Spaeth, 1961). Still other studies have suggested additional roles, some of which may reflect the type of group studied (Cloyd, 1964b; Redl, 1942; Thrasher, 1927; White & Lippitt, 1960). What produces such differentiated roles? In part, these appear to reflect roles that participants perform in other contexts (Davis *et al.*, 1961; Freese & Cohen, 1973; Strodbeck & Mann, 1956) or general role expectations associated with age, sex, or social class (Maas, 1954; Torrance, 1954a). But in part, also, they appear in response to tasks that are accepted by the group or problems that develop through group interaction.

Most real-life social groups disband and then reassemble at regular intervals, and "older" groups are characterized by their own conceptual structures. The more group members interact, presumably, the more accurate their beliefs about one another will be, the more likely they are to develop a sense of identification with the group, the firmer will be their shared norms for group members, the more they will like one another (and dislike outsiders), and so on (Sherif, 1956). This bundle of ideas is sometimes summarized by the term *cohesiveness,* which denotes the tendency of the group to stick together as an entity in the face of threats or other challenges from without (Festinger, Back, Schachter, Kelley, & Thibaut, 1950). Identification with the group, collective commitment to the tasks taken on by the group, positive cathexes for group members, a sense of collective identity or "we-feeling," and various other factors reflect cohesiveness—whereas deviancy by group members, the attraction of other activities and persons, punishment for deviancy, and the like all tend to lower it. The interesting fact is that many of these variables associated with cohesiveness exhibit reversible relationships with one another, thus group identification facilitates mutual liking of members and vice versa. To the extent that they exhibit cohesiveness, then, and to the extent that the phenomena we associated with this term affect the behaviors of these members, "older" social groups are different kinds of entities altogether from the artificial assemblies of subjects found in experimental social psychology.

Groups are ubiquitous, malleable, and have the potential for changing a person's habitual roles and self-concept. Given these latter properties, groups are often used in therapy, and "encounter group" experiences have been argued to have a number of positive effects. Moreover, some enthusiasts have claimed that group roles and processes appear to mirror the roles and processes of more complex social systems, that findings from research on groups may apply directly to communities or organizations. Such claims should be examined closely. "Encounter group" experiences are known to have negative as well as positive effects (Lieberman, Yalom, & Miles, 1973), and it seems unlikely that the ontogeny of social groups resembles the phylogeny of larger systems in which interaction is no longer face-to-face.

In summary, then, social groups are defined by a specific form of activity—interaction. Most groups disband and reassemble at regular intervals. Groups may or may not exhibit role and positional differentiation and a conceptual structure, but each of these becomes more likely as the group ages. Social groups may be found in many contexts and are often imbedded within more complex social systems. Much research has been carried out on the roles, functions, and other properties of social groups, as is indicated by the mammoth bibliographies of Hare (1962, 1976) and Raven (1961, *et seq.*).   J. H. Davis (1969), Hare (1962, 1976), R. D. Mann (1959), McGrath and Altman (1966), Raven and Rubin (1976), and Shaw (1971) provide useful summaries of knowledge concerning this social system form.

Communities

The term *community* is used in at least three senses in contemporary social science. The first is that shared characteristics, interests, or sentiments—a community consisting of those alike in some fashion (the black community, the Jewish community, etc.). Communities in this first sense are merely shared identities and have been discussed as such throughout the text. Communities, however, may also consist of persons and roles that are physically compact in space. Finally, communities may be built around shared patterns of interaction and identification. Let us discuss these latter two concepts.

Earlier, the concept of *setting* was defined as a structured environmental context for one or more roles that is not characteristically relocated or deformed by those roles. As we know, many settings constitute places or venues within the Euclidean three-dimensional space inhabited by ourselves and our behaviors. Let us term these latter **locations**. As a rule, the boundaries of a location must be set statistically, for the density of roles-within-places will be but a relative thing. Within our society, morning activities—such as getting out of bed, washing, shaving, brushing one's teeth, getting dressed, and so on—are more likely to occur within the home or hotel than they are in the school, church, or downtown street corner. But however unlikely the event, if we observe long enough sooner or later we will find some demented soul who brushes his (or her) teeth or changes from his pajamas on the street corner, so we must use statistical criteria to establish the boundaries of those locations wherein the roles we are concerned with are dense. By the same token, if a particular role is not associated with any place but is instead spread evenly around, there is no location associated with it. Locations are physically compact when compared with the entire space in which they are found.

Since various grounds exist for which roles may be differentiated from one another, various types of locations may also be recognized. It is possible for locations to be *person differentiated* (teachers do not normally appear in police stations, whereas policemen are not often found within classrooms), *activity differentiated, functionally differentiated,* and so forth. Locations may also be characterized by artifacts or other environmental cues that enable actors to recognize them or carry out the roles with which they are typically associated.

Now let us return to the concept of community. In simplest terms, a **community** consists of a population of persons and a location that is the locus of some associated subset of their roles. By convention, the usual criterion used for defining community is that of "residential activities." Moreover, this preference is reinforced by laws that assign primacy to "residence" for the purpose of establishing voting rights, taxation liabilities, and the like. But work activities, recreational activities, and even functional classifications for roles have occasionally been used for establishing community boundaries. These various definitions have given rise to a vocabulary of community types—residential communities, recreational communities, and so forth.

Until this century it would not have been necessary to differentiate between residential, work, and recreational communities. Primitive communities and European and American communities of earlier centuries constituted but a single location in which nearly all of the roles carried on by residents were to be found. Given modern forms of transportation, however, residential locations provide only a portion of the needs of citizens who commute from their residences to work, engage in recreation, educate themselves, or meet other needs. Thus, the modern city features a variety of locations wherein portions of the role structure are carried on. The concentric zone theory of Park and Burgess (1921), for example, suggested that at the center of the metropolis one finds the high-rise buildings in which labor the leaders of commerce, around them are found circles of slum housing, heavy industry, and so on, while scattered toward the perimeter of the region appear educational locations, recreational locations, and other venues for specialized roles. Even this picture is incomplete, however, since modern societies require us to travel great distances to carry out some of our roles, and there are few communities these days that provide all of the needs of their citizens.

In the sense defined above, communities throughout the Western world are similar in both their roles and locational structures. Most authors who discuss community roles have used a functional analysis—terming the differentiated activities of the community **institutions**. For examples, many communities exhibit institutions concerned with education, law enforcement, decision making, distribution of goods, maintenance activities, and so forth (Friedenberg, 1966). When communities are small, a single actor may participate from time to time in roles from various institutions—as when the fire company is manned by volunteers. But with increasing size these institutions tend to become more complex and to be personed by specialists only. As a rule, then, the larger community offers a wider variety of more specialized institutions, but fewer demands are placed upon citizens to participate in the large city. This conundrum explains both why it is that persons are tempted to move to the city and why they are ambivalent about remaining there. It also tends to hold for other social system forms, such as larger schools (Barker & Gump, 1964).

Two institutions have seemed to fascinate community scholars more than any others—those of decision making and social class. A number of studies (for examples, Hunter, 1953; or Lynd & Lynd, 1929, 1937) have shown that community decision making may be controlled by a small group of powerful persons who manipulate the superficial forms of democracy either for their own benefit or for what they conceive to be the benefit of the community. (On the other hand, somewhat different persons appear to be community "leaders," depending on the criteria one uses for judging leadership—Freeman, Fararo, Bloomberg, & Sunshine, 1963). Other studies (Hollingshead, 1949; Warner, Meeker, & Eells, 1949) have concentrated on the social class structures of communities and have shown that subsets of the community population persist who have differential access to desiderata and exhibit quite different roles within the community. (We return to the topic of social class in the next section.)

Good evidence concerning community roles is hard to gather, given the problems of conducting formal behavior observation in field settings. Most community studies have depended on participant observation and interviews for their data, thus their findings may be biased. In addition, anthropologists who have done consider-able field work in communities abroad have often focused their attention on the enfolding society rather than on the community per se. Perhaps the best exceptions to these generalizations are to be found in the work of Roger Barker and his associ-ates (Barker, 1963, 1968; Barker & Schoggen, 1973; Barker & Wright, 1955). These investigators developed methods for studying community roles and a host of facets for expressing role content, but to date their work has been confined to small communities.

So far we have defined the concept of community in terms of a single criterion —role density. This does not help us much when our task is that of differentiating regions within a metropolis. When is Hyde Park a community and when is it merely a locality? Are block councils representative of community spirit? Is it possible to build primary relationships into the urban setting through functional equivalents of the long-lost total community? If roles such as those of residence are widely dif-fused within a vast region, and the individual has but minimal participation in deci-sion making among millions, that person may feel lonely, isolated, and helpless in his or her battle to control the environment of the city.

This leads us to a second definition of the community. Let us begin with a community defined as before—a set of persons who share roles, some of the latter also associated with a location. Let us now also specify that the location be physi-cally compact in two senses: (*a*) that it be constituted of a single, contiguous set of places; and (*b*) that it be small enough that its members can get from any point to any other point in it in a short time using some form of transportation that brings people face-to-face—usually by walking. Finally, let us establish some means for communicating within this location, a socially recognized system for interacting: that is open to all who wish to participate in it; that meets regularly; that is known to exist; and that constitutes a social group when it does assemble. Under these con-ditions I shall term the persons, roles, location, and interaction system as a **local community**.

The concept of local community is relatively new and has sprung from citizens' felt needs for regaining control within the anomic, urban city. At least two theories have been suggested for viewing the local community, the first expressing the no-tion that local communities can be utilized for organizing social action to change or disrupt existing (inequitous) institutions within the larger community (Alinsky, 1946), the latter suggesting that local communities can serve the person by provid-ing him or her an opportunity for identification, education, and collective participa-tion with others in community problem solving (W. W. & L. J. Biddle, 1965). These two viewpoints reflect differences in the theory of social integration, to which we return at the end of the chapter. There can be no doubt, however, that it is difficult for the individual to contend with the vast problems of megalopolis. And new sources of identification and participation—local communities, professional associations, volunteer associations, and others—will have to be developed to meet the needs for integration and control within our increasingly complex society (Goode, 1957; Gusfield, 1976).

In summary, then, communities are assembled of persons whose roles occupy at least one location. Once upon a time our residential, work, recreational, and other roles all occupied the same location, which constituted a total community for its members. However, today a given population occupies various locations, hence lives in many communities, depending on the roles we choose to examine. But commutation has its price, and urban residents complain of loss of control and a lack of primary relations in the big city. As a result, some urban dwellers have attempted to set up local communities within the metropolis that consist of a (residential) location and an interaction system that provides them both primary relationships and some control over their environment. All communities exhibit role and positional differentiation, and most analysts have associated these with the functions accomplished by community roles—terming such associations institutions. Those who live in small communities tend to be involved in many institutions, whereas those from larger cities play more specialized roles in a narrower range of institutions. Two institutions—decision making and social class—have attracted more attention to date than most others, although formal observation of community roles is hard to conduct.

Societies

Societies and communities are similar to one another and are sometimes confused by both the social scientist and the layman. Both involve propinquity, and in both it is presumed that some form of common interests tie together the fabric of social life. Nevertheless, the concept of community usually focuses on propinquity itself, whereas societies are normally differentiated from one another not because they are compact but rather because they are culturally distinct.

Let us convert this latter distinction into a definition. Assume that one has isolated a population of persons who share one or more unique elements of structure. The elements they share might involve behaviors, conceptions, the use of symbols, or any other structural components. By definition, such persons will be more alike one another in the structural elements they share than they are alike their near neighbors. Let us then term the structures they share a **culture**, and the population of persons who share that culture a **society**.

This is a broad definition and suggests that many different criteria may be used for establishing the boundaries of a society—roles, activities, artifacts, functions, beliefs, norms, values, or whatnot. For example, by this definition Germans and Frenchmen constitute different societies because they speak a different language.

But southerners and Yankees are also different societies becasue they have different accents, ditto blacks and whites in America, children and adults, and so on. Although the concepts of society and culture are indeed used in this vague sense in the vernacular, we usually think of these terms as applying to groups of people who are physically compact or to nationality groups. Let us therefore extend the definition of society slightly so as to get rid of trivial examples.

Let a **compact society** consist of a population of persons meeting simultaneously the criteria for both society and community; that is, for whom a set of roles exist, forming part of their behavioral culture, that are performed within a limited location. Although this second definition appears restrictive, it still does not specify that the boundaries of the compact location and behaviaral culture must coincide. For example, within a single city a black and white culture may coexist. One judges the appearance of a black society, however, only when blacks have at least one location that is "their own"; i.e., Harlem. Another example is that of the Jews and Israel. Since Jews now have a homeland, they constitute a compact society, although many of them are found elsewhere. If we further restrict the definition so that the boundaries of society, culture, and territory coincide, let us term the resulting concept a **national society.**

Great reification has been attached to the concept of society. Race and ethnicity may be decried, social class by deplored, religion be seen as an "opiate of the masses," and family, kinship, organizations, games, and associations be viewed as conveniences—but most social scientists seem to accept without question the idea that the society forms a significant context to which we *must* accommodate in our behaviors. Is this reification justified? Do societies have the determinative impact on behavior we often assume?

In support of this assumption, there can be no doubt that national societies may differ from one another in literally thousands of ways. When we enter another country we may be surprised, delighted, or shocked to discover a wide range of new roles we had never before considered possible. Somehow, the differences between ourselves and Thais, Italians, or Ugandans seem to involve more realms of life than do the differences between Democrats and Republicans, men and women, or those from different regions of the country. Moreover, roles within any given society appear to be interdependent and to proceed from assumptions widely held within that society concerning the appropriate ways of solving problems. Nor are those roles adventitious. Most societies feature institutions that are concerned with socialization, religion, the maintenance of order, the allocation of goods and services, and so forth. Thus, societies tend to be similar in the functions they accomplish for their citizens, although the roles and activities with which these functions are accomplished may be unique. Finally, it also appears that societies tend to follow evolutionary sequences in their development (White, 1959). As they do so, the "evolutionary stage" to which a society has progressed appears to constrain forms for the constituent social systems (such as families) found in that society.

On the negative side, modern societies also exhibit great variation in the structural forms appearing within them. To some extent factory workers (or students, or doctors) are more similar to their counterparts in neighboring societies than they are to those in different occupations within the same society. One wonders, also, to what extent our idea that societies are important is merely a reflection of the fact that certain people are found to speak a language that is different from their neighbors. Anthropologists sometimes make the convenient assumption that those sharing a language are ipso facto members of a common society, but this assumption appears tenable only when other roles played by those persons are interdependent and distinct from the roles played by others elsewhere. The fact is that we do not yet know much about which roles are distinct and which shared across a broad range of societies (however, see Aberle, 1961; and Murdock, 1937) [B&T, Selection 30]. Modern societies (like modern cities) are becoming more interdependent, and it is more difficult to believe in societal boundaries when they are regularly breached by commerce or travel by citizens. Perhaps the day will come when the boundaries of our political, economic, educational, recreational, and order-maintaining regions no longer coincide—in which case the concept of national society will have become obsolescent. (Something like this seems to have appeared in Europe with the formation of the Common Market.)

Many variables have been suggested for differentiating societies, perhaps the most pervasive of which is a continuum stretching from the primitive, preliterate, localized *folk society* to the vast, mechanized, literate *urban civilization* (Redfield, 1930, 1941). In most discussions of this continuum, the prototype of the folk society is that of the isolated and self-sufficient community, whereas that of the urban civilization is a Western European country. Urban civilizations offer significant advantages to their members, such as a longer life span, modern forms of communication and transportation, and that cultural universal—Coca Cola. Most of the world's people opt for urbanization when given a chance. Nevertheless, urban civilizations offer a life style that is clearly different from that of folk societies, and some of the characteristics of this style may not be unmixed blessings.

1. The folk society offers only a few social positions and roles, whereas the urban civilization provides uncountably many ways of identifying oneself and of occupying one's time. Members of a folk society can hold the complete inventory of positions and roles available in their society in their heads, but this is impossible for those living in an urban society.

2. Roles and activities of the folk society are generally simple to understand, whereas those of the urban civilization are often too complex for their members (or social scientists!) to comprehend, predict, or control properly. Although the urban dweller uses the electronic, atomic, and medical marvels of society, he or she hasn't a clue as to how they work or how they were produced.

3. Complex roles require socialization. The warrior or shaman may perform a

role that is difficult and demanding, but such roles are easier to understand and learn than those of the physician or engineer. Formal education and the prolongation of adolescence are characteristic of urban civilizations—to the intense frustration of young men and women who are physically mature for some years before they are able to practice their careers.

4. Given the smaller number of persons and positions in the folk society, relationships among persons have a primary character. Other persons are known more intimately, and it is rare that one interacts with a member of a position whom one does not also know personally. In contrast, urban dwellers must interact with many persons whom they know only by positional membership. Life is both complex and impersonal—witness the well-known ability of New Yorkers to ignore unconscious persons lying on street corners.

These factors pose limits upon the degree of urbanization a population will tolerate—a limit already exceeded in our city ghettos. They also challenge us to engineer an environment that provides the advantages of an urban society and still provides for the social needs of its members. Clearly, if we plan social systems merely in terms of their economic profitability we are lost. On the other hand, if we take care to provide sufficient education, social forms that allow primary relations (such as communes or attrative residential communities), and ways of working out the energy and idealism of citizens, we can live to enjoy the benefits of urban life.

Urban civilizations are complex, and theorists have long searched for concepts that would help them to analyze such societies in simple terms. Perhaps the best such concept is *social class,* which we first met a few pages back. Let us now define the social class concept formally. In Chapter Four we discussed the distinction between *achieved* and *ascribed* positions—the former is associated with actions taken by members, the latter with accidents of birth, social experience, or maturity. We also noted that positions can be ranked against one another in terms of various criteria of *status* if they regularly receive more or less of some form of sanction than other positions. The concept of social class requires that we combine these distinctions. Thus, a **social class** constitutes an achieved position within a society whose members have higher or lower status than do comparable positions.

Several comments are in order concerning this definition.

1. Nothing has been suggested within it concerning the identification of social classes by their members. Americans tend to deny the existence of social classes, thus within the United States social classes tend to be membership positions. Europeans are more class conscious, and for them social class is usually a social position.

2. Nothing in the definition requires that societies must be differentiated into social classes or that a given number of social classes must appear within each society. Analysts have differed on the number of classes that should be recognized and

how class membership should be measured. Some analysts have focused on "subjective" class membership, others have studied "objective" indices.

3. Although nearly any form of reward or punishment might be used to set up and maintain a social class structure if administered faithfully, most analysts have insisted that class structures are dominated by only a few sanctions, specifically those of prestige, wealth, and authority (Lasswell, 1936; Weber, 1925). Any of these three might be used to set up a social class system, and within a pluralistic society in which these desiderata were not highly correlated, a different class system would result depending on the desideratum chosen. Not surprisingly, most analysts view the social class concept to be more legitimate when correlations among these desiderata are high (Landecker, 1963).

4. Nothing has yet been said about the grounds upon which social class membership is achieved. Karl Marx (1867) argued that class membership resulted from the way in which one participates in the economic system and distinguished three social classes: the *aristocracy,* the *bourgeoisie,* and the *proletariat.* Moreover, he noted that because of the differential sanctions applied to them, membership in these three classes persisted from generation to generation. Marx further argued that problems inherent within capitalism would worsen the lot of the proletariat and eventually cause them to rebel and set up a communist state. Recent theorists have argued with Marx on several grounds. It has been suggested that Marx did not anticipate the large number of persons who would become managers or provide human services, that the problems Marx foresaw for capitalism have not yet materialized, and that there is more intergenerational class mobility than Marx thought likely. Moreover, the close tie that Marx presumed between economic activity and sanctions received has been questioned. To illustrate, many unionized industrial workers in America receive higher wages than nonunionized professionals, and thus are able to enjoy a life style that was not anticipated by Marx.

Despite these quarrels, investigators have discovered strong links beween occupation and prestige (Inkeles & Rossi, 1956), thus it has seemed reasonable to measure social class by assessing the occupation practiced by the head of household (Hollingshead, 1949; Warner, Meeker, & Eells, 1949). Moreover, literally thousands of studies have now appeared in which social class, so measured, was found related to differentiated roles, treatments, or other phenomena. To illustrate, once we know a person's (occupational) class, we can make better-than-chance predictions about his or her choice of housing, clothes, tastes in liquor, political practices, recreational behavior, modes of family interaction, educational attainment, indeed life expectancy! In this sense, information about a person's social class is as useful as information about age, sex, race, or other demographic variables. This does not mean that social classes are "real." Correlations are not really high between prestige, wealth, and authority, and it is not clear when one should use these or other criteria for distinguishing societal positions.

Social classes are sometimes contrasted with **castes,** the latter term referring to ascribed positions within a society whose members have higher or lower status in contrast with other such positions. Castes are not widely recognized in Western countries, and Americans are generally shocked by the notion of caste (despite the fact that racial and sexual positions are surely castes in the United States). Moreover, there can be no doubt that castes are a tragedy for those who are "out-castes" (such as the Indian untouchable) and for those having talents that cannot be developed due to an overly rigid social structure. In addition, a caste system tends to resist social change. But by the same token, participants in a caste system have the security of a firm definition of the situation and the support of others in their caste when troubles overwhelm. Because of their greater rigidity and reification, British social classes have some of the qualities that go to make up castes; and even Americans are intrigued by the insufferable assurance of upper-class Englishmen and women.

Caste and class are not the only concepts used for discussing societal roles. Other distinctions are sometimes made that are also based on *occupation* (see Chapter Eight). The United States census differentiates, for example, between farmers, self-employed persons, and professionals—each an occupational classification that may cut across several social classes. Miller and Swanson (1960) argue that in modern, urban America the differences between *mass* and *bureaucratic* occupational experiences will determine more of one's life experiences than will traditional social classes. Some societal analysts use sex, race, age, or ethnicity for discussing societal roles. Some also are concerned with *regionalism* (Odum, 1947), for within urban societies one may find geographic regions wherein roles, activities, and beliefs are somewhat distinct, such as the South or New England in the United States, or the Maritimes and Prairie provinces in Canada.

As is true for the field of small groups, a large literature has appeared discussing societal roles. Most of this literature is speculative, given the difficulties involved in collecting observational data for an entire country. A general review of theories of society may be found in Parsons, Shils, Naegele, and Pitts (1961; also see Marsh, 1967). An example of comparative analysis of the political social system of four societies, drawn from Gallup Poll data, may be found in Alford (1963). A promising development for societal analysis has been the appearance of the Human Relations Area File (Murdock, 1957), which contrasts characteristics for several hundred societies known either from historical or ethnographic accounts. Data from such files may be used for studying relationships among various structural characteristics across societies (Coult & Habenstein, 1965).

In summary, then, societies are assemblies of persons who share elements of culture that are somewhat distinct when compared with the cultures of their neighbors. Societies may or may not be physically compact, but most of the societies with which we are familiar occupy a compact setting. Societies are discussed endlessly by both sociologists and anthropologists, and more reification is given to this social form than to any other. Folk societies may be differentiated from urban civilizations, the latter exhibiting not only a higher standard of living, but also a complex, differentiated, specialized, and impersonal structure of roles and activities. Various analytic concepts have been used to discuss the roles of urban civilizations, among them the notions of social class, caste, and regionalism. To date much of the literature on societies has been speculative, but empirical studies are now becoming more likely as we develop better sources of comparative data.

POSITIONAL STRUCTURE

We are, in fact, anthropoid apes trying to live like termites, and, as any philosophical observer can attest, not doing too well at it.
                                                                —*Ralph Linton*

We turn next to the concept of **positional structure** and to social systems that are defined positionally. It is possible, of course, for social systems to form around the individual, and sometimes the analyst finds such systems of interest. Attention has been given to the social systems created by "great" men, and tomes have appeared concerning procedures that evolved in the Napoleonic court or the command bunker of Hitler's Third Reich. But "little" people are also imbedded in social systems, and investigators have also begun to look at the micro-ethnography of one person's family (Henry, 1971; Lewis, 1959) or one teacher's classroom (Smith & Geoffrey, 1968). To establish the identity of participants in social systems such as these is not problematic, since each person in the system is known by name to all others.

More often analysts have studied systems that were larger and persisted in time despite shifts in personnel. Within these latter the identity of participants is much at issue, for when one person in the system is replaced by another all concerned must be provided means for recognizing the replacement. In most persisting systems this problem is solved by providing a set of identity terms to persons. By definition, such terms constitute *social positions*. Providing they are also characteristic of the system in which they appear, we shall say that those *positions are structured* for that system.

How is the positional structure of the system related to the roles or other overt features that are also structured for it? In many cases positions are associated with roles, of course. Thus where positional differentiation appears as a social system feature, we would also expect to find that members of those positions also exhibited roles that were somewhat differentiated. This does not mean that all structured roles of the system are position associated. Office managers and their secretaries may have quite different activities when at their desks, yet both may eat in the same cafeteria. A second possibility is that the positions of the system may not be associated with differentiated roles. Something like this occurs when positional designations are recognized within the system that were once associated with roles which have disappeared due to technological advance. Some armies still recognize cavalry ranks that once related to the care of horses, although horses have long since been replaced with tanks and mobile artillery. In time, however, positional distinctions that are not role associated tend to disappear from most systems. Finally, some nascent social systems are defined as positional structures, but whether these latter actually become social systems or not depends on whether those structures become role associated. Kinship, social class, ethnic, or astrological structures are only considered social systems when the positional classifications they offer are also associated with differentiated roles.

It would be convenient if each person who participated in a social system were assigned a single identity term within that system and there were a common basis for making all such assignments. Unfortunately, this is not always the case. Naturally occurring social systems feature various means by which participants may be identified, and one of the first tasks of the analyst is to establish the identity terms —and their bases—that are used by members for designating one another. Within a preliterate community a given man may hold: a political designation, a term specifying clan membership, a title denoting religious status, an honorific concerned with prowess in battle, a name designating his mother's family, and perhaps more than a score of other identities that are widely recognized. Use of these terms will often vary, depending on the context in which members find themselves. Worse, it may also happen that different terms are used for designating members of a single position, depending on the identity of the speaker.

To learn to use such a multitude of titles is both demanding and fun. It is also inefficient, and planners of social systems have usually opted for a simpler means of identifying participants. Normally this is done by structuring a *single facet of counter positions* as part of the system. It may be recalled from Chapter Four that counter positions are defined as those whose membership does not overlap, and when a set of counter positions exhausts a population of persons, those positions may be said to constitute a facet. Within the business office, for example, a single system of occupational titles is ordinarily used, none of the titles subtends any of the others, and every participant is assigned to one (and not more than one) of the titles. There is no reason why a planned system *must* have a single positional facet, however. Some planned systems have ambiguous positions, some have more than one facet, some have no positional structure at all. Factories, for example, often feature two titular systems, one stemming from the company, and another from its union, whereas some social groups have no positional structure at all. It is also true that even within the most formal of planned systems, participants sometimes "louse up" the designative system by devising their own terms to refer to one another. In time these latter may also become widely known, hence become a structured feature of the social system.

It is also worthwhile remembering another point first made in Chapter Four—that the characteristic defining a position need not coincide with the grounds on which a person enters, remains a member of, or leaves that position. Of these, the most interesting for the system analyst is the criterion of positional entrance. As a rule, explicit procedures for positional assignment are likely to appear whenever persons are considered replaceable within the social system. This is true for both planned social systems (such as formal organizations) and for nonplanned systems (such as communities). It is less true for systems that are defined in terms of positional distinctions (such as kinship systems). Within the latter the grounds for establishing a person's membership in a position are normally sufficient, and no additional procedure is needed for making positional assignments. However, procedures are necessary when one wants to "change" a positional assignment in the system—hence adoption ceremonies.

Kinship Systems

We turn next to two social system forms that are defined primarily through positional criteria. Anthropologists have long stressed the importance of kinship relations for determining roles in folk societies. Within some preliterate societies, kinship may determine status, wealth, residence, occupation, recreation, association—indeed whether one is allowed to live or die! Kindreds also persist in modern civilizations, and although kin relationships may lie dormant for months or years for the urban dweller, in times of crisis they may serve to organize that person's roles (Sussman & Burchinal, 1962).

Formally, a **kinship system** constitutes a single facet of counter positions that are defined in terms of three related criteria: sexual identity, marriage, and descent. As we have already seen, **sexual identity** is a form of positional classification that is based on physical features and is recognized in all societies. The significance of sexual identity for kinship lies in the physical fact that it takes one (each) man and woman to generate a child—a fact that appears known in most societies.

Marriage is a semipermanent union among two or more adult persons that has at least three bases: (*a*) it is socially recognized; (*b*) it involves sexual license; and (*c*) it is exclusive. This does not deny that other bases for marriage may appear within a given society, for example, mutual help, support, family maintenance, child rearing, etc. But the definitional basis for marriage is that of a "permanent" sexual union between persons. This implies that marriages are recognized concretely and are supported by treatment from other persons not involved in the marriage. It is, in fact, the social recognition of marriage that enables us to differentiate marriages from other forms of sexual liaison.

Let us explore the concept of marriage a bit further. First, marriage is a social form that is recognized within a given society. Its exact form depends on the customs of the society, and although marriages are recognized, by courtesy, from one Western society to another, this convention is strained when forms of marriage are radically different. Muslims, for example, are advised to leave their "extra" wives at home when visiting the United States. Since marriages are contracted only within a given society, it is at least theoretically possible for one person to be married twice if he commutes between two societies—shades of *Captain's Paradise!*

Second, marriage refers to the "entire" union that ties together the adults of the household rather than to the single bond between one husband and one wife. In the polygamous marriage, for example, should a second wife (or second husband) join the union, the marriage bond has been expanded to include this additional person. Many forms of marriage have appeared in different societies, including monogamy, polyandry, polygyny, and group marriage forms. Some societies recognize marriages between persons of the same sex. In other cases, for some purposes, even former spouses now dead or divorced must be considered to be members of the marriages.

Third, marriages involve expectations for both roles and treatments that are not applied to nonmarried persons. Sexual license is granted those who are married. In addition, those who marry are often given a new name, wear different cloting, live in a new location, use new terms for addressing others, enjoy additional legal responsibilities, or shift their productive roles. Others in the community must also adjust their treatments of the newly married persons. In fact, to enter into marriage may involve more shifts in roles and treatments than any other act the person may take in his or her lifetime! Most societies set up ceremonies for establishing a marriage, thus impressing its importance on both those who are to be married and others. However, not all persons are willing to subject themselves to marriage ceremonies, and many societies also have ways of establishing the rights of persons who live as though married, such as laws pertaining to common-law marriage.

Marriages are socially recognized, thus they constitute social positions in which membership is established through ceremony rather than through subsequent behavior. Like sexual identity, then, marriage provides a means for classifying persons that is conceptually independent of behavior. This is also true for the third criterion used for establishing kinship, **descent**. Physically, descent is established through sexual reproduction. Children are descended from their father because he conceived them and from their mother because she gave them birth. Descent, thus, is based on prior experience, and those who are related by descent need have no subsequent behavioral relationship with one another.

Let us also explore the concept of descent. First, it turns out that giving birth is a much more difficult, singular, and public act than those involved in conception. For this reason, descent of the child from his or her mother is somewhat easier to establish than descent from the father. This does not mean that societies are disinterested in descent from the father. Far from it, in patrilineal societies (such as our own) descent from the father may be more significant than descent from the mother. Such societies usually establish customs tying legal descent to the husband-of-record, regardless of who done the deed. And it was not so many years ago that reigning monarchs in Europe were required to perform conception-related activities with their wives in public view!

Second, many societies have generalized upon the physical facts of descent and have provided additional grounds whereby persons might be said to be descended from others who are not their physical parents. When Rachel dicovered she was barren, she persuaded Jacob to "go in unto" her handmaid, Bilhah. When the latter bore a son, Rachel claimed him as her own, named him Dan, and Dan claimed descent from Rachel thereafter. In some polygamous societies, descent is reckoned from the senior husband (or wife) of the marriage. If these customs seem strange, consider our own customs concerning adoption, or that many Christians hold beliefs concerning the descent of Jesus that would appear to be—at the very least—improbable. In general, where rules of descent violate the physical facts of reproduction, these rules establish a relationship between descent and marriage. Thus, the physical fact of sexual reproduction is replaced by a set of socially recognized beliefs tying putative reproduction to marriage.

Now let us put these notions together to construct kinship systems. Let us adopt the conventional symbols of ♂ for a male person and ♀ for a female, and let us symbolize the act of conception with a broken line ——— and descent by a solid line with an arrow head ⟶. Using these symbols, the simplest kinship system we can imagine is one that ties together the child and the two parents into a positionally structured graph:

But there is no reason why the system must stop with this simple relationship. The same two parents may have more than one child:

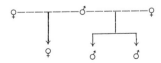

Or one of the parents may have conceptional relationships with more than one other person.

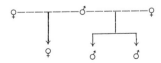

Or we may wish to consider relationships across three or more generations.

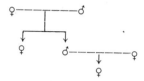

The preceding graphs are based on the facts of physical parentage. But we have already discovered that physical descent is of less significance than social descent, that marriage is more important than sexual reproduction for determining kinship relations. For this reason, conventional kinship graphs are normally constructed by symbolizing descent and marriage, rather than descent and conception, with marriage indicated by a solid, double line ====. A simple graph of a husband and wife and their three children appears thus:

As suggested earlier, kinship systems normally constitute a simple facet of counter positions in which each person has one, unambiguous position. Such systems have a simple, orderly branching structure that is called a *tree* by mathematicians (Harary, Norman, & Cartwright, 1965; White, 1963). As we shall see, positional structures in other social systems may be less orderly. Kinship systems appear as crescive or "natural" features in all known societies. This does not mean that such systems are always associated with role behaviors. As it turns out, kinship distinctions are strongly associated with roles in some societies, whereas in other societies kinship is less important in terms of behavior.

There are but few natural bounds to a kinship system. Sometimes a descent line is terminated through unwillingness of the younger generation to get married or to have children. (Despite the fact that he had 21 children, descent from J. S. Bach terminated within three generations.) Sometimes, also, one is known to have descended from a bastard—in the technical sense—thus to have no progenitors in the previous generation. These conditions aside, if one pushes back the generations, it turns out that each of us is distantly related to nearly everyone else in the society. Nevertheless, most of us are unwilling to carry information in our heads concerning our relationships-by-descent with thousands of other persons.

Several mechanisms are used for controlling kinship information. One of these is to use terms for designating persons who have a specific relationship with oneself within the kinship system. In English our male parent is termed a "father," our female parent a "mother," our female sibling a "sister," and so forth. However, we are apt to term our father's brother an "uncle," and to use the same term to refer to our mother's brother, and the spouses of both our father's and mother's sisters. Worse, the term "cousin" is used in a strict sense to refer to the sons or daughters of our father's or mother's siblings, and it is also used in a vernacular sense to refer to other persons known to be more distantly related to us. English has relatively few kinship terms, and these are sloppily applied—a condition applying to most Western languages. Some primitive societies offer a much more differentiated and exacting kinship vocabulary (Buchler & Selby, 1968).

Various distinctions have been suggested for analyzing kinship terms. For example, Service (1960) [B&T, Selection 5] suggests two, cross-cutting classifications. *Egocentric* terms are those that are used uniquely by the individual and designate the relationship he or she holds with the other, whereas *sociocentric* terms are those that may be used by anyone. *Terms of address* are those used when speaking to another; *terms of reference* are those one uses when describing the other to a third party. The term *kindred* is also used, albeit loosely, to refer to the total set of positions who are recognized by a person to have relationships-by-descent with him or herself, although some persons of the kindred may be known only as *kinfolk* and not by specific relationship with the person we are studying. Various types of kindreds appear, depending on the society we are studying. For example, some societies are organized by *clans* whose putative descent is from a common, mythical ancestor.

All of which leads us to the significance of kinship systems. Kinship relations are not mere curiosities; rather they are associated with role expectations that prescribe rights and obligations we owe to our various relatives (Farber, 1971; Lévi-Strauss, 1949). In our society, for example, rights of husbands and wives, parents and children, are set forth in laws; and if we violate those laws we can be sent to jail. Moreover, although they may not be codified in law, if we mistreat our nephews, cousins or other more distant relatives we may earn opprobium from those who know the situation. Some of us would not turn out even a distant cousin who came to us in need, despite the neolocality of our urban civilization.

Kinship relations are of greater significance in primitive societies. Many such societies feature sexual recognition, avoidance, or extensive responsibilities among kin relatives. Some societies demand residential locality for the newly married couple—in matrilocal societies with the relatives of the bride, in patrilocal societies with the groom's kin. Where the "Levirate" prevails, the surviving brother has an obligation to marry the widow of his deceased brother. Consanguineal relatives often owe responsibilities of mutual support and historical enmity to others who are not of the kindred. How significant indeed were kinship relations to the Australian aborigine who lived in a harsh land where his or her ability to survive depended on claims for water rights made to someone who was his or her tenth cousin!

That norms should be attached to kinship should not surprise us. Birth, death, and those activities associated with procreation are of vital interest to all. Our inheritance, our lives, our fortunes, our sacred honor, indeed the names with which we are addressed—are all tied to kinship. There can be few experiences more shattering within a traditional society than bastardy, and most civilized societies have laws attempting to protect the rights of those who are born "without names." Though kinship may be less significant for the urban dweller who has community, nation, occupation, and television to entertain him or her, kinship is still a major source of identity.

In summary, then, kinship systems are defined by the criteria of sexual identity, marriage, and descent. Thus they are positional structures, are "natural," and are characterized by invariant membership. Since the forms of marriage change from society to society, kinship systems also exhibit different forms; however, most kinship systems exhibit a simple branching structure. Kinship systems may be indefinitely large, but most societies recognize only a portion of the systems in the kindred that are known to be related to a given person. Kinship systems are important because they control role expectations for sexual behavior, property rights, obligations for support, and personal identity. Kinship systems have been studied extensively by anthropologists. The notion of kinship is an abstract one, however, and does not refer to any specific setting or activity. For this reason, the study of behavioral roles of kindred members is normally confined to a more specific context—such as the family.

Families

As used in the common language, the term *family* has three connotations, those of kinship, primary relationships, and cohabitation. For convenience, we use the first two of these criteria to define the concept of family. The third will then costitute a variable that differentiates families from one another.

A family, then, consists of a set of persons who are related to one another by means of kinship and who regularly engage in primary activities. Although primary activities involve more intense relationships than does simple interaction, in at least two senses the family forms a more weakly bonded structure than does the social group. First, members of the family need not engage in primary activities at the same time. Within the family having teen-age children, for example, siblings may not see one another at home for several days at a time, and yet each maintains primary relationships with parents when he or she is at home and with one another at the same high school. Second, it is not uncommon for two persons within a large family not to be on speaking terms, although each of them maintains primary relationships with all other family members. Thus it is not necessary that all family members have primary relationships with all others in the family, but merely that the primary activities be relatively dense.

Families may involve as few as two members and as many as several dozen persons. For some purposes it is useful to discriminate between larger and smaller families, and the usual way in which this is done is by identifying *nuclear families*. Let us define a **close family** to be one whose members exhibit kinship ties that are not greater than length one in the kinship graph. For example, siblings form a close family, as do a mother and her children—since bonds in the kinship graph run directly from one of the persons to the others. Close families may or may not exhibit a marriage; if they do they are termed **nuclear families**. A nonclose family form is known as an **extended family**. For example, a household that includes two parents, their children, and a grandmother is an extended family. Again, the nuclear families of two brothers jointly form an extended family.[5]

Now, what about the business of living together? Families may or may not occupy a compact setting—such as a home or a set of adjacent buildings. If they do, they may be called a **compact family**. It is clear from this definition that the concepts of compactness and nuclearity are independently defined. A family can be compact without being close, or vice versa. Obviously, these two variables tend to be correlated, but one would predict different effects for one than the other. Members of a nuclear family owe one another certain rights and obligations that will be exercised even though they may be separated by many miles—witness the demand for funds made by university students of their parents. Members of compact families invariably affect one another even though their degree of kin relatedness may be minimal—such as the impact of the maiden aunt or drunken cousin who moves in for an extended stay.

The archetypical American family is both nuclear and compact. To say this is not to imply that Americans have always lived in nuclear, compact families, nor that this is necessarily the "best" form of family, nor even that the majority of Americans now live in such a family. During the nineteenth century and earlier more Americans lived in extended families. However, with the advent of industrialization, it is argued (Parsons, 1943) that married couples were more likely to become neolocal, hence to form isolated nuclear families. At present much of the popular protrayal of American families involves the nuclear, compact form, and Americans who opt for a different life style are sometimes stigmatized or made to feel guilty. But isolated, nuclear families have weaknesses. Among others, such families provide few remedies for inadequate role performance on the part of parents and few resources to help meet financial or medical emergencies. For these and related reasons, nuclear, compact families are now being questioned (Casler, 1974), the divorce rate for marriages reflecting this family form is skyrocketing, and many Americans are thinking about, or actively exploring, other styles of life. It remains to be seen whether the nuclear, compact family will survive this century or will be replaced with other family forms, if not alternative living arrangements that do not involve the family at all.

Like societies, families have attracted both reification and attention from social scientists. Nuclear families are one of the few social system forms that is found in

---

[5] The concepts of nuclear and extended family do not exhaust distinctions that can be made based on kinship. Murdock (1957) distinguished "extended," "independent," "lineal," and "stem" families (also see Chu & Hollingsworth, 1969).

all societies. Moreover, families are the locus of much of our adult, personal behavior, and they are the system in which initial socialization of the young takes place. For these reasons, the roles of family members have been viewed as an important subject by psychologists as well as by sociologists and anthropologists. Many studies have appeared that are concerned with the roles of family members and the effects of parental roles on the roles of children or vice versa (for examples, see Adams, 1971; Lee, 1977; Nye, 1976; or Sears, Maccoby, & Levin, 1957), and good summaries of the field are available (Hoffman & Hoffman, 1964; Kinton, 1975).

Most discussions of family roles begin with the notion that activities of the husband and wife are differentiated. In traditional, Victorian families, for example, the husband earned a living and maintained the external property, while the wife was mistress of the household and had primary responsibility for child care. Naive persons presumed that this division of labor was invariant, possibly generated by temperamental differences between the sexes. And yet, as one goes from our society to others, one encounters other divisions of family roles (Murdock, 1937) [B&T, Selection 30]. In her classic study of *Sex and Temperament*, Margaret Mead (1935) suggested that male and female roles were culturally arbitrary and reversible, a thesis that is basic to the women's movement today. Those who discuss contemporary American families have suggested that the roles of husband and wife are becoming more amalgamated—possibly to the point where both parents will hold jobs and both will share equally in household maintenance and child care. This is an attractive thesis, and if true we may be on the threshold of an era in which roles within the family are based on preference rather than on restrictive norms associated with kinship. In terms of data, however, Blood and Wolfe (1960) [B&T, Selection 31] suggest that in the typical American family the roles of father and mother are still quite differentiated, although there is open discussion and allocation of tasks to be accomplished.

It is surely reasonable to believe that parental roles affect those of children. Nearly all indices of maladjustment in the later lives of children (criminality, drunkenness, schizophrenia, and so forth) correlate positively with disruption of parental roles (McCord & McCord, 1957) [B&T, Selection 46]. In addition, we are offered a variety of theories suggesting the effects of specific parental roles on personality development in children. Deleterious consequences are presumed to result from maternal deprivation, early and severe weaning or toilet training, absence of the father due to work pressures and commutation, parental psychosis, and maternal overprotection. Indeed, one of the Great American Pastimes of the twentieth century is making mothers feel guilty about their child-rearing techniques, since obviously they are to blame for any personal problems that their children will suffer later (see Ginott, 1965, for example).

The only difficulty with these theories is that they lack empirical support. Studies of families in which the roles of members were actually observed are few and far between (for exceptions, see Barker & Wright, 1955; Henry, 1971; Strodbeck, 1951). Moreover, when a particular index of parental role disruption is measured, it often turns out to be correlated with other indices. Thus, mothers who deprive their children of love at an early age are also likely to be overdemanding when the same children are teen-agers, and parental drunkenness and psychosis are correlated with the brutal facts of poverty. As a result, sorting out the definitive effects of any specific parental role on childhood personality development is extraordinarily difficult. It may also be a fruitless task in the long run. Presumably the sequence and patterning of family roles (including the roles played by children) are more important in determining personality than are parental roles per se. (We return to this topic in Chapter Eight.)

In summary, then, a family consists of a set of persons who are closely related to one another and who engage in primary activities. Some families are extended, but others are close or nuclear. Families also may or may not be compact in that they live within a compact setting, and presumably their patterns of interaction depend upon both compactness and nuclearity. The archetypal American family is both nuclear and compact, and considerable reificiation has been given to this form in American folklore. Many theories are now available concerning role differentiation in the family and the effects of parental roles upon the roles and later development of children. Most of these stress differentiation of the roles of fathers and mothers (although there is evidence that these roles are becoming more amalgamated in contemporary societies) and the deleterious effects upon children of disruption of parental roles. However, little behavioral evidence has been accumulated to date concerning actual family interaction.

CONCEPTUAL STRUCTURE

> *A corporation cannot blush.*
> —*Howel Walsh*

We turn, at last, to the concept of **conceptual structure** and to social systems that are defined in conceptual terms. Most social systems feature conceptual elements that are held concerning those systems or their components. Expectations are held concerning the roles of system participants; the system itself may be identified, approved, or denigranted; tasks may be set for the system, or jobs for its indiviudal participants, and so forth. Conceptual elements such as these are structured when they are found to be characteristic of the system and affect or are affected by one or more structured roles of the system in some way. Some social theorists (particularly those influenced by Talcott Parsons) argue that the conceptual elements of a system must be shared among participants in that system, thus they argue that chracteristicness implies consensus. As we shall show in this section, conceptions need not be consensually held and still may be characteristic.

Structured conceptions may appear for almost any kind of social system, both those that occur naturally and those that are planned. Such conceptions constitute explanations of the system for participants and are presumed both to reflect the ongoing structure of behaviors within the system and to influence participants by providing them with orientation and motivation to participate. Thus, changes in either the behaviors or conceptions that are structured for a system should lead, in time, to changes in the other component set.[6]

Some social systems are also defined for us through the appearance of conceptual elements. Ceremonies of religion, magic, pomp, games, formal organizations, law courts, wars (both hot and cold) all persist as social entitites because of our acceptance of them—because we give credence to such social forms and to the roles, actitivies, and functions they perform. As a rule, *planned* social systems are more likely to have foundational definitions that include conceptual elements. At least some of those elements will have predated the appearance of behavioral components, so reification is likely to be given to conceptions for planned systems. However, unless we can bring ourselves to accept the viability of plans, the system will not come into being. Governments, as well as currencies, depend upon acceptance by their constituents.

Components of Conceptual Structure

STRUCTURED EXPECTATIONS

Let us now examine some of the concepts frequently used for discussing conceptual structure. Surely the most popular of these concepts is the covertly held expectation. Beliefs, norms, and preferences may all be structured for a social system. Structured conceptions may be held for any behavioral component of the system and for the actions of individuals as well as for those of sets of persons. However, if analysts have usually concerned themselves with systems in which the participants were members of structured social positions, it is not surprising that attention has also been given to expectations for those positions. Where appropriate, I shall refer to expectations that are structured for roles of positions in a social system as **role expectations**—a term that may possibly be familiar to readers.

Great importance is attached by some analysts to the concept of role expectation, and it is commonly argued that such expectations will normally mirror the behavioral events they purport to represent. (Role beliefs should be accurate in the main; role norms and role preferences should be aligned with their role models.) In fact, role expectations need not mirror roles at all! Let us consider four possible relationships that may appear between a role expectation and its behavioral model.

[6] Theorists are remarkably vague about how these changes come about and when we should expect change or resistance to change in the behavioral or conceptual structures. We return to these problems at the end of the chapter.

1. The expectation may be present and accurate or aligned in the main. Provided that the subject and object persons are in frequent interaction, it is reasonable to believe that expectations concerning that interaction will appear and will come, in time, to reflect or generate behavior. Thus, accuracy and alignment of role expectations should tend to characterize small social systems (such as the family).

2. The role expectation may be missing. Several arguments suggest that this condition is likely for larger social systems. As Goffman (1959) has suggested, sometimes too much knowledge may ruin the person's appreciation of another's performance or may disrupt role adjustment. Again, information concerning how portions of the system operate may sometimes be denied to unbelievers, noninitiates, or to those who have not received "top secret clearance." Above all, we neither need, nor are we interested in maintaining, complex expectations concerning the activities of persons who are distant from ourselves. Most of us hold detailed expectations concerning those with whom we interact frequently, stereotypic expectations concerning the behaviors of "important" persons in the system whom we do not know personally, and few-to-no expectations for others in the system.

Given this argument, it seems unlikely that role expectations (or other structured conceptions) will be held consensually throughout a complex social system. Rather we should conceive of most role expectations as concepts that are shared among small sets of persons in the system, whereas the total structure of expectations will consist of partially overlapping fields of beliefs, norms, and preferences. What does this imply for the concept of characteristicness? As a rule, structured expectations are characteristic of their systems not because they are consensually held, but rather because they persist in identifiable form over time. Usually that form involves overlapping fields of partial consensus, but some social systems also feature nonconsensual or even conflicting role expectations that are characteristic. If these aspects of the system persist and affect other system components in some way, we judge them to be structured for that system.

3. Role expectations may be distorted. In Chapter Six the term *pluralistic ignorance* was used to refer to broadly held expectations that are either inaccurate or nonveridical. Earlier it was suggested that distorted expectations are normally assumed to be individual events, deviations from conditions that are required for social stability, and soon to be cured. When distorted expectations are held by large sets of persons, however, and when they persist over time, one looks for social mechanisms that will perpetuate them. As we know, conditions of pluralistic ignorance have appeard when pressures to conceptualize were present and opportunities for behavioral observation were denied. How often pluralistic ignorance will appear as a structural feature of social systems is not now known, but one suspects that it is fairly common.

4. Role expectations may occasionally be present but the roles with which they are concerned are missing. Something like this occurs during periods of rapid social change, when older persons retain memories of how things used to be and are

confused by new forms. Such conditions might prove irrelevant to social system analysis—if the role expectations in question had no discriminable effect on subject behavior. But some social systems seem to organize considerable effort around role expectations that appear vacuous to outsiders—witness activities of the ultraright, paramilitary cell group. Regardless of such examples, this last condition should be rare.

The concept of role expectation is a popular one in sociological thought and appears, in one form or another, in nearly every introductory text for that field. Many distinctions have been suggested for such expectations. One of these differentiates *folkways* from *mores* (Sumner, 1906)—the former referring to role expectations that are traditional but involve only the descriptive modality, the latter equally traditional but generally involving cathectic or prescriptive modality (so that persons "feel more strongly" about mores than about folkways). Folkways and mores are alike, however, in that violation of them leads to but informal or nonconsensual enforcement. They are to be contrasted with *laws,* which involve the imposition of explicit sanctions for nonconformity. Laws, in turn, may be categorized into *customary* (or *common*) *laws,* which are explicitly sanctioned although the laws themselves are not written down, and *enacted laws* wherein the laws also appear as symbolic records. (The game of cricket illustrates a number of customary laws or "traditions" that are well respected although not inscribed in rule books—hence the phrase, "That's not cricket!" For example, under the written rules it is quite legal for the bowler to knock off the bails without delivering the ball, and should the runner be out of his crease at that moment he may be declared out. However, "That's not cricket," since the bowler—if he is a gentleman—is supposed to warn the runner of the latter's infraction, and in cases where this customary law is violated the bowler can expect to receive opprobrium.)

Such distinctions suggest that beliefs, norms, and preferences may not be equally structured for a given social system. Little data are available on the subject, but it seems reasonable to postulate that within most social systems beliefs are the most likely to be structured, followed by norms, and then preferences, in that order. Why should beliefs be important to the system? Because a structured "definition of the situation" appears requisite for most complex forms of interaction, and in fact some rather complex systems appear to operate through the structuring of beliefs alone. (To illustrate, laboratory experiments in social psychology often operate through instructions to subjects that are presented in the descriptive mode.) Considerable importance has been given to the functioning of role norms in social systems, and dozens of distinctions have been suggested for role expectations in this mode (Benoit-Smullyan, 1944; Davis, 1949) [B&T, Selections 3 and 7]. Most theories concerned with the conceptual integration of social systems have stressed the importance of norms. Sometimes these theories assume that participants perceive that sanctions will follow from nonconformity to norms. Sometimes, too, it is assumed that participants internalize structured norms as personal values. Students who first encounter such explanations are apt to conclude that civilization is largely constrained by structured norms. If this were all that civilization offered we should all become hippies. However, as Skinner reminds us in *Walden Two* (1948), it is not necessary for persons to share norms in order to generate conformity. A less painful way is to ensure that they share preferences, for then they will conform because it pleasures them to do so. A less odious way is to provide them all the same, persuasive set of beliefs that suggest utility and reward for those behaviors desired. Thus, although structured norms *can* induce conformity, we need not believe that these are the only forms of expectations that can do the job. (We return to this argument, too, at the end of the chapter.)

Nevertheless, it is reasonable to believe that most social systems in Western societies *do* structure at least some norms for their participants. If we are to be good group members, worshippers, husbands or wives, workers, or politicians our behaviors will to some extent reflect norms structured for our positions. This does not mean that the normative structure is homogeneous. Homans (1950) reminds us that some systems offer both an "official system" of norms that are codified and an "informal system" of norms that are imposed by local convention. Nor does it mean that the norms are immutable or rationally determined. Some norms appear to be historical accidents and are unrelated to other characteristics of the system such as the tasks it accepts, the functions it accomplishes, or the satisfactions of its members. Persons in some religious orders are expected to wear uniforms that reflect standards of dress from bygone days and are in fact quite uncomfortable. And yet, we tend to protect normative structures and can find all sorts of reasons for resisting changes in mores.

Preferences seems less likely to be structured than either beliefs or norms. Folk wisdom in Western societies suggests that control of behaviors is difficult to maintain by preferential means alone. Whether this is objectively true is not at issue. Most of us seem to think it is true, hence we spend little time setting up and preserving preferential structures in the systems of which we are members. Thus when structured preferences appear, they are often unanticipated. However, beware the structured preference! Participants who suddenly discover that they share unhappiness with features of the system are not likely to sit on their hands if they have the means to change the form.

SOCIAL SYSTEM IDENTITY

Structured expectations are not the only conceptual element that may appear within a social system. Another important element is the **identity of the system.** Like persons, positions, roles, activities, or other system components, social systems can be associated with identity terms by which they are referenced by their members and others. In fact, most of the social systems with which social scientists are concerned are so identified. My family is generally referred to as "the Biddles," my usual employing organization "the University of Missouri," my community "Columbia, Missouri," and so on. In addition, other terms are also available to us that serve to reference types or classifications of social systems—namely, families, organizations, communities, games, and the like. Terms used for identifying social systems, then, also vary in the degree of their familiarity and abstractness.

There are at least two advantages in having a term with which participants and others can recognize a social system. On the one hand, designation of the system allows persons to deal with it as a referential entity, to concern themselves with its welfare, for instance, to attach reification to its existence, to approve or disapprove it, and so forth. On the other, the existence of an identity term allows persons to consider themselves as members, or to deny that they are members, of the system. Elsewhere we have allowed for the possibility that individuals might identify themselves with terms that designated persons, positions, roles, and activities. We now extend this notion so as to allow identification with families, communities, nation-states, organizations, and other social system forms.

Let us pursue this matter of membership in the social system a bit. How does one go about establishing those who are "in" and "not in" the system? Given the greater complexity of the social system, this is a more difficult question to answer than was that of establishing positional membership. In practice, two kinds of answers have been given: those based on behavior of other overt evidence, and those based on identification. As an example of the former, we take the definition of Brown (1960), who accepts as members of a formal organization those who take part in the "development, manufacture, and sale"of the commodity produced by that organization. Definitions based on overt events also are characteristic of experimental social psychology wherein small-group membership is induced by bringing strangers together in a confined space to engage in interaction.

The second type of answer, based on identification, is suggested by Holmes (1966) who argues that membership should be seen as reflecting identification with and commitment to the social system. Definitions of this latter sort also characterize field studies in sociology wherein membership in the system is established by asking respondents to nominate the system of which they are members. These two answers have differing implications, one of which is illustrated by Holmes with those who occupy the position of client, such as passengers on board a ship, patients in a hospital, or prisoners in a jail. From the viewpoint of behavioral structure, clients are "materials" whose processing is a major function of the system. In terms of conceptual structure, long-term clients are likely to identify with the system and even to instigate characteristic activities within it because of that identification. It would seem unprofitable to force a choice between these two orientations, but let us remember that objective and subjective membership in a social system may not coincide.

TASKS

Some social systems are also characterized by yet another type of conceptual structure, *tasks*. Task and function are similar concepts. Both are concerned with the effects of activity, and the two have similar roots in history. In contemporary role theory, however, these two terms have distinct meanings. Whereas the concept of function applies to the observable consequences of activity (whether such consequences were intended, and whether or not the participants are aware of them), the concept of task refers to shared intentions for activity that appear within the system (whether or not they are accomplished). Functional analyses can be performed for any social system, since whenever a system exists there also we will find structured activities that have effects. Functional analysis is ex post facto; in the beginning there was the system, but only after it exists will its functions become clear. Tasks, however, precede the system, and systems may be planned to accomplish tasks. In terms of modality, functions are *descriptive* and are discovered by the social scientist; tasks are *prescriptive* and are accepted by and applied to participants in the system. It is possible, however, for a system member to recognize both the tasks set for the system and its functions; moreover, he or she may tell us under certain circumstances that they are at variance with one another. In formal terms, a **task** consists of a shared prescription for a state of affairs that is to result from the structured roles or activities of the system.

Tasks may be stated for the social system as a whole, or they may be stated for individuals within the system. When necessary to differentiate, I shall use the term **jobs** to refer to tasks for individuals. For example, we may read in the job specifications for a particular worker on an assembly line that he or she must: (*a*) solder not less than 1000 units per day; (*b*) maintain his or her equipment in working order; and (*c*) keep his or her workbench and surrounding area clean. On the other hand, the worker's firm may set for itself the task of "producing color television sets of a high standard to be sold within the medium-price range."

Tasks are referential statements, and many of our earlier discussions concerning properties of referential phenomena may be applied to their analysis. Tasks are prescriptive in mode, but they may apply to all sorts of phenomena, including human behavior, events in the physical environment, or even observable conditions such as covert processes presumed to operate within persons or transcendental happenings. In the latter case, we would have no objective means for judging whether or not the task was ever met by social system activity—which seems to be the case for some tasks that are set by the preacher for his parishioners or for the classroom teacher by educational philosophy.

Since tasks may be stated in the form of references to human behavior, some confusion has appeared within role theory concerning the relationship between this concept and that of expectation (e.g., see the definition of task suggested by Oeser & Harary, 1962) [B&T, Selection 6]. To illustrate this difference, a norm for a teacher might specify, "Teachers should use the Smith-and-Jones textbook for fifth-grade mathematics," whereas a task might be stated, "Teachers should endeavor to have all of their fifth-grade pupils attain not less than a passing grade on the Smith-and-Jones achievement examination," or even "Teachers should strive to 'do their best' at all times." Norms, then, set forth means without necessarily telling us what is to be accomplished in the doing; tasks tell us ends without necessarily telling us how this is to be accomplished.

Tasks are also sometimes confused with goals. Although I will not use the term *goal* in a formal sense in this book, it is useful to distinguish these two concepts. Goals are states of affairs that are desired by the person—thus they are individualistic and cathectic. Tasks are states of affairs that are intended collectively by social system members—their orientation is consensual and prescriptive. In some writings about small groups one finds the phrase "group goal" used as a rough synonym for the task concept. This usage is poor. It confuses the cathectic and prescriptive modes; one is never sure whether *group* refers to the fact that the concept is held by members in consensus or applies to members collectively (or both); and this same phrase has been used by other authors to refer to external functions of the group. For these reasons, *task* is surely to be preferred.

Like functions, tasks can also appear in sequences, and some task specifications set forth a complex sequence of events that must appear in order. This is particularly true in ceremonies and in organizations that exhibit an assembly line in which products are to move from one location to another—acquiring nuts, bolts, motors, panels, paint, and the like while en route. If some person in the middle fails to perform his or her job, either the product is faulty or the assembly line comes to a halt. Because of this similarity, tasks may be subjected to some of the same analytic techniques that are employed in functional analysis. The analyst must make clear to us, however, whether he or she is analyzing functions or tasks, since one is a description of observed effects whereas the other concerns prescriptions for accomplishment.

STRUCTURED INSCRIPTIONS

Inscriptions may also be structured within a social system provided that their use is characteristic. Not all systems feature inscriptions, of course. Systems in preliterate societies have no such features, and many simple social systems in urban civilizations are not associated with documents. In general, however, the more complex the behavior of a system, the more difficult it will be for members of the system to maintain knowledge of it in their heads. This suggests that complex system forms are dependent on inscriptions and will not appear without them. For example, one can think of few examples of formal organizations that appeared in preliterate societies, although the commercial empire of the Incas might be an exception (wherein records were kept in the form of knots tied in cords).

For this reason, elements of conceptual structure tend to drift into codification over time. If unchecked, this process creates endless red tape and the overspecification of roles and activities, so that eventually the rules must be ignored or the system will bog down in triviation. Such a process is more likely when those who make the rules are physically separated from those for whom the rules are made. Although the endstate of this process is madness, and although we have understood for years the danger of unfettered documentary expansion (witness *Parkinson's Law, Catch 22,* or *Up the Down Staircase*), we seem unable to resist the lure of inscriptions in certain social system forms, such as in the federal government or our major universities.

Social systems may be differentiated from one another in the degree to which this drift toward codification has taken place. In addition, analyses may be made of the types of elements that are expressed as inscriptions. Some systems feature documents for roles but not for tasks—as in professional codes of conduct. Other systems feature documents specifying ends but not means—as in battle orders. Some structured inscriptions are prescriptive in the main, others are mainly descriptive, and a few are cathectic. Some systems are defined through inscriptions—such as corporations—although for most systems documentation appears to be adjunctive rather than definitive.

In sum, we have reviewed three elements of conceptual structure: role expectations, social system identity, and tasks—and the idea of structured inscriptions with which these are often codified. These concepts do not exhaust the topic of conceptual structure, of course. Great importance is attached to conceptual structure by some role theorists, for it is argued that one reason why complex social forms are able to persist is "because" of the structured ideas participants hold concerning those phenomena. At the same time, few details are really known today about the ideas concerning social systems that are actually held by participants, nor do we yet know much about how people go about forming, responding to, or changing those ideas.

Games

We turn now to two social system forms—games and organizations—that are defined in terms of conceptual structure. Social groups, societies, and kinship systems are alike in that their occurrence is "natural." Given the normal course of human affairs, such systems seem to appear spontaneously, without much thought or planning on the part of participants. By the time social planners appear on the scene, examples of these systems are available to be examined, and normally we accommodate them rather than seek to change their forms.

This is less true for games and organizations. These latter begin as "planned" or artificial contrivances that are assembled for the functions they accomplish. Games antedate organizations and are as old as the human species or older. But every year brings the appearance of new games, industries have sprung up to invent and sell us the latest in game fads, and it is rare that we find ourselves playing a game whose history goes back more than a centruy or two. Thus games and organizations are more like artifacts, whereas groups, communities, societies, and families are more like settings. We accept the former for the time being only, reserving in our hearts the right to alter their rules if they no longer suit us, but few of us would think of attempting to change the rules governing the society or kinship system into which we were born.

There are several differences between games and organizations. Perhaps the most basic has to do with the task for which the social system is mobilized. Organizations are set up to accomplish ends within the external environment, whereas in games the task is an internal, arbitrary state (i.e., winning) that pleases participants. The organization is thus instrumental, the game consummatory. The former develops leisure time, the latter consumes leisure time. In the words of Mark Twain, "Work consists of whatever a body is *obliged* to do, and Play consists of whatever a body is not obliged to do." Although the playing of games may have functional consequences for the community, and thus the game is encouraged or discouraged by others, the game task is a contrived one having no functional significance in and of itself—which is one of the reasons why William James suggested the game as a "moral equivalent of war." These statements are less true, of course, for professional sports, which combine some of the features of both games and organizations. Within professional golf or football, for example, the task of winning is still maintained and is presumably an enjoyable state for the players. But professional sport is also organized for other tasks within the external environment, and success crowns the brows of its heroes with more than leaves of myrtle.

Games are the one social system form for which we may always presume the existence of shared norms. Indeed, games appear only when players are willing to subject their conduct to a common structure of norms. This normative structure is invariant for a given game type and forms the definitional foundation for the game. Players are always assumed to know this structure and (within limits) to honor it in their behavior. Norms for simple games may be negotiated, on the spot, among potential players; however, norms for more complex games are usually supported by written rules. Within some games players are "on their honor" to conform to the norms which define the game. In other games a referee is provided who is to enforce conformity. Whichever method is used, it is the presence of this shared normative structure that differentiates our concept of game from other gamelike forms in which one person is manipulating another for profit (such as a "con-game"), encounters that are governed by pathological needs (such as those discussed by Eric Berne), or free play.

In addition, games are also provided an identity term. Such a term enables players to think about the game and to announce (to themselves and to others) when they are and are not "playing." This is necessary because the same behavior may be viewed quite differently, depending on whether it is judged in terms of game norms or in terms of other standards for behavior. Within a football game, for example, it is quite legitimate to tackle and knock down another player who is holding a football in his arms. Such a behavior would be strongly disapproved in most other contexts.

For our purposes, then, a **game** constitutes an identifiable social system that is conducted for an arbitrary, internal task having positive cathexis for participants. Games must also be characterized by shared norms for conduct. Games are fun, but they are also organized. Prototypic game forms may be observed in the frolicking of dogs or the romping of small children. But to frolic or romp is not necessarily to play the game—as Piaget assures us. Rather, the gameplayer subjects his or her performances to standards that are set for them in the norms (or rules) of the game, and should he or she not do this, the attainment of the game task will be tainted and of less value to the person and others. This tells us that participants must also have the ability to internalize game rules, for without this ability there would be little reason for them to play—apart from the joy of frolic.

Many distinctions have been suggested for games, only a few of which can be reviewed here, and a sophisticated mathematics has been devised for game analysis that also has application to economic behavior and conflict situations (Howard, 1971; von Neumann & Morgenstern, 1947). In most games those involved participate either as individual *players* or as multiperson *teams*, and if the latter there may also be an explicit, positional facet specified for each team. Games are classified in terms of the number of players (or teams) allowed; thus, a two-person game (chess), a four-person game (bridge), a three- to seven-person game (poker), and so on. Games may also be termed *zero-sum* if the total of all scores allocated to participants must always be a fixed amount, or *non-zero-sum*. Game rules always specify forms of tolerated interaction among players and often lay down conventions governing cooperation or secret dealing among players. Rules may also be stated for relationships among players on teams, the recruitment or replacement of players, the duties of an umpire or referee, artifacts necessary for playing the game, the behavior of spectators, and so forth.

So much for the conceptual structure of the game. But game players also behave, and their roles have also been studied in both game and nongame contexts. Investigators have studied the effects of game rules upon player roles (Gump & Sutton-Smith, 1955), the functions games perform in the lives of players (Goffman, 1967), and the relationship between game forms and other characteristics of the society (Silver, 1978). Attention has also been given to designing games that would provide contexts for experiments in social psychology (Christie & Geis, 1968; Deutsch & Krauss, 1960; Kelley, 1965; Rappoport & Chammah, 1965; Shure, Meeker, & Hansford, 1965); and games have been used as "painless" means for instructing participants in the intricacies of real-life tasks such as decision making in the business world or international relations (Guetzkow, Alger, Brody, Noel, & Snyder, 1963; Kibbee, Craft, & Nanus, 1961; Robinson, 1966; Zuckman & Horn, 1973).

In summary, games are identified systems of organized fun in which players subject themselves to a normative structure and an arbitrary, internal task that is positively valued. Games are "planned" social systems whose rules are conveniences and are subject to periodic negotiation. Many different game forms are known, and mathematics have been developed for analyzing game rules. Roles of game players have been studied along with other game features. Games have also been designed as means for investigating interaction and for purposes of instruction.

Organizations

Organizations are similar to games in that they are identified and are planned for task accomplishment. They differ from games, however, in several ways. For one, the tasks for which an organization is conducted constitute tangible changes in the environment. In addition, the typical organization is more complex than the typical game—involves more participants, more tasks, more equipment, more roles and activities. Since it is larger, the organization is not generally characterized by face-to-face interaction among its participants, hence norms in the organization are only partially shared. As a result of these characteristics, integration of the organization is more difficult than integration of the game. Most organizations provide this integration through three means: (*a*) a formal arrangement of jobs so that tasks are accomplished; (*b*) a chain-of-command or authority system through which the jobs, tasks, roles, and activities of the organization are tied together; and (*c*) a set of written documents that pin down portions of its conceptual structure.

For our purpose, then, an **organization** consists of an identified social system that is conducted for one or more tangible tasks in the external environment. Organizations are usually characterized by partially shared norms, a task structure, an authority structure, and written documents that support the enterprise.[7]

We illustrate these characteristics by describing a small (hypothetical) organization, the J. J. Jones Corporation. This organization sets for itself the task of manufacturing electrical switching equipment for both home and industry (although it generates many other functions, including the provision of jobs within its community and pollution of the atmosphere through its smokestack). Jobs within the firm include those of stamping out metal enclosures, assembly of switches, sol-

---

[7] Some major contributors to role theory have dealt primarily with organizations and have suggested theories that were focused upon authority, task accomplishment, role expectations, and conformity to norms (for examples, see Gross, Mason, & McEachern, 1958; Katz & Kahn, 1966; Oeser & Harary, 1962, 1964; Preiss & Ehrlich, 1966). Such emphases are less useful when we are interested in other social system forms that do not have the characteristics of organizations.

dering connections, sweeping floors, keeping account books, supervising weekly meetings of personnel, and planning social events for employees. The firm also exhibits an authority structure: a president, a treasurer, various secretaries, foremen and line workers, janitors, and a computer operator. All of these persons are controlled by norms, some of which are set forth in written rules, some of which are merely shared among sets of employees who have common experiences.

The concept of organization involves two additional notions that we have not yet considered: authority and task structures. We consider each of these briefly.

AUTHORITY STRUCTURE

Chapter Four introduced the notions of power, authority, and legitimacy. To paraphrase that discussion, *power* denotes the ability of a person to influence another, however that influence is accomplished. *Authority* denotes power that stems from positional membership. Some authoritative power is rationally based. For example, you are likely to "follow the doctor's orders" when ill, because you presume that your pysician is sufficiently well trained to prescribe medication that will make you well again. However, in some cases we follow the directives of others for no explicit, rational reasons other than that they hold a superordinate position to ours within a social structure. Within organizations, the president has the "right" to order the vice president around—not because he or she is wiser or more moral, nor because his or her decisions are always going to have a positive effect—merely because his or her position is superordinate. This latter form of authority is termed *legitimacy*.

Those of us who have grown up in a society that is dominated by organizations are used to authority. However, representatives of preliterate societies (or New Left advocates) find it difficult to understand why it is that we take orders from those whose positions within an army, university, or business firm are hierarchically superior to our own. Well, why do we? Once again, several answers may be given to this question. Within the army or prison it is likely that we take orders because should we not do so we lay ourselves open to immediate punishment. Some of our willingness to follow directives may also reflect our appreciation of the difficulties of organizing collective effort. Thus, when entering a new situation where all hands are turning to the accomplishment of a task, some of us will ask, "Who's in charge here?" and then inquire of that person if our help is needed. But some of us defend the dictates of authority as if they were delivered by Jehovah on Mt. Sinai. We have all been infuriated by clerks or librarians who were unable to make reasonable exceptions to an order they were given. A couple of years ago a captain for Eastern Airlines was fired for dumping unburned fuel from his jet engines into a bucket on the apron. Although his act saved pollutants from being disbursed into the air, he was dismissed because his airline "could not afford to trust a man who would not follow orders" (according to an official of the firm). Earlier we reviewed research by Milgram in which innocent subjects were willing to follow orders that called for them to "hurt" and "injure" others. For some of us, then, following orders has become a way of life, the organization an entity *sui generis,* an object of secular worship.[8]

For whatever reasons, Westerners are generally familiar with the theory of order giving and order taking, see these processes as endemic to the organization of collective effort, and are willing to cast themselves into either of these roles if the situation warrants. This general willingness to participate in the authority game is sometimes summarized with the terms of **leader** and **follower,** which I will define for purposes of this exposition as persons who are assigned the jobs, respectively, of saying what is to be done and of doing it. Or, to put it another way, within the organization the leader has authority over the follower by virtue of their respective positions which are assigned to them structurally.[9] In some cases the leader will also be assigned explicit sanctions that can be used to enforce his or her orders; in other cases no such powers will be structured.

In preliterate communities (and in some laboratory experiments of the social psychologist) leadership and followership grow from the personal characteristics of persons who are present. However, such haphazard assignment of leaders is untrustworthy. Instead, most organizations take upon themselves to assign authority in an explicit and public fashion by providing a broad conceptual structure in which positions for the organization are clearly set forth. In the typical table of organization for a factory, for example, we find a president who has authority over several vice presidents and a treasurer, who in turn supervise section chiefs, district managers, foremen, and so one on down the line to the workers who have authority over no one else. Such an arrangement is termed an **authority structure.**[10]

Two variables are often discussed in the literature on authority. The first of these is the **domain of authority,** which is defined as the range of facets expressing the follower's behavior over which the leader has authority. (Domain of authority is comparable to the notion of breadth of role that we encountered in Chapter Three.) Except in rare organizations whose control over their members is "total" (as has been claimed for fanatical religious cults), the domain of behaviors for which authority is specified is usually quite narrow and limited to task-related events. Foremen should exert authority over the worker's output, care of tools, safety, and the like—but should have nothing to say about the worker's home life, recreational habits, choice of foods, or church membership. Organizations differ,

---

[8] The psychoanalyst would tell us that our willingness to accept or resist authority stems from our relationships with our fathers. The educational philosopher makes similar claims for our experiences with teachers in classrooms. Both may be partly right (see Chapter Eight).

[9] Leadership is sometimes confused with *charisma,* which describes the ability of the individual to exert influence over others (see Chapter Four). The former is based on authority, the latter on personal characteristics (again, see Chapter Eight).

[10] Although peculiarly characteristic of the organization, authority structures may also appear in other social system forms, particularly games, communities, and societies.

however, in the breadth of domains over which they characteristically exert authority. Teachers complain that authority is exerted over them within regions that are extrinsic to the tasks set for the school—such as standards for their behavior when in the home or marketplace. American firms often prescribe a wider domain of conformity for business leaders than is prescribed for equivalent positions within British firms, reflecting beliefs about the education of upper-class persons in the two countries.

The second variable discussed for authority is **span of control**, which refers to the number of persons over whom a given leader has authority. As a rule, breadth of domain and span of control are negatively related. That is, when the domain of activities for which authority is specified is broad, it becomes difficult for the leader to supervise more than a few followers. Research done on army infantry squads since World War II, for example, resulted in reducing squad size from nine to five men, since it was discovered that a squad leader had difficulty in exerting effective control over the larger number under battlefield conditions (Torrance, 1954b).

Authority structures may be expressed in graphical format, basic rules for which are discussed as "structural role theory" by Oeser and Harary (1962, 1964) [B&T, Selection 6]. Let us examine some of the properties of authority graphs for organizations. First, we normally presume that the organization has but a single domain of authority, but this is not prescribed by definition. In fact, some organizations exhibit two or more unrelated domains—each of which generates its own authority graph. Such a situation appears, for example, within school systems where there is an inspectorate that is responsible to a central authority and not to the school's principal. Another example appears in totalitarian armies where the "political commissar" or "gestapo" representative may have authority unrelated to that of the nominal commanding officer. However, most organizations have found that it reduces blood pressure and aids in efficient decision making if there exists only a single authority structure.

Second, most authority structures consist of a single connected graph. Should the organization feature two independent authority structures these might operate at cross-purposes, and most organizations tend to close up gaps in the authority structure. Third, most authority structures feature a single "top boss." It would be quite possible to have two or more bosses at various points within the authority structure, as is illustrated in Figure 7.1. However, most organizations would consider this an additional source of confusion, and so they add the restriction that the graph must have a least upper bound in some person. This is equivalent to making the authority graph a "semilattice," as is illustrated in Figure 7.2 (Friedell, 1967). For example, the president of the firm will usually demand that all members of the board support him (or her) unequivocally and cease their individual efforts to undermine his authority by exerting their own over persons nominally his subordinates. However, even within this structure it is possible for some positions to have

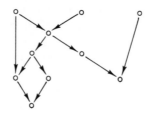

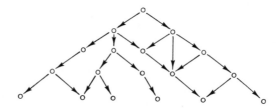

Figure 7.1. An illustrative, nonrestricted authority structure.

Figure 7.2. An illustrative authority structure as a semilattice.

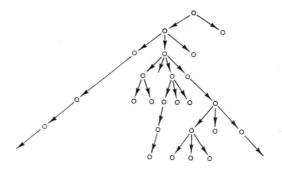

Figure. 7.3. An illustrative authority structure as a tree.

more than a single leader. If we state as an additional requirement that no position shall have more than one leader, this converts the structure into a "tree," as illustrated in Figure 7.3.[11]

---

[11] Recently a number of organizations have begun to experiment with authority structures having different properties than those listed here. In "team organization" or "project management" separate authority structures may be set up for different jobs, or a group of persons may share authority jointly (Golembiewski, 1967). Perhaps unfortunately, these concepts are more often discussed than implemented.

Additional terms have been developed for describing authority structures. For example, *line positions* within an authority structure are those having authority over others, whereas *staff positions* provide services to a supervisor but do not themselves have authority. Organizations may be found wherein many, or few, staff positions appear. *Pyramidal organizations* are those having few top leaders and a long chain of command, whereas within *flat organizations* there are more top positions and fewer levels of authority. Research has been conducted on the effects of various types of authority structure on organizational productivity, morale, and other desirable effects (Haas & Drabek, 1973; Thompson, 1967).

One intriguing effect of authority stems from the way positions in an authority structure are normally filled. Most people find the exercise of authority pleasurable and are reluctant to appoint persons to positions of responsibility (and pleasure) unless those persons have demonstrated that they could handle jobs of lesser responsibility (and pleasure). Thus, positions in many organizations are characteristically filled by choosing among candidates who are performing lower-level roles satisfactorily. Each person moves up within the organization, from position to position, as long as he or she is doing well. When the person does not do well, he or she is left in that job. Thus, the authority structure is also a position sequence (see Chapter Four), and the only persons stabilized in positions are those who perform poorly. In time each person finds his or her "level of incompetence," and the organization smothers in burgeoning bureaucratic boobery—otherwise known as *The Peter Principle* (Peter & Hull, 1969).

TASK STRUCTURE

Organizations are also characterized by a **task structure**. Such a structure exists when an overall task is recognized, jobs are set forth for its accomplishment, and jobs are assigned to individuals. Characteristically, jobs are assigned to positions within the organization. For example, the parish church may be staffed by two priests, a sexton, several sisters, and so on. The pastor has managerial responsibilities, must hear confession, must conduct certain masses, and the like. His assistant may be charged with youth leadership. The sexton is to maintain the physical property of the church and parish house; the sisters are to teach Sunday school. Each expected role supports a set of jobs to be performed, the jobs bearing functional relationships to the general task of maintaining the spiritual welfare of the congregation, while the roles in turn are assigned to positional titles that are to be filled by different persons from time to time. This does not mean that other functions are not performed by the organization that are not specified in the task structure, nor must the jobs set forth be performed well or even at all. Nor need jobs, if performed, actually contribute to task accomplishment, nor need the sequence of jobs set forth be the "best" way of accomplishing the task. Archaic forms of worship may drive parishioners away from the church, a given pastor may be incompetent or drunken, or the church may perform additional good works in the community not specified in its tasks. The behavioral roles and functions of any organization may or may not correspond with its task structure, although correspondence is likely in the well-run organization.

Task structures may also be graphed, as may authority structures, and this latter is often done as an aid in job analysis. Jobs performed within a given role must often be performed in sequence, whereas jobs from two related roles may also be functionally interdependent (Trahair, 1967). If the organization is to prosper, steps must be taken to assign jobs to roles that mesh well together, to integrate the jobs of interdependent roles, and to assign persons to positions who are motivated and trained to perform the roles for which they are responsible. Thus, tasks of *management* appear within nearly all organizations. In fact, management is more important in larger organizations, and one of the hallmarks of large organizations is the amount of their effort that is spent in management. (Contrast the small managerial structure of the private college with the enormous managerial assembly of the university. The latter consumes a much larger proportion of the educational dollar.) The significance of managerial tasks has led analysts to propose classifications for organizational tasks along managerial lines. Thus, tasks such as personnel allocation, training, resource procurement, management of employee motivation, safety, and the like are recognized. Needless to say, in the small organization such tasks may be performed by a single manager, by workers themselves, or may be ignored.

The fact that jobs and roles are typically differentiated within the organization is usually denoted by the term *specialization*. In Chapter Three we differentiated between two aspects of specialization. A *diffuse* role or job is one that involves many or all of the domains of behavior encountered within the system; whereas a *nondiffuse* role is one involving but a limited domain. A *singular* role or job is one that is performed by a single person within the social system; a *nonsingular* one is performed by several persons. Diffuseness and singularity have different implications for the organization. Singular roles are generally performed by those who have special training and can command a higher salary. By the same token, such persons are sorely missed when ill or when their positions are vacated. For these reasons, organizations tend to avoid singularity. Diffuse roles are harder to learn, to supervise, to evaluate, and thus tend to be eschewed by the task-oriented organization, despite the fact that they are more rewarding to individuals who perform them. But the greater the number of nondiffuse roles in the organization, the more one needs a system of control and integration. In the archetypical organization, then, there is a drift toward defining roles so that they are *non*diffuse and *non*singular, together with endless expansion of the managerial system—tendencies satirized by C. N. Parkinson (1957).

Specialization is a necessity, of course. Surely a Saturn moon rocket could not be assembled without enormous specialization of roles and automated machinery. Organizational roles require both expert performance and years of training. Moreover, productivity expands when roles are assembled into a production line. However, specialization has its disadvantages. One of these is that specialized roles can become insufferable in their triviality and boredom. Another is that specialists tend to know only their jobs and be ignorant or intolerant of the importance of others' jobs. Thus, in embracing specialization we may also buy into an occupation that is warped and paper-thin—having sold our humanity for job security and the comforts of a high civilization. Taken at its worst, the life of the organizational member can be an ugly thing indeed; for he or she is afflicted with a boring though complex task, a myopic outlook, an incompetent superior, and a complex authority structure that must be honored if he or she is to keep his or her job. This bundle of ideas is anathematized with such terms as *bureaucracy* and *red tape*. But to rail at a phenomenon is not to solve it. Organizations, and the bureacracies they engender, are one of the most significant inventions of human beings, and few of us would be willing to abandon the high civilization they engender. However, Linton (and Kafka) are right in that bureaucracy tends to reduce us all to insectivorous forms. Too often we rationalize organizations for their products; we must also learn to humanize their proceedings.

Is it possible to have an organization without a task structure? For that matter, is it possible to have an organization without an authority structure? Clearly, some social systems appear with but one of these. The Masons constitute a persisting social system with a magnificent authority structure and only minimal tasks, if any. Task-oriented social systems without authority are harder to come by, but such a state is claimed for some utopian communities or recent communes. It is difficult to think of these as examples of organizations. However, organizations that have temporarily lost their task or authority structures are easy to find. Consider the March of Dimes organization, which survived a major crisis a decade or so ago when the task that hat been set for the organization—namely the eradication of polio— was suddenly accomplished! One can imagine the consternation in The Head Office when rumors of the successful Salk and Sabine vaccines were verified. Here was a magnificent, successful, functioning organization about to become bankrupt—because of success! But fear not, Leadership Was Equal To The Challenge, and a new task was selected—eradication of birth defects—which could assure continuance of the organization.

This example serves to remind us that organizations are social systems and are manned by individuals who have their own needs and definitions of the situation.[12] Persons retain membership in organizations because it pleases them to do so, and they will not abandon their positions or suffer the destruction of the organization gladly. Although organizations are characterized by task and authority, they survive through accomplishment and rewards for their participants.

---

[12] Barr (1958, pp. 34–35) illustrates this point by satirizing the university in which

There's no common purpose. The trustees want to prevent subversion and stay solvent. . . . The president wants to get publicity and, eventually, if it isn't too late, a

ORGANIZATIONAL VARIABLES

A substantial literature has now appeared discussing variables that may be used to differentiate organizations, many of which have also been used by other authors to "define" organizations (Benson, 1977; Etzioni, 1961; Haas & Drabek, 1973; Katz & Kahn, 1966; March, 1965; March & Simon, 1958). One of the most primitive of organizational variables is simply size. Many organizational phenomena are related to size, such as bureaucracy, productivity, morale, and the like (Thomas, 1959) [B&T, Selection 16]. Why is this so? What difference does it make to the employee who is working in a room with 30 other persons whether the organization has 300 or 3000 members in all? Unlike the small group, the organization is but weakly connected by bonds of authority and task, and we have not presumed these bonds to change as a function of size. Size, then, must be a marker variable that just happens to correlate with other variables that determine organizational effects. Many of these have already been discussed. Larger organizations tend to be more role differentiated, more specialized, more bureaucratized, less sensitive to the needs of employees, and so forth. Although each of these is a tendency, the relationship with size is not invariant (Haas, Hall, & Johnson, 1963; Hall, Haas, & Johnson, 1967). Fifty thousand Egyptian slaves hauling granite blocks for a pyramid are less role differentiated than 500 employees on a modern assembly line. Moreover, regardless of size the modern secondary school is surely more specialized in its roles than the primary school.

Another set of variables is associated with the task of the organization. As we have already suggested, some organizations process products, others people. The processing of products is a simpler task, since tangibles are produced, shaping those tangibles is less likely to be constrained by morality or law, and success may be measured in economic terms. The processing of people involves complex relationships between staff and clients, and success is more difficult to judge. Some organizations also attempt to set a vastly complex structure of jobs, leaving as little to the initiative of the individual as possible—whereas other organizations set minimal job specifications and give autonomy to the participant (Katz, 1968). Some organizations set narrow tasks for themselves and are vulnerable to decline in need for that task—as when buggies or cuspidors are no longer needed.

Other variables are associated with the authority structure. Within some or-

---

bigger job somewhere else. The department heads want to raid each other for students, especially for majors, and thereby enlarge their departments. The professors want to publish, get promoted, get famous, and meanwhile stave off their creditors. . . . The wives of the professors . . . are socially ambitious and go in for cutthroat competition. The men students try to make fraternities, make athletic teams, avoid study, and then graduate somehow or other. The girls try to make sororities and find a husband. The parents of the students hope their offspring won't 'get ideas.' The dean of women hopes the girls won't conceive anything more dangerous than a conᶜept before they find husbands. And the alumni hope the teams will win, and hunt promising high school athletes to send us.

ganizations authority is based on explicit sanctioning, as in the army, whereas in business firms and universities authority is more likely to reflect loyalty and charisma. Some organizations rely on complex written rules for job specifications; in others jobs are defined by shared norms that are "understood" by all. And if written rules are used, these may either be revised, appropriate, and up-to-date, or they may be archaic and a subject for annoyance, laughter, or avoidance. Within a few organizations (such as family businesses or acrobatic teams) roles are attached to individuals, and when those persons die the organization will either go out of business or a painful period of readjustment is forced on the survivors. Within most organizations, however, roles and authority are given to social positions, and formal procedures are set for recruiting persons to these positions. Some organizations will recruit "anybody" to their ranks; others have complex programs of selection, assignment, and training for new members.

Still other variables are associated with behavioral structure in the organization. Some organizations have high morale, warm social relationships, and are "a good place to work"; others include ulcers or overt ethnic conflict among their functions. Again, patterns of interaction within the organization may take place along lines of authority or task structures, or may appear among friends who are not structurally related to one another at all. The vice president in charge of sales may play poker on Friday evenings with his old buddies who are in a different division of the firm, thus exchanging information between these two divisions that would not normally be exchanged. Moreover, such unplanned-for interactions may either hinder or enhance the functioning of the organization. In the organization, as in other large social systems, it is also likely that social groups will appear (Golembiewski, 1965), and when they do these groups can create their own conceptual structures that supplement, or are sometimes even at odds with, the official rules of the organization—hence Homans' (1950) distinction between the "official" and "informal" norms of the organization. And, lest we forget, organizations are laid within larger social contexts and are supported or attacked for the functions they perform within that context. Organizations may be lauded for their "social responsibility" when staff members devote energies to civic improvement, or may be rubbished when they fail to provide social services for their employees or dispose of their by-products in a nonpolluting fashion.

In summary, then, organizations are identified social systems that are set up for the accomplishment of tangible tasks. Most organizations are complex and are integrated through task and authority structures and through the use of written documents. To say that the organization has a task structure means that there exists at least one overall task to which the organization is committed and that jobs within the organization are assigned to individuals in facilitation of that task. To say that authority is structured means that the organization will exhibit a chain of command, a set of leaders and followers, whose ability to influence stems from membership in the organization rather than from functional consequences of the orders given. Because of their complexity, organizations often depend on written rules for specifying task and authority, although the "official" system of rules may be supplemented and modified by "informal" norms that also govern behavior. Although the following conditions will not always obtain, in most organizations: jobs are reflected in roles; jobs and roles are attached to social positions; and individuals are assigned to positions by formal procedures. Many organizational variables have been studied, including those applying to task structure, authority structure, behaviors of organization members, and others.

Organizations are an invention of modern, urban persons, and it is difficult to imagine high civilization without organizations to accomplish its tasks. Nevertheless, organizations tend to drift toward specialization and bureaucratization, and being a member of an organization is no guarantee of happiness. A major problem faced by urban civilization is to design organizations that are both effective and humane, for if we do not accomplish the latter, it is we who are serving the organization and not vice versa. It is intriguing that some of us solve this problem by worshiping "the organization," and find meaning in our lives through service to the golem that is both our creation and our tormentor. Others of us view the spectre of the organization with horror. Chaplain, Orwell, Whyte, and Galbraith have provided us nightmares of a future that is organization dominated and robotized. And yet, organizations (being instrumental) are among the most malleable of social forms. Organizations are different today from what they were yesterday, and most observers suggest that the rate at which organizations are changing is accelerating. Indeed, Bennis and Slater (1968) have suggested that the authority-ridden, highly specialized organization may be obsolete, and other social forms may have to be evolved to cope with the evolving needs of humankind.

ENVOI

This chapter began with a discussion of the assumptions one must make when applying role concepts to social systems. As noted, many theorists build assumptions concerning sanctioning, consensus, accuracy, veridicality, or conformity to role expectations into their discussions of social systems. Not only are such assumptions not necessary, they are substantially in error for many social systems. It *is* necessary, however, to build assumptions concerning characteristicness and interdependence into the discussion, and this was done through use of the concept of structure. In this chapter, then, social systems were considered to be systems of structured (i.e., characteristic and interdependent) behaviors. It was also noted that many social systems have other structured features (such as role expectations, tasks, or position complements). Finally, social system forms are defined by foundations of structured elements that may or may not include behaviors.

Concerning this last point, three rough classes of social systems were reviewed: (*a*) those defined primarily in terms of structured behaviors (including social groups, communities, societies); (*b*) those defined in terms of structured positions (kinships and families); and (*c*) those defined as normative structures (games and organizations). As it turns out, a rough relationship occurs between this set of distinctions and another concerning the planning of social systems. As we know, social systems may either be "natural" phenomena that develop and evolve in response to forces within the social environment, or they may be "artificial," planned events that are set up by their participants for explicit purposes. As a rule, systems that are defined behaviorally or in terms of positional structure are more likely to be "natural," whereas those defined normatively are more likely to be planned.

Actually, this distinction is overly simple. Someone must have provided the inventions that survive as contemporary social forms, thus our institutions are in part "the relics of past struggles among 'suffering, striving, doing' men" (Bendix, quoting Weber, 1962). Moreover, once organizations are set up, it would appear that they are as much driven by the irrational needs and local viewpoints of their participants as they are by rational considerations (Galbraith, 1967).

To what extent, then, are we the authors or the victims of our social systems? Must we accommodate evolving ways, or can we take arms against our troubles and build a better world for tomorrow? The term *experiment* is used to describe both the testing of predicted hypotheses and the manipulation of independent variables (or both). Marxism is either a theory of social evolution or a prescription for radical social change (or both). Those who attempt to describe evolutionary processes in social systems (such as Toynbee) are viewed as prophets of doom or as deniers of free will. The facts would appear to be that we are *both* authors and victims, both sculptors and clay. Much of our lives is spent in accommodating to existing ways, and those of us who find our customs unjust or immoral have a difficult time persuading others that these must be abandoned. Change appears to be torpid, and social systems seem to respond more to impersonal forces than to rational planning. However, it is also true that social systems are planned. Particularly in times of crisis, people are willing to contemplate the planning of new ways. Unfortunately, we do not yet have much general knowledge concerning either evolutionary or planned social change. Role theory provides a good vocabulary for describing social systems and for discussing problems that must be faced by individuals who participate in them. So far, however, role theorists have concerned themselves more with structure than with change.

This does not mean that role theory is without implications for social action. On the contrary, several general explanations have been advanced by those who use role concepts to account for the appearance of social systems, and these hold implications for organizing social change. The first of these, which I shall call the **normative orientation**, views social relationships in terms of mutual obligations that are governed by expectations. Crucial to this orientation are such issues as socialization, consensus, conformity of behavior to norms, and the association between norms, roles, and positions. This orientation is probably shared by more role theorists than any other, and throughout this text I have complained about those who build its assumptions into definitions of basic concepts for the role field. We confronted this orientation when we asked why it was that the individual was willing to accept a system of authority, and why it was that some persons appear to conform to injunctions for no apparent reasons. We will meet it again in the next chapter when we discuss the formation of the self. Given the normative orientation, should we want another to follow our wishes, we must convince the other that the behavior called for is morally right. Again, given this orientation, social change is unlikely unless one can convince others that present practices are wrong. Believers in the normative orientation include many religious figures and those who practice nonviolence. The most important social scientist preaching the normative orientation today is probably Piaget (1932), but others have also taught it, including Freud (1922), and of course Parsons (1951).

The second theory, which I shall call the **functional orientation**, sees social activity as a series of events that have explicit consequences. Social systems are constrained by their requisites and effects, and roles within them are organized for their functions. Stress is given to the importance of ecology and to the contribution each constituent social system makes to the total society. Further, each social system is quite literally a "system," and the performance of any given role has consequences for the roles of others. Role expectations are not so much prescriptions for action as they are rationalizations of behavior patterns that have already been set by necessity. Given the functional orientation, should we want another to follow our wishes, it is merely necessary to place that other within a context that constrains the behavior we are looking for. Moreover, the biggest obstacle to social change is that nearly anything we attempt to alter has consequences that disturb the equilibrium of other elements. Critics of organizations have preached this orientation from time immemorial, as have those who despair of federal programs for social betterment. On the positive side of the ledger, the Tennessee Valley Authority exhibits changes that can take place when a major, ecological feature is altered (Selznick, 1949). Social scientists concerned with this orientation have included Davis (1949), Levy (1952), and Merton (1949).

A third theory, which I shall call the **pragmatic orientation**, views human beings as reality assessors. Each of us enters contexts whose features we recognize, and our behaviors may be predicted from a knowledge of how we view those situations. Within this theory persons are seen not as moralists or as environmental chaff, but rather as reality assessors. Why does the pedestrian wait at the curb in the face of onrushing traffic? Not because of his or her moral scruples or because of the impact of that act upon others' behavior, but rather because he or she understands the consequences of stepping off the curb. Social systems are to be understood as concoctions of persons whose understandings are but limited to their own immediate situations; thus misunderstanding, deception, and malintegration are normal features of social organization. Moreover, since human beings are individuals with unique perspectives, it would be disastrous to attempt to enforce conformity on all.

Consensus is a fiction with which we comfort or alarm ourselves, not a behavioral reality. Given the pragmatic orientation, should we want another to follow our wishes, it is necessary to show the other that it is in his or her own interests—or perhaps our collective interests—to do so. According to this orientation, the biggest obstacle to social change is that participants cannot conceive of another way of organizing behaviors that would be an improvement on the present system, and were they presented with it they would accept the change proposed. Those who engage in explicit social planning often follow this orientation, as do managers of many large organizations. This orientation was set forth by the philosophers of pragmatism such as James (1890) and Dewey (1922), but its strongest contemporary advocates may be found among the symbolic interactionists such as Blumer (1969), Goffman (1959), Rose (1962), Stone and Farberman (1970), and Turner (1956, 1962).

Nor do these three orientations exhaust the available postures concerning social systems, although others have less often been advocated by those using role concepts. Another theory is the **exchange orientation**, as exemplified by such authors as Blau (1964) or Homans (1961, 1974). Within this orientation, individuals are seen as contributing to social systems and receiving, in return, things that they value. According to the exchange orientation, if we want another to follow our wishes, it is advisable to convince the other that sanctions will follow, depending on his or her conformity. Still another is the **conflict** or **power orientation**, which views social systems in terms of resource procurement, power differentials among participants, and the process of social conflict. Early conflict theorists included Marx (1867) and Simmel (1908), whereas modern proponents of this orientation would include Dahrendorf (1959, 1967), Coser (1956, 1967) and others. According to the power orientation, another follows our dictates because he or she has no alternative other than so doing. Within either of these theories, social change is unlikely unless one makes the status quo an unpleasant condition. Union leaders of a generation ago and "responsible" campus radicals of the present generation appear to adopt the exchange orientation, as they threaten to strike or demonstrate unless a specific change of policy is instituted. Revolutionaries embrace the power orientation, particularly with regard to the control over force and the institutions of social control (such as the press). Nor should we ignore the **cathectic orientation**, which suggests that it is not necessary to use force, moralization, or even understanding in order to obtain comformity—but rather that conformity results most painlessly from cathexes. In other words, if we can but control the preferential processes in others, we will achieve their conformity because they will "want" to do what we have planned them to want to do. Propagandists and advertisers illustrate the use of this orientation, for what is advertising but the programming of our desires? "Brainwashing" is another illustration (Schein, 1961). Advocates of the cathectic orientation have ranged from propagandists to J. B. Watson (1930), but a particularly strong case is made in Skinner's *Walden Two* (1948).

Well, which of these theories is right? Which best handles human behavior and the organization of social systems? Which offers the best prescription for social innovation? Observation suggests that each of these orientations is valid—from time to time. There can be no doubt, for example, but that many people with wealth, power, and prestige are capable of rationalizing their blessed states with a morality that would justify differential rewards. But, on the other hand, some wealthy people give it all away and enter the monastery. America exemplifies the success of pragmatism, and yet many Americans are becoming unhappy with their material success and feel they have left their moral roots behind. Advertising is a multi-billion-dollar success story, but it takes a lot of time to change people's preferences, and the society changes so rapidly that we do not have the time to properly condition ourselves to the newest devices available this year.

Each of these orientations is only partially adequate, then. Nevertheless, those who have preached them have in the main been unable to contemplate the existence of other orientations, since all theories seemed to be complete in themselves. Adherents of each orientation have tended to view others "with the blank disregard reserved for the peddler of irrelevance" (Holmes, 1966). As a result, the serious proponent of social change is left in some confusion as to his or her best strategy—whether to argue, cajole, threaten, seek structural changes in the environment, offer rewards, or riot in order to gain the attention of others. What is needed now is an amalgamation of these orientations and serious empirical work on the problem of social change.

Chapter Eight

The Person in a Social Context

Conscience is, in most men, an anticipation of the opinions of others.

—Sir Henry Taylor

As we learned in the last chapter, some role theorists view the person as a cog in a social machine. With excessive concerns for sanctioning, authority, and shared norms, some who write in the role genre have turned away from the individual. But if we are to predict human behavior only from context and positional identity, how then can we account for individual differences? How do we explain the genius, the deviant, the dropout, the social planner?

These are serious questions for the social scientist, and unless role theory discusses them it is merely a means for describing static social systems. As it turns out, other role theorists have addressed these very questions, and to their efforts we now turn. At the beginning of Chapter Seven we asked two questions: "Wherein lies the real environment?" and "Which came first, the social system or the individual?" To both of these we now answer, "Within the individual." Chapter Seven showed us how such concepts as role, position, and expectation could be used to describe social systems. Now, paradoxically, we will discover that these same concepts may also be used to describe the socialization, accommodation, adjustment, and leadership of individuals who live in a social world. In so doing, we shall explore one of the major promises of role theory—namely, its claim to provide an explanation of human behavior in concepts that also account for phenomenal experience.

SOCIALIZATION AND OTHER EXPLANATIONS

> *To summarize: The function of socialization is to transform the human raw material of society into good working members. . . . Role acquisition is probably the most important aspect of adult*
>
> *—Orville Brim*

A good place to begin is with a question. How are roles generated? How do we explain similar behaviors that appear in persons who share membership in a social position or who enter similar contexts? Moreover, why do exceptions to roles occur? Why do some persons fail to conform? How do we account for deviancy and creativity in role performance?

Socialization

Most role theorists use the concept of socialization to explain the appearance of roles. Roles, they argue, appear because persons are taught appropriate ways to behave by others. Moreover, the major way in which roles are taught is through the medium of role expectations. Thus, persons are exposed to experiences that would lead them to form similar expectations for their own and others' roles, and these in turn lead them to exhibit or encourage appropriate role behavior.

Some confusion has appeared among the related concepts of *learning, socialization,* and *education.* The broadest of these concepts is learning, which refers to any nonfacilitated change in the behavior or conceptual state of the person that can be shown to have followed from an environmental condition. Many things can be learned: things that are relevant or irrelevant, good habits and bad habits, behaviors that lead to the death of the person and the disruption of others, or behaviors that lead to harmony, discovery, and a better life for all. In contrast, socialization refers to those learning processes that lead to greater ability of the person to participate within a social system—either through understanding it or by conforming to it inadvertently. However, socializing experiences may either be accidental or planned, may be found within explicit social structure or may occur accidentally and inadvertently. Thus, it is also useful to differentiate education to be those portions of socialization that are deliberate, where one person intends to instruct another (Wilson, 1965).

For our purposes, then, **socialization** may be defined as changes in the behavioral or conceptual state of the person that follow from an environmental condition and lead to the greater ability of the person to participate in a social system. Socialization involves two notions: that of learning and that of accommodation. Within the socialization model, then, the environment is an independent variable, the person dependent. Socialization is successful to the extent that appropriate role expectations or behaviors are induced in the person. This does not mean that conformity to role expectations is the only successful form of socialization. Indeed, to survive in most social systems requires an ability to innovate, and some educators strive to induce such an ability. But within the socialization model, the person is conceived as a recipient rather than as an initiator or co-participant.

Socialization may be divided into the learning of overt phenomena (such as role behaviors) and covert processes (such as role conceptions). These two kinds of socialization differ in their implications. When we set out to discuss overt socialization we use concepts such as those of imitation, sanctioning, or reinforcement which make no assumptions about the covert processes presumed to stand behind behavior. In fact, the person who has learned a role may or may not have an understanding of the behaviors involved, may or may not appreciate their functional significance, may or may not understand others' expectations concerning them, or may not even be aware that he or she is exhibiting them at all.

Most theorists assume that roles are explained by conceptions, however, thus they have concerned themselves with the socializing of covert processes. When discussing covert socialization we must account not only for the processes whereby conceptions are learned but also for the ways in which they affect behavior, lest our person is (like Tolman's rat) to remain lost in thought. Thus, theories of covert socialization make additional assumptions about responses to conceptions. Not all theorists are willing to make these assumptions. Some prefer to discuss socialization in overt terms only, some make innocent (or stupid) assumptions about one-to-one relationships between conceptions and behaviors, and some use other theories altogether to explain the appearance of roles. (We return to these latter shortly.)

Types of Socialization

INITIAL SOCIALIZATION.

Several types of socialization have been discussed. Of these, perhaps the most important is the distinction between initial, later, and resocialization. **Initial socialization** refers to learning the person experiences when he or she is a child and is discovering how things are for the first time. Initial socialization involves many components, and any discussion of it must accommodate at least four facts. First, the child is growing physically during the period of intital socialization, and at later times during his or her growth can accomplish tasks that were impossible at a younger age. For example, control of the anal sphincter is beyond the ability of the 6-month-old infant, although the 2-year-old can usually do quite well at this task. Second, children are exposed to only a few types of social systems during initial socialization. These systems assume forms that are characteristic for a given society—forms that are determined by tradition and pressures from without rather than from the needs of the child. Most children in Western countries receive the bulk of their initial socialization in familes and schools, and adjustment to these forms may also determine adjustment to other social systems the person later encounters as an adult.

Third, within initial socialization the child is learning conceptions for the first time. The child is thus faced with the task of forming conceptual structure as he or she goes along, rather than that of adapting existing conceptual structure to new purposes. The process of initial socialization also begins well before the child is able to verbalize such events adequately. Moreover, the child has no preconceived standards or biases left over from other roles to unlearn. This suggests that initial role learning is likely to be more lasting, more wholistic, more central, more likely to determine later role learning, and less under verbal control than are those roles learned later in life.

However, evidence for these processes is hard to come by, not only because experimenting with children is viewed as immoral, but also because, fourth, the experiences to which the infant is exposed during initial socialization are also likely to persist as stimuli during later childhood and adolescence. To illustrate, Freud suggested that isolated, traumatic events in infancy (such as an episode of maternal rejection) would affect the whole course of personality development in later years; but this is hard to verify because the infant who has suffered trauma at a given stage of development is also likely to suffer similar traumas as an older child, since he or she is living within the same family, social class, and community.

That these four facts all appear within initial socialization has led to some confusion among those who would discuss this period of the person's life. Freud based his theories of personality primarily on concepts of physical development and parental behavior. Parsons and Bales (1955) stressed the social system of the family in their theory. McClelland (1951) focused upon the facts of initiality, and so it goes. Common to most such discussions, however, is the notion that initial socialization goes through *phases*. It is asserted that certain types of learning come first and that only after these have been accomplished (or the child has matured, or new portions of the environment have been encountered) does the child then turn to other learnings. This notion of the phases of initial socialization is basic in Freud's writing and is commonly expressed with the phrase "developmental tasks" (after Duvall & Hill, 1945; Havighurst, 1952, 1953).

Associated with the idea of phases in initial socialization is the proposition that problems associated with each phase must be properly mastered or the person will retain "scars" in his or her personality that will harm later development. What conditions are likely to promote the solving of developmental tasks? Most commentators stress that the basic environmental condition must be a warm, loving, and supportive home, although Bettelheim (1950) has pointed out that "love is not enough," and that the child needs predictability too.[1]

LATER SOCIALIZATION.

The boundaries between initial and **later socialization** are arbitrary, but for convenience let us place them at that point in the person's life when he or she begins to make self-conscious choices about identities or social positions. Within Western societies, at least, this usually takes place during adolescence. At about the age of puberty the young person begins to realize that decisions must be made about education, occupation, and life style, and that these decisions will affect greatly the course of his or her life. This does not mean that all persons are equally involved in identity selection. On the contrary, few identity choices may be open within the caste-ridden society. For some boys in our society choice of a career may be preprogrammed by parental reinforcement, whereas for some girls the selection of a career may be thought secondary to the problem of finding a husband. Nevertheless, the task of choosing identities for oneself is widely experienced and is distinct from those involved in initial socialization. Indeed, so central is this task that adolescence in Western societies is sometimes described as a time of "identity crisis" (Erikson, 1968).

Later socialization differs from initial socialization in other respects, too. Physical maturation is nearly completed. The youth is exposed to a wider range of social systems, hence the home and school have diminishing influence. Since the experiences an adolescent receives during later socialization are secondary, his or her response to them is filtered through the forest of earlier learnings that were acquired as a child. In part the person builds on these experiences, but in part they hamper his or her growth if the new conceptions called for violate assumptions that were learned earlier.

Partly for these reasons, and partly because of the youth's developing sexual drives, the period of later socialization is characterized by idealism, great energy, and a rejection of parental authority. Throughout the ages young persons have

---

[1] For that matter, not all of us share the belief that childhood happiness is a good thing.

Mendelssohn, the aristocrat born 'with a silver spoon in his mouth' . . . had yet another handicap. He had a happy, healthy childhood and a happy, healthy life. . . . True, he had problems and worries . . . but these superficial unpleasantnesses cannot be compared with the sufferings of a Mozart, Beethoven or Schubert. Hence, fate withheld from him those sources of deep and intense emotion, the expression of which makes the music of these great masters so dramatically moving, alternately discordant and conciliatory, restive and resigned (Kenton, no date).

Alas, poor Mendelssohn!

quarreled with their parents, sought to establish their own standards of dress and deportment, have left home, engaged in crusades, and sought release in competitive athletics and physical mobility. Some ages have offered an outlet for this idealism and energy—although, tragically, the usual outlet has been war. At other times no outlet has been offered, and then appears the recurrent and familiar theme of intergenerational conflict—as the men and women of the society find the excesses of their sons and daughters as tormenting as the latter had hoped they would be.

RESOCIALIZATION.

Adolescence also terminates, of course, and eventually the maturing person passes into adulthood when, presumably, the crises of identity are solved and idealism, energy, and rejection of authority have been tamed by marriage, career involvement, and indebtedness. When do these events occur? In traditional societies within a year or two of puberty, thus restricting later socialization to but a year or two. In modern societies, marriage and career entry may not take place until the mid-twenties, thus prolonging later socialization by a decade or more.

By conventional wisdom, socialization ceases with the entry of the person into adulthood. But does it? At least some changes in position and role have always been required of adults, but these have clearly expanded in modern societies. Many persons are required to make changes in their identities and roles when new technologies or social forms appear. Some of us make these changes easily, but others have difficulty in adjusting to new conditions. The newspapers are filled with advertisements for computer programmers, engineers, and other trained specialists, while at the same time high rates of unemployment persist in our urban ghettos and former coal fields.

To solve problems of this sort we are now building educational programs that will aid citizens to change jobs. Similar programs have also been advocated for other adult changes in role or identity, such as those associated with disability (Wright, 1960) [B&T, Selection 15] or aging (Cavan, 1962). In short, whenever the person must enter a new place in life, and that place requires new skills or a different outlook, it should be possible to smooth that entry with education.

But are the phenomena of later socialization and **resocialization** all that different? Time was when education was seen as a terminable process. For a while one subjected oneself to the rigors of an unpleasant school, then (what blessed relief!) one escaped to the consummatory pleasures of adult life. Today this concept if fading. More Americans are participating in formal education each year, perhaps as much as a third of the population. Classes for postgraduate degrees are filled with older persons who have returned for additional qualifications, and other opportunities are being offered in adult education that lead to no other outcomes than participative learning. If this be the case, then formal preparation for new roles may come to be seen as a life-long, cyclic process. Education is becoming consummatory rather than simply instrumental—an acceptable alternative to idleness, drug addiction, or rioting—resocialization a way of life (Biddle & Rossi, 1966).

Socialization Processes

Within many social systems, socialization of the new member is carried out informally and in the context of normal sequences of interaction. However, other social systems exhibit explicit activities that are concerned with member socialization, and some social systems are operated primarily for the task of socialization.

Organizations whose primary fuction was socialization have traditionally been called "schools," "colleges," and "universities," and the institution of which they are a part, "education." Lately this usage has been eroded due to the acceptance of additional functions by schools and the appearance of other types of socializing agencies that do not identify themselves with education. As for the multiplication of goals in education, consider the many-faceted contributions of Clark Kerr's "multiversity" or the fact that public high schools of today are called on to provide driver training, adult education, a winning football team, attractive courses that will keep teen-agers off the streets, sex education, and employment opportunities for citizens who serve as "teacher aids." In addition, various agencies have now appeared whose function is resocialization such as counseling bureaus, social work agencies, halfway houses, pathway organizations, chapters of Alcoholics Anonymous, vocational rehabilitation centers, physiotherapeutic establishments, and on and on (Empey & Rabow, 1961; Landy, 1960a; Landy & Wechsler, 1960) [B&T, Selection 47]. Let us refer to the entire bundle of such organizations, both schools and others, as **socializing agencies.**

Many distinctions have been suggested for the activities of explicit socialization including schooling, lecturing, coaching, training, apprenticeship, and so forth. As a rule, *instruction* occurs whenever one person attempts to socialize another. *Schooling* refers to the appearance of organized instructional activity in which the position of teacher is differentiated from other positions in the system and given the explicit task of socializing neophytes. Within schooling one may distinguish *lecturing,* when the person provides the other information, from *coaching,* when the person helps the other to practice his or her new role (Strauss, 1959, pp. 100-118) [B&T, Selection 43]. In *training* the neophyte is placed under the supervision of one who is already a member of the position but is not positionally differentiated from the latter, whereas in *apprenticeship* the neophyte is given a separate positional membership that will lead to joining the ranks of journeymen only when sufficient skill has been reached or time has passed.

Other distinctions have been suggested for the classification of socializing processes that occur informally. One of these is **cooptation,** which refers to the ways in which a group imposes its standards and values on the person who sets out to enter or change it (Michels, 1911; Selznik, 1949). For example, an early study by Merei (1949) documented cooptation in groups of young children, in that those who would "lead" had to adopt the expressive norms of the group in order to get along with other members and eventually to achieve actual "leadership."

Another process is **assimilation** which concerns the interaction between a person and a social system (or, more often, an immigrant and host populations) such that in the process they become more alike (Taft, 1966). Involved in assimilation are such processes as accommodation, adaptation, and adjustment, with the end-state of assimilation being reached when the person is no longer distinct from other members of the social system into which he or she is passing. Assimilation is greatly facilitated when the entering person carries no identifying stigmata, such as racial features or an accent, that make him or her stand out from others. It is also aided by the reduction of prejudice toward the stranger, the acceptance of the task of assimilation by all concerned, the presence of supporting social systems, and the absence of threat. Weinstock (1963), for example, argues that "the higher the immigrant's position on the occupational prestige scale in the country of origin, and the greater the transferability of his skill, the more acculturated he is likely to become in the country where he settles." Porter (1965) points out that within Canada the assimilation of immigrant populations has not proceeded as fast as it has in the United States, because the goal of the "melting pot" has never been widely accepted, and because unassimilated, ethnic communities have been encouraged.

Other Explanations for Roles

Although it is popular, some theorists do not accept the concept of socialization as sufficient to explain the appearance of roles. While not denying that socialization occurs, these latter theorists find it unable to account for some role phenomena. A number of different theories have appeared from these latter, three of which should be noted.

1. Some theorists argue that roles arise in part from *instinctive or physiological processes* that lie within the person. For example, ethologists have suggested that sex roles, aggressiveness, and territoriality are induced through nonlearned processes. Psychoanalysts have sometimes argued that sexual behavior, dominance, mastery, and various other roles are inherited. Trait theorists in psychology sometimes presume an inherited base for roles that reflect intelligence, motor skills, or energy level. Such arguments are based on several beliefs: (*a*) that socialization is insufficent to explain roles that are truly general; (*b*) that "obvious" physiological differences in persons are bound to be reflected in behavior; (*c*) that certain forms of behavior are easier for some persons to learn than for others; and (*d*) that some animal roles are known to be based on instinct, ergo. . . . Arguments such as these have not been popular in the United States, particularly among minority groups. At their worst, such arguments imply that female sub-servience and war are inevitable.

At their best, they suggest uncomfortable "facts" to which we must accommodate in our social plans. We return to this explanation presently in our discussion of general roles.

2. Other theorists conceive roles in part to be *coerced by social processes* over which the person has little control. Some Marxists, for example, argue that the roles of the bourgeosie or proletariat are dictated by the structural features of the society. Social evolutionists sometimes state that a given technological base "requires" the appearance of certain positions and roles within the society, and so on. Arguments such as these tend to ignore the mechanisms by which the person goes about accommodating the roles of the system. In effect they say that whether persons like the situation or not, certain functions *must* be accomplished, hence roles must be performed within the system, and persons will be found who are willing to take these up. Once again, such arguments are not popular within the individualistic and capitalistic ethos of American society.

3. Finally, still other theorists see roles as *evolving from the interplay* of a person's needs and situational demands. For symbolic interactionists such as Turner (1962), roles are largely idiosyncratic, and to the extent that two or more persons exhibit similar roles, this similarity presumably reflects the fact that they have had similar experiences *and* face similar problems. After some years, those who study leadership have come to the conclusion that leadership roles reflect both the person and the context (Stogdill, 1974). Arguments such as these assign a more active place to the person than do arguments based on either instinct or social imperative—or arguments based on socialization for that matter. Within them the person is viewed as an independent variable, to some extent the master of his or her own fate; and for this reason this last explanation sits well within the mainstream of pragmatic, American thought. The explanation appears strongest when we are attempting to understand roles in small social systems where the person is able to exercise some control. It appears weaker when we are attempting to deal with roles in the large organization or society where the person has little power. We return to this explanation at several points in the discussion that follows.

These, then, are the major explanations offered for the appearance of positions, roles, and role expectations. Let us now see how these ideas have been applied in discussions of specific role phenomena.

INDIVIDUALITY

There's more to the self than Mead's the "I."

—*Wayne Wheeler*

Role theorists have used various concepts for viewing the person as an individual. Let us examine four of these: the self, general roles, deviancy, and love.

The Self

Major theorists concerned with the self have appeared within the symbolic interactionist tradition. This interest is usually traced to G. H. Mead (1934), who separated the self into two components, the self as an agent (the "I"), and the self as an object of reflection and judgement (the "Me").[2] The first of these, the "I," concerns the self as an actor, an independent agent, an individual who experiences, values, thinks, wants. It was this concept of self to which Descartes referred when he asserted "Cogito, ergo sum." For Mead, the "I" consists of "the impulsive tendency of the individual. It is the initial, spontaneous, unorganized aspect of human experience. It represents, then, the undisciplined, unrestrained, and undirected tendencies of the individual" (Meltzer, Petras, & Reynolds, 1975, p. 60). In terms of epistemology, we are surer of ourselves in the sense of Mead's "I" than we are of any other phenomenon, although to assert the independent existence of the "I" and a physical world leads us toward a philosophy of dualism, and it is probable that even this perception of ourselves as independent identities is a reflection of the individualistic stance taken in Western languages and social beliefs.

The second component of the self suggested by Mead was the "Me" which represents the person as an object, as a physical body and locus of social properties, as a recipient of behaviors from others, and as one to whom standards for conduct apply. Suppose I were asked to describe myself. I would likely begin with identity labels: "I am an American, a husband, a tennis player, a university professor, a social psychologist, a father of three children," and so on. In so doing I would be providing information about the conceptions I hold for myself as an object person. I would tell even more about "Me" if I also told about the preferences and norms I hold for myself: "I like to eat peanut butter"; "One should always clean a wound thoroughly." Altogether these constitute the "**Me**," which we may define as the set of all covert identities and expectations held by the person pertaining to him or herself as an object person. As we shall see, some of these expectations are formed through direct experience, but others—and a substantial number—are formed by internalizing expectations first voiced by other persons.

Although not to be found in the work of Mead as such, some of those influenced by Mead have also suggested a third component of the self to involve the characteristics of the person that are displayed to others. The best discussion of this concept, which I shall term the *image,* appears in Goffman's *The Presentation of Self in Everyday Life.* Goffman suggests that the person has an interest in controlling "the conduct of others, especially their responsive treatment of him. This control is achieved largely by influencing the definition of the situation which

[2] Actually, the distinction between "I" and "Me" was first suggested by William James (1890, pp. 291, 371).

the others come to formulate, and he can influence this definition by expressing himself in such a way as to give them the kind of impression that will lead them to act voluntarily in accordance with his own plan" (1959, pp. 1-16). To illustrate, let us consider the behaviors of several men who are trying to sell us life insurance. One of these men has mannerisms that suggest competency in fiscal affairs, another implies that he is concerned for our welfare, another wears a lapel pin identifying him as a Rotarian, another is "all business." Each of these men has a different **image**, which we may define as the set of identities and expectations for the person that are structured by context or are implied by the behaviors the person displays. Some aspects of a person's image are revealed inadvertently, by accident, or in response to unexpected events. But (as Goffman reminds us) the management of an image may be quite deliberate, in which case one is left to wonder which is the "real" self, the set of identities or expectations a person holds for him or herself, or those that he or she reveals to us in behavior?

What are the relationships among these three kinds of self-concepts? Mead suggests that there is a continual dialogue between the "I" and the "Me." As phrased by Meltzer (1967), "Every act begins in the form of an 'I' and usually ends in the form of the 'Me.' For the 'I' presents the initiation of the act prior to its coming under control of the definitions or expectations of others (the 'Me'). The 'I' thus gives propulsion while the 'Me' gives *direction* to the act. Human behavior, then, can be viewed as a perpetual series of initiations of acts by the 'I' of acting-back-upon the act (that is, guidance of the act) by the 'Me' " (pp.11-12; also see Meltzer *et al.*, 1975). It should also be clear that whereas the concept of "Me" is but a simple extension of other concepts that have appeared in role theory, the concept of "I" involves new assumptions not heretofore considered. When we conceive of the "I," we are in effect differentiating that aspect of the person which "wants" and "initiates action" from the conceptions of self formed and stored. Should we make use of a computer analogy for the mind, the "I" consists of those units in the computer that "takes action and makes decisions." The "Me" is those units that "store data" and in particular "data concerning the nature of the computer." The third concept of self, the *image,* can be added to this analogy by positing that the computer exhibits behavior so as to cause us to develop ideas concerning its structure or functioning (as we did for the computer "Hal" in *2001: A Space Odyssey).* The "I" and the "Me" are laid within the person only; the image requires an audience who are to respond to the behaviors of the person.

Although frequently theorized about, the "I" has attracted little research, possibly because of its awkward assumptions. Much of the literature on person perception may be conceived as related to the concept of image, but little of this effort was generated by the image concept. The "Me," however, fits well within the mainstream of role thought, is easy to operationalize, and has generated a good deal of research. Studies of self-referent identities are represented by a research tradition that has used Manfred Kuhn's *Who Am I?* (or *Twenty Statements Test)* inventory

(Kuhn & McPartland, 1954). For general reviews of these studies, see Mulford and Salisbury (1964) and Spitzer, Couch, and Stratton (no date). Studies of self-referent expectations for behavior are literally without end, but a general review of those compatible with the concept of "Me" may be found in Wylie (1968). For these reasons I shall concentrate on the "Me" from here onward in discussing the self.

Now, how does the person come to develop self-referent expectations? How does he or she learn identity terms for self and expectations for behavior that are thereafter his or her own? Various answers have been suggested to these questions by theorists such as Mead, Freud, Sarbin (1952), Piaget (1932, 1959) and Kohlberg (1968). Most of these answers have stressed that self-development proceeds through stages, with a number of developmental tasks that must be solved by the child, more or less in invariant order. Let us consider some of these.

1. The child must learn to differentiate his or her body from other objects. As readers may be aware, really young infants appear puzzled over the limits of their body and seem surprised to discover the sensations aroused when sucking or biting a foot. Once the child is able to make this distinction, a primitive (nonsymbolic) identity may be said to exist in the differentiation of *me* from *not-me*.

2. The child must learn to differentiate persons from other objects. Since persons are selective, whimsical, and dynamic, the child finds it necessary to differentiate them from more stable components of the environment. Interaction with others begins, and differential response to "significant others" may be observed. Given such distinctions, primitive (nonsymbolic) expectations may be said to exist for the behaviors of others that are not held for impersonal objects.

In addition, *role playing* may now be practiced. As we know from Chapter Six, role playing refers to the imitation of other persons' roles. Through role playing the child gains information about role performance and eventually gains insight into the situation in which the other stands (Mann & Mann, 1959) [B&T, Selection 23]. Why do children imitate? Partly because they are encouraged to do so by others and partly because imitation seems to be biologically programmed (Berelson & Steiner, 1964; Meltzoff & Moore, 1977). Whatever may be the reasons, role playing appears early in the life of the person, increases in complexity as the child matures, and persists as a major strategy of socialization throughout the person's life.

3. The child must learn the use of verbal symbols, and in so doing develops the capacity to reference him or herself as a person. Persons have names, and these names may be built into sentences in which the speaker and others are referenced. The child also has a name, and he or she learns to use that name as others have used it. A symbolic identity has been achieved for the first time, but it is inflexible. The child has no understanding of the relativity of symbol use and references him or herself as do others; for example, "John wants milk."

4. The child must learn to attribute sentience to others. Through trial and error

the child learns that some sentences spoken by others are repeated and relate in a predictable manner to actions taken by those others, particularly to sanctions imposed on him or herself for misbehavior. Eventually the child tumbles to the idea that the others' behaviors may be explained by assuming the presence of internal states that match those sentences. Attributed conceptions are now present, and given the fact that others are presumed to be sentient, the child is now capable of thinking of himself or herself in the same sentient terms. The child now recognizes his or her own self-formed conceptions for what they are; the person has become self-aware.

In addition, *role taking* may now be practiced. As we learned in Chapter Six, role taking derives from the veridicality concept and means that the person is able to (correctly) attribute conceptions to others. In role taking the person places him or herself "in another's shoes" and gains appreciation for how the world looks from that perspective. In the beginning, the child presumes that conceptions held by others are constant and independent of context. Later, as we shall see, he or she learns to attribute different conceptions depending on context. Once learned, however, role taking also persists throughout the person's lifetime and constitutes a major strategy for understanding, thus predicting the reactions of others.

5. The child must learn to internalize others' expectations for him or herself. Whereas at an earlier date the child learned of the norms for his or her conduct that were held by *significant others,* the child now incorporates those standards into his or her own expectations for self through the process of **internalization.**[3] In this process, attributed norms are first assigned to a *generalized other* and then are incorporated into the child's own normative system. What was once, "My mother does not approve of me eating with my fingers," becomes, "Everyone who is important disapproves my eating with my fingers," and eventually, "*I* must not eat with my fingers." In short, the child now has a conscience. In addition, some (but presumably not all) norms thus incorporated are also subject to **cathectic conversion** (Parsons, 1951) so that the child now "prefers" the prescribed behavior. This takes the sting out of the standard. The child no longer conforms because he or she "must" do so, but rather because he or she "chooses" to do so. Thus the child delights in being a "good" boy or girl. The self now formed includes not only expectations that are self-generated, but also expectations that were originally expressed for the child by others. The child's identity has now been expanded to include membership in the referential position constituting the *generalized other.* The self is still inflexible, however, for the child lacks understanding of social systems and the contextual character of roles.

Internalization has additional implications worth noting. For one, when expecta-

---

[3] "Internalization" is Freud's term (1933); while Piaget (1932) used "interiorization" for the same concept. The term, "generalized other" was first used by Mead (1934). Sullivan (1940) seems to have coined the term "significant other."

tions are assigned to a generalized other, the child is in effect attributing consensus. This suggests that the assumption of consensus which so often appears in social theories is a reflection of a stage of growth we have all experienced. For another, parents will often restrict the generalized other to members of a specific social class, ethnic group, race, or nationality. In effect, the child is being taught to differentiate "one of us" from "the dangerous stranger." In this sense, the learning of prejudice may also reflect the way in which internalization is conducted. For another, norms that are merely internalized have somewhat different implications from those that are converted to preferences. To take the latter step reduces resentment in the child but also may lead to less flexibility in the self when the child reaches adulthood.

6. The child must learn that certain roles (and role expectations) vary depending on context and identity. Thus, "When on a picnic it is alright to eat with one's fingers," and "Only Jews must fast on Yom Kippur." Once the child gains this understanding, he or she is able to participate in simple social systems (such as games). In so doing, the child also learns the rules by which social systems are organized for the first time. At last some expectations become attached to social positions (rather than to persons). The child also learns that he or she can take up (and in some cases put down) membership in social positions. As a result, the self now includes part-time as well as full-time identities, and expectations that are context specific as well as expectations that are general.

At this stage of development, internalized expectations are still absolutes, given products of a universal culture, a catechism of norms, preferences, and beliefs that are conceived of as being invariant and given by authority, or God. The self is differentiated by unbending. Piaget (1932) suggests that at this stage the child cannot conceive of any other rules for the game than the ones he (or she) knows; his expectations are the monarch and he their subject. Presumably some persons do not progress beyond this point (Kohlberg, 1968). (In Chapter Seven we met examples of persons who appear to worship the organization.) However, some persons clearly do, and additional developmental tasks are mastered.

7. The youth (no longer a child) should learn that internalized expectations are not inviolate. Rules for conduct are not absolute and invariant. Rather, they are conveniences—products of the actions of others—suitable for being ignored when appropriate. In Piaget's terms, the youth should now become autonomous.

Several processes seem to be involved in meeting this task. First, the person discovers that many forms are culturally relative and that different standards for conduct apply in other families, other churches, other nations. This information may be gained either through direct experience of other social systems or through education that provides such experiences vicariously. It is possible, of course, that the person may experience cultural relativity as a curiosity that has no relevance to him or herself. However, most persons learn to adopt somewhat different norms for themselves when entering a radically different context. For example, some young men learn indolence, chicanery, and theft while in the army, because norms for such conduct are prevalent in that context.

Second, many persons develop an ability to rationalize their norms in terms of values to which they may be logically related. **Value** is another of those wonderful terms in the social sciences that has scores of meanings. I shall use it here to mean a prescriptive statement that is accepted by the person as an absolute. It is characteristic of values that they need not be "explained"; rather they *are* "explanations" for norms or conduct. When first learned by the child, norms may constitute values in and of themselves. For example, the child may learn the norm, "I must never drink alcohol," without any understainding of why this norm might be appropriate. The more mature person develops an ability to derive at least some norms from values and beliefs. Thus, should an adult hold the value, "A person must not injure oneself," and the belief, "Drinking alcohol is likely to cause injury to the body," it is possible for him or her to derive the norm, "I must not drink alcohol." As this ability develops, then, some of the norms the person learned as isolated cognitive elements when a child become anchored with values. Other, unanchored norms are abandoned, and still others, new norms, are developed by the person as he or she thinks about the implications of values held.

Many distinctions have been suggested for the value concept, one or two of which are relevant to our discussion here. Values include both prescriptions for human behavior (as were illustrated above) and prescriptions for other states of affairs. Some values are cognitively isolated; others may be integrated into belief-value systems (such as a religious ideology). In breadth, values are similar to tasks. However, tasks are set forth explicitly and consensually for collective attainment within social systems, whereas values may be implicit and idiosyncratic to the person.

One approach to the classification of values has been suggested by anthropologists who tend to assume that major values are shared within a society. Thus, one might read in the typical ethnographic report that a particular society stressed "sacred" or "economic" or "body image" values in the explanations given by its members for their conduct. Such interpretations reflect a variety of concept systems. Perhaps the best known of these is the *pattern variable* classification first suggested by Parsons (1951). Many studies are now available in which two or more countries have been contrasted for their values using one or more pattern variables.

The self we have now described is probably sufficient when the person lives in a stable, traditional society. With it the person is able both to understand and to accommodate existing ways. But Western societies require yet another skill. Since contemporary social systems change rapidly, to be masters of their fates citizens must learn to change and control the systems of their societies. Thus, for adults, an additional task appears.

8. The adult (no longer a youth) should learn how to change and control the features of the social systems in which he or she participates. Social systems are no longer conceived as existencies to be accommodated, but rather as conveniences whose parts may be altered if there are good reasons for so doing. The self is no longer a passive accommodator, but is now conceived as a social planner and doer.

This task has limits. Most of us are willing to alter only certain of our social systems and are likely to feel upset when someone suggests changes in our nationality, ethnicity, social class, race, or family. But most of us eventually come to the conclusion that at least some of our social systems should and may be modified when their functions are dangerous, unpleasant, or immoral.

Once again, several processes seem to be involved in meeting this task. For one, strategies for manipulating the social system are teachable, and persons are more likely to conceive themselves as planners and doers when taught. City managers, business executives, community developers, and—increasingly—social workers, clinical psychologists, educators, and ministers are taught such skills within formal education. Revolutionaries, guerrillas, and partisans are provided similar training under less formal auspices—which serves to remind us that the renovation of social systems is not always popular. Among those skills required of the innovator are the abilities to persuade and cooperate with others.

For another, some of us plan social systems in which norms may be abandoned in favor of cathexes as tools for shaping behavior (Bredemeier & Stephenson, 1962). In such contexts a person need no longer concern him or herself with what "ought" to be done but rather concentrate on what he or she and others "want" to do. Utopian communities have been created with this end in mind during both the nineteenth and twentieth centuries, although (sadly) most such communities have failed to carry out the grubby tasks of physical maintenance. Another distorted example appears in the behavior of tyrants who exercise their unfettered preferences by stating (and enforcing) demands upon others. But perhaps the best example is to be found in the interaction of persons who love and trust one another. In such a context, behavior may be governed not only by each person's own preferences, but also by preferences each person attributes to the other, thus patterns of conduct and shared preferences develop interdependently within a negotiated order. Such a system evolves in a flexible manner, and its governing expectations involves preferences as well as norms. (We return to this prospect shortly.)

To summarize, then, the self has been viewed in many ways, but for our purposes we may conceive it as composed of identities and expectations that are held by the person for him or herself. Some of these are developed by the person from his or her own needs and thoughts, but others (perhaps the majority) are internalized from the expressions of other persons. The self develops in stages as the person meets a variety of developmental tasks. Each stage leads to better symbolization, greater differentiation, or more understanding of the relationship between the self and the social environment.

Is the self complete with the accomplishment of the last task we have discussed? Surely not. Philosophers and autobiographers assure us that they have experienced profound changes in self-concept at later times in their lives (e.g., St. Augustine). It is not common to speak of these as "stages" of development, however, since changes in the self during maturity are more likely to be idiosyncratic than shared. Major changes in the self also appear less likely during maturity than the specific learning of new roles. And for these reasons, few discussions have appeared of the development of self during adulthood.

General Roles

Another approach to socialization makes use of the notion of *general role*. As was suggested in earlier chapters, some roles and positions are context specific. Others, in contrast, are not confined but apply to all or nearly all contexts within a society. Few contexts appear within the United States in which race and sex are not salient identities—in which they do not affect behavior in some ways. How do we account for the appearance of such general roles? If learned, how are such common patterns of behavior induced? If not learned, then how else might such general roles be explained?

Like so many ideas in role theory, the notion of general role includes several different concepts that are useful to separate. (Unfortunately this is not always done, and authors who write about general roles may confuse their readers, or themselves, by alliding two or more concepts.) Let us begin by noting that some identity terms apply to many persons and contexts within a given society. Such terms denote **general positions** that are structured for the society in which they appear (see Chapter Seven). Positions reflecting sex, race, and age are all but ubiquitous in their impact within the United States, and identities based on ethnicity, the nuclear family, and obvious states of infirmity are nearly as general (Emmerich, 1961) [B&T, Selection 45]. In other societies these latter general positions may not be recognized, but others may appear that are associated with caste or social class, kinship, body size, or mystical experiences. In still other societies occupational, political, or skill-related identities may be structured as general positions.

Closely associated with the concept of general position is that of **general role**, which denotes those unique patterns of behavior that characterize members of a general position. Some aspects of a general role tend to appear regardless of context. Within the United States men tend to be more aggressive and women more sensitive, blacks to be less "up tight" than whites, children to be more impulsive than adults—regardless of context. In contrast, other aspects of a general role will be limited to a specific context. Girls learn to read more quickly in American primary schools than do boys (Gates, 1961; Maccoby, 1966; Stroud & Lindquist, 1942). (This difference does not appear at all, or is even reversed, in primary schools within other countries—see Kagan, 1969; Preston, 1962). American blacks tend to excel in professional athletics and popular music, American Jews and WASPs to be overrepresented within higher education.

In addition, members of the society may also maintain *general role expectations* for the members of general positions. As we know (again from Chapter Seven), role expectations are those that are structured for the positions of a social system. Provided that expectations associated with a general position are structured for a given society, we shall call them **general role expectations** for that position. Americans generally prefer women to wear "feminine" clothing, to approve of deference in children, to believe that those of Irish descent are skilled in politics. These illustrate, respectively, sex-role, age-role, and ethnic-role expectations.

The concept of general role expectation appears a straightforward one, but we should be wary of its apparent simplicity. For one thing, as we know (once again, from Chapter Seven), role expectations need not be consensually held to be structured for a given social system. General role expectations, then, may be held consensually within the society or may appear with nonconsensual features that are structured. (Men and women characteristically maintain somewhat different role expectations for men, as they do for women. Moreover, a person characteristically has somewhat different role expectations for him or herself as a person than for his or her sexual position—see Deaux, 1976.) For another, general role expectations may be held either *for* members of a general position or *by* members of a general position. Discussions of the former are more common, for example the term *sex-role expectations* usually refers to expectations held *for* men and women; but examples of the latter may also be found. Differences in the role behaviors of men and women are sometimes "explained" by positing that men and women hold somewhat different role expectations for themselves.

Like general roles, general role expectations may apply to specific contexts or may not be limited by context boundaries. And like other expectations, general role expectations need not be accurate or aligned. (Ethnic expectations are often stereotypic, and many are inaccurate.) General role expectations may also involve all three modes of expression as well as expectations that are held by subjects themselves and, in addition, those that are characteristically attributed to others. It all sounds quite complex, now, does it not? Perhaps we can reduce the confusion by noting that "most" authors who write about general role expectations assume consensus, discuss expectations *for* position members, are concerned primarily with noncontextualized behaviors, and confine their discussions to beliefs or norms that are held by subjects themselves. Those who write about expectations for the role of women, for example, are usually concerned with consensually held norms or stereotypic beliefs that are held about women regardless of context.

Whatever may be their bases, general roles appear in all societies. How do we account for the appearance of such phenomena? How do we explain the widespread and common differences in the behaviors of men and women, those who belong to different ethnic groups, or persons who differ in race or age? Once upon a time most of these general roles were explained by assuming the presence of inherited, physiologically based processes. According to this explanation, men were more aggressive than women because it was "in their nature" to be more aggressive, Jews had an inherited "instinct" for miserliness, blacks were "inherently" more musical, etc. Since the appearance of Margaret Mead's *Sex and Temperament* (1935), however, most social scientists have come to feel that general roles (except those associated with age and native ability) are learned and not innate.[4] Men and women, Jews and WASPs, blacks and whites, thus are assumed to behave differently because they have been appropriately socialized; and differences in role behavior are supported, if not induced, by differential expectations for those behaviors that are also learned.

How, then, do children go about learning to differentiate the general positions of their society and the behaviors and expectations that may be appropriate to each? Let us begin with roles and expectations that are associated with the child's *own* general positions. How does the young girl, for example, come to recognize her identity as a woman and come to act and think in ways that are appropriately "feminine"? A good discussion of this problem appears in Maccoby and Jacklin (1974), whereas Katz, Bowermaster, Jacobson, and Kessell (1977) review studies concerned with early sex-role socialization. In general, it is argued that those adults concerned with the young girl—her parents, teachers, and others—adopt behaviors that are explicitly designed to produce just these effects. Several such behaviors have been identified (Hartley, 1964) [B&T, Selection 44]. One of these is *molding,* which may be defined as the differential treatment of children before they are even aware of their general identities—"gentling" female or "rough-housing" male infants. Another method is *canalization* (Murphy, 1947), which refers to the differential manipulation of the environment for the child, as in the provision of sex-relevant toys. Another is the *differential manipulation of symbols* such as the use of sexually relevant terms of address ("good girl") with the child. Still another is *differential activity exposure,* when the child is taken to witness activities that are relevant to his or her future identity, such as football matches for the young boy. All of these behaviors and others appear within the typical family and are supported by similar behaviors that appear in the school and other contexts entered by the child. In this argument, then, general positions, roles, and role expectations are largely induced in the child through environmental pressure.

Another argument is based on the concept of **identification,** which may be defined as the attachment of positive cathexis by the child to an adult as a representative of a position that the child may enter. To illustrate, the daughter identifies with her mother if she approves her mother as a woman, or the university

[4] Current advocacy for the inheritance of general roles comes mostly from ethologists (for example, see Tiger, 1969). The idea that general roles might reflect instincts that had survival value for our primitive ancestors is attractive to some scholars (such as Wilson, 1975). Unfortunately, such ideas are often used as a basis for repressive laws or for resisting calls for equal rights. Moreover, evidence often opposes the assertions of the instinctivists. Tiger's hypothesis that men are instinctively more likely to "bond" in groups was contradicted in data collected by Booth (1972).

student identifies with his or her instructor if the latter is approved as a professional. It is argued that once the child has formed an identification with an adult, he or she will find it easier to learn the role exhibited by that person. The child will do so by imitating that role in his or her own behavior and will learn expectations by taking the role of the other with whom identification has taken place.[5]

This argument is similar to that advanced for the "significant other" earlier in the chapter, but identification requires the appearance of an older person who is positionally appropriate for the child. The mother, for example, is the "wrong" sex as far as the young boy is concerned, and it would be difficult for him to learn appropriate behaviors and conceptions for the male role from her alone. This leads to the general prediction that the child will find it easier to learn general roles and expectations when there is an appropriate other within the family or school with whom identification can be formed (Heiss, 1968). To illustrate, Roe (1953) suggests that forming an identification with an older mentor may be the most important experience determining the career of the young scientist. Boys whose fathers are clearly inadequate as role models, or girls whose mothers are unappealing as women, are argued to have more difficulty in later adjustments to their sex roles.[6]

Expectations for one's general positions form an important aspect of the self. But how *central* is each general identity? How important are sex roles, ethnic roles, or age roles to the person? In Chapter Five we noted that expectations are central to the degree that they are important to the person and dominate his or her behavior (also see Lewin, 1936; and Rokeach, 1962). Identities may also be considered **central** when they are strongly defended by the person, are bolstered by associated beliefs and values, and affect a wide range of the person's behaviors. To my knowledge this important topic has not been studied directly. It is often assumed, however, that those identities that are learned early in the person's life are also more likely to be central, and studies have been published that are concerned with the order in which general identities are learned. To illustrate, Foa, Triandis, & Katz (1966) presented data indicating that sexual identity is learned at an early age in several contrasting societies, hence sex roles should be quite central to the self. Racial identities also appear to be learned at an early age (Clark & Clark, 1947; Goodman, 1952). In contrast, religious and ethnic identities seem to be learned at a later age, thus should be more malleable when the child becomes an adult.

But what about expectations for general positions of which the child is not to become a member? Clearly, young girls learn about men as well as women, blacks

---

[5] The concept of identification may also be extended to reference positions. Some boys identify with athletes generally; some girls model themselves after actresses.

[6] Since children are more likely to be socialized by women in America, that is by mothers and female teachers, it is sometimes argued that girls form more realistic sex-role expectations, whereas boys form expectations that are more influenced by cultural stereotypes. Implications of these differences are discussed by Lynn (1962), who summarizes research on the topic (also see Vener & Snyder, 1966).

learn of whites as well as blacks, and so on. How does one learn about counter positions and their roles? Information of this latter sort is learned either through hearsay or direct experience with others. As we know, expectations formed through hearsay may be shallow and inaccurate. Hearsay also allows few opportunities for role taking, hence less integrated understanding of others or of roles that the child might perform in relationship to the other. In general, then, children should learn more about sex roles in families where children of both sexes are present and in coeducational schools (Brim, 1958). Religious, racial, and ethnic roles should be learned with greater accuracy, sympathy, and understanding when the child is provided supportive exposure to others representing different religions, races, and ethnic groups. Educators are well aware of this argument, hence their desire to provide schools that are religiously, racially, and ethnically integrated. Unfortunately, token integration and hostile interaction with members of counter positions may produce more problems than they solve (Bank, Biddle, Keats, & Keats, 1977). One gains little in replacing an unfriendly stereotype with an ugly reality.

Of studies of general roles and role expectations there is literally no end. Scores of books have appeared on sex roles alone during the past 3 or 4 years, and much of the published research on prejudice, attitudes, and attitude change concerns expectations for racial, religious, and ethnic identities. Clearly, general roles are an abiding interest of social scientists. One suspects that part, at least, of this interest is generated by our ambivalent feelings about general roles. To accept membership within a general position is to provide oneself with a set of ready-made expectations for behavior that become part of the self. To illustrate, the author (who is a male) habitually wears trousers and would not think of appearing in a skirt, except perhaps at a costume party. "The wearing of trousers" is appropriate for males in our society, and an expectation for this behavior has also become part of my self-concept. To accept expectations such as these is convenient and frees us from worry over what is after all a trivial matter.

On the other hand, when general roles lead to discrimination, or general role expectations conflict with the person's needs and ambitions, then identity becomes an albatross. It is surely immoral to deny a person access to education, careers, equal pay for equal work, recreation, or housing because of one's membership in a general position. General roles of one sort or another have appeared in all known societies. One hopes that we will be humane enough in the future to confine their impact to matters of style rather than substance.

Deviancy

Up to this point I have dealt with successful role learning and the development of an adequate self-concept. But not all persons develop selves and roles that are appropriate for adult participation. In fact, more persons than we normally care to think about are headed for criminality, mental disease, alcoholism, chronic illness, or other careers of maladjustment. If we are to understand the roles of real persons, we must also discuss events leading to these latter, less desired outcomes.

Once again, some definitions are in order. In broad terms, the concept of deviancy derives from nonconformity. Any behavior may be considered deviant when it does not conform to shared expectations. There is a sharp difference between the concepts of deviant behavior and deviant identity, however. All of us perform deviant acts from time to time, but only some of us are labeled as deviant persons. Let us sort out these two concepts formally.

For our purposes, a **deviant behavior** may be defined as one that violates expectations that are structured within a given social system. Deviant acts are normally defined only within a context, and what may be deviant within one classroom, social group, or family may not be deviant within the community, another social group, or the society at large. In most classrooms, for example, speaking without first raising one's hand and being called on by the teacher is a deviant act, and clapping at the end of a sermon would be deviant in most churches. Such acts would not be deviant in the theater. Note also that a behavior may not be equally deviant to all persons in the system. Within many American families, parents are more likely to judge pot smoking an act of deviancy than are adolescent children. Also note that persons may respond differently when witnessing an act of deviancy. Some may punish the miscreant, some may attempt other forms of influence, some may frown, some may do nothing at all (although they are aware of the deviant character of the act).

To define the concept of deviant identity, let us return to distinctions that were first made in Chapter Four. As we know, identities may be defined using various foundations. Let us consider those defined by trait. As we know, some behaviors (traits) are presumed to transcend situations, thus to be generally characteristic of those persons who exhibit them. Of these, some traits violate expectations and tend to provoke punishments from others when they appear. Those identities that are defined by traits which attract punishments that are structured for a given society I shall call **deviant identities**. To illustrate, the terms *genius* and *thief* both denote identities based on traits, but only the latter is deviant.

Most, if not all, deviant identities are social positions. Moreover, since they are based on the trait concept, deviant identities are generally "explained" by processes presumed to be characteristic of the person. Thus, a "thief" is thought to have poor impulses or habits, whereas a person who is "insane" is presumed unable to distinguish right from wrong. Some authors also expand the concept of deviant identity to apply to any position having low status. Thus, blacks, women, or handicapped persons may also be said to be "deviants." This seems unwise to me. Low status is simply not the same thing as structured punishment.

How does one become a deviant? Through what processes does one acquire such identities as criminality, insanity, or stupidity? Such labels are pejorative, and many social systems set up procedures to guard against their promiscuous application. For example, in nearly all societies there are formal processes of law through which one must pass before being declared a felon. Hearings are now required before a board of experts before one is declared insane or in need of special education, and some persons would seek to extend the protection of formal hearings to all forms of pejorative judgement (such as university grading procedures). On the other hand, some deviancy labels are protected by neither law nor custom. One may acquire the reputation of a "drunkard," "loser," or "loose woman" on little evidence and without much recourse. Nevertheless, these latter identities will also provide the victim punishments and will affect the way the person so labeled thinks about him or herself.

Given the pejorative nature of deviancy labeling, it is not surprising that social scientists have begun to study this topic. To illustrate one such interest, Szasz (1960) argues that to label a person "mentally ill" is likely to exacerbate that person's problems. This contrasts sharply with the usual medical practice of basing treatment upon a firm diagnosis that is understood by the patient and others. Normally we assume that the patient will be better off if he (and others) are aware of high blood pressure, ulcers, gout, or Buerger's Disease. To provide such diagnoses may reduce the patient's anxiety and should lead to cooperation in treatment. But if diagnosis involves the application of deviancy labels, the patient may actually be worse off if the diagnosis is made! One wonders to what extent this argument also applies to other quasi-medical deviancy labels, such as alcoholic and homosexual.[7]

Why then does the person become a deviant? What leads the person to become a criminal, an alcoholic, stupid, or insane? Three broad explanations for deviancy have appeared, based on innate processes, socialization, and interactive notions. Let us consider each of these briefly.

Nearly all forms of deviancy have been thought innate at one time or another, and today many social scientists believe in an inherited basis for intelligence, schizophrenia, homosexuality, or alcohol addiction. Evidence supporting such beliefs is shaky, since we are unwilling to conduct experiments that would allow us to separate inheritance from environment. Nevertheless, beliefs about the inheritance of at least some forms of deviancy are widespread and have several implications. For one, such beliefs argue against attempting to "cure" the deviant. Homosexuals may welcome such a belief, since it implies that they need not feel guilty about their impulses. Politicians may use such beliefs to avoid funding programs for criminal or addictive rehabilitation. Such beliefs also argue for eugenic planning, and advocates are sometimes found who would sterilize those who are stupid, insane, or "criminogenic."

Two theories have been set forth that would explain deviancy through socialization. The first, **inadequate socialization**, suggests that the child becomes a deviant

---

[7] For that matter, several authors have begun to study "illness" as a form of deviancy (Freidson, 1966; Mechanic, 1962; Twaddle, 1973, 1974). Shades of *Erewhon*!

because of failure of the environment to provide necessary experiences that are enjoyed by other children or failure of the child to utilize those experiences provided. Many environmental features may be missing and have been associated with later deviancy. Children who have no parent with whom to identify appear more prone to later deviancy; children of impoverished familes exhibit more deviancy than children of the well-to-do; children higher in birth order (hence, attracting less attention from their parents) show greater rates of deviancy, and so on. Such experiences, it is argued, are not in and of themselves the "causes" of adult deviancy. But once the child begins to exhibit signs of deviant behavior, his or her membership in a deviant identity may become a self-fulfilling prophecy in that the person generates treatments by others that will reinforce deviant ways of behaving (Schafer, 1967). The aggressive bully may be shunned by other boys (and their parents) thus encouraging him to strike even harder. The withdrawn child stimulates fewer and fewer contacts with others, contacts he or she badly needs. Thus, it is argued, deviancy may become a vicious cycle that entraps the child whose initial socialization was only minimally inadequate.

A second theory, **inappropriate socialization**, argues that the child is unlikely to be entrapped into deviancy inadvertently. Rather, the child is socialized *for* deviancy in that he or she is exposed to deviant persons with whom he or she can identify. This may take place deliberately or accidentally. Fathers who are professional thieves may train their sons to follow in their footsteps (or footpads, in this case), and specific forms of deviancy may be taught in some "reform" schools (a la Fagin!) or in adolescent gangs (Cloward & Ohlin, 1960) [B&T, Selection 13]. However, the child who is exposed to a drunken father or an anxious and withdrawn mother may learn how to play the roles of "drunkenness" or "anxious withdrawal" even though the parents involved would give anything to prevent this from happening. In support of this general argument, it is known that the children of criminals are more likely to become criminals themselves, particularly if the criminal's parent is of the same sex (McCord & McCord, 1957) [B&T, Selection 46]. Children of drunken parents are more likely to drink to excess, children of disturbed parents are more likely to exhibit disturbance, and so forth. It would be easy to oversell this evidence, however. For one thing, it might as easily be used to argue for genetic causes of deviancy. For another, nearly all of these forms of deviancy on the part of parents also lead to increased rates in *other* forms of deviancy on the part of children too. This suggests that the deviant parent may affect his or her child in two ways: by providing an inadequate environment so that the child has greater difficulty generally; and by providing a role model for specific deviancy should the child choose to identify with the parent. That these two processes should operate simultaneously requires ambivalence on the part of the child, for the child is likely to resent inadequacy in his or her home environment, whereas the theory of inappropriate socialization requires the child to identify with the parent. Needless to say, the evidence enabling us to differentiate inadequate from inappropriate socialization is not yet adequate (or appropriate).

Theories that would explain deviancy in terms of childhood socialization are enormously popular. For more than a century reformers have argued that poverty breeds crime and addiction, and if there is one legacy that Freud left us above all others, it is the idea that parents are responsible for the sins of their children. In a sense, the concept of socialization has become part of the myth culture of our civilization, and much of the activities of child psychologists, remedial educators, juvenile court officials, and those who operate correctional institutions may be said to reflect this general idea. And yet, there are difficulties with theories that would explain deviancy solely in terms of socialization.

For one, the evidence favoring such theories may be questioned. Granted that the child from an impoverished home is more likely to exhibit adult deviancy, does this mean that the stresses of that home "caused" later deviancy? Other explanations are surely possible. Those who grow up in poor homes are also more likely to be poor when adults, thus to be subjected to greater pressures toward deviancy when adults and to be less protected from prosecution when detected in deviant acts. Again, childhood poverty is often associated with membership in a racial or ethnic position for which stereotypic expectations for deviant behaviors are maintained by others. Would not these latter also be likely to cause deviancy through discriminatory treatment? To provide clear evidence for theories based on socialization one would have to conduct controlled experiments with children, but as we know such experiments are not likely.[8]

For another, such theories assume a passive role on the part of the child as well as a broad agreement on the definition of deviancy within the wider society. Both assumptions are questionable. Our pluralistic society involves a multitude of norms for conduct that often conflict. Conduct that might cause one to be labeled as a deviant among one group of persons may be entered into with impunity within a second group or may be *de rigeur* in a third. And surely the child is in part an active agent of his or her own destiny. The early application of some deviancy labels may be rejected by the child who then takes pains to eschew all traces of behavior that would be associated with that identity. Deviancy labels, thus, may either be a trap or a goad, and reactions to their application will differ depending on other aspects of the person's character.

Given these difficulties, some theorists have begun to develop theories concerning deviancy that reflect an interactive perspective. Within some of these latter, behavior that is viewed by some persons as deviant is seen as a reasonable, coping response on the part of the person (Becker, 1963). Thus, the prostitute enters into her profession because (among other things) it pays her far better than would a

---

[8] Moreover, when conducted, such experiments may produce surprising results. Joan McCord (1978) reports an early study in which urban boys were provided several years of counseling designed to prevent delinquency. Thirty years later, when these boys had become men, the program was discovered to have *increased* delinquency! (McCord suggests that such intervention programs may have the inadvertent effect of altering subjects' self-concepts for the worse.) However interpreted, such results pose a challenge to socialization theories of deviancy.

secretarial job. The person who exhibits emotional disturbances does so (in part) because such behavior provokes expressions of sympathy or acquiescence from others. The alcoholic enjoys relief from responsibilities and anxiety, the pleasure of other drinkers' company, and forgiveness from nondrinkers when at last he or she sobers up (Berne, 1964). Such theories view the person as a responder to the current environment rather than as a victim of early socialization.

A second interactionist perspective is *labeling theory*, which we first encountered in Chapter Four. Labeling theorists presume that the deviant is well aware of his or her identity, and focus on the processes and debilitating effects associated with labeling (Erikson, 1962; Lemert, 1951, 1967; Scheff, 1966). Entry into deviancy is said to result from public discovery of one or more acts of "primary deviancy." Once discovered, the person may be subjected to a "ceremony of status degradation" that announces membership in the deviant identity. Thereafter, the person and others come to think of the person in terms of the deviancy label, and the person is subjected to experiences that may lead to "secondary deviancy." To illustrate, once the criminal has served a sentence, he or she is presumably free to return to civilian life. But the criminal may find it difficult to find a job, may still be thought of as a criminal, is likely to associate with ex-cons, and may be tempted to further crime. Such theories again view the person as a responder to the current environment, but that person is viewed as a victim rather than as a coper who happens to see the world in somewhat different terms than we are used to. Theories of this latter sort suggest that deviant behavior can be modified if we are able to change the ways in which others view or treat the deviant, hence they have become popular among some clinical psychologists, social workers, and community psychiatrists. Unfortunately, support for this perspective is weak (Gove, 1975).

Well, which approach is right? To what extent is deviancy inherited, socialized, or a result of interaction? Chances are that all three explanations are partly right. It seems reasonable to believe that some persons are affected by inherited chemistry, some carry scars from poor socialization, and some are primarily coping with an ugly environment. Some forms of deviancy probably reflect more of one of these factors than the others, but in the long run, theories of deviancy will probably have to contend with factors from all three explanations.

Loving Others

Role theory also provides a means for discussing experiences that enlarge the individual. To illustrate this potential, let us look at the complex business of loving one another. I take up this topic with diffidence. The varieties of love are many, and wiser persons than I have discussed them for years. In the final analysis only those who have experienced love will know what I am talking about, and each is likely to believe that his or her experiences with love were unique and that it is impossible to generalize from them. Nevertheless, role concepts offer a unique perspective on love, and we might learn a bit by considering it.

For openers, let us decide what we are talking about. The term *love* is used for various purposes. It expresses affection, sexual attraction, the warm feelings a person might have for infants or pets, identification, dependency, and a host of other pleasant emotions. As used by Christians, it concerns our willingness to trust and care for one another. As used by song writers and suitors, it expresses intense attraction and the desire to have sexual relations and live with another. Although these uses cover many meanings, they appear to focus upon two basic ideas: love as an emotional state, and love as a process.

As an emotional state, love involves strong feelings of attachment. In terms of concepts we have used in this text, the person who loves another will be found to prefer strongly to be with that other and to do many things in the other's presence. It is possible, of course, for preferences such as these to appear in one person, but most of us would presume that some sort of reciprocation is a necessary precondition for love. Thus, when strong preferences for the other are shared among two (or more) persons, I shall say that those persons are **affectively bonded**. Clearly, affective bonding is one of the conditions of love. With all due respect to the song writers, however, it is not the only condition. Those who admire one another from a distance can scarcely be said to love, no matter how strong may be their mutual attraction. Love that is not expressed in behavior is mere potential energy—passion that is as yet unfulfilled. We must also build process into our definition of love.

In terms of process, love may be considered a form of primary relationship. As we know from Chapter Seven, primary activities are those in which interaction is face-to-face, is frequently repeated among the same actors, and involves many behavioral facets. Not all primary activities constitute love, however, not even all of those conducted among persons who are affectively bonded. In some cases, control over primary activities is vested mainly in one of the partners, but few would consider such asymmetrical cases examples of love. In other cases the partners may punish rather than reward each other, but this is surely not love either. And in some cases the relationship is not sufficiently intense. Consider a man and a woman who are strongly attracted to each other. If constrained by personal or social circumstances, the two may interact closely for years but not express love. In the fullness of time, however, they may begin to see more of each other, escalate behaviors that are mutually rewarding, discuss a wider variety of topics, exercise influence over each other, and view themselves in terms that include the other. Their relationship has become more intense; they are now in love. As we shall see shortly, love relationships may vary in intensity along a number of dimensions. But for the moment let us define **love** as an intense, mutually influenced, and mutually rewarding relationship of primary interaction between persons who are affectively bonded.

Let us explore this definition a bit. We normally think of love as something that happens between a man and a woman, for this is the most common way in which love is expressed in Western countries. However, there is no reason why two persons of the same sex cannot form a love relationship, nor need love be confined to two-person groups. Love is difficult to maintain in larger groups, however, because of the problems involved in sustaining primary-level interactions among all participants. Sexual activities are common in the expression of love (partly because of their mutually rewarding character), and many of us use the experience of sex as a signal that love has "arrived." This is foolish. Sexual relations can occur between persons who despise each other, and loving relationships have surely formed among some persons who are unwilling or uanable to consummate their affair. Others of us assume that "declarations of love" are necessary and that persons are not truly in love unless they recognize and express this state to one another. Although common, such declarations are also not needed. Some truly splendid love affairs have evolved slowly between persons who came to understand that they were in love only some time after the relationship had formed.

Some theorists insist that love forms best among persons who are approximately equal in power, and it cannot be denied that love often dies when one of the partners grows through experience or education while the other does not. But love has occasionally formed between two persons who are rich and poor, or healthy and chronically ill, provided that both partners are able to control aspects of the relationship. Love involves feedback between process and emotional state, for to the extent that the partners manage to provide pleasure for each other through their activities, they will also increase their fondness for each other, hence seek to expand those activities. Conversely, when activities go sour, it takes careful management to ensure that fondness for one another does not also flee. For this reason love is not an easy state to maintain, and it is common for those who love one another to experience crises in which they must change their roles and activities so as to meet new demands of the environment and the evolution of their own and others' needs. Love is *not* something that happens to a single person, however, no matter how strongly he or she may feel about another. Instead, love is an evolving relationship in which two (or more) strongly attracted persons interact frequently, intensely, reciprocally and rewardingly, thus providing experiences for themselves that cannot be achieved outside of the relationship.

Let us now consider the concept of **intensity**. What do we mean when we say that a love relationship is intense? At the risk of reducing some very complex processes to triviality, let us presume that intensity can be expressed in at least three different ways: in *breadth, openness,* and *depth.* A few love relationships may be intense in all three of these aspects; most exhibit intensity in one or two; it is difficult if not impossible to conceive love without intensity in at least one of these senses. What, then, do we mean by breadth, openness, and depth?

As readers may recall from Chapter Three, roles are considered broad when they include a wide range of behaviors. This concept may easily be generalized to the concept of love. In general, then, the **breadth** of love may be defined as the range of behaviors involved in its characteristic activities. Broad (intense) relationships are ones in which the partners characteristically spend a good deal of time together and in which they solve a majority of life's problems collectively. Within narrow relationships, the love affair is confined to some restricted aspects of the partners' lives. By way of illustration, marriages in which the husband and wife work together in a common context are normally broader than those in which the partners are employed separately.

When love relationships are first formed, they are of course narrow. Those who love one another normally seek to expand the range of their shared activities, so love relationships tend to expand until they meet one or more barriers. Some of those barriers are associated with the partners. Some persons have but a limited repertory of behaviors; some have obnoxious personal habits that the other chooses to avoid; some have individual interests that they cannot or choose not to share with the other. Other barriers are associated with the environment. Employment, travel, or illness may reduce the breadth of love, and clandestine love relationships are always limited in breadth by the dangers associated with disclosure. In general, the broader a love relationship the greater its potential for rewarding participants and the more difficult its management. Because of the latter, most lovers choose eventually to set limits on the breadth of love. These constraints are usually in the form of norms that mark the boundaries of the relationship. In well-managed love relationships these norms are set through discussion and mutual agreement; in less-well-managed affairs they are signaled through the imposition of sanctions on one another.

Which brings us to the second aspect of intensity. Love relationships also vary in the range of topics that the partners discuss, a quality I shall refer to as **openness.** In open (intense) relationships the partners characteristically discuss a wide range of topics, whereas in closed ones their discussion is confined to limited effort or few topics of conversation. One suspects that breadth and openness will normally be associated with each other, but exceptions can be thought of for this generalization. The taciturn farm couple may share a broad range of activities yet communicate only rarely with each other. When one partner in a love relationship that is both broad and open is temporarily hospitalized, the other may take great pains to maintain its open character by bringing "all the news" to bedside on a daily basis.

Love relationships begin by being relatively closed, of course, and also tend to become more open with the passage of time. Unlike the case of breadth, however, most barriers to openness seem to lie within the partners. Persons who are not used to open discussions, those who are bored or chronically fatigued, those who are threatened or unhappy in the relationship, and those who do not share broad backgrounds of agreement with their partners all appear less able to maintain openness. Many theorists have stressed the importance of maintaining openness if the love relationship is to prosper. Some naive persons think that "once our problems are solved" there will be few reasons to keep an open pattern of discussion and that the love affair can slide into comfortable, consensual silence. Such assumptions are tragic. Life is too complex in its challenges, and each of us grows and changes his or her needs and views of events as time passes. These challenges require adjustment in the roles and activities that constitute love, and clearly the best way of attaining that adjustment is through open discussion. As was suggested above, norms for conduct appear in nearly all love relationships. When partners are able to discuss these openly, trust in each other will grow. Unfortunately, many of us are too busy with our own affairs, or too used to the soporific passivity of television, to make the effort.

Love relationships may be both broad and open and still lack depth. To define this third aspect of intensity adequately, we must have some means for discussing the way in which love penetrates into core aspects of the partners (Altman & Taylor, 1973). To do this I shall make use of the concept of centrality. As we discussed earlier in the chapter, identities and expectations are considered central to the extent that they are important to the person and tend to dominate his or her behavior. **Depth**, then, refers to the degree to which the love relationship incorporates identities and expectations that are central to the partners. Within a shallow love, the central identities and expectations of the partners are not affected, nor are their self-concepts greatly challenged. Within a deep (intense) love, however, central identities and expectations are challenged, reworked, and reinvested. Core aspects of the self are changed and become committed to the relationship; the person becomes transformed and builds a new sense of his or her identity within love. A particularly vivid example of this process occurred between Elizabeth Barrett and Robert Browning. As readers may know, prior to the building of their love, Elizabeth Barrett was dominated by a willful, Victorian father and considered herself a bedfast cripple. As part of the process of developing love with Robert Browning she threw off her father's influence and left her sickbed behind. One striking aspect of depth is its feedback effect upon trust. Trust in the other promotes depth, and successful self-exposure multiplies trust and commitment. In time this process may lead those who love deeply to abandon norms in favor of preferences to control their activities. Although it is highly rewarding, such preferential management requires both effort and sensitivity to maintain.

New love relationships are even less likely to be deep than they are to be broad or open. In fact, real depth of love is undoubtedly a rare event. Few of us have the ability to question core aspects of ourselves, few are willing to do so, and few are willing to place sufficient trust in another to allow those core aspects to be challenged openly. Deep love demands that the person be capable of self-analysis and be willing to face even neurotic fears. Like openness, depth of love requires the commitment of energy, and persons entering into a deep love must be willing to evolve shared definitions of reality with their partners. As a result, those who love deeply are more vulnerable to the illness or death of their partners than are those who establish less intense relationships. For all of these reasons, deep love is undoubtedly a rare event. Most of us prefer to reserve core aspects of ourselves to private con- templation and to limit what we will commit to a love relationship. (To provide an illustration, most of us begin love relationships with traditional sex-role expecta- tions. Such expectations are central. Contextual pressures, ideology, and the devel- oping needs of the partners may call for a questioning of these central expectations. Those who love deeply are willing to question such expectations and may work out new and mutually satisfying ways of dividing labor that are not based on traditional sex-role concepts—see Heiss, 1962. Most persons seem unwilling to raise these ques- tions.) And yet, those among us who have evolved depth of love seem to glow, and those who have written about this experience seem to feel that it has been the most rewarding of their lives. Perhaps they know something the rest of us do not.

How, then, do persons learn to love one another? First of all, let us note that learning to love is a multiperson process (Levinger & Snoek, 1972). Two (or more) mutually attracted persons will come together and evolve a set of roles and activi- ties that affords them pleasure, thus reinforcing their desires to continue the rela- tionship. The socialization model seems particularly inappropriate to describe such a process. It is certainly true that early childhood experiences may set limits on our willingness to participate in love. (Those who were exposed to parents or others who exhibited a given form of love seem likely thereafter to conceive love for them- selves in its terms. Those with high levels of anxiety, neuroticism, or rigidity are probably less able to express love than others.) But in the final analysis, that which is evolved between the partners is a product of their *interaction*. To provide a posi- tive example those who love creatively are constantly learning from each other (and their relationship) new ways to pleasure each other. In negative terms, let us suppose that two persons are fond of each other and would like to evolve a love relationship. The first person desires a relationship that is broad and open, the second person wants one that is less broad and more closed. If the former cannot persuade the latter of the advantages of the more intense form, he or she will have to settle for a more superficial relationship. It takes two to tango.

Second, love is not a static state but instead evolves as a function of experience and may be expected to go through phases of expansion and contraction. Breadth, openness, and depth are not fixed conditions but rather should be conceived as equilibria that may be affected by forces both external and internal to the love rela- tionship. Each depends on the willingness of partners to trust one another, to engage in intimacies, to commit time and energy to joint activities; and the latter, in turn, will depend in part on whether earlier experiences of breadth, openness, and depth were or were not successful. When they were not, it takes creativity and man- agerial skill to keep love afloat. Separation from the other, demands from children or members of extended families, occupational problems, customs, laws, illness—all are likely to place pressures on the relationship. Love is, or should be, a live and lively business, and where love becomes static it is also likely to stultify and die.

To say the least, love is not always conceived in such flexible terms. In fact, love is sometimes confused with marriage. As we know from Chapter Seven, marriages constitute socially recognized unions that involve sexual license. Presumably marriages were instituted in the first place to control sexual jealousy, protect the rights of women and children, and provide for secure primogeniture. Nothing in any of these notions requires the partners in a marriage to love each other. In fact, the concept of love is not recognized in all societies, although marriage–in one or another of its forms–appears to be universal. It is surely a beautiful thing when those who have been married for years are also able to love one another, but this is in no way guaranteed, nor should we condemn those to whom it does not happen. Marriage is a legally recognized union, love a creative relationship between persons who are strongly attracted to one another. Margaret Mead has suggested that several forms of marriage be recognized, thus allowing greater legal flexibility to accommodate the forms of love. Perhaps we should be listening.

There is much more to the business of loving than I have indicated, of course. Serious investigators have been remarkably hesitant to conceive love in researchable terms or to study the ways in which people learn to love and live with one another (however, see Rubin, 1973). Perhaps it is time we turned our attention from conflict, prejudice, addiction, and poverty to some of the experiences that make life worth living.

OCCUPATIONS AND ROLE CHANGING

> *I would live all my life in nonchalance and insousiance were it not for making a living, which is rather a nouciance.*
>
> *—Ogden Nash*

We turn now to adult roles–as exemplified by occupations and role changing– and in so doing we move away from the concept of socialization as an explanatory mechanism. As we shall see, the evolution of adult roles seems to involve a good deal more than simply the training of a person to follow expectations. Rather, those who discuss adult roles usually conceive the person in a more active mode– accommodating, enjoying or suffering from, sometimes even changing, the social systems in which he or she participates.

It is intriguing to note that if we were positing a role theory for traditional societies this section of the chapter would probably disappear. Changes in identity and role during adulthood are universal experiences, but in simple societies such changes involve fewer problems than they do for the person who lives in an urban civilization. In simple societies the person knows from an early age the complement of positions and roles within the society and can contemplate from childhood onward those which he or she may presently enter. In a real sense, the person learns as a child "all about" the roles he or she will play as adults, although performance of those roles may be demanding indeed, and entry into positions of adult responsibility may require both effort on the part of the person and hard-won acceptance by others.

In modern societies the complement of positions and roles is far too numerous for this form of contemplation. As the person enters a new occupation, as he or she moves to a new community, as more and more of the society's institutions are entered—the person constantly encounters positions and roles for which he or she had no prior knowledge. Adulthood, then, becomes a life-long process of discovering new roles. This is all the more true because the society itself is changing so rapidly. New technological developments appear, and with them new organizational forms, occupations, avocations, and revocations of earlier ways of conducting affairs. For urban men and women, role changing becomes a way of life.

What do we know about these processes? What has role theory contributed to our understanding of adult life? Let us first take up the concept of occupation.

Occupations and Professions

The concept of occupation has a central place in the thinking of many role theorists. Beginning with the contributions of Hughes (1937, 1945) a series of studies have appeared dealing with recruitment, identification, personal problems, role conflicts, characteristic roles and activities, and a host of other phenomena associated with occupations and professions. [Numerous occupations are represented in the titles of studies cited in the B&T bibliography.]

Interest in occupations is a reasonable one for role theorists, for the concept of occupation involves some of the central concerns of the role field. Clearly an occupation is a social position, for members of the occupation share an identity that is recognized widely. Moreover, occupations have their definitional basis in a role (rather than in physical features or background experiences). However, this does not differentiate occupations from other role-based positions, such as those associated with recreation, criminal behavior, bad habits, or neurotic symptoms.

In contrast with these others, occupations are defined by employment. When a person engages in an occupation, he or she does so in order to receive money from others for his or her services. But what is money? In some primitive societies the concept of money is unknown. Artifacts are valued only for their intrinsic value, and social systems can be organized only in terms of barter. However, high civilizations feature a set of environmental units, *money*, in terms of which other units are valued. The basic characteristic of these units we call money is that they have but few intrinsic uses, and the acceptance of their value as a universal standard of exchange forms part of the shared, expectational system of the society. The concept of money, thus, is a complex one, and children have to be taught to use and value it in order to participate adequately in high civilization. (Interestingly, racoons and other nonspeaking animals can also be taught the use of money, if one is patient enough.)

The concept of money enables us to provide a formal definition for **occupations,** which are social positions whose foundation is a role that is performed to obtain money from the environment. Note that the concept of occupation involves a transaction between its members and the environment. Occupations are embedded within a social system that provides a financial reward. Most occupations are associated with complex organizations, but some occupational roles (such as that of the beggar) are merely performed on the street corner to attract money from passersby. The fact that occupations are defined monetarily does not mean that occupational roles do not have other functions, nor that all occupational role performance must be financially rewarded, nor even that members perform their role solely in order to obtain financial reward. None of these conditions is true. The assembly-line worker produces automobiles as well as a paycheck, country doctors may accept chickens or preserves in lieu of a fee, and many people tell us that they work "for the love of the job" (although they are also paid). However, the definition does tell us that it would be difficult to discriminate occupational positions from other role-based positions in a society that had no money.

Another characteristic is sometimes associated with the occupation concept. Occupations are said to be "achieved" rather than "ascribed" (see Chapter Four). In fact, this is not a necessary condition at all. In some caste systems, for example that of India, castes are associated with occupations such as carpentry, animal husbandry, or metal working; and members born into a caste cannot change their occupation, nor can others who are not members of that caste perform it. However, the definition of occupation remains, because even under such a system those who perform the role are paid for their services.

Discussions of occupations often differentiate professions from other occupational forms. In general, **professions** are occupations whose roles involve interaction with human beings (clients), whose performance is based upon a long period of training and is accounted "expert," for which the associated roles tend to be performed in private, and for which an explicit code of conduct in the form of rules governing the role are set and enforced by its members. Exceptions may be found for each of these conditions, and yet when all or most of them are met we are likely to consider the occupation for which this is the case a profession. (To take an illustrative case, let us see whether we would consider the occupation of *teacher* a profession. Teaching certainly involves interaction with clients; it is based on some years of training; and most of its role is performed without benefit of (adult) supervision. However, do teachers set and enforce a code of ethics for their own behavior? This condition is rarely met, thus in one respect at least teachers are not typically professional.)

Role Changing

How does one enter an occupation? What processes are involved in the recruitment and training of those who will fill professional roles? Moreover, what does it feel like to be an apprentice, a journeyman, a master, and later a retiree? Such questions are vital to understanding adult roles in Western societies. Let us now examine them. In doing so we will discover that concepts useful for describing occupational entry may also be used for entry into other types of adult positions.

The scope of our concerns may be illustrated with a conundrum that has plagued much of the literature concerning the analysis of professional careers. A number of studies have contrasted the role expectations of teacher-trainees with those of practicing teachers in primary and secondary schools. Without exception these studies have shown that teacher-trainees have expectations that are more "optimistic," "liberal," "democractic," and "progressive" than are those of practicing teachers. At least four explanations for this phenomenon have been advanced. First, it has been suggested that we are today selecting and recruiting a different group of persons for teachers than was true a generation ago. Second, it has been argued that those who become teachers experience personal changes when they come up against the realities of the social system in which they must work. Third, it has been advocated that the young people of today have not yet had time to effect the changes in the social system of education that they will now undertake. Fourth, it has been pointed out that those who are truly unhappy with teaching will either leave the profession or will be fired, thus leaving only those behind who can tolerate the system. These four explanations form a convenient way of discussing the phenomena involving the person as he or she accommodates new identities and roles.[9]

SELECTION AND RECRUITMENT

Selective processes operate in many social systems, and often persons are themselves involved in the process of selecting among possible positions to enter or roles to play. Thus when people are to enter a new social system two analytically distinct processes of **selection** operate, often in conjunction with one another: *social selection* and *personal selection.*

By **social selection** (or allocation) we mean that the social system into which the person is to enter exercises control over those who are allowed entry. Most universities open their doors only to those who pass a matriculation examination or have a good academic record from high school; professional societies restrict entry to those who have desired qualifications; organizations use complex tests to choose employees and to assign the right person to the right job; the U.S. Army restricts entry to those who are healthy and can meet a minimal qualification for intelligence. Most of these illustrations concern entrance qualifications that are explicit and are generated by tasks undertaken by the social system. It is also possible for social selection to reflect standards that are not made explicit (as in the case of

[9] Some of the terms, insights, and illustrations in this section of the chapter are adapted from Thomas (1968).

some restrictive covenants that deny residence or club membership to persons of the "wrong" religion or race) or are but vaguely known even to those who perform the act of selection. For example, Argyris (1954) reports that bank officials habitually recruit a quiet, passive, obedient, cautious, and careful type of employee, although they are only partially aware that they are so doing.

Social selection is not always practiced within the social system. One enters a family or kinship through accidents of birth. Entry into most recreations is under the sole control of its participants—one become a recreational fisherman by demonstrating its characteristic role. Thus, we may distinguish social systems that practice social selection from those that do not. Social selection is more likely to appear when roles are difficult to perform, require prior training, and are felt to be important.

A second distinction pertaining to social selection was discussed in Chapters Four and Seven. Some social systems select personnel through use of a *position sequence* (in Merton's terms, a "status sequence") such that positions are ordered within the system, and those entering a new position of the sequence must perforce have been a member of those positions preceding it in the sequence. A good example of this is provided by the sequence of age-graded positions: infant, child, adolescent, adult, elderly. Another is suggested by the typical, closed bureaucracy wherein one must "rise through the ranks" in order to enter a position of greater authority and responsibility. As we suggested in Chapter Seven, if the tie between authority and position sequencing is too tight, the organization may end up retaining persons in positions whose jobs they cannot perform. For this reason, most organizations seek additional criteria for selection beyond those of the position sequence. Position sequences are viewed as "fair," however, and are sometimes demanded by unions.

Personal selection consists of the processes a person goes through in determining whether or not he or she is to enter a position. There are several ways of thinking about personal selection. For one thing, these processes are both covert and overt. Sometimes the person considers various alternatives for future action and then chooses among them to the best of his or her ability, as may be the case when the adolescent is choosing among available career opportunities. However, personal selection also involves the differentiation of behavior by the person, since the choice process must be communicated to others. Personal selection is also both advertent and inadvertent—or in most cases involves some elements of both since the person has but imperfect knowledge of the social system being considered for entry. He or she may also be unaware of some of the functions of activities that indicate selective processes. For example, Hare and Bales (1963) found that males, and persons high in dominance, were more likely to select central seats at the beginning of discussion sessions in classrooms, thus to communicate more directly to others, and thereby become "leaders." Several models have appeared for the complex processes of career decision making, suggesting such concerns as those of congruence between self and role (discussed later) and the effects of childhood experiences (Bordin, Nachmann, & Segal, 1963; Nachmann, 1960). It has also been suggested that personal selection is basically a serial process involving successive acts of decision making, which provide partial entry into the social system, which in turn provide greater knowledge that suggests the need for supplementary decision making, and so on.

Evidence has also appeared suggesting the importance of identification in resocialization. This process may be either advertent (in which case both the person and the other are aware of the latter's status as a model) or inadvertent (in which case the person may choose an identity through accidental exposure to an attractive figure). Roe (1953) established that scientists were often recruited to their professions through the personal attention of a university instructor. Sherman (1963) found that those choosing a career in teaching had been influenced by both well-liked and disliked (!) teachers to whom they had been exposed (see also Jackson & Moscovici, 1963). Lofland and Stark (1965) found identification an important component of religious conversion.

Although social and personal selective processes are analytically separable, in many social systems they both occur and are intertwined. Consider entry into the priesthood. The initial decision to enter a seminary involves personal selection and is presumably based on factors in the person's self-concept, expectations concerning the role of the priest, values regarding the best way to spend one's life, and so forth. However, during his training years at the seminary the novice is scrutinized by his mentors to establish whether he should enter the profession, and if so what specialized role he should play in it. Those who are not accepted as priests will be counseled-out so that the person will not be crushed by his rejection. Similar processes occur in the medical school (Becker, Geer, Hughes, & Strauss, 1961; Merton, Reader, & Kendall, 1957), the teachers' college, and other formal institutions of education. However, social systems differ in the degree to which personal selection is allowed. The British Eleven-Plus Examination, for example, assigned pupils to secondary schools mainly through social selection, whereas American education allows greater scope for personal selection—at least in theory.

PERSONAL CHANGE

The notion that we should change our personalities when assuming a new identity is not new. It forms a favorite theme in literature, as in *The Rise of Silas Lapham*. It is also contended that those elected to the presidency "rise to the occasion," that marriage to a "good woman" can turn a wastrel into an honest citizen, and that those of us who are accountants, bankers, barristers, or librarians carry with us the marks of our professions. Surely there is something in these notions. The person who enters a new station in life may be called upon to don a new uniform, to master skills, or to learn a new vocabulary. Such expected roles are often enforced on the neophyte through socialization. Much of this is informal. Older members of the position will often be observed "showing the ropes" to or frowning at inappropriate role behavior in the neophyte. But are informal experiences sufficient to produce appropriate roles and adjustment for the recruit? Sometimes not, hence the need for new educational institutions that can help those taking on a new occupation, trying to recover from addiction or imprisonment, or facing retirement.

But not all **personal change** is induced by others. Neophytes may also exceed the requirements of the expected role and adopt the manners, clothing, accents or other accidental role behaviors that are nevertheless characteristic of position members—even to the point of aping the neurotic foibles of others (Etzioni, 1964). This suggests that personal change may be due as much to pressures originating within as without the person. Additional evidence for this notion is provided by **anticipatory socialization**, a concept first suggested by Merton (1949) [B&T, Selection 42]. In this phenomenon, the person who anticipates entering a new position will be found to take on aspects of its role prior to assuming membership. The person hoping for a promotion within a bureacracy may change his or her hair style, adopt a new wardrobe, change his or her circle of friends, or even buy a "more appropriate" automobile. In systems where social selection takes place, such behaviors have two functions. On the one hand, they enable the person to practice the new role so that he or she will not be incompetent when appointed to the post, while on the other, demonstrations of role-playing adequacy may lead others to choose him or her for the position. Concepts such as anticipatory socialization imply that the socialization model can account for only a fraction of the events of personal change, and that we will have to study the interaction between the person and the environment in order to predict how his or her new role will evolve.

SOCIAL SYSTEM CHANGE

Persons may also effect **social system change**. For historical examples of this process one can cite the careers of Benjamin Franklin, Napoleon, or Disraeli. But not all of us are such monumental sources of influence on the social fabric. A more limited perspective on the impact of the individual on the system is suggested by such concepts as injunction, power, influence, and leadership, for all of us are capable of exerting these in the smaller social systems of which we are members.

But unfettered power can lead to dictatorship or anarchy. For this reason, most social systems have homeostatic mechanisms that defend the system against those who attempt to change it. The operation of such mechanisms in the political sphere is well known. Within American legislatures many reasons exist for doing little or nothing about requests for action, until legislators become convinced that the problem is "truly serious." The police occupy positions whose role is concerned largely with the maintenance of social control and the frustration of those who exhibit deviation. Observational studies suggest that social groups react to deviant behaviors by first attempting to influence deviants toward conformity and then seeking to oust the offender from their midsts (Schachter, 1951).

For these reasons, some people who seek to change customs, such as an unjust war, capitalism, or racial prejudice may feel that it is impossible to create "real" social change without recourse to violence. Lacking the ability, the clout, and often the understanding necessary to work change in the complex society "responsible" for these evils, they may conclude that noise, threats, and terrorism will create the changes they desire. As was suggested at the end of Chapter Seven, this conclusion is dubious. Violence leads to repression as well as to change, and most demonstrations appear to have few effects.

But this does not answer the question posed by our critics. How can the individual effect a change in the social system, a change that "makes a difference," one that is not immediately overcome by homeostasis? Two answers have been suggested to this problem, both of which are associated with the term, *leadership*. As we know from Chapter Seven, within some social systems, persons whom we term *leaders* appear who are given explicit responsibility for setting rules, tasks, and other structural features of the system. Examples of such persons include the politicians and statesmen of a country, the elected officials and influential families of a community, and those near the top of the authority structure in an organization. In the oligarchy, such as a totalitarian regime, a single person may have enormous powers over the system and may be able to change its structural features almost at will. Within a democratic society and most modern organizations, in contrast, leaders have only limited powers. For example, one leader may be given the task of initiating a proposal, which is then reviewed and modified by others, only to have a council of responsible persons who pass on it eventually. Decision making within a legislature is even more complex, with many interests being represented and many roles being played (Wahlke, Eulau, Buchanan, & Ferguson, 1962) [B&T, Selection 28].

One answer for the critic who wants to affect the system, then, is for him or her to join it and rise within it to a position of leadership. This route has several difficulties, however. For one, effective participation in leadership is delayed for years if not decades. For another, those who participate in the system for a number of years may "buy into" its assumptions and become unwilling to contemplate changing it because of their commitment to the status quo. Indeed it may be argued that some persons in positions of leadership are chosen because is is known that they are unlikely to "rock the boat," although Whyte (1956) claims that this is true primarily for lower-echelon leadership within the organization. Such arguments have more force, of course, when the system of choosing designated leaders is based on tenure rather than on election or qualification.

The second use of the leadership concept, which we shall call **personal leadership**, is that associated with the person who characteristically exerts influence over others (regardless, or in defiance, of authority). A good deal of research has now been carried out on personal leadership, much of which is summarized by Stogdill (1974). This research appears to have gone through three phases. Once upon a time, investigators assumed that personal leadership was associated with individual characteristics, such as intelligence, energy, knowledge of the social system, emotional balance, and so forth. Research within this first model ranged from studies of historical accounts of "great men" to investigations of personal leadership within small groups. At a later point in time investigators, despairing of finding universal traits of personal leaders, turned to the analysis of social system characteristics, suggesting that different styles of leadership were necessary depending on the structural characteristics of the system. More recently these two streams of thought have come together, thus it may be possible after all to establish characteristics making for effective personal leadership within specific types of social systems (Fiedler, 1967).

How does the effective personal leader operate within the social group? Within smaller social systems, this is done by facilitating the task accepted by group members and by meeting the needs of individual participants. But can this proposition generalize to more complex social systems? How does the person exert personal leadership in the community, the organization, the modern urban society? These are complex questions. It appears that various personal leadership roles are possible that differ in their potentialities for generating social change and depend on system characteristics (again see Wahlke *et al.,* 1962) [B&T, Selection 28]. Thus, opportunities may be available within social systems for the individual who has qualities making for personal leadership, but those qualities useful in one context may not be equally useful in another.

None of the preceding discussion provides an adequate answer for the person who has legitimate desires to rectify injustice, stupidity, or venality in the world, for we have not said in specific terms what he or she is to do. To provide such information it would be necessary to discover the problems the person is concerned with, the social systems of which they are a part, and the possibilities for entering positions of leadership or exerting personal leadership within them. Moreover, it may (occasionally) be the case that the best route for promoting social change is that of creating uproar and public dispute, but often other strategies (such as persuasion, encouragement, suggesting alternative activities, and so forth) have greater potentials for producing change.

WINNOWING

We have now reviewed three of the four processes suggested to account for differences between positional recruits and positional incumbents. The fourth process is **winnowing,** or the selective departure of persons from positional membership due to death, lack of personal satisfaction, actions taken by the system, or because persons have gone on to better things.

As was suggested for recruitment and selection, winnowing can be broken into those factors associated with individuals—**personal winnowing**—and those stemming from the social system—**social winnowing.** Indeed, many of the distinctions made for selection may be repeated for winnowing. Personal winnowing, for example, can involve both covert and overt events. Those who leave a position are generally less likely to have had their needs met within it than those who remain behind (Ross & Zander, 1957). As a specific instance of this, several studies have shown that role conflict is likely to promote personal winnowing (Kahn, Wolfe, Quinn, Snoek, & Rosenthal, 1964).

Social winnowing occurs when the social system moves to weed out undesirables from positional membership. Examples of this include dismissal from jobs, disownment, demotion, transfer, being "kicked upstairs," and so forth (Etzioni, 1964; Lemert, 1967). Social winnowing also occurs negatively when the system selects individuals for promotion, and it is often suspected that persons who have exceptionally long tenure in a single position are unfit for other jobs. Once again, the processes of social winnowing are different from social system to social system and will vary depending on whether the system exhibits a positional sequence or not.

Interaction between the processes of personal and social winnowing is inevitable. The person having low morale may behave in such a manner as to encourage the boss to fire him or her, whereas the employee who is doing well in the eyes of his or her superiors may be encouraged by them to make extra effort that increases the probability of promotion.

In summary, then, four processes have been suggested for discussing the effects of role changing—selection, personal change, social change, and winnowing. All of these processes operate in the adult social world we inhabit. Moreover, each affects the others in ways we are only now coming to appreciate. To return to our original question, why are teacher-trainees different from practicing teachers? Possibly because we are recruiting a different group of young people into teaching today, possibly because the new group of trainees has yet to suffer the indignities of the system, possibly because the new group has not yet had time to change the system, and possibly because those who have inappropriate expectations have yet to depart. None of these explanations offers a complete solution to the problem, indeed they appear to be interlocked. An adequate exploration of their interrelationships would require a longitudinal study of some magnitude. Unfortunately, such studies are difficult to find—in education or elsewhere.

ADJUSTMENT AND THERAPY

> *If you treat an individual as he is, he will stay as he is, but if you treat him as if he were what he ought to be, he will become what he ought to be and could be.*
>
> *—Johann von Goethe*

Western civilization is complex, rapidly changing, and often crisis ridden. Such a civilization offers many different positions and roles. However, not all of these positions are equally attractive. And some of the roles we are called on to play are unpleasant, demanding, and anxiety provoking. Such roles would be difficult to perform had we a lifetime to learn and practice them. But roles for which we were originally trained may have changed as the society evolves, which leaves us unprepared for the new demands we must now meet. As a result, many persons are maladjusted for their positions and roles.

Endless evidence may be cited for maladjustment. Between one and three million Americans are alcoholics. More than one-third of all marriages now end in divorce. One out of every ten of us will seek psychiatric or psychological help, and two others could probably benefit from it. More than half of us suffer from some form of stress-induced disorder (Leighton, Harding, Macklin, Macmillan, & Leighton, 1963; Srole, Langer, Michael, Opler, & Rennie, 1962). The children of many Americans from minority groups—blacks, Chicanos, Indians, Appalachian highlanders, and others—are provided with inferior schools, and as adults are less able to cope than are those who apparently "deserved" a better education. Moreover, all of us have been exposed to a curriculum that stressed academic achievement, vocational training, and the Protestant Ethic—and are therefore "unfit" to enjoy a society that offers increasing opportunities for leisure. Truly, we are *all* somewhat maladjusted for the world now appearing.

Role theory cannot solve these problems, of course. It can, however, provide concepts for discussing maladjustment and therapy. And to these we now turn.

Adjustment

The term *adjustment* has many connotations: adaptation, ability to perform, flexibility, satifaction, and others. As used by therapists, adjustment seems to imply any condition characterized by lack of unhappiness or neurotic symptoms. As used by nearly everyone else, adjustment connotes an ability to cope with demands that are placed on us by others, and it is this latter concept that I shall deal with here.

For our purposes, **adjustment** may be considered the person's ability to accommodate his or her social positions and expected roles. The adjusted person likes his or her identities and enjoys and performs well the roles that are expected of him or her. Persons are maladjusted when they are unhappy with their positions or dissatisfied with or unable to perform well roles that are expected of them. To be maladjusted is not necessarily a bad thing. Creative scientists and artists are often dissatisfied with the expectations of earlier generations. But maladjustment is always associated with tension, hence it is assumed to be problematic for the person. Maladjusted persons are motivated to do something about that condition, thus maladjustment predicts both personal and social change. To illustrate this proposition, Margaret Mead (1956) argues that social change is more likely in societies where children are happy and adults unhappy than in societies wherein the reverse obtains. (If Mead is correct, surely we are in for a generation of social upheaval.)

STRUCTURAL PROBLEMS

Maladjustment may be generated by problems in the environment or in the person, and both have been studied by role theorists. Among structural problems, perhaps the most serious occurs when the person is mired within a social position that has low prestige, wealth, or legitimacy. Social psychologists have known for years that low status is associated with maladjustment (for a summary of the evidence see Lindzey & Byrne, 1968, pp. 485–488). This association is surely greater when the person cannot resign from that low-status position. Is is one thing to be an apprentice or a medical student. Even though such positions have low status, persons in them expect better times in the future. It is quite another thing to be a black, a woman, or a member of some despised minority group. Membership in these latter positions is conferred through physical features or prior experience, and individuals who are their members have few options for improving their status. Various authors have commented upon the stress induced in persons who are members of low-status, ascribed positions (for blacks see Dai, 1945; Elkins, 1961; Grier & Cobbs, 1968; for women—Epstein, 1970; Harrison, 1964; Knudsen, 1969; for ethnic minorities—Abel & Hsu, 1949; DeVos, 1955, 1961). Moreover, one cannot but applaud (and join) the efforts of those who would abolish status differentials based on ascribed positions. Nevertheless, membership in low-status positions does not always cause maladjustment. Gove (1972) shows that maladjustment is greater among women who are *married* than among women who are not married or men who are married or single. Jaco (1959), Opler (1959), Meadow and Stoker (1965), and many others have suggested that members of minority groups have unique strengths, based on cultural traditions, that enable them to cope differently with stress. Clearly, membership in a low-status position does not always cause maladjustment.

Other structural problems are associated with roles. One of these is *role conflict,* which we reviewed in Chapter Six. As was suggested there, a role conflict may appear when polarized dissensus is held (or is presumed to be held) for object persons. Various studies have found role conflicts in organizations, and these seem to have the potential for disturbing persons who are exposed to them. People differ in their tolerance for role conflict, and some of the personality correlates of this tolerance are known. Nevertheless, role conflict is generally associated with loss of morale, lowered productivity, and other deleterious effects. For this reason, most theorists have interpreted role conflict as a problem to be overcome in organizations, and research has been conducted on the strategies a person may use to resolve the role conflicts he or she experiences.

Another structural problem is **role ambiguity**, which appears when shared specifications set for an expected role are incomplete or insufficent to tell the incumbent what is desired or how to do it. Kahn, Wolfe, Quinn, Snoek, and Rosenthal (1964) found ambiguity to be a source of unhappiness for persons within the organization, but Katz (1968) has argued that "autonomy" must be provided for employees if they are to solve the shifting, daily problems of their jobs. It seems unclear at present, then, under what conditions the person will seek additional structure for his or her role and when he or she will resent that structure.

Other structural problems are associated with the role set the person carries. One of these is **role overload,** which occurs when the person is faced with a role set that is too complex. The idea that persons will encounter stress when faced with too many roles has been argued by several theorists (Coser & Coser, 1974; Goode, 1960; Merton, 1957a; Slater, 1963, Snoek, 1966). This proposition seems to be based on the assumption that persons have but limited time and energy and will be distressed when too many demands are placed on them. The busy mother, for example, may find it difficult to take on executive responsibility within the PTA because she "does not have time" for this new role. Recently this notion has been challenged (Marks, 1977; Sieber, 1974). For one thing, human energy does not seem finite in any simple sense, and persons seem quite able to take on additional roles in which they are truly interested. For another, persons may also become bored when faced with a too-simple role set.

Another problem reflecting role set is **role discontinuity.** This concept was first suggested by Ruth Benedict (1938) and refers to lack of integration in the various roles a person is called upon to perform in sequence. Benedict's illustration of this concept was with age-graded positions, and she suggested that problems faced by the adolescent are more a product of discontinuities resulting from prior role training than of physiological factors. The concept of role discontinuity has now been applied to various positional sequences: to the resocialization of prisoners of war (Wilson, Trist, & Curle, 1952), to halfway houses (Landy, 1960b) [B&T, Selection 47], to the planning of retirement (Donahue, Orbach, & Pollack, 1960), and so forth.

Yet another problem is *role malintegration.* As was suggested in Chapter Three, it may be difficult for the person to accommodate roles that require great physical effort with those that require thought, or administrative responsibilities with creativity. Such role sets are malintegrated—and stressful.

PERSONAL PROBLEMS

The six concepts discussed above do not exhaust the subject of structural problems that may place pressures on the person. Stress may also be induced by insecure tenure, irregular pacing, threats to safety, unwelcome responsibility, inadequate information for making decisions, the necessity for public performance, and a host of other conditions. These latter are more the province of industrial psychology than of role theory per se. However, role theorists have developed concepts for personal problems that may be associated with maladjustment, and to a sample of these latter we now turn briefly.

One set of concepts reflect the idea that persons with more talent are more likely to cope with structural problems. Thus, those with greater **role skill** are able to perform more complex roles and thus avoid stress. What characteristics make for role skill? Several general traits have been suggested, such as intelligence, flexibility, and emotional maturity—most of which reflect the roles of modern, industrial society. Other characteristics have been advanced for primitive societies (such as tolerance for pain), while authors of science fiction have speculated endlessly about qualities that would have survival value in outer space or following an atomic holocaust. One special ability that has attracted research is *role-taking adequacy*. As was suggested earlier, persons who are able to take the role of the other should find interaction an easier task and experience less stressful (Milgram, 1960). One may question the limits of this line of reasoning, however. Persons with great skill may also become unhappy when given roles that involve few challenges.

This suggests that adjustment of the person may be best when there is a match between the expected role and personal characteristics of the incumbent, or **self-role congruence**. As was suggested by Thomas (1968), experiences of at least minor self-role incongruence are common. New entrants into positions normally face a period of adaptation and learning before they can perform roles adequately. However, persisting incongruity poses problems for the person. Thomas summarized research on incongruence under seven headings: *motive malfit* (Atkinson & Hoselitz, 1958), *incentive malfit* (Wilensky, 1956), *skill malfit, capacity malfit* (Argyris, 1957), *identity malfit, performance malfit* (Borgatta, 1961), and *value malfit* (Wilensky, 1956). Belief in the notion of self-role congruence is widespread in industry, and many corporations use a battery of placement tests to determine whom they will hire and to what job each person is to be assigned. Nevertheless, persons always grow and change with new experience, and in some cases lack of congruence may provoke persons to seek a change in the expected role they are performing. Once again, then, propositions about self-role congruence may have limited applicability.

ROLE STRAIN

Persons who experience stress associated with positions or expected role are said to experience **role strain** (Goode, 1960; Marks, 1977; Merton, 1957a; Snoek, 1966). What follows from the experience of role strain? Does the person break down, curse, weep, resign from the position (or from the human race)? Such reactions are not likely in the short run. More often the person indicates his or her awareness of the transgression by being embarrassed. Thus, embarrassment provides clues that tell us something about the requirements of roles (Goffman, 1956; Gross & Stone, 1964). Embarrassment may also be used by recruiters as a "test" of fitness for a demanding role. How does the person handle occasions when requirements of the role cannot be met? Does he or she become embarrassed, and if so, how does he or she then behave? Another "test" of role strain appears in the ritualistic game of "playing the dozens" or "Joning," which takes place betwen two black, urban American men with an audience. The game involves a series of creative, though ritualized, insults that must be given and taken in good humor. If one of the players "loses his cool" and offers to fight he has lost the game (Berdie, 1947; Dollard, 1939; Golightly & Scheffler, 1948).

In longer terms, of course, role strain places considerable burden on the person. If uncorrected, such strains may lead to frustration, the experience of failure, feelings of insecurity, or eventually to ulcers and early death (Argyris, 1957; Mitchell, 1958). But persons need not tolerate role strain forever. In some cases, persons are able to restructure expectations for their positions or roles. Indeed, therapy with married couples often involves explicit restructuring of role expectations (Glasser, 1963; Rapoport & Rosow, 1957) [B&T, Selection 26]. In other cases, resigning from the position may be the best strategy. Still other coping strategies are open to those who choose to cope with a difficult position or expected role, including reduced *involvement* and use of *role distance.*

Involvement concerns the degree to which the person invests effort or is organismically engaged in role performance. Sarbin (1954) [see also B&T, Selection 20] suggests a seven-stage model for involvement. At one end of this model are casual roles, such as those of the customer in a supermarket, in which the person is just minimally involved. At the other end we find roles that are so involving that they create physiological responses within the body that seriously affeet the person, as in psychosomatic illness or instances of ritualistic cursing and "voodoo death." Interstingly, within some contexts structured norms appear concerning the "proper" level of involvement a person should exhibit for a given role. When "listening to another," for example, one should emit cues to signal that one is paying attention. Football players are supposed to be "psyched up" for important games. Clearly, one defense against role strain is to reduce one's level of involvement. The executive with high blood pressure is often advised to "take it easy" and "leave his or her job in the office" at 5:00 p.m. (Unfortunately, not all of us are able to follow such good advice.)

Involvement has both social as well as personal effects, and should one signal too great a level of involvement in the performance of difficult or demanding roles, one may give the impression to others that one is in danger of making mistakes in performance. In such cases, Goffman (1959) suggests that the person may defend him or herself from the appearance of overinvolvement by adopting a casual air or otherwise exhibiting **role distance**. The surgeon, for example, may joke with assistants or nurses during the operation, the president makes a display of confidence when making a decision that he (or she) knows to be risky. Such displays tend to reduce tension in others and may help the responsible person to relax a bit.

These concepts do not exhaust the subject of adjustment to roles. Indeed, research into this complex subject is just beginning, and it will be some time before we are able to state powerful theories for this topic. Nevertheless, Cottrell (1942) suggested a series of propositions concerning adjustment of the person to age and sex roles that probably have wide relevance. Readers are encouraged to examine his classic paper on this subject.

Counseling and Therapy

A striking fondness for role concepts has appeared among those who practice the clinical professions. As was suggested earlier, clinical agencies may be viewed as engaging in socialization, hence they are similar in some respects to schools and colleges. However, most of the clinical professions have arisen during the twentieth century, during the same decades that saw the rise of role terminology. As a result, leading practitioners of these professions have contributed to the development of role theory, and role terminology has often been used to express the beliefs of clinicians.

SOCIAL SYSTEMS IN CLINICAL PRACTICE

Role concepts are used in several ways within the clinical professions. One of these has been to analyze the social systems represented by the client, his or her family, the therapeutic session, the clinical agency, and the clinical professions. Considerable effort has now been expended on conceptualizing and studying the role of the person who is ill. Some of this effort has concerned illness behavior in general (Freidson, 1970; Gordon, 1966; Mechanic, 1961; Parsons, 1951, 1958; Twaddle, 1969, 1972). Other authors have concentrated on the role of mental illness (Goffman, 1961a; Gove, 1975; Laing, 1967; Laing & Esterson, 1964; Leifer, 1969; Perrucci, 1974; Rosenhan, 1973; Sarbin, 1967a,b; Scheff, 1966, 1970; Szasz, 1961, 1970). Common to such contributions are descriptions of the role of the ill person, treatments of that person by others, expectations that are held for illness, and conditions leading to entry into and departure from the ill position. Common also are challenges to the notion that illness is produced mainly (if not exclusively) by biological events. In these studies it is pointed out that we all hold expectations for the roles of those who are ill and those who will care for the ill, and our responses when ill may reflect these ideas as much as they reflect our fever, nausea, pain, anxiety, or physical disability. Taken to their extreme—as is often done with mental illness—such arguments suggest that illness is myth, that the person apparently suffering from schizophrenia, for example, is merely responding to role expectations and coping with the pressures of his or her life. Such exaggerations are contradicted by evidence indicating that some forms of mental illness, including schizophrenia, are associated with chemical imbalance and can be alleviated with medication. Nevertheless, they alert us to the fact that illness roles may indeed reflect expectations and treatment from others as well as the physical conditions the person suffers.

Effort has also gone into analyzing the role relationships among clients and their families or associates (Glasser & Glasser, 1962; Henry, 1971), and studies have examined the pathologies of role conflict, lack of judgement, unclarity, or other problems associated with the family roles of patients. And as we know, studies of work environments have also been conducted using role concepts that have thereafter been interpreted for the problems they generate for the person. Used in this way, role theory can provide descriptive tools for the clinician that enable one to understand, and perhaps eventually to manipulate, the roles of the client *in situ*.

A third application of role concepts concerns analysis of the therapy session. Traditional therapeutic interviews have involved two persons—a therapist and a patient—and literally hundreds of studies have been published using role concepts for the analysis of this traditional system (Lennard & Bernstein, 1960; Overall & Aronson, 1963 [B&T, Selections 18 and 19]; for a review, see Corsini, 1966). Other types of therapy can involve multiple therapists, multiple clients (group therapy), the use of specialists, milieu therapy, and various other forms. These, too, have received attention from investigators who use role concepts (for an example, see Lieberman, Yalom, & Miles, 1973).

Clinical professions and agencies have also been given their share of attention. The clinical professions have received the same sort of scrutiny as has been accorded to teachers, doctors, or businessmen. Mental hospitals have been examined (Zander, Cohen, & Stotland, 1957) together with general hospitals (Visser, 1976), social work agencies (Thomas, 1959) [B&T, Selection 16], and other clinical settings. Moreover, clinical organizations have received many of the same criticisms as have other forms of organizations—for they, too, may suffer from bureaucratization, rigidity, anomie, loss of morale, and the like.

Role concepts also provide the clinical practitioner with a vocabulary for discussing the problems faced by the client during the course of his or her resocialization. Not only does the client face problems in his or her home or therapeutic session, but the client also has a personality that is expressed in role expectations and behaviors. Much of the course of therapy may be charted in the growth of conceptions that are held by the client and are attributed by the client to others. Thus, role theory also provides a vocabulary for discussing the client as a unique human being.

CLINICAL USES OF ROLE PLAYING

Role concepts have also received another application in the clinical professions. This latter involves the use of role playing as a strategy for dealing with clients. In Chapter Six *role playing* was defined as imitation by the person of another's role. In role playing, the person not only gains information about the role, but also understanding of the situation in which the other stands. As it turns out, role playing has also been used extensively in therapy. Enthusiasm for the therapeutic use of role playing is widespread and has occasionally seemed to be a cult. Use of this technique was pioneered by J. L. Moreno and his students, but the same sorts of extravagant claims have been made for role playing as have sometimes been made for Chiropractic, Dianetics, or Hadacol. And for this reason, noninitiates tend to view with scepticism the antics of the "role playing movement."

Nevertheless, there are strong reasons for advocating the use of role playing in therapy. Role playing is a natural phenomenon that is practiced by children in the process of growing, therefore it forms part of the normal repertoire of roles that are performed and enjoyed by everyone. The client who plays roles in therapy may provide insights concerning roles that are played elsewhere by others or by him or herself. The therapist and other clients (if present) can also gain insight or add their interpretations in the role-playing session. Role playing also allows the client to practice alternative roles (rather than simply talk about them). It is also inherently a "dramatic" technique (indeed, the form of role playing in which the individual plays him or herself before an audience is often known as *psychodrama*—after Moreno), which implies that the client may have "peak experiences" when deeply involved with role playing. These experiences can also lead to insights or to the reliving and resolving of painful episodes from the client's past.

This argument suggests that role playing may be used for many purposes, and a list of these is suggested by Lippitt and Hubbell (1956), who also provide a bibliography on the topic. First, Lippitt and Hubbell claim that role playing may be used for "improving interpersonal and intercultural relations" in various settings including the classroom, the hospital, the family, the social work agency, and in industry. Second, role playing may be useful for "changing attitudes and behavior" among different positions including teachers, boy scout leaders, industrial leaders, military officers, and prisoners. Third, it is claimed that role playing "stimulates group participation, involvement in training, and interest in academic subjects" among group members, students, industrial trainees, conference participants, trainee counselors, mental patients (and their attendants), social workers, nurses, rabbis, and students of all kinds. Fourth, role playing presumably "develops spontaneity" in children and others. Fifth, role playing may "serve as a technique for personnel selection and situational diagnosis," and has been so used by the military agencies, therapists, marital counselors, and others. Sixth, role playing is claimed to "help individuals with inner conflicts and problems," particularly those who are seriously ill with emotional disturbances. And, seventh, role playing is also used for "research."

Is there any experimental evidence that these claims are justified? Unfortunately, the evidence is weak. In 1956 J. H. Mann published a review of experimental evidence for role playing conducted to that date. In his words,

Perhaps the most striking impression to be gained from a review of the experimental studies of role playing is their scarcity. Except for the few studies reported here, effort among practitioners of role playing seems to have been devoted to the exploitation of its various applications. . . . With reference to personality assessment, there is some sound evidence for believing that reliable and valid role playing tests can be developed. Such tests are, however, still in their infancy. . . . With reference to personality change, it can only be said that there is as yet little supportive evidence (p. 233).

Proponents of role playing have not been daunted by such lukewarm reviews (any more than have teachers, social workers, or psychiatrists by similar lacks of evidence concerning their efforts). Instead, a panoply of applications of role playing in therapy has now been devised. Perhaps the best integrated presentation of these latter appeared in Corsini (1966). This author differentiated "straight role playing" (in which the client plays his or her own role against someone who plays another's role), from four other variations. In "role reversal" the client plays the role of his or her antagonist while another (usually the therapist) role plays the client. In the "alter ego format," the client plays his or her own role, another plays the role of an alter, and a third person pretends to reveal to the client what the alter is "really thinking" about the client and his or her behavior. In the "mirror technique" the client looks on while two persons play roles—one of them role playing the client, the other role playing the alter. Finally, in "doubling" the client plays him or herself, but another person—usually another client in a group session—attempts to speak for the client and to express out loud what the client is feeling.

Nor does this exhaust the variations. Additional techniques were also suggested by Lippitt and Hubbell (1956). In "soliloquy" the client shares with the group or therapist his or her normally censored feelings and thoughts. In "multipe role playing" the therapist shifts the identities of the players from time to time to give them additional insights. In "replaying" a particular episode is repeated. In "chair auxiliary ego" the shyness of a client (who might be a child, for example) is overcome by playing the role to a chair—which might have the therapist behind it for appropriate response. The use of a "silent auxiliary ego" has been attempted with patients who are not responding to verbal techniques, and "hypnodrama" has been used to warm up clients and to uncover fertile fields for investigation.

It should be emphasized that even among its most vigorous proponents the technique of role playing is used only as one of several strategies for resocialization. Others often used in conjunction with role playing include interviewing, group discussion, interpretation, cathartic release, structuring, and so forth. It should also be emphasized that clinical role playing is a highly involving business. Since clients may be seriously involved or disturbed by their experiences during role-playing sessions, these must be handled with intelligent and thoughtful care. As is true for most psychotherapeutic techniques, role playing can be dynamite in the wrong hands—which is even true for that social analogue of role playing, the game of Charades.

The fact that little evidence is available to support claims for role playing in therapy does not mean that role playing has been avoided by researchers. On the contrary, several studies have shown that covert expectations may be modified through role playing (for examples, see Culbertson, 1957; Elms, 1969; and Janis & King, 1954). More recently a controversy has arisen concerning the use of role playing in experimental studies conducted by social psychologists. Reacting to the questionable morality of subjecting subjects to stress (as in Milgram, 1965), several authors have suggested that role playing might be an appropriate substitute for deception in laboratory studies (Brown, 1965; Kelman, 1967; Mixon, 1972). This proposition was attacked by other authors (Aronson & Carlsmith, 1968; Freedman, 1969) and has since been subjected to studies comparing deception with role playing (for a review, see Miller, 1972). As a rule, these studies have shown that results from the two techniques are similar but not identical.

As is often the case, evidence has not quieted the controversy. Instead, other authors have begun to advocate role playing as a technique having independent validity for experimental research (Cooper, 1976). To illustrate its usefulness, consider the recent study by Zimbardo, Haney, Banks, and Jaffe (1972) in which Stanford undergraduates were asked to play the roles of prisoners and guards in a realistic simulation of a prison. Within a short time, participants in the simulation were deeply involved in the action—guards were behaving in a vicious manner, prisoners were depressed and rebellious. Indeed, so realistic was the simulation that the investigators had to call it off before its scheduled close so as to protect participants! Such demonstrations show the power of identity, the ubiquity of certain role expectations, and the fact that role playing can be deeply involving. Recent reviewers suggest that some degree of role playing appears in all manipulative experiments that involve human subjects and urge that additional research be conducted on its effects—see particularly a symposium edited by Hendrick (Alexander & Scriven, 1977; Baron, 1977; Hendrick, 1977; Krupat, 1977; Mitchell, Kaul, & Pepinsky, 1977; Mixon, 1977; Mohavedi, 1977).

To summarize, then, role concepts have been used for discussing many of the phenomena associated with clinical practice, particularly for a description of the social systems of the client, the clinical session, and the clinical agency. It also has application in describing the adjustment and problems faced by the client and the progress of his or her therapy or resocialization. Finally, a specific technique has been developed in conjunction with role concepts—the clinical use of role playing— that has generated enthusiasm among clinicians in many fields and a wide range of claimed applications, for which there is little good evidence. Despite this lack, role playing has attracted attention and is known to be highly involving.

ENVOI

At the beginning of the chapter we considered an accusation that is sometimes leveled against role theory—that it dehumanizes the person and reduces him or her to but a cog within a social machine. Is this a valid contention?

On balance, the charge seems false. Far from ignoring the singularity of the individual, role concepts provide us with a vocabulary for discussing the formation of the self. Deviants have not been ignored by those interested in roles, nor have problems involved in adult resocialization and adjustment. Nor have we failed to appreciate the problems faced by the person who must accommodate his or her position and role within the social system.

If the contention has any validity, it resides in the problem of individual integration that has plagued us throughout the book—that of providing an appropriate, autonomous, and self-fulfilling role for the person within a complex and ever-changing world. There can be no doubt that organizations and urban societies have the ability to defend themselves against change; but change they do. Nor can there be doubt that factors inducing change are often beyond the ability of the individual to comprehend or control. Nor can it be questioned that we have entered into the second half of the twentieth century with inadequate means for socializing that leave many of us crippled and unable to adjust to the complex roles we are called upon to play.

The difficulty faced by urban dwellers is that they feel helpless in the face of numbers, complexity, environmental degradation, homeostatic mechanisms, complex roles, and rampant social change. Although such persons may be unhappy in their identities or roles, they can alter their lives only with difficulty. Thus, if role theorists have appeared to acquiesce in the dehumanization of contemporary men and women, it is possible that they are merely reflecting their own feelings of dehumanization.

But if role theory has not acquiesced in dehumanization, can it help to solve this complex problem? Let us take a Durkheimian position in answering this question. Human behavior may be understood, and human social systems evolve in response to understandable social forces. Much of human behavior is described by role concepts, and as we develop a propositional theory for the role field, we should —by the same token—be gaining the ability to make rational plans for ourselves and our society. Of course, role theory cannot provide the whole answer. As we shall see in the final chapter, there are significant shortcomings to the role orientation. And even if there were not, social planning requires that we agree on ends as well as understand the means. But surely concepts such as those suggested within the role corpus are necessary if we are to control social systems and understand the experiences and behaviors of those who live within them.

Chapter Nine

Ultima Rolle

> *We have many concepts but few confirmed theories; many points of view, but few theorems; many "approaches" but few arrivals. Perhaps a shift in emphasis would be all to the good.*
> —*Robert K. Merton*

Once upon a time, in Chapter One, we defined the subject matter of role theory to concern behaviors that are characteristic of persons within contexts and the various processes that are used to predict and explain those behaviors. Now we have had opportunity to find out what those words meant. We have studied the concepts of *behavior, role, identity, position,* and *expectation.* We have seen how contexts may affect the behaviors of persons and how those behaviors may have subsequent functions. We have noted that role theory provides concepts for both overt events (such as behaviors) and covert processes presumed to explain those events (expectations). Finally, we have examined fields of application that have been the traditional interests of role theorists—the analysis of social systems, individual behavior, and the clinical use of role concepts.

Now it is time to stand back and take a look once more at role theory as a whole. What are the strengths and weaknesses of this approach? How well does role theory accomplish its presumed objectives? Are those objectives reasonable? To what extent can role theory help to solve the pressing problems generated in our complex, brawling civilization?

WHERE WE ARE NOW

> *In common-sense psychology (as in scientific psychology) the result of an action is felt to depend on two sets of conditions, namely factors within the person and factors within the environment.*
>
> *—Fritz Heider*

Role theory is a lively field with a good many strengths and some fairly impressive weaknesses. Some of these were suggested in Chapter One; others have been discussed elsewhere in the text. Let us recapitulate these briefly.

SUBJECT MATTER AND STANCE

Above all, role theory is popular because of its basic subject matter. As we have noted, it is a fact that human beings behave in ways that are to some extent predictable and consistent and that their behaviors are similar to the behaviors of others who share identities with them and appear in similar contexts. To study and explain these behavior patterns (or *roles*) is a key problem of the social sciences. Hence, role theory is central to the interests of many.

Role theory is also popular because it accommodates a variety of explanations for role behavior. As we have seen, it it possible to assume that roles are based on instincts, are induced by culture, are socialized, are produced by sanctions or threats of sanctions, evolve in interaction, or stem from the integration of values within the person. Each of these orientations, and others, fits comfortably within the role framework, and to this extent the role field offers a common arena in which anthropologists, ethologists, sociologists, and psychologists of various persuasions can come together.

Another advantage of role theory is that it accommodates both behaviorism and phenomenology. Since behaviors are differentiated from expectations, role theory enables the investigator to appose thoughts and deeds. It flatters the person by casting him or her as an active thinker about events and suggests that if the person does not have free will in any absolute sense, he or she is at least capable of integrating and deciding among those behavioral alternatives conceived. Because of its dualistic stance, role theory appeals to pragmatists and persons with social concerns, and it has been widely adopted by educators and clinicians.

At the same time, the eclectic stance of role theory has its disadvantages. Few role theorists seem to recognize the breadth of the field. As we know, role theorists tend to build questionable assumptions (such as those concerning consensus, simple formation, sanctioning, conformity, or structurality) into their basic definitions of role concepts. The assumptions chosen by the theorist will vary depending on his or her training. But since these assumptions are not made by others, misunderstanding and arguments over the meaning of terms have characterized the role field. Critics have also praised or damned role theory for assumptions made by a given theorist, failing to recognize that others who use role concepts would not make those assumptions.

USE OF COMMON LANGUAGE

Another feature of the role field is that much of its vocabulary is taken from words common in Western languages. Such a vocabulary carries surplus connotations that we learned at an early age. We all recognize words such as expectation, role, function, conformity, and sanction, and their technical use in role theory is clearly an extension of common-language use. For this reason, social scientists can use the role vocabulary and appear to communicate with one another without ever really agreeing over the precise meaning of terms. And for the same reason, the technical terms of the role field may be used by social scientists to communicate with subjects and clients. When interested in measuring expectations, for example, the role theorist may ask the subject, "What are your expectations?" rather than go to the bother of constructing indirect instruments for searching out the mystery. Research reports from the role field are often written in its technical vocabulary, in the apparent hope that funding agencies or the public will follow the argument. Because of its use of common terms, role theory has an immediate appeal to the neophyte and appears "natural" to even the hard-bitten iconoclast from related disciplines.

Use of common terms has its price, of course, and critics have noted that role theory has been characterized by terminological and conceptual confusion. As was suggested in Chapter One, this confusion reflects at least three processes: (a) the use of key terms within role theory for different concepts; (b) denotation of the same concepts by different terms, and (c) obscurity and the use of superfluous assumptions in writings within the role field. We should not be too surprised at this confusion, for if the discourse within role theory has been carried partly by surplus connotation, it should also follow that theorists will differ from one another when they try to make their efforts explicit and denotative. Another way of putting the problem is to suggest that heretofore role theory has been characterized by a partially articulate vocabulary rather than by an integrated conceptual system.

EMPIRICAL ORIENTATION

Role theory is an empirical science and has been commended for the vigor of its empirical research. Much is known today about such topics as conformity, role conflict, imitation, accuracy and veridicality, stereotypy, status equilibration, and the like. Role theory is also popular because of its methodological neutrality. With the possible exception of clinical role playing (which was developed for therapy rather than for research), role theory has produced no methodological departures.

Rather, its practitioners have adopted existing instruments and have used a variety of strategies for operationalizing role concepts.

And yet, the empirical picture is not entirely rosy. To say that role concepts have been operationalized in various ways suggests confusion in the empirical effort. Studies presumed by their authors to concern role conflict, for example, may turn out (upon examination) to concern a dozen or more quite different concepts. Or studies presumed by their authors to concern quite different concepts (such as conformity, status equilibration, and modeling) may turn out to be operationally indistinguishable. Coverage of interesting topics within role theory is also spotty. Little is known today about the breadth of roles, ambiguity and cue clarity in positions, or centrality of expectations. Surprisingly important processes in role theory (such as consensus) seem to have attracted little empirical attention to date. Above all, few investigators have yet taken up basic research in the role field; indeed, little agreement has yet surfaced over what that basic research might concern.

SCOPE AND FORMALIZATION

Role theory is not only eclectic in stance, it is also broad in scope. Those who use role concepts have concerned themselves with a striking array of social problems, and theorists have tied central role concepts to a wide variety of other phenomena. Role concepts appear in contemporary discussions of sexism, racism, and classism; they surface in articles concerned with disaster, international relations, ecology, the population explosion, communes, commuting, communication, and communism; and role concepts are found within the technical education of professionals who are being trained to meet these concerns. Sources may also be found in which role expectations, for example, are argued to reflect unconscious impulses, motives, attitudes, instincts, physiology, space, time, temperature, artifacts, the weather—if not the phases of the moon. As a result, role theory tends to be both broad and shallow, popular and superficial.

To put this matter another way, to date there has been little formalization in role theory. Several critics have noted that role theory lacks an integrative, propositional structure. Despite the fact that propositional summeries are available for subfields of the role orientation, these have not yet been tied together with a single structure of basic propositions. In addition, formal discussion of theory has not appeared for many interesting role concepts. We know very little, for example, about how expectations are formed in the first place, nor have we as yet much evidence on the strategies selected by persons when they want another to change his or her behavior, nor do we know the limits of the consensus and conformity paradigms, nor the competitive strengths of the various theories of social integration. The difficulty is not that role theory does not exhibit propositions. Rather, the problem is that it has so few propositions concerning basic processes, and these propositions are so vital to the integrative promise of role theory.

In sum, then, present-day role theory should be given a mixed report card.

Immensely popular, eclectic and broad in stance, and characterized by both practical application and empirical research, role theory seems to have a bright future. And yet, at present its terminology is sloppily applied, its concepts only partially articulate, its findings and knowledge only partially formalized. Clearly, problems of these latter sorts must be dealt with if role theory is to realize its bright promise.

WHAT WE MIGHT DO ABOUT IT

> *No wise fish would go anywhere without a porpoise.*
> —*Lewis Carroll*

What, then, should be done for role theory? Assuming that this field holds the promise of fulfilling Kurt Lewin's criterion for a good theory (namely, that it is practical), what might one do to help?

Clearly, part of the answer lies in continuing the vigorous empirical effort that has characterized the role field. Literally thousands of studies have now been published concerning role processes, but these are a drop in the bucket of need. No matter how well researched a given topic within the role arena may be, definitive knowledge is not yet at hand. Are you interested in veridicality, conformity, pluralistic ignorance, socialization, general roles, or role conflict resolution? Welcome aboard! There is a lot to be learned about each of these topics, and as you develop your own plans for research you will discover similar interests in other researchers.

Clearly too, those who have applied role ideas to the discussion of human problems should be encouraged to continue the effort. Role theory *is* relevant to human affairs, and application of role notions holds the promise of gaining at least partial control over the problems that threaten us. In addition, the more successful we are in applying role ideas to practical problems, the more likely we are to stimulate agencies to fund needed basic research in role theory.

But what about the confusions, inadequacies, and shortcomings of the role field? What might be done about these?

Tasks to Be Undertaken

Several tasks are in order if we are to straighten out affairs within the role realm.

A CONCEPTUAL SYNTHESIS

Surely the first requirement needed for systematizing role theory is adoption of a single system of terms and concepts for the role field. As readers may by now have detected, one of the author's motives in writing this text was to set forth such a system. Whether my system will be accepted is not for me to predict, but clearly some form of systematic treatment of role concepts must eventually appear. As was noted in Chapter One, it may be argued that during the formative state of a discipline there is heuristic value in preserving confusion. With all due respect to this argument, role theory has already explored enough realms to boggle the mind! Surely it is now time that the role field adopt a single, integrated structure of terms and concepts and begin to take seriously its promise as an integrative science.

KNOWLEDGE RETRIEVAL

A second task concerns control of knowledge from the role field. Let us assume that you, the reader, wanted to find out what was presently known about some topic in role theory, for example, *conformity*. How would you go about finding this information? Clearly the best way to begin would be to consult standard reverence sources for research that are catalogued under the term *conformity* or its synonyms. But as we know, *conformity* has been used to reference a number of different concepts, many of which will be irrelevant to your interests. Thus, any term-based search of the literature will generate a number of studies that are useless (for you). Worse, some research of interest to you will not be catalogued under *conformity* at all but will appear under other terms and phrases—"role conflict resolution," "attitude," "attitude change," "consistency," "motivation," "adjustment," and many more. Without spending literally hundreds of hours in the library, how are you going to find these other references?

As serious as these problems may be, let us assume that you have solved them. You now have before you several scores of studies on conformity and would like to assess them. You begin to read them and a host of new problems appears. The studies vary in design, operations, subjects, content, and contexts. Standards for reportage differ, and information you would need in order to assess the validity of results is often missing. Concepts and propositions stated may or may not be matched to operations. Above all, most investigators make claims for the interpretation or applicability of their findings that transcend the limits of their data. Which, then, is knowledge from the role field: the specific and limited findings of data, or the broader and fuzzier "explanations" of results offered by the investigator? Both appear to be valuable, but for different reasons, and in the meantime which are you to believe?

If you are like most investigators, sooner or later one or more of these problems will defeat you, and you will give up on trying to keep abreast of research that is relevant to your interests. Instead, you will probably confine your reading to one or two journals, or look for articles that express problems in a vocabulary that you know is relevant, or confine your attention only to studies that are produced by certain other investigators. All of which leads to scholasticism and to fissioning the role field into isolated sets of investigators and effort. Clearly, role theory needs a common system for storage and retrieval of knowledge.

Interestingly, such a system becomes feasible once one has an integrated structure of terms and concepts for the role field. Such a system requires that we "translate" all propositions and arguments, all operations and findings into a single, standardized vocabulary. Once this is done, the computer may be used for storing and retrieving information for any topic in role theory. To illustrate how this might be done, Barbara Bank, I, and others recently built a retrieval system for articles concerned with comparison concepts (Bank, Biddle, Griffin, Johnson, Kang, & Törnblom, 1972). The system stores articles in the computer in the form of standardized abstracts. Each abstract provides: (*a*) a reference citation; (*b*) information about the design of the study; (*c*) information about the setting in which data were collected and the subjects of the investigation; (*d*) a listing of variables used in the research and their operations; and (*e*) a listing of propositions and findings reported together with their supporting evidence. All this information is coded with English-language words and phrases that are given explicit and standardized definitions. As a result, the abstract file may be addressed with requests for available information concerning any given variable, proposition, or other features of the studies coded. Systems such as these may be extended to retrieve knowledge in related fields—provided only that those fields have an integrated structure of terms and concepts.

Use of systems such as these is cumbersome at present. Since there is little standardization of terminology or format for publishing, considerable labor is required to translate articles into standardized abstract format. In the future I would suggest that such standardized abstracts be prepared as part of the process of journal publishing. Indeed, to publish such abstracts on a regular basis would alert editors, reviewers, authors, and readers to the need for standardized information in research reports. Costs for such an undertaking might be underwritten by the professional associations or the federal government as a necessary service for those seeking knowledge from the social sciences.

BASIC RESEARCH

Another task concerns the conduct of basic research. At several points in the text I have noted the lack of basic research in role theory and have suggested that little was yet known about issues of central importance. Lacking basic research, for example, it is difficult to know the limits of assumptions we might want to make about consensus, sanctioning, or the simple formation of expectations. Nor will we truly understand *why* a person conforms or deviates from role expectations without basic knowledge concerning the occurrence, etiology, and effects of holding such expectations. But what delimits the class of "basic" research in role theory? Is research on status equilibration "basic"? What about role conflict resolution? Role casting? Span of control? The clinical effects of role playing?

As important as these topics are, they do not concern basic issues in role theory. Instead, I shall argue that basic research concerns the central concepts upon which role theory is erected: roles, identities (or positions), and expectations. These

Table 9.1
SELECTED, BASIC TOPICS FOR RESEARCH IN ROLE THEORY

Concept class	Basic research issues	Illustrative variables for research
Roles	How are roles to be studied? When do roles appear? Which roles are associated with contexts, which with persons? What causes roles? How do roles evolve? What are the functions of roles? How are persons affected by roles? How do roles affect other roles?	Generality (contextualization, personalization) Complexity (breadth, difficulty, coherence) Uniqueness Visibility Specialization (diffuseness, singularity) Integration (complementarity, interdependence, reciprocation) Role strain (overload, discontinuity, congruence, involvement, role distance)
Identities and positions	How are identities to be studied? When do social positions appear? Which are associated with behaviors, features, traits, prior experiences, treatments, social structure? How are positional members recognized? What causes social positions? How do positions evolve? What are the functions of positions? How are persons affected by identity?	Conditions of entry (achievement, ascription) Conditions of maintenance and exit Status (prestige, wealth, authority) Generality Ambiguity (cue clarity) Centrality Identification (reference other) Deviancy (labeling)
Expectations	How are expectations to be studied? When do expectations appear? How are enunciations, conceptions, and inscriptions related? When are prescriptions, cathexes, and descriptions differentiated? Which expectations are associated with contexts, which with persons? When are expectations shared?	Modality Form Person (subject, object, sentient) Content Contextualization Strength and amount Generality (personalization, contextualization) Clarity (ambiguity, diffuseness) Consonance Formality

Concept class	Basic research issues	Illustrative variables for research
	What causes expectations? How are expectations learned, how are they altered by experience? What are the functions of expectations? How do they affect persons?	Legitimacy Stereotypy Centrality (imbeddedness, internalization, saliency) Comparison concepts Consistency Concordance

are the core concerns of the field, and until we have useful information about the forms, conditions of occurrence, causes, and effects of these events it is unlikely that role theory can grow as an integrated science.

Let me expand this argument a bit. Table 9.1 presents a list of issues and topics for basic research in the role field. As can be seen, three columns appear within this figure. The first, or left-hand, column lists the three central concepts for which basic research is conceived. The second column notes typical issues for basic research. The third column provides a partial listing of basic variables that may be investigated for the concept given.

One or two examples may help to illustrate Table 9.1. As readers may recall from Chapter Three, studies of actual roles are hard to find. Many investigators have studied role expectations, and limited research is now available concerning behaviors that are characteristic of a few contexts such as classrooms or decision-making groups. Despite these few exceptions, it is difficult to find studies of the actual behaviors of nurses, hobos, mothers-in-law, social drinkers, or community leaders. As a result, much of what we think we know about these roles reflects personal experience or hearsay. Worse, we do not really know yet how to go about the task—how, for example, to observe behavior efficiently in most contexts or how to establish whether or not a given behavior is characteristic. Solving problems of this sort are crucial to the conduct of studies concerned with the occurrence, genesis, evolution, or functions of roles.

Again, in Chapter Five I suggested that it is useful to distinguish three modes of expectation. But is the issue of modality really that clear-cut? Under what conditions do persons differentiate their beliefs, norms, and preferences? Or is it possible that additional modes are sometimes differentiated, and if so what are they? What experiences lead to the forming of expectations that differ in mode, and what does the person *do* when he or she holds a norm rather than a preference? Are expectations that differ in mode equally likely to be held for oneself, for another person, for a reference position? Issues such as these are crucial to understanding the place of expectations in human affairs.

EXPLANATORY THEORY

Unintegrated findings do not a science make, and role theory cannot realize its potential until propositional theory is developed that will tie its concepts, predictions, and empirical evidence into coherent wholes. Thus there is a fourth task for role theorists, to press for formal and explanatory theory.

In addition to the problems we have already discussed, several factors make this task difficult. For one thing, funding agencies have shown little interest in supporting basic research in the social sciences, let alone efforts to form explanatory theory. In the United States, at least, there is a confusion between science and engineering, and activities of the role theorist may only be supported if he or she promises to provide answers to some practical problem. Some social scientists, too, seem to value evidence more highly than explanation and to presume that once a relationship has been established for one set of subjects within one context that it is likely to hold for all persons and all times and places. Needless to say, the serious role theorist finds such presumptions questionable.

If roles are conceived, in part, to reflect identity and context, then the role theorist will always question whether a given finding about human behavior does or does not generalize. Such questions are not always asked by social scientists. Many psychologists or sociologists are likely to believe that a laboratory demonstration or survey result that was obtained for middle-class Americans will also generalize to working-class Americans or to citizens of other countries. Scientists of such persuasions tend to express their findings in simple propositions—namely, "When persons are subjected to condition A they will do X." Role theorists, who are more concerned with the effects of identity and context, are likely to reason: "From the evidence given, I would judge that within context C, when those who hold identity P are subjected to condition A they will do X—and I am not sure what others would do in a different context." Such a stance is more bloody-minded and should lead, eventually, to more accurate predictions about human affairs. It also poses difficulties for those who would formalize role theory. For one, multivariate (or contingent) propositions are difficult to think about or to integrate into theory. For another, we often have little evidence concerning the impact of variations in identity or context on the effect in which we are interested. For a third, theories that would provide us classifications for indentities and contexts are hard to find. Clearly, such classifications are needed if we are to formalize propositions about roles—which makes the work of investigators such as Barker, Cattell, and Foa so important for the role theorist.

Again, to construct formal theory for the role field will remain difficult as long as boundaries of that field are so diffuse. If defined broadly, role theory might be conceived an integrating perspective that subsumes most of the social sciences. But in so doing, one gives up all hope of establishing theory that is unique to the role field. On the other hand, if narrower boundaries are set, some agreement must be established among role theorists over core concepts, issues, and phenomena for which the role field is responsible.

Despite these problems, establishment of explanatory theory for the role field is necessary, and those interested in the role field should be encouraged to devote effort to this task.

Boundaries and Unsolved Problems

The question of boundaries of role theory may also be viewed as a substantive issue. Clearly, the core concerns of role theory involve only a fraction of the wide range of concepts traditionally associated with the social sciences. In addition, certain other problems that are traditionally ignored by role theorists are necessary to consider when formalizing theory for the role field. Let us examine some of these issues.

TIME, SPACE, AND FORMALIZATION

One of the first difficulties with the role orientation is its cavalier treatment of time. At several points in the text it was noted that we had made assumptions about time. One such assumption suggests that events will stand still long enough for us to measure them, to find out what their characteristic aspects were, or to form expectations about them. It was pointed out, for example, that the concepts of personality, role, and culture are time binding and assume that minimal change is taking place during the period of our observation. Moreover, we make basic assumptions within role theory about the invariance of human beings and their physical features.

The problem is even worse than these assumptions suggest, for sloppiness concerning time is built into our language. Consider our terms for activities that recur periodically. A single meeting of a group suffices to establish its identity, but when its members reassemble after the lapse of a week is it still the "same" group? Our common language would have it so. Since sloppiness concerning time is built into our common language, it is no wonder that it appears commonly in the social sciences. And those of us who are concerned with temporal processes, such as learning or social change, have difficulty communicating even with other members of our professions.

A similar sloppiness appears in our treatment of the physical environment in which human behavior is conducted. Much of role theory is oblivious to the environment, and when we must speak of the environment we do so grudgingly with such general terms as *artifact, environmental unit,* or *setting.* And yet, human beings are physical events, as are their features, their behaviors, the contexts to which they respond, and the functions that those responses produce. There is no great mystery surrounding the impact of human action on the physical environment or vice versa. When housebuilding or baking a cake are taking place, these events can be described in clear and unambiguous physical terms—whether the action is being accomplished through human muscle power or the agency of a machine. Only a few social scientists today are truly concerned about the physical environment: archeologists, industrial psychologists, ecologists, and a few others. The rest of us appear to ignore the physical environment whenever possible—since most of us are indifferently trained in the physical sciences, and since the physical environment is also often ignored by our subjects themselves, even though it affects their behaviors.

The problems of time and space come together when one attempts to formalize role concepts and propositions. Anyone who attempts to write an algebra for role theory will shortly discover the need to denote time. Moreover, it is difficult to discuss such subjects as behavioral control, sanctioning, innovation, and social change without formal concepts for treating the environment. However, to allow time and space into role theory forces us to abandon well-entrenched conventions and necessitates that role theory be recast into a system of symbols that would no longer be familiar to neophytes. I suspect that the time for formalizaing role theory is coming soon, but when this step is taken, role theory will no longer have the broad appeal it now generates through its common language vocabulary.

SEMANTICS

Another difficulty with the coverage of role concepts appears when we attempt to study the overt expression of expectations by persons. Clearly, expectations *are* enunciated from time to time. However, expectational enunciation is but one of many semantic forms that appear in everyday speech. Other semantic forms appear that share common elements with expectations. They too may exhibit references to human characteristics, modality of the expression, statements concerning contextualization or contingency, and the like. All of which suggests that the concept of expectation may be but one of a number of semantic forms we might use as models for cognitive processes.

Unfortunately, the study of semantics is as yet in its infancy. Traditional linguistics concerned itself with dialectical analysis and the evolution of languages, whereas recent developments in structural linguistics have stressed the analysis of lexical, phonemic, and order characteristics of language—whether or not these had any relevance to the meaning of the enunciation. Only since the mid-1960s or so have linguists begun to turn serious attention to the formal analysis of meaning in symbolic expression (for example, see Chomsky, 1972; Rommetveit, 1974). Such efforts will have a significant effect on role theory.

MOTIVATION

Role theory is "weak" on motivation, and often the explanations of role analysts leave us confused as to why anyone takes action at all. (Perhaps Milgram was right, and the basic reason why subjects respond is simply because the experimenter tells them to do so!) Well, what about this shortcoming? Do we need a concept of motivation, and if we need one, how can it be built into role theory?

Let us consider first the possibility that role theory can get along without an explicit concept of motivation. This is not an unattractive possibility. Dewey (1922) and others have argued that human beings are active naturally. If this is so, our explanatory task is not that of accounting for the genesis of behavior but rather that of explaining why a person does one thing and not another. That which we perceive as motive in the person's behavior may be either a product of our expectations for it, of identity (Foote, 1951), or of the person's attempt to rationalize that behavior in terms he or she can use to organize subsequent behaviors (Mills, 1940).

Another argument suggests that a concept for motivation is not needed in role theory because the issue is already dealt with in basic propositions. To illustrate, in Chapter Five I suggested that unopposed preferences for oneself should lead to conforming behavior, whereas norms for the self should produce conformity if accompanied by fears of sanctions or if viewed as legitimate. Such propositions may easily be converted into motivational format. So can propositions concerning the effects of role conflict, status equilibration, concordance, perceived consensus, identification, and involvement. The fact is that role theorists do not usually speak of these states as having motivational properties. But they might easily do so.

Arguments such as these provide at least a partial solution for the problem and enable us to accommodate those portions of the motivation concept that are related to phenomenal experience. Thus, they appear to encompass Lewin's concepts of "force" and "need tension," and Gordon Allport's ideas about "functionally autonomous" motives. They are not sufficient, however, for other theories that use the motive concept to discuss biological states, emotions, or unconscious drives. Concepts of these latter sorts appear difficult to build into role theory in its present form. Role theorists have ignored physiology and emotion as often as they have ignored time and space, and acceptance of the assumption of phenomenal equivalence has led most role theorists to avoid dealing with the unconscious. In the long run, role theory will have to deal with these latter problems too.

In short, then, there are several ways in which the problem of motivation can be dealt with in role theory: by defining it away; by recognizing that role propo-

sitions may be restated in motivational forms; and by introducing additional concepts for physiolgoy, emotion, and unconscious processes. Some of these solutions
are easier to accommodate than others.

SOCIAL CHANGE

Role theory is also "soft" on social change. With the possible exceptions of
Turner and Warren, I know of no role theorists who have advanced systematic propositions concerning social change, nor have many role studies been published that
are concerned with the topic. In part, role theory presumes that quasi-stationary
forms of human behavior exit—roles, activities, social systems—about which subjects built expectations and to which they are socialized to accommodate in their
behavior. But in part, role theory also appears to reflect a general tendency in
American social science that lays greater stress on social structure than on social
process.

And yet, our is an era of unbridled social change. A host of phenomena that
once characterized our society are no longer with us. Lynching has passed away; the
gold standard has been abolished; witchcraft trials are a thing of the past; occupations such as blacksmithing are obsolescent; conditions that brought forth the
speakeasy, the WPA, and legal slavery are gone—and few would mourn their passing.
But what of today's social arrangements—nuclear families, inflation, professional
football, and institutionalized racism—are these to remain permanent features of
our society, or will they too pass into the limbo of history?

As of the moment, role theorists are no more able to answer this question than
are social scientists of other persuasions. Clearly, role theory offers an approach to
individual change. And clearly, too, role theory can tell us something about the
integration and malintegration of social systems—and in a general way, we would
predict that those social systems that were malintegrated would either change their
forms or go out of business. But predicting the likelihood of change is a far different thing from predicting which way the change will go. Presumably White (1959)
is right when he claims that the major force driving social change is technological
innovation. If we were wise enough to know those technological innovations that
were "just about" to be invented, and if we had a bit more control over the impact
of technologies on our social forms, perhaps we could begin to solve the problem of
predicting social change. But for the moment, role theory can only account for
social changes that have already taken place—after the fact.

In the long run, one would surely want role theory to accommodate the phenomena of social change, as well as time, space, and the other problems just reviewed. Whether this is necessary in the short run depends on how one chooses to
set boundaries for the field.

THE SOCIAL USE OF ROLE THEORY

People who live in chateaux shouldn't throw tomateaux.
—Morton

So much for what role theory is and might become. But what is the *use* of role theory? What can role theory do for us in the real world? Given its strengths and weaknesses, what can role theory accomplish today, and what are its prospects for tomorrow?

For one thing, role theory provides us with a vocabulary for discussing human affairs and the way in which people think about those affairs. Role theory parades as a relevant social science. Indeed, given its basic subject matter and eclectic stance, we would be hard pressed to find any field within the social sciences that has broader appeal than role theory. Role concepts have already been applied to scores of institutions, events, and problems in contemporary life—from conformity to deviancy, individuals to social systems, vocations to avocations, socialization to resocialization, stability to disaster, love to war. And each month brings new examples of the practical application of role ideas.

Many of these applications are also supported by empirical data, thus role theory also provides us a means for collecting data that are directly relevant to human affairs. Concepts such as role, position, and expectation appear easy to operationalize, and data concerning them have an immediate appeal not only to investigators, but also to human subjects and clients who support research. Moreover, a lot of practical knowledge has already been gathered by role investigators concerning both abstract topics such as conformity or role conflict resolution and practical concerns such as industrial morale, entry into professions, or counseling.

At the same time, application of role theory to the study and solving of human problems has been spotty. Role theory has already contributed to the clinical professions, but its potential has yet to be realized in other realms. Consider law. As we have seen, a number of role concepts are based on legal models, but most of these models were developed years ago. Role theory has much to contribute to contemporary debates on social responsibility, juvenile delinquency, the theory of deterrence, the conditions under which the application of threats and sanctions is likely to be effective, alternative explanations for deviancy, and so forth. Thus role theory could repay its conceptual heritage with information that would be useful in the formulation of laws and improvement of our legal system. But this would require both an expansion of relevant research and a broadening of dialogue between role theorists and those concerned with the law.

Our record with regard to social planning is a little better, but still spotty. By now we are used to the notion of using empirical knowledge to plan certain kinds of social systems. Some industries conduct research on their organizational structures, and a few also study their impact on the surrounding community. Some "model" communities are now planned, and the rules of games are deliberately altered to improve the game or give it greater audience appeal. But most programs for social betterment are not based on research; indeed, to propose research on programs for "socialized" medicine or the redistribution of wealth would be viewed by some as politically unfeasible. Research is inadequate for planning within education today, nor do we base programs for the elimination of racism, classism, sexism, or ethnic bigotry upon research. Gross injustice still persists in our country—with decaying cities, rural poverty, discrimination against blacks, Indians, or Puerto Ricans, and other blights that make a mockery of our claims of enlightenment and social justice. Such problems are amenable to research and to alleviation through programs of public action. But unfortunately, public action is viewed as a political matter in America, rather than as a fit subject for scientific investigation and a moral necessity. Role theory has much to contribute to programs of social betterment, but until that contribution is understood and desired by others, role theorists will remain partially "unemployed."

Role theory is not the only discipline that can contribute toward effective social planning. We also need the help of ecolgoists, demographers, architects, physsiologists, engineers, educators, physicians. But surely role theorists can also contribute their concepts and specialized knowledge concerning socialization, conformity, consensus, the effects of expectations, deviance, and creativity. In part, that contribution will depend on research conducted in the near future. But even today the role theorist has enough knowledge and insight to make a contribution. Role theory may not yet be the integrated, propositional structure we would like it to be. But this is no excuse for indolence in applying its knowledge to the alleviation of human misery.

In seeking to apply that knowledge, the role theorist walks a narrow line. When requesting funds for research, we must argue with enthusiasm—yet not make false promises. When conducting research, we must strive for empirical validity—while also maintaining compassion for our subjects. When reporting results, we must distinguish findings from explanations—and be willing to limit the former to those subject identities and contexts for which we collect data. Role theorists bear burdens because of the relevance of their discipline. Role theory offers the serious social scientist an opportunity to understand and contribute to human affairs, but it also lays upon his or her shoulders the yoke of honesty. The role of the role theorist involves restraint as well as research, reason, and social responsibility.

References

Abel, T. M. & Hsu, F. L. K., 1949. Some aspects of personality of Chinese as revealed by the Rorschach test. *Rorschach Research Exchange, 13:* 285-301.

Abelson, R. P., 1972. *Attitudes, conflict and social change: Are attitudes necessary?* New York: Academic Press.

Aberle, D. F., 1961. Culture and socialization. In F. L. K. Hsu (Ed.), *Psychological anthropology.* Homewood, Ill.: Dorsey.

Aberle, D. F., Cohen, A. K., Davis, A. K., Levy, M. J., Jr., & Sutton, F. X., 1950. The Functional prerequisites of a society. *Ethics, 60:* 100-111.

Ackerman, N. W., 1951. "Social role" and total personality. *American Journal of Orthopsychiatry, 21:* 1-17.

Acock, A. C. & DeFleur, M. L., 1972. A configurational approach to contingent consistency in the attitude-behavior relationship. *American Sociological Review, 37:* 714-726.

Adams, D. N., 1971. *The American family: A sociological interpretation.* Chicago: Markham.

Adams, J. S., 1963. Toward an understanding of inequity. *Journal of Abnormal and Social Psychology, 67:* 422-436.

Adams, R. S. (Ed.), 1970. Symposium on teacher role in four English-speaking countries. *Comparative Education Review, 14:* 5-6.

Adams, R. S. & Biddle, B. J., 1970. *Realities of teaching: Explorations with video tape.* New York. Holt.

Adorno, T. W., Frenkel-Brunswik, E., Levinson, D. J., & Sanford, R. N., 1950. *The Authoritarian Personality.* New York: Harper.

Ajzen, I., 1971. Attitudinal versus normative messages: An investigation of the differential effects of persuasive communications on behavior. *Sociometry, 34:* 263-280.

Ajzen, I. & Fishbein, M., 1969. The prediction of behavioral intentions in a choice situation. *Journal of Experimental Social Psychology, 5:* 400-416.

Ajzen, I. & Fishbein, M., 1970. The prediction of behavior from attitudinal and normative variables. *Journal of Experimental Social Psychology, 6:* 466-487.

Ajzen, I. & Fishbein, M., 1972. Attitudes and normative beliefs as factors influencing behavior intentions. *Journal of Personality and Social Psychology, 21:* 1-9.

Alexander, C. N., Jr. & Campbell, E. Q., 1962. Peer influences on adolescent drinking. *Quarterly Journal of Studies on Alcohol, 28:* 444-453.

Alexander, C. N., Jr. & Scriven, G. D., 1977. Role playing: An essential component of experimentation. *Personality and Social Psychology Bulletin, 3:* 455-466.

Alford, R. R., 1963. *Party and society: The Anglo-American democrats.* Chicago: Rand McNally.

Alinsky, S. D., 1946. *Reveille for radicals.* Chicago: University of Chicago Press.

Allen, V. L., 1965. Situational factors in conformity. In L. Berkowitz (Ed.), *Advances in experimental social psychology* (Vol. 2). New York: Academic Press, 133-175.

Allen, V. L., 1975. Social support for nonconformity. In L. Berkowitz (Ed.), *Advances in experimental social psychology* (Vol. 8). New York: Academic Press.

Allport, F. H., 1924. *Social psychology.* New York: Houghton Mifflin.

Allport, F. H., 1934. The j-curve hypothesis of conforming behavior. *Journal of Social Psychology, 5:* 141-153.

Allport, G. W., 1935. Attitudes. In C. Murchison (Ed.), *A Handbook of social psychology.* Worcester, Mass.: Clark University Press.

Allport, G. W., 1954. *The Nature of Prejudice.* Cambridge, Mass.: Addison-Wesley.

Alluisi, E. A. & Morgan, B. B., Jr., 1976. Engineering psychology in human performance. In *Annual review of psychology* (Vol. 27). Palo Alto, Calif.: Annual Reviews.

Altman, I. & Taylor, D., 1973. *Social penetration: The development of interpersonal relations.* New York: Holt.

Altmann, S. A., 1962. Social behavior of anthropoid primates: Analysis of recent concepts. In E. L. Bliss (Ed.), *Roots of behavior.* New York: Harper.

Amir, Y., 1969. Contact hypothesis in ethnic relations. *Psychological Bulletin, 71:* 319-342.

Anderson, A. R. & Moore, O. K., 1957. The formal analysis of normative concepts. *American Sociological Review, 22:* 9-17.

Anderson, H. H. & Anderson, G. L., 1961. Image of the teacher by adolescent children in seven countries. *American Journal of Orthopsychiatry, 31:* 481-492.

Angell, R. C., 1958. *Free society and moral crises.* Ann Arbor: University of Michigan Press.

Ardrey, R., 1961. *African genesis.* New York: Atheneum.

Ardrey, R., 1966. *The territorial imperative: A personal inquiry into the animal origins of property and nations.* New York: Atheneum.

Argyle, M., 1957. Social pressure in public and private situations. *Journal of Abnormal and Social Psychology, 54:* 172-175.

Argyris, C., 1954. The fusion of an individual with the organization. *American Sociological Review, 19:* 267-272.

Argyris, C., 1957. *Personality and organization: The conflict between system and the Individual.* New York: Harper.

Aronson, E., 1969. The theory of cognitive dissonance: a current perspective. In L. Berkowitz (Ed.), *Advances in experimental social psychology* (Vol. 4). New York: Academic Press.

Aronson, E. & Carlsmith, J. M., 1963. Effect of the severity of threat on the devaluation of actual performance. *Journal of Abnormal and Social Psychology, 66:* 584-588.

Aronson, E. & Carlsmith, J. M., 1968. Experimentation in social psychology. In G. Lindzey & E. Aronson (Eds.), *Handbook of social psychology* (2nd ed, Vol. 2). Reading, Mass.: Addison-Wesley.

Aronson, E. & Mills, J., 1959. The effect of severity of initiation on liking for a group. *Journal of Abnormal and Social Psychology, 59:* 177-181.

Asch, S. E., 1956. Studies of independence and submission to group pressure: I. A minority of one against a unanimous majority. *Psychological Monographs, 70,* No. 9 (Whole No. 417).

Asher, S. R. & Allen, V. L., 1969. Racial preference and social comparison processes. *The*

Journal of Social Issues, 25: 157-166.

Atkinson, J. W. & Hoselitz, B. F. 1958. Entrepreneurship and personality. *Explorations in Entrepreneurial History, 10:* 107-112.

Bales, R. F., 1950. *Interaction process analysis: A method for the study of small groups.* Cambridge, Mass.: Addison-Wesley.

Bales, R. F., 1958. Task roles and social roles in problem-solving groups. In E. E. Maccoby, T. M. Newcomb, & E. L. Hartley (Eds.), *Readings in social psychology* (3rd ed.). New York: Holt.

Bales, R. F. & Slater, P. E., 1955. Role differentiation. In T. Parsons & R. F. Bales, *The family socialization and interaction process.* Glencoe, Ill.: The Free Press.

Bandura, A., 1965. Vicarious processes: A case of no-trial learning. In L. Berkowitz (Ed.), *Advances in experimental social psychology* (Vol. 2). New York: Academic Press.

Bandura, A., 1969. *Principles of behavior modification.* New York: Holt.

Bandura, A., 1973. *Aggression: A social learning analysis.* Englewood Cliffs, N. J.: Prentice-Hall.

Bandura, A. & Walters, R. H., 1963. *Social learning and personality.* New York: Holt.

Bank, B.J., 1968. *The utility of role theory: The case of the advertising salesman.* Unpublished master's thesis. Iowa City: University of Iowa.

Bank, B. J., Biddle, B. J., Griffin, J. T., Johnson, D. L., Kang, J., & Törnblom, K., 1972. *A propositional coding system for role theory.* (Technical Report No. 49). Columbia: Center for Research in Social Behavior, University of Missouri.

Bank, B. J., Biddle, B. J., Keats, D. M., & Keats, J. A., 1977. Normative, preferential, and belief modes in adolescent prejudice. *Sociological Quarterly, 18:* 574-588.

Banton, M., 1965. *Roles: An introduction to the study of social relations.* New York: Basic Books.

Barker, R. G. (Ed.), 1963. *The stream of behavior: Explorations of its structure and content.* New York: Appleton-Century-Crofts.

Barker, R. G., 1968. *Ecological psychology: Concepts and methods for studying the environment of human behavior.* Stanford, Calif.: Stanford University Press.

Barker, R. G. & Gump, P. V., 1964. *Big school, small school: High school size and student behavior.* Stanford, Calif.: Stanford University Press.

Barker, R. G. & Schoggen, P., 1973. *Qualities of community life.* San Francisco: Jossey-Bass.

Barker, R. G. & Wright, H. F., 1955. *Midwest and its children: The psychological ecology of an American town.* Evanston, Ill.: Row, Peterson.

Baron, R. M., 1977. Role playing and experimental research: The identification of appropriate domains of power. *Personality and Social Psychology Bulletin, 3:* 505-513.

Barr, S., 1958. *Purely academic.* New York: Simon and Schuster, 34-35.

Bass, B. M., 1961. Conformity, deviation, and a general theory of interpersonal behavior. In I. A. Berg & B. M. Bass (Eds.), *Conformity and deviation.* New York: Harper.

Bates, F. L., 1956. Position, role, and status: A reformulation of concepts. *Social Forces, 34:* 313-321.

Becker, H. S., 1963. *Outsiders: Studies in the sociology of deviance.* New York: The Free Press.

Becker, H. S., Geer, B., Hughes, E. C., & Strauss, A. L., 1961. *Boys in white: Student culture in medical school.* Chicago: University of Chicago Press.

Bem, D. J., 1964. *An experimental analysis of beliefs and attitudes.* Unpublished doctoral dissertation. Ann Arbor: University of Michigan.

Bendix, R., 1962. *Max Weber: An intellectual portrait.* New York: Doubleday.

Benedict, B., 1969. Role analysis in animals and men. *Man, 4:* 203-214.

Benedict, R., 1934. *Patterns of culture.* Boston: Houghton Mifflin.

Benedict, R., 1938. Continuities and discontinuities in cultural conditioning. *Psychiatry, 1:* 161-167.

Bennis, W. G., Berkowitz, N., Affinito, M., & Malone, M., 1958. Authority, power, and the ability to influence. *Human Relations, 11:* 143–155.

Bennis, W. G. & Slater, P. E., 1968. *The temporary society.* New York: Harper.

Benoit-Smullyan, E., 1944. Status, status types, and status interrelations. *American Sociological Review, 9:* 151–161.

Benson, J. K., 1977. Innovation and crisis in organizational analysis. *Sociological Quarterly, 18,* 3–16.

Berdie, R. F., 1947. Playing the dozens. *Journal of Abnormal and Social Psychology, 42:* 120–121.

Berelson, B., 1952. *Content analysis in communication research.* Glencoe, Ill.: The Free Press.

Berelson, B., Lazarsfeld, P. F., & McPhee, W. N., 1954. *Voting.* Chicago: University of Chicago Press.

Berelson, B. & Steiner, G., 1964. *Human behavior.* New York: Harcourt, Brace.

Berger, J., Zelditch, M., Jr., & Anderson, B., 1966. *Sociological theories in progress.* Boston: Houghton Mifflin.

Bergin, A. E. & Suinn, R. M., 1975. Individual psychotherapy and behavior therapy. *Annual Review of Psychology, 26:* 509–556.

Berkowitz, L., 1962. *Aggression: A social psychological analysis.* New York: McGraw-Hill.

Berkowitz, L., 1972. Social norms, feelings, and other factors affecting helping and altruism. In L. Berkowitz (Ed.), *Advances in experimental social psychology* (Vol. 6). New York: Academic Press.

Berkowitz, L. & Daniels, L., 1963. Responsibility and dependency. *Journal of Abnormal and Social Psychology, 66:* 429–436.

Berkowitz, L. & Walster, E. (Eds.), 1976. Equity theory: Toward a general theory of social interaction. *Advances in experimental social psychology,* (Whole Vol. 9). New York: Academic Press.

Berne, E., 1964. *Games people play: The psychology of human relationships.* New York: Grove Press.

Bertrand, A. L., 1972. *Social organization: A general systems and role theory perspective.* Philadelphia: F. A. Davis.

Bettelheim, B., 1943. Individual and mass behavior in extreme situations. *Journal of Abnormal and Social Psychology, 38:* 417–452.

Bettelheim, B., 1950. *Love is not enough: The treatment of emotionally disturbed children.* Glencoe, Ill.: The Free Press.

Biddle, B. J., 1961. *The present status of role theory.* Columbia: University of Missouri Press (Mimeographed).

Biddle, B. J., 1970. Role conflicts perceived by teachers in four English speaking countries. In Symposium on teacher role in four English-Speaking countries. *Comparative Education Review, 14:* 30–44.

Biddle, B. J., Bank, B. J., & Marlin, M., 1978. *Legitimacy, discovery, and other mediators of normative influence on adolescent drinking* (Technical Report No. 128). Columbia: Center for Research in Social Behavior, University of Missouri.

Biddle, B. J., Bank, B. J., & Marlin, M., in press a. Parental and peer influence on adolescents. *Social Forces.*

Biddle, B. J., Bank, B. J., & Marlin, M., in press b. What they think, what they do, and what I think and do: Social determinants of adolescent drinking. *Journal of Studies on Alcohol.*

Biddle, B. J., Rosencranz, H. A., & Rankin, E. F., Jr., 1961. *Studies in the role of the public school teacher.* Columbia: University of Missouri Press (Mimeographed).

Biddle, B. J., Rosencranz, H. A., Tomich, E., & Twyman, J. P., 1966. Shared inaccuracies in the role of the teacher. In B. J. Biddle & E. J. Thomas (Eds.), *Role theory: Concepts and research.* New York: Wiley.

Biddle, B. J. & Rossi, P. H., 1966. Educational media, education, and society. In P. H. Rossi & B. J. Biddle (Eds.), *The new media and education.* Chicago: Aldine.

Biddle, B. J. & Thomas, E. J., 1966. *Role theory: Concepts and research.* New York: Wiley.

Biddle, B. J., Twyman, J. P., & Rankin, E. F., Jr., 1962. The role of the teacher and occupational choice. *School Review, 70:* 191-206.

Biddle, W. W. & Biddle, L. J., 1965. *The community development process: The rediscovery of local initiative.* New York: Holt.

Bills, R. E., Vance, E. L., & McLean, O. S., 1951. An index of adjustment and values. *Journal of Consulting Psychology, 18:* 135-137.

Blake, J. & Davis, K., 1964. Values and sanctions. In R. E. Faris (Ed.), *Handbook of modern sociology.* Chicago: Rand McNally, 456-484.

Blau, P. M., 1964. *Exchange and power in social life.* New York: Wiley.

Blau, P. M. (Ed.), 1975. *Approaches to the study of social structure.* New York: The Free Press.

Block, J. & Thomas, H., 1955. Is satisfaction with self a measure of adjustment? *Journal of Abnormal and Social Psychology, 51:* 254-259.

Blood, R. O. & Wolfe, D. M., 1960. *Husbands and wives: The dynamics of married living.* New York: The Free Press.

Blumer, H., 1969. *Symbolic interactionism.* Englewood Cliffs, N. J.: Prentice-Hall.

Blumstein, P. W., 1973. Subjective probability and normative evaluations. *Social Forces, 52:* 98-107.

Booth, A., 1972. Sex and social participation. *American Sociological Review, 37:* 183-193.

Bordin, E. S., Nachmann, B., & Segal, S. J., 1963. An articulated framework for vocational development. *Journal of Counseling Psychology, 10:* 107-117.

Borgatta, E. F., 1955. Attitudinal concomitants to military statuses. *Social Forces, 33:* 342-347.

Borgatta, E. F., 1961. Role-playing specification, personality and performance. *Sociometry, 24:* 218-233.

Bowerman, C. E. & Kinch, J. W., 1959. Change in family and peer orientation of children between the fourth and tenth grades. *Social Forces, 37:* 206-211.

Bowers, W. J., 1968. Normative constraints on deviant behavior in the college context. *Sociometry, 31:* 370-385.

Brannon, R., Cyphers, G., Hesse, S., Hesselbart, S., Keane, R., Schuman, H., Viccaro, T., & Wright, D., 1973. Attitude and action: A field experiment joined to a general population survey. *American Sociological Review, 38:* 625-636.

Braun, C., 1976. Teacher expectation: Sociopsychological dynamics. *Review of Educational Research, 46:* 185-213.

Bredemeier, H. C. & Stephenson, R. M., 1962. *The analysis of social systems.* New York: Holt.

Brehm, J. W., 1956. Postdecision changes in the desirability of alternatives. *Journal of Abnormal and Social Psychology, 52:* 384-389.

Brehm, J. W. & Cohen, A. R., 1962. *Explorations in cognitive dissonance.* New York: Wiley.

Brigham, J. C., 1971. Ethnic stereotypes. *Psychological Bulletin, 76:* 15-38.

Brim, O. G., Jr., 1958. Family structure and sex role learning by children: A further analysis of Helen Koch's data. *Sociometry, 21:* 1-16.

Brittain, C. V., 1963. Adolescent choices and parent-peer cross-pressures. *American Sociological Review, 28:* 385-391.

Brophy, J. E. & Good, T. L., 1970. Teachers' communication of differential expectations for children's classroom performance: Some behavioral data. *Journal of Educational Psychology, 61:* 365-374.

Brophy, J. E. & Good, T. L., 1974. *Teacher-student relationships: Causes and consequences.* New York: Holt.

Broverman, I., Vogel, S., Broverman, D., Clarkson, F., & Rosenkrantz, P., 1972. Sex-role stereotypes: A current appraisal. *Journal of Social Issues, 28:* 59-78.

Brown, R., 1962. Models of attitude change. In R. Brown, E. Galanter, E. H. Hess, & G. Mandler (Eds.), *New directions in psychology* (Vol. 1). New York: Holt.

Brown, R., 1965. *Social Psychology.* New York: The Free Press.

Brown, W., 1960. *Exploration in management: A description of the Glacier Metal Company's concepts and methods of organization and management.* New York: Wiley.

Bruner, J. S. & Tagiuri, R., 1954. The perception of people. In G. Lindzey (Ed.), *Handbook of social psychology,* (1st ed. Vol. 2). Reading, Mass.: Addison-Wesley, 634–654.

Buchler, I. R. & Selby, H. A., 1968. *Kinship and social organization: An introduction to theory and method.* New York: Macmillan.

Buckley, W., 1967. *Sociology and modern systems theory.* Englewood Cliffs, N. J.: Prentice-Hall.

Burchard, W. W., 1954. Role conflicts of military chaplains. *American Sociological Review, 19:* 528–535.

Burdick, H. A. & Burnes, A. J., 1958. A test of "strain toward symmetry" theories. *Journal of Abnormal and Social Psychology, 57:* 367–370.

Butler, J. M. & Haigh, G. V., 1954. Changes in the relation between self-concepts and ideal concepts consequent upon client-centered counseling. In C. R. Rogers & R. F. Dymond (Eds.), *Psychotherapy and personality change.* Chicago: University of Chicago Press.

Cain, M. E., 1968. Some suggested developments for role and reference group analysis. *British Journal of Sociology, 19:* 191–205.

Calder, B. J. & Ross, M., 1973. *Attitudes and behavior.* Morristown, N. J.: General Learning Press.

Caldwell, B. M., 1964. The effects of infant care. In M. L. Hoffman & L. W. Hoffman (Eds.), *Review of child development* (Vol. 1). New York: Russell Sage Foundation.

Campbell, A., Converse, P. E., Miller, W. E., & Stokes, D. E., 1960. *The American voter.* New York: Wiley.

Campbell, D. T., 1947. *The generality of social attitudes.* Unpublished doctoral dissertation. Berkeley: University of California.

Campbell, D. T., 1961. Conformity in psychology's theories of acquired behavioral dispositions. In I. A. Berg & B. M. Bass (Eds.), *Conformity and deviation.* New York: Harper.

Cannell, C. F. & Kahn, R. L., 1968. Interviewing. In G. Lindzey & E. Aronson (Eds.), *The handbook of social psychology* (2nd ed., Vol. 2). Reading: Mass.: Addison-Wesley.

Caplan, N., 1968. Treatment intervention and reciprocal interaction effects. *Journal of Social Issues, 24:* 63–88.

Caplow, T., 1954. *The sociology of work.* Minneapolis: University of Minnesota Press.

Carlson, A. R., 1968. *The relationship between a behavioral intention, attitude toward the behavior, and normative beliefs about the behavior.* Unpublished doctoral dissertation. Urbana: University of Illinois.

Casler, L., 1974. *Is marriage necessary?* New York: Human Sciences Press.

Cattell, R. B., 1946. *Description and measurement of personality.* New York: World Books.

Cattell, R. B., 1950. *Personality: A systematic and factual study.* New York: McGraw-Hill.

Cattell, R. B., 1963. Personality, role, mood, and situation-perception: A unifying theory of modulators. *Psychological Review, 70:* 1–18.

Cauthen, N. R., Robinson, I. E., & Krauss, H. H., 1971. Stereotypes: A review of the literature 1926–1968. *The Journal of Social Psychology, 84:* 103–125.

Cavan, R. S., 1962. Self and role in adjustment during old age. In A. M. Rose (Ed.), *Human behavior and social processes: An interactionist approach.* Boston: Houghton Mifflin.

Chapanis, N. P. & Chapanis, A., 1964. Cognitive dissonance: Five years later. *Psychological Bulletin, 61:* 1–22.

Charters, W. W., Jr., 1952. *A study of role conflicts among foremen in a heavy industry.* Unpublished doctoral dissertation. Ann Arbor: University of Michigan.

Cheong, G. S. & DeVault, M. V., 1966. Pupils' perceptions of teachers. *The Journal of Educational Research, 59:* 446–449.

Child, I. L., 1963. Problems of personality and some relations to anthropology and sociology. In S. Koch (Ed.), *Psychology: A study of a science* (Vol. 5). New York: McGraw-Hill, 593–638.

Chomsky, N., 1959. A review of B. F. Skinner's verbal behavior. *Language, 35:* 26–58.

Chomsky, N., 1965. *Aspects of the theory of syntax.* Cambridge, Mass.: M.I.T. Press.

Chomsky, N., 1972. *Studies on semantics in generative grammar.* The Hague: Mouton.

Chowdhry, K. & Newcomb, T. M., 1952. The relative abilities of leaders and non-leaders to estimate opinions of their own groups. *Journal of Abnormal and Social Psychology, 47:* 51–57.

Christie, R. & Geis, F. L., 1968. Machiavellian game playing. In R. Christie & F. L. Geis (Eds.), *Studies in Machiavellianism.* New York: Academic Press.

Chu, H. J. & Hollingsworth, J. S., 1969. A cross-cultural study of the relationships between family types and social stratification. *Journal of Marriage and the Family, 31:* 322–327.

Cicourel, A. V., 1970. Language as a variable in social research. *Sociological Focus, 3:* 43–52.

Clark, K. B. & Clark, M. P., 1947. Racial identification and preference in Negro children. In T. M. Newcomb & E. L. Hartley (Eds.), *Readings in social psychology.* New York: Holt, 169–178.

Cline, V. B., 1964. Interpersonal perception. In B. A. Maher (Ed.), *Progress in experimental personality research* (Vol. 1). New York: Academic Press.

Cloward, R. & Ohlin, L. E., 1960. *Delinquency and opportunity–A theory of delinquent gangs.* New York: The Free Press.

Cloyd, J. S., 1964a. Functional differentiation and the structure of informal groups. *Sociological Quarterly, 5:* 243–250.

Cloyd, J. S., 1964b. Patterns of role behavior in informal interaction. *Sociometry, 27:* 161–173.

Cobb, P. R., 1952. High school seniors' attitudes towards teachers and the teaching profession. *Bulletin of the National Association of Secondary School Principals, 36:* 140–144.

Coleman, J., Katz, E., & Menzel, H., 1966. *Medical innovations: A diffusion study.* Indianapolis: Bobbs-Merrill.

Collins, B. E. & Hoyt, M. F., 1972. Personal responsibility for consequences: An integration and extention of the "forced compliance" literature. *Journal of Experimental Social Psychology, 8:* 558–593.

Collins, B. E. & Raven, B. H., 1969. Group structure: Attraction, coalitions, communication, and power. In G. Linzey & E. Aronson (Eds.), *The handbook of social psychology* (2nd ed., Vol. 4). Reading, Mass.: Addison-Wesley.

Cooley, C. H., 1902. *Human nature and the social order* (Rev. ed., 1922). New York: Scribner's.

Cooper, H. M., in press. Pygmalion grows up: A model for teacher expectation, communication, and performance influence. *Review of Educational Research.*

Cooper, J., 1976. Deception and role playing: On telling the good guys from the bad guys. *American Psychologist, 31:* 605–610.

Cooper, W. W., Leavitt, H. J., & Shelly, J. H., III (Eds.), 1964. *New perspectives in organization research.* New York: Wiley.

Corsini, R. J., 1966. *Roleplaying in psychotherapy: A manual.* Chicago: Aldine.

Coser, L. A., 1956. *The functions of social conflict.* Glencoe, Ill.: The Free Press.

Coser, L. A., 1967. *Continuities in the study of social conflict.* New York: The Free Press.

Coser, L. A. (with Coser, R. L.), 1974. *Greedy institutions.* New York: The Free Press.

Cottrell, L. S., 1942. The adjustment of the individual to his age and sex roles. *American Sociological Review, 7:* 617–620.

Coult, A. D. & Habenstein, R. W., 1965. *Cross tabulations of Murdock's World Ethnographic*

Sample. Columbia: University of Missouri Press.

Cronbach, L. J., 1955. Processes affecting scores on "Understanding of others" and "Assumed similarity." *Psychological Bulletin, 52:* 177-193.

Cronbach, L. J., 1958. Proposals leading to analytic treatment of social perception scores. In R. Tagiuri & L. Petrullo (Eds.), *Person perception and interpersonal behavior.* Stanford, Calif.: Stanford University Press.

Culbertson, F. M., 1957. Modification of an emotionally held attitude through role playing. *Journal of Abnormal and Social Psycholgoy, 54:* 230-233.

Cummings, L. L. & El Salmi, A. M., 1970. The impact of role diversity, job level and organizational size on managerial satisfaction. *Administrative Science Quarterly, 15:* 1-10.

Dahl, R. A., 1957. The concept of power. *Behavioral Science, 2:* 201-218.

Dahrendorf, R., 1958. Homo Sociologicus: Ein Versuch zur Geschichte, Bedeutung und Kritik der Kategorie der sozialen Rolle. (Homo sociologicus: An essay on the history, meaning, and critique of social role.) *Kölner Zeitschrift für Sociologie und Sozial-Psychologie, 10,* 178-208.

Dahrendorf, R., 1959. *Class and conflict in industrial society.* Stanford, Calif.: Stanford University Press.

Dahrendorf, R., 1967. *Essays in the theory of society.* Stanford, Calif.: Stanford University Press.

Dai, B., 1945. Some problems of personality development among Negro children. *Proceedings of the Twelfth Institute of the Child Research Clinic of the Woods Schools, 12:* 67-105.

Darwin, C., 1872. *The expression of the emotions in man and animals.* London: J. Murray.

Davis, J., 1930. A study of 163 outstanding communist leaders. *Proceedings of the American Sociological Society, 24:* 42-55.

Davis, J. A., Gebhard, R. U., Huson, C., & Spaeth, J. L., 1961. *Great books and small groups.* New York: The Free Press.

Davis, J. H., 1969. *Group Performance.* New York: Addison-Wesley.

Davis, K., 1949. *Human Society.* New York: Macmillan.

Davis, K. E., 1965. Tactics of ingratiation and persuasion. Boulder: Department of Psychology, University of Colorado (Mimeographed).

Deaux, K., 1976. *The behavior of women and men.* Monterey, Calif.: Brooks/Cole.

DeFleur, M. S. & Westie, F. R., 1958. Verbal attitudes and overt acts: An experiment on the salience of attitudes. *American Sociological Review, 23:* 667-673.

DeFleur, M. L. & Westie, F. R., 1963. Attitude as a scientific concept. *Social Forces, 42:* 17-31.

DeFriese, G. H. & Ford, W. S., 1969. Verbal attitudes, overt acts, and the influence of social constraint in interracial behavior. *Social Problems, 16:* 493-504.

Deutsch, M. & Collins, M. E., 1951. *Interracial Housing.* Minneapolis: University of Minnesota Press.

Deutsch, M. & Gerard, H. B., 1955. A study of normative and informational social influences upon individual judgment. *Journal of Abnormal and Social Psychology, 51:* 629-636.

Deutsch, M. & Krauss, R. M., 1960. The effect of threat upon interpersonal bargaining. *Journal of Abnormal and Social Psychology, 61:* 181-189.

Deutsch, M. & Krauss, R. M., 1965. *Theories in social psychology.* New York: Basic Books.

Deutscher, I., 1966. Words and deeds: Social science and social policy. *Social Problems, 13:* 235-254.

Deutscher, I., 1967. *On adding apples and oranges: Making distinctions and connections in social science.* Paper presented at the annual meeting of the Midwest Sociological Society, Des Moines, Iowa.

Deutscher, I., 1973. *What we say/what we do: Sentiments and acts.* Glenview, Ill.: Scott, Foresman.

DeVos, G. A., 1955. A quantitative Rorschach assessment of maladjustment and rigidity in acculturating Japánese Americans. *Genetic Psychology Monographs, 52:* 51-87.

DeVos, G. A., 1961. Symbolic analysis in the cross-cultural studies of personality. In B. Kaplan (Ed.), *Studying personality cross-culturally*. Evanston, Ill.: Row, Peterson.

Dewey, J., 1922. *Human nature and conduct: An introduction to social psychology*. New York: Carlton House.

Dienstbier, R. A., 1972. A modified belief theory of prejudice emphasizing the mutual causality of racial prejudice and anticipated belief differences. *Psychological Review, 79:* 146-160.

Dinitz, S., Angrist, S., Lefton, M., & Pasamanick, B., 1962. Instrumental role expectations and post-hospital performance of female mental patients. *Social Forces, 40:* 248-254.

Dollard, J., 1939. The dozens: Dialectic of insult. *American Image, 1:* 3-25.

Donahue, W., Orbach, H. L., & Pollack, O., 1960. Retirement: The emerging social pattern. In C. Tibbitts (Ed.), *Handbook of social gerontology: Societal aspects of aging*. Chicago: University of Chicago Press.

Doob, L. W., 1940. Some factors determining change in attitude. *Journal of Abnormal and Social Psychology, 35:* 549-565.

Doob, L. W., 1947. The behavior of attitudes. *Psychological Review, 54:* 135-156.

Doyle, L. A. 1958. Convergence and divergence in the role expectations of elementary teachers. *Michigan State University College of Education Quarterly, 4:* 3-9.

Drabick, L. W., 1967. Perceivers of the teacher role: The teacher educator. *Journal of Teacher Education, 18:* 51-57.

Duijker, H. C. & Frijda, N. H., 1960. National character and national stereotypes: A trend report prepared for the International Union of Scientific Psychology. *Confluence, 1.* Amsterdam: North–Holland.

Dulany, D. E., 1961. Hypotheses and habits in verbal "operant conditioning." *Journal of Abnormal and Social Psychology, 63:* 251-263.

Dulany, D. E., 1968. Awareness, rules, and propositional control: A confrontation with S-R behavior theory. In D. Horton & T. Dixon (Eds.), *Verbal behavior and S-R behavior theory*. Englewood Cliffs, N.J.: Prentice-Hall.

Dunkin, M. J. 1966. *Some determinations of teacher warmth and directiveness*. Unpublished doctoral dissertation. Brisbane, Australia: University of Queensland.

Dunkin, M. J. & Biddle, B. J., 1974. *The study of teaching*. New York: Holt.

Durkheim, E., 1897. *Le Suicide*. Paris: F. Alcan.

Dusek, J., 1975. Do teachers bias children's learning? *Review of Educational Research, 45:* 661-684.

Duvall, E. M. & Hill, R., 1945. *When you marry*. Boston: D. C. Heath.

Eagly, A. H. & Himmelfarb, S., 1978. Attitudes and opinions. In M. R. Rosenzweig & L. W. Porter (Eds.), *Annual review of psychology* (Vol. 29). Palo Alto, Calif.: Annual Reviews.

Ehrlich, H. J., 1973. *The social psychology of prejudice: A systematic theoretical review and propositional inventory of the American social psychological study of prejudice*. New York: Wiley.

Ehrlich, H. J., Rinehart, J. W., & Howell, J. C., 1962. The study of role conflict: Explorations in methodology. *Sociometry, 25:* 85-97.

Eibl-Eibesfeldt, I., 1970. *Ethology: The biology of behavior*. New York: Holt.

Elashoff, J. & Snow, R., 1971. *Pygmalion reconsidered*. Worthington, Ohio: Charles A. Jones.

Elkins, S., 1961. Slavery and personality. In B. Kaplan (Ed.), *Studying personality cross-culturally*. Evanston, Ill.: Row, Peterson.

Elms, A. C. 1969. *Role playing, reward, and attitude change*. New York: Van Nostrand.

Emmerich, W., 1961. Family role concepts of children ages six to ten. *Child Development, 32:* 609-624.

Empey, L. T. & Rabow, J., 1961. The Provo experiment in delinquency rehabilitation. *American Sociological Review, 26:* 679–696.

English, H. B. & English, A. C., 1958. *A comprehensive dictionary of psychological and psychoanalytical terms: A guide to usage.* New York: Longmans, Green.

Epstein, C., 1970. *Woman's place.* Berkeley: University of California Press.

Erikson, E. H., 1956. The problem of ego identity. *Journal of the American Psychoanalytic Association, 4:* 56–121.

Erikson, E. H., 1963. *Childhood and society* (2nd ed.). New York: Norton.

Erikson, E. H., 1968. *Identity, youth and crises.* New York: Norton.

Erikson, K. T., 1962. Notes on the sociology of deviance. *Social Problems, 9:* 307–314.

Etzioni, A. (Ed.), 1961. *Complex organizations: A sociological reader.* New York: Holt.

Etzioni, A., 1964. *Modern organizations.* Englewood Cliffs, N.J.: Prentice-Hall.

Ewens. W. L. & Ehrlich, H. J., 1972. Reference-other support and ethnic attitudes as predictors of intergroup behavior. *Sociological Quarterly, 13:* 348–360.

Farber, B., 1971. *Kinship and class: A midwestern study.* New York: Basic Books.

Feather, N. T., 1967. A structural balance approach to the analysis of communication effects. In L. Berkowitz (Ed.), *Advances in experimental social psychology* (Vol. 3). New York: Academic Press.

Fendrich, J. M., 1967. Perceived reference group support: Racial attitudes and overt behavior. *American Sociological Review, 32:* 960–970.

Festinger, L., 1954. A theory of social comparison processes. *Human Relations, 7:* 117–140.

Festinger, L., 1957. *A theory of cognitive dissonance.* Stanford, Calif.: Stanford University Press.

Festinger, L. (Ed.), 1964. *Conflict, decision and dissonance.* Stanford, Calif.: Stanford University Press.

Festinger, L., Back, K., Schachter, S., Kelley, H. H., & Thibaut, J. W., 1950. *Theory and experiment in social communication.* Ann Arbor, Mich.: Research Center for Group Dynamics, Institute for Social Research.

Festinger, L. & Carlsmith, J. M., 1959. Cognitive consequences of forced compliance. *Journal of Abonormal and Social Psychology, 58:* 203–210.

Festinger, L. & Kelley, H. H., 1951. *Changing attitudes through social contact.* Ann Arbor, Mich.: Research Center for Group Dynamics, Institute for Social Research.

Festinger, L., Riecken, H. W., & Schachter, S., 1956. *When prophecy fails.* Minneapolis: University of Minnesota Press.

Fiedler, F. E., 1967. *A theory of leadership effectiveness.* New York: McGraw-Hill.

Finlayson, D. S. & Cohen, L., 1967. The teacher's role: A comparative study of the conceptions of college of education students and head teachers. *British Journal of Educational Psychology, 37:* 22–31.

Fishbein, M., 1967. Attitude and the prediction of behavior. In M. Fishbein (Ed.), *Readings in attitude theory and measurement.* New York: Wiley, 477–492.

Fishbein, M., 1973. The prediction of behaviors from attitudinal variables. In C. D. Mortensen & K. K. Serno (Eds.), *Advances in communication research.* New York: Harper.

Fishbein, M. & Ajzen, I., 1975. *Belief, attitude, intention and behavior: An introduction to theory and research.* Reading, Mass.: Addison-Wesley.

Fishbein, M. & Raven, B. H., 1962. The AB scales: An operational definition of belief and attitude. *Human Relations, 15:* 35–44.

Fishburn, C. E., 1962. Teacher role perception in the secondary school. *Journal of Teacher Education, 13:* 55–59.

Fishburn, C. E., 1966. Learning the role of the teacher. *The Journal of Teacher Education, 17:* 329–331.

Flanders, N. A., 1970. *Analyzing teaching behavior.* Reading, Mass.: Addison-Wesley.

Foa, U. G., 1958. Behavior, norms, and social rewards in a dyad. *Behavioral Science, 3:* 323–334.

Foa, U. G., 1965. New developments in facet design and analysis. *Psychological Review, 72:* 262–274.

Foa, U. G. & Foa, E. B., 1971. Resource exchange: Toward a structural theory of interpersonal communication. In A. W. Siegman & B. Pope (Eds.), *Studies in dyadic communication.* Elmsford, N.Y.: Pergamon, 293–327.

Foa, U. G. & Foa, E. B., 1974. *Societal structures of the mind.* Springfield, Ill.: Thomas.

Foa, U. G., Triandis, H. C., & Katz, E. W., 1966. Cross-cultural invariance in the differentiation and organization of family roles. *Journal of Personality and Social Psychology, 4:* 316–327.

Foote, N., 1951. Identification as the basis for a theory of motivation. *American Sociological Review, 16:* 14–21.

Forslund, N. A. & Gustafson, R. J., 1970. Influence of peers and parents and sex differences in drinking by high-school students. *Quarterly Journal of Studies on Alcohol, 31:* 868–875.

Foskett, J. M., 1967a. *The normative world of the elementary school principal.* Eugene: Center for the Advanced Study of Educational Administration, University of Oregon.

Foskett, J. M., 1967b. *The normative world of the elementary school teacher.* Eugene: Center for the Advanced Study of Educational Administration, University of Oregon.

Freedman, J. L., 1969. Role playing: Psychology by consensus. *Journal of Personality and Social Psychology, 13:* 107–114.

Freedman, R., Hermalin, A., & Chang, M., 1975. Do statements about desired family size predict fertility? The case of Taiwan, 1967–70. *Demography, 12:* 407–416.

Freeman, H. E. & Simmons, O. G., 1963. *The mental patient comes home.* New York: Wiley.

Freeman, L. C., Fararo, T. J., Bloomberg, W., Jr., & Sunshine, M. H., 1963. Locating leaders in local communities: A comparison of some alternative approaches. *American Sociological Review, 28:* 791–798.

Freese, L. & Cohen, B. P., 1973. Eliminating status generalization. *Sociometry, 36:* 177–193.

Freidson, E., 1966. Disability as social deviance. In M. B. Sussman (Ed.), *Sociology and rehabilitation.* Washington, D.C.: American Sociological Association.

Freidson, E., 1970. *Profession of medicine: A study of the sociology of applied knowledge.* New York: Dodd, Mead.

French, J. R. P., Jr. & Raven, B., 1959. The bases of social power. In D. Cartwright (Ed.), *Studies in social power.* Ann Arbor: Institute for Social Research, University of Michigan.

Freud, S., 1922. *Group psychology and the analysis of the ego.* London: International Psychoanalytic Library.

Freud, S., 1933. *New introductory lectures on psychoanalysis.* New York: Norton.

Friedell, M. F., 1967. Organizations as semilattices. *American Sociological Review, 32:* 46–54.

Friedenberg, E. Z., 1966. New value conflicts in American education. *School Review, 74:* 66–94.

Friedman, C. J. & Gladden, J. W., 1964. Objective measurement of social role concepts via the semantic differential. *Psychological Reports, 14:* 239–274.

Fromm, E., 1941. *Escape from freedom.* New York: Rinehart.

Furst, E. J., 1965. A factor analysis of preferences in teacher role-behavior. *Journal of Experimental Education, 33:* 379–382.

Gabrenya, W. K., Jr. & Biddle, B. J., 1978. *Personal norms in social decision making: Construct validity and delimiting conditions.* (Technical Report No. 137). Columbia: Center for Research in Social Behavior, University of Missouri.

Gage, N. L. & Cronbach, L. J., 1955. Conceptual and methodological problems in interpersonal perception. *Psychological Review, 62:* 411–422.

Galbraith, J. K., 1967. *The new industrial state.* Boston: Houghton Mifflin.

Gamson, W. A., 1968. *Power and discontent.* Homewood, Ill.: Dorsey.

Gates, A., 1961. Sex differences in reading ability. *Elementary School Journal, 61:* 431–434.

Geen, R. G., 1977. Some effects of observing violence upon the behavior of the observer. In B. Maher (Ed.), *Progress in experimental personality research* (Vol. 8). New York: Academic Press.

Geen, R. G. & Quanty, M. B., 1977. The catharsis of aggression: An evaluation of a hypothesis. In L. Berkowitz (Ed.), *Advances in experimental social psychology* (Vol. 10). New York: Academic Press.

Getzels, J. W., 1958. Administration as a social process. In A. W. Halpin (Ed.), *Administrative theory in education.* Chicago: Midwest Administrative Center, University of Chicago, 150–165.

Getzels, J. W. & Guba, E. G., 1954. Role, role conflict, and effectiveness: An empirical study. *American Sociological Review 19:* 164–175.

Getzels, J. W. & Guba, E. G., 1955a. Role conflict and personality. *Journal of Personality, 24:* 74–85.

Getzels, J. W. & Guba, E. G., 1955b. The structure of roles and role conflict in the teaching situation. *Journal of Educational Sociology, 29:* 30–40.

Getzels, J. W. & Guba, E. G., 1957. Social behavior and the administrative process. *School Review, 65:* 423–441.

Gibbs, J. P., 1965. Norms: The problem of definition and classification. *American Journal of Sociology, 70:* 586–594.

Ginott, H. G., 1965. *Between parent and child: New solutions to old problems.* New York: Macmillan.

Glasser, P. H., 1963. Changes in family equilibrium during psychotherapy. *Family Process, 2:* 245–264.

Glasser, P. H. & Glasser, L. N., 1962. Role reversal and conflict between aged parents and their children. *Marriage and Family Living, 24:* 46–51.

Goethals, G. R. & Nelson, R. E., 1973. Similarity in the influence process: The belief–value distinction. *Journal of Personality and Social Psychology, 25:* 117–122.

Goffman, E., 1952. On cooling the mark out: Some aspects of adaptation to failure. *Psychiatry: Journal for the Study of Interpersonal Relations, 15:* 451–463.

Goffman, E., 1956. Embarrassment and social organization. *American Journal of Sociology, 62:* 264–271.

Goffman, E., 1959. *The presentation of self in everyday life.* New York: Doubleday.

Goffman, E., 1961a. *Asylums: Essays on the social situation of mental patients and other inmates.* New York: Doubleday.

Goffman, E., 1961b. *Encounters: Two studies in the sociology of education.* Indianapolis: Bobbs-Merrill.

Goffman, E., 1967. *Interaction ritual: Essays on face-to-face behavior.* Chicago: Aldine.

Goldhamer, H. & Shils, E. A., 1939. Types of power and status. *American Journal of Sociology, 45:* 171–182.

Goldman, M. & Fras, L. A., 1965. The effects of leader selection on group performance. *Sociometry, 28:* 82–88.

Goldman, R., Jaffa, M., & Schachter, S., 1968. Yom Kippur, Air France, dormitory food, and the eating behavior of obese and normal persons. *Journal of Personality and Social Psychology, 10:* 117–123.

Golembiewski, R. T., 1962. *The small group: An analysis of research concepts and operations.* Chicago: University of Chicago Press.

Golembiewski, R. T., 1965. Small groups and large organizations. In J. G. March (Ed.), *Handbook of organizations.* Chicago: Rand McNally.

Golembiewski, R. T., 1967. *Organizing men and power: Patterns of behavior and line-staff models.* Chicago: Rand McNally.

Golightly, C. L. & Scheffler, I., 1948. Playing the dozens. *Journal of Abnormal and Social Psychology, 43:* 104-105.

Good, T. L. & Brophy, J. E., 1977. *Educational psychology: A realistic approach.* New York: Holt.

Goode, W. J., 1957. Community within a community: The professions. *American Sociological Review, 22:* 194-200.

Goode, W. J., 1960. A theory of role strain. *American Sociological Review, 25:* 483-496.

Goodman, M. E., 1952. *Race awareness in young children.* Reading, Mass.: Addison-Wesley.

Goranson, R. E., 1970. Media violence and aggressive behavior: A review of experimental research. In L. Berkowitz (Ed.), *Advances in experimental social psychology* (Vol 5). New York: Academic Press, 2-31.

Gordon, G., 1966. *Role theory and illness: A sociological perspective.* New Haven, Conn.: College and University Press.

Gouldner, A. W., 1960. The norm of reciprocity: A preliminary statement. *American Sociological Review, 25:* 161-178.

Gove, W. R., 1972. The relationship between sex roles, marital status, and mental illness. *Social Forces, 51:* 34-44.

Gove, W. R., 1975. *The labeling of deviance: Evaluating a perspective.* New York: Wiley.

Gratch, H. (Ed.), 1973. *Twenty-five years of social research in Israel: A review of the Israel Institute of Applied Research 1947-1971.* Jerusalem: Jerusalem Academic Press.

Greenhoe, F., 1940. Community contacts of public school teachers. *Elementary School Journal, 40:* 497-506.

Greenwald, A. G., Brock, T. C., & Ostrom, T. M. (Eds.), 1968. *Psychological foundations of attitudes.* New York: Academic Press.

Grier, W. H. & Cobbs, P. M., 1968. *Black rage.* New York: Basic Books.

Griffin, J. T., 1972. *Influence strategies: Theory and research. A study of teacher behavior.* Unpublished doctoral dissertation. Columbia: University of Missouri.

Gross, E. & Stone, G. P., 1964. Embarrassment and the analysis of role requirements. *The American Journal of Sociology, 70:* 1-15.

Gross, N., Mason, W. S., & McEachern, A. W., 1958. *Explorations in role analysis: Studies of the school superintendency role.* New York: Wiley.

Guetzkow, H., Alger, C. F., Brody, R. A., Noel, R. C., & Snyder, R. C., 1963. *Simulation in international relations.* Englewood Cliffs, N.J.: Prentice-Hall.

Gullahorn, J. T., 1956. Measuring role conflict. *American Journal of Sociology, 61:* 299-303.

Gullahorn, J. T. & Gullahorn, J. E., 1963. Role conflict and its resolution. *Sociological Quarterly, 4:* 32-48.

Gump, P. V. & Sutton-Smith, B., 1955. The "It" role in children's games. *The Group, 17:* 3-8.

Gusfield, J. R., 1976. *Community: A critical response.* New York: Harper.

Guttman, L., 1954. A new approach to factor analysis: The radex. In P. F. Lazarsfeld (Ed.), *Mathematical thinking in the social sciences.* Glencoe, Ill.: The Free Press, 258-348.

Haas, J. E. & Drabek, T. E., 1973. *Complex organizations: A sociological perspective.* New York: Macmillan.

Haas, J. E., Hall, R. H., & Johnson, N. J., 1963. The size of the supportive component in organizations: A multi-organizational analysis. *Social Forces, 42:* 9-17.

Habenstein, R. W. (Ed.), 1970. *Pathways to data: Field methods for studying ongoing social organizations.* Chicago: Aldine.

Habenstein, R. W. & Christ, E. A., 1955. *Professionalizer, traditionalizer, and utilizer.* Columbia: University of Missouri Press.

Haer, J. L., 1953. The public views the teacher. *Journal of Teacher Education, 4:* 202–204.

Hage, J. & Marwell, G., 1968. Toward the development of an empirically based theory of role relationships. *Sociometry, 31:* 200–212.

Hall, E. T., 1959. *The silent language.* New York: Doubleday.

Hall, R. H., Haas, J. E., & Johnson, N. J., 1967. Organizational size, complexity, and formalization. *American Sociological Review, 32:* 903–912.

Hamilton, D., 1971. A comparative study of five methods of assessing self-esteem, dominance, and dogmatism. *Educational and Psychological Measurement, 31:* 441–452.

Hammond, S., 1952. Stratification in an Australian city. In G. E. Swanson, T. M. Newcomb, & E. L. Hartley (Eds.), *Readings in social psychology* (Rev. ed.). New York: Holt, 288–299.

Harary, F., Norman, R. Z., & Cartwright, D., 1965. *Structural models: An introduction to the theory of directed graphs.* New York: Wiley.

Hare, A. P., 1962. *Handbook of small group research.* New York: The Free Press.

Hare, A. P., 1976. *Handbook of small group research* (2nd ed.). New York: The Free Press.

Hare, A. P., & Bales, R. F., 1963. Seating position and small group interaction. *Sociometry, 26:* 480–486.

Harrison, E., 1964. The working women: Barriers in employment. *Public Administration Review. 24,* 78–85.

Harsanyi, J. C., 1962. Measurement of social power, opportunity costs, and the theory of two-person bargaining games. *Behavioral Science, 7:* 67–80.

Hartley, R. E., 1964. A developmental view of female sex-role definition and identification. *Merrill-Palmer Quarterly, 10:* 3–16.

Hastorf, A. H., Schneider, D. J., & Polefka, J., 1970. *Person perception.* Reading, Mass.: Addison-Wesley.

Havighurst, R. J., 1952. *Developmental tasks and education.* New York: McKay.

Havighurst, R. J., 1953. *Human development and education.* New York: Longmans, Green.

Heberlein, T. A. & Black, J. S., 1976. Attitudinal specificity and the prediction of behavior in a field setting. *Journal of Personality and Social Psychology, 33:* 474–479.

Heider, F., 1944. Social perception and phenomenal causality. *Psychological Review, 51:* 358–374.

Heider, F., 1946. Attitudes and cognitive organization. *Journal of Psychology, 21:* 107–112.

Heider, F., 1958. *The psychology of interpersonal relations.* New York: Wiley.

Heider, F., 1960. The gestalt theory of motivation. In M. R. Jones (Ed.), *Nebraska symposium on motivation* (Vol. 8). Lincoln: University of Nebraska Press.

Heise, D. R., 1973. *Attitudinal construction of expectations: Working papers.* Chapel Hill, N.C.: unpublished manuscript.

Heiss, J. (Ed.), 1968. *Family roles and interaction: An anthology.* Chicago: Rand McNally.

Heiss, J. S., 1962. Degree of intimacy and male–female interaction. *Sociometry, 25:* 197–208.

Helmreich, R., Aronson, E., & LeFan, J., 1970. To err is humanizing—sometimes: Effects of self-esteem, competence, and a pratfall on interpersonal attraction. *Journal of Personality and Social Psychology, 16:* 259–265.

Helmreich, R. & Collins, B. E., 1968. Studies in forced compliance: Commitment and magnitude of inducement to comply as determinants of opinion change. *Journal of Personality and Social Psychology, 10:* 75–81.

Helson, H., 1964. *Adaptation-level theory: An experimental and systematic approach to behavior.* New York: Harper.

Hendrick, C., 1977. Role-taking, role-playing, and the laboratory experiment. *Personality and Social Psychology Bulletin, 3:* 467–478.

Henry, J., 1971. *Pathways to madness.* New York: Random House.

Herriott, R. E., 1963. Some social determinants of educational aspiration. *Harvard Educational Review, 33:* 157–177.

Heyerdahl, T., 1950. *Kon-Tiki: Across the Pacific by raft*. Chicago: Rand McNally.

Himmelfarb, S. & Eagly, A. H. (Eds.), 1974. *Readings in attitude change*. New York: Wiley.

Hodge, R. W., Siegel, P. M., & Rossi, P. H., 1964. Occupational prestige in the United States, 1925-1963. *American Journal of Sociology, 70:* 286-302.

Hoffman, M. L. & Hoffman, L. W. (Eds.), 1964. *Review of child development research*. New York: Russell Sage Foundation.

Hollander, E. P., 1958. Conformity, status, and idiosyncrasy credit. *Psychological Review, 65:* 117-127.

Hollingshead, A. B., 1949. *Elmtown's youth*. New York: Wiley.

Holmes, R., 1966. *Power and consent: A social-psychological analysis of organizations*. (Technical Report No. 14). Columbia: Center for Research in Social Behavior, University of Missouri.

Homans, G. C., 1950. *The human group*. New York: Harcourt, Brace.

Homans, G. C., 1961. *Social behavior: Its elementary forms*. New York: Harcourt, Brace.

Homans, G. C., 1974. *Social behavior: Its elementary forms* (Rev. ed.). New York: Harcourt, Brace.

Hovland, C. I., 1954. Effects of the mass media of communication. In G. Lindzey (Ed.), *Handbook of social psychology* (Vol. 2). Reading, Mass.: Addison-Wesley.

Hovland, C. I. & Rosenberg, M. J. (Eds.), 1960. *Attitude organization and change*. New Haven, Conn.: Yale University Press.

Howard, N., 1971. *Paradoxes of rationality: Theory of metagames and political behavior*. Cambridge, Mass.: M.I.T. Press.

Howells, J. M. & Brosnan, P., 1972. The ability to predict workers' preferences: A research exercise. *Human Relations, 25:* 265-281.

Hughes, E. C., 1937. Institutional office and the person. *American Journal of Sociology, 43:* 404-413.

Hughes, E. C., 1945. Dilemmas and contradictions of status. *American Journal of Sociology, 50:* 353-359.

Hughes, E. C., 1958. *Men and their work*. New York: The Free Press.

Hunt, J. G. & Hunt, L. L., 1977. Dilemmas and contradictions of status: The case of the dual-career family. *Social Problems, 24:* 405-416.

Hunter, F., 1953. *Community power structure: A study of decision makers*. Chapel Hill: University of North Carolina Press.

Huntley, C. W., 1940. Judgments of self based upon records of expressive behavior. *Journal of Abnormal Social psychology, 35:* 398-427.

Hutchins, E. B. & Fiedler, F. E., 1960. Task-oriented and quasi-therapeutic role functions of the leader in small military groups. *Sociometry, 23:* 393-406.

Hyman, H. H., 1942. The psychology of status. *Archives of Psychology, 38:* 1-94.

Hyman, H. H. & Singer, E., 1968. *Readings in reference group theory and research*. New York: Wiley.

Inkeles, A. & Rossi, P. H., 1956. National comparisons of occupational prestige. *American Journal of Sociology, 61:* 329-339.

Insko, C. A., 1967. *Theories of attitude change*. New York: Appleton-Century-Crofts.

Jackson, J. M., 1960. Structural characteristics of norms. In N. B. Henry (Ed.), *The dynamics of instructional groups: Sociopsychological aspects of teaching and learning*. Yearbook of the National Society for the Study of Education, *59*, Part II: 136-163.

Jackson, J. M., 1975. Normative power and conflict potential. *Sociological Methods and Research, 4:* 237-263.

Jackson, P. W., 1968. *Life in classrooms*. New York: Holt.

Jackson, P. W. & Moscovici, F., 1963. Teachers-to-be: A study of embryonic identification with a professional role. *School Review, 71:* 41-65.

Jaco, E. G., 1959. Mental health of the Spanish Americans in Texas. In M. K. Opler (Ed.), *Culture and mental health.* New York: Macmillan.

Jacobson, A. H., 1952. Conflict of attitudes toward the roles of the husband and wife in marriage. *American Sociological Review, 17:* 146-150.

Jacobson, E., Charters, W. W., Jr., & Lieberman, S., 1951. The use of the role concept in the study of complex organizations. *Journal of Social Issues, 7:* 18-27.

Jahoda, M., 1964. Stereotype. In J. Gould & W. L. Kolb (Eds.), *A dictionary of the social sciences.* New York: The Free Press.

James, W., 1890. *The principles of psychology.* New York: Holt.

Janis, I. L., 1968. Attitude change via role playing. In R. P. Abelson, E. Aronson, W. J. McGuire, T. M. Newcomb, M. J. Rosenberg, & P. H. Tannenbaum (Eds.), *Theories of cognitive consistency: A sourcebook.* Chicago: Rand McNally.

Janis, I. L. & King, B. T., 1954. The influence of role playing on opinion change. *Journal of Abnormal and Social Psychology, 49:* 211-218.

Jensen, G. F., 1972. Parents, peers and delinquent action: A test of the differential association perspective. *American Journal of Sociology, 78:* 562-575.

Jessor, R., Graves, T., Hanson, C., & Jessor, S., 1968. *Society, personality and deviant behavior.* New York: Holt.

Jones, E. E., 1964. *Ingratiation.* New York: Appleton-Century-Crofts.

Jones, E. E., Davis, K. E., & Gergen, K. J., 1961. Role playing variations and their informational value for person perception. *Journal of Abnormal and Social Psychology, 63:* 302-310.

Jones, E. E. & Gerard, H. B., 1967. *Foundations of social psychology.* New York: Wiley.

Jones, K. V., 1967. *Conformity as a response to ambiguity in a non-sanctioned situation.* Unpublished master's thesis. Columbia: University of Missouri.

Juster, F. T., 1964. *Anticipations and purchases: An analysis of consumer behavior.* Princeton, N.J.: Princeton University Press.

Kagan, J., 1969. Personality and intellectual development in the school-age child. In I. Janis (Ed.), *Personality: Dynamics, development, and assessment.* New York: Harcourt, Brace.

Kahn, L. A., 1951. The organization of attitudes toward the Negro as a function of education. *Psychological Monographs, 65:* 1-39.

Kahn, R. L., Wolfe, D. M., Quinn, R. P., Snoek, J., & Rosenthal, R. A., 1964. *Organizational stress: Studies in role conflict and ambiguity.* New York: Wiley.

Kandel, D., 1974. Interpersonal influences on adolescent drug use. In E. Josephson & E. E. Carroll (Eds.), *Drug use: Epidemiological and sociological approaches.* New York: Halsted Press.

Kandel, D. B. & Lesser, G. S., 1972. *Youth in two worlds.* San Francisco: Jossey-Bass.

Kanfer, F. H. & Phillips, J. S., 1970. *Learning foundations of behavior therapy.* New York: Wiley.

Kang, J., 1971. *Recency in forming an impression: The effects of a linear combination of symbolic and observational information.* Unpublished doctoral dissertation. Columbia: University of Missouri.

Karcher, E. K., Jr., 1952. *The first sergeant in the United States Air Force: A perceptual component approach to the analysis of leadership and organizational positions* (Technical Report No. 7). Chapel Hill: Institute for Research in Social Science, University of North Carolina.

Katz, D. & Kahn, R. L., 1966. *The social psychology of organizations.* New York: Wiley.

Katz, E. & Lazarsfeld, P. F., 1955. *Personal influence.* Glencoe, Ill.: The Free Press.

Katz, F. E., 1968. *Autonomy and organization: The limits of social control.* New York: Random House.

Katz, L. G., Bowermaster, J., Jacobson, E., & Kessell, L., 1977. *Sex role socialization in early childhood*. ERIC Clearinghouse on Early Childhood Education. Urbana: University of Illinois.

Katz, P. & Zigler, E., 1967. Self-image disparity: A developmental approach. *Journal of Personality and Social Psychology, 5:* 186–195.

Kelley, H. H., 1965. Experimental studies of threats in interpersonal negotiations. *Journal of Conflict Resolution, 9:* 79–105.

Kelley, S. & Mirer, T. W., 1974. The simple act of voting. *American Political Science Review, 68:* 572–591.

Kelman, H., 1958. Compliance, identification, and internalization: Three processes of attitude change. *Journal of Conflict Resolution, 2:* 51–60.

Kelman, H., 1961. Processes of opinion change. *Public Opinion Quarterly, 25:* 57–78.

Kelman, H. C., 1967. The human use of human subjects: The problem of deception in social-psychological experiments. *Psychological Bulletin, 67:* 1–11.

Kenton, E. F., no date. Notes for recordings of Mendelssohn chamber music. VOX SBVX 581.

Kibbee, J. M., Craft, G., & Nanus, B., 1961. *Management games: A new technique for executive development.* New York: Reinhold.

Kiesler, C. A., 1971. *The psychology of commitment: Experiments linking behavior to belief.* New York: Academic Press.

Kiesler, C. A., Collins, B. E., & Miller, N., 1969. *Attitude change.* New York: Wiley.

Kiesler, C. A., Mathog, R., Pool, P., & Howenstine, R., 1971. Commitment and the boomerang effect: A field study. In C. A. Kiesler (Ed.), *The psychology of commitment: Experiments linking behavior to belief.* New York: Academic Press.

Killian, L. M., 1952. The significance of multiple-group membership in disaster. *American Journal of Sociology, 57:* 309–314.

Kilpatrick, F. P. & Cantril, H., 1960. Self-anchoring scaling: A measure of individuals' unique reality worlds. *Journal of Individual Psychology, 16:* 158–173.

Kinsey, A. C., Pomeroy, W. B., & Martin, C. E., 1948. *Sexual behavior in the human male.* Philadelphia: W. B. Saunders.

Kinton, E. R., 1975. *Family structures and roles in crises: An annotated bibliography.* Aurora, Ill.: Social Science and Sociological Resources.

Kirkland, K. D. & Thelen, M. H., 1977. Uses of modeling in child treatment. In B. B. Lahey & A. E. Kazdin (Eds.), *Advances in child clinical psychology* (Vol. 1). New York: Plenum.

Klapp, O. E., 1962. *Heroes, villains and fools: The changing American character.* Englewood Cliffs, N.J.: Prentice-Hall.

Klapp, O. E., 1969. *Collective search for identity.* New York: Holt.

Knudsen, D., 1969. The declining status of women: Popular myths and the failure of functionalist thought. *Social Forces, 48:* 183–193.

Kohlberg, L., 1968. The child as a moral philosopher. *Psychology Today, 2:* 25–30.

Koopman, M. O., 1946. What one midwestern community thinks of its teachers. *Educational Research Bulletin, 25:* 34–41.

Kothandapani, V., 1971. Validation of feeling, belief, and intention to act as three components of attitude and their contribution to prediction of contraceptive behavior. *Journal of Personality and Social Psychology, 19:* 321–333.

Kounin, J. S., 1970. *Discipline and group management in classrooms.* New York: Holt.

Krasner, L., 1971. Behavior therapy. *Annual Review of Psychology, 22:* 483–532.

Krasner, L., Knowles, J. P., & Ullman, L. P., 1965. Effects of verbal conditioning of attitudes on subsequent motor performance. *Journal of Personality and Social Psychology, 1:* 407–412.

Krebs, D. L., 1970. Altruism—An examination of the concept and a review of the literature. *Psychological Bulletin, 73:* 258–302.

Krupat, E., 1977. A re-assessment of role playing as a technique in social psychology. *Personality and Social Psychology Bulletin, 3:* 498–504.

Kuhn, A., 1974. *The logic of social systems.* San Francisco: Jossey-Bass.

Kuhn, M. H., 1964. Major trends in symbolic interaction theory in the past twenty-five years. *The Sociological Quarterly, 5:* 61–84.

Kuhn, M. H. & McPartland, T. S., 1954. An empirical investigation of self-attitudes. *American Sociological Review, 19:* 68–76.

LaForge, R. & Suczek, R., 1955. The interpersonal dimension of personality: Ill. An interpersonal check list. *Journal of Personality, 24:* 94–112.

Laing, R. D., 1967. *The politics of experience.* New York: Ballantine.

Laing, R. D. & Esterson, A., 1964. *Sanity, madness, and the family.* London: Tavistock.

Laing, R. D., Phillipson, H., & Lee, A. R., 1966. *Interpersonal perception: A theory and a method of research.* London: Tavistock.

Landecker, W. S., 1963. Class crystallization and class consciousness. *American Sociological Review, 28:* 219–229.

Landy, D., 1960a. Rehabilitation as a sociocultural process. *Journal of Social Issues. 16:* 3–17.

Landy, D., 1960b. Rutland Corner House: Case study of a halfway house. *Journal of Social Issues, 16:* 27–32.

Landy, D. & Wechsler, H., 1960. Common assumptions, dimensions, and problems of pathway organizations. *Journal of Social Issues, 16:* 70–78.

LaPiere, R. T., 1934. Attitudes versus actions. *Social Forces, 13:* 230–237.

Lasswell, H. D., 1936. *Politics: Who gets what, when, how.* New York: McGraw-Hill.

Laulicht, J., 1955. Role conflict, the pattern variable theory, and scalogram analysis. *Social Forces, 33:* 250–254.

Lee, G. R., 1977. *Family structure and interaction: A comparative analysis.* New York: Lippincott.

Leifer, R., 1969. *In the name of mental health.* New York: Science.

Leighton, D. C., Harding, J. S., Macklin, D. B., Macmillan, A. M., & Leighton, A. H., 1963. *The character of danger: Psychiatric symptoms in selected communities.* New York: Basic Books.

Leik, R. K., 1966. A measure of ordinal consensus. *The pacific Sociological Review, 9:* 85–90.

Lemert, E. M., 1951. *Social pathology.* New York: McGraw-Hill.

Lemert, E. M., 1967. *Human deviance, social problems, and social control.* Englewood Cliffs, N.J.: Prentice-Hall.

Lennard, H. L. & Bernstein, A., 1960. *The anatomy of psychotherapy.* New York: Columbia University Press.

Lenski, G., 1954. Status crystallization: A non-vertical dimension of social status. *American Sociological Review, 19:* 405–413.

Lerner, D., 1961. An American researcher in Paris: Interviewing Frenchmen. In B. Kaplan (Ed.), *Studying personality cross culturally.* New York: Harper, 427–442.

Leventhal, G. S., 1976. The distribution of rewards and resources in groups and organizations. In L. Berkowitz & E. Walster (Eds.), *Advances in experimental social psychology* (Vol. 9). New York: Academic Press.

Leventhal, H., Jones, S., & Tembly, G., 1966. Sex differences in attitude and behavior change under conditions of fear and specific instruction. *Journal of Experimental Social Psychology, 2:* 387–399.

Leventhal, H., Singer, R. P., & Jones, S., 1965. The effects of fear and specificity of recommendation. *Journal of Personality and Social Psychology, 2:* 20–29.

Leventhal, H., Watts, J. C., & Pagano, F., 1967. *Effects of fear and specificity of recommendations on smoking behavior.* New Haven: Department of Psychology, Yale University (Mimeographed).

Levinger, G. & Snoek, J. D., 1972. *Attraction in relationships: A new look at interpersonal attraction.* Morristown, N.J.: General Learning Press.

Lévi-Strauss, C., 1949, *Les structures élémentaires de la parenté.* Paris: Mouton/De Gruyte. (*The elementary structures of kinship.* Boston: Beacon Press, 1969.)

Levy, L. H., 1956. The meaning and generality of perceived and actual-ideal discrepancies. *Journal of Consulting Psychology, 20/* 396–398.

Levy, M. J., 1952. *The structure of society.* Princeton, N.J.: Princeton University Press.

Lewin, K., 1936. Some social-psychological differences between the United States and Germany. *Character and Personality, 4:* 265–293.

Lewis, O., 1959. *Five families: Mexican case studies in the culture of poverty.* New York: Basic Books.

Lieberman, M. A., Yalom, I. D., & Miles, M. B., 1973. *Encounter groups: First facts.* New York: Basic Books.

Lifton, R. J., 1963. *Thought reform and the psychology of totalism.* New York: Norton.

Lindgren, H. C., 1962. *Educational psychology in the classroom* (2nd ed.). New York: Wiley.

Lindzey, G. & Byrne, D., 1968. Measurement of social choice and interpersonal attractiveness. In G. Lindzey & E. Aronson (Eds.), *The handbook of social psychology* (2nd ed., Vol. 2). Reading, Mass.: Addison-Wesley.

Linton, R., 1936. *The study of man.* New York: Appleton-Century.

Linton, R., 1945. *The cultural background of personality.* New York: Appleton-Century.

Lippitt, Rosemary & Hubbell, A., 1956. Role playing for personnel and guidance workers: Review of literature with suggestions for application. *Group Psychotherapy, 9:* 89–114.

Lippitt, R., Polansky, N., Redl, F., & Rosen, S., 1952. The dynamics of power: A field study of social influence in groups of children. In G. Swanson, T. Newcomb, & E. Hartley (Eds.), *Readings in social psychology* (Rev. ed.). New York: Holt.

Lippman, W., 1922. *Public opinion.* New York: Harcourt, Brace.

Liska, A. E., 1974. Emergent issues in the attitude–behavior consistency controversy. *American Sociological Review, 39:* 261–272.

Liska, A. E., 1975. *The consistency controversy: Readings on the impact of attitude on behavior.* New York: Wiley.

Lockwood, D., 1964. Sanction. In J. Gould & W. L. Kolb (Eds.), *A dictionary of the social sciences.* New York: The Free Press.

Lofland, J. & Stark, R., 1965. Becoming a world-saver: A theory of conversion to a deviant perspective. *American Sociological Review, 30:* 862–874.

Lorenz, K., 1963. *Das Sogenannte Böse: Zur Naturgeschichte der Aggression.* Vienna: G. Borotha-Schoeler Verlag. (Translated as *On aggression.* New York: Harcourt, Brace, 1966.)

Lynd, R. S. & Lynd, H. M., 1929. *Middletown: A study in contemporary American culture.* New York: Harcourt, Brace.

Lynd, R. S. & Lynd, H. M., 1937. *Middletown in transition: A study in cultural conflicts.* New York: Harcourt, Brace.

Lynn, D. B., 1962. Sex-role and parental identification. *Child Development, 33:* 555–564.

Maas, H. S., 1954. The role of members in clubs of lower-class and middle-class adolescents. *Child Development, 25:* 241–251.

Macauley, J. & Berkowitz, L. (Eds.), 1970. *Altruism and helping behavior.* New York: Academic Press.

Maccoby, E. E., 1966. *The development of sex differences.* Stanford, Calif.: Stanford University Press.

Maccoby, E. E. & Jacklin, C. N., 1974. *The psychology of sex differences.* Stanford, Calif.: Stanford University Press.

Mack, R. W., 1956. Occupational determinateness: A problem and hypotheses in role theory. *Social Forces, 35:* 20–25.

Mann, J. H., 1956. Experimental evaluations of role playing. *Psychological Bulletin, 53:* 227–234.

Mann, J. H., 1959. The relationship between cognitive, affective, and behavioral aspects of racial prejudice. *Journal of Social Psychology, 49:* 223–228.

Mann, J. H. & Mann, C. H., 1959. The effect of role-playing experience on role-playing ability. *Sociometry, 22:* 64–74.

Mann, R. D., 1959. A review of the relationship between personality and performance in small groups. *Psychological Bulletin, 56:* 241–270.

March, J. G. (Ed.), 1965. *Handbook of organizations.* Chicago: Rand McNally.

March, J. G. & Simon, H. A., 1958. *Organizations.* New York: Wiley.

Marks, S. R., 1977. Multiple roles and role strain: Some notes on human energy, time, and commitment. *American Sociological Review, 42:* 921–936.

Marsh, R. M., 1967. *Comparative sociology: A codification of cross-society analysis.* New York: Harcourt, Brace.

Marwell, G., 1968. Role allocation and differentiation through time in medium sized groups. *The Journal of Social Psychology, 74:* 225–231.

Marwell, G. & Hage, J., 1970. The organization of role-relationships: A systematic description. *American Sociological Review, 35:* 884–900.

Marwell, G. & Schmitt, D. R., 1967a. Compliance-gaining behavior: A synthesis and model. *Sociological Quarterly, 8:* 317–328.

Marwell, G. & Schmitt, D. R., 1967b. Dimensions of compliance-gaining behavior: An empirical analysis. *Sociometry, 30:* 350–364.

Marx, K., 1867. *Das Kapital: Kritik der Politischen Ökonomie* (Vol. I). Hamburg: Meissner. (*Capital.* New York: Modern Library, 1936.)

McClelland, D. G., 1951. *Personality.* New York: William Sloane.

McCord, J., 1978. A thirty-year follow-up of treatment effects. *American Psychologist, 33:* 284–289.

McCord, J. & McCord, W., 1957. The effects of parental role model on criminality. *Journal of Social Issues, 13:* 66–75.

McDougall, W., 1908. *An introduction to social psychology.* London: Methuen.

McGrath, J. E. & Altman, I., 1966. *Small group research: A synthesis and critique of the field.* New York: Holt.

McGuire, W. J., 1969. The nature of attitudes and attitude change. In G. Lindzey & E. Aronson (Eds.), *The handbook of social psychology* (2nd ed., Vol. 3). Reading, Mass.: Addison-Wesley.

Mead, G. H., 1934. *Mind, self and society.* Chicago: University of Chicago Press.

Mead, M., 1935. *Sex and temperament.* New York: Morrow.

Mead, M., 1956. *New lives for old: Cultural transformation—Manus, 1928-1953.* New York: Morrow.

Meadow, A. & Stoker, D., 1965. Symptomatic behavior of hospitalized patients. *Archives of General Psychiatry, 12:* 267–277.

Mechanic, D., 1961. Stress, illness behavior and the sick role. *American Sociological Review, 26:* 51–58.

Mechanic, D., 1962. The concept of illness behavior. *Journal of Chronic Dieseases, 15:* 189–194.

Meeker, B. F., 1971. Decisions and exchange. *American Sociological Review, 36:* 485–495.

Meltzer, B. N., 1967. Mead's social psychology. In J. G. Manis & B. N. Meltzer (Eds.), *Symbolic interaction: A reader in social psychology.* Boston: Allyn & Bacon.

Meltzer, B. N., Petras, J. W., & Reynolds, L. T., 1975. *Symbolic interactionism: Genesis, varieties and criticism.* London: Routledge.

Meltzoff, A. N. & Moore, M. K., 1977. Imitation of facial and manual gestures by human neonates. *Science, 198:* 75–78.

Merei, F., 1949. Group leadership and institutionalization. *Human Relations, 2:* 23–39.

Merton, R. K., 1949. *Social theory and social structure: Toward the codification of theory and research.* Glencoe, Ill: The Free Press.

Merton, R. K., 1957a. The role-set: Problems in sociological theory. *British Journal of Sociology, 8:* 106–120.

Merton, R. K., 1957b. *Social theory and social structure* (Rev. ed.). Glencoe, Ill.: The Free Press.

Merton, R. K., & Kitt, A. S., 1950. Contributions to the theory of reference group behavior. In R. K. Merton and P. F. Lazarsfeld (Eds.), *Continuities in social research.* Glencoe, Ill.: The Free Press.

Merton, R. K., Reader, G. G., & Kendall, P. L., (Eds.), 1957. *The student physician: Introductory studies in the sociology of medical education.* Cambridge, Mass.: Harvard University Press.

Messinger, S. L., Sampson, H., & Towne, R. D., 1962. Life as theater: Some notes on the dramaturgic approach to social reality. *Sociometry, 25:* 98–110.

Michels, R., 1911. *Zur Soziologie des Parteiwesens in der Modernen Demokratie: Untersuchungen über die Oligarchischen Tendenzen des Gruppenlebens.* Leipzig: W. Kinkhardt. (Translated as *Political parties: A sociological study of the oligarchical tendencies in modern democracy.* New York: The Free Press, 1949.)

Milgram, N. A., 1960. Cognitive and empathetic factors in role-taking by schizophrenic and brain damaged patients. *Journal of Abnormal Social Psychology, 60:* 219–224.

Milgram, S., 1965. Some conditions of obedience and disobedience to authority. *Human Relations, 18:* 57–76.

Milgram, S., 1974. *Obedience to authority: An experimental view.* New York: Harper.

Miller, A. G., 1972. Role playing: An alternative to deception? A review of the evidence. *American Psychologist, 27:* 623–636.

Miller, D. C. & Shull, F. A., Jr., 1962. The prediction of administrative role conflict resolutions. *Administrative Science Quarterly, 7:* 143–160.

Miller, D. R. & Swanson, G. E., 1960. *Inner conflict and defense.* New York: Holt.

Mills, C. W., 1940. Situated actions and vocabularies of motive. *American Sociological Review, 5:* 904–913.

Minard, R. D., 1952. Race relationships in the Pocahontas coal field. *Journal of Social Issues, 8,* No. 1: 29–44.

Mishler, E. G., 1951. *Personality characteristics and the resolution of role conflicts.* Unpublished doctoral dissertation. Ann Arbor: University of Michigan.

Mishler, E. G., 1953. Personality characteristics and the resolution of role conflicts. *Public Opinion Quarterly, 17:* 115–135.

Miskimins, R. W. & Braucht, G., 1971. *Description of the self.* Fort Collins, Col.: Rocky Mountain Behavioral Science Institute.

Mitchell, E. V., Kaul, T. J., & Pepinsky, H. B., 1977. The limited role of psychology in the role-playing controversy. *Personality and Social Psychology Bulletin, 3:* 514–518.

Mitchell, J., 1966. Cons, square-johns, and rehabilitation. In B. J. Biddle & E. J. Thomas (Eds.), *Role theory: Concepts and research.* New York: Wiley.

Mitchell, W. C., 1958. Occupational role strains: The American elective public official. *Administrative Science Quarterly, 3:* 210–228.

Mixon, D., 1972. Instead of deception. *Journal for the Theory of Social Behavior, 2:* 145–177.

Mixon, D., 1977. Temporary false belief. *Personality and Social Psychology Bulletin, 3:* 479–488.

Mohavedi, S., 1977. Role playing: An alternative to what? *Personality and Social Psychology Bulletin, 3:* 489–497.

Money, J. & Ehrhardt, A. A., 1972. *Man & woman, boy & girl: The differentiation of gender identity from conception to maturity.* Baltimore: Johns Hopkins University Press.

Montagu, M. F. A. (Ed.), 1968. *Man and aggression.* London: Oxford.

Moore, W. E., 1969. Social structure and behavior. In G. Lindzey & E. Aronson (Eds.), *Handbook of social psychology* (2nd ed., Vol. 4). Cambridge, Mass.: Addison-Wesley.

Moore, W. E. & Tumin, M. M., 1949. Some social functions of ignorance. *American Sociological Review, 14:* 787–795.

Moreno, J. L., 1934. *Who shall survive?* Washington, D.C.: Nervous and Mental Disease Publication. (Rev. ed., New York: Beacon House, 1953.)

Moreno, J. L. (Ed.), 1960. *The sociometric reader.* Glencoe, Ill.: The Free Press.

Morgan, C. L., 1896. *Habit and instinct.* London: Arnold.

Morris, R. T., 1956. A typology of norms. *American Sociological Review, 21:* 610–613.

Mulford, H. A. & Salisbury, W. W., II., 1964. Self-conceptions in a general population. *Sociological Quarterly, 5:* 35–46.

Murdock, G. P., 1937. Comparative data on the division of labor by sex. *Social Forces, 15:* 551–553.

Murdock, G. P., 1957. World ethnographic sample. *American Anthropologist, 59:* 664–687.

Murphy, G., 1947. *Personality: A biosocial approach to origins and structure.* New York: Harper.

Musgrove, F., 1961. Parents' expectations of the junior school. *Sociological Review, 9:* 167–180.

Musgrove, F. & Taylor, P. H., 1965. Teachers' and parents' conceptions of the teacher's role. *British Journal of Educational Psychology, 35:* 171–178.

Mussen, P. H., 1950. Some personality and social factors related to changes in children's attitudes toward Negroes. *Journal of Abnormal and Social Psychology, 45:* 423-441.

Myrdal, A. & Klein, V., 1956. *Woman's two roles, home and work.* London: Routlege and Kegan Paul.

Nachmann, B., 1960. Childhood experience and vocational choice in law, dentistry, and social work. *Journal of Counseling Psychology, 7:* 243–250.

Nadel, S. F., 1957. *The theory of social structure.* Glencoe, Ill.: The Free Press.

Naegele, K. D., 1960. Superintendency versus superintendents: A critical essay. *Harvard Educational Review, 30:* 372–393.

Neiman, L. J. & Hughes, J. W., 1951. The problem of the concept of role–A re-survey of the literature. *Social Forces, 30:* 141–149.

Newcomb, T. M., 1947. Autistic hostility and social reality. *Human Relations, 1:* 69–86.

Newcomb, T. M., 1950. *Social psychology.* New York: Dryden.

Newcomb, T. M., 1953. An approach to the study of communicative acts. *Psychological Review, 60:* 393–404.

Newcomb, T. M., 1956. The prediction of interpersonal attraction. *American Psychologist, 11:* 575–586.

Newcomb, T. M., 1959a. Individual systems of orientation. In S. Koch (Ed.), *Psychology: A study of a science* (Vol.3). New York: McGraw-Hill.

Newcomb, T. M., 1959b. The study of consensus. In R. K. Merton, L. Broom, & L. S. Cottrell, Jr. (Eds.), *Sociology today: Problems and prospects.* New York: Basic Books, 277–292.

Newcomb, T. M., 1961. *The acquaintance process.* New York: Holt.

Newcomb, T. M., 1963. Stabilites underlying changes in interpersonal attraction. *Journal of Abnormal and Social Psychology, 66:* 376–386.

Norman, R., 1975. Affective-cognitive consistency, attitudes, conformity, and behavior. *Journal of Personality and Social Psychology, 32:* 83–91.

Nye, F. I., 1976. *Role structure and analysis of the family.* Beverly Hills, Calif.: Sage Publications.

Odum, H., 1947. *Understanding society: The principles of dynamic sociology.* New York: Macmillan.

Oeser, O. A. & Harary, F., 1962. A mathematical model for structural role theory. *Human Relations, 15:* 89–109.

Oeser, O. A. & Harary, F., 1964. A mathematical model for structural role theory, II. *Human Relations, 17:* 3–17.

O'Leary, K. D. & O'Leary, S. G., 1971. *Classroom management: The successful use of behavior modification.* New York: Pergamon.

Opler, M. K., 1959. Cultural differences in mental disorders: An Italian and Irish contrast in schizophrenia–U.S.A. In M. K. Opler (Ed.), *Culture and mental health.* New York: Macmillan.

Ort, R. S., 1950. A study of role conflicts as related to happiness in marriage. *Journal of Abnormal and Social Psychology, 45:* 691–699.

Ort, R. S. 1952. A study of role-conflicts as related to class level. *Journal of Abnormal and Social Psychology, 47:* 425–432.

Osgood, C. E., 1960. Cognitive dynamics in the conduct of human affairs. *Public Opinion Quarterly, 24:* 341–365.

Osgood, C. E., 1962. Studies on the generality of affective meaning systems. *American Psychologist, 17:* 10–28.

Osgood, C. E., Suci, G. J., & Tannenbaum, P. H., 1957. *The measurement of meaning.* Urbana: University of Illinois Press.

Osgood, C. E. & Tannenbaum, P. H., 1955. The principle of congruity in the prediction of attitude change. *Psychological Review, 62:* 42–55.

Ostrom, T. M., 1969. The relationship between the affective, behavioral, and cognitive components of attitude. *Journal of Experimental Social Psychology, 5:* 12–30.

Overall, B. & Aronson, H., 1963. Expectations of psychotherapy in patients of lower socioeconomic class. *American Journal of Orthopsychiatry, 33:* 421–430.

Paloma, M. M., 1972. Role conflict and the married professional woman. In C. Safilios-Rothschild (Ed.), *Toward a sociology of women.* Lexington, Mass.: Xerox.

Park, R. E., 1927. Human nature and collective behavior. *American Journal of Sociology, 32:* 733–741.

Park, R. E. & Burgess, E. W., 1921. *Introduction to the science of sociology.* Chicago: University of Chicago Press.

Parkinson, C. N., 1957. *Parkinson's law.* Boston: Houghton Mifflin.

Parsons, T., 1942. Age and sex in the social structure of the United States. *American Sociological Review, 7:* 604–616.

Parsons, T., 1943. The kinship system of the contemporary United States. *American Anthropologist, 45:* 22–48.

Parsons, T., 1951. *The social system.* Glencoe, Ill.: The Free Press.

Parsons, T., 1958. Definitions of health and illness in the light of American values and social structure. In E. G. Jaco (Ed.), *Patients, physicians, and illness.* New York: The Free Press.

Parsons, T. & Bales, R. F., 1955. *Family, socialization, and interaction process.* Glencoe, Ill.: The Free Press.

Parsons, T. & Shils, E. A., 1951. *Toward a general theory of action.* Cambridge, Mass.: Harvard University Press.

Parsons, T., Shils, E., Naegele, K. D., & Pitts, J. R., 1961. *Theories of society: Foundations of modern sociological theory.* New York: The Free Press.

Parton, D. A., 1976. Learning to imitate in infancy. *Child Dvelopment, 47:* 14–31.

Perrucci, R., 1974. *The circle of madness: On being insane and institutionalized in America.*

Englewood Cliffs, N.J.: Prentice-Hall.
Peter, L. J. & Hull, R., 1969. *The Peter principle.* New York: Morrow.
Phillips, B. N., 1955. Community control of teacher behavior. *Journal of Teacher Education, 6:* 293–300.
Piaget, J., 1932. *The moral judgment of the child.* London: Kegan, Paul, Trench, & Trubner.
Piaget, J., 1959. *The language and thought of the child.* Atlantic Highlands, N.J.: Humanities Press.
Polansky, N., Lippitt, R., & Redl, F., 1950. An investigation of behavioral contagion in groups. *Human Relations, 3:* 319–348.
Porter, J., 1965. *The vertical mosaic: An analysis of social class and power in Canada.* Toronto: University of Toronto Press.
Preiss, J. J. & Ehrlich, H. J., 1966. *An examination of role theory: The case of the state police.* Lincoln: University of Nebraska Press.
Premack, D., 1962. Reversibility of the reinforcement relation. *Science, 136:* 255–257.
Premack, D., 1971. Language in chimpanzee? *Science, 172:* 808–822.
Preston, R. C., 1962. Reading achievement of German and American children. *School and Society, 90:* 350–354.
Radcliff-Brown, A. R., 1934. Sanction, social. In *Encyclopedia of the social sciences* (Vol. 13). London: Macmillan, 531–534.
Rapoport, A., 1960. *Fights, games and debates.* Ann Arbor: University of Michigan Press.
Rapoport, A. & Chammah, A., 1965. *Prisoner's dilemma.* Ann Arbor: University of Michigan Press.
Rapoport, R. & Rapoport, R., 1969. The dual-career family: A variant pattern and social change. *Human Relations, 22:* 2–30.
Rapoport, R. & Rapoport, R., 1971. *Dual-career families.* London: Penguin.
Rapoport, R. & Rosow, I., 1957. An approach to family relationships and role performance. *Human Relations, 10:* 209–221.
Raven, B. H., 1961. *Bibliography of small group research.* Los Angeles: Department of Psychology, University of California. (Additional editions appeared subsequently.)
Raven, B. H. & French, J. R. P., Jr., 1958a. Group support, legitimate power, and social influence. *Journal of Personality, 26:* 400–409.
Raven, B. H. & French, J. R. P., Jr., 1958b. Legitimate power, coercive power, and observability in social influence. *Sociometry, 21:* 83–97.
Raven, B. H. & Rubin, J. Z., 1976. *Social psychology: People in groups.* New York: Wiley.
Redfield, R., 1930. *Tepoztlan: A Mexican village.* Chicago: University of Chicago Press.
Redfield, R., 1941. *The folk culture of Yucatan.* Chicago: University of Chicago Press.
Redl, F., 1942. Group emotion and leadership. *Psychiatry, 5:* 573–596.
Rescher, N., 1966. *The logic of commands.* New York: Dover.
Reynolds, V., 1968. Kinship and the family in monkeys, apes and man. *Man, 3:* 209–223.
Reynolds, V., 1970. Roles and role change in monkey society: The consort relationship of rhesus monkeys. *Man, 5:* 449–465.
Rhea, B., 1964. *Organizational analysis and education: An exercise in sociological theory.* Unpublished doctoral dissertation. Columbia: University of Missouri.
Riley, M. W., Riley, J. W., Jr., & Moore, M. E., 1961. Adolsecent values and the Riesman typology: An empirical analysis. In S. M. Lipset & L. Lowenthal (Eds.), *Cultural and social character.* Glencoe, Ill.: The Free Press.
Robinson, J. A., 1966. Simulation and games. In P. H. Rossi & B. J. Biddle (Eds.), *The new media and education.* Chicago: Aldine.
Robinson, J. P. & Shaver, P. R., 1973. *Measures of social psychological attitudes* (Rev. ed.). Ann Arbor: Institute for Social Research, University of Michigan.

Rocheblave-Spenlé, A.-M., 1962. *La notion de rôle en psychologie sociale: Etude historico-critique.* (The concept of role in social psychology: An historical-critical study). Paris: Presses Universitaires de France (Revised, 1969).

Rodgers, D. A., 1959. Spontaneity and specificity in social role relationships. *Journal of Personality, 27:* 300–310.

Rodman, H., 1966. Illegitimacy in the Caribbean social structure. *American Sociological Review, 31:* 673–683.

Roe, A., 1953. *The making of a scientist.* New York: Dodd, Mead.

Rogers, C. R. & Dymond, R. (Eds.), 1954. *Psychotherapy and personality change.* Chicago: University of Chicago Press.

Rogers, E. M., 1962. *Diffusion of innovations.* New York: The Free Press.

Rokeach, M., 1962. *The open and closed mind.* New York: Basic Books.

Rokeach, M., 1968. *Beliefs, attitudes, and values. A theory of organization and change.* San Francisco: Jossey-Bass.

Rokeach, M., Smith, P. W., & Evans, R. I., 1960. Two kinds of prejudice or one? In M. Rokeach (Ed.), *The open and closed mind.* New York: Basic Books.

Rommetveit, R., 1954. *Social norms and roles.* Minneapolis: University of Minnesota Press.

Rommetveit, R., 1974. *On message structure: A framework for the study of language and communication.* New York: Wiley.

Rose, A. M., 1962. A systematic summary of symbolic interaction theory. In A. M. Rose (Ed.), *Human behavior and social processes: An interactionist approach.* Boston: Houghton Mifflin.

Rosen, B. C., 1955. Conflicting group membership: A study of parent-peer group cross-pressures. *American Sociological Review, 20:* 155–161.

Rosenberg, M. J. & Abelson, R. P., 1960. An analysis of cognitive balancing. In M. J. Rosenberg, C. I. Hovland, W. J., McGuire, R. P. Abelson, & J. W. Brehm (Eds.), *Attitude organization and change.* New Haven, Conn.: Yale University Press.

Rosenberg, S., 1968. Mathematical models of social behavior. In G. Lindzey & E. Aronson (Eds.), *The handbook of social psychology* (2nd ed.). Reading, Mass.: Addison-Wesley.

Rosenhan, D. L., 1973. On being sane in insane places. *Science, 179:* 25–258.

Rosenshine, B., 1971. *Teaching behaviors and student achievement.* London: National Foundation for Educational Research.

Rosenthal, R., 1966. *Experimenter effects in behavioral research.* New York: Appleton-Century-Crofts.

Rosenthal, R., 1967. Covert communication in the psychological experiment. *Psychological Bulletin, 67:* 356–367.

Rosenthal, R. & Jacobson, L., 1968. *Pygmalion in the classroom: Teacher expectation and pupils' intellectual development.* New York: Holt.

Rosenthal, T. L., 1976. Modeling therapies. In M. Hersen, R. M. Eisler, & P. M. Miller, (Eds.), *Progress in behavior modification* (Vol. 2). New York: Academic Press.

Rosenthal, T. L., Rogers, C., & Durning, K., 1972. Sequence of extreme belief-incongruent versus neutral information in social perception. *Australian Journal of Psychology, 24:* 267–273.

Rosnow, R. L. & Robinson, E. J. (Eds.), 1967. *Experiments in persuasion.* New York: Academic Press.

Ross, I. C. & Zander, A., 1957. Need satisfactions and employee turnover. *Personnel Psychology, 10:* 327–338.

Rubin, Z., 1973. *Liking and loving.* New York: Holt.

Sample, J. & Warland, R., 1973. Attitude and the prediction of behavior. *Social Forces, 51:* 292–304.

Sampson, E. E., 1969. Studies of status congruence. In L. Berkowitz (Ed.), *Advances in experimental social psychology* (Vol. 4). New York: Academic Press.

Santee, R. T. & VanDerPol, T. L., 1976. Actor's status and conformity to norms: A study of students' evaluations of instructors. *The Sociological Quarterly, 17:* 378–388.

Sarbin, T. R., 1950. Contributions to role-taking theory: Hypnotic behavior. *Psychological Review, 57:* 255–270.

Sarbin, T. R., 1952. Contributions to role-taking theory: III. A preface to a psychological analysis of the self. *Psychological Review, 59:* 11–22.

Sarbin, T. R., 1954. Role theory. In G. Lindzey (Ed.), *Handbook of social psychology* (Vol. 1). Cambridge, Mass.: Addison-Wesley.

Sarbin, T. R., 1967a. On the futility of the proposition that some people be labeled "mentally ill." *Journal of Consulting Psychology, 31:* 447–453.

Sarbin, T. R., 1967b. The scientific status of the mental illness concept. In S. Plog (Eds.), *Determinants of mental illness: A handbook.* New York: Holt.

Sarbin, T. R. & Allen, V. L., 1968. Role theory. In G. Lindzey & E. Aronson (Eds.), *Handbook of social psychology* (2nd ed., Vol. 1). Cambridge, Mass.: Addison-Wesley.

Schachter, S., 1951. Deviation, rejection, and communication. *Journal of Abnormal and Social Psychology, 46:* 190–207.

Schafer, W. E., 1967. Deviance in the public school: An interactionist view. In E. J. Thomas (Ed.), *Behavioral science for social workers.* New York: The Free Press.

Schanck, R. L., 1932. A study of a community and its groups and institutions conceived of as behaviors of individuals. *Psychology Monographs, 43:* 1–133.

Scheff, T. J., 1966. *Being mentally ill: A sociological theory.* Chicago: Aldine.

Scheff, T. J., 1967. Toward a sociological model of consensus. *American Sociological Review, 32:* 32–46.

Scheff, T. J., 1970. Schizophrenia or ideology, *Schizophrenia Bulletin, 2:* 15–19.

Schein, E., 1961. *Coercive persuasion.* New York: Norton.

Schelling, T. C., 1966. *Arms and influence.* New Haven, Conn.: Yale University Press.

Schlenker, B. R., Bonoma, T., Tedeschi, J. T., & Pivnick, W. P., 1970. Compliance to threats as a function of the wording of the threat and the exploitativeness of the threatener. *Sociometry, 33:* 394–408.

Schmitt, R. L., 1972. *The reference other orientation: An extension of the reference group concept.* Carbondale and Edwardsville: Southern Illinois University Press.

Schofield, J. W., 1975. Effect of norms, public disclosure, and need for approval on volunteering behavior consistent with attitudes. *Journal of Personality and Social Psychology, 31:* 1126–1133.

Schopler, J., 1965. Social power. In L. Berkowitz (Ed.), *Advances in experimental social psychology* (Vol. 2) New York: Academic Press.

Schopler, J. & Thompson, V., 1968. Role of attribution process in mediating amount of reciprocity for a favor. *Journal of Personality and Social Psychology, 10:* 243–250.

Schuman, H. & Johnson, M. P., 1976. Attitudes and behavior. In A. Inkeles, J. Coleman & N. Smelser (Eds.), *Annual review of sociology* (Vol. 2). Palo Alto, Calif.: Annual Reviews.

Schwartz, S. H. & Tessler, R. C., 1972. A test of a model for reducing measured attitude-behavior discrepancies. *Journal of Personality and Social Psychology, 24:* 225–236.

Scott, W. A., 1957. Attitude change through reward of verbal behavior. *Journal of Abnormal and Social Psychology, 55:* 72–75.

Scott, W. A., 1959a. Cognitive consistency, response reinforcement, and attitude change. *Sociometry, 22:* 219–229.

Scott, W. A., 1959b. Attitude acquisition by response reinforcement: Replication and extension. *Sociometry, 22:* 328–335.

Sears, D. O., 1969. Political behavior. In G. Lindzey & E. Aronson (Eds.), *Handbook of social psychology* (2nd ed., Vol. 5). Cambridge, Mass.: Addison-Wesley.

Sears, R. R., Maccoby, E., & Levin, H., 1957. *Patterns of child rearing.* Evanston, Ill.: Row, Peterson.

Sebeck, T. A., Hayes, A. S., & Bateson, M. C. (Eds.), 1964. *Approaches to semiotics.* The Hauge: Mouton.

Sechrest, L., Webb, E. J., Campbell, D. T., & Schwartz, D., 1966. *Unobtrusive measures: Nonreactive research in the social sciences.* Chicago: Rand McNally.

Seeman, M.. 1953. Role conflict and ambivalence in leadership. *American Sociological Review, 18:* 373-380.

Selznick, P., 1949. *TVA and the grass roots.* Berkeley: University of California Press.

Service, E. R., 1960. Kinship terminology and evolution. *American Anthropologist, 62:* 747-763.

Shaw, M. E., 1971. *Group dynamics: The psychology of small group behavior.* New York: McGraw-Hill.

Shaw, M. E. & Costanzo, P. R., 1970. *Theories of social psychology.* New York: McGraw-Hill.

Sherif, M., 1936. *The psychology of social norms.* New York: Harper.

Sherif, M., 1956. Experiments in group conflict. *Scientific American, 195:* 54-58.

Sherif, M. & Hovland, C. I., 1961. *Social judgment: Assimilation and contrast effects in communication and attitude change.* New Haven, Conn.: Yale University Press.

Sherman, B., 1963. Teachers' identifications of childhood authority figures. *School Review, 71:* 66-78.

Sherwood, C. E. & Walker, W. S., 1960. Role differentiation in real groups: An extrapolation of a laboratory small-group research finding. *Sociology and Social Research, 45:* 14-17.

Shibutani, T., 1961. *Society and personality.* Englewood Cliffs, N.J.: Prentice-Hall.

Shils, E., 1965. Charisma, order, and status. *American Sociological Review, 30:* 199-213.

Shure, G. H., Meeker, R. J., & Hansford, E. A., 1965. The effectiveness of pacifist strategies in bargaining games. *Journal of Conflict Resolution, 9:* 106-117.

Sieber, S. D., 1974. Toward a theory of role accumulation. *American Sociological Review, 39:* 567-578.

Silver, B. B., 1978. Social structure and games: A cross-cultural analysis of the structural correlates of game complexity. *Pacific Sociological Review, 21:* 85-102.

Simmel, G., 1908. Der Streit. In *Sociologie: Untersuchungen über die Formen der Vergesellschaftung.* Leipzig: Verlag von Duncker und Humbolt. (*Conflict.* Published together with *The web of group affiliations.* Glencoe, Ill.: The Free Press, 1955.)

Simmons, O. G. & Freeman, H. E., 1959. Familial expectations and posthospital performance of mental patients. *Human Relations, 12:* 233-242.

Singer, J. D., 1963. Internation influence: A formal model. *The American Political Science Review:* 420-430.

Skinner, B. F., 1948. *Walden two.* New York: Macmillan.

Skinner, B. F., 1953. *Science and human behavior.* New York: Macmillan.

Skinner, B. F., 1957. *Verbal behavior.* New York: Appleton-Century-Crofts.

Skinner, B. F., 1960. Teaching machines. In A. A. Lumsdaine & R. Glaser (Eds.), *Teaching machines and programmed learning.* Washington, D.C.: National Educational Association.

Skinner, B. F., 1971. *Beyond freedom and dignity.* New York: Knopf.

Skinner, B. F., 1974. *About behaviorism.* New York: Knopf.

Slater, P. E., 1955. Role differentiation in small groups. *American Sociological Review, 20:* 300-310.

Slater, P. E., 1963. On social regression. *American Sociological Review, 39:* 467-478.

Smith, B. O., Meux, M., Coombs, J., & Nuthall, G., 1964. *A tentative report on the strategies of teaching.* Urbana: Bureau of Educational Research, University of Illinois.

Smith, E. E., 1957. The effects of clear and unclear role expectations on group productivity and defensiveness. *Journal of Abnormal and Social Psychology, 55:* 213-217.

Smith, L. M. & Geoffrey, W., 1968. *The complexities of an urban classroom: An analysis toward a general theory of teaching.* New York: Holt.

Smith, T. E., 1965. The image of high-school teachers: Self and other, real and ideal (should teachers be seen and not heard?) *The Journal of Educational Research, 59:* 99-104.

Snoek, J. D., 1966. Role strain in diversified role sets. *American Journal of Sociology, 71:* 363-372.

Soles, S., 1964. Teacher role expectations and the internal organization of secondary schools. *The Journal of Educational Research, 57:* 227-238.

Sommer, R. & Killian, L. M., 1954. Areas of value differences, I: A method for investigation. *Journal of Social Psychology, 39:* 227-235.

Sorenson, A. G., Husek, T. R., & Yu, C., 1963. Divergent concepts of teacher role: An approach to the measurement of teacher effectiveness. *Journal of Educational Psychology, 54:* 287-294.

Spitzer, S., Couch, C., & Stratton, J., no date. *The assessment of self.* Iowa City: Escourt-Serroll.

Srole, L., Langer, T. S., Michael, S. T., Opler, M. K., & Rennie, T. A., 1962. *Mental health in the metropolis: The Midtown Manhattan Study.* New York: McGraw-Hill.

Staats, A. W., 1964. *Human learning: Studies extending conditioning principles to complex behavior.* New York: Holt.

Staats, A. W. & Staats, C. K., 1963. *Complex human behavior: A systematic extension of learning principles.* New York: Holt.

Staub, E., 1972. Instigation to goodness: The role of social norms and interpersonal influence. *Journal of Social Issues, 28:* 131-150.

Stech, F. J., McClintock, C. G., Fitzpatrick, N. J., & Babin, C. A., 1976. When a cultural prohibition is effective: A field investigation. *Journal of Applied Social Psychology, 6:* 211-227.

Stein, M., Vidich, A. J., & White, D. M. (Eds.), 1960. *Identity and anxiety.* Glencoe, Ill.: The Free Press.

Stogdill, R. M., 1974. *Handbook of leadership: A survey of theory and research.* New York: The Free Press.

Stone, G. P. 1962. Appearance and the self. In A. M. Rose (Ed.), *Human behavior and social process.* Boston: Houghton Mifflin, 93-94.

Stone, G. P., & Farberman, H. A., 1970. *Social psychology through symbolic interaction.* Waltham, Mass.: Ginn-Blaisdell.

Stouffer, S. A., 1949. An analysis of conflicting social norms. *American Sociological Review, 14:* 707-717.

Stouffer, S. A. & Toby, J., 1951. Role conflict and personality. *American Journal of Sociology, 56:* 395-406.

Strauss, A. L. 1959. *Mirrors and masks.* New York: The Free Press.

Strodbeck, F. L., 1951. Husband–wife interaction over revealed differences. *American Sociological Review, 16:* 468-473.

Strodbeck, F. L., 1957. Social status in jury deliberations. *American Sociological Review, 22:* 713-719.

Strodbeck, F. L. & Mann, R. D., 1956. Sex role differentiation in jury deliberations. *Sociometry, 19:* 3-11.

Stroud, J. & Lindquist, E., 1942. Sex differences in achievement in the elementary and secondary schools. *Journal of Educational Psychology, 33:* 657-667.

Stryker, S., 1957. Role-taking accuracy and adjustment. *Sociometry, 20:* 286–296.

Stryker, S., 1962. Conditions of accurate role-taking: A test of Mead's theory. In A. Rose (Ed.), *Human behavior and social processes: An interactionist approach.* Boston: Houghton Mifflin.

Sullivan, H. S., 1940. *Conceptions of modern psychiatry.* Washington, D.C.: W. A. White Psychiatric Foundation.

Sumner, W. G., 1906. *Folkways.* Boston: Ginn.

Sussman, M. & Burchinal, L., 1962. Kin family networks: Unheralded structure in current conceptualizations of family functioning. *Marriage and Family Living, 24:* 320–332.

Sutcliffe, J. P. & Haberman, M., 1956. Factors influencing choice in role conflict situations. *American Sociological Review, 21:* 695–703.

Szasz, T. S., 1960. The myth of mental illness. *American Psychologist, 15:* 113–118.

Szasz, T. S., 1961. *The myth of mental illness: Foundations of a theory of personal conduct.* New York: Harper.

Szasz, T. S., 1970. *The manufacture of madness: A comparative study of the inquisition and the mental health movement.* New York: Harper.

Taft, R., 1955. The ability to judge people. *Psychological Bulletin, 52:* 1–23.

Taft, R., 1966. *From stranger to citizen.* London, Tavistock.

Tagiuri, R., 1969. Person perception. In G. Lindzey & E. Aronson (Eds.), *The handbook of social psychology* (2nd ed., Vol. 3). Reading, Mass.: Addison-Wesley.

Tarde, G., 1903. *The laws of imitation.* New York: Holt.

Thibaut, J. W. & Kelley, H. H., 1959. *The social psychology of groups.* New York: Wiley.

Thibaut, J. W. & Riecken, H. W., 1955. Some determinants and consequences of the perception of social causality. *Journal of Personality, 24:* 113–133.

Thomas, D. L., Franks, D. D., & Calonico, J. M., 1972. Role-taking and power in social psychology. *American Sociological Review, 37:* 605–614.

Thomas, E. J., 1959. Role conceptions and organizational size. *American Sociological Review, 24:* 30–37.

Thomas, E. J., 1968. Role theory, personality and the individual. In E. F. Borgatta & W. W. Lambert (Eds.), *Handbook of personality theory and research.* Chicago: Rand McNally.

Thomas, K., 1971. *Attitudes and behavior.* Middlesex, England: Penguin.

Thomas, W. I. & Znaniecki, F., 1918. *The Polish peasant in Europe and America.* Boston: Badger.

Thompson, J. D., 1967. *Organizations in action.* New York: McGraw-Hill.

Thrasher, F. M., 1927. *The gang.* Chicago: University of Chicago Press.

Thurstone, L. L., 1931. The measurement of attitudes. *Journal of Abnormal and Social Psychology, 26:* 249–269.

Tiger, L., 1969. *Men in groups.* New York: Random House.

Tönnies, F., 1887. *Gemeinschaft und Gesellschaft: Abhandlung des Communismus und des Socialismus als Empirischer Culturformen. (Community and organization: The development of communism and of socialism as empirical forms of culture.)* Leipzig: Fues's Verlag (R. Reisland).

Torrance, E. P., 1954a. Some consequences of power differences on decision making in permanent and temporary three-man groups. Washington State College, *Research Studies, 21:* 262–265.

Torrance, E. P., 1954b. The behavior of small groups under the stress of conditions of "survival." *American Sociological Review, 19:* 751–755.

Trahair, R. C. S., 1967. *Structural role theory and the definition of the worker's situation: An empirical study* (Technical Report No. 23). Columbia: Center for Research in Social Behavior, University of Missouri.

Trahair, R. C. S., 1968. The workers' judgment of their job as a variable in work role analysis. *Human Relations, 21:* 141–162.

Trahair, R. C. S., 1969. Dynamics of a role theory for the workers' judgement. *Human Relations, 22:* 99–119.

Trahair, R. C. S., 1970. The workers' judgment of pay and additional benefits: An empirical Study. *Human Relations, 23:* 201–223.

Triandis, H. C., 1977. *Interpersonal behavior.* Monterey, Calif.: Brooks/Cole.

Tuckman, B. W., 1965. Developmental sequence in small groups. *Psychological Bulletin, 63:* 384–399.

Turner, J. H., 1974. *The structure of sociological theory.* Homewood, Ill.: Dorsey. (Rev. Ed. 1978).

Turner, R. H., 1956. Role taking, role standpoint, and reference-group behavior. *American Journal of Sociology, 61:* 316–328.

Turner, R. H., 1962. Role-taking: Process versus conformity. In A. M. Rose (Ed.), *Human behavior and social processes: An interactionist approach.* Boston: Houghton Mifflin.

Turner, R. H., 1968. Role: Sociological aspects. In D. L. Sills (Ed.), *International encyclopedia of the social sciences* (Vol. 13). New York: Macmillan.

Turner, R. H., 1973. Unresponsiveness as a social sanction. *Sociometry, 36:* 1–19.

Turner, R. L., 1965. Characteristics of beginning teachers: Their differential linkage with school-system types. *School Review, 73:* 48–58.

Twaddle, A. C., 1969. Health decisions and sick role variations: An exploration. *Journal of Health and Social Behavior, 10:* 105–115.

Twaddle, A. C., 1972. The concepts of the sick role and illness behavior. *Advances in Psychosomatic Medicine, 8:* 162–179.

Twaddle, A. C., 1973. Illness and deviance. *Social Science and Medicine, 7:* 751–762.

Twaddle, A. C., 1974. The concept of health status. *Social Science and Medicine, 8:* 29–38.

Twyman, J. P. & Biddle, B. J., 1963. Role conflict of public school teachers. *Journal of Psychology, 55:* 183–198.

van de Vliert, E., 1974. *Rolgedrag in de organisatie.* (Role behavior in the organization). Deventer, Netherlands: Kluwer.

van de Vliert, E., 1979. Gedrag in rolkonfliktsituaties: 20 jaar onderzoek rond een theorie. (Behavior in role conflict situations: 20 years of research concerning a theory). *Nederlands Tijdschrift voor de Psychologie. 34:* 125–145.

van de Vliert, E. & Cottrell, D. A., in press. The validity of the moral and expedient role orientation test. *Journal of Social Psychology.*

Vener, A. M. & Snyder, C. A., 1966. The preschool child's awareness and anticipation of adult sex-roles. *Sociometry, 29:* 159–168.

Vickers, G., 1971. Institutional and personal roles. *Human Relations, 24:* 443–447.

Vidulich, R. N. & Krevanick, F. W., 1966. Racial attitudes and emotional response to visual representations of the Negro. *Journal of Social Psychology, 68:* 85–93.

Visser, A. P., 1976. *Role relationships in general hospitals.* Amsterdam: Department of Social Psychology, The Free University.

von Neumann, J. & Morgenstern, O., 1947. *The theory of games and economic behavior* (2nd ed.). Princeton, N.J.: Princeton University Press.

Vroom, V. H., 1969. Industrial social psychology. In G. Lindzey & E. Aronson (Eds.), *The handbook of social psychology* (2nd ed., Vol. 5). Reading, Mass.: Addison-Wesley.

Wahlke, J. C., Eulau, H., Buchanan, W., & Ferguson, L. C., 1962. *The legislative system: Explorations in legislative behavior.* New York: Wiley.

Walker, E. L. & Heyns, R. W., 1962. *An anatomy for conformity.* Englewood Cliffs, N. J.: Prentice-Hall.

Walster, E., Aronson, E., & Abrahams, D., 1966. On increasing the persuasiveness of a low prestige communicator. *Journal of Experimental Social Psychology, 2:* 325-342.

Walster, E., Berscheid, E., & Walster, G. W., 1973. New directions in equity research. *Journal of Personality and Social Psychology, 25:* 151-176.

Wankel, L. M. & Thompson, C., 1977. Motivating people to be physically active: Self-persuasion versus balanced decision making. *Journal of Applied Social Psychology, 7:* 332-340.

Warner, L. G. & DeFleur, M. L., 1969. Attitude as an interactional concept: Social constraint and social distance as intervening variables between attitudes and action. *American Sociological Review, 34:* 153-169.

Warner, W. L., Meeker, M., & Eells, K., 1949. *Social class in America: A manual of procedure for the measurement of social status.* Chicago: Science Research Associates.

Warren, R. L., 1949. Social disorganization and the interrelationship of cultural roles. *American Sociological Review, 14:* 83-87.

Washburne, C., 1957. The teacher in the authority system. *Journal of Educational Sociology, 30:* 390-394.

Watson, J. B., 1930. *Behaviorism* (Rev. ed.). New York: Norton.

Weber, M., 1925. *Wirtschaft und Gesellschaft* (2nd ed.). Tubingen: J. C. B. Mohr. (Translated as *Economy and Society.* New York: Bedminster, 1968.)

Weick, K. E., 1968. Systematic observational methods. In G. Lindzey & E. Aronson (Eds.), *The handbook of social psychology* (2nd ed., Vol. 2). Reading, Mass.: Addison-Wesley.

Weinstein, E. A. & Deutschberger, P., 1963. Some dimensions of altercasting. *Sociometry, 26:* 454-466.

Weinstock, S. A., 1963. Role elements: A link between acculturation and occupational status. *British Journal of Sociology, 14:* 144-149.

Weiss, R. F., 1962. Persuasion and acquisition of attitudes: Models from conditioning and selective learning. *Psychological Reports, 11:* 709-732.

West, J., 1945. *Plainville U.S.A.* New York: Columbia University Press.

Westie, F. R., 1965. The American dilemma: An empirical test. *American Sociological Review, 30:* 527-538.

Wheeler, S., 1961. Role conflict in correctional communities. In D. R. Cressey (Ed.), *The prison: Studies in institutional organization and change.* New York: Holt.

White, H., 1963. *An anatomy of kinship: Mathematical models for structures of cumulated roles.* Englewood Cliffs, N. J.: Prentice-Hall.

White, L. A., 1949. *The science of culture.* New York: Farrar, Straus.

White, L. A., 1959. *The evolution of culture.* New York: McGraw-Hill.

White, O. K., 1972. Constituting norms and formal organization of American churches. *Sociological Analysis, 33:* 95-109.

White, R. K. & Lippitt, R., 1960. *Autocracy and democracy.* New York: Harper.

Whyte, W. H., Jr., 1956. *The organization man.* New York: Simon Schuster.

Wicker, A. W., 1969. Attitudes versus actions: The relationship of verbal and overt behavioral responses to attitude objects. *Journal of Social Issues, 25:* 41-78.

Wilcox, A. & Fritz, B., 1971. Actual-ideal discrepancies and adjustment. *Journal of Counseling Psychology, 18:* 166-169.

Wilensky, H. L., 1956. *Intellectuals in labor unions: Organizational pressures vs. professional roles.* Glencoe, Ill.: The Free Press.

Wilensky, H. L., 1964. The professionalization of everyone? *American Journal of Sociology, 70:* 137-158.

Wilson, A. T. M., Trist, E. L., & Curle, A., 1952. Transitional communities and social reconnection: A study of the civil resettlement of British prisoners of war. In G. E. Swanson, T. M. Newcomb, & E. L. Hartley (Eds.), *Readings in social psychology* (Rev. ed.). New York: Holt.

Wilson, E. D., 1975. *Sociobiology.* Cambridge, Mass.: Belknap Press of Harvard University.

Wilson, H. C., 1965. On the evolution of education. In B. J. Biddle, R. S. Adams., P. F. Green, F. E. Katz, P. C. Rosenblatt, R. Videbeck, & H. C. Wilson, *Essays on the social systems of education.* Columbia: University of Missouri Press (mimeographed).

Wispé, L. G., 1955. A sociometric analysis of conflicting role experiences. *American Journal of Sociology, 61:* 134–137.

Wolff, W., 1933. The experimental study of forms of expression. *Character and Personality, 2:* 168–176.

Wolff, W., 1935. Involuntary self-expression in gait and other movements: An experimental study. *Character and Personality, 3:* 327–344.

Wolff, W., 1943. *The expression of personality: Experimental depth psychology.* New York: Harper,

Worchel, P. 1957. *Adaptability screening of flying personnel: Development of a self-concept inventory for predicting maladjustment* (USAF Report No. 52-62). Randolph AFB, Texas: School of Aviation Medicine.

Wright, B. A., 1960. *Physical disability—A psychological approach.* New York: Harper.

Wrong, D. H., 1961. The oversocialized conception of man in modern sociology. *American Sociological Review, 26:* 183–193.

Wylie, R., 1968. The present status of self theory. In E. F. Borgatta & W. W. Lambert (Eds.), *Handbook of personality theory and research.* Chicago: Rand McNally.

Wylie, R., 1974. *The self-concept, Revised Edition* (Vol. 1). Lincoln: University of Nebraska Press.

Yates, A. J., 1970. *Behavior therapy.* New York: Wiley.

Zajonc, R. B., 1960. The concepts of balance, congruity, and dissonance. *Public Opinion Quarterly, 24:* 280–296.

Zajonc, R. B., 1965. Social facilitation. *Science, 49:* 269–274.

Zajonc, R. B., 1966. *Social psychology: An experimental approach.* Belmont, Calif.: Wadsworth, 13–14.

Zander, A., Cohen, A. R. & Stotland, E., 1957. *Role relations in the mental health professions.* Ann Arbor: Institute for Social Research, University of Michigan.

Zetterberg, H. L., 1965. *On theory and verification in sociology* (3rd enl. ed.). Totowa, N.J.: Bedminster.

Zimbardo, P. G. & Ebbesen, E. B., 1969. *Influencing attitudes and changing behavior.* Reading. Mass.: Addison-Wesley.

Zimbardo, P. G., Ebbesen, E. B., & Maslach, C., 1977. *Influencing attitudes and changing behavior* (Rev. ed.). Reading, Mass.: Addison-Wesley.

Zimbardo, P. G., Haney, C., Banks, W. C., & Jaffe, D., 1972. *Stanford prison experiment.* Stanford, Calif.: Philip G. Zimbardo, Inc. (Tape Recording).

Zimmerman, B. J. & Rosenthal, T. L., 1972. Concept attainment, transfer, and retention through observation and rule-provision. *Journal of Experimental Child Psychology, 14:* 139–150.

Zuckman, D. & Horn, R. E., 1973. *A guide to simulation/games for education and training.* Cambridge, Mass.: Information Resources.

Glossary of Key Terms and Concepts

Acceptance: An expectation is *acceptant* when it is similar to and determined by another's expectation. [189]

Accuracy: A descriptive expectation is *accurate* when it is similar to and determined by a characteristic of an object person. [182]

Achieved position: A position that is entered through effort on the part of members. [103]

Activity: A temporary but characteristic co-occurrence of two or more interdependent roles. [68, 228]

Adjustment: The ability of the person to accommodate his or her social positions and expected roles. [322]

Advertence: One or more behaviors indicating that a person intends to affect another's behavior. [46]

Affective bonding: A state in which two or more persons share strong preferences for doing things with one another. [307]

Alien position: An object position of which the subject person is not a member. [125]

Alignment: A prescriptive or cathectic expectation is *aligned* when it is similar to and determined by a characteristic of an object person. [182]

Alter: One or more members of a counter position. [100]

Alter position set: A listing of the positions within a social system with whom a person has role relations. [101]

Ambiguity of an expectation: An expectation is *ambiguous* if we can not identify the subject who holds or enunciates it. [154]

Ambiguity of a position: Lack of clarity concerning a position or its members [108]

Ambiguity of a role: An expected role is *ambiguous* when expectations within it are incomplete or insufficient to guide behavior. [154]

Amount of expectation: An expectation is *high in amount* if "a lot" of the object-person characteristic is expected. [152]

Amount score: A response given to a facet-alternative instrument that presumably measures an expectation. [143]

Analytic position: A position designated by a term that is recognized by social scientists. [92]

Anticipatory socialization: Adoption of roles and role expectations appropriate to a new position by a person before the person enters that position. [318]

Applicability of an expectation: An expectation is *applicable* to a given person when that person (or his or her position) is the object person. [156]

Appraisal: An inscribed cathexis. [132]

Approval: A scale presumed to underlie judgements of prescriptive modality. Approval assumes both positive and negative values. [134]

Artifact: A structured physical context for one or more associated roles that *is* characteristically relocated or deformed by those roles. [230]

Ascribed position: A position that is entered through accidents of birth, social experience, or maturity. [103]

Assertion: An overtly expressed description. [132]

Assessment: An overtly expressed cathexis. [132]

Assimilation: Interaction between a person and a social system (or an immigrant and host population) such that in the process they become more alike. [288]

Assumption of conformity: The questionable assumption that roles are inevitably generated by role expectations. [117-118]

Assumption of correspondence: The questionable assumption that persons share roles or role expectations throughout the social system. [117-118]

Assumption of phenomenal equivalence: The questionable assumption that persons are phenomenally aware of the role expectations they hold. [117-118]

Assumption of sanctioning: The questionable assumption that persons conform to role expectations (solely) out of concern for sanctions. [117-118]

Assumption of simple formation: The questionable assumption that role expectations are modeled soley after injunctions for behavior enunciated by others or after observation of behaviors. [117-118]

Attitude: A diffuse, preferential conception. [154]

Attributed consensus: Occurs when a person assigns to others the same expectations that he or she also holds. [192]

Attributed expectation: An extended expectation whose leading expectation is in the descriptive mode. [147]

Audience (person): Another in whose presence a stimulus behavior has occurred. [34]

Authority: Power that is associated with positional membership. [106]

Authority structure: A facet of persons or counter positions that are related by means of authority; a formal arrangement of leaders and followers. [268]

Behavior: Undefined, primitive concept. (Any overt, relatively transitory action of a human being.) [24]

Behavioral conformity: Imitation that is (presumably) induced through social influence. [44]

Behavioral contagion: Imitation that is (presumably) induced through reduction of expected sanctions that normally restrain behavior. [44]

Behavioral impact: The impinging of a person's behavior upon another. (Three types of behavioral impact are discriminated: *behaviors occurring in the presence* of the other; *behaviors directed* toward the other; and *behaviors affecting* the other.) [34-35]

Behavioral linkage: A behavior is *linked* to another behavior if the performance of the first affects the probability of the second. (Three types of linkage are discriminated: *facilitation, reward,* and *reinforcement.*) [37]

Behavioral response: Alteration of subsequent behavior by the other such that it is reasonable to presume recipience of a stimulus behavior. (Three conditions for behavioral response are discriminated: *reflexive, unambiguous,* and *probabilistic.*) [36]

Behaviors affecting another: Behaviors known to be "received" by one or more others. (Three conditions for recipients are discriminated: *recognition response; prepotent behavior;* and *behavioral response.*) [35]

Behaviors directed toward another: Behaviors that are "cast" toward one or more others. [34]

Behaviors occurring in the presence of another: Behaviors emitted in the presence of another. [34]

Belief: A covertly held description. [132]

Breadth of a relationship: A relationship is *broad* when it involves a wide range of characteristic activities. [308]

Breadth of a role: The range of characteristic behaviors appearing within a role. [73]

Caste: An ascribed position within a society whose members have higher or lower status than do comparable positions. [244]

Cathectic conversion: The conversion of an internalized norm into a preference. [293]

Cathectic orientation: A general explanation for social systems that views human beings as manipulators of preferences. [279]

Cathexis: An expectation that tells how the subject feels about an object-person characteristic. [126]

Centrality of an expectation: An expectation is *central* to the degree that it is important to the person and dominates his or her behavior. [158]

Centrality of an identity: An identity is central when it is strongly defended by the person, is bolstered by beliefs and values, and affects a wide range of the persons's behaviors. [300]

Characteristicness: Correspondence among "a significant proportion" of two or more events (such as behaviors). [59]

Charisma: Power that is associated with an individual. [106]

Clarity of an expectation: An expectation is *clear* if its object person, referenced characteristic, mode, and sentient person are not vague. [153]

Close family: A family whose kinship ties are not greater than length-one. [252]

Cognitive dissonance: Occurs when a person holds inconsistent conceptions, at least one of which concerns that person's behavior. [202]

Coherence of a role: The degree to which the characteristic behaviors of a role fit well together. [74]

Community: A population of persons and a location that is the locus of some associated subset of their roles. [236]

Compact family: A family that occupies a compact setting. [253]

Compact society: A population of persons who share a culture and a common location for one or more of their roles. [240]

Comparability: Observable events (such as behaviors) are *comparable* if they are both mapped nonvacuously into a facet. [33]

Comparability of expectations: Expectations are *comparable* with one another (or with behaviors) if they agree in each of the following aspects: their object persons, the characteristic they discuss and the facet in which this is expressed, their modality, and their context. [163]

Comparison concept: A concept that expresses a condition of identicality or similarity among two or more expectations, or expectations and behaviors. It may or may not involve assumptions about determination. [164, 206]

Complement of positions: Should a focal position and one or more counter positions exhaust the universe of persons with which we are generally concerned, these positions constitute a *complement*. [100]

Complete method: A means of measuring expectations formally. Asks subjects to provide a modality rating for each of the facet categories for an object-person characteristic. [142]

Complexity of a role: A role, has greater *complexity* when it is broad, difficult, or noncoherent. [73]

Compliance: A behavior is *compliant* if it conforms to an expectation held or enunciated by another. [172]

Conception: A covertly held expectation. [121]

Conceptual structure: The elements of a social system that are structured and covert. [255]

Concordance: Occurs when comparable expectations of contrasting modalities are found to be similar. [205]

Conflict (or power) orientation: A general explanation for social systems that views human beings as aggressors or as brokers of power. [279]

Conformity: A behavior *conforms* to an expectation if it is both similar to and determined by the latter. [165]

Consensus (also **sharing, common consensus,** or **simple consensus**): Occurs when two or more persons share expectations (that is, hold comparable expectations that are identical or similar). [154. 191, 192]

Consistency (of a behavior): A behavior is *consistent* if it conforms to an expectation held by the subject person. [167]

Consonance of expectations: Extended expectations are *consonant* whenever their component expectations have forms or elements of the same type. [156]

Constituting expectation: An expectation that is both widely shared and generally applicable. [155]

Content-specific role: A role defined in terms of behaviors representing a specified set of facets. [71]

Context: Any condition or state of affairs that affects behavior. [52]

Contextual role: A role defined as those behaviors characteristic of a context. [67, 72]

Contextualization of a role: A role is *contextualized* when its behaviors are circumscribed by the boundaries of a context. [72]

Contextualized expectation: An expectation whose applicability is circumscribed by explicit, contextual boundaries. [145]

Cooptation: Occurs when a group imposes its standards and values on the person who sets out to enter or change it. [287]

Correspondence: Two or more events (such as behaviors) *correspond* if their mappings into an arbitrarily chosen set of facets are either similar or identical. [33]

Counter position(s): One or more positions upon which we do not focus for purposes of analysis, whose members do not belong to the focal position or other compared counter positions. [100]

Cue clarity of a position: A position has *cue clarity* when its positional signs are unambiguous and observable. [109]

Culture: A structure of social elements some of which are unique; that is, are shared among a population of persons but not among others. [239]

Demand: An overtly expressed prescription. [132]

Depth of a relationship: A relationship is *deep* when it incorporates identities and expectations that are central to the participants. [310]

Descent: A positional tie established through sexual reproduction; a child descends from the father because he has conceived the child, and the mother because she has given birth to the child. [248]

Description: An expectation that makes objective statements about an object-person characteristic. [126]

Determinateness of a position: A position is *determinate* when it has elaborate conditions for entry and maintenance of membership. [104]

Determination: One expectation (or behavior) is said to *determine* another if its appearance affects the occurrence of the other in some way (usually unspecified). [164]

Deviant behavior: A behavior which violates expectations that are structured within a social system. [302]

Deviant identity: An identity whose foundation is a trait that attracts structured punishments within a given society. [302]

Differentiation: Two or more events (such as behaviors) are *differentiated* if one or more of their mappings into an arbitrarily chosen set of facets are distinct. [33]

Difficulty of a role: The degree to which skill and energy are required to perform a role. [74]

Diffuse dissensus: A dissensus in which the expectations compared do not fall into two or more distinct modes. [196]

Diffuseness of an expectation: An expectation is *diffuse* if it comprises a set of unclear, though associated, components. [154]

Diffuseness of a role: A *diffuse* role is one that involves many or all of the domains of behavior encountered within a social system. [77]

Direct injunction: A demand or assessment for another's behavior that is expressed by a person to the other (a form of behavior indicating advertence). [46]

Dissensus: Occurs when two or more persons do not share expectations (that is, hold comparable expectations that are not identical or similar). (Antonym of consensus.) [195]

Distinctness: Observable events (such as behaviors) are *distinct* if they are comparable and have nonvacuous, nonidentical mappings that are significantly different for the facet(s) compared. [33]

Distinctness of expectations: Comparable expectations (or expectations and behaviors) are *distinct* if they have distributional forms that are significantly different. [163]

Domain of authority: The range of facets expressing the follower's behavior over which the leader has authority. [268]

Ego: One or more members of a focal position. [99]

Empathy: The (presumed) ability of some persons to attribute veridical expectations to any or all sentient others. [187]

Empty position: A social position that is temporarily without an incumbent. [102]

Entry condition: A criterion for entry into a social position. [103]

Enunciation: An overtly expressed expectation. [119]

Environmental unit: Undefined, primitive concept. (A unit of the physical world that can be relocated or deformed through behaviors, as a result of which the probability of subsequent behaviors appearing is affected.) [37]

Exchange orientation: A general explanation for social systems that views human beings as bargainers. [279]

Exit condition: A criterion for departure from a social position. [103]

Expectation: A statement that expresses a (modal) reaction about a characteristic of one or more persons. [119, 132]

Expectation for other: An expectation held for another person or an alien position. [125]

Expectation for self: An expectation held for the subject person or for the subject person's position. [124]

Expected profile: The set of expectations for the nonbehavioral characteristics of identified object persons that are consensually held by one or more subject persons (or are attributed by them to sentient others). [210]

Expected role: The set of expectations for the behaviors (in context) of identified object persons that are consensually held by one or more subject persons (or are attributed by them to sentient others). [210]

Expected sanction: An expectation concerning sanctioning; that is, for the appearance of one or more behaviors constituting rewards or punishments for the other and for which performance by the person is more or less likely, depending on performance of stimulus behavior by the other. [174]

Expected treatment: The set of expectations for the behaviors (in context) directed toward identified object persons that are consensually held by one or more subject persons (or are attributed by them to sentient others). [210]

Extended expectation: Two or more simple expectations arranged in a chain so that later expectations in the sequence are the referenced characteristics of those that precede it. [146]

Extended family: A family that is not close. [253]

Facet: A set of categories, or sometimes a set of ordered alternatives, or even an interval scale, against which one can make ratings for an aspect of the events being studied (such as behaviors). [27]

Facet alternative method: A means of measuring expectations formally. Asks subjects to discriminate among responses expressing facet categories for an object-person characteristic. [143]

Facilitation: When one behavior enhances the probability of another by means of environmental manipulation (that is, through deformation or relocation of environmental units). [38]

Family: A set of persons who are related to one another by kinship and who regularly engage in primary activities with one another. [252]

Feature (physical): Undefined, primitive concept. (Any overt, relatively enduring state of a human being.) [23]

Focal position: A position upon which we focus for purposes of analysis, whose membership does not exhaust the universe of persons with which we are generally concerned. [99]

Follower: A person for whom response to authority is structured; that is, to whom is assigned the job of doing what another says is to be done. [268]

Formality of an expectation: An expectation is *formal* when it is long winded, full of semantic qualification, exact, and rule expressed. [156]

Formalization of a role: An expected role is *formalized* to the extent that its expectations are inscribed, complex, and subject to qualification. [214]

Foundation of a position: The defining criterion of a position—those characteristics positional members are presumed to have in common. [98]

Function: Any condition or state of affairs that results from behavior. [51]

Functional inconsistency: Two expectations are *functionally inconsistent* if their joint performance would produce effects that are logically inconsistent or would require meeting logically inconsistent conditions. [202]

Functional orientation: A general explanation for social systems that views social activity as a series of events that have explicit consequences. Crucial to this orientation are such issues as roles and activities, contexts, functions, and functional requisites. [278]

Functional role: Behaviors that are involved in the accomplishment of a specific function. [71]

Game: An identified social system that is conducted for an arbitrary, internal task having positive cathexis for participants. [265]

General position: A social position that is widely recognized and applies in all or nearly all contexts. [297]

General role: Patterns of behavior that characterize members of a general position. [297]

General role expectations: Expectations for the behaviors of members of a general position that are structured for the society. [298]

Generality of an expectation: An expectation is *general* if it refers to many object persons and contexts. [153]

Generality of a position: The degree to which a position applies to many persons and contexts. [107]

Generality of a role: A role has greater *generality* when it is performed by a wider group of persons or upon more occasions. [72]

Group (or **social group**): A set of two or more persons who are linked through interaction. [233]

Hindrance: When one behavior decreases the probability of another by means of environmental manipulation (that is, through deformation or relocation of environmental units). (Antonym of *facilitation.*) [38]

Human being (person, other, individual): Undefined, primitive concept. (Any observable member of the species *Homo sapiens.*) [22]

The "I": The person as an actor; the impulsive tendency of the person (a component of the self). [290]

Identicality: Observable events (such as behaviors) are *identical* if they are comparable and have the same, nonvacuous mapping for the facet(s) compared. [33]

Identicality of expectations: Comparable expectations (or expectations and behaviors) are *identical* if they have the same distributional forms. [163]

Identification: The attachement of positive cathexis by a person to another as a representative of a position that the person may enter. [299]

Identity: A symbol used for designating one or more human beings. [89]

Identity of a social system: A symbol that is used for designating the social system. [259]

The Image: The set of identities and expectations for the person that are structured by context or are implied by the behaviors the person displays (a component of the self). [291]

Imbedding of an expectation: An expectation is *imbedded* in a belief or value system when it is logically tied to other elements of that system. [158]

Imitation: A behavior *imitates* another if it is linked to and corresponds with the other. [43]

Inadequate socialization: Induction of deviancy through failure to provide socializing events that *are* experienced by others. [303]

Inappropriate socialization: Induction of deviancy through provision of socializing events that are not experienced by others. [304]

Inclusional inconsistency: Two expectations are inclusionally *inconsistent* if they agree in mode, are distinct, and one expemplifies conditions appearing in the other. [202]

Inconsistency (of expectations): Two expectations are *inconsistent* when one of them implies some event that is denied by the other. [201]

Indirect injunction: A behavior expressed by a person to another that references phenomena other than the other's behavior but nevertheless has logical implications for it or its functions. (A form of behaving indicating advertence.) [46]

Individual: A single human being. [22]

Individual expectation: An expectation (presumed) held or expressed by a single subject person. [123]

Influence: A person *influences* another when the person's behavior affects one or more behaviors of the other and we have evidence of advertence on the part of the person. [46]

Initial socialization: Socialization in childhood. [283]

Injunction: An enunciation expressed by the person to another that encourages or discourages the other's behavior (a form of behavior indicating advertence). [46]

Inscription: An expectation expressed in written form. [121]

Institution: The roles and activities of a community that are associated with a given function. [237]

Intensity: Any of several conditions that may characterize a primary relationship among persons. Relationships are judged intense if they are *broad, open,* or *deep.* [308]

Intention: An assertion that concerns events that will presumably appear in the future. [129]

Interaction: A condition existing between two or more persons such that each exhibits one or more behaviors affecting the other(s) during the period of our observation. [233]

Internalization: The process whereby norms that are first expressed by *significant others* for the child, are later attributed to a *generalized other,* and then incorporated into the child's own expectational system. [293]

Internalization of an expectation: An expectation is *internalized* to the extent that a subject holds it him or herself instead of attributing it to others. [158]

Involvement in a role: The degree to which the person invests effort or is organismically engaged in role performance. [326]

Job: A task that is set for an individual. [261]

Kinship system: A facet of counter positions that are defined in terms of sexual identity, marriage, and descent. [247]

Later socialization: Socialization in adolescence and young adulthood. [285]

Leader: A person for whom authority is structured; that is, to whom is assigned the job of saying what is to be done. [268]

Legitimacy: Authority that is conferred through social structure rather than through functions produced. [107]

Legitimacy of an expectation: An expectation is *legitimate* when viewed as "right and proper."[157]

Length of an extended expectation: The number of simple expectations comprising the chain of which an extended expectation is composed. [146]

Liking: A scale presumed to underlie judgements of cathectic modality. Liking assumes both positive and negative values. [134]

Linking: Two behaviors are *linked* if the performance of the first affects the probability of the performance of the second. [37]

Local community: A set of persons who inhabit a compact, contiguous setting, their roles, and a socially recognized interaction system that ties them together. [238]

Location: A setting that is a place within the Euclidean three-dimensional space inhabited by human beings and their behaviors. [236]

Logical inconsistency: Two expectations are *logically inconsistent* if they are identical in form and distinct. [202]

Love: An intense, mutually influencing, and mutually rewarding relationship of primary interaction between persons who are affectively bonded. [307]

Maintenance condition: A criterion for retaining membership in a social position. [103]

Marriage: A semipermanent relationship among two or more adult persons that is socially recognized, involves sexual license, and is exclusive. [247]

The "Me": The set of all covert identities and expectations held by the person pertaining to him or herself as an object person (a component of the self). [290]

Membership position: A position designated by a term that is not familiar to persons in the subject population. [92]

Modal strength method: A means of measuring expectations formally. Asks subjects to discriminate among response alternatives along a modality scale. [142]

Modality: That aspect of an expectation which denotes the reaction expressed by the subject concerning object-person characteristics. Expectations may be descriptive, prescriptive, or cathectic in mode. [126]

Modeling: Imitation that is (presumably) induced through identification. [45]

National society: A population of persons who share a culture and a common location for many or most of the unique elements of that culture. [240]

Negative advertence: Occurs when advertent behaviors of the person (such as injunctions or sanctions) are designed to discourage behavior in the other. [46-47]

Negative reinforcer: A behavior that decreases the probability of a criterion response through reinforcement. [41]

Nonsimple expectation: An expectation containing one or more modality or reference components that may be decomposed into simple expectations without semantic loss. [144]

Norm: A covertly held prescription. [132]

Normative orientation: A general explanation for social systems that views social relations in terms of mutual obligations that are governed by expectations. Crucial to this orientation are such issues as socialization, consensus, conformity of behavior to norms, and the association among norms, roles, and positions. [277]

Nuclear family: A close family that exhibits a marriage. [253]

Object person: A (referenced) person whose characteristics are at issue in an expectation. [122, 148]

Occupation: A social position whose foundation is a role that is performed to obtain money from the environment. [314]

Openness of a relationship: A relationship is *open* when it involves discussion of a wide range of topics. [309]

Organization: An identified social system that is conducted for one or more tangible tasks in the external environment. [266]

Other: One (or more) human beings. [22]

Other-reference of an expectation: An extended expectation is *other-referenced* when its sentient and object positions are conjoint. [156]

Overt structure: The elements of a social system that are structured and observable. [227]

Own position: An object position of which the subject person is a member. [124]

Person: One (or more) human beings. [22]

Person-associated role: The behaviors that are characteristic of a set of persons. [65]

Personal change: Changes in roles and role expectations assumed by the person when entering a new position. [318]

Personal expectation: An expectation applying to a single object person. [124]

Personal leadership: Exertion of influence through charisma rather than through authority. [319]

Personal role: The behaviors that are characteristic of an individual. [66]

Personal selection: Mechanisms in which a person exercises control over whether he or she will join a social system. [316]

Personal winnowing: Mechanisms in which a person exercises control over whether he or she will leave a social system. [320]

Personalization of a role: A role is *personalized* when its performance is limited to just one or a few persons. [73]

Pluralistic ignorance: A consensus that is either inaccurate, nonaligned, or nonveridical. [192]

Polarized dissensus: A dissensus in which the expectations compared fall into two or more distinct modes. [196]

Position: An identity used for designating two or more persons who presumably share one or more overt characteristics (also, by convention, those persons so designated). [91]

Position set: The collection of social positions characterizing a given person. [101]

Positional differentiation: The fact that a set of collective identities is socially recognized and used clearly within a population. [102]

Positional expectation: An expectation applying to an object position. [124]

Positional role: The behaviors that are characteristic of a social position. [65]

Positional sequence: A complement of positions arranged so that membership in one is a requisite for entry into the next, and so on through the sequence. [101]

Positional sign: Overt behavior that announces membership in a position; it may or may not be identical with the positional foundation. [109]

Positional structure: The positional elements characteristic of a social system. [245]

Positive advertence: Occurs when advertent behaviors of the person (such as injunctions or sanctions) are designed to encourage behavior in the other. [46–47]

Positive reinforcer: A behavior that increases the probability of a criterion response through reinforcement. [41]

Power: The ability to exert influence. [106]

Pragmatic orientation: A general explanation for social systems that views human beings as reality assessors. Crucial to this orientation are such issues as beliefs, negotiation, and the evolution of roles from interaction. [278]

Preference: A covertly held cathexis. [132]

Prepotent behaviors: Behaviors whose force is so great that no human being receiving them and having normal facilities can be other than aware of them. [35]

Prescription: An expectation that approves or requests an object-person characteristic. [126]

Prestige of a position: The degree to which members of a position attract deferential behavior from others. [105]

Primary activity (or relationship): An activity in which interaction is face-to-face, is frequently repeated among the same actors, and involves many behavioral facets. [228]

Prior experience: One or more roles or treatments the person is known (or presumed) to have experienced in the past. [96].

Profession: An occupation whose roles involve interaction with human beings (clients), whose performance is based on a long period of training and is accounted "expert," for which associated roles tend to be performed in private, and for which an explicit code of conduct is set and enforced by its members. [314]

Profile: Nonbehavioral characteristics of a set of persons. [61]

Promise: An indirect injunction warning of the likelihood of a positive sanction being given and making clear its contingent relationship with the stimulus behavior of the other. [47]

Punishment: A behavior that presumably decreases the probability of another because it is a prepotent stimulus (and normally evokes recognition responses indicating pain). (Antonym of *reward*.) [39]

Recipient (person): Another known to have been affected by a stimulus behavior. [35]

Recognition response: Behavior by another in which that other volunteers awareness of the stimulus behavior. [35]

Reference position: A term of identity for two or more persons that appears as a referential element within an expectation (sometimes called a *reference group* by other authors). [148]

Reinforcement: Occurs when one behavior enhances or decreases the probability of another through recipience (that is, facilitation and hindrance have been ruled out and a probabilistic relationship occurs). [41]

Relationality of a position: The degree to which a given position is paired with counter positions. [104]

Report: An assertion which concerns events that took place in the past. [129]

Representation: An inscribed description. [132]

Resocialization: Socialization in adulthood. [286]

Reward: A behavior that presumably enhances the probability of another because it is a prepotent stimulus (and normally evokes recognition responses indicating pleasure). [39]

Role: Those behaviors characteristic of one or more persons in a context. [58]

Role ambiguity: An expected role is *ambiguous* when expectations within it are incomplete or insufficient to guide behavior. [323]

Role complement: The set of roles appearing within a social system. [76]

Role complementarity: Roles are *complementary* when they fit together in that specific functions are accomplished through their joint performance. [78]

Role conflict: Any condition of common or attributed polarized dissensus which poses (usually unspecified) problems for object persons. [196]

Role differentiation: Two roles are said to be *differentiated* if they have but few behaviors in common. [75]

Role discontinuity: Lack of integration in the roles a person is called upon to perform in sequence. [324]

Role distance: Defense against the appearance of role involvement through casualness, confidence, or humor. [326]

Role expectations: Expectations that are structured for the roles of positions within a social system. [256]

Role integration: A system is *role-integrated* when its roles fit well together. [77]

Role interdependence: Roles are *interdependent* when they mutually facilitate or hinder one another. [78]

Role overload: Appears when the person is faced with a role set that is too complex. [324]

Role playing: Occurs when a person (correctly) imitates the role of another. [189]

Role reciprocality: Roles are *reciprocal* when some of the characteristic behaviors of one act as sanctions for the other, and vice versa. [78]

Role sector: Those protions of a positional role consisting of behaviors directed toward (or affecting) members of a specific counter position. [60]

Role set: The set of roles performed by a given person. [76]

Role skill: The ability of the person to perform complex roles. [325]

Role specialization: When differentiated roles within a social system are performed by different persons, they are *specialized*. [77]

Role strain: Experiences of stress associated with positions or expected roles. [325]

Role taking: Occurs when a person holds veridical expectations that (correctly) map the expectations of a sentient other. [189]

Role theory: A science concerned with the study of behaviors that are characteristic of persons within contexts and with various processes that presumably produce, explain, or are affected by those behaviors. [4]

Rolecasting (altercasting): Encouraging or projecting a role for the person as part of the treatment given him or her by another. [63]

Rule: An inscribed prescription. [132]

Saliency: Reports of conceptions are *salient* when they are volunteered first in response to open-ended questions. [215]

Sanction: A behavior of a person constituting a reward or punishment to another, exhibition of which is more or less likely depending on exhibition of a stimulus behavior by the other. (A form of behavior indicating advertence.) [47]

Secondary activity: An activity that is not primary (that is, involves less intense and less personalized forms of interaction). [229]

Selection: Mechanisms involved in adding a person to a social system. [315]

Self-reference of an expectation: An extended expectation is *self-referenced* when the subject person is a member of a sentient position whose expectations are cited. [156]

Self-role congruence: Appears when role expectations and role skill are approximately matched. [325]

Sentient clarity of an expectation: An extended expectation is *sentient clear* if the sentient person to whom it is attributed is not vague. [155]

Sentient person: A referenced person whose expectation is cited in an extended expectation. [148]

Sentient personalization of an expectation: An extended expectation is *sentient personalized* if it is attributed to only a single sentient person. [155]

Setting: A structured physical context for one or more associated roles that is *not* characteristically relocated or deformed by those roles. [230]

Sexual identity: A universally recognized form of positional classification based on physical features (that is, primary and secondary sexual characteristics). [247]

Shared consensus: Occurs when two or more persons both share and are aware that they share expectations. [192]

Sharing of expectations: Expectations are *shared* if they are (presumably) held or enunciated in common by two or more subject persons. [123, 154]

Similarity: Observable events (such as behaviors) are *similar* if they are comparable and have nonvacuous, nonidentical mappings that are insignificantly different for the facet(s) compared. [33]

Similarity of expectations: Comparable expectations (or expectations and behaviors) are *similar* if they have distributional forms that are identical or insignificantly different. [163]

Simple expectation (own expectation): An expectation involving a single modal reaction about one characteristic of an object person. [144]

Singularity of a role: A *singular* role is one that is performed by just one or a few persons within a social system. [77]

Social class: An achieved position within a society whose members have higher or lower status than do comparable positions. [242]

Social facilitation: Imitation that is (presumably) induced by the sheer presence of others. [44]

Social position: A position designated by a term that is familiar to persons in the subject population. [91]

Social selection: Mechanisms in which a social system exercises control over those who will be allowed to become members. [315]

Social system: A structured set of behavioral elements—alternately, a characteristic set of interdependent roles. (Concrete examples of social systems are defined by foundations of structured elements that may or may not include behaviors.) [225]

Social system change: Changes induced in the social system due to activities of one or more persons. [318]

Social winnowing: Mechanisms in which a social system exercises control over who will be separated from a social system. [320]

Socialization: Environmentally induced changes in the behavior or conceptual state of the person that lead to greater ability to participate in a social system. [282]

Socializing agency: An organization whose task is the socialization of persons. [287]

Societal role: Behaviors that are characteristic of persons in a given society. [65]

Society: A population of persons who share a culture. [239]

Span of control: The number of persons over whom a given leader has authority. [269]

Status equilibration: The tendency for persons to equate criteria for status (such as prestige, wealth, and authority). [107]

Status of a position: A position has higher *status* if its members have (or are presumed to have) more of some characteristic that is positively sanctioned, or if it regularly receives (or is presumed to receive) more of some positive sanction than some other position. [105]

Stereotypy of expectation: An expectation is *stereotypic* to the degree that it is based on hearsay rather than on evidence. [157]

Stereotypy of a role: An expected role is *stereotypic* when a substantial portion of the expectations of which it is composed are sterotypic in origin. [214]

Strength of an expectation: An expectation is *strong* if it generates a "high" modal score. [152]

Strength score: A response given to a modal-strength instrument that presumably measures an expectation. [142]

Structural position: A position whose existence is stipulated by social structure. [92]

Structure (social): A set of social elements that are characteristic of a given social system and are interdependent. [225]

Structured context: A context is *structured* for a social system form if it is characteristic of and is found to affect one or more of the characteristic roles of that form. [229]

Structured function: A function is *structured* for a social system form if it is characteristic of and is affected by one or more of the characteristic roles of that form. [231]

Structured position: A position is *structured* for a social system form if it is characteristic of that form. [225]

Subject person: A person who enunciates or holds an expectation. [122]

Subjective probability: A scale presumed to underlie judgements of descriptive modality. Subjective probability assumes positive values only (and zero). [134]

Successful influence: Occurs when positive advertence results in an increase in the behavior of the other or negative advertence results in a decrease in the behavior of the other. [47]

Target (person): Another toward whom a stimulus behavior is directed. [35]

Task: A shared prescription for events that are to result from the structured roles and activities of a social system. [261]

Task structure: A facet of persons or counter positions that are related by means of jobs; a formal arrangement of norms that are assigned to persons for task accomplishment. [271]

Threat: An indirect injunction warning of the likelihood of a negative sanction being given and making clear its contingent relationship with the stimulus behavior of the other. [47]

Trait: A behavior that is (presumed to be) characteristic of a person, regardless of context. [96]

Treatment: Those behaviors characteristically directed toward persons in a context. [62]

Treatment sector: Those portions of a positional treatment consisting of behaviors directed toward (or affecting) persons by members of a specific counter position. [62]

Uniformity: Behaviors that correspond are said to be *uniform*. [33]

Uniqueness of a role: The proportion of behaviors making up a role that are dissimilar to the behaviors of other roles with which we make a comparison. [74]

Unsuccessful influence: Occurs when advertent behaviors are not successful in changing the behavior of the other. [47]

Value: A prescriptive statement that is accepted by the person as an absolute. [295]

Veridicality: An extended expectation is *veridical* when it is similar to and determined by a simple expectation. [187]

Visibility of a role: The degree to which a role is performed in the presence of an audience. [75]

Wealth of a position: The number of commodities its members are given or are allowed to control. [106]

Winnowing: Mechanisms involved in separating a person from a social system. [320]

Author Index

Subject Index

(Note that terms appearing in boldface type are also defined in the Glossary.)

411